Entrepreneurship Development and Small Business Enterprises

Second Edition

Poornima M. Charantimath
Karnataka Law Society's Institute of Management Education and Research, Belgaum

PEARSON

Assistant Editor–Acquisitions: Pradeep Kumar Bhattacharjee
Senior Editor–Development: Priya Christopher *Editor–Production*: M. R. Ramesh

ISBN 978-81-317-6226-4

First Impression, 2014

Published by Pearson India Education Services Pvt Ltd, CIN: U72200TN2005PTC057128,formerly known as TutorVista Global Pvt Ltd, licensee of Pearson Education in South Asia.

Head Office: 7th Floor, Knowledge Boulevard, A-8(A), Sector 62, Noida 201 309, UP, India.
Registered Office: Module G4, Ground Floor, Elnet Software City, TS-140, Block 2 and 9, Rajiv Gandhi Salai, Taramani, Chennai 600 113, Tamil Nadu, India. Fax:080-30461003, Phone: 080-30461060, www.pearson.co.in, Email: companysecretary.india@pearson.com

Compositor: Chennai Publishing Services
Digitally Printed in India by Repro Knowledgecast Limited, Thane in the year of 2016.

To my parents,

Late Sri. Veeresh Kambalimath

and

Smt. Ganga Kambalimath

About the Author

Poornima M. Charantimath is Professor and Head of the Centre for Entrepreneurship Development at Karnataka Law Society's Institute of Management Education and Research, Belgaum. Dr Charantimath has been actively involved in teaching, research, and consultancy in a distinguished career spanning more than 20 years.

She received her master's degree in management studies from the University of the West of England, Bristol, the United Kingdom, and her Ph.D. in management from the Department of Management Studies, Karnataka University, Dharwad.

Dr Charantimath has served as Deputy Director at the Indian Institute of Materials Management, Bangalore, and Director at KLS Institute of Management Education and Research, Belgaum. She is a fellow of the Institution of Engineers (India) and served as a member of the Board of Studies at Visvesvaraya Technological University, Belgaum. She is also a Ph.D. guide for the research students of Jawaharlal Nehru Technological University, Hyderabad and CMJ University, Meghalaya. She is the author of *Total Quality Management* (Pearson Education, 2011).

Dr Charantimath has been awarded the Association of Overseas Technical Scholarship (AOTS) and has attended a workshop on total quality management and strategic management at Osaka, Japan. She has been recognized by the Deshpande Center for Social Entrepreneurship as a pioneering faculty member engaged in promoting entrepreneurship education. A recipient of the Distinguished Engineer Award from the Institution of Engineers, Belgaum, and the Achiever of the Year Award from Round Table India, she is also an assessor for the CII-EXIM Bank Award for Business Excellence and the Ramakrishna Bajaj National Quality Award. Dr Charantimath has also conducted training programmes for several organizations such as Tata Motors, the Aditya Birla Group, Hindustan Latex Limited, and G5 Solution in the areas of total quality management and strategic management.

Contents

Foreword xiii
From the Academia xiv
From the Industry xv
Preface xvii

PART 1: ENTREPRENEURIAL PERSPECTIVES

1 Entrepreneurship 2

Introduction 3
Evolution of the Concept of Entrepreneurship 4
- Richard Cantillon 4
- Adam Smith 5
- Jean-Baptiste Say 5
- Francis Walker 5
- Joseph Schumpeter 5

Entrepreneurship Today 5
- Who Is an Entrepreneur? 6
- How Do I Become an Entrepreneur? 6
- Advantages of Being an Entrepreneur 7

Types of Entrepreneurs 7
Intrapreneurship 8
- Difference Between a Manager and an Entrepreneur 8

Entrepreneurial Competencies 10
Capacity Building for Entrepreneurs 14
Summary 16
Key Terms 16
Case Study 17
Discussion Questions 18
Activity 18
Project 18
Endnotes 18

2 Entrepreneurial Development and Training 20

Introduction 21
Entrepreneurial Environment 21
- Global Entrepreneurship Environment 21
- Business Climate in India 22
- Environmental Factors Affecting Entrepreneurial Growth 24
- Creating a Favourable Environment for Entrepreneurship 27

Models of Entrepreneurial Development 28
- Psychological Models 28
- Sociological Models 29
- Integrated Models 30

Entrepreneurial Motivation 31
- Need for Achievement (nAch) 32
- Thematic Apperception Test (TAT) 32
- Entrepreneurship Motivation Training (EMT) 32

Entrepreneurship Training Methods 34
- Lecture Method 34
- Participative Methods 35

The Process of Entrepreneurial Development 36
Summary 38
Key Terms 38
Case Study 39
Discussion Questions 39
Activity 40
Project 40
Endnotes 40

3 Women Entrepreneurs 42

Introduction 43
Women's Entrepreneurship in Asia 46
Women's Entrepreneurship in India 46
Challenges Faced by Women Entrepreneurs 49
- Microsphere 49
- Mesosphere 49
- Macrosphere 49

Strategies for the Development of Women Entrepreneurs 50
- Encouraging Home-based Businesses 50
- Widespread Business Education 51
- Better Financial Assistance 51
- Wider Access to Technology 51
- Group Entrepreneurship/Grassroots Entrepreneurship Through Self-help Groups 51

Institutions Supporting Women Entrepreneurs in India 54
- Consortium of Women Entrepreneurs of India (CWEI) 54
- Federation of Indian Women Entrepreneurs (FIWE) 55
- FICCI Ladies Organization (FLO) 55
- Women's India Trust (WIT) 56
- Association of Women Entrepreneurs of Karnataka (AWAKE) 56

Special Bank Schemes Promoting Women's Entrepreneurship 56
- Cent Kalyani of Central Bank of India Credit Scheme 56
- National Bank for Agriculture and Rural Development (NABARD) 57
- Small Industries Development Bank of India 58

Women Entrepreneurs from Around the World 58
- Mary Kay Ash 58
- Jenna Jameson 59
- Anita Roddick 59
- Oprah Winfrey 59
- Madame C. J. Walker 59
- Coco Chanel 59
- Debbi Fields 60
- Estée Lauder 60
- Arianna Huffington 60

Women Entrepreneurs in India 60

Kiran Mazumdar-Shaw 61
Ritu Kumar 62
Women's Empowerment Through Entrepreneurship 63
The Gender and Development Approach 63
Shri Mahila Griha Udyog Lijjat Papad (SMGULP) 64
Summary 65
Key Terms 65
Case Study 66
Discussion Questions 67
Activity 67
Project 67
Endnotes 67

4 Family Business 70

Introduction 71
Role and Importance of the Family Business 71
Contributions of Family Businesses in India 73
Stages of Development of a Family Business 73
Characteristics of a Family-owned Business in India 74
Various Types of Family Businesses 74
Roles, Responsibilities, and Rights of Family Members in a Family Business 75
Founder 75
Owners (Shareholders) 75
Directors (Board of Directors) 75
Family Members 75
The Three-circle Model of Family Business 75
Challenges Faced by Family-owned Businesses 77
Succession in Family Business 79
Improving the Performance of a Family Business 80
Summary 82
Key Terms 82
Case Study 82
Discussion Questions 83
Activity 83
Project 83
Endnotes 84

5 Micro, Small, and Medium Enterprises 86

Introduction 87
Role and Importance of Micro, Small, and Medium Enterprises 88
Concepts and Definitions of MSME 90
The MSMED Act, 2006 91
Government Policy Initiatives Since 1948 93
Report of the Task Force on MSME 95
Growth and Development of MSME in India 96
Current Schemes for MSME 98
Credit Guarantee Trust for Micro and Small Enterprises (CGTMSE) 99
Technology Upgradation Schemes 99
Marketing Assistance Scheme 99
Certification Scheme 99
Credit Rating Scheme 99
The Fourth All-India Census of MSME 100
Problems Facing the MSME Sector 102
Role of Clusters in Promoting MSME 104
Summary 105
Key Terms 105
Case Study 106
Discussion Questions 107
Activity 107
Project 107
Endnotes 108

PART 2: NEW VENTURE CREATION

6 Identification of Business Opportunities 110

Introduction 111
What Defines a Good Business Opportunity? 111
When Is an Idea an Opportunity? 113
How to Generate Business Ideas 113
What Leads to the Creation of Opportunities 115
How to Identify a Business Opportunity 117
Mobility of Entrepreneurs 118
Geographical Mobility of Entrepreneurs 118
Occupational Mobility 119
Business Opportunities in India 119
Models for Opportunity Evaluation 120
The RAMP Model 121
Mullins's Seven-domain Framework 121
Summary 123
Key Terms 123
Case Study 124
Discussion Questions 126
Activity 126
Project 127
Endnotes 127

7 Project Management and Financing 130

Introduction 131
Project Manager 132
Project Life Cycle 133
Project Scheduling 134
Gantt Charts 134
Network Techniques 135
Project Management Software 138
Microsoft Project 138
InstaPlan 138
Yojana 139
PRISM Project Manager 139
PRIMAVERA 139
Capital Budgeting 140
Generating an Investment Project Proposal 140
Project Analysis 140
Market Analysis 141
Technical Analysis 141
Financial Analysis 141
Economic Analysis 142
Ecological Analysis 142

Project Evaluation and Selection 142
- The Payback Period 142
- Accounting Rate of Return (ARR) 142
- Net Present Value (NPV) 143
- Internal Rate of Return (IRR) 144
- Benefit–Cost Ratio (BCR) 145

Project Financing 147
- Equity Financing 147
- Angel Investing 148
- Debt Financing 148
- Miscellaneous Sources 149

Project Implementation Phase 149
Capital Structure and Cost of Capital 149
Detailed Project Report 150
Summary 152
Key Terms 152
Case Study 153
Discussion Questions 154
Activity 155
Project 155
Endnotes 155
Annexure 155

8 Business Plans 158

Introduction 159
Purpose of a Business Plan 159
Contents of a Business Plan 160
- Cover Page and Table of Contents 160
- Executive Summary 161
- Business Concept 161
- Business Strategy 161
- Management Summary 161
- Marketing Plan 162
- Operations Plan 162
- Financial Plan 162
- Appendix 162

Presenting a Business Plan 163
- Oral and Visual Presentation 164

Why Do Some Business Plans Fail? 164
Procedure for Setting Up an Enterprise 166
- Selection of a Project 166
- Decide on the Constitution 168
- Obtain Registration 168
- Obtain Clearances from Departments as Applicable 168
- Arrange for Land/Shed 168
- Arrange for Plant and Machinery 170
- Arrange for Infrastructure 170
- Prepare Project Report 171
- Apply for and Obtain Finance 172
- Implement the Project and Obtain Final Clearances 172

Summary 173
Key Terms 173
Case Study 174
Discussion Questions 177
Activity 177
Project 177
Endnotes 177
Annexure 178
Business Plan I: Micro, Small, and Medium Enterprises (MSME) Clinic 178
Business Plan II: Fragrance House 191

9 Institutions Supporting Business Enterprises 204

Introduction 205
Central-level Institutions 206
- National Board for Micro, Small, and Medium Enterprises (NBMSME) 206
- The Khadi and Village Industries Commission (KVIC) 207
- The Coir Board 207
- MSME–DO 208
- National Small Industries Corporation (NSIC) 208
- National Science and Technology Entrepreneurship Development Board (NSTEDB) 209
- National Productivity Council (NPC) 209
- Entrepreneurship Development Institute of India (EDI) 210
- National Research Development Corporation of India (NRDCI) 211
- National Entrepreneurship Development Institutes 212

State-level Institutions 215
- State Directorate of Industries and Commerce 215
- District Industries Centres (DIC) 215
- State Financial Corporation (SFC) 216
- State Industrial Development Corporation (SIDC) 216
- State Industrial Area Development Board (SIADB) 216

Other Institutions 217
- National Bank for Agriculture and Rural Development (NABARD) 217
- Housing and Urban Development Corporation (HUDCO) 218
- Technical Consultancy Organization (TCO) 219
- Small Industries Development Bank of India (SIDBI) 220
- Export Promotion Councils (EPCs) 220
- Industry Associations 221
- Non-Governmental Organizations (NGOs) 222
- Business Incubators 223

Summary 226
Key Terms 226
Case Study 227
Discussion Questions 228
Activity 228
Project 228
Endnotes 228

10 Business Organizations and Business Laws 230

Introduction 231
- Sole Proprietorship 231
- Joint Hindu Family Business 232
- Partnership 232
- Limited Liability Partnership (LLP) 233
- Joint Stock Company 234
- Corporate Governance 238
- Cooperative Society 238
- Franchising 239

Business Laws 241
- The Indian Contract Act, 1872 243
- The Sale of Goods Act, 1930 244
- The Indian Partnership Act, 1932 244

The Limited Liability Partnership Act, 2008 245
The Indian Companies Act, 1956 245
The Negotiable Instruments Act, 1881 246
The Information Technology Act, 2000 247
Intellectual Property Rights 249
The Patents Act, 1970 249
The Copyright Act, 1957 249
The Trade Marks Act, 1999 250
The New Designs Act, 2000 251
The Consumer Protection Act, 1986 251
The Right to Information Act, 2005 252
The Competition Act, 2002 252
The Foreign Exchange Management Act (FEMA), 1999 253
Summary 254
Key Terms 254
Case Study 255
Discussion Questions 256
Activity 257
Project 257
Endnotes 258

PART 3: MANAGEMENT OF ENTERPRISES

11 Preventing Sickness in Enterprises 260

Introduction 261
Specific Management Problems 262
Management Deficiency 262
Finance 262
Manufacturing and Technical Problems 262
Product Planning 263
Selection of Equipment, Plant, and Machinery 263
Human Resource Development 263
Technical Know-how 263
Preparation of Project Report 263
Industrial Sickness 263
Definition of Sickness 264
Definition of Sick Enterprises—Micro and Small Enterprises 264
Sick Industrial Companies Act, 1985 265
National Company Law Tribunal (NCLT) 266
National Company Law Appellate Tribunal (NCLAT) 266
Industrial Sickness in India 267
Sickness in Micro, Small, and Medium Enterprises 267
Causes of Industrial Sickness 269
Symptoms of Industrial Sickness 270
Prediction of Sickness 271
Process of Industrial Sickness 272
Normal or Healthy 272
Tending Towards Sickness 273
Incipient Sickness 273
Complete Sickness 273
Rehabilitation of Sick Units 274
Technical Appraisal 274
Commercial Appraisal 274
Management Appraisal 274
Financial Appraisal 275
Turnaround Strategy 275
Winding Up of a Company 276
Exit Strategy 278
Initial Public Offering 278
Summary 279
Key Terms 280
Case Study 281
Discussion Questions 282
Activity 282
Project 282
Endnotes 282

12 Financial Management in Enterprises 284

Introduction 285
Functions of Financial Management 285
Accounting and Bookkeeping 286
Process of Accounting 287
Types of Accounting 288
Generally Accepted Accounting Principles 288
Types of Books of Accounts 288
Financial Statements 289
Balance Sheet 290
Profit and Loss Account 292
Cash Flow Statements 292
Working Capital Management 294
Calculation of Working Capital Cycle 295
Ratio Analysis for Working Capital Management 296
Sources of Working Capital 296
Break-even Analysis 298
Financial Ratio Analysis 299
Liquidity Ratios 300
Activity/Turnover Ratios 300
Debt/Solvency Ratios 301
Profitability Ratios 301
Capital Market Ratios 302
DuPont Analysis 303
Summary 304
Key Terms 305
Case Study 306
Discussion Questions 309
Activity 309
Project 309
Endnotes 310

13 Operations and Human Resource Management in Enterprises 312

Introduction 313
Operations Management 313
Operations Strategy 314
Demand Forecasting 315
Forecasting Models 315
Technology Management 316
Production Management 317
Production Planning and Control (PPC) 317
Work Content and Capacity Determination 318
Supply Chain Management 319

Materials Management 320
Inventory Management 322
Inventory Costs 322
Inventory Control Techniques 322
Benefits of Inventory Control 325
Productivity 325
Total Quality Management 325
Prerequisites for TQM 326
Benefits of TQM 326
Quality Management System (QMS) 327
Maintenance 327
Occupational Health and Safety Advisory Services 330
Benefits of OHSAS 18001 Registration 331
National Safety Council of India (NSCI) 332
Environmental Management System 333
Benefits of Environmental Management System 333
Human Resource Management 334
HRM Policy 335
Functions of HRM 335
Industrial Relations 338
Employee Engagement 339
Labour Laws 340
Indian Factories Act, 1948 341
Payment of Wages Act, 1936 341
Minimum Wages Act, 1948 342
Payment of Bonus Act, 1965 342
Industrial Employment Act, 1946 342
Industrial Disputes Act, 1947 (82 and 84) 343
Trade Unions Act, 1926 344
Child Labour Act, 1986 344
The Equal Remuneration Act, 1976 344
Sexual Harassment of Women at Their Workplace (Prevention) Act, 2003 345
Laws Relating to Environment and Pollution Control 345
Social Security Laws 346
Employees' Provident Fund and Miscellaneous Provisions Act, 1952 347
Payment of Gratuity Act, 1972 347
Maternity Benefit Act, 1961 348
Miscellaneous Legislation 348
Summary 349
Key Terms 349
Case Study 350
Discussion Questions 352
Activity 353
Project 353
Endnotes 353

14 Managing Marketing and Growth in Enterprises 356

Introduction 357
India's Growing Services Sector 357
Common Marketing Problems Faced by Enterprises 358
Differences Between Product and Services Marketing 358
Intangible Nature of the Service Product 359
Trust Aligned with the Product 359
Product Positioning 359
More Contacts Between Customers and Service Personnel 359
Customer Involvement in Production 359
Interactions Among Marketing, Operations, and Human Resources 359
Problems in Controlling Product Quality and Consistency 360
Absence of Inventories 360
Importance of the Time Factor 360
Structure of Distribution Channels 360
Essential Marketing Mix of Services Marketing 360
People 360
Process 361
Physical Evidence 361
Key Success Factors in Services Marketing 361
Marketing Process 362
Market Research 362
Marketing Planning 362
Marketing Mix 364
Implementation and Control 366
Costing and Pricing 366
Cost Ladder 367
Branding 367
New Techniques of Marketing 368
Internet Marketing 368
Direct Marketing 368
Niche Marketing 368
Ambush Marketing 369
Green Marketing 369
Social Marketing 369
Relationship Marketing 370
Viral Marketing 370
Rural Marketing 371
Global Marketing 371
International Trade 373
Tariff Barriers to Trade 373
Non-tariff Barriers to Trade 373
Facilitators 374
International Marketing Environment 375
Export Procedure and Documentation 376
Organizational Life Cycle 378
Growth Strategies 379
Organic Growth 379
Inorganic Growth 380
Essence of Business Ethics and Corporate Social Responsibility 382
Corporate Social Responsibility 384
Social Responsibility Strategies of Enterprises 384
Summary 385
Key Terms 386
Case Study 388
Discussion Questions 389
Activity 389
Project 391
Endnotes 391

Index 393

Foreword

Entrepreneurship is a mandatory subject of study at most business schools in India. It is also a current fad to hold entrepreneurship seminars, summits, and conferences as an extra-curricular activity.

But is entrepreneurship just another subject on the B-school menu—like marketing, finance, or operations? I believe that entrepreneurship is an attitude—a complete philosophy, a manner of thinking, and a way of life. An entrepreneur looks at a problem and wants to solve it in a new and interesting way. He (or she) is a creator in the truest possible sense.

For long, the purpose of attending a B-school has been to become industry-ready and to "fit in" to the requirements of large conglomerates that require young managers. Entrepreneurship, on the other hand, requires one to think out of the box, to take risks, and enter unknown territory both mentally and physically.

It is a paradigm shift that few are prepared for. Yet, I believe that teaching entrepreneurship at B-schools is important. Only a few may take the bold step of starting their own ventures. But the qualities of entrepreneurship—which include passion, purpose, and perseverance—are applicable to every endeavour in life. These qualities will stand the young manager in good stead and potentially create many intrapreneurs.

Dr Poornima Charantimath's book provides a blend of theoretical and practical knowledge that will expose young minds to new thoughts and ideas. I commend the author for undertaking this important work and I am sure it will guide and inspire students everywhere.

Rashmi Bansal
Writer, entrepreneur, and youth expert

From the Academia

Many countries, including India, lost their spirit of entrepreneurship during the long period of colonial rule. Entrepreneurship development did not receive adequate attention for several decades post independence. This is particularly so in the context of educational institutions that provide the transformational energy to individuals to take unexplored career paths. It is only in the past decade or so that we have started experiencing a new wave of enthusiasm to promote entrepreneurship among college students.

While organizations such as the Society of Entrepreneurship Educators (SEE) and the National Entrepreneurship Network (NEN) have done pioneering work in this regard, the need for good quality study materials has not been fully met.

This edition of Dr Poornima M. Charantimath's book, *Entrepreneurship Development and Small Business Enterprises*, is an excellent contribution to fill this void. The mix of conceptual material and case studies will help the readers build entrepreneurial capabilities.

Kavil Ramachandran
Clinical Professor and Associate Dean—Academic Programmes
Thomas Schmidheiny Fellow of Family Business and Wealth Management
Indian School of Business, Hyderabad

From the Industry

I first met Dr Charantimath in a TiE (The Indus Entrepreneurs) event hosted by the Deshpande Foundation in Hubli, Karnataka. I was invited to speak about my journey in founding redBus.in. When I received this invitation, I was happy, motivated, and intrigued. I was happy to learn that entrepreneurship fever has reached Tier II towns in India; motivated to do my bit to contribute to the knowledge of entrepreneurship in Tier II towns; and intrigued thinking about who the audience might be.

I was very pleased to see the diversity in the audience—there were students, academicians, young entrepreneurs, established business persons, government employees, and social-sector volunteers. The variety of questions that were asked during the session made me realise that the audience was very curious and interested in learning about entrepreneurship.

After my presentation, Dr Charantimath approached me, introduced herself as the head of the Centre for Entrepreneurship Development at KLS Institute of Management Education and Research, Belgaum, and congratulated me on my success. The existence of a centre for entrepreneurship development in a college at Belgaum is testimony to the spread of entrepreneurship research and education across the country.

When I returned to Bangalore, I received an e-mail from Dr Charantimath inviting me to her institute. I learnt more about her background in research and her keen interest in entrepreneurship development. After a few months, I had the pleasure of reviewing chapters of the second edition of her book, *Entrepreneurship Development and Small Business Enterprises*.

Dr Charantimath's book is well-researched and focuses on the life cycle of entrepreneurship. This book is ideal for academic teaching of entrepreneurship in India because, unlike other books that are aimed at a Western audience, this book is written in the Indian context with Indian case studies and examples, which will surely help students learn with ease.

Given the enthusiasm I saw in the audience at the TiE event, especially among the students and academicians, I believe that there is significant interest in entrepreneurship education in India. This book has been aptly written to serve this need. I would like to thank all the academicians who are contributing to the emergence of a new India where cutting-edge, innovative enterprises emerge out of graduate institutions.

Phanindra Sama
Founder and CEO
www.redBus.in

Preface

The first edition of *Entrepreneurship Development and Small Business Enterprises* was published in 2006—a time when entrepreneurship development was considered a vehicle to create wealth and jobs in the country. Entrepreneurs now play a key role in driving our economy by enhancing employment opportunities, driving savings and per capita income, and generating additional revenue for the government in the form of taxes and duties. Acknowledging the increasing importance of entrepreneurship development, many business schools now devote greater attention to the subject in their curricula. The second edition of this book has been written in response to the changing requirements of the students and academic fraternity.

FOCUS AND APPROACH

Entrepreneurship Development and Small Business Enterprises (2e) has resulted from the continuous testing of alternative ideas, concepts, and pedagogical design with students of business schools and engineering colleges, entrepreneurs from diverse industries, and research scholars. The book aims to introduce the subject to students and provides a thoughtful, practical guide to the process of successfully launching and growing an entrepreneurial venture. It strives to make learners more excited about the venture creation process.

This book is mainly written for students and instructors of business schools and engineering colleges. It will also be useful for trainers who support entrepreneurship development through seminars and workshops. A student-centric approach has been followed, which will stimulate classroom discussion and idea exchange. A large number of inspirational vignettes and examples have been used to develop employment providers rather than employment seekers.

Another highlight of the book is the discussion of the entrepreneurial scenario and challenges peculiar to India. Students will be able to easily relate to the wealth of examples and guidelines provided in the Breakthrough Entrepreneurship, World of Entrepreneurs, and Checklist for Entrepreneur boxes. The activities and projects provide opportunities for further experiential learning and research.

NEW TO THE SECOND EDITION

The second edition, while retaining the key features of the first edition, builds on it by introducing new material relevant for today's readers to enhance and sharpen their learning. The pedagogy of the book has been expanded to make learning easier and interesting. The highlights are:

- **Coverage:** The book provides a thorough coverage of the conceptual framework of entrepreneurship development, and causal and effectual entrepreneurship.
- **Balanced coverage of the manufacturing and service sectors:** The manufacturing and service sectors have been covered in greater detail by showcasing real-world examples and case studies from Indian and global enterprises.
- **Six new chapters:** The new edition comprises fourteen chapters inclusive of six new chapters—Entrepreneurial Development and Training; Micro, Small, and Medium Enterprises; Identification of Business Opportunities; Project Management and Financing; Business Plans; and Business Organizations and Business Laws.
- **Sixteen new case studies:** Sixteen end-of-chapter case studies drawn from diverse sectors reflect current thinking and practice in the Indian context.
- **Additions to the end-of-chapter exercises:** New activities and projects bring students closer to the real-life applications of the theories discussed in the chapters. The two real-life business

plans added at the end of Chapter 8 give an insight into how business plans can be drafted and funding obtained for the new venture.

- **Comprehensive supplement package:** A complete supplement package comprising an instructors' manual and PowerPoint lecture slides support interactive teaching and learning.

STRUCTURE OF THE BOOK

Entrepreneurship Development and Small Business Enterprises (2e) comprises 14 chapters, which are divided into three parts.

Part 1: Entrepreneurial Perspectives focuses on the conceptual framework of entrepreneurship development. This part consists of five chapters that discuss the basic concepts of entrepreneurship, functions, challenges, training and development, women entrepreneurs, family business, and the importance and role of micro, small, and medium enterprises.

Part 2: New Venture Creation comprises five chapters that focus on the identification of business opportunities, preparation of business plans, project management and financing as well as the legal framework and institutional support for new venture creation.

Part 3: Management of Enterprises includes four chapters that provide an insight into the prevention of industrial sickness, exit strategies, and financial, operations, and human resource management in new enterprises. The chapter on human resource management discusses the importance of industrial relations and gives an overall picture of the labour laws relevant to enterprises. The marketing and growth strategies to be followed throughout the life cycle of a venture are also discussed in detail.

KEY FEATURES

Chapter-opening vignettes introduce the key concepts of a chapter by correlating them to the contribution of an entrepreneur/ enterprise to socioeconomic transformation.

Kiran Mazumdar-Shaw is the founder, chairman, and managing director of India's leading biotechnology enterprise, Biocon Limited. She founded Biocon in 1978 by partnering with an Irish firm to make industrial enzymes. The photograph shows Kiran Mazumdar-Shaw accepting the prestigious Padma Bhushan award from former President A. P. J. Abdul Kalam in 2005.

Breakthrough Entrepreneurship relates chapter concepts to innovative practices and real-world examples from the entrepreneurial arena.

BREAKTHROUGH ENTREPRENEURSHIP 3.2 Harpreet Ahluwalia—Green Entrepreneur

Harpreet Ahluwalia has turned her passion for art and nature into a successful business. Harpreet's entrepreneurial journey began when she ordered a few custom-designed pots for her home in Noida. She decorated her home with potted plants in a way that sent out a message of passion and love. People who came to visit her liked her pottery designs and she began receiving requests for them. Finding herself in business, Harpreet launched her first venture—Earthly Creations Inc.

Harpreet's interaction with the potters who work for her gives her insights into their lives. The interactive nature of Harpreet's venture not only helps her to discover the talent of these economically poor but aesthetically wealthy potters but also helps her to financially support them.

Harpreet has come a long way since the launch of Earthly Creations Inc. She is now a regular participant in over 40 exhibitions across India. Additionally, she is a syndicated columnist with gardening journals and environmental talk shows. She presently runs four businesses successfully: Earthly Creations, Excalibre, Alluring Fantasies, and Healings. Earthly Creations specializes in terracotta garden decorations; Excalibre engages in a range of consulting services, including the coaching and mentoring of executive management teams; Alluring Fantasies deals in artefacts; and Healings focuses on holistic healing. Her message remains "Love animals and gift a piece of nature."

Source: Kumar, Rajen (2010). "Harpreet Ahluwalia's Tryst with Nature: Creating Green Space in Your Life," *SME World*, July, 3 (7): 32–34, available at ww.smeworld.org/story/cover-stories-105/creating-green-space-in-your-life-97.php (last accessed in March 2013). Reproduced with permission.

Checklist for Entrepreneurs provides practical guidelines and to-do lists for entrepreneurship development.

CHECKLIST FOR ENTREPRENEURS 1.3 How to Set SMART Goals

SMART is an acronym for a goal-setting technique that is popular among entrepreneurs because of its simplicity and effectiveness. The acronym stands for "Specific, Measurable, Achievable, Realistic, Timely." Set your goals according to the following set of criteria:

- **Specific:** "Specific" is the what, why, and how of the SMART model. Ensure that your goals are very specific and easy to understand. For example, instead of setting a vague goal, like starting a restaurant, set a more specific goal, like setting up a Chinese fine-dining restaurant.
- **Measurable:** If you can't measure your goal, you can't manage it. Choose a goal with measurable progress, so that you can see the changes occurring. Establish concrete criteria for measuring progress toward the achievement of your goal. You can track your progress on a daily, weekly, monthly, or quarterly basis, or by increases in rupee or percentage of market share. For example, instead of setting a goal to increase the market share of your business by the end of the financial year, set a measurable goal stating that you will increase your market share from 20 to 25 per cent by the end of the financial year.
- **Achievable:** Set the bar high enough for a satisfying achievement but, at the same time, get an understanding of how big this challenge actually is for you. Have you ever done anything like it before? Has anyone else? Yes, there's always someone who's first, and you may be that person, but make sure you know the true difficulty level of the goal you're setting before you get started. When you set a goal, start figuring out ways to achieve that goal. You need to develop knowledge, attitude, skills, and financial capability to reach them.
- **Realistic:** The goal set by you should be realistic and should yield results.
- **Timely:** Set a time frame for the goal. If you don't set a time frame, the commitment is too vague and it gives you the opportunity to procrastinate. For example, instead of setting a goal simply to start a venture, set a specific goal stating that you will be starting your venture by, say, January 2014.

Source: www.goal-setting-guide.com (last accessed in March 2013). Reproduced with permission.

World of Entrepreneurs discusses the latest developments and interesting stories relating to entrepreneurship development.

WORLD OF ENTREPRENEURS 13.6 Employees First, Customers Second

Employees First, Customers Second is a bestselling business book written by Vineet Nayar, the CEO of HCL Technologies. In the book published in 2010, Nayar describes his revolutionary philosophy of configuring and managing an enterprise by focusing on its value creators (frontline employees) to achieve remarkable growth and profits.

HCL Technologies Ltd (HCLT) is one of India's fastest-growing global information technology services companies. Vineet Nayar joined HCL in 1985 and became the CEO in 2007. He led a remarkable turnaround in the company over the next five years.

The book discusses Nayar's experiences leading HCL Technologies, and its turnaround from a $70 crore company that was losing market share to a $200 crore company at the forefront of its business. Nayar provides a clear and frank discussion of the issues he faced, his personal thought processes, and his learning journey during the transformation. The main factor behind the turnaround was Nayar's belief that employees are the biggest assets of an organization. Therefore, companies should strive for both employee satisfaction as well as customer satisfaction.

Nayar recognized that the asset base of an organization is increasingly coming to reside in the talent and creativity of its employees. He provides a new configuration of approaches putting employees first to create a new style of organization. He provides tried and tested tools that are helpful for understanding what you can do to change your enterprise. The main tools included in the book are value zone, mirror/mirror, transparent zone, zero tickets, and true 360-degree evaluation and feedback.

HCL Technologies has been recognized around the world for its innovative and transformative management practices. In 2009, HCLT was named the best employer in India and one of the top twenty-five best employers in Asia by Hewitt Associates. *BusinessWeek* has also listed HCLT as one of the five emerging companies in the world to watch out for.

Source: Nayar, Vineet (2010). *Employees First, Customers Second: Turning Conventional Management Upside Down*. Boston, Massachusetts: HBP.

The **summary** recapitulates the main points discussed in the chapter.

SUMMARY

A woman entrepreneur may be defined as a confident, innovative, and creative woman capable of achieving economic independence individually or in collaboration, generating employment opportunities for others through initiating, establishing, and running the enterprise by keeping pace with her personal, family, and social life. Women's entrepreneurship helps to reduce poverty, promote gender equality, and empower women. Some factors that contribute to women becoming entrepreneurs are the desire for economic independence, availability of technology, a desire for the establishment of an identity, and the achievement of excellence. Some common traits of successful women entrepreneurs are ambition, confidence, transparency, willingness to learn, financial acumen, teamwork, loyalty, and a sense of social responsibility.

The overall context of women's entrepreneurship can be described in three different spheres: microsphere, mesosphere, and macrosphere. The challenges in the path of women's entrepreneurship are an initial lack of confidence due to sociocultural barriers, market-oriented risks, poor knowledge of business administration, lack of awareness about possible sources of financial assistance, and lack of exposure to training programmes. There are many organizations in India supporting women entrepreneurs, and almost all public-sector banks have special loan schemes for women entrepreneurs. There are inspirational examples of successful women entrepreneurs in India and abroad. A special mention may be made of Shri Mahila Griha Udyog Lijjat Papad (SMGULP), a unique and successful cooperatively-managed organization and a symbol of the progress of women in developing countries like India.

A **case study** at the end of each chapter enables readers to apply their learning from the chapter to real-life problems and situations.

CASE STUDY

Shahnaz Husain

I do not sell products. I sell an entire civilization in a jar.

—*Shahnaz Husain*

Shahnaz Husain, CEO of Shahnaz Husain Group, is a successful Indian woman entrepreneur, best known for her herbal cosmetics and for her pioneering role and leadership in promoting the herbal care industry in India. The Shahnaz Husain Group, based in New Delhi, is one of the largest manufacturers of herbal products in the world, creating and marketing over 350 products for various beauty and health needs worldwide.

Shahnaz Husain belongs to a royal Muslim family, which originally came from Samarkhand, Pakistan. Her family members held high positions in the princely kingdoms of Bhopal and Hyderabad in the pre-Independence days. During her childhood, Shahnaz had the privilege of receiving a modern education, which groomed her into a well-rounded personality. Shahnaz did her schooling from an Irish convent and her father Chief Justice N. U. Beg instilled in her a love of poetry and English literature. Married at 15, she became a mother by the time she was 16.

When Shahnaz's husband was posted to Tehran, Iran, Shahnaz accompanied him. During her stay in Tehran, she developed a keen interest in beauty treatments and decided to study cosmetology. To support the expenses of the cosmetology course, she wrote articles for the *Iran Tribune* on various topics. While pursuing her studies, she learned that chemical cosmetics harmed the human system as well as the environment in the long run. This turned her attention to Ayurveda, which she believed was the best alternative to chemical cosmetics.

After leaving Tehran, she trained extensively in cosmetic therapy for a period of 10 years from some of the leading institutes in Paris, London, New York, and Copenhagen. On completion of her training in 1977, she returned to India. In the same year, she set up her first beauty salon at her house in Delhi with an initial investment of ₹35,000. In contrast to other salons offering chemical cosmetics, she made use of Ayurvedic products with natural formulations that could be safely used on the human body. By doing this, she ushered in an era of herbal cosmetics and herbal therapy. On setting up her first salon in New Delhi, she had put up a banner with her qualifications on it. Within days, she was booked six months ahead. She says, "I removed the banner and since then I have never advertised. I have let my products speak for themselves."

The features **Activity** and **Project** enable students to broaden their knowledge of the subject through practical application.

ACTIVITY

1. Study the Fourth All-India Census on MSME and prepare a brief report containing the summary of the results and prepare a PowerPoint presentation for the class (20 minutes).

PROJECT

1. Conduct a SWOT analysis of MSME in India and prepare a brief report.
2. Your instructor will divide the class into small groups consisting of four to six members. Each group will visit a nearby micro/small/medium enterprise, study the problems of the enterprise, and under the supervision of their instructors, prepare a 15 minute PowerPoint presentation on the problems faced by the enterprise. Each group will then make their presentation in front of a panel consisting of three instructors. After all the presentations are over, the panel will announce the winning group and the first and second runners-up.

THE TEACHING AND LEARNING PACKAGE

The teaching and learning package includes an instructors' manual and PowerPoint lecture slides, which can be downloaded from the book's companion Web site, www.pearsoned.co.in/poornimam-charantimath.

- **Instructors' Manual:** The instructors' manual provides an analysis of all the case studies as well as the answers to the chapter-ending exercises.
- **PowerPoint Slides:** PowerPoint lecture slides designed for each chapter provide an overview of the important concepts discussed in the chapter.

ACKNOWLEDGEMENTS

I thank all those who have helped, encouraged, and supported me all through the project. I am grateful to Rashmi Bansal, writer and entrepreneur, for agreeing to write the Foreword. I thank Kavil Ramachandran, Clinical Professor and Thomas Schmidheiny Fellow of Family Business and Wealth Management at the Indian School of Business, Hyderabad, and Phanindra Sama, founder and CEO, redBus.in, for enriching the book with their perspectives on entrepreneurship.

I thank all the members of the Board of Management, Karnataka Law Society, Belgaum, for their support and encouragement. The working environment provided at my institution, the Institute of Management Education and Research (IMER), greatly facilitated my work on this book. My students at IMER have always been a source of motivation. I would like to thank all the authors quoted here whose research and ideas have enriched this book. I am indebted to many entrepreneurs for their valuable comments.

My husband Manoj N. Charantimath, son Amit, and daughter-in-law Chandana have been pillars of support and have been very accommodating of my odd routines.

My thanks are also due to my publisher Pearson Education, the editorial team, and all the reviewers of the book for their constructive suggestions. I acknowledge the efforts of Subhasree Patra, Priya Christopher, A. Maran, Pradeep Kumar Bhattacharjee, and M. R. Ramesh who worked hard to give this book its present form. Readers may please e-mail their feedback and suggestions to drcharantimath@klsimer.edu.

Poornima M. Charantimath

Entrepreneurial Perspectives

1. **Entrepreneurship**
2. Entrepreneurial Development and Training
3. Women Entrepreneurs
4. Family Business
5. Micro, Small, and Medium Enterprises

Part 1

"I keep revising my vision. Only when you can dream it, you can do it."

—Dhirubhai Ambani

Dhirubhai Ambani founded the Reliance Group—India's largest private-sector enterprise and the first Indian company to feature in the Fortune *500 list. He is remembered as someone who rewrote Indian corporate history and built a truly global corporate group. He is often credited with creating an equity cult in the Indian capital market. He gave few public speeches, but the words he spoke are still remembered for their value. Ambani once famously said, "I am deaf to the word 'no'."*

Entrepreneurship

1

LEARNING OBJECTIVES

Upon completion of this chapter, you should be able to:

1. Understand the role and importance of the entrepreneur in economic development.
2. Introduce the evolution and concepts of entrepreneurship.
3. Identify the various types of entrepreneurs and their functions.
4. Recognize entrepreneurial competencies.
5. Explain the myths of entrepreneurship.
6. Identify the factors required for capacity building for entrepreneurs.

INTRODUCTION

Historically, entrepreneurs have altered the direction of national economies, industries, and markets. In addition to increasing national income through job creation, entrepreneurship has always served as a bridge between innovation and the marketplace. Many innovations have altered our pattern of living, and many services have been introduced to alter or create new service industries such as commercial banking, medical treatment, logistics, information systems, and insurance. Let us look at some ways in which entrepreneurs can participate in the development of an economy.

1. **Contribution to GNP and per capita income:** Entrepreneurship contributes to economic stability by introducing new products and services in the market and encouraging effective resource mobilization. This helps in increasing the gross national product as well as per capita income of the people in the country. Economic stability leads to increased institutional investment for productive activities and is a sign of economic growth.
2. **Employment generation:** The government is limited in its ability to create employment opportunities for the country's population. Entrepreneurs play an effective role in reducing the problems of unemployment in the country. Entrepreneurs are not only self-employed but also provide employment to others. Entrepreneurial activities lead to other activities, generating a multiplier effect in the economy. For example, when the information technology boom occurred in India, it led to several successful entrepreneurial ventures. This provided employment to many and also led to the launch of a number of engineering colleges, development of real-estate and hospitality ventures, and infrastructural facilities. Such developments, in their turn, encourage further entrepreneurship.

3. **Balanced regional development:** The development of enterprises in less-developed regions promotes balanced regional development in the country. In addition, entrepreneurship stimulates the distribution of wealth and income to more and more individuals (such as stakeholders) and geographical areas, thus benefiting larger sections of society.
4. **Promotion of export and trade:** Entrepreneurship promotes the country's export trade and earns foreign exchange. When required, this earning can help combat the country's import dues requirements. International trade brings economic strength and techno-economic reliance.
5. **Improvement in the standard of living:** Entrepreneurs bring a wide variety of products and services into the market. This increases competition in the market and makes it possible for people to avail of a better quality of products and services at lower and more competitive prices, resulting in an improvement of the country's overall standard of living.
6. **Increased innovation:** With the liberalization of the Indian economy, the increased competition in the domestic and international market has encouraged entrepreneurs to be more creative.
7. **Overall development of the economy:** Entrepreneurs create new technologies, products, processes, and services that become the next wave of new industries, and these in turn drive the economy. Entrepreneurs are change agents in society. They create wealth and value, and generate employment in society. This naturally leads to social and economic growth.

The Nobel Prize Committee has played its own role in the recognition of entrepreneurship.[1] The work of two economists, Dr Edmund S. Phelps from the United States and Dr Muhammad Yunus from Bangladesh (also the founder of Grameen Bank), who received the Nobel Memorial Prize in Economic Sciences (2006), makes a case for entrepreneurship. One of Phelps' main arguments is that the creativity of entrepreneurs serves to transform the work environment in firms developing an innovation as also in those dealing with the innovation.[2]

Unsurprisingly, every *Fortune* 500 enterprise in existence is the result of an entrepreneur's resourcefulness and perseverance. According to Karl Vesper, a leading chronicler of entrepreneurship research, entrepreneurs are viewed by those who favour market economy as the pillars of industrial strength—the movers and shakers who constructively disrupt the status quo. *Forbes* comes out with a list of the world's and India's richest persons every year. Prior to the 1970s, this list used to be dominated by monarchs and heirs of family fortunes built up over years. Today, many of the world's richest, like Bill Gates and Bernard Arnault, are entrepreneurs.

EVOLUTION OF THE CONCEPT OF ENTREPRENEURSHIP

How an entrepreneur is perceived and defined by society has changed several times over the last few centuries. The word entrepreneur originally stems from French and, literally translated, means someone who undertakes a difficult task. An early example of an entrepreneur is Marco Polo, who attempted to establish trade routes from Venice to the Far East. In Europe, during the Middle Ages, the term entrepreneur was used to describe both an actor and a person who managed large production projects, such as someone in charge of great architectural works, such as castles and fortifications, public buildings, abbeys, and cathedrals. Later, in seventeenth-century Europe, an entrepreneur began to be regarded as a person bearing risks of profit or loss in a fixed contract with the government.

Richard Cantillon

Richard Cantillon, a noted Irish–French economist, developed one of the early theories of entrepreneurship. He authored *Essai sur la Nature du Commerce en Général* (*Essay on the Nature of Trade in General*) around 1730 and is regarded by some as the founder of the term "entrepreneur" in its modern sense.[3] In this book, he argued that entrepreneurs made conscious decisions about resource allocations, seeking higher yields for their money and other investments. Cantillon divided society into two major classes—fixed income earners and non-fixed income earners. He viewed entrepreneurs as non-fixed income earners with known costs of production but uncertain incomes (as they must depend on the market and the demand for their products), and therefore operating at a risk.

Adam Smith

In 1776, Adam Smith published *An Inquiry into the Nature and Causes of the Wealth of Nations*, where he stated that an entrepreneur has all the knowledge necessary to become a great merchant, and is hindered from becoming one only by insufficient capital. Adam Smith argued that in order to create an effective capitalist system, individuals must pursue both selfish and social interests. He introduced the concepts of liberal and entrepreneurial capitalism.

Jean-Baptiste Say

Jean-Baptiste Say (born in 1767) believed that entrepreneurs behaved with exceptional insight to fulfil society's needs through the process of taking risks. Say defined an entrepreneur as a person able to recognize opportunities and manage them effectively. He also differentiated the person bearing risk—the entrepreneur—from the one supplying the capital—the venture capitalist. Inventors like Thomas Edison and Eli Whitney developed new technologies for commercial use but were unable to finance their projects themselves. So, as entrepreneurs they used capital provided by venture capitalists. A venture capitalist was viewed as a professional money manager who made investments from a pool of equity in order to obtain a high rate of return on the investment.

Francis Walker

Francis Walker, in *The Wages Question: A Treatise on Wages and the Wages Class*, published in 1876, distinguished between those who supplied funds and received interest, and entrepreneurs, i.e. those who made a profit through managerial capabilities. He defined an entrepreneur as one who is endowed with more than average capacity to organize and coordinate factors of production like land, labour, capital, and enterprise. According to him, an entrepreneur is a pioneer, a leader, and a captain of the firm. Hence, any profit that the firm makes depends on his efficiency and superior talent.

Joseph Schumpeter

In the late-nineteenth and early-twentieth century, entrepreneurs were frequently not distinguished from managers and were viewed mostly from an economic perspective. In the middle of the 20th century the notion of *an entrepreneur as an innovator*, an individual developing something unique, was established. Joseph Schumpeter (1883–1950) in his work *The Theory of Economic Development* extended the concept of entrepreneurship to include the importance of innovation. In his words, "the function of entrepreneurs is to reform or revolutionize the pattern of production by exploiting an invention or, more generally, an untried technological possibility for producing a new commodity or producing an old one in a new way, by opening up a new source of supply of materials or a new outlet for products, by reorganizing an industry and so on. This [entrepreneurial] function does not essentially consist in inventing anything or otherwise creating the conditions which the enterprise exploits. It consists in getting the job done."[4] The Schumpeterian view of an entrepreneur is that of an innovator playing the role of a dynamic businessman, often adding material growth to economic development.

ENTREPRENEURSHIP TODAY

The scope of what entrepreneurship involves will continue to change and evolve with global economic, social, and political changes. Although there have been a number of generally acceptable definitions, most of which vary in focus and scope, there is no official definition of entrepreneurship. However, increased academic interest in entrepreneurship is bringing a sharper focus to bear upon the subject.

Who Is an Entrepreneur?

The word "entrepreneur" is derived from the French verb *enterprendre* ("to undertake"). The word was originally used to describe people who "take on the risk" between buyers and sellers or who "undertake" a task such as starting a venture.[5] The fifth edition of the Oxford Advanced Learner's Dictionary defines an entrepreneur as a person who starts or organizes a commercial enterprise, especially one involving financial risk. The process of creation of a business enterprise is called entrepreneurship.

The twentieth century saw a predominance of the personal perspective in the conceptualization of entrepreneurship. In his book *The Entrepreneurial Mind*, Jeffry Timmons defined entrepreneurship as "the ability to create and build something from practically nothing."[6] His definition captures the idea that entrepreneurs are like magicians, creating thriving organizations out of good ideas, hard work, business dealing, and personal skills. Timmons's words hint at the myths inherent in the common understanding of entrepreneurship. Entrepreneurship is the dynamic process of creating incremental wealth. The wealth is created by individuals who assume the major risks in terms of equity, time, and/or career commitment or provide value for some product or service. The product or service may or may not be new or unique but value must somehow be infused by the entrepreneur through receiving and locating the necessary skills and resources.[7]

How Do I Become an Entrepreneur?

The road to becoming an entrepreneur comprises the following steps:

Step 1: Generating business ideas and identifying business opportunities—Business opportunities must first be identified through an evaluation of business ideas. A business opportunity is a favourable set of circumstances that creates a need for a new product, service, or business. Business ideas may be generated in the following ways:

- **Observing trends:** Social and economic trends, technological developments, and political and regulatory changes often create opportunities for entrepreneurship. For example, a social trend like more women entering paid employment creates the need for more child care centres.
- **Finding gaps in the market:** A lack of a product or service in the market is a barely-disguised opportunity for entrepreneurs.

You will learn more about the identification of business opportunities in Chapter 6. Once a business opportunity is identified, the entrepreneur must conduct a feasibility analysis.

Step 2: Conducting a feasibility analysis—A feasibility analysis is the process of determining the validity of a business idea. The important facets of a feasibility analysis are market analysis, technical analysis, financial analysis, economic analysis, and ecological analysis. If the proposed business is found to be feasible after the conduct of a feasibility study, then a business plan is sketched out.

Step 3: Making a business plan—A business plan is a written document, typically 20–30 pages in length, which describes what a venture intends to accomplish and how it plans to achieve its goals. It serves a dual purpose both inside and outside the firm. Inside the firm, it enables the company to develop a roadmap to follow in executing its strategies. Outside the firm, it introduces potential investors and other stakeholders to the business opportunity and how it is pursued. It also provides the business model of the firm.

Step 4: Arranging funds—Once a project is selected, the two most common sources of funding for a venture are equity and debt financing. Equity financing means exchanging ownership in a firm for funding. The various forms of equity financing are angel investing, venture capital, private equity, personal savings, and investments from family and friends. In debt financing, money is borrowed to run a business. The various forms of debt financing are: funding through bank loans, financial institutions, and credit cards.

Step 5: Setting up an enterprise and building a venture team—To set up an enterprise, building a new venture team is very important. A venture team, also called promoters of the venture, is made up of the people who will transform an idea of a venture into a fully functioning firm. While setting up an enterprise, it is important to ensure the following things:

- **Smooth management of the enterprise:** The different facets of managing an enterprise comprises managing, finance, strategy, markets, operations, technology, and human resources.
- **Nurturing growth:** Once the business is set up and sustainability is assured, the entrepreneur should look at growing the business organically or inorganically. Organic growth is achieved through internally-driven strategies that rely on efforts generated within the firm itself, such as new product development, internal expansion, and diversification. Inorganic growth is the result of external growth strategies and relies on establishing relationships with third parties, such as licensing, mergers, strategic alliances, joint ventures, and franchising.
- **Exit strategies:** An exit strategy involves planning for the termination of one's ownership of a company. There are several reasons for an entrepreneur to want to exit his venture. It is wise to think of an exit strategy while setting up the enterprise itself. In case an entrepreneur wants to close the existing business and start a new business, he has to wind up the existing business. In case he wants to retire, he should have a succession plan in place.

Advantages of Being an Entrepreneur

There are many advantages of being an entrepreneur. Some of them are listed below:

- An entrepreneur is an independent person who makes his/her own decisions and acts on them.
- An entrepreneur has enough scope for innovation.
- An entrepreneur often has the opportunity of realizing dreams .and achieving excellence while simultaneously contributing to the welfare of society.
- An entrepreneur usually has immense job satisfaction.
- An entrepreneur can bring about the socioeconomic transformation of a region by generating employment for others and creating wealth.
- An entrepreneur can make a significant contribution to the development of the country.

TYPES OF ENTREPRENEURS

Innovation is one of the most important characteristics of an entrepreneur. Entrepreneurs may be classified on the basis of functional characteristics, personality types or schools of thought. Based on nine personality types, entrepreneurs may be classified as the improver, the advisor, the superstar, the artist, the visionary, the analyst, the fireball, the hero, and the healer.[8] Again, based on schools of thought on entrepreneurship, we can classify entrepreneurs as belonging to the "great person" school of entrepreneurship (focusing on intuitive ability, vigour, good instincts, etc.), the psychological characteristics school of entrepreneurship, the classical school of entrepreneurship (focusing on the innovative streak in entrepreneurs), the management school of entrepreneurship (focusing on the idea of creating entrepreneurs by training them to be good managers), the leadership school of entrepreneurship (focusing on leadership qualities of entrepreneurs), and the intrapreneurship school of entrepreneurship (focusing on developing entrepreneurial traits in managers in an organization).[9] Let us look at how entrepreneurs may be classified according to functional characteristics:

- **Innovative entrepreneur:** Innovative entrepreneurs are innovative in their approach to business and introduce new products, new production methods, or discover new markets or new forms of organization in their enterprise.

- **Imitative or adoptive entrepreneur:** Entrepreneurs belonging to this category imitate products, production methods, and new forms of organization in their enterprise. This category of entrepreneurs can be found especially in developing and underdeveloped countries, partly due to a lack of investment in research and development.
- **Fabian entrepreneur:** Fabian entrepreneurs are not proactive in nature and do not respond very much to changes in the environment. Instead, they change only when there is a threat to the existence of their enterprise.
- **Drone entrepreneur:** Drone entrepreneurs are conservative and complacent in nature and like to maintain the status quo. These entrepreneurs may incur losses and have to close down their enterprises.

SNAPSHOT

- An entrepreneur is a person who creates an enterprise. The process of creation is called entrepreneurship.
- The word "entrepreneur" is derived from the French verb *enterprendre,* meaning "to undertake."

INTRAPRENEURSHIP

Intrapreneurship, or corporate entrepreneurship, is the process by which teams within an established company conceive, foster, launch, and manage a new business that is distinct from the parent company but leverages the parent's assets, capabilities, market position, and other resources. Intrapreneurs are employees within an organization who use their entrepreneurial spirit to introduce new products, new processes, new methods, and new forms within the corporation.[10] Intrapreneurship describes the innovation that occurs inside established companies through the efforts of creative employees. For example, Arthur Fry, an employee of 3M, invented Post-it® note pads, which turned out to be a very profitable product for 3M. The company's policies and work environment have fostered intrapreneurship, resulting in a win–win strategy for both 3M and its employees.

In 2001, with global economic recession, Wipro Technologies initiated a unique programme. Instead of laying off their IT professionals, who were not being assigned to projects due to decrease in number of projects from clients, the company invited employees to develop business ideas and submit proposals in various technology domains either individually or in a team. A committee of cross-functional teams from various functions such as technology, finance, marketing, and operations was formed. The proposals submitted by employees were scrutinized for feasibility. The selected proposals were initiated based on mutually-decided timelines and profit sharing. Employees were also trained in the area of Intellectual Property Rights, encouraged, and guided to file patents under joint ownership with the company. This programme enabled Wipro to tap the entrepreneurial potential of its employees and to use the vast pool of its trained technical talent by intrapreneurship.

Intrapreneurship is a top-down approach, wherein the top management plays the role of a facilitator and empowers employees to effectively utilize resources and try out new ideas. The top management must devise and put in place a system that would unleash employees' potential and build a reward and recognition mechanism for them. Table 1.1 lays out the differences between entrepreneurs and intrapreneurs.

Difference Between a Manager and an Entrepreneur

It has become clear in recent years that the ideal manager will be one who will know how to combine certain traits of the professional manager, such as order and discipline, with entrepreneurial

Table 1.1 Entrepreneur Versus Intrapreneur

Criteria	Entrepreneur	Intrapreneur
Dependency	Independent in his operations	Dependent on the entrepreneur/owner
Fund raising	Raises funds required for the enterprise	Funds are not raised
Risk taking	Fully bears the risk involved in the business	Does not fully bear the risk involved in the business
Operation	Operates from outside	Operates within the organization
Primary motive	Goal-oriented, self-reliant, and self-motivated	Access to corporate resources and also responds to corporate rewards and recognition

characteristics, such as quick reaction to business opportunities, creativity, and the ability to fill employees with a sense of vision and challenge. Entrepreneurship is really more than just business start-ups and high-growth small businesses. Big companies look for people with an entrepreneurial mindset.

The role of an entrepreneur is different from the role of a manager. The most exciting part of entrepreneurship is being one's own boss. Let us look at the differences between a manager and an entrepreneur:

- The entrepreneur starts a venture and is the owner of the enterprise, whereas the manager is an employee in an enterprise.
- The entrepreneur starts an enterprise and creates wealth and generates profit. The manager receives a salary for the services rendered to the enterprise.
- An entrepreneur is an employer whereas a manager is an employee.
- An entrepreneur is a job provider whereas a manager is a job seeker.
- An entrepreneur assumes more risk and uncertainty than a manager does.
- Entrepreneurs take mainly strategic decisions, whereas managers take operational decisions.

WORLD OF ENTREPRENEURS 1.1 B-schools Nurture Students for Entrepreneurship

Entrepreneurship is becoming a popular career choice among the youth. As a result, we see a growing number of curricular innovations in the syllabi of many business schools as they make "entrepreneurship education" a part of their curriculum. Earlier, mainly senior managers would undertake an MBA course to climb up the corporate ladder.

Harvard Business School graduates become entrepreneurs by the time they are 15 years out of school, and London Business School's full-time MBA programme includes six entrepreneurship electives. In India, entrepreneurship education is gradually picking up. The not-for-profit organization National Entrepreneurship Network (NEN) was launched in 2003 by the Wadhwani Foundation, and cofounded by IIT Bombay, IIM Ahmedabad, BITS Pilani, S.P. Jain Institute of Management and Research, Mumbai, and the Institute of Bioinformatics and Applied Biotechnology, Bangalore. NEN is a catalyst for entrepreneurial activity across India.

IIM Ahmedabad believes that entrepreneurship education seeks to provide students with the knowledge, attitude, and skills required to encourage entrepreneurial success, and lays down conditions and solutions to the challenges that one might foresee in a venture. The N. S. Raghavan Centre for Entrepreneurial Learning (NSRCEL), established through a generous endowment from N. S. Raghavan at IIM Bangalore, is also a catalyst for entrepreneurial activity.

DISCUSSION FORUM

- Discuss with examples how entrepreneurs can bring about socioeconomic transformation in a region.
- Distinguish between (a) entrepreneur and intrapreneur; (b) entrepreneur and manager.
- Name the various types of entrepreneurs.

ENTREPRENEURIAL COMPETENCIES

The term entrepreneurial competencies refers to the key characteristics that should be possessed by successful entrepreneurs in order to perform entrepreneurial functions effectively. Entrepreneurs are often unique people. They often see things that others fail to notice. They endeavour to bring about change and foster growth. They believe in themselves. Entrepreneurship drives them to move forward and reach where they want to be. Entrepreneurs are men and women of all sizes, ages, shapes, religions, colours, and backgrounds. However, most successful entrepreneurs do share the competencies given below:

- **Creativity and innovation:** Creativity is the ability to develop new ideas and to discover new ways of looking at problems and opportunities; *thinking* new things. On the other hand, innovation is the application of creative solutions to problems or opportunities to enhance or to enrich people's lives, or *doing* new things. A person may therefore conceive of something new and envision how it will be useful, but not necessarily take the necessary action to make it a reality. Drucker[11] thus describes the entrepreneur as an innovator.

  Ideas usually evolve through a creative process whereby imaginative people bring them into existence, nurture them, and develop them successfully. The creative process for an idea involves five stages—germination, preparation, incubation, illumination, and verification.

- **Leadership and team building:** Leadership is the basic quality of an entrepreneur. This spirit keeps him paces forward in any field. The quality of leadership should be demonstrated in networking and problem-solving ability, generating resources, and building teams. Good business leaders are great visionaries. They create a vision for the company, share the vision passionately, own a vision, and relentlessly drive it towards completion.

  An entrepreneur should have an ability to build a team. A team is a group of individuals with a common mission, focused and aligned to achieve a specific task or set of outcomes. A good team will be able to share knowledge, core competency, and goals. With mutual trust in place, collaborative work breeds the organizational climate needed for developing a perfect team. Collaboration and consensus bring about a synergetic effect in the enterprise.

- **Opportunity seeking and initiative:** Entrepreneurs can pursue opportunities in any industry at any time. For example, some entrepreneurs build successful new companies by contributing to the founding of a new industry, such as Robert Swanson, who co-founded the biotechnology giant Genentech Inc. and became a pioneering entrepreneur in the field of biotechnology. Other entrepreneurs build new companies in old and mature industries, such as Sam Walton who founded Walmart, did in the field of retailing. Let us take the example of Captain Gopinath, whose first venture was in the field of sericulture but who soon identified an opportunity in the airline business. Later, Captain Gopinath launched a cargo airline and managed to rope in Reliance Industries as an investor into his express cargo business. In short, he is constantly identifying new opportunities across various industries.

  Along with being able to identify business opportunities, an entrepreneur needs to have the urge to take initiatives. The initiative to start a business can't be enough—entrepreneurs

BREAKTHROUGH ENTREPRENEURSHIP 1.2 National Innovation Foundation

The National Innovation Foundation (NIF) was set up in March 2000, by the Department of Science and Technology (DST), Government of India, under the chairmanship of Dr R. A. Mashelkar, Director General, Council for Scientific and Industrial Research and Secretary, Department of Scientific and Industrial Research, Government of India. Professor Anil K. Gupta, President, Society for Research and Initiatives for Sustainable Technologies and Institutions (SRISTI), Founder of Honey Bee Network and Professor, Indian Institute of Management Ahmedabad, is the Executive Vice Chairperson of NIF. It is an autonomous society based in Ahmedabad, Gujarat, India.

The mission of NIF is to make India an innovative global leader in sustainable technologies without social and economic handicaps affecting the evolution and diffusion of green grassroots innovations. The objective is to provide a platform to those in Indian society who have solved a technological problem without any help from external agencies. Grassroots technological innovations by definition are need-based, simple, cost-effective and sustainable. The experience of NIF shows that many grassroots innovations happen without any or with very limited external assistance. These innovations address the key needs of grassroots consumers, which have not been met by existing products and services. There is a need to build a value chain around these innovations and to provide incubation support, if the benefits from these innovations have to be disseminated to a large chunk of consumers. NIF is pursuing, scouting, documenting, spawning, augmenting, adding value, protecting intellectual property rights, and disseminating on commercial as well as non-commercial basis.

The Honey Bee database of 10,000 innovations, collected and documented by SRISTI, would be part of the national register of innovations to be managed and supported by NIF. Grassroots Innovations Augmentation Network (GIAN) scales up innovation, from the Honey Bee database of innovations, through value additions in innovations to sustain creativity and the ethics of experimentation. GIAN was conceived at the International Conference on Creativity and Innovation at Grassroots (ICCIG), jointly organized by IIM Ahmedabad and SRISTI. IGNITE, an innovative idea competition, has been initiated by NIF for promoting creativity and innovation among school children. The best ideas in the competition are awarded.

The primary objectives of NIF are to create an entrepreneurial society in India by providing institutional support for scouting, spawning, and sustaining grassroots innovations through the application of information technology in time-bound programmes to bring about a socioeconomic transformation of society. NIF is developing an innovation park for potential grassroots innovators to convert the best ideas into actual projects.

Source: www.nif.org.in (last accessed in March 2013).

must have the initiative to continue to grow and expand not only the business but their own minds.

- **Risk-taking and decision-making ability:** Great business ideas have sometimes started as a hunch that enterprising individuals have acted upon. There is always the risk of loss in any endeavour, and entrepreneurs have just the right amount of confidence to take calculated risks to achieve their objective. However, an entrepreneur's risk-taking does not depend on luck, but on sheer effort and hard work.

  An entrepreneur performs the function of calculated risk-bearing. Risk-bearing and decision-making call for absolute clarity of thought and action. The focus should always be on the market. The progress of an entrepreneur depends increasingly on effective knowledge and continuous updating of market conditions and the proper utilization of resources. A good entrepreneur should avoid excessively high as well as low risk situations. Low-risk investment often provides a return not exceeding 10 per cent, moderate risk of 20 per cent and a high risk up to 100 per cent. It is left to individual entrepreneurs to choose the degree of risk they would like to or can afford to take.

  It is generally difficult to assess risk factors in the small-scale sector. Most business failures appear to occur within five years of founding. A long history of gradually shrinking sales and profits needs careful consideration.

- **Tolerance of ambiguity and uncertainty:** Schere argued that a tolerance of ambiguity is an important characteristic for entrepreneurs because the challenges and potential for success associated with business start-ups are by nature unpredictable.[12] Budner defined an ambiguous situation as "one which cannot be adequately structured or categorized by an individual because of the lack of sufficient clues."[13] Tolerance of ambiguity is the ability to respond positively to ambiguous situations, and this is an important quality for entrepreneurs to have because they continually face more uncertainty in their everyday environment than do managers of established organizations.

  Apart from being tolerant of ambiguity and uncertainty, entrepreneurs also need to be comfortable with conflict. Start-up entrepreneurs usually do not receive revenue in the beginning. To make matter worse, lack of customers is a common feature. For an entrepreneur of a start-up company, change is the way of life. New customers, co-workers, and staff add to the stress of everyday life. Setbacks and surprises are inevitable, with hardly enough time to respond to situations. Successful entrepreneurs maximize the effect of good "high performance" results and minimize the stress of exhaustion and frustration.

- **Motivation to excel:** Entrepreneurs are motivated primarily by the desire to create something new, the desire for autonomy, wealth and financial independence, the achievement of personal objectives, and the propensity for action ("doing"). The excitement and the thrill of starting a new venture is another major motivator. Importantly, most entrepreneurs stress that the objective was never money for its own sake. They wanted to leave a legacy in the form of a profitable long-lasting business.

  Within the research domain of characterizing a successful entrepreneur, the concept of need for achievement (nAch) has received much attention. McClelland[14] argued that individuals who are high in nAch are more likely than those who are low in nAch to engage in activities or tasks that have a high degree of individual responsibility for outcomes, require individual skill and effort, have a moderate degree of risk, and include clear feedback on performance.

- **Problem solving:** Successful entrepreneurs are *problem solvers*. A formal problem-solving model helps entrepreneurs solve problems in a logical manner. The model consists of six steps:

  1. Define the problem.
  2. Gather information.
  3. Identify various solutions.
  4. Evaluate alternatives and select the best option.
  5. Take action.
  6. Evaluate the action taken.

- **Goal orientation:** Goal setting is the process of setting both long-term and short-term objectives for the successful performance of an entrepreneur. A clear set of goals helps to measure the performance standards of employees. In addition, everyone needs to feel that they have a worthwhile goal to reach with the resources and leadership available. Without goals, different members may move in different directions, which may give rise to difficulties.

  Firstly, goals must be defined and the purpose and necessity of the specified goals must be explained to every team member. Goals must be measurable or as specific as possible so that employees are able to feel a sense of achievement when a goal is attained. Once goals are achieved, team members should receive feedback on their performance.

- **Self-efficacy and adaptability:** Self-efficacy is the belief in one's ability to muster and implement personal resources, skills, and competencies to attain a certain level of achievement on a given task. In other words, self-efficacy can be seen as task specific self-confidence. Self-efficacy for a specific task has been shown to be a robust predictor of an individual's performance in that task and helps to explain why people of equal ability can perform differently.

CHECKLIST FOR ENTREPRENEURS 1.3 How to Set SMART Goals

SMART is an acronym for a goal-setting technique that is popular among entrepreneurs because of its simplicity and effectiveness. The acronym stands for "Specific, Measurable, Achievable, Realistic, Timely." Set your goals according to the following set of criteria:

- **Specific:** "Specific" is the what, why, and how of the SMART model. Ensure that your goals are very specific and easy to understand. For example, instead of setting a vague goal, like starting a restaurant, set a more specific goal, like setting up a Chinese fine-dining restaurant.
- **Measurable:** If you can't measure your goal, you can't manage it. Choose a goal with measurable progress, so that you can see the changes occurring. Establish concrete criteria for measuring progress toward the achievement of your goal. You can track your progress on a daily, weekly, monthly, or quarterly basis, or by increases in rupee or percentage of market share. For example, instead of setting a goal to increase the market share of your business by the end of the financial year, set a measurable goal stating that you will increase your market share from 20 to 25 per cent by the end of the financial year.
- **Achievable:** Set the bar high enough for a satisfying achievement but, at the same time, get an understanding of how big this challenge actually is for you. Have you ever done anything like it before? Has anyone else? Yes, there's always someone who's first, and you may be that person, but make sure you know the true difficulty level of the goal you're setting before you get started. When you set a goal, start figuring out ways to achieve that goal. You need to develop knowledge, attitude, skills, and financial capability to reach them.
- **Realistic:** The goal set by you should be realistic and should yield results.
- **Timely:** Set a time frame for the goal. If you don't set a time frame, the commitment is too vague and it gives you the opportunity to procrastinate. For example, instead of setting a goal simply to start a venture, set a specific goal stating that you will be starting your venture by, say, January 2014.

Source: www.goal-setting-guide.com (last accessed in March 2013). Reproduced with permission.

An individual with high self-efficacy for a given task will exert more effort for a greater length of time, persist through setbacks, set and accept higher goals, and develop better plans and strategies for the task. A person with high self-efficacy will also take negative feedback in a more positive manner and use that feedback to improve their performance. These attributes of self-efficacy may be important to the entrepreneurial process because it often entails ambiguous situations in which effort, persistence, and planning become important.

Successful entrepreneurs are adaptive and resilient. Change is inevitable, and there will be plenty of times when entrepreneurs need to correct course and modify plans so that business isn't left behind. It is essential to accommodate changes in the marketplace and not to be rigid and so miss opportunities for growth and improvement. Entrepreneurs should not be afraid of failure. Mistakes and failure come with the territory of being successful entrepreneurs, and if they are not making mistakes, they are probably engaging in a very easy task, where there is little chance of failure.

- **Internal locus of control:** Do you control your destiny or are you controlled by it? Some people believe that they hold the power to control the outcome of their actions. Other people feel that the outcome of their actions is determined by external factors. Locus of control refers to how a person perceives the causes of events in one's life. Individuals high on the internal locus of control assume that any success or failure they experience is due to their personal actions and that they have the ability to influence events. When someone perceives events as under the control of others, fate, luck, the system or their boss, they have an external locus of control. What is your locus of control? And what forces are responsible for your successes and failures? These important attitudes affect your motivation, expectations, self-esteem, risk-taking behaviour, and the actual outcome of your actions. Successful leaders and entrepreneurs typically show a high internal locus of control.[15]

- **Persistence, persuasion, and networking:** Entrepreneurs display persistence, and are not discouraged into quitting by difficulties and problems that come up in business or in their personal life. Entrepreneurs with a track record of success are much more likely to succeed than first-time entrepreneurs. In essence, they have exhibited persistence in selecting the right industry and the right moment to start new ventures.

  Networking is something all successful entrepreneurs are good at. Networking, is not an option but a pre-requisite for survival in this world of intense competition. While networking, it is important to open all avenues by getting involved in every kind of social media, to build relationships by being open-minded, and to follow through any business opportunity you may have identified with personal interaction. Businesses have always relied on networks of clients, suppliers, associates and contacts to spread the word about their work and their products. But it is not enough to simply network. A successful entrepreneur usually uses deliberate strategies to persuade and influence others.

DISCUSSION FORUM

- What are entrepreneurial competencies?
- Discuss the functions of an entrepreneur.

CHECKLIST FOR ENTREPRENEURS 1.4 — Entrepreneurial Competencies

- Take initiative.
- Identify and act on business opportunities.
- Demonstrate high quality of work by setting standards of excellence.
- Show commitment to work contract.
- Practice efficiency orientation.
- Plan systematically and develop persistence to reach goals.
- Develop a problem-solving approach.
- Have self-confidence.
- Be assertive.
- Learn to be persuasive.

CAPACITY BUILDING FOR ENTREPRENEURS

In order to become a developed nation, India needs more entrepreneurs with a managerial mindset. This is because in order to create wealth, the economy must create jobs that, in turn, are fuelled by entrepreneurial activity. This needs a supportive regulative environment, venture capital activity, and a strong capital market. So in order to build an entrepreneurial society, we need to focus on the following five areas.

- **Create the right eco-system:** There is a need to scale up and enrich the ecosystem. The various elements of the ecosystem for commercialization are venture capitalists, institutional support systems, government schemes, and incubators. An ecosystem is a system of interconnected stakeholders—institutions and individuals whose linkages enable efficient production, and the spread of new and economically useful knowledge. There is a need to kill silos and capitalize on the power of collaboration.

- **Build skills:** Experiential learning is a part of entrepreneurship. The five most important skills needed for an entrepreneur are personal skills, communication skills, negotiation skills, leadership skills, and sales skills. The education system in India can ensure that the curriculum in schools, colleges, and universities is modified to address business needs and to build centres of entrepreneurial excellence in institutions that will actively support entrepreneurship.
- **Provide access to capital:** For a long time, Indian entrepreneurs have faced a shortage of capital. Determining capital requirements, crafting financial and fund-raising strategies, and managing the financial process are critical to a new venture's success. Government policy should be congenial for foreign investors, financial institutions, venture capitalists, and angel investors to enable them to invest in new ventures.
- **Enable networking and exchange:** In professional or business networking, people use their personal contacts for succeeding in their businesses. A network serves to provide a lot of support to the entrepreneurial enterprise in times of crisis. Some ways to network are through social networking Web sites, business associations, alumni networks, and during trade fairs.

DISCUSSION FORUM

- Comment on the statement, "It is not all that rosy to start your own business, so before you take the plunge with an overdose of optimism, be sure you do not fall for any of these myths."
- Discuss popular myths of entrepreneurship and why they are more fantasy than fact.

CHECKLIST FOR ENTREPRENEURS 1.5 ✓ Myths About Entrepreneurship

Certain myths have grown up around entrepreneurs over the years. Here is a list of some common myths that entrepreneurs should guard against:

- **Entrepreneurs are born, not made:** In reality, the making of an entrepreneur occurs through education, training, experience, and experiential learning.
- **Entrepreneurs are academic and social misfits:** The reality, however, is that today, many business schools are offering formal education in entrepreneurship and most entrepreneurs are highly educated and very professional in their approach
- **All you need is money to be an entrepreneur:** In reality, money is only one of the ingredients in the success of the venture.
- **All you need is luck to be an entrepreneur:** In reality, what may appear to be luck to others is often in fact a planned manipulation of events and circumstances
- **A great idea is the only ingredient in a recipe for business:** In reality, a great idea may stay just that if it is not backed by adequate finance, demand for the product, and, most importantly, good management.
- **My best friend will be a great business partner:** In reality, it is wrong to assume that people with whom you have great personal ties will make good business partners.
- **Having no boss is great fun:** In reality, entrepreneurs are far from independent and have to work with various stakeholders in the business, including partners, investors, suppliers, customers, creditors, employees, and various other agencies involved in the business. They have to work longer hours and handle many complex situations.
- **I can start making lots of money immediately:** In reality, it is often months, if not years, before an entrepreneur starts making money.

- **Create tax benefits, incentives, and simplify the bureaucratic process:** One way to encourage entrepreneurial activity would be to allow entrepreneurs to keep more of what they earn by lowering tax rates. Incentives to entrepreneurs, such as reduction of legal costs to hiring, would be beneficial. A reduced requirement of government mandated paperwork at various points while running a business could be desirable.

DISCUSSION FORUM

- Discuss the problems faced by entrepreneurs during various stages of the venture.
- Explain how to build entrepreneurial capacity.

SUMMARY

Entrepreneurs are the lifeblood of any economy. Entrepreneurs are classified into various types. Creativity, innovation, leadership, opportunity seeking and initiative, risk taking and decision making ability, tolerance of ambiguity and uncertainty, motivation to excel, problem solving, goal orientation, self-efficacy and adaptability, locus of control, persistence, persuasion and networking are the competencies of a successful entrepreneur. The functions of an entrepreneur are identifying business opportunities, turning ideas into action, feasibility study, resourcing, setting up of the enterprise, managing the enterprise, growing the enterprise, and closing the venture. In order to build capacity for entrepreneurs: create the right environment for success; ensure that entrepreneurs have access to right skills and capital; enable networking and exchange; create tax benefits; incentives; and simplify the bureaucratic process.

KEY TERMS

Corporate Entrepreneurs/Intrapreneur: Employees within an organization who use their entrepreneurial spirit to introduce new products, new processes, new methods, and new forms within the corporation.

Drone Entrepreneur: Entrepreneurs who are conservative and complacent in nature and like to maintain the status quo.

Entrepreneur: A person who creates an enterprise.

Entrepreneurship: The process of creating or seizing an opportunity and pursuing it regardless of the resources currently controlled.

Fabian Entrepreneur: Entrepreneurs who change only when there is a threat to the existence of their enterprise.

Imitative or Adoptive Entrepreneur: Entrepreneurs who imitate products, production methods, and new forms of organization in their enterprise.

Innovative Entrepreneur: Entrepreneurs who are innovative in their approach to business and introduce new products, new production methods, or discover new markets or new forms of organization in their enterprise.

CASE STUDY

Entrepreneurship, Luck or Persistence?

When Deepak Joshi was 18 years old, he sampled ice cream at a store and thought that he could make it better. He made his own recipe and began selling ice cream bars, cones, and cups in his hometown Belgaum. People began asking him for more.

Deepak got himself trained at Central Food Technological Research Institute (CFTRI), Mysore, and developed skills to prepare ice creams of different flavours and compositions. Using meagre profits and his mother's kitchen, Deepak Joshi began making large batches of ice creams. He then designed his own wrappers and developed a commission system for friends who sold ice creams at several schools.

Business was so good that it became an obsession. Deepak worked after college, weekends, and holidays, aside from a brief period when the health department suspended his operations until he obtained proper permits to make ice creams. He made different types of ice creams by trying his own methods until he graduated from college. At first, he could meet the demand without purchasing special equipment or sacrificing other activities, but when he began providing ice creams for college fundraising events and fun fairs, demand exceeded capacity, and Deepak started buying professional equipment, hiring helpers, and purchasing bulk supplies.

Looking back, Deepak recalled the obsession, the long hours, and the drive to learn about the business. Deepak set about placing orders with local stores and developing contacts with dozens of schools, colleges, caterers, hotels, and civic organizations. His business soon consumed his entire family and closest friends. He registered the company and set up an ice-cream parlour. During the first month, he had 18,000 orders, and by the time he graduated, Deepak was distributing specialty ice creams to retail stores in three states.

At the age of 26, Deepak repositioned his company as a major distributor of specialty ice creams and began planning a chain of upscale ice-cream parlours, which would complement his current ice cream manufacturing and distribution system. When he paused to think about his plans, he realised that to launch a regional or national chain would mean major changes in his organization. He and his family could not handle all the responsibilities, and the nature of Deepak's ice-cream business would change. Although the idea of pursuing a major business was exciting, Deepak could not help feeling apprehensive.

Reflecting upon his business, Deepak realised that many people considered his success to be no more than the luck of a personable young man who made good ice creams and had accidentally stumbled upon a few good markets. In fact, he had worked extremely hard to attract clients. Most of his customers had not been comfortable buying from a young college student, and customers seldom took him seriously until they had dealt with him for a long time. Winning over customers had always been a challenge to Deepak, not a roadblock, and creating unusual ice creams had been exciting.

He was not anxious to become a corporate manager, and although he had always worked well with others, Deepak liked being independent. Running a company would mean sacrificing his autonomy. Yet the idea of a chain of stores selling his specialty ice creams had been a dream for years. At the same time, expansion would mean financial risk, and Deepak had always avoided debt. He dealt in cash and had always carefully calculated his expenses to avoid even the slightest loss. He realised that he was at a major crossroads in his young career. The choice seemed to be whether to follow his dream and expand or to be content with his existing business.

Questions:

1. Identify the entrepreneurial characteristics of Deepak Joshi. How do they match the characteristics described for successful entrepreneurs?
2. Take a position regarding the decision facing Deepak. Should Deepak expand his business and open a chain of ice-cream parlours.
3. Based on what you know about Deepak and what you believe his characteristics to be, would you say his success was due to luck or persistence? Explain. How does luck play a role in any new venture?

DISCUSSION QUESTIONS

1. Explain the concept of entrepreneur. How does an entrepreneur differ from a manager?
2. Explain the characteristics of a successful entrepreneur.
3. Discuss the evolution of the concept of entrepreneurship.
4. Describe, with examples, various sources of innovation.
5. Comment on the statement, "Developing countries are a fertile ground for imitative rather than innovative entrepreneurs."

ACTIVITY

Purpose: To identify entrepreneurial competencies.

Time: 45 minutes

Procedure:

1. The instructor will divide the class into a maximum of six groups.
2. Each group should select and invite a local entrepreneur to the class to share his or her experience. Make the session as interactive as possible.
3. Each group should correlate the characteristics of a successful entrepreneur discussed in this chapter to the personality of the entrepreneur invited by it to the class.

PROJECT

1. Visit any local enterprise. Interview the entrepreneur; study his entrepreneurial journey; and prepare the profile of the entrepreneur not exceeding 2,000 words.

ENDNOTES

1. There is no separate Nobel Prize for entrepreneurship, but the importance of entrepreneurship has been recognized by Nobel recipients like Dr Edmund S. Phelps. On 10 October 2006, the front page of *The Wall Street Journal* carried the headline "The New Nobel Prize Winner Makes a Case for Entrepreneurship." In the accompanying article, Dr Phelps discoursed on the importance of entrepreneurship.
2. Timmons, Jeffrey A. and Stephen Spinelli, Jr (2009). *New Venture Creation: Entrepreneurship for the 21st Century*. The McGraw-Hill Companies, Inc. International Edition, p. 5.
3. Even though the term "entrepreneur" was used earlier, one of Richard Cantillon's remarkable contributions to the field of economics was that he was the first to stress and analyse the term "entrepreneur" and to fully consider the critical role of entrepreneurship in an economy.
4. Schumpeter, Joseph (1952). *Can Capitalism Survive?* New York: Harper and Row, p. 27.
5. Bolton, B. and J. Thompson (2002). *Entrepreneurs: Talent, Temperament, Technique*. London: Elsevier Butterworth–Heinemann.
6. Timmons, Jeffrey A. (1989). *The Entrepreneurial Mind*. Harvard Business School: Brick House Publishing Company.

7. Ronstadt, Robert C. (1984). *Entrepreneurship*. Dover, MA: Lord Publishing Company, p. 28.
8. Zahorski, Darrell, "The Nine Personality Types of Entrepreneur," available at http://sbinformation.about.com/cs/development/a/personality.htm (last accessed in March 2013).
9. Kuratko, Donald F. and Richard M. Hodgetts (2009). *Entrepreneurship: Theory, Process, Practice*. Mason, OH: South Western Cengage Learning.
10. The word "intrapreneurship" was coined by Gifford Pinchot III.
11. Drucker, Peter F. (1985). *Innovation and Entrepreneurship*. New York: Harper & Row.
12. Schere, J. (1982). "Tolerance of Ambiguity as Discriminating Variable Between Entrepreneur and Managers." *Proceedings of the Academy of Management*. 42: 404–408.
13. Budner, S. (1962). "Intolerance for Ambiguity as Personality Variable." *Journal of Personality*, 30: 29–50.
14. McClelland, David (1961). *The Achieving Society*. Princeton, NJ: D. Van Nostrand.
15. Lee, D. Y. and E. W. K. Tsang (2001). "The Effects of Entrepreneurial Personality, Background and Network Activities on Venture Growth." *Journal of Management Studies*. June, 38 (4): 583–602.

Entrepreneurial Perspectives

1. Entrepreneurship
2. Entrepreneurial Development and Training
3. Women Entrepreneurs
4. Family Business
5. Micro, Small, and Medium Enterprises

"Nobody talks of entrepreneurship as survival, but that's exactly what it is."
—Anita Roddick, founder of The Body Shop

Shiv Khera is a motivational expert and a successful entrepreneur—the founder of Qualified Learning Systems, Inc., USA. An educator, author, business consultant, and successful entrepreneur, he helps motivate people to realise their true potential. Shiv Khera's impressive client list includes, among others, Lufthansa, Nestlé, Gillette, Johnson & Johnson Limited, National Panasonic, DHL, HSBC and many more.

Entrepreneurial Development and Training

2

LEARNING OBJECTIVES

Upon completion of this chapter, you should be able to:

1. **Understand the significance of the entrepreneurial environment.**
2. **Discuss the models of entrepreneurial development.**
3. **Explain entrepreneurial motivation.**
4. **Discuss the entrepreneurship training methods.**
5. **Identify the phases of entrepreneurial development.**

INTRODUCTION

An entrepreneur may not only be born, but also be made. In this chapter, we will learn about various training methods that help aspiring entrepreneurs to develop certain traits. We will also discuss the environment suitable for the development of entrepreneurship, the various economic, political, legal, social, cultural, psychological, and technological factors affecting entrepreneurial growth, the business climate in India, the various models for promoting entrepreneurial development, and theories of entrepreneurial motivation.

ENTREPRENEURIAL ENVIRONMENT

The term entrepreneurial environment refers to a combination of factors that play a role in the development of entrepreneurship. Entrepreneurs need to understand the business environment, including growth prospects, political stability, bureaucratic set-ups, and judiciary effectiveness in the region in which their business operates. It is observed that countries having policies encouraging a minimalist approach to rules and regulation, offering incentives like tax benefits and subsidies, and providing training, development and counselling services to starting, supporting and sustaining business ventures are often perceived as having an entrepreneurship-friendly environment. Factors such as the availability of financial resources and investment in research and development increases the rate of new venture creation.

Global Entrepreneurship Environment

Two academicians—Zoltán Ács of George Mason University, Virginia, and Láazló Szerb, University of Pécs, Hungary—have developed a dynamic tool, the global entrepreneurship development index (GEDI), which allows measurement and comparison of the extent of entrepreneurial activities on a global level.[1] GEDI is an index that captures the contextual features of entrepreneurship and offers a measure of the quality and quantity of the business formation process in various countries. It is presently the only measure of entrepreneurship reflecting its multidimensional nature and has overcome the shortcomings of the various other measures of entrepreneurship like the global entrepreneurship monitor, which is primarily based on the number of businesses regardless of the degree of their success from a financial perspective, job creation, or improvement of the local knowledge base. The GEDI captures the contextual features of entrepreneurship by focusing on three broad areas that form sub-indices—entrepreneurial attitude or how society sees entrepreneurship; entrepreneurial activity or what individuals are actually doing to improve the quality of human resources and technological efficiency; and entrepreneurial aspirations or how much entrepreneurial activity is being directed toward innovation, high-impact entrepreneurship, and globalization. The dimension of entrepreneurial aspirations is particularly important to the study of emerging companies across borders as it incorporates the efforts of the early-stage entrepreneur to introduce new products and services, develop new production processes, penetrate foreign markets, substantially increase the number of firm employees, and finance the business with formal or informal venture capital, or both. The entrepreneurial attitude sub-index aims to identify attitudes associated with the entrepreneurship-related behaviour of a country's population. The indicators are opportunity perception, start-up skills, non-fear of failure, networking, and cultural support. The entrepreneurial activity sub-index is principally concerned with measuring start-up activities with a high potential for growth. This high growth potential is indicated by good business opportunities, the degree to which a sector is technology intensive, the quality of human resources, and the uniqueness of the product or service offered to meet the competition.

The GEDI of 71 countries for 2010 is given in Table 2.1. The index shows that entrepreneurship and the degree of a country's development are correlated. Developed countries, such as Denmark, the United States, Canada, Sweden, Iceland, and Norway, are among the top ten. Likewise, developed countries like Australia, Ireland, and Switzerland are all good performers in the area of entrepreneurship. The most populous countries, such as China and India, are in the middle part of the ranking list. Developing countries like Jamaica, Bosnia-Herzegovina, Venezuela, Brazil, the Philippines, Iran, Bolivia, Ecuador, and Uganda rank lowest in the list.

Business Climate in India

In the last few years, India has consistently registered an impressive gross domestic product (GDP) growth rate and has been considered to be one of the largest economies of the world. India houses a population comprising a workforce of highly-skilled and well-trained young people in the age group of 20–35 years. Its middle class consists of 32–35 crore people and has considerable spending power.

The ever-increasing spending power of India's population of more than 700 billion makes it one of the most attractive markets globally for investing in various types of products and services. India has recently joined the "trillion dollar GDP" club, an unofficial classification of the world's major economies with a GDP of over USD 1 trillion per year.[2]

Many sectors of the economy traditionally owned and monopolized by the government are now opening up to private ownership, creating a void that can be filled by entrepreneurs. Some examples of such sectors are hospitality, retail, infrastructure, banking, and insurance. Apart from these sectors, opportunities also exist in niche markets for micro, small, and medium entrepreneurs. Additionally, with a vibrant democracy, India has also enjoyed relatively higher stability in comparison with other countries in its neighbourhood.

Bureaucratic issues, like a company's registration period, paperwork, licensing issues, and taxation issues, can often be a discouraging factor for entrepreneurs in India. For instance, the procedure for incorporation of a company in India comprises over 10 steps and takes, on an average, about 35 days. To simplify certain bureaucratic procedures, single-window clearances are available for certain industries. The procedures are not very different for foreign citizens looking to establish businesses in India.

Table 2.1 The Global Entrepreneurship Development Index Ranking

GEDI Rank	Country	Gross Domestic Product (GDP)	GEDI Rank	Country	Gross Domestic Product (GDP)
1	Denmark	35,890	37	Poland	14,095
2	Canada	34,926	38	Croatia	15,599
3	United States	44,474	39	Peru	7,558
4	Sweden	36,358	40	China	5,087
5	New Zealand	26,773	41	Colombia	8,336
6	Ireland	44,402	42	South Africa	9,565
7	Switzerland	40,183	43	Turkey	12,747
8	Norway	49,014	44	Mexico	14,135
9	Iceland	35,490	45	Dominican Republic	7,709
10	Netherlands	38,083	46	Indonesia	3,459
11	Australia	34,073	47	Hungary	18,639
12	Belgium	34,584	48	Romania	13,217
13	Finland	33,869	49	Macedonia	9,632
14	United Kingdom	34,726	50	Egypt	5,383
15	Singapore	39,508	51	Jordan	5,092
16	Germany	34,512	52	Panama	11,947
17	Puerto Rico	20,223	53	India	2,656
18	France	33,412	54	Brazil	9,376
19	Slovenia	24,913	55	Venezuela	11,333
20	Korea	25,481	56	Thailand	7,974
21	Israel	25,868	57	Russia	14,121
22	Austria	36,836	58	Tunisia	7,758
23	Hong Kong	39,089	59	Morocco	4,248
24	United Arab Emirates	39,900	60	Jamaica	6,848
25	Czech Republic	22,110	61	Algeria	7,887
26	Chile	13,609	62	Serbia	10,853
27	Italy	30,248	63	Kazakhstan	10,477
28	Spain	31,241	64	Bosnia and Herzegovina	8,077
29	Japan	33,288	65	Iran	10,625
30	Saudi Arabia	23,428	66	Ecuador	7,597
31	Malaysia	12,681	67	Bolivia	4,242
32	Latvia	15,574	68	Syria	4,476
33	Portugal	22,595	69	Guatemala	4,661
34	Greece	28,024	70	Philippines	3,186
35	Uruguay	10,844	71	Uganda	918
36	Argentina	12,769			

Source: Zoltàn J. Àcs and László Szerb, "Global Entrepreneurship Development Index (GEDI)," paper presented at the Summer Conference 2010 on "Opening Up Innovation: Strategy, Organization, and Technology," Imperial College, London Business School, 16–18 June 2010, available at http://www2.druid.dk/conferences/viewpaper.php?id=502261&cf=43 (last accessed in August 2012). Reproduced with permission.

The Indian judiciary has an unimpressive record in law enforcement. Firstly, contract enforcement and legal recourse are usually cumbersome as the procedures are often lengthy and plagued by red tape. Although efforts are being made to set up courts exclusively catering to consumer concerns and business issues, it may be a long time before such set-ups become functional. So entrepreneurs operating in the Indian environment are advised to reduce their reliance on contracts if damages from violation are expected to be very high. Secondly, as far as intellectual property is concerned, the scope of recognition of patents is limited, so entrepreneurs may have to use other legal resources to protect their innovations. On the brighter side, however, the litigation costs—insurance and liability costs—in India are extremely low as consumer courts do not usually award high penalties for damages, effectively reducing the cost of doing business in India.

Entrepreneurs also need to be aware of the great linguistic and cultural diversity in India while expanding their businesses. India consists of 28 states and seven union territories, each state or union territory having its own set of culturally-different communities. Although Hindi is the official language of the country, there are 21 official languages, including Bengali, Telugu, Marathi, Urdu, and Gujarati. English is widely used in national, political, and commercial communication.

The World Bank's Doing Business project provides objective measures of business regulations and their enforcement in 183 economies and selected cities at the sub-national and regional level. The indicators provided in the Doing Business reports can be used to analyse specific regulations that enhance or constrain investment, productivity, and growth. These reports aim to provide an objective basis for understanding and improving the regulatory environment for business all over the world.[3] Table 2.2 breaks down the ease of doing business into several factors in the context of India.

Environmental Factors Affecting Entrepreneurial Growth

One of the secrets of the success of most developed countries is an entrepreneur-friendly environment and the presence of a large number of dynamic entrepreneurs who provide room for newer and better inventions.[4] Less-developed countries, on the other hand, are confronted by a situation where aspiring entrepreneurs are hard to find and existing ones tend to leave their countries in search of better opportunities due to the lack of a favourable environment for entrepreneurship. Certain

Table 2.2 Business Climate in India

Topic Rankings	DB 2012 Rank	DB 2011 Rank	Change in Rank
Starting a business	166	166	No change
Dealing with construction permits	181	181	No change
Getting electricity	98	109	↑ 11
Registering property	97	96	↓ -1
Getting credit	40	37	↓ -3
Protecting investors	46	44	↓ -2
Paying taxes	147	165	↑ 18
Trading across borders	109	107	↓ -2
Enforcing contracts	182	182	No change
Resolving insolvency	128	140	↑ 12

Source: The World Bank, Doing Business 2012, avilable at www.doingbusiness.org/data/exploreeconomies/india (last accessed in March 2013). The World Bank authorizes the use of this material subject to the terms and conditions on its Web site, www.worldbank.org/terms.

nations like Japan, however, are bound by strong traditions with a conservative outlook that promote entrepreneurship. In the drive for development, countries like China and India have changed their laws and policies to favour entrepreneurship.

Several researchers have carried out studies to identify the factors that motivate people to start business enterprises. In his pioneering study, R. A. Sharma[5] classified all the factors motivating entrepreneurs into two types:

- **Internal factors:** This includes educational background, occupational experience, desire to do something pioneering and innovative, desire to be free and independent, and family background.
- **External factors:** This includes assistance from the government, financial assistance from institutions, availability of technology or raw materials, encouragement from big business units, and heavy demand for product.

The environment may have both positive and negative influences on the emergence of entrepreneurship. Economists agree that the lack of entrepreneurs is not caused by economic conditions alone as it was believed earlier.[6] It is also due to the whole set of sociocultural and institutional conditions prevailing in our society. Several environmental factors affect entrepreneurial growth and development—economic, political and legal, social and cultural, psychological, and technological.

Economic Environment The economic environment comprises the following:

- **Capital:** Capital is one of the prerequisites for the establishment of an enterprise. The cost of capital depends upon the interest the entrepreneur has to pay to financial institutions as well as on government policies regarding the cost of capital.
- **Labour:** The availability of skilled labour is a critical factor in the emergence of entrepreneurship. In underdeveloped and developing countries, where cheap labour is available, the quality of labour can be improved by skill development. On the other hand, in developed countries such as the United States of America, the disadvantage of high-cost labour may be dealt with by introducing labour-saving innovations.
- **Raw material:** In the absence of raw materials, neither any enterprise can be established nor can an entrepreneur emerge. The supply of raw materials depends on other opportunity conditions. The more favourable these conditions are, the more likely is the raw material to have its influence on entrepreneurial emergence.
- **Market:** The fact remains that the potential of the market constitutes the major determinant of probable rewards from the entrepreneurial function. Both the size and composition of the market influence entrepreneurship in their own ways.
- **Infrastructure:** The availability of infrastructural facilities such as land, transportation, communication, and industry associations make valuable contributions towards promoting and sustaining entrepreneurship in the economy.

Political Environment The political environment includes national and international political factors that can affect the operations of an enterprise. A politically stable government can affect entrepreneurial activities in a positive manner as the government is largely responsible for ensuring the availability and accessibility of required resources for entrepreneurship. Government policies affecting prices, availability of capital, labour, demand structure, taxation, income distribution, and various incentives and subsidies also affect entrepreneurial growth and performance to a large extent. At the same time, some government policies relating to licenses, regulations, and bureaucracy are undesirable for the growth of business enterprises.

Social and Cultural Environment Social and cultural factors strongly affect the kind of behaviour that contributes to entrepreneurial growth. The main components of the social and cultural environment are religion, family background, education, social status, values, and behaviour acceptable within the society.

Sociologists claim that caste and religion do have an impact on the environment. For example, the Protestant ethics that emerged among the Western Christian population from the Protestant Reformation of the sixteenth century were favourable to capitalism, business, and entrepreneurship. The trading classes in the United States and the family business concerns of France have also distinguished themselves as entrepreneurs. In India, the Parsis of Maharashtra, and the Jains of Rajasthan and Gujarat have been mainsprings of entrepreneurial activity.

Family background greatly affects the entrepreneurial environment and maintenance of the social system. Family background includes the size of family, the type of family (joint or nuclear), and the economic status of the family. Having a family background in manufacturing provides a starting point for industrial entrepreneurs.

In any society, the system of education plays a significant role in inculcating entrepreneurial values. In India, however, the present education system trains students to become job seekers rather than job providers.

Entrepreneurial growth requires proper motives like profit-making or the acquisition of prestige and social status. The strength of these motives depends upon the culture of the society. If the culture is wealth-creation oriented, entrepreneurship would be applauded and praised, as wealth accumulation as a way of life would be appreciated. The absence of proper economic motives is a general characteristic of agrarian societies in which people do not attach value to industrial growth and business acumen.

Psychological Environment Societies that are dynamic and promote change by encouraging innovations and novelties encourage entrepreneurial activities. The most important psychological theory of entrepreneurship was put forward by David McClelland in his theory of achievement motivation. The theory states that people with a high need for achievement are distinctive in several ways. Entrepreneurship becomes the link between the need for achievement and economic growth. Societies that are able to identify achievers, motivate them, and reward them would be able to create an entrepreneurial climate.

Technological Environment Rapid advancement of technology has enabled the development of technology entrepreneurs globally in the area of information technology (IT), information technology enabled services (ITES), software technology, and hardware technology. Information and communication technology has become a key enabler for promoting entrepreneurial activities.

SNAPSHOT

Factors affecting entrepreneurship growth:

- Economic environment
- Political and legal environment
- Social and cultural environment
- Psychological environment
- Technological environment

DISCUSSION FORUM

- Discuss the global entrepreneurship environment.
- Explain the factors affecting entrepreneurship growth.

WORLD OF ENTREPRENEURS 2.1 **Bangalore: The Silicon Valley of India**

Bangalore, the capital of the state of Karnataka in southern India, is popularly nicknamed the "Silicon Valley of India," in comparative reference to the original Silicon Valley, based around Santa Clara Valley, California, a major hub for IT firms in the United States. Today, most IT majors have a presence in Bangalore. There are several IT clusters in various parts of the city, but the biggest clusters are located in Electronic City and Whitefield.

In 1976, the Government of Karnataka encouraged the electronics industry through the establishment of the Karnataka State Electronics Development Corporation Limited (KEONICS). KEONICS entered into production on its own as well as with joint-venture initiatives with domestic and foreign industrial houses. Between 1981 and 1985, KEONICS established the first Software Technology Parks of India (STPI) in Electronics City (an electronics industrial complex). During this time, Electronics City attracted companies like HP, Siemens, WIpro, Infosys, Motorola, Tata, and others.

A significant step in the transformation of the city into an IT hub was the entry of the US semiconductor company Texas Instruments (TI) to set up an R&D centre in 1984. The presence of TI attracted the attention of many major IT global players such as IBM and Intel in the early 1990s. During 1992, DoT set up satellite earth stations for high-speed communications. The world-class IT Park developed in Whitefield, called the International Technology Park Limited, was another significant step in transforming the city into a major IT hub. Bangalore also houses GE's biggest R&D centre outside the US—the Jack Welch Technology Center and Philips Innovation Campus.

Today, large IT firms like Infosys Limited and Wipro are headquartered in Bangalore. The city also houses major IT giants like Microsoft, Oracle, Dell, Sun Microsystems, Motorola, Inc., Hewlett-Packard Development Company, Cisco Systems, Inc., Nortel, and Nokia. Bangalore has been ranked one of the top five "global hubs of technological innovation" by the United Nations. It may safely be said that Bangalore provides a very favourable environment to entrepreneurs in terms of availability of technology, people, and resources.

Sources: www.keonics.com/history.php (last accessed in March 2013); Chengappa, Bidanda (2011), "The Origin and Evolution of India's Silicon Valley," Daily News and Analysis (DNA), November 2, available at www.dnaindia.com/analysis/column_the-origin-and-evolution-of-indias-silicon-valley_1606305 (last accessed in March 2013); Basant, Rakesh (2006). "Bangalore Cluster: Evolution, Growth and Challenges," working paper presented in May, W. P. No. 2006-05-02, IIM Ahmedabad, available at www.iimahd.ernet.in/publications/data/2006-05-02rbasant.pdf (last accessed in March 2013).

Creating a Favourable Environment for Entrepreneurship

In India, budding entrepreneurs face a greater degree of uncertainty while starting businesses when compared to developed countries. There is a need to create an ecosystem that will foster and support entrepreneurial development in India. India is an emerging economy, and in order to become a developed nation, there is a need to reduce unemployment. To create jobs, everything possible must be done to promote entrepreneurship and self-employment.

An entrepreneur must comply with several laws. Direct and indirect taxes and various duties to be paid by an entrepreneur include income tax, professional tax, service tax, value added tax (VAT), sales tax, and excise. Additionally, the entrepreneur has to comply with labour laws, pollution control norms, and various other statutes and regulations. India needs to develop policies focusing on the following areas to foster entrepreneurship:

- **Entrepreneurship education:** Entrepreneurship should be considered a career choice. The present Indian education system is mainly examination-oriented, with limited scope for creativity and innovation. Entrepreneurship education should involve creative, experiential learning and should be taught at the school and college level as it is best to identify potential entrepreneurs early. Such an education can be provided by selecting, motivating, training, and supporting potential students with the help of a curriculum designed by people from various industries. It would also be good to institutionalize mechanisms for mentoring and guidance by networks of experienced people working in various industries.

- **Availability of finance:** There is a need to institutionalize and streamline the supply of equity and debt capital to entrepreneurs by establishing more organized networks of angel investors and venture capitalists. There needs to be facilitation of buy-outs, closure, and restructuring and the enactment of labour reform to iron out issues preventing the growth and expansion of businesses.
- **Infrastructure:** There is a need to improve the physical infrastructure that directly impacts the ability of small firms to access more national and international markets, and to do so across all regions.
- **Technology:** There is a need to facilitate commercialization of research and development through increased private–public partnerships and incentives for subcontracted research. There should be an improvement in technology transfers among universities, government, and entrepreneurs.
- **Governance and reduction of complex bureaucratic procedures:** There is a need to improve the quality of governance and leverage technology to reduce effort, cost, and time to set up new enterprises. There should be structural changes to simplify and streamline bankruptcy proceedings, and to change perceptions about bankruptcy and its impact on social status. The government should also emphasize the social responsibility and philanthropic aspects of entrepreneurs' success, not just wealth creation.

  Indian entrepreneurs view bureaucracy as a major obstacle. There are a large number of procedures to be followed and clearances to be obtained to start and operate a business. Each of these procedures can take a long time. Corruption is widespread in some government departments and private-sector companies. There is a need to rein in corruption and reduce the complexity of bureaucratic procedures.

MODELS OF ENTREPRENEURIAL DEVELOPMENT

The models of entrepreneurial development are broadly classified into three categories:

- Psychological models
- Sociological models
- Integrated models

Psychological Models

The psychological model is based on the psychological approach to entrepreneurship. The essence of psychological theory is an understanding of the difference in individuals' attitudes. According to this theory, the internal attitude and ability to judge and forecast any situation lead a person to become a successful entrepreneur. David McClelland's theory on need for achievement is the most important among the various psychological theories on entrepreneurship. In his theory, McClelland emphasized the relationship of need for achievement or achievement motivation to economic development via entrepreneurial activities. He considers "achievement motivation" to be the major determinant of entrepreneurial development.

McClelland's Theory of Achievement Motivation David McClelland has explained entrepreneurial development from a psychological perspective. He considers entrepreneurs as people who do things in a better way and make decisions in times of uncertainty. He argues that motivation is an important determinant for entrepreneurial growth. The dream to achieve big things overpowers monetary or other external incentives. The McClelland Theory of Achievement Motivation holds that people have the following three motives for accomplishing things:

- Need for Power (nP), or the drive to influence others and any given situation.
- Need for Affiliation (nAff), or the drive for interpersonal relationship.
- Need for Achievement (nAch), or the drive to excel, advance, and grow.

McClelland suggests that all of these three needs may simultaneously act on an individual. However, in the case of an entrepreneur, the need for achievement is found to dominate.

Theory of Withdrawal of Status Respect (1964) Everett Hagen's concept of the entrepreneur is that of a "creative personality" interested in accelerating change and driven by a motivation to achieve. According to Hagen, entrepreneurial growth has been very gradual and may or may not even occur in the same generation. In his theory of withdrawal of status respect, Everett Hagen's argument is that certain social changes may disrupt the stability of traditional society and cause psychological changes in a group or in an individual. The withdrawal of status respect may occur when a traditional, group is displaced from its previous status or on migration to some other place or to a new society.[7] Hagen uses the case of Japanese history to substantiate his argument.

Internal–External Locus of Control Theory Professor J. D. Rotter of Ohio University introduced the Internal–External Locus of Control Theory, which highlights the self-confidence of a person, and the dependency on fortune and external environment for becoming an entrepreneur. According to this theory, the internal locus of control comprises self-confidence, extreme belief in one's own ability, and initiatives taken by an individual. Locus of control determines whether a person perceives a potential goal to be attainable through one's own actions (internal locus of control) or through uncontrollable external factors (external locus of control).

Sociological Models

The sociological theory of entrepreneurship holds social cultures to be the driving force behind entrepreneurship. The entrepreneur becomes a role performer in conformity with the role expectations of society. Such role expectations are based on religious beliefs, taboos, and customs. Max Weber, Hozelist, Thomas Cochran, and Frank W. Young all advocated a sociological explanation for the development of entrepreneurship.

Max Weber's Theory of Religious Beliefs According to Max Weber, religious beliefs are the driving or restraining forces for entrepreneurial activity. For one thing, religious beliefs play a crucial role in determining the attitude of the entrepreneur towards generating or limiting profits. Weber took the position that entrepreneurial growth is dependent upon the ethical values (due to religion) of society.

Weber stressed the spirit of capitalism, which promotes a favourable attitude in society towards the acquisition of wealth. Capitalism thrives under the Protestant work ethic that advocates hard work, honesty, and discipline. The spirit of capitalism, coupled with the motive of profit, results in the creation of a large number of successful business enterprises.

Weber distinguished between the "spirit of capitalism" and the "adventurous spirit." The spirit of capitalism is influenced by a strict discipline, whereas the adventurous spirit comes from the free force of impulse. The right combination of discipline and impulse defines the successful entrepreneur.

Hozelist's Sociocultural Theory According to Hozelist, a specific social culture leads to growth in entrepreneurship. Social sanctions, cultural values, and role expectations are responsible for the emergence of entrepreneurship. He also propounded that entrepreneurship grows in societies that permit variability in choice of paths of life and non-standard socialization of individuals. Hozelist's approach emphasizes the theory of deviance and assumes that those who introduce changes must be deviants since they reject the traditional way of doing things.

Thomas Cochran's Theory of Entrepreneurial Supply Thomas Cochran, in agreement with Hozelist, believed that the environment in which an individual is brought up determines his entrepreneurial urge. According to him, the supply of entrepreneurs in society needs to be seen with reference to prevailing child-rearing practices. He stated that the performance of the entrepreneur might be seen in reference to his own attitudes towards an occupation. Values and role expectations of the particular social group to which he belongs are the most important determinants in the performance of business entrepreneurial roles.

Frank W. Young's Theory of Group Level Pattern Frank W. Young's theory of entrepreneurship is one of change based upon society's incorporation of relative sub-groups within society. He said that groups can be reactive in two ways: If a group experiences low status recognition and denial of access to important social networks, and if the group possesses a greater range of institution resources than other groups at the same system level. These two factors bring development to the society. A group without anything will compete with other groups and also try to acquire societal recognition. A sub-group that has a relatively low status in a larger society will lead to entrepreneurial behaviour if the group has better institutional resources than others in that society at the same level. Young's model of entrepreneurship suggests the creation of supporting institutions in society, such as the family, as the determinant of entrepreneurship.

Integrated Models

In search of an integrated approach, the behaviourists tried to synthesize psychology and sociology to explain entrepreneurship. However, there has been a dominant influence of psychological parameters in their interpretation of entrepreneurial behaviour. In Udai Pareek and T. V. Rao's theoretical framework for analysing entrepreneurship, they argue that there are some sequential propositions in human behaviour that lead to entrepreneurship. According to them, these propositions, which occur in sequence, ultimately end up in entrepreneurial development.[8] According to T. V. Rao, the optimal presence of the following factors, which are additive in nature, leads to the initiation of entrepreneurship:

- Need for motive (achievement motivation)—the dynamic which is the main thrust behind entrepreneurial action.
- Long-term involvement in thought and action to achieve the goal in entrepreneurial activity.
- Personal, social, and material resources favourable to entrepreneurial activity.
- Sociopolitical system suitable for the establishment, development, and expansion of an enterprise.

BREAKTHROUGH ENTREPRENEURSHIP 2.2 The Kakinada Experiment

According to the findings of David McClelland's research, "the need for achievement" motivated people to work hard and money-making was incidental. In order to find out whether this need for achievement could be induced, McClelland conducted an experimental study for five years in a place called Kakinada in Andhra Pradesh, India, in collaboration with Small Industries Extension and Training Institute (SIET). SIET is now known as the National Institute for Micro, Small, and Medium Enterprises (NI-MSME).

The Kakinada experiment was begun in January 1964. The main objective of the experiment was to break the barrier of limited aspirations by inducing achievement motivation. Under the Kakinada experiment, 52 young people were selected, put through a three-month training programme, and motivated with a set of fresh goals. The trainees were asked to think, talk, and act positively among themselves and imitate their role model or those who performed well. They were asked to imagine themselves in need of challenges. The achievement motivation training had a positive impact on the participants. The participants were mostly unemployed youth, and after training, some started enterprises and some joined enterprises as employees. From the Kakinada experiment it was concluded that suitable training could provide necessary motivation to entrepreneurs.

The Kakinada experiment led people to appreciate the need for an entrepreneurship development programme to induce motivation and competence among young and potential entrepreneurs.

WORLD OF ENTREPRENEURS 2.3 **RUDSETI Rural Entrepreneurship Development Model**

Rural Development and Self-Employment Training Institute (RUDSETI), a unique initiative to promote self-employment among unemployed youth, was founded in 1982 jointly by the Sri Dharmasthala Manjunatheshwara Educational Trust, Syndicate Bank, and Canara Bank under the leadership of Dr D. Veerendra Heggade. It is located in Ujire, Dharmasthala, in Karnataka. The Institute has been providing training programmes oriented towards self-employment for the last 30 years. In the field of entrepreneurship, the RUDSETI model has become a brand name in addressing the unemployment problems among rural youth. It has caught the attention of the Central Government and has become a replicable model.

According to the RUDSETI model, any unemployed youth in the age group of 18–45 years, irrespective of caste, creed, religion, gender, and economic status, having the aptitude to take up self-employment, can undergo free training. RUDSETI offers more than 60 types of entrepreneurship development programmes in varying areas of expertise. All the programmes are of short duration, ranging from one to six weeks. The cutting edge of RUDSETI training is the post-training follow-up for sustained motivation among the trainees. RUDSETI bazaars are organized to provide marketing support to RUDSETI-trained entrepreneurs. Each unit organizes at least one bazaar every year during fairs, exhibitions, and special occasions in their area. This facilitates the trainees to get an insight into market trends and customer behaviour.

Continuous experimentation has enabled RUDSETI to evolve a versatile training module combining its result-oriented practices and the best aspects of entrepreneurship development modules practised in India in the backdrop of researches made by social scientists and management experts. Each RUDSET institute is assisted by the Local Advisory Committee (LAC)—an advisory body with representatives from sponsors, government officials, and eminent personalities. It periodically reviews and monitors the progress of RUDSETI.

Encouraged by its success, RUDSETI has now set up 26 units in 16 states. Up to June 2012, RUDSETI has trained about 2.92 lakh youth, of which 2.07 lakh trainees have settled with their self-employment ventures. RUDSETI's collaboration with developmental agencies, institutions, voluntary organizations, and government agencies to achieve common objectives has proved to be mutually beneficial. The methodology followed and results obtained by RUDSETI have motivated banks, NGOs, and the government to advocate and replicate the model in various parts of the country.

Sources: www.rudsetitraining.org (last accessed in March 2013) and the RUDSETI training manual.

SNAPSHOT

The models suggested for the development of entrepreneurship are:

- Psychological models
- Sociological models
- Integrated models

ENTREPRENEURIAL MOTIVATION

Motivation is an important determinant for entrepreneurial growth. McClelland emphasized the importance of achievement motivation as the basis of entrepreneurial personality.[9] Motivation becomes a cause of economic and social development through entrepreneurship by fulfilling the following needs:

- Need for Power (nP), or the drive to influence others and any given situation.
- Need for Affiliation (nAff), or the drive for interpersonal relationship.
- Need for Achievement (nAch), or the drive to excel, advance, and grow.

McClelland suggests that all these three needs may simultaneously act on an individual. However, in the case of an entrepreneur, the need for achievement is found to dominate. Let us discuss the need for achievement in further detail.

Need for Achievement (nAch)

The need for achievement (nAch) is defined as the disposition to achieve something excellent. The need to achieve is closely linked to entrepreneurship and acts as a motivating factor for the success of an entrepreneur as someone who is motivated to excel is usually able to identify situations in which success is likely. Again, in order to motivate employees and ensure the smooth functioning and success of an enterprise, an entrepreneur or a manager has to put forward some objectives before every employee and encourage the employee to achieve them. An employee can be motivated by creating a desire to achieve the objectives set. In this way, achievement motivation is useful for the success of entrepreneurs and their enterprises. People with a predominant need for achievement exhibit the following characteristics:

- They find achievement to be more important than reward.
- They set their own goals, which are moderately challenging.
- They pursue goals for which they can obtain feedback about their success.
- They are constantly competing with standards of excellence.
- They have self-efficacy (belief in one's own ability) and an internal locus of control (the belief that their actions affect outcomes).

Thematic Apperception Test (TAT)

The thematic apperception test (TAT) is a projective psychological test developed by the American psychologist Henry A. Murray and the American psychoanalyst Christiana D. Morgan in the 1930s. McClelland used the TAT[10] as a tool to measure individual needs and motivating factors in people. During a TAT, an individual is asked to look at a series of pictures for a short period of time and describe what they think is happening in the picture. This is a test of imagination where a story for each picture is spontaneously generated by the individual looking at it. This test is administered on the assumption that the individual will illustrate their own (presumably hidden) needs and motivations into the story they generate. The test also determines the individual's score for each of the three needs—need for power, need for affiliation, and need for achievement. The scores may be used to suggest the types of roles the individual is well suited for.

Entrepreneurship Motivation Training (EMT)

Experiments conducted by David McClelland and his associates in India and abroad (1960) revealed that people can acquire motives and develop through training and education. McClelland emphasizes the achievement syndrome, self-study, goal setting, and interpersonal skills in a training course. The entrepreneurial development programme, with the entrepreneur as its focus, has to tap into entrepreneurial potential and transform visions into action. These programmes are conducted with the help of EMT labs. These labs provide entrepreneurs with experimental learning situations, which help them to examine their outlook and attitude towards entrepreneurship and to practice newly learned behaviour. The EMT labs are based on the psycho-dynamic theories of personality formation, personality development, and motive acquisition. The objectives of EMT are:

- To enhance the entrepreneurial spirit and improve the entrepreneurial competence of the participants by emphasizing motivation, planning, and cooperative efforts.
- To help the participants to examine their own self and relate their images of themselves with their environment.
- To make them aware about their own style of influencing people and situations.
- To enable them to recognize their creative and innovative potential.

EMT is an integrated part of an entrepreneur development programme (EDP) and enables the enhancement of motivation and commitment of the participants. EMT is a specialized training programme that requires expertise on the part of the trainer and there is no single accepted model of training applicable in all situations. It is a trainee-centred programme and aims to facilitate change in participants through their own experiences generated during the training. The training mainly depends on the trainer, who conceives plans and implements them to effect an enduring positive transformation in the entrepreneurial motivation of participants. The trainer's role is to create conditions where a real-life experience may be generated and then to facilitate the participants to learn from such experiences. Inferences are drawn from actual experiences generated in the group. EMT is carried out under three major headings:

- Developing a curriculum plan for EMT
- Implementing EMT
- Evaluating EMT

Developing a Curriculum Plan for EMT In EMT, specific objectives may be formulated for areas such as achievement syndrome, influence competence, risk taking, personal efficiency, goal setting, coping strategy, tolerance of ambiguity, problem-solving, and creativity. The elements of the course curriculum are viewed in terms of:

- The target group
- Training need identification
- Objective
- Duration
- Content
- Methods
- Material required
- Course calendar
- Evaluation

Implementing EMT A well-prepared course curriculum allows a smooth implementation of the programme. However, attention may be paid to the following aspects for the effective implementation of EMT:

- Choice of a trainer
- Preparation of training material
- Selection of the venue

Evaluating EMT There are three steps involved in evaluation:

- Deciding on the criteria for evaluation
- Deciding on the level of evaluation
- Deciding on the methods and process of evaluation

The criteria for evaluation indicate the targets or standards against which the performance could be measured. Actually, it's difficult to set any quantitative target for evaluating EMT. So the objectives of EMT become the standard for evaluating the programme. EMT may be evaluated at the participant's level by considering their reaction to the programme. Some things that are commonly considered in obtaining the participants' reactions are overall impression of the course, general interest, trainer's organization, presentation, and handling of sessions.

SNAPSHOT

- According to McClelland, a person has three types of needs at any given time—need for achievement, need for power, and need for affiliation.
- The need for achievement is the highest for entrepreneurs.
- EMT is carried out under three major headings: developing a curriculum plan for EMT, implementing EMT, and evaluating EMT.

DISCUSSION FORUM

- Explain McClelland's achievement motivation theory.
- Which are the three major phases for implementing EMT?

CHECKLIST FOR ENTREPRENEURS 2.4 — Entrepreneurial Motivation

Here are suggestions to help boost your motivation:

- **Dare to dream big:** Have the courage to dream big. Give shape and colour to your dreams. This will help you plan out the details of how to realise your dream.
- **Own your vision:** Create a vision for your life. Passionately own your vision and relentlessly drive it to completion.
- **Aim high:** All rags-to-riches stories revolve around people who aimed high. Evaluate your strengths. Get an understanding of your potential and unleash it to try to fulfil those aims.
- **Do what you are passionate about:** Do what you are passionate about, and you will enjoy what you are doing and show excellence.
- **Watch, read, and listen to success stories:** Practice positive thinking techniques. Watching, reading, and listening to success stories and motivational movies will boost your motivation level.
- **Celebrate every success:** Reflect on your achievement so far, even if it is small. Every victory should be celebrated. Reward yourself by celebrating every small success. Share your happiness at your success with family and friends in order to boost your self-esteem.

ENTREPRENEURSHIP TRAINING METHODS

Entrepreneurship training involves a learning process. The training methods that facilitate the learning process lead to involvement and participation and finally result in changes in the behavioural pattern of people at a cognitive or operational level. Thus, the various methods used during the training programme have a special significance. Let us discuss some popular training methods used during entrepreneurship training programmes to create learning situations.

Lecture Method

The lecture method of training is one of the oldest and most widely-used training methods. A lecture may be defined as an informative discourse delivered to an audience. It clearly implies a one-way communication to a number of people by someone who is knowledgeable in his subject. The method is used to deliver the majority of content in training programmes. In entrepreneurship training programmes, this method is widely used in combination with other methods like those involving seminars, conferences, panel discussions, workshops, buzz groups, the syndicate method, the case method, role play, the simulation method, and the laboratory method. Modern technology provides a wide range of aids to the speaker with the help of which the lecture method could be made more interesting, absorbing, and meaningful.

Participative Methods

The participative training method incorporates discussion of the content of training programmes, participation, understanding of the group process, and overall facilitation of things like belief, attitudes, knowledge, and sharing of experiences between people—all of which are imperative for broadening the general perspective as well as in business. Participation leads to a climate in which the trainees feel responsible, have their own views, knowledge, and experience. Let's discuss the various participative training methods:

- **Conference:** This method may effectively be used where the objective is to develop a perspective and insight into the subject conferred on, and where it is important to collect ideas from many before embarking on a project. The usual procedure adopted for conducting conferences is to prepare the agenda notes and working paper and invite experts to contribute papers for the conference. The plenary session, which is held in the beginning to spell out the objectives, purposes, the scope, and specific topics for discussion in the conference, provides a general forum for the participants and also helps in sharpening the focus of discussions. The chairman is the key figure in the conference.

- **Seminar:** A seminar is a formal presentation by a small group of people on a particular topic of common interest. In a seminar, participants present their views on a specific topic, followed by discussion and conversation. A seminar enables exchange of thoughts and ideas and the findings of the discussion are recorded for future action.

- **Panel discussion:** A panel discussion is designed to provide an opportunity to participants to hear the viewpoints of different people who are knowledgeable on a specific topic. A panel usually comprises 4–5 panel members. The discussion is led by a moderator. The role of the moderator is very important for opening the discussion, leading the discussion, closing the discussion, and concluding the discussion. The moderator should inform the panel members of the objective of the panel discussion and the time allotted for the panel discussion.

- **Workshop:** A workshop is product-centred and focuses on the specificity of the task to be accomplished. It is a method of designing training activities around identified work problems in order to find solutions to them. The objective is to obtain contributions from all affected individuals and optimize the resources available to solve the problems and to plan future action. The workshop differs from other group methods only in that it is set up to tackle specific operational problems. The participants play a key role in making the workshop a success. The workshop ends with a definite plan of action for the solution of a particular problem or task.

- **Buzz group:** Buzz groups are sub-divisions of a large group. The focus of this method is to provide an opportunity to everyone to express an opinion on the topic. The interaction is confined to a limited number of participants ranging from five to ten. The deliberation takes place in a small group on a given topic, which is presented by the leader of the sub-group.

- **Syndicate method:** This method is suitable for learning at a higher level. This method is widely used in teaching–learning situations, especially in top-level management training. This method requires a competent trainer and should have a core group of co-trainers equally competent in handling different assignments given to them. The participants should be divided into small groups consisting of eight to ten participants. This small group is known as a "syndicate." Generally, each syndicate is given a brief and carefully prepared background paper by the instructor. The syndicate discusses the issues involved in the subject area assigned to it and prepares a paper. The leader of each syndicate presents his report separately, followed by questions raised by each syndicate on the recommendation of other syndicates. The trainer acts mainly as a resource person in providing necessary information and facilitating their thinking on a particular topic. The participants learn from their own participation and from the experiences the trainers and other members bring to syndicate discussions.

- **Case method:** The case method has long been accepted as an important method for training entrepreneurs. It facilitates active participation and participative learning. If properly administered, it has the advantage of improving the knowledge, attitude, and skills of the trainees. The effectiveness of the case method depends upon the preparation of the case and the leading of the case in a classroom situation by the trainer. The trainer is expected to perform the role of facilitator.
- **Role play:** Trainees are made to enact a particular role so as to give a real feel of the roles given to them. This enables participants to understand the behaviour of others as well as their own feelings and emotions. The trainer must brief the trainees on the theme or situation and what is expected of them. This is a common and very effective technique for bringing into the classroom real-life situations concerning entrepreneurship. Sometimes the script is given to the team, while at other times the trainees prepare their own script around a given situation.
- **Simulation method:** Simulation methods try to replicate various activities in "real life" in the form of a game. In the simulation method, a "near real-life situation" is created providing an opportunity to trainees to experience. The trainees experience the impact of their behaviour on the situation. The simulation technique is carried out to generate response and reactions based on the real feelings of the participants, which are subsequently analysed by the trainer. Simulation games can result in very effective learning but trainers who administer them need considerable competency and good preparation.
- **Laboratory method:** The laboratory method of training is process-oriented learning wherein the participants learn by sharing their experiences, particularly those generated in the group. The method is also termed as sensitivity training, T-group, D-group, L-group, etc. The basic assumption in this method is that the efficiency and productivity of the group depends more often on the manner in which people work together than on their technological skill. The laboratory method offers a climate conducive to open discussion and learning, and encourages trusting behaviour. A major goal of such a method is to contribute towards personal growth through increased self-awareness and inter-personal competence.

THE PROCESS OF ENTREPRENEURIAL DEVELOPMENT

Most definitions of entrepreneurship indicate some need for planning. The process of helping a person to develop into an entrepreneur comprises the following three phases:

- **Stimulatory phase:** The stimulatory phase involves implementing stimulatory activities for creating interest and awareness in potential entrepreneurs. These activities prepare the foundation for the emergence of entrepreneurship in society. This phase involves various activities such as planned publicity for entrepreneurial opportunities, providing entrepreneurial education, counselling and motivational training to new entrepreneurs, identification of potential entrepreneurs through scientific techniques, providing guidance in selection of product/service and preparing project reports, creating entrepreneurial forums, and recognizing and rewarding existing entrepreneurs.
- **Support phase:** The support phase involves implementation of support activities that help in new venture creation. Support activities nurture and promote entrepreneurship. This phase involves various activities such as registration of enterprises; development of the product prototype; arrangement of finance, land, shed, power, and common facility centre; offering

management consultancy services and marketing support; guidance for selecting plant and machinery; and getting approvals and licenses.

- **Sustenance phase:** The sustenance phase involves the implementation of sustaining activities that help in the continuous and efficient functioning of enterprises within a society. This phase involves various activities such as modernization, diversification, expansion, getting additional finance, and research and development support to help an enterprise survive, develop, and grow after it is set up.

SNAPSHOT

- Entrepreneurship training programme methods are: lecture method, participative method, syndicate method, case method, role play, simulation method, and laboratory method.
- The various phases in the entrepreneurial development cycle are: stimulatory activities, support activities, and sustaining activities.

DISCUSSION FORUM

- Discuss training methods used in entrepreneurship training programmes.
- Explain the entrepreneurial development cycle.

BREAKTHROUGH ENTREPRENEURSHIP 2.5 Effectual Entrepreneurship

Aspiring entrepreneurs in business schools are taught principles and tools such as goal setting, market research, forecasting, and business planning to develop managerial thinking based on the causal approach. The causal reasoning approach is a step-by-step process in which the emphasis is on pre-set goals or opportunities; expected return; avoiding surprises; competitive analysis; forecasting; and predicting the future. The main focus of academic research on entrepreneurship had been on the causal action of entrepreneurs.

The research conducted by Saras D. Sarasvathy from the University of Virginia's Darden School found that expert entrepreneurs use the effectual reasoning approach when compared to the causal reasoning approach. Effectuation is a heuristic (trial and error) problem-solving approach. It is a logic of entrepreneurial expertise that both novice and experienced entrepreneurs can use in the highly unpredictable start-up phase of a venture to reduce failure costs for the entrepreneur. The effectual reasoning approach is a speculative and self-led investigation where the emphasis is on starting within your means; focusing on the downside risk; leveraging contingencies; forming partnerships; and controlling the future.

The syllabi in most business schools in India are designed to develop managers rather than entrepreneurs. Managers are often good at causal reasoning. They set a goal and diligently find the best way to achieve it. Entrepreneurs need to be and are often good at effectual reasoning. They start without concrete goals and constantly improve and react creatively to contingencies.

Management educators need to revolutionize the way entrepreneurship is taught throughout the world. Effectuation is a part of an "entrepreneurial method" where "effectual logic" can be used as the fuel to create more effective experiments by entrepreneurs testing their theories in the real world. In the early stages of venture creation, effectual and causal logic is necessary for growth and expansion. There is a need to add effectuation in the syllabi of business schools to develop and promote entrepreneurship in society.

Source: Read, Stuart, Saras D. Sarasvathy, Nicholas Dew, Robert Wiltbank, and Anne-Valerie Ohlsson (2011). *Effectual Entrepreneurship*. Oxford: Rutledge.

SUMMARY

Entrepreneurial environment is the result of a dynamic interaction among entrepreneurial attitudes, entrepreneurial activity, and entrepreneurial aspirations and varies across stages of economic development. The environmental factors affecting entrepreneurial growth are economic, political, legal, social and cultural, psychological, and technological. The global entrepreneurship and development index (GEDI) is a unique measure of entrepreneurship and its supporting conditions and offers a qualitative and quantitative measure of the business formation process.

David McClelland emphasized the importance of achievement motivation as the basis of the entrepreneurial personality. Entrepreneurship helps economic and social development by fulfilling the need for power, affiliation, and achievement. The need for achievement is the highest among entrepreneurs. Entrepreneurship motivation training (EMT) involves developing a curriculum plan for EMT, implementing EMT, and evaluating EMT. Some of the methods used during entrepreneurship training to create a learning situation are the lecture method, participative method, syndicate method, case method, role play, simulation method, and laboratory method.

The entrepreneurship development models fall into three categories—psychological, sociological, and integrated. The entrepreneurial development process involves three phases— stimulatory activities, support activities, and sustaining activities.

KEY TERMS

Economic Environment: The main components of economic environment are capital, labour, raw materials, market, and infrastructure.

Entrepreneurship Environment: The environment suitable for the development of entrepreneurship in the society.

Global Entrepreneurship Development Index (GEDI): An index that captures the contextual features of entrepreneurship and offers a measure of the quality and quantity of the business formation process in various countries. It is a unique measure of entrepreneurship and its supporting conditions worldwide.

Need for Achievement: The disposition to achieve something excellent.

Need for Affiliation: The drive for interpersonal relationships.

Need for Extension: The need to pursue goals that are likely to help a large number of persons.

Need for Power: The drive to influence others and any given situation.

Political Environment: National and international political factors that can affect the operations of an enterprise. The main components of political environment are: political stability, government policy regarding FDI, incentives, subsidies, licenses, regulations, taxation, etc.

Psychological Environment: Societies that are dynamic and promote change by encouraging innovations and novelties encourage entrepreneurial activities. The main components of psychological environment are the attitude of society, innovation, novelties, and achievement motivation.

Social and Cultural Environment: Social and cultural factors that strongly affect the kind of behaviour that contributes to entrepreneurial growth. The main components of social and cultural environment are religion, family background, education, social status, values, and behaviour acceptable within the society.

Technological Environment: The environment in which the technological advancement has become a catalytic agent in the promotion of entrepreneurial growth in industrial and allied services.

CASE STUDY

The Story of Silicon Valley

The phenomenal success of Silicon Valley, 45 miles southeast of San Francisco in California, the United States of America, has become iconic of the American entrepreneurial spirit. Silicon Valley houses the world's largest technology corporations. The main catalysts that led to the development of Silicon Valley were the institutional support of Stanford University, venture capital and generous stock options for employees, the information technology revolution, and a favourable entrepreneurial climate for risk-taking.

Professor Frederick Terman of Stanford University, who is widely credited (together with William Shockley) as being the father of Silicon Valley, encouraged faculty and graduate students to start their own companies. He persuaded his students William Hewlett and David Packard to start the Hewlett-Packard Company. Terman's real contribution was the creation of a sound ecosystem and the culture of entrepreneurship. The efforts of Professor William Shockley, who also taught at Stanford University, to commercialize a new transistor device led to the Silicon Valley becoming a hotbed of electronics innovation. In this way, Silicon Valley received the institutional support of Stanford University in its early days.

Silicon Valley has a strong networking system in combination with business angels and venture capital firms willing to support promising start-ups. This was made possible by the favourable political, economic, and intellectual climate prevailing in the United States. The Valley is a testimony to the concerted international efforts and contributions made by people from diverse cultural and racial backgrounds. In the early years of the Valley's development, the US government granted it military research funding. Successful entrepreneurs also supported its development by using their profits to become venture capitalists for the Silicon Valley. Many professionals were keen to work for a new venture at substantially reduced remuneration, as it provided a greater scope for entrepreneurship and job satisfaction compared to established firms. There was also the offer of generous stock options to employees in order to attract and retain talent in the Valley. Companies such as Netscape, Intel, Cisco, and Yahoo, have turned many of their employees into millionaires. This is mainly regarded as one of the foundations for the success of enterprises in Silicon Valley.

As Silicon Valley evolved and grew, it started attracting the best talent from all over the world. It has the largest concentration of brilliant computer professionals and the best supporting services globally. It was here that the silicon-based integrated circuit, microprocessor, and microcomputer—at the root of the information technology revolution—were developed.

America fostered a culture where failures were treated as learning experiences and failure held no terror (ideally). As such, risk-taking is considered a part-and-parcel of the entrepreneurial spirit and no stigma is attached to a failed effort. Immigrants have accounted for one-third of the scientific and engineering workforce in Silicon Valley. Prominent among them are Chinese, Indians, and Singaporeans. Firms are easily created, successfully developed, and frequently fail.

Questions:

1. What makes Silicon Valley a unique entity?
2. "Silicon Valley is a magnet for the new immigrant entrepreneur." Comment.
3. Is it possible to emulate the Silicon Valley Model?

Source: Lewis, Michael M. (2001). *The New New Thing: Silicon Valley Story*. New York: Penguin Books and Gregory Gromov, "Silicon Valley History," available at www.netvalley.com/silicon_valley_history.html (last accessed in March 2013).

DISCUSSION QUESTIONS

1. What are the factors that motivate people to go into business?
2. According to you, what are the factors hindering the development of entrepreneurship in India?

3. What is meant by entrepreneurial motivation? Is it necessary for a successful entrepreneur? Discuss.
4. What do you understand by achievement motivation? How can achievement motivation be developed?
5. Explain the factors that motivate people to become entrepreneurs.
6. Discuss the concept, objectives, and stages of entrepreneurship development programmes (EDPs).
7. List out the entrepreneurship development programmes available in India. Describe any one programme in detail.
8. Give an overview of the progress of entrepreneurship development programmes in India.

ACTIVITY

Understanding Yourself

Introduction: This activity represents a projective technique to understand your potential. This exercise enables you to understand your strengths and weaknesses for self-awareness and motivation. A person with higher self-esteem has higher self-awareness—both of strengths as well as weaknesses.

Objective: To help the participant to introspect and identify his strengths, weaknesses, and goals.

Time: 1 hour 30 minutes

Instructions: Fill in the following worksheet by writing five strengths and five weaknesses and your goals for each year. Next, within 250–300 words, write about yourself and what you want to be five years from now. Interested participants can present their story in front of the class.

Sl No.	Strengths	Weaknesses	Goals	Action
	List your skills, knowledge, and attitude	List areas where you lack skills, knowledge, and attitude		
1.			For next year	
2.			For second year	
3.			For third year	
4.			For fourth year	
5.			For fifth year	

PROJECT

1. Interview an entrepreneur in your region and make a list of the factors that motivated the entrepreneur to start an enterprise. In class, compare your notes with others and prepare a list of the common motivating factors among all entrepreneurs.

ENDNOTES

1. Àcs, Zoltàn J., László Szerb, and Edward Wlgar (2011). *Global Entrepreneurship and Development Index 2011*. Cheltenham, UK: Edward Elgar Publishing Limited.

2. Chaudhary, Vanshika (2011). "The Great Indian Middle Class: An Economy Driver," *Youth Ki Awaaz: Mouthpiece for the Youth*, November 5, available at www.youthkiawaaz.com (last accessed in March 2013); www.planningcommission.nic.in/plans; and Karnik, Gaurav (ed.) (2011). *Doing Business in India*. Ernst and Young, available at www.ey.com/Publication/vwLUAssets/Doing_business_in_India_2011/$FILE/Doing_business_in_India_2011.pdf (last accessed in March 2013).
3. www.doingbusiness.org/about-us (last accessed in March 2013).
4. Porter, Michael (1990). *The Competitive Advantage of Nations*. New York: The Free Press.
5. Sharma, R. A. (1980). *Entrepreneurial Change in Indian Industry*. New Delhi: Sterling Publishers Pvt. Ltd.
6. Casson, Mark (1982). *The Entrepreneur: An Economic Theory*. Totowa, NJ: Barnes and Noble Books.
7. Hagen, Everett E. (1964). *On the Theory of Social Change*. London: Tavistock, p. 557.
8. Rao, T. V. and Udai Pareek (eds.) (1978). *Developing Entrepreneurship*. New Delhi: Learning Systems, pp. 355–367; Pareek, Udai (1978). "Evaluation of Training," *Vikalpa*, October 4, 3 (4): 289–299.
9. McClelland, D. C. (1967). *The Achieving Society*. New York: Free Press; London: Collier-Macmillan.
10. McClelland D. C. (1965). "Toward a Theory of Motive Acquisition," *American Psychologist*, 20 (5): 321–333.

Entrepreneurial Perspectives

1. Entrepreneurship
2. Entrepreneurial Development and Training
3. **Women Entrepreneurs**
4. Family Business
5. Micro, Small, and Medium Enterprises

"When women move forward, the family moves, the village moves, the nation moves."
—Pundit Jawaharlal Nehru

Kiran Mazumdar-Shaw is the founder, chairman, and managing director of India's leading biotechnology enterprise, Biocon Limited. She founded Biocon in 1978 by partnering with an Irish firm to make industrial enzymes. The photograph shows Kiran Mazumdar-Shaw accepting the prestigious Padma Bhushan award from former President A. P. J. Abdul Kalam in 2005.

Women Entrepreneurs

3

LEARNING OBJECTIVES

Upon completion of this chapter, you should be able to:

1. **Understand the role of entrepreneurship in the empowerment of women.**
2. **Describe the concept of women's entrepreneurship.**
3. **Identify the factors influencing the development of women entrepreneurs and the challenges in the path of women's entrepreneurship.**
4. **Explore strategies for the development of women entrepreneurs and identify institutions supporting women's entrepreneurship in India.**
5. **Discuss successful women entrepreneurs from India and around the world.**

INTRODUCTION

It is imperative to recognize that in the modern dynamic environment, the woman entrepreneur is an important part of the global quest for sustained socioeconomic progress. A strategy aimed at economic development will not be effective without the participation of women, who constitute nearly half of the world population and an important part of the workforce. The participation of women in economic activities is necessary not only from a human-resource point of view but also for raising the status of women in society. The economic status of women is now accepted as an indicator of a society's stage of development. Therefore, it becomes imperative for the government to frame policies for the development of entrepreneurship among women. The long-term objectives of development programmes for women should be to raise their economic and social status in order to bring them into the mainstream of national life and development. For this, due recognition must be accorded to the role and contribution of women in the various social, economic, political, and cultural fields.

The Indian government defines a woman entrepreneur's enterprise as one "owned and controlled by a woman having a minimum financial interest of 51 per cent of the capital and giving at least 51 per cent of the employment generated by the enterprise to women."[1] Women's entrepreneurship has gained momentum in the last three decades with an increase in the number of enterprises run by women and a consequent increase in women's contribution to economic growth. Industrial development, technological innovations, foreign direct investments, and export potential have helped bring a wide range of socioeconomic opportunities to women entrepreneurs. Moreover, with more and more women pursuing professional, technical, and higher education and with the advent of mass media, women are now more aware of their right to be economically independent. Naturally, most business sectors—from *papad*-making to the manufacturing of power cables—have seen an increase in the proportion of women employees.

Women make excellent entrepreneurs as they tend to be good at multitasking, deftly handling home and business. It has often been observed that women entrepreneurs are great communicators and are naturals when it comes to building relationships. Moreover, women are also good problem-solvers and calculated risk-takers.[2]

Certain common traits bind many women entrepreneurs together. Successful women entrepreneurs are often ambitious in their desire for personal achievement, which drives them to great heights in their careers. It is generally observed that they are optimistic, confident of their own abilities, know their strengths and weaknesses, and stick to their own judgement in the face of opposition or an initial absence of success. They can take bold risks as well as responsibility for their own actions. They are often innovative, flexible, adaptable to changing market trends and business methods, and willing to learn, unlearn, and relearn. They feel compelled to produce high-quality work at a competitive cost. They value teamwork and loyalty and are conscious of their responsibility toward society.[3]

Kamal Singh defines a woman entrepreneur as a "confident, innovative and creative woman capable of achieving economic independence individually or in collaboration, generates employment opportunities for others through initiating, establishing and running the enterprise by keeping pace with her personal, family, and social life."[4] Today, India is full of success stories of women entrepreneurs. Kiran Mazumdar-Shaw started Biocon with a seed capital of only

WORLD OF ENTREPRENEURS 3.1 The "10,000 Women" Initiative

The Goldman Sachs Foundation, in partnership with the United States Department of State, launched the "10,000 Women" initiative on 8 March 2008 on the 100th anniversary of International Women's Day. "10,000 Women" is part of Goldman Sachs's global initiative to increase the number of women entrepreneurs in the business world and to expand entrepreneurial talent and the managerial pool among women in developing and emerging economies.

Goldman Sachs's initiative is a $5.5 crore worldwide campaign to drive economic growth by providing 10,000 women with a business and management education as well as access to capital, networks, and mentors. This programme has already reached more than 3,500 women in more than 20 countries. This shows that a partnership among education, development, and business experts can help bring about significant change and improved business education for women. The initiative has six important components to meet its goals. They are to:

- Enable 10,000 women to receive a business and management education over a period of five years.
- Build quality and capacity through partnerships with business schools around the world.
- Provide mentoring and post-graduation support for women entrepreneurs.
- Work with leading research and women's development organizations.
- Develop partnerships in the USA to help disadvantaged women.
- Commit sufficient resources to the initiative.

The Indian School of Business (ISB), Hyderabad, is an academic partner for the "10,000 Women" initiative in India. To ensure that the most deserving women entrepreneurs receive the maximum benefit of this initiative, the programme targets those who, for more than a year, have been running a business venture of their own with excellent growth potential and an annual revenue of ₹5 lakh to ₹50 lakh. Over the last three years, more than 300 women entrepreneurs have successfully completed Goldman Sachs's "10,000 Women Entrepreneurs Certificate Programme" across Delhi, Mumbai, Pune, Bangalore, and Hyderabad.

Sources: "Goldman Sachs 10,000 Women Initiative," available at www.gbsnonline.org/programs/current/goldman-sachs-10000-women-initiative.html (last accessed in March 2013); "The Goldman Sachs 10,000 Women Initiative and United States Department of State Announce New Partnership," 08 March 2011, available at http://www2.goldmansachs.com/media-relations/press-releases/current/10k-w-partnership.html (last accessed in March 2013); "Goldman Sachs 10,000 Women Entrepreneurs Certificate Programme," available at www.isb.edu/10000women/ (last accessed in March 2013); http://womeninbusiness.about.com/od/challengeswomenface/a/10k-women.htm (last accessed in March 2013); and http://jay-parkhe.posterous.com/Word-Press-402 (last accessed in March 2013).

₹10,000 and has seen it grow into a global provider of pharmaceuticals. Shri Mahila Griha Udyog, the organization that makes the famous Lijjat Papad, began with just seven women working on a cooperative basis in a building with a seed capital of ₹80 and has expanded into a company that currently employs over 42,000 sister-members throughout India.[5] Shahnaz Husain began her entrepreneurial journey in a single beauty parlour in Delhi and now has a global presence. Ekta Kapoor's success with Balaji Telefilms has set a good example for young women entrepreneurs in the television industry. Wherever they have set foot, Indian women entrepreneurs have written a new chapter. Women entrepreneurs have been able to excel in their fields for the following reasons[6]:

- **The need for economic independence:** Most women start businesses because they feel the need to be economically independent or supplement their family incomes. Financial independence often becomes a necessity for single women and widows. Growing urbanization and industrialization have encouraged and often necessitated women's entrepreneurship. In certain cases, women are forced to shoulder the responsibility of earning for their families.
- **Technology:** Technology has enabled many women to work from home or start home-based businesses, making it easier for them to balance their careers and family life. Technology, such as the Internet, also connects women entrepreneurs across the globe and helps them work effectively, efficiently, and productively.
- **Achievement of excellence:** Women with achievement motivation crave a challenging career, such as one involving entrepreneurship, rather than an ordinary job. Most women start business enterprises not only to make money but also to experience a sense of accomplishment and achievement.
- **Establishing an identity:** Many women pursue a career for self-fulfillment. Entrepreneurship fulfiles women's need to establish their own identities and make a mark in society. It channelizes their talents and helps them make the best use of their education. Many women work for corporate companies for a certain period of time to acquire skills and experience and later choose to start their own enterprises.

BREAKTHROUGH ENTREPRENEURSHIP 3.2 Harpreet Ahluwalia—Green Entrepreneur

Harpreet Ahluwalia has turned her passion for art and nature into a successful business. Harpreet's entrepreneurial journey began when she ordered a few custom-designed pots for her home in Noida. She decorated her home with potted plants in a way that sent out a message of passion and love. People who came to visit her liked her pottery designs and she began receiving requests for them. Finding herself in business, Harpreet launched her first venture—Earthly Creations Inc.

Harpreet's interaction with the potters who work for her gives her insights into their lives. The interactive nature of Harpreet's venture not only helps her to discover the talent of these economically poor but aesthetically wealthy potters but also helps her to financially support them.

Harpreet has come a long way since the launch of Earthly Creations Inc. She is now a regular participant in over 40 exhibitions across India. Additionally, she is a syndicated columnist with gardening journals and environmental talk shows. She presently runs four businesses successfully: Earthly Creations, Excalibre, Alluring Fantasies, and Healings. Earthly Creations specializes in terracotta garden decorations; Excalibre engages in a range of consulting services, including the coaching and mentoring of executive management teams; Alluring Fantasies deals in artefacts; and Healings focuses on holistic healing. Her message remains "Love animals and gift a piece of nature."

Source: Kumar, Rajen (2010), "Harpreet Ahluwalia's Tryst with Nature: Creating Green Space in Your Life," *SME World*, July, 3 (7): 32–34, available at ww.smeworld.org/story/cover-stories-105/creating-green-space-in-your-life-97.php (last accessed in March 2013). Reproduced with permission.

WOMEN'S ENTREPRENEURSHIP IN ASIA

Entrepreneurship has emerged as a major focus of attention in the last few decades. It has expanded beyond the scope of an owner-manager to include professional managers in large corporations and conglomerates who play the role of entrepreneurial managers. Being synonymous with creativity and innovation, entrepreneurship is believed to be an economic panacea for problems such as unemployment and lopsided development.

There is high focus on entrepreneurship in Asia. Entrepreneurs are believed to be determining factors in the creation of new wealth in society. In many developing countries, such as in India, there is a concentration of small- and medium-sized companies and family businesses. Women's entrepreneurship development in Asian countries has the potential to empower women and create a socio-economic transformation of the region to which these women belong. In some Asian countries, especially where the level of economic development is reflected by the low level of per capita income and the degree of industrialization, this potential remains largely untapped. Less than 15 per cent of entrepreneurs in South Asia, comprising Bhutan, India, Bangladesh, Maldives, Nepal, Pakistan, and Sri Lanka, are women. It has also been found that there are three categories of women entrepreneurs: "chance," "forced," and "created entrepreneurs." These three categories are based on how their businesses got started or the main reasons or motives behind starting their own businesses.[7]

Self-employment is emerging as a very important source of livelihood for women in Asia. This is due to the scarcity of employment opportunities in this part of the world. Additionally, many types of paid employment here are felt to be more suitable for males than for females (for example, mining, construction). Furthermore, many women are less educated, having fewer technical skills.

The 1970s saw women setting up enterprises across Asia. They had begun to chop away at one of the last and most enduring bastions of male dominance—the no-women's land of business entrepreneurship, risk taking, and financial adventure. In India, the 1990s was the decade of entrepreneurial explosion. Today, women are taking to business entrepreneurship not only in metropolitan cities such as Delhi, Mumbai, Kolkata, Bangalore, and Ahmedabad but also in backward areas like Bihar and in smaller towns. This trend has risen mainly because of changes in social attitudes in urban areas, the break-up of the traditional joint family system, a rising standard of living, opportunities for higher education for women, growing awareness of the need for economic independence, consciousness of women's potential, and credit and other facilities provided by the government to set up enterprises.

In a study conducted in Southeast Asian countries, women were found to make up a significant part of those classified as employers and self-employed. On an average, women classified as employers or self-employed form 23 per cent to 30 per cent of the total number of women workers in Indonesia, Malaysia, the Philippines, and Thailand. In sections such as manufacturing, trading, and community services in these countries, a substantial number of entrepreneurs are female. Moreover, the percentage share of women who are employers or self-employed is rising all over Southeast Asia.[8] Over two decades, from the 1970s to the 1980s, while the percentage of employers and self-employed in the labour force remained stable in all Southeast Asian countries, the percentage of women classified as employers or self-employed rose in virtually all sectors.

Entrepreneurship requires the presence of economic opportunity, sympathetic cultural forces, supportive government action, and strong personal values. Most of these facilitating factors are certainly not in favour of women. While it appears relatively easy for women in the more advantaged (but typically smaller) segments of the population to set up and sustain enterprises of their own, the real challenge in developing countries is in bringing the vast majority of disadvantaged women into the mainstream of economic activity.

In times to come, the knowledge economy will offer women newer opportunities in entrepreneurship.

WOMEN'S ENTREPRENEURSHIP IN INDIA

The emergence of women entrepreneurs and women-owned firms, and their significant contributions to the economy, is visible in India. These businesses are ready for continued growth in the future.

The new generation of women-owned enterprises is actively seeking capital for its businesses, using modern technology to find and create a niche in both the domestic and export markets. While women-owned businesses possess the potential and are capable of contributing much more, it is essential to formulate strategies to invigorate, support, and sustain their efforts in the right direction.

Surveys demonstrate that women's primary entrepreneurial activity is focused on the micro, small, and medium enterprises (MSME) sector. Among the total number of women entrepreneurs in the country, approximately 61 per cent are small-scale entrepreneurs, 18 per cent are large-scale manufacturers, and the remaining are involved in cottage and village enterprises.[9] They work in a wide range of sectors—from trade and services to tailoring, beauty parlours, and at printing presses. However, the involvement of women entrepreneurs in the production sector is minimal and the development of this sector is rather slow.

Studies show that women contribute significantly to the running of family businesses, mostly in the form of unpaid effort and skills. Moreover, many enterprises that are defined as being run by women (businesses in which women hold the controlling share) are in fact run in their names by men who control the operations and decision-making. Programmes meant to help women entrepreneurs can succeed only if note is taken of such problematic situations as well as of the familial and social conditioning that undermines the confidence, independence, and mobility of women. Programmes encouraging entrepreneurship among women will require a change in societal attitudes rather than a mere creation of additional employment opportunities for women. These programmes should also go beyond subsidies and credit allocation to change in attitude, group and association formation, training in both managerial and technical skills, and other support services. One way to do this would be to begin training in entrepreneurial attitudes at the high-school level through well-designed courses. Furthermore, appropriate skill-development training still remains the key for a programme to successfully develop entrepreneurship among women. NGOs like the Rural Development and Self-Employment Training (RUDSET) Institute in Karnataka have been successful in achieving reasonably high levels of success in this regard.

Apart from training, the availability of finance and other necessities like land, industrial plots, and sheds is often a constraint that many women-owned businesses face. Funding is not easily available for primary activities. Banks and moneylenders are reluctant to lend money to women entrepreneurs due to the risk and high operational costs involved in these businesses. However, schemes like the Integrated Rural Development Programme (IRDP) and the Prime Minister's Rozgar Yojana (PMRY), and organizations like the Small Industries Development Bank of India (SIDBI) do extend assistance in trade, even in trade finance.

Most women entrepreneurs find it difficult to market their products successfully. Marketing requires both mobility and confidence in dealing with the external world, both of which women have been discouraged from developing by social conditioning. Organizations promoting women entrepreneurs arrange frequent exhibitions to showcase the products and services developed by women entrepreneurs. Some NGOs even use mobile marketing vans. However, these are not long-term arrangements and quality control is inadequate. The long-term strategy should be to teach marketing skills to women entrepreneurs in order to make them responsive to the market. This means that market surveys of selected products should be made part of the training programme for women entrepreneurs and professional marketing advice should be shared with them. The use of professional marketing expertise is essential to identify marketing channels for the products made by women entrepreneurs. Industrial estates could also provide marketing outlets for the display and sale of products made by women.

The Centre for Women's Development Studies (CWDS) indicates that while the participation of women in the workforce is high and on the increase, the general status of women and their control over resources is not increasing at the same pace. According to the CWDS, the basis of gender inequalities is the restriction of women from exercising control over the means of production—whether land or capital—in spite of being usually allowed to engage in subsistence-level income generation, The CWDS believes that governments must try harder to bring in sensitizing policies to address these concerns.[10]

The UNDP has initiated a project, Science and Technology Applied for Rural Transformation (START), which operates through a network of technology development centres and resource centres. Each technology centre develops a network of small NGOs and women-dominated enterprises to implement the project and to fulfill the twin objectives of increasing productivity using the natural resources of the region and using technology to enhance opportunities.

The following are a few facts about women entrepreneurs in India:

- A majority of women entrepreneurs are married and have small families.
- Many women entrepreneurs belong to the low-income group.
- Many women become entrepreneurs out of economic necessity.
- Unmarried women and women from low-income groups face difficulties in getting financial support to launch their enterprises.
- A large number of women with little or no education enter into business without undergoing any training. Most of these practising women entrepreneurs lack vocational education.
- Women from the low-income group exercise greater freedom in making the decision to start a business as compared to middle-class women who suffer from cultural constraints.
- Support systems often do not effectively carry out the development of vision, confidence, business orientation, and skills.
- Gender discrimination is often encountered at every stage of business development.
- Women entrepreneurs often prefer diversification to specialization, stabilization of income and minimization of risk to maximization of income, and are security-oriented rather than growth-oriented.
- It is still not uncommon to find enterprises owned by women but run by men, although this trend is slowly fading.
- In the field of technology, women entrepreneurs have made a conscious decision to set up technology-based enterprises. Many have ventured into hi-tech areas such as manufacturing of solar thermals, vacuum reactors, television boosters, air compressors, voltage stabilizers, and amplifiers. However, for most women, their businesses remain microenterprises.

DISCUSSION FORUM

- Define the term "women entrepreneur."
- Illustrate the role of women entrepreneurs in the economic development of society with examples.

BREAKTHROUGH ENTREPRENEURSHIP 3.3 Vidya Murkumbi—Sugar Entrepreneur

Born in 1955, Vidya Murkumbi is a star in the Indian sugar industry. Although she was initially involved in the trading and distribution of various Tata and Parle products, she later moved into the manufacturing and marketing business. A chemistry graduate, Vidya established Murkumbi Bioagro Private Limited and Murkumbi Industries Private Limited in 1988. In 1998, she co-founded Shree Renuka Sugars Limited along with her son Narendra.

Vidya's entrepreneurial experience with Shree Renuka Sugars Limited began when she and her son Narendra bought a loss-making sugar mill in 1998, paying for it with loans and (uniquely) the money obtained from the sale of company shares to sugarcane farmers living around the sugar mill. Under the leadership of Vidya and her son Narendra, Shree Renuka Sugars—which is among the country's fastest growing sugar companies—has gone public, diversified into electricity generation, and even acquired a Brazilian sugar company. Today, its sugar refining capacity of 4,000 tonnes per day is the largest in India. Currently, Vidya and Narendra own three sugar refineries. The mother–son duo is ranked 93rd in *Forbes's* list of India's richest 100 published in 2009. According to *Forbes*, Vidya and her son Narendra have a net worth of $49 crore.

Source: "Vidya Murkumbi's advice to start-ups," *Economic Times*, 12 February 2010, available at www.peerpower.com/et/196/Vidya-Murkumbi-s-advice-to-startups (last accessed in March 2013); and www.forbes.com/lists/2009/77/india-billionaires-09_Indias-Richest_Rank.html (last accessed in March 2013).

CHALLENGES FACED BY WOMEN ENTREPRENEURS

The challenges that women entrepreneurs face extend to the different environments that they operate in.[11] The overall context of women's entrepreneurship development can be described in the form of the following three different spheres.

Microsphere

Women entrepreneurs operating in a microsphere are mainly confined to the local environment and obliged to live close to the family. For example, in many South Asian countries, women entrepreneurs are expected to carry out household work, childcare, and other tasks in addition to their businesses. In such an environment, women entrepreneurs find it difficult to travel to procure supplies and meet customers and are often unable to grow and expand their businesses freely.

Mesosphere

Women entrepreneurs operating in the mesosphere work at a regional or national level. There are a large number of organizations involved in implementing policies and programmes as well as in providing support services to entrepreneurs operating within the mesosphere. However, for a variety of reasons, many of these organizations tend to act as barriers when it comes to providing assistance to women entrepreneurs operating within this environment. In some cases this can be attributed to a lack of awareness about women's concerns and insensitivity towards gender issues. The State might formulate gender-progressive laws and policies, but the resistance offered by the bureaucracy, judiciary, and other official organizations often hinders the implementation of these measures.

Macrosphere

Women entrepreneurs operating in the macrosphere find themselves working at a global level. The macro-environment within which they develop and grow comprises many interconnecting structures and dynamics, such as laws and regulations, economy, international trade, market liberalization and globalization, availability of finance and credit, labour market, human capital resources, technology, physical infrastructure, and natural resources.

The business environment has an impact on all enterprises, large and small, run by both women and men. There is much evidence to indicate that women are at a greater disadvantage than men in relation to the opportunities and obstacles arising from these environmental structures and dynamics. This is partly because the extent to which women can negotiate in the labour market is critically affected by predominant gender ideology and practices. Negotiation takes place over wages, conditions of work, and workers' rights. However, women who negotiate in the workplace are sometimes constrained not only by gender gaps in skills and education but also by employers' assumptions regarding their abilities, work commitment, efficiency, and needs, all of which is further exacerbated by the unequal sharing of family responsibilities at the micro level.[12]

Within their environments, women entrepreneurs face major challenges. A major obstacle in the path of women's entrepreneurship is that women entrepreneurs often find it difficult to access funds from various financial institutions as they do not possess tangible security and credit in the market. When they are able to access funds, the complex and complicated procedures of many financial institutions (including banks) and the delay in obtaining loans make it difficult for women to arrange the working capital to finance the day-to-day operation of their enterprises. This chronic shortage of working capital leaves women entrepreneurs extremely vulnerable to competition and other emergencies.

Globalization, heavy competition in the marketplace, limited mobility, and inadequate training in marketing skills often induce women entrepreneurs to depend on middlemen who pocket a major chunk of the profit for marketing their products and services. Most women entrepreneurs lack information on changing market dynamics and face difficulty in payment collection.

Women often also lag in acquiring and mastering the technical skills necessary to manage their enterprises.

Many women are low on self-confidence, and this could be another barrier to successful entrepreneurship by women. Women's lack of confidence in their own abilities stems from various socio-cultural factors. In our society, women are often discouraged from receiving higher education and vocational training, and those who do have the opportunity for higher studies often feel pressured to pursue stereotypical career options for women (such as being a doctor, teacher, nurse, or government employee) instead of business. As women have long accepted a subordinate role, society—including, sometimes, women themselves—are usually sceptical about women's capabilities. This is quite apparent in the family's reluctance to finance a woman's venture, bankers' reluctance to take risks on projects set up by women, and individuals' unwillingness to stand guarantee for loans to a woman. Entrepreneurship is also made difficult by the general expectation of society that a woman, irrespective of her career as a working woman or an entrepreneur, will perform what society perceives to be her family duties. Women are usually accepted as experts in their field only after they have proven themselves to be excellent at their work. So in order to demonstrate credibility, women entrepreneurs need to be confident of their strengths and abilities and demonstrate excellence in their work.[13]

STRATEGIES FOR THE DEVELOPMENT OF WOMEN ENTREPRENEURS

The following efforts can be made to promote the development of women entrepreneurs in the country [14]:

Encouraging Home-based Businesses

By operating her business from home, a woman can coordinate her household and business responsibilities more easily, and be on the path to achieving work–life balance.

BREAKTHROUGH ENTREPRENEURSHIP 3.4 Revathi Siddhartha Roy—Forsche Cabs

Revathi Siddhartha Roy, who is a graduate of St Xavier's College, Mumbai, and holds a Ph.D. in economics, is the founder of Forsche—a women-only cab service operating in Mumbai and Delhi. Forsche cabs are driven exclusively by women drivers and accept only women customers. Revathi still recalls how the idea of starting an exclusive ladies' cab service occurred to her at a traffic signal in Mumbai on a December night in 2006 when she was put off by the irresponsible driving of her local cab driver. Some examples of similar women's cab services around the world are Dubai's "Women's Taxi," Britain's "Pink Ladies," and Moscow's "Pink Taxi."

An avid rally-driver, Revathi launched Forsche Cabs on Women's Day in 2007. Although Revathi has had her share of trouble with credit institutions, she is not unduly worried about capital as she believes that NGOs, women's organizations, and sponsors will come to the aid of Forsche if necessary. Instead, she believes that her greatest challenge at this stage is to get women drivers to join, train, and stay in the company. In spite of the challenges, Forsche, which began with just a single cab plying the streets of Mumbai, has grown to a fleet of over 65 cabs across Mumbai and Delhi. Revathi accessorizes the cabs by adding small feminine touches such as make-up kits, bigger mirrors, and nail polish removers. Additionally, women cab drivers are trained in driving, etiquette, conversation skills, and martial arts before being assigned to the fleet.

Source: Based on Bhatt, Neha and Smita Mitra (2011). "Wheeling Into New Frontiers," 28 February, available at www.outlookindia.com/article.aspx?270516 (last accessed in March 2013); Manu, A. (2010). "How She Became an Entrepreneur, Against All Odds," 6 August, available at www.rediff.com/business/slide-show/slide-show-1-meet-the-founder-of-forshe-cabs/20100806.htm (last accessed in March 2013); and IANS (2010), "Banks Shut Door on All-Women's Cab Service," 19 September, available at www.sify.com/finance/banks-shut-door-on-india-s-all-women-cab-service-news-default-kjtmubehfai.html (last accessed in March 2013).

Widespread Business Education

Workshops, counselling services, vocational training, seminars, and conferences should be organized frequently for women entrepreneurs. They should undergo training in effective communication and management skills and practices to handle human resources as well as in the legal aspects of running a business. Non-governmental organizations should be involved in training women entrepreneurs at the grassroots level. Efforts should be taken to include entrepreneur education at the school level. Gender sensitization programmes should be conducted for officials and trainers dealing with women entrepreneurs.

Better Financial Assistance

A separate and independent bank for women along the lines of Venezuela's Women's Development Bank (WDB) should be established in our country to provide low-interest loans to women. Procedures for financial assistance by banks and government organizations should be simplified. Women inspectors, if available, should be asked to inspect women's enterprises.

Wider Access to Technology

Women entrepreneurs should acquire relevant training in the use of technology and in the functioning of their plant and machinery. Effective and efficient use of technology such as the Internet can help them acquire information about the variety, range, and quality of competing products, and provide a platform for the publicity and marketing of their own products and services.

Group Entrepreneurship/Grassroots Entrepreneurship Through Self-help Groups

Group entrepreneurship is a collaborative approach to enterprise creation that benefits a community. It is a viable option for the weaker sections of society and can help women overcome their poverty. It empowers women and inspires them with confidence in themselves.

A scheme for group entrepreneurship is the self-help group (SHG), which enables the rural poor to earn their own livelihood while participating in the process of development. The SHG scheme has been extensively used by voluntary agencies for a long time but it has now been incorporated into the conventional development process.

A self-help group is a small, voluntarily-formed, economically-homogeneous, and significant group of rural/urban poor who mutually agree to contribute to a common fund from which money is agreed to be lent out to its members according to group decisions.

A typical rural women's SHG is a good example of capacity building for prospective entrepreneurs. Its aims include enabling members with no educational, industrial, or entrepreneurial background to become self-reliant; developing and enhancing the decision-making capacity of members; instilling in members the strength and confidence to solve their problems; and providing poor people with a forum where they can learn about collectively mobilizing and managing money and matters. Table 3.1 shows the status of women's SHGs in India for the years 2008–2010. Note that on an average, around 80 per cent of total SHGs in India were women's SHGs during this period of time.

In an SHG, women are organized into small groups. The group formation helps to generate peer group support and solidarity. The group meets regularly, initially for awareness generation. After selecting a project, some members of the group attend training. At this stage, regular and timely attendance at meetings becomes very important. The quantum of weekly saving is also decided upon at this stage and each member is expected to contribute and participate. The initial contribution is usually made by an NGO, a funding agency, or the government.

SHGs directly help women increase their income by providing loans for productive enterprises. There are also other indirect ways in which SHGs can help increase income. For

Table 3.1 Position of Women SHGs in India

Particulars	Year	Total SHGs		Exclusive Women's SHGs		Percentage of Women's SHGs to Total SHGs	
		Number	Amount	Number	Amount	Number	Amount
Saving-linked SHGs	31.03.2009	6,121,147	5,545.62	4,863,921	4,434.03	79.5	80.0
	31.03.2010	6,953,250	6,198.71	5,310,436	4,498.56	76.4	72.6
Loans disbursed	2008–09	1,609,586	12,253.51	1,374,579	10,527.38	85.4	85.9
	2009–10	1,586,822	14,453.30	1,294,476	12,429.37	81.6	86.0
Loans outstanding	31.03.2009	4,224,338	22,679.84	3,277,355	18,583.54	77.6	81.9
	31.03.2010	4,851,356	28,038.28	3,897,797	23,030.36	80.3	82.1

Source: NABARD, "Status of Microfinance in India—2009–10." Reproduced with permission.

example, they help avoid the interest rate of moneylenders and equip women to face possible loss of assets like cattle and goats through insurance. However, SHGs cannot be considered as just a credit or a savings group. Indeed, these groups form the basis for solidarity, strength, and collective action.

It needs to be mentioned that the SHG's involvement in self-employment activities certainly contributes to group entrepreneurship at the grassroots level. Group entrepreneurship offers an opportunity for the rural poor to learn basic managerial skills and values. This is useful not only to the poor but to society as a whole. Hence, group entrepreneurship through SHGs is an investment in the poor as well as an engine of development.

A brief review of the credit-based NGO activities suggests that they can be classified into four categories:

- NGOs acting as financial intermediaries between government schemes and the poor.
- NGOs lending directly to the poor.
- NGOs promoting self-help thrift and savings groups.
- NGOs functioning as non-governmental cooperative banks for the poor.

What Makes SHGs Work? SHGs work because of the following factors:

- **The self-help group addresses a felt need and a common interest:** When people share a common problem that can be addressed by group action, they are more likely to mobilize themselves and work with support agencies to change the situation than if the problem applies to only a few members. Social cohesion tends to break down as groups grow or spread over large areas. For this reason, as groups expand, they either create subgroups or formalise regulations and delegate decision making to smaller working groups.
- **The benefits of working together outweigh the costs:** The benefits may be economic (cash savings, increased production, income and time saving), social capital formation (increased ability to collectively solve problems), increased individual capacity (knowledge and skills), psychological (sense of belonging and confidence), or political (greater access to authority, greater authority, and reduced conflict).
- **The group is embedded in the local social organization:** Community organizations are most successful when based on existing relationships and groupings or when members share a common identity such as kinship, gender, age, caste, or livelihood.
- **The group has the capability, leadership, knowledge and skills to manage the tasks:** As noted above, special attention needs to be given to ensuring that groups have the necessary capacities for the tasks at hand. Those in leadership positions need to be respected and honest in

their dealings. In some cases, safeguards may need to be put in place to ensure that these leaders are accountable to the group's members.

- **The group owns and enforces its rules and regulations:** Internalized rules and regulations that are known to its members characterize all successful groups and associations. Group members should be able to participate in determining the rules and the enforcement mechanisms.

The SHG System A self-help group is a collection of about 10 to 20 people from a similar class or region who come together to form a savings and credit organization. They often pool financial resources to make small interest-bearing loans to their members. This process creates a code of ethics that focuses on saving. The setting of terms and conditions and the accounting of loans are done in the group by designated members.

A self-help group may receive support from a non-governmental organization (NGO), a microfinance organization (MFO) or a bank. Alternatively, it could evolve from a traditional rotating savings and credit association (ROSCA) or other locally initiated groups. The process of formal linkage to an MFO or a bank usually goes through the following stages, which may take anywhere between a few months and years:

- The SHG members decide to make regular savings contributions. These may either be kept by their elected head in cash or kind or banked.
- The members start to borrow individually from the SHG for various purposes on terms and interests rates decided upon by the group.
- The SHG members open a savings account in the group's name with the MFO or bank for funds that are not needed by members or in order to qualify for a loan from the bank.
- The MFO or bank sanctions a loan to the SHG in the name of the group. This loan is then used by the group to supplement its own funds in lending money to its members.
- Members are generally married women between the ages of 25 and 50, to ensure a permanent address and thereby the security of the loans.
- Members are selected from the same community so that they are mutually accountable and understand the cooperative nature of the savings/loan plans. These voluntary SHGs are formed of women of different faiths and communities.
- The SHG has no alignment to any political parties or programmes. Politics is not allowed to be discussed at meetings.
- The SHG is willing to be initiated into a 12-month small mutual savings plan, which works like an orientation for a bigger Micro-Finance Institution (MFI) or an ICICI Bank microcredit programme to follow. By this time, members of the SHG have demonstrated a proven ability to save funds and pay interest.

Various SHG Activities to Promote Entrepreneurship SHGs carry out various activities to encourage entrepreneurship. They set up microenterprises. which are very small business units manufacturing finished or semi-finished products. Their activities may include desktop publishing, making greeting cards, book manufacturing, creating handicrafts, mono bloc units, shops, and so on. Other activities that SHGs may carry out with the assisted funds are improvised mat weaving, handlooms, fibre rope making, poultry farming, dairy farming, and gem cutting and polishing.[15]

DISCUSSION FORUM

- Discuss with suitable examples how entrepreneurship can help in the empowerment of women.
- Explain how self-help groups can develop entrepreneurship at the grassroots level.

BREAKTHROUGH ENTREPRENEURSHIP 3.5 **Sabala: Exporting Indian Handicrafts Through SHGs**

Sabala is a voluntary organization established in 1986 in the arid district of Bijapur in North Karnataka. It is registered under the Karnataka Societies Registration Act, 1960, and is governed by a governing council. Mallamma S. Yalwar is the founder and chief executive of Sabala. Sabala's vision is to empower women and other marginalized communities to access sustainable livelihood and opportunities. Sabala works with widows, destitute women, tribals, physically-challenged girls and women, and economically backward women.

Sabala creates opportunities for women to learn a skill and to use these skills to generate income. Over time, Sabala has striven to help the income generation of people in marginalized communities through the revival of various traditional forms of crafts such as Banjara and Kasuthi crafts. The Banjara community is a tribal community believed to have descended from the Roma gypsies of Europe. The Banjara art, characterized by mirror work, is an original art form passed down from one generation to the next. Sabala has trained and supported more than one thousand Banjara women from villages situated in Bijapur district in handicraft work by developing self-help groups.

Sabala's drive to organize the poor to work profitably stems from the conviction that there is tremendous potential within the poor to help themselves and that this potential can be harnessed by organizing them. For example, Sabala will help tribal women from Bijapur district form an SHG comprising 20 members. After this, they will send trainers to train the selected women in the art of making handicrafts. After the development of skills, the group members will begin to generate income. The SHG members will then open a savings bank account in the name of the group and members may decide to make regular savings contributions from their incomes. The formation of such SHGs at Sabala has resulted in the empowerment of women from marginalized communities to have access to sustainable livelihood opportunities.

Sabala produces a wide range of products, including export-quality jewellery, ethnic hand bags, cushion covers, gift items, kurtas, and wall hangings. In 1998, Sabala established the Craft Development Centre to revive traditional craft, promote self-employment and entrepreneurship among artisans, check migration, build the capacity and networking of artisans by self-help groups, and provide marketing facilities to ensure regular income and sustainability.

Source: www.sabalaindia.com (last accessed in March 2013). Reproduced with permission.

INSTITUTIONS SUPPORTING WOMEN ENTREPRENEURS IN INDIA

There are various institutions in India that are devoted to promoting women's entrepreneurship. They have several schemes to help start, sustain, and support women entrepreneurs. The office of the Development Commissioner of the Ministry of Micro, Small, and Medium Enterprises of the Government of India has opened a women's cell to provide assistance to women entrepreneurs. There are also several income generating government schemes, implemented by the Department of Women and Child Development, that provide assistance in setting up training-cum-income-generating activities for needy women. This section lists the institutions supporting women's entrepreneurship in India.

Consortium of Women Entrepreneurs of India (CWEI)

CWEI is a registered civil society and a voluntary organization that works for the economic empowerment of women in India and all over the world, and aims to eradicate poverty and unemployment among women. It consists of NGOs, voluntary organizations, self-help groups, institutions and individual enterprises, both from rural and urban areas, which collectively support and benefit from the activities taken up by the consortium. CWEI has a representation in policy-making at the Ministry of Small-Scale Industries (SSI), Government of India. It is based in New Delhi and acts as a springboard for promoting entrepreneurship at the grassroots level.

SNAPSHOT

Some institutions supporting women's entrepreneurship in India are:

- Consortium of Women Entrepreneurs of India (CWEI)
- Federation of Indian Women Entrepreneurs (FIWE)
- FICCI Ladies' Organization (FLO)
- Women's India Trust (WIT)
- Association of Women Entrepreneurs of Karnataka (AWAKE)

CWEI acts as a catalyst to bring marginalized and displaced women, including tribal women, into the mainstream of economic activity by encouraging entrepreneurship and self-employment. It promotes self-help groups, facilitates technology transfer, and explores marketing linkages within and outside India. It does so by organizing buyer–seller meets, fairs and exhibitions, international women entrepreneurs' meets, training sessions, and conferences.[16]

Federation of Indian Women Entrepreneurs (FIWE)

FIWE was founded in 1993 following the decisions taken at the Fourth International Conference of Women Entrepreneurs held in Hyderabad in December. Today, it is one of India's premier institutions for women and is completely devoted to entrepreneurship development. It is a formation of an umbrella group of local organizations with a large membership base of 15,000 individual members/professionals and 28 member associations spread throughout the country. Small-scale entrepreneurs account for approximately 60 per cent of FIWE combined membership, with large firms representing 15 per cent and the remaining being microenterprises.[17]

FIWE aims to foster the economic empowerment of women, particularly those belonging to the small and medium enterprises (SME) segment, by helping them become successful entrepreneurs and integrating them into the mainstream industry. It endeavours to provide a networking platform, technical know-how, industry research and expertise, and skill development training to women. The organization provides a common forum for businesswomen and ensures that their opinions, ideas, and visions are taken into account by policy makers and by various other agencies for the development of women's enterprises.

FICCI Ladies Organization (FLO)

FLO is the women's wing of the Federation of Indian Chambers of Commerce and Industry (FICCI)—the apex body of industry and commerce in India. FLO was formed in 1983 as a national-level forum for women with the objective of "women's empowerment." FLO aims to promote the socio-economic advancement of women by promoting entrepreneurship and professional excellence. It has established chapters in major cities all over India, with the head office in Delhi. The members comprise entrepreneurs, professionals, and corporate executives. FLO conducts seminars, workshops, panel discussions, training programmes, and conferences on a wide range of subjects to empower women entrepreneurs and professionals.

FLO works at three levels. At the grassroots level, it conducts entrepreneur development programmes for women in the low income group, working with them and advising them how to start a business, and following it through with some help in vocational training. At the middle level, it conducts seminars, workshops, and training programmes on capacity building and skill development for women running micro, small, and medium enterprises. At the senior level, FLO conducts advanced management programmes for women at the helm.

Young FICCI Ladies Organisation (YFLO) is an offshoot of FLO with the goal of empowering young women at various levels across the different strata of Indian society. YFLO was formed to address the hopes, desires, and aspirations of young women in India. FICCI, along with FLO and YFLO, is working towards bringing forth a socioeconomic transformation in society.[18]

Women's India Trust (WIT)

In 1968, Kamila Tyabji, a lawyer by profession, founded a charitable organization, Women's India Trust (WIT), in Mumbai. Since then, it has grown into a large organization with two shops in Mumbai and a training and production centre known as the Kamila Tyabji WIT Centre in Panvel, 40 km from Mumbai. The Kamila Tyabji WIT Centre, along with a hostel for girls, was built in 1983. Encouraged by the success of WIT in Mumbai, the Kamila Trust, UK, was set up in the early 1990s with the aim of selling in England items produced by the WIT family of women in India. At first, friends held "home sales" in London and Yorkshire, and then in 1994 the Kamila Trust opened its own shop, KASHI, in London. Every year, WIT trains 150 girls in areas such as block printing, screen printing, nursing, toy-making, and catering. The WIT *bazaar* showcases some of the products made by women who have been trained at WIT.

WIT's mission is to help women from less privileged backgrounds help themselves by providing unskilled and disadvantaged women a platform for advancement and empowerment. WIT offers training and employment opportunities to any needy woman, irrespective of age, caste, or religion. To this day, WIT remains dedicated to the original aim of its founder—to help less privileged women overcome adversity and achieve stability in their lives.[19]

Association of Women Entrepreneurs of Karnataka (AWAKE)

AWAKE was established in December 1983 by seven enterprising women: Madhura Chatrapathy, Kiran Majumdar, Lekha Chand, Shandrila Naidu, Indrajeet Sahani, Aban Minochar, and Supanya Datta. Based in Bangalore, it is one of India's premier institutions for women entrepreneurs. The name of the organization is reminiscent of Swami Vivekananda's famous exhortation: "Arise, awake and stop not till the goal is reached." AWAKE began with the mission of economically empowering women through entrepreneurship. AWAKE's vision is to reach out to as many women as possible and create entrepreneurs who will be role models for emulation worldwide. AWAKE is a non-profit and non-governmental organization (NGO). It is a registered society accredited by the ISO 9001 Quality Management System.

AWAKE comprises members who are women entrepreneurs. These members guide women who want to start or improve their businesses by counselling, training, sharing their experiences and expertise, and by providing them with peer group support. AWAKE promotes entrepreneurship through business incubators as well as with entrepreneurship-training and skill development. The members of AWAKE extend their services every Thursday.

An affiliate of Women's World Banking, AWAKE has built up a powerful support network with national and international development agencies—both governmental and non-governmental. Such networking facilitates technology transfer, skill building, product development, project management, and the development of the various kinds of expertise needed to promote entrepreneurship among women.[20]

SPECIAL BANK SCHEMES PROMOTING WOMEN'S ENTREPRENEURSHIP

Almost all public-sector banks have special loan schemes for women entrepreneurs. Table 3.2 lists the special schemes available with banks for promoting women's entrepreneurship.

Cent Kalyani of Central Bank of India Credit Scheme

Cent Kalyani has been specially introduced to offer financial assistance to women entrepreneurs for economic pursuits in industry, agricultural and allied activities, or business. Central Bank, with

Table 3.2 Schemes for Women Entrepreneurs

Bank	Scheme
Bank of India	Priyadarshini Yojana
Canara Bank	CAN Mahila
Central Bank of India	Cent Kalyani
Dena Bank	Dena Shakti
Oriental Bank of Commerce	Oriented Mahila Vikas Yojana
Punjab National Bank	Mahila Udyam Nidhi Scheme
Punjab and Sind Bank	Udyogini Scheme
State Bank of India	Stree Shakti Package
State Bank of Mysore	Stree Shakthi Package
Small Industries Development Bank of India	Mahila Udyama Nidhi
Tamilnad Mercantile Bank	Mahalir Loan
Vijaya Bank	V Mangala
Union Bank of India	Viklang Mahila Vikas Yojana
UCO Bank	Nari Shakti
ICICI Bank	Women's Account
NABARD	Arwind, Mahima

branches throughout the country, welcomes women entrepreneurs who wish to avail financial assistance for pursuing vocations of their choice. Credit facilities are available for women entrepreneurs under the following heads:

- **Small business:** For entrepreneurs who intend to provide service (not professional service) such as setting up a small lunch canteen, mobile restaurant, circulating library, and so on.
- **Professional and self-employed:** For entrepreneurs who are specially qualified/skilled and experienced like doctors, chartered accountants, engineers, or trained in art or craft and so on.
- **Retail trade:** For entrepreneurs who intend to engage in retail trading of various commodities.
- **Village and cottage/tiny industries:** For entrepreneurs who are engaged in manufacturing, processing, preservation, and services such as handloom weaving, handicraft, food processing, garment manufacturing in villages and small towns with a population not exceeding 50,000 and utilizing locally available resources/skills.
- **Small-scale industries:** For entrepreneurs to start a unit engaged in manufacture, processing, or preservation of goods.
- **Agriculture and allied activities:** For women entrepreneurs who are engaged/intend to engage in agricultural and allied activities, such as farming, floriculture, maintaining fisheries, bee-keeping, maintaining plant nurseries, sericulture, and trading in agricultural inputs.
- **Government-sponsored programmes:** Women entrepreneurs are also financed under various government sponsored programmes where capital subsidies are available.

National Bank for Agriculture and Rural Development (NABARD)

The National Bank for Agriculture and Rural Development seeks to remove the barriers of credit to women. It aims to treat women as risk-free, bankable clients, provide linkages along with credit, identify appropriate economic activities for women, promote women's self-help groups, and link them with the formal banking system. NABARD has evolved exclusive schemes for women such as Assistance to Rural Women in Non-farm Development (ARWIND) and Marketing of Non-farm Products of Rural Women (MAHIMA) as well as support in the form of grant assistance for setting up "women development cells" by Regional Rural Banks (RRBs)/ cooperative banks. ARWIND has both credit and grant components. It is envisaged that a women's group organized or sponsored by a suitable agency could avail of bank credit normally not exceeding ₹50,000 per woman member for an own account activity or group activity, with 100 per cent refinance support from NABARD. MAHIMA seeks to create a niche or pro-woman market and assists in credit by way of 100 per cent refinance up to ₹10 lakh.[21]

Small Industries Development Bank of India

SIDBI is assisting the entire spectrum of the SSI sector including village and cottage industries through suitable schemes tailored to meet the requirements of setting up of new projects, expansion, diversification, modernization, and rehabilitation of existing units. SIDBI has two women-specific schemes.

Under Mahila Vikas Nidhi (MVN), well-managed NGOs with a good track record and linkages with financial institutions are eligible to borrow. It is a specially designed fund for economic development of women, providing them avenues for training and employment opportunities. A judicious mix of loan and grant, the basic activity involves setting up of training-cum-production centres. The assistance is basically catalytic and only the really well-run NGOs can secure grants. Assistance may be in the form of loans. Repayment is normally within five years and the initial moratorium is of one year or 18 months.

The Mahila Udhyam Nidhi scheme is for enterprising women entrepreneurs to set up new projects in the tiny and small-scale sector, and for the rehabilitation of viable, sick small-scale industry units. This scheme serves to eliminate the gap in equity. The scheme is operated through the State Financial Organization's twin-function industrial design centres/scheduled commercial banks/ scheduled urban cooperative banks. The cost of the project should not exceed ₹10 lakh.

DISCUSSION FORUM

- Explain the institutional framework for supporting women entrepreneurs in India.
- Discuss the various schemes of SIDBI in supporting women entrepreneurs in India.

WOMEN ENTREPRENEURS FROM AROUND THE WORLD

Historically, entrepreneurship has been a male-dominated pursuit, but many of today's most memorable and inspirational entrepreneurs are women.[22]

Mary Kay Ash

Born in 1918, Mary Kay Ash is recognized as one of America's greatest women entrepreneurs. The founder of Mary Kay Cosmetics created a business that has helped nearly half a million women around the world fulfill their dreams of business ownership. Mary Kay Ash worked in various corporate positions for 25 years. In 1969, with the help of her 20-year-old son and her life savings of $5,000, she started Mary Kay Inc., her first 500 sq. ft store in Dallas, with nine independent beauty consultants. In 1996, Mary Kay started the Mary Kay Ash charitable foundation. A best-selling author of three books and a powerful motivational speaker, she was named the "Most Outstanding Woman in Business in the 20th Century" by Lifetime Television in 1999.

Jenna Jameson

Jenna Jameson is an American entrepreneur and former pornographic star who has been called the world's most famous adult-entertainment performer. Jameson's adult-entertainment Internet company ClubJenna, formed in 2000 and sold to *Playboy* in 2006, earned an estimated revenue of $30 million with 50 per cent profits in 2005.[23] During her career, she manipulated the business model in her industry to her own advantage before diversifying into a range of other products. Jameson's story of powerful branding, tightly-controlled distribution, and multiple streams of passive income contains lessons for entrepreneurs in any industry.

Anita Roddick

Anita Roddick was a British businesswoman who founded The Body Shop. The Body Shop is a store that purchases natural ingredients from disadvantaged communities for a line of cosmetics, helping these disadvantaged communities generate income while providing women with superb cosmetics. Roddick was known as one of the most outspoken social activists in the business world. She created Children on the Edge (COTE) in the UK in 1990 and then expanded it globally to help disadvantaged children affected by conflicts, natural disasters, disabilities, and HIV/AIDS over the course of their early lives. The Body Shop still adheres to the core values laid out by Roddick. She authored the book *Take It Personally*, encouraging equality and an end to the exploitation of workers and children in underdeveloped countries.

Oprah Winfrey

Oprah Winfrey is an American television host, actress, producer, and philanthropist, best known for her self-titled, multi-award winning talkshow, which has become the highest-rated programme of its kind in history.

She has been ranked the richest African American of the 20th century and the greatest black philanthropist in American history. The power of Winfrey's opinions and endorsement to influence public opinion, especially consumer purchasing choices, has been dubbed "The Oprah effect." The animal-rights group People for the Ethical Treatment of Animals (PETA) named Winfrey the "2008 Person of the Year," crediting her with using her fame and listening audience to help animals. Winfrey used "The Oprah Winfrey Show" to highlight the cruelty-free vegan diet that she tried and to uncover horrific cases of cruelty to animals in puppy mills and on factory farms.

Madame C. J. Walker

Madame C. J. Walker was an African-American businesswoman, hair-care entrepreneur, and philanthropist. She made her fortune by developing and marketing a hugely successful line of beauty and hair products for black women under her company Madam C. J. Walker Manufacturing Company. A daughter of former slaves and orphaned at the age of seven, Walker built a thriving beauty products business in the early 20th century, eventually employing over 3,000 people. Her hard work, honest business dealings, and quality products led her to become the first self-made female African-American millionaire. "There is no royal flower-strewn path to success," she once commented. "And if there is, I have not found it for if I have accomplished anything in life it is because I have been willing to work hard."

Coco Chanel

Coco Chanel, who was as bold and distinctive as her signature fragrance, was one of the major innovators of 20th century fashion. She appropriated styles, fabrics, and articles of clothing that were worn by men and introduced them into women's fashion to create a distinctively simple, yet elegant style. The first perfume to bear Chanel's name, Chanel No. 5, became her signature fragrance after it was launched in 1923 and is still one of the best-selling fragrances in the world. Coco Chanel introduced her signature cardigan jacket in 1925 and the signature "little black dress" in 1926. Most of her fashions had staying power, and didn't change much over time.

Debbi Fields

At 20 years of age, Debbi Fields was a housewife with no business experience or college degree, but a good chocolate chip cookie recipe and a dream. Today, Mrs. Fields Cookies is one of the world's most recognizable dessert franchises, with over 600 stores in the USA and in 10 other countries.

Besides being a Harvard Business School case study on business efficiency, Debbi Fields has authored various books, including *Mrs. Fields Cookie Book: 100 Recipes from the Kitchen of Debbi Fields*—the first cookbook to make it to the top of the *New York Times* bestseller list. Debbi Fields is a shining example of a woman who, from a humble beginning, went on to make it big. She persevered and achieved something that most around her believed impossible—a successful cookie business.

Estée Lauder

Estée Lauder was a philanthropist and a successful entrepreneur. She was born in New York, USA, in 1908. Along with her husband Joseph, she founded Estée Lauder Companies Inc. in 1946. The company has its headquarters in Midtown Manhattan, New York City. The company is a manufacturer and marketer of skin care, perfume, and hair-care products. Estée Lauder Inc. sells its products in department stores across the world and has a chain of free-standing retail outlets. By the early 21st century, the company was worth about ₹55,000 crore. Estée was responsible for converting her family business into an empire.[24]

Estée Lauder, a creative visionary, through extraordinary ambition, perseverance, impeccable taste, and innovative marketing, became the wealthiest self-made woman in America. She was a woman with a mission and focused in the pursuit of her dream. She was a creative entrepreneur, who changed the beauty business. She has received many honours, including the French Legion of Honour.

SNAPSHOT

Some famous women entrepreneurs:

- Mary Kay Ash
- Jenna Jameson
- Anita Roddick
- Oprah Winfrey
- Madame C. J. Walker
- Coco Chanel
- Debbi Fields
- Estée Lauder
- Ariana Huffington

Arianna Huffington

Arianna Huffington is the president and editor-in-chief of *The Huffington Post*, a nationally syndicated columnist, and the author of 13 books. Arianna Huffington originally comes from Greece but moved to England at the age of 16. She launched *The Huffington Post*, a news and blog site, in May 2005. *The Huffington Post* soon became a very widely-read, linked-to, and frequently-cited media brand on the Internet, making Arianna a very successful Internet entrepreneur. In 2006, she was named in *Time* magazine's list of the world's 100 most influential people.[25]

WOMEN ENTREPRENEURS IN INDIA

There are several women entrepreneurs in India who have created and set standards for their industries.[26] Their stories are inspiring and motivating, and have generated a lot of interest not

CHECKLIST FOR ENTREPRENEURS 3.6 ✓ Women Entrepreneurs—Points to Remember

Here are five key points for women entrepreneurs to remember on their road to success:

- Do what you are passionate about. After you have identified your area of interest, get advanced training in the area before you start your own business venture.
- Remember that many women balance both a career and a family. Clearly, it is possible for women to balance the personal and the professional. Set your priorities and mould the family environment to make this possible. Take your family into confidence and find a way to balance your career with your work life.
- Believe in yourself. Do not underestimate your abilities. To succeed in business, you must believe in yourself before you can inspire others to work for you or to invest in your business.
- Prepare your mindset. Remember that success has no gender. Groom yourself to face every challenge positively.
- Dare to dream, and dare to act on the basis of that dream. Take every opportunity that comes your way.

only in India but also across the globe. This section will give you a glimpse into the lives and achievements of some of the most successful women entrepreneurs from various sectors in India.

Kiran Mazumdar-Shaw

A successful technocrat of global standing, Kiran Mazumdar-Shaw is the founder, chairman, and managing director of India's leading biotechnology enterprise, Biocon Limited. She is highly respected in the corporate world and has received, besides numerous other national and international awards, the prestigious national civilian awards Padmashree in 1989 and Padma Bhushan in 2005 for her pioneering efforts in industrial biotechnology. Her contributions to industrial biotechnology have drawn global attention to the Indian biotechnology industry as well as to Biocon. In 2004, *Forbes* named her India's richest woman.

Early Life Born in Bangalore on 23 March 1953, Kiran Mazumdar-Shaw did her schooling from Bishop Cotton Girls' School, Bangalore, and later studied at Mount Carmel College, Bangalore. After obtaining a bachelor's degree in zoology from Bangalore University, she did her post-graduation in malting and brewing from Ballarat University in Melbourne, Australia, and qualified as a master brewer in 1975. In her choice of profession, she received encouragement from her father, who was a master brewer himself.

Career and Success In 1974, Kiran started her professional career as trainee brewer in Carlton and United Breweries, Melbourne. After returning to India, she worked in technical positions in Kolkata and Vadodara. In 1978, she joined Biocon Biochemicals Limited of Ireland as a trainee manager. In the same year, in collaboration with the same Irish firm, she founded Biocon in the garage of her rented house in Bangalore with a capital of ₹10,000. In 1980, the company acquired 20 acres of land in Bangalore and shifted operations to the new location. Initially, Kiran faced many credibility challenges as a young woman entrepreneur with an untested business model. Her loan applications were turned down by various banks as, among other reasons, biotechnology was a new field in India, and her company had few assets to boast of. However, Kiran overcame these challenges with her extraordinary perseverance and hard work. In 1989, Unilever acquired Biocon Biochemicals Limited of Ireland and merged it with its subsidiary, Quest International. Nine years later, after Unilever agreed to sell its shareholding in Biocon to Indian promoters, Biocon became an independent entity.

Biocon's initial operation was to extract an enzyme from papaya. Under Kiran's stewardship, Biocon, recognized today as India's pioneering biotechnology enterprise, transformed itself from an industrial enzymes manufacturing company to an integrated biopharmaceutical company with a well-balanced business portfolio of products and strategic research initiatives. In 2004, Biocon came

BREAKTHROUGH ENTREPRENEURSHIP 3.7 — Patricia Narayan—Turning Hobby into Business

Patricia Narayan's entrepreneurial journey started 30 years ago—selling pickles and jams, samosas, bajjis, and coffee on Marina beach. Today, she owns a chain of restaurants. Patricia had never dreamed of becoming an entrepreneur. Both her parents were government employees. She was very passionate about cooking and trying out new recipes.

Faced with the challenge of battling a failed marriage and with two small children to support, Patricia decided to turn for survival to what she most liked doing—cooking. With the support of her parents and a small investment, she started to make pickles, jams, and squashes at home and sell them. The demand for her products gradually increased. In 1982, she placed her mobile cart at the Anna Square on Marina beach (near which she lived) and started selling cutlets, samosas, bajjis, fresh juice, coffee, and tea there. On the first day, she ended up selling only one cup of coffee worth 50 paise and came away disappointed. However, she went back to her business the next day, and from that day, of course, there was no looking back. Patricia ran this business from 1982 to 2003 and during this period her maximum turnover was ₹25,000 in one day.

Patricia was soon offered the opportunity to run the canteen for the slum clearance board at their office with a proper kitchen. She accepted the offer and managed a roaring business with a profit of ₹20,000 per month on an average. Later, she began to run the canteen for the Bank of Madurai, serving around 300 people per day. The next offer came from the National Institute of Ports Management, Chennai, where she served three meals each day to about 700 students. By this time, she was earning almost ₹1 lakh per week. She worked at this canteen until 1998.

In 2006, Patricia and her son launched their first restaurant "Sandeepha." Today, the sale from the 14 outlets of Sandeepha across Chennai average approximately ₹2 lakh daily, and Patricia, who started her first business with only two people, now has 200 people working for her. In 2010, she received the "FICCI Woman Entrepreneur of the Year" award.

Patricia's advice to young entrepreneurs is never to compromise on quality, never to lose self-confidence, always to believe in one's product, and always to stick to what one knows.

Source: http://business.rediff.com/slide-show/2010/jun/08/slide-show-1-from-50-paise-to-rs-2-lakh-a-day-success-story.htm (last accessed in March 2013). Reproduced with permission.

up with an initial public offering (IPO) and the issue was over-subscribed by over 30 times. Post-IPO, Kiran Mazumdar Shaw held close to 40 per cent of the stock of the company and was regarded as India's richest woman with an estimated worth of ₹2,100 crore.

Ritu Kumar

Ritu Kumar is a leading Indian designer who is credited with merging the ancient traditions of Indian craftsmanship with modern sensibilities. She was the first woman to bring the boutique culture to India. She has demonstrated that handmade products can be as profitable as and even more glamorous than those made by machine.

Early Life Ritu Kumar was born on 11 November 1944, in Amritsar, Punjab. Her family moved to Delhi, and Ritu graduated in 1964 from Lady Irwin College, Delhi. After her graduation, she married and moved from Delhi to Kolkata, where she joined an amateur theatre group. In 1966, she completed a course on artistry from Briarcliff College, New York.

Career and Success Ritu began her entrepreneurial journey in her 20s in the post-independence era with hand block printers in a small village near Kolkata. Her journey was difficult and involved forging a new road where none existed. Back then, cottage industry was a very small industry in India, and Ritu soon found that she had hardly any retailers/buyers for the end products that she was helping to create. In response to this problem of the lack of retailers, she opened the country's first boutique in 1966 in Delhi. Her boutique was a small store that sold the items created under her supervision by villagers in their villages. There was no organized marketing for her products. Information about her unique venture was passed on mostly by word of mouth.

In the course of her entrepreneurial journey, Ritu has helped revitalize the lost or fading traditional art of textile crafts and design, and enabled artisans skilled in them to continue to work in their own environments. Today, Ritu's boutiques usually display garments and accessories that draw on the textile and embroidery heritage of India while appealing to women across the globe. To give an example, her Indo-Western fusion wear achieves an aesthetic balance by merging elements of Indian block prints, embroidery, and craft inputs with a Western style. She has 34 outlets in all the major cities of India and one outlet in the USA.

WOMEN'S EMPOWERMENT THROUGH ENTREPRENEURSHIP

A woman is often described as the better half of man. But the actual condition of women in the world does not match up to this description. By and large, across the world, women have not achieved equality with men. In India, women constitute about 48 per cent of the population but their participation in economic activity is only 34 per cent.[27] There is a continuing concentration of women in low-paid and low-status occupations, indicating that women are marginalized in the labour force. There is a common assumption that men are the breadwinners of the family and that women work either as a hobby or to obtain only a supporting income for the household.

The major reason for the marginalization of women and their work is the social prejudice that a woman's world is required to be focused on the family and the household. In addition to this, in the rural areas of India, there is a lack of education and effective employment opportunities for women. Such constraints and social traditions largely inhibit the emergence of the vast potential of women, which remains the nation's greatest untapped resource.

The Gender and Development Approach

The gender and development (GAD) approach to perceiving women's position in development is influenced by social feminism and post-modern and post-colonial theories. It takes into account the totality of women's lives, rejecting the public/private dichotomy that undermines women's work at home. The focus of the GAD approach on seeing development from a woman's perspective makes women the "subjects" rather than the "objects" of development and agents of change rather than recipients of welfare. The GAD approach works to move women from the margin to the centre of developmental discourse by allowing them to gain a sense of control over their lives (empowerment).

Employment gives economic status to women. Economic status gives way to social and political status and thereby empowerment. Entrepreneurial activities for women are clearly within the GAD framework as development cannot be sustained unless the people for whom it is intended are at the centre of developmental activity.

Women have a unique position in the economy. In India, with an unfavourable woman–man ratio and strong patriarchal roots, entrepreneurship and access to funds have been difficult. It is, therefore, immensely creditworthy that cooperatives have been created that have encouraged women to seek self-reliance and economic freedom. There are also associations like the Federation of Indian Women Entrepreneurs that seek to foster the economic empowerment of women by helping them to become successful entrepreneurs.

It is not always easy for women to find jobs that are compatible with family responsibilities and household chores. So, many women are attracted by the idea of self-employment in enterprises adjoining their house premises. This allows flexible hours, which helps them take care of both home and business. Small-scale enterprises represent an important means of income for women in developing countries. They provide employment and income to alleviate poverty.

Shri Mahila Griha Udyog Lijjat Papad (SMGULP)

Shri Mahila Griha Udyog Lijjat Papad (SMGULP) is a cooperative organization that demonstrates the empowerment that women can achieve through entrepreneurship. SMGULP began in 1959 with just seven semi-literate sister-members on the terrace of a building in Mumbai, and a seed capital of just ₹80 borrowed from a local money lender and social worker. From such meagre beginnings, SMGULP has grown so phenomenally that it now employs over 42,000 sister-members and has achieved sales of over ₹829 crore. It has a central office in Mumbai and 75 branches across India.

Background SMGULP was the brainchild of seven semi-literate Gujarati housewives from Mumbai, who launched the initiative with the production of four packets of *papad*. As the members adopted a policy of self-reliance (seeking no monetary help from any external source), production began on a commercial note. The group was mentored by Chaganlal Karamsi Parekh, a local money lender and social worker who had lent the women ₹80 for their investment. He advised them to run the organization as a business enterprise without compromising on quality. The group got considerable publicity through word of mouth and articles in vernacular newspapers. By the end of the third year, the organization had more than 300 members. As the membership increased to a number that was too large for the terrace to accommodate, the kneaded flour began to be distributed among the members to take to their homes. Once made, the *papads* were brought back for quality checking, weighing, and packaging.

In 1962, the organization adopted the name Shri Mahila Griha Udyog Lijjat Papad (SMGULP) and chose Lijjat as the brand name for its products. In 1966, SMGULP registered itself under the Bombay Public Trust Act, 1950, and under the Societies Registration Act, 1860, and was recognized by the Khadi and Village Industries Commission as a village industry.

Following the tremendous success of the *papad* business, Lijjat began producing other products such as *khakhra, masala, vadi*, wheat *atta,* and bakery products. In 1979, the group also initiated some more ventures such as leather making, matches, and incense making. Lijjat now has an annual turnover of around ₹829 crore, with ₹36 crore in exports.[28]

Innovative Business Model Based on Values The chief values that hold SMGULP together are self-esteem and respect for others. There is no place in this organization for social or religious prejudice, and democracy in its truest form is encouraged. Every woman earns according to the labour that she puts in and the profits are shared equally. SMGULP does not accept donation or charity and it is run like a business organization. Valuing people and understanding their problems have helped create a sound and sustainable business model.

The business model of Lijjat is based on the philosophy of *sarvodaya* (trust) and collective ownership. All its working members are owners—essentially women—and have equal shares in both profit and loss. Men may only become salaried employees. The managing committee consists of 21 members comprising the president, vice-president, two secretaries, and two treasurers. The office bearers of the managing committee, as well as those in charge of various branches and divisions, are chosen from among the members on the basis of a consensus every three years. Additionally, each branch has a committee of 11 members chosen by consensus. Decisions are made in a democratic manner on the basis of consensus.

Any woman who pledges to adopt the organization's values and respects quality can become a member and a co-owner of this organization. Members with a clean house and the requisite space to dry *papad* can take the job of rolling and the drying of the *papad* while those who do not have this facility may take up the responsibility of kneading and packaging. Packed *papads* are sealed in a box and are transported to the depot belonging to the area. The distributors pay cash and pick up the *papad*. Each branch then calculates its profit and divides it equally among all its members on a daily basis.

Awards SMGULP has received many awards over the years for its outstanding contribution to the empowerment of women. Some of them are the Best Village Industries Institution Award from the Khadi and Village Industries Commission in March 2003, The *Economic Times* Award for

Corporate Excellence in 2002, and The Brand Equity Award from PHD Chamber of Commerce and Industry.

SUMMARY

A woman entrepreneur may be defined as a confident, innovative, and creative woman capable of achieving economic independence individually or in collaboration, generating employment opportunities for others through initiating, establishing, and running the enterprise by keeping pace with her personal, family, and social life. Women's entrepreneurship helps to reduce poverty, promote gender equality, and empower women. Some factors that contribute to women becoming entrepreneurs are the desire for economic independence, availability of technology, a desire for the establishment of an identity, and the achievement of excellence. Some common traits of successful women entrepreneurs are ambition, confidence, transparency, willingness to learn, financial acumen, teamwork, loyalty, and a sense of social responsibility.

The overall context of women's entrepreneurship can be described in three different spheres: microsphere, mesosphere, and macrosphere. The challenges in the path of women's entrepreneurship are an initial lack of confidence due to sociocultural barriers, market-oriented risks, poor knowledge of business administration, lack of awareness about possible sources of financial assistance, and lack of exposure to training programmes. There are many organizations in India supporting women entrepreneurs, and almost all public-sector banks have special loan schemes for women entrepreneurs. There are inspirational examples of successful women entrepreneurs in India and abroad. A special mention may be made of Shri Mahila Griha Udyog Lijjat Papad (SMGULP), a unique and successful cooperatively-managed organization and a symbol of the progress of women in developing countries like India.

KEY TERMS

Gender and Development (GAD): The theory of gender and development focuses on the socially-constructed basis of difference between men and women and emphasizes the need to challenge existing gender roles and relations.

Glass Ceiling: The unseen barrier that keeps minorities and women from rising to the upper rungs of the corporate ladder, regardless of their qualifications or achievements.

Group Entrepreneurship: A collaborative approach to enterprise creation that benefits a community.

Self-Help Group (SHG): A small, voluntarily-formed, economically-homogeneous, and significant group of rural/urban poor who mutually agree to contribute to a common fund from which money is agreed to be lent out to its members according to group decisions.

Woman Entrepreneur: A woman entrepreneur may be defined as a confident, innovative, and creative woman capable of achieving economic independence individually or in collaboration, generating employment opportunities for others through initiating, establishing, and running the enterprise by keeping pace with her personal, family, and social life.

Woman Entrepreneurship: An enterprise owned and controlled by a woman having a minimum financial interest of 51 per cent of the capital and giving at least 51 per cent of the employment generated by the enterprise to women.

Women's Empowerment: An approach to perceiving women's position in development, influenced by social feminism and post-modern and post-colonial theories, which takes into account the totality of women's lives, rejecting the public/private dichotomy that undermines women's work at home.

CASE STUDY

Shahnaz Husain

I do not sell products. I sell an entire civilization in a jar.

—*Shahnaz Husain*

Shahnaz Husain, CEO of Shahnaz Husain Group, is a successful Indian woman entrepreneur, best known for her herbal cosmetics and for her pioneering role and leadership in promoting the herbal care industry in India. The Shahnaz Husain Group, based in New Delhi, is one of the largest manufacturers of herbal products in the world, creating and marketing over 350 products for various beauty and health needs worldwide.

Shahnaz Husain belongs to a royal Muslim family, which originally came from Samarkhand, Pakistan. Her family members held high positions in the princely kingdoms of Bhopal and Hyderabad in the pre-Independence days. During her childhood, Shahnaz had the privilege of receiving a modern education, which groomed her into a well-rounded personality. Shahnaz did her schooling from an Irish convent and her father Chief Justice N. U. Beg instilled in her a love of poetry and English literature. Married at 15, she became a mother by the time she was 16.

When Shahnaz's husband was posted to Tehran, Iran, Shahnaz accompanied him. During her stay in Tehran, she developed a keen interest in beauty treatments and decided to study cosmetology. To support the expenses of the cosmetology course, she wrote articles for the *Iran Tribune* on various topics. While pursuing her studies, she learned that chemical cosmetics harmed the human system as well as the environment in the long run. This turned her attention to Ayurveda, which she believed was the best alternative to chemical cosmetics.

After leaving Tehran, she trained extensively in cosmetic therapy for a period of 10 years from some of the leading institutes in Paris, London, New York, and Copenhagen. On completion of her training in 1977, she returned to India. In the same year, she set up her first beauty salon at her house in Delhi with an initial investment of ₹35,000. In contrast to other salons offering chemical cosmetics, she made use of Ayurvedic products with natural formulations that could be safely used on the human body. By doing this, she ushered in an era of herbal cosmetics and herbal therapy. On setting up her first salon in New Delhi, she had put up a banner with her qualifications on it. Within days, she was booked six months ahead. She says, "I removed the banner and since then I have never advertised. I have let my products speak for themselves."

The year 1980 was a milestone in the entrepreneurial journey of Shahnaz. She represented India at the Festival of India in London, where she was given a counter in the perfumery section of Selfridges. Her team sold an entire consignment in three days and broke the store's record for cosmetics sales for the year. As a result, Shahnaz was allotted a permanent counter in Selfridges and her products entered the global market. Shahnaz's custom-made natural products for skin and hair problems quickly became successful.

During the last three decades, the Shahnaz Husain Group has acquired a tremendous global presence, having sold in prestigious stores like the Galleries Lafayette (Paris), Bloomingdales (New York), Harrods and Selfridges (London), the Seibu chain (Japan), La Rinascente (Milan), as well as in other exclusive outlets and clinics worldwide. The group has salons and outlets in prominent locations all over the world, which have extended on a unique franchise system.

Shahnaz pioneered the commercialization of Ayurvedic cosmetic products. She identified the market for Ayurveda as a niche market and introduced the novel concept of "natural care and cure." With the professional infrastructure to support the demands of product and publicity, and tremendous goodwill, the Shahnaz Husain Group has also gone global with its other ventures like the Shahnaz Husain Forever Beautiful lifestyle shops, beauty training institutes, Ayurvedic health resorts, Ayurvedic centres for Dhara, Panchakarma, and Kerala massage, and Shahnaz Husain medi-spas. In fact, Shahnaz is now focusing her attention on developing products that can prove to be beneficial for astronauts. To sell her products, Shahnaz has always relied on quality, innovation, and word of mouth, rather than on advertisements.

The Shahnaz Husain product range has over 350 exclusive products in 20 distinct categories for skin, hair, and body care. Innovative, dynamic, and determined to taste success, Shahnaz Husain has become a legend in her own lifetime.

Shahnaz Husain operates a chain of training centres that provides education and training in Ayurveda and cosmetology. Shahnaz Husain International Beauty Academy, based in New Delhi, provides diploma and post-graduate courses in beauty therapy as well as various short-term tailor-made and need-based vocational courses.

Questions:

1. Examine the qualities of Shahnaz Husain as an entrepreneur and their contribution to her success in business.
2. What, in your opinion, was the turning point in Shahnaz Husain's career as an entrepreneur?
3. What can an aspiring woman entrepreneur learn from this case study on Shahnaz Husain?

Source: www.shahnaz.in/company.asp (last accessed in March 2013).

DISCUSSION QUESTIONS

1. Define a woman entrepreneur. Discuss the importance of women entrepreneurs.
2. Explain the factors influencing the development of women entrepreneurs and strategies needed for the development of women entrepreneurs in India.
3. Give an account of the growth of women entrepreneurs in India.
4. Discuss the challenges in the path of women's entrepreneurship.
5. Discuss the institutions supporting women's entrepreneurship in India.

ACTIVITY

Purpose: To learn about inspirational women entrepreneurs.

Time: 45 minutes

Procedure:

1. Your instructor will separate class members into a maximum of six groups.
2. Each group member should choose, visit, and prepare the profile of one successful women entrepreneur in their area.
3. Each group should make a presentation in class on the successful woman entrepreneur.

PROJECT

1. Select any successful woman entrepreneur of your choice and study her profile. Identify the challenges she has faced and how she has overcome those hurdles to become a successful woman entrepreneur.

ENDNOTES

1. Fielden, Sandra and Marilyn Davidson (2006). "Women Small Business Owners in India," *International Handbook of Women and Small Business Entrepreneurship, Part 4*. Cheltenham, UK: Edward Elgar Publishing Limited.

2. Dhameja, S. K. (2001). *Women Entrepreneurs*. New Delhi: Deep & Deep Publications.
3. Vinze, M. (1987). *Women Entrepreneurs in India*. New Delhi: Mittal Publications.
4. "A Look at the Development of Women Entrepreneurs in India," in Prosenjit Datta (ed.), *The SME Whitebook 2010–11: Essential Handbook for Small and Medium Enterprises,* 2nd ed., p. 38.
5. www.lijjat.com/Content.asp?id_Section=7 (last accessed in March 2013).
6. Ganesan, S. (2003). *Status of Women Entrepreneurs in India*. New Delhi: Kanishka Publishers.
7. Tambunan, Tulus (2009). "Women Entrepreneurship in Asian Developing Countries: Their Development and Main Constraints," *Journal of Development and Agricultural Economics*, 1 (2): 27–40, available at www.academicjournals.org/jdae/PDF/Pdf2009/May/Tambunan.pdf (last accessed in March 2013).
8. www.ilo.org/wcmsp5 (last accessed in March 2013).
9. Ministry of Small, Medium, and Micro Enterprises, Government of India (2010–11). "Annual Report," p. 25, available at http://msme.gov.in/MSME-Annual-Report-2010-11-English.pdf (last accessed in March 2013).
10. Majumdar, Swapna (2003). "Social Monitor: Seven Markers for Gender Balance," *The Tribune*, 16 March, available at www.tribuneindia.com/2003/20030316/herworld.htm#3 (last accessed in March 2013).
11. Moore, D. and E. Buttner (1997). *Women Entrepreneurs: Moving Beyond the Glass Ceiling*. Thousand Oaks, CA: Sage.
12. Mohiuddin, A. (1983). "Entrepreneurship Development Among Women: Retrospect and Prospect." *SEDME,* 10 (2).
13. Raghavulu, M. V. (2003). "Women Entrepreneurship in Backward Areas," *SEDME,* 30 (4).
14. Birley, S. (1989), "Female Entrepreneurs: Are They Really Any Different?," *Journal of Small Business Management,* 27 (1).
15. Key, Thelma (2003). "Empowering Women Through Self-help Microcredit Programmes," *Bulletin on Asia-Pacific Perspectives, Asia-Pacific Economies: Sustaining Growth Amidst Uncertainties. Bangkok: UNESCAP,* available at www.unescap.org/drpad/publication/bulletin%20 2002/ch6.pdf (last accessed in March 2013).
16. www.cwei.org (last accessed in March 2013).
17. www.fiwe.org/ (last accessed in March 2013).
18. www.ficciflo.com/ (last accessed in March 2013).
19. www.wit.org.in (last accessed in March 2013).
20. http://awakeindia.org.in (last accessed in March 2013).
21. www.nabard.org/ (last accessed in March 2013).
22. http://entrepreneurs.about.com/od/famouswomenentrepreneurs/Famous_Women_Entrepreneurs.htm (last accessed in March 2013).
23. Miller, Matthew (2005). "The (Porn) Player," *Forbes*, 7 April, www.forbes.com/free_forbes/ 2005/0704/124.html (last accessed in March 2013).
24. www.history.co.uk/encyclopedia/lauder-este.html (last accessed in March 2013).
25. www.huffingtonpost.com/arianna-huffington (last accessed in March 2013).
26. www.indiatvnews.com (last accessed in March 2013).
27. Suganthi, J. (2009). "Influence of Motivational Factors on Women Entrepreneurs in SMEs," Asia-Pacific Business Review, January–March, available at http://findarticles.com/p/articles/ mi_6771/is_1_5/ai_n31974125/ (last accessed in March 2013).
28. www.lijjat.com/Organisation/AboutUs.aspx (last accessed in March 2013).

Entrepreneurial Perspectives

1. Entrepreneurship
2. Entrepreneurial Development and Training
3. Women Entrepreneurs
4. **Family Business**
5. Micro, Small, and Medium Enterprises

"Successors can't learn from their mistakes if they are never allowed to make any."
—Leon A. Danco

Dabur India Ltd is a classic example of a professionally-managed, family-owned business. Dabur was born in 1884 in a small pharmacy in Calcutta, where Dr S. K. Burman launched his mission of making traditional ayurvedic products. In 1986, Dr Burman expanded his operations by setting up a manufacturing plant and Dabur became a public-limited company while retaining its core values and its customary focus on health care products. There is a family council to take care of the family's interests. Corporate governance and transparency in action are of high priority at Dabur. During 2011–12, Dabur India Ltd crossed the billion-dollar-turnover mark. Today, the sixth generation of Burmans has entered the family business.

Family Business

4

LEARNING OBJECTIVES

Upon completion of this chapter, you will be able to:

1. Understand the role and importance of the family business and the basic concepts needed to understand the mechanism of family businesses.
2. Trace the history of the family business in India and learn about some of the country's particular and specific family businesses.
3. Explain the roles, rights, and responsibilities of family members in a family business.
4. Identify the types and models of family businesses as well as the challenges faced by family-owned businesses.
5. Discuss the succession plan in family businesses.
6. Discuss strategies for improving the performance of a family business.

INTRODUCTION

We can define a family business in various ways.[1] However, in general, a family-business is one that satisfies any one of the following criteria:

- There is management or ownership control by direct descendants of the founders.
- A number of generations of the same family are involved in management or ownership.
- Two or more extended family members influence the business through the exercise of kinship ties, management roles, and ownership rights, which the owner intends to pass to a family heir.
- A high percentage of share capital is owned by a family member, either jointly or individually, and family members are employed in the highest decision-making posts.
- There is an expression of intent to maintain family involvement in the future.

ROLE AND IMPORTANCE OF THE FAMILY BUSINESS

Families are vital and supportive environments for entrepreneurial behaviour. Some of the world's largest family-owned firms are Wal-Mart Stores, Inc., Ford Motor Company, Samsung, the Fiat Group, L'Oréal, IKEA, the Tata Group, Havells, and McCain Foods. It has been observed that family support and the presence of self-employed parents are important influences in venture initiation and business ownership.

Families rule the world of business. About a third of all *Fortune* 500 companies are family businesses. Family businesses account for over half of the United State's GDP and about 78 per cent of all new job creation there. In India, around 95 per cent of the registered firms are family businesses while over 90 per cent of the registered firms in Pakistan are estimated to be family businesses. Family business groups like the Tata, Birla, and Godrej Groups have dominated the private sector in India ever since the British regime. As a result, many affiliated firms have been established under these groups, headed by a family member.

Family businesses from every trade imaginable have been around for centuries—from shoemakers and confectioners to farmers. Some of the world's oldest firms are family owned. Did you know that the world's oldest documented continuing family business is Hoshi Ryokan, a Japanese hotel set up in 717 AD, spanning 46 generations of family ownership? Some of the world's largest businesses, such as Wal-Mart Stores, Inc., are also family owned.

Family businesses range in size from small to large businesses in terms of employees and turnover and can be placed in two different categories. The first category comprises businesses having only family members as its stakeholders, such as Birlas, Kirloskars, Wadias, etc. The second category comprises businesses in which the family has a majority stake and controls the company, such as Wal-Mart Stores, Nestlé, Ferrari, Fiat, Ford, Hyundai, Nike, the Virgin Group, the Reliance Group, Wipro, and Havells. Belonging to a single family culture and having a strong set of values, family businesses have certain inherent strengths, such as the ability to withstand economic shocks, make quick decisions, maintain good business relations, and ensure leaders with time-proven leadership qualities. Often, long-term strategic thinking resulting in prudent business decisions enables family businesses to become sustainable. In an ever-changing business world with constant technological advancements, new business approaches, new managerial practices, and emerging market trends, family businesses generally remain flexible, adaptable, and innovative.

In India, family-owned businesses have played and will continue to play a central role in the growth and development of the country. Indian business firms such as Havells India, the Aditya Birla Corporation, and Tata Sons are making acquisitions abroad and expanding their businesses globally.[2] Individual associations and relationships can complicate the management and negatively affect the objectives of the family business. The issue of succession can cause immense strain within a family business. It is not surprising then that, on an average, only three out of ten family businesses survive to the second generation and only one to the third generation. As more and more family businesses are handed down from one generation to the next, more and more family legacies are lost due to lack of planned transitions.[3]

Most commercial enterprises are born as family-owned and family-managed businesses. Many remain this way, while a smaller number need access to public equity capital and in the process can no longer remain in the ownership of the family. Still others could remain family-owned but professionally managed, either due to the family's lack of interest or practical necessity. Unfortunately, there is no clear distinction in India between a business that is owned and managed by the family and a business that isn't so. For the sake of simplicity, let us assume that a firm where members of one or more particular families exert significant influence over the firm's strategy and its destiny is family-owned and firms where family members—unless professionally qualified—do not hold executive positions are professionally managed. Box 4.1 discusses the story of Kongõ Gumi, the Japanese temple-building company that was the world's oldest continuously operating family business until its assets were purchased by Takamatsu Corporation in 2006.

Family businesses have certain advantages over other businesses. Some of these are listed below:

- The family culture is a source of great pride for family and non-family employees alike.
- There is a long-term orientation in business objectives as the continuity of the firm is of great concern to the family.
- A family firm functions in a less bureaucratic manner and is not impersonal in dealing with employees and customers.
- A family firm shows greater willingness to weather bad times by ploughing back profits.
- It is structured to impart training to the members of the family from a young age.

WORLD OF ENTREPRENEURS 4.1 Oldest Family-owned Firm in the World

Japanese temple builder Kongō Gumi succumbed to excess debt and an adverse business environment in 2006—1,428 years after its founder Shigemitsu Kongō came to Japan in search of work.

The story of the beginning of Kongō Gumi is simple. In 578 AD, the carpenter Shigemitsu Kongō travelled from the Korean kingdom of Paekche to Japan in search of work. In Japan, he helped in the construction of several great buildings such as the Buddhist complex Shitennō-ji. Soon, he set up his own company. Thus was born Kongō Gumi, the company that came to be known as the world's oldest continuously-operating family business untill its liquidation in 2006.

Over the centuries, Kongō Gumi participated in the construction of many famous buildings, including the sixteenth-century Osaka Castle. Before its assets were purchased by Takamatsu Corporation in 2006, it was run by Masakazu Kongō—the 40th Kongō to lead the 1,428-year-old company.

Kongō Gumi survived fourteen centuries because of a strong family value system, which was reflected in the work culture of the family business. Secondly, temple-building, the core business of Kongō Gumi, was considered a stable industry. Thirdly, the Kongō Gumi family always had a clear succession plan, with the successor being chosen on the basis of merit. Lastly, the family found a strong sense of pride in the work of temple building, which they considered holy.

Source: http://archiver.rootsweb.ancestry.com/th/read/FHSA/2007-12/1198732310 (last accessed in March 2013).

CONTRIBUTIONS OF FAMILY BUSINESSES IN INDIA

India has a rich and glorious history of family-owned enterprises.[4] Some influential families, such as the Tatas, Birlas, and Godrej, have run their businesses for over a hundred years and influenced the economic and political situation of the country. Over time, family businesses have done more than simply pay taxes and employ people. During the last one hundred years or so, Indian family businesses have made significant contributions in several areas. Their first contribution was to the Indian freedom movement. In the early years, firms were created specifically to pursue goals such as import substitution and economic freedom from the colonists. The Godrej enterprise, for instance, was started by Ardeshir Godrej in 1897 with a vision to promote India's economic freedom. Their second contribution was to keep the spirit of enterprise alive even through the 40 years of quasi-socialism, when the government imposed onerous taxation and repeatedly tried to smoothen the "concentration" of economic power. The third contribution of Indian family businesses has been their philanthropic efforts, or giving back to the community. To the average Indian, the names of many large Indian business groups are synonymous with philanthropic efforts in education, environment, health, culture, and heritage conservation. Numerous small and medium family enterprises have also actively supported foundations engaged in charitable work.

STAGES OF DEVELOPMENT OF A FAMILY BUSINESS

While strategic, operational, and financial transformation is a given for any corporation that hopes to survive the trauma of competing in the post-liberalization marketplace, India's business houses have started rewriting the role of the family in business. The typical family business goes through four stages in its development.

1. **Entrepreneurial**: In this phase, someone in the family starts a business after having identified a business opportunity. At this stage, the business is customer-centric. The entrepreneurial vision develops and a mission is set for the organization.
2. **Functionally specialized**: This is the growth phase for the family business. In this phase, the organization is divided into various functions and priority is given to growth and increasing the scale of operation. The organization becomes more flexible during this phase and the use of control measures is limited.

3. **Process-driven**: In the process-driven phase, a family business is system-oriented and processes are set. The greatest attention is given to core competencies and to competing with other businesses in achieving customer satisfaction.
4. **Market-driven**: During this phase, the family business matures and is completely driven by market forces. The business enters various markets and crosses geographical boundaries by strategic alliances.

CHARACTERISTICS OF A FAMILY-OWNED BUSINESS IN INDIA

Indian business is overwhelmingly owned and managed by the *Bania* families of the traditional trading castes. Characteristics of family-owned businesses in India are:

- **Importance of family relationship**: Family relationship is the most important factor in determining the position a person holds in the business.
- **Composition of the board of directors**: Family members, including those who are neither contributing nor involved in the business, are on the board of directors.
- **Loyalty:** Members of the extended family and relatives have a very strong sense of loyalty to the family and this, by default, translates into loyalty to the business.
- **Dedication of family members**: As the family's fortunes are usually tied to that of the family business, the owning family shows great dedication and single-mindedness in ensuring the continued survival and success of the business.
- **Male-dominated**: Sons and male members are more likely to hold higher positions and succeed as the CEO of the company. The role of women is often that of a facilitator and a mother figure to family members and employees.
- **Dominance of certain trading communities**: Some communities have been very successful in business and are synonymous with family-owned businesses in India.

SNAPSHOT

- Over 75 per cent of all registered companies in the industrialized world are family businesses.
- One-third of *Fortune* 500 companies have families at their helm. Family companies employ about 50–60 per cent of the workforce in the industrialized world.

DISCUSSION FORUM

- Explain the importance of the family business.
- Discuss in small groups the contributions made by Indian family businesses with examples.
- Identify the characteristics of family-owned businesses in India.

VARIOUS TYPES OF FAMILY BUSINESSES

Family businesses can be of the following types:

- **Family-owned business**: It is a for-profit enterprise owned by members of a single extended family.

- **A family-owned and managed business**: It is a for-profit enterprise owned by members of a single extended family. The business also has the active participation of at least one family member in the top management of the company. This enables family members to set policies and objectives and implement them.
- **A family-owned and led business**: It is a for-profit enterprise owned by members of a single extended family. The business has the active participation of at least one family member in the top management as well as on the board of directors of the company. This enables family members to set the company's direction, culture, and strategies.

ROLES, RESPONSIBILITIES, AND RIGHTS OF FAMILY MEMBERS IN A FAMILY BUSINESS[5]

In a family business, it is essential to have clarity regarding the roles, responsibilities, and rights of family members in order to avoid conflict of interest. A clear understanding of role enables family members to work within a common framework of goals and to contribute more effectively to the development of the business.

Founder

In a family business, the founder identifies the business opportunity and establishes the business. The roles and responsibilities of the founder of a family business include launching an enterprise, building it, directing and guiding family members and employees, engaging family members in the business, and succession planning. The founder has maximum control in the family business and has rights in all the business transactions. The founder is also responsible for the development of ground rules as well as a mission for the enterprise.

Owners (Shareholders)

Owners are the shareholders in the family business and have several roles and responsibilities. The owners are responsible for building an environment of trust and motivating the employees to achieve the objectives of the enterprise.

Directors (Board of Directors)

The position of board membership in a family business is reserved for members of the family. In a few cases, it may be given to competent and well-trusted members of the family. This practice is usually necessary to keep the family's control of the business. Most of the business decisions are taken by the family-member directors.

Family Members

Family members can have different responsibilities, rights, and expectations from their businesses. Family members are usually assigned different roles and responsibilities based on their competency. Some family members may be groomed in a certain way based on career and succession planning. Family businesses should establish the necessary communication channels and institutions to keep all family members informed about business strategy, challenges, and direction.

THE THREE-CIRCLE MODEL OF FAMILY BUSINESS

In a family business, the business, family, and ownership need governance. The Three-circle Model of family business was developed by Professors Renato Tagiuri and John A. Davis at Harvard Business School as a simple, powerful, and generally accepted model for family businesses. The model comprises the governance of three systems—the family system, the business system, and the ownership system.

- **Governance of the family system:** During the founding stage, the family business is governed by family meetings, which are usually informal. At a later stage, the family is governed by a formal family assembly (also called a family forum) that meets once or twice in a year. As the business matures, the family develops a family council that focuses on the needs of the family business and governs the family circle. The family council is to the family what the board of directors is to the business.

  The family council should have a good representation from every branch of the family. It usually consists of 5–9 members and meets 2–6 times in a year. The selection criteria of the members are defined by the family. The family council defines the vision, mission, and values of the family business as well as the roles, rights, and responsibilities of family members involved in the business. It sets goals for the career and succession of family members and ensures the healthy involvement of the family in social activities. The family council also formulates a family constitution, which is a written document stating the family vision, mission, values, and policy.
- **Governance of the business system:** The governance structure of the business is centred on the management team. The management team would consist of key managers in the business, including family and non-family members. The team develops a business plan, budget, and strategic plan for the approval of the board of directors. The team evaluates potential successors for management, including family and non-family members.
- **Governance of the ownership system:** The governance model for ownership is centred on the board of directors. The board monitors the company performance, advises the CEO, and takes decisions regarding dividend reinvestment of profits. The board develops the strategic direction of the business and prepares the continuity plan, contingency plans, and the succession plan.

Anyone involved in a family business system can be located in a particular spot in the Three-circle Model. Within the three circles, there are seven potential positions that intersect and overlap and that various individuals can hold. Each of the following positions is marked out in Figure 4.1.

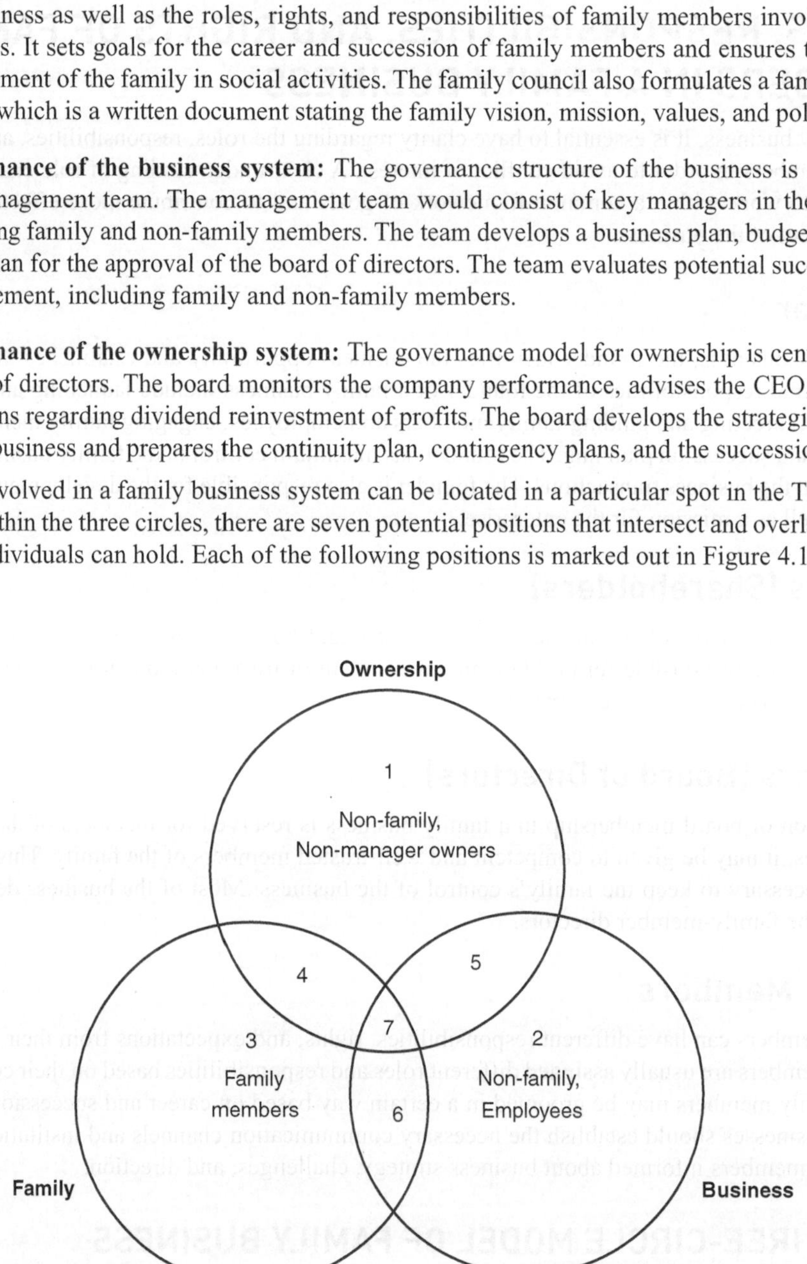

Figure 4.1 The "Three-circle" Model of Family Business

Source: Adapted from R. Tagiuri and John A. Davis (1982). "Bivalent Attributes of the Family Firm," reprinted (1996) in the classic section of *Family Business Review*, Volume IX, Number 2, Summer, 199–208. Reproduced with permission.

- **Position 1:** As shown in Figure 4.1, this position falls under "ownership." Individuals who occupy this position are external investors who own part of the business but do not work in it and are not members of the family.
- **Position 2:** This position falls under "business." Individuals who occupy this position are non-family members involved in management.
- **Position 3:** This position falls under "family." Individuals who occupy this position are family members who are not actively involved in the business either as employees or owners.
- **Position 4:** As shown in Figure 4.1, this position falls in the overlapping area between "family" and "ownership." Individuals who occupy this position are family members who own shares in the business but are not employees.
- **Position 5:** This position falls in the overlapping area between "ownership" and "business." Individuals who occupy this position are non-family owners and employees.
- **Position 6:** This position falls in the overlapping area between "family" and "business." Individuals who occupy this position are family members who work in the business but who do not own shares.
- **Position 7:** This position falls in the overlapping area among "ownership," "family," and "business." Individuals who occupy this position are family members who are owners and who also work in the business.

DISCUSSION FORUM

- Define family business and explain various types of family businesses.
- Discuss in small groups the roles, responsibilities, and rights of family members in a family business.
- Explain the Three-circle Model of family business.

SNAPSHOT

- A family-owned business is one in which the enterprise is owned, controlled, and operated by members of one or more families.
- Business communities are some socioeconomic classes or castes that have been traditionally associated with the business.
- The Three-circle Model of family business has three systems: business system, family system, and ownership system
- There are three components of family governance: family forum, family council meeting, and a family constitution.

CHALLENGES FACED BY FAMILY-OWNED BUSINESSES

The challenges faced by family-owned businesses vary according to the size of the company and its degree or stage of development.[6] It is generally difficult for Indians to maintain business relationships and communicate freely with family members in a family business without any regard to the complexity of the relationship shared with that family member because the family has always held centre stage in India. This inability to communicate freely with family members about such things as their role in the business has resulted in conflicts that have ruined the growth of family businesses. Some of the major challenges faced by family-owned businesses are:

- **Non-participating family members:** Every family-owned business has some participating members, i.e. those who are actively involved in the business and some non-participating members, i.e. those who are stakeholders but are not actively part of the business. These non-participating members are interested only in dividends and earnings and not in the growth of the business. As such, they are often unable to comprehend the problems of operating a business. The participating and non-participating members may have different viewpoints about the business, which may lead to conflict in many instances.
- **Family emotions:** Emotion is a major factor in family-owned businesses as close family members such as father and children, or brothers and sisters, all work together. Emotional outbursts among family members may lead to quarrels and ill feelings among relatives, and this negativity may spread in the organization and engulf non-family employees too.
- **Family versus business:** India, as a country, is very family oriented. As family members are usually trusted more than outsiders, there is often a tendency to give away jobs and responsibilities to family members—even if the individuals are incompetent. This adversely affects the business and its bottom line.
- **Defining authority:** It is very difficult in family businesses to define authority. Younger family members usually find it difficult to eschew the role of obedient youngsters with respect to older family members. So a younger family member, if made the CEO, may find it difficult to tell senior family members to change their working styles. Many members in the family tend to undermine the authority of younger members even if they are in positions of authority. This makes it difficult for the younger generation to manage family businesses.
- **"Fair to all" approach:** The philosophy of giving equal shares to all the family members may lead to rivalry if some family members contribute more to the operation of the business than others.
- **Retaining non-family professionals:** It is a huge challenge to retain non-family professionals in family-owned businesses because promotions that are closed to them at the top level may be given to family members, even if less competent. In some cases, family members can demoralize the organization by their behaviour at the workplace. For example, they may be idle, avoid unpleasant tasks, or make critical errors without being asked to account for it. As the company grows and the family finds that they can't hold all the positions, some non-family professionals are recruited to hold these top positions. However, they are not empowered to make decisions. Instead, they act as mere implementers of decisions taken by other family members. As such professionals feel underutilized and powerless; it becomes a challenge to retain their services.
- **Change management:** Change is something that does not happen very often in family-owned businesses in India, and when it does happen, it is usually very slow. Amidst rapid changes in the global business environment, however, family businesses must learn to face the challenge of quickly adapting to the changing environment.
- **Decision making:** The majority of family-owned companies operate like extended family units. All decisions are centralized and taken behind closed doors and guarded from everyone. The management of the business is closely held by a few members of the family, which means that decision making may be biased.
- **Succession planning:** Succession planning is almost absent in family-owned businesses in India. This may lead to huge problems of succession after the death of the leading individual. In

India, Reliance Industries Limited was torn apart after the death of Dhirubhai Ambani due to the absence of a clear succession plan.

SUCCESSION IN FAMILY BUSINESS

How best to pass on the business to the next generation is the greatest challenge for a family business. There is a need to make the right decisions for the family and the business. The succession process involves preparing a succession plan, choosing a successor, grooming the successor, and handing over the business.[7]

- **Preparing a succession plan**: Every succession plan is different. It is essential to hire the most competent advisors to facilitate the succession planning process. The succession planning should include key goals for the succession process, a schedule of the transition stage, and contingency plans (strategies to counter the death or incapacitation of key managers from the family). The schedule should furnish the details of when a succession may occur. It is important that the family members know the succession plan. Over a period of time, the successor will begin to make business decisions and may have to take the business in different directions due to changes in the business environment.
- **Choosing a successor:** It is essential to evaluate a competent successor who can fulfil the family and business mission. The family council can help in the choosing of a successor. The succession process does not happen quickly and may take several years to complete. It is important, while the person heading the company is still alive, to spell out succession plans as family quarrels over succession may have several adverse consequences for the company.
- **Grooming the successor:** Grooming primarily involves passing on leadership skills, business secrets, and various skills required to run the business. During the grooming stage, some authority must be granted to the successor to enable on-the-job learning before the actual passing on of the baton. At this stage, the successor should become familiar with the nature of the business and should be introduced to the various stakeholders and business associates. The successor's progress in developing skills and competencies should be extensively measured and documented by advisors on a regular and continuous basis.
- **Deciding on the role of the founder:** The role of the former founder after stepping down from the business should be clearly stated. The company also should make sure that the retiring business founder will have everything necessary to live a comfortable life. The founder should work with advisors to ensure that the business is transferred to the successor in as tax-efficient a manner as possible. For this, it is essential to carry out business valuation. Business valuation also enables buying shares from and selling shares to family members and tracking the progress of business plans toward the achievement of results. It is essential to agree upon future boundaries for the founder before the succession is formalized. Clear documentation of all agreements among constituents will lead to clear ideas of rights and responsibilities. A very important document is the will of the founder, which determines the shares of the family members.

SNAPSHOT

- Family quarrels over succession can have several adverse consequences for the company.
- It is important, while the person heading the company is still alive, to spell out the succession plans.
- Family councils can discuss the business issues and draw up a family constitution.
- It is important that the family members know the succession plan.

CHECKLIST FOR ENTREPRENEURS 4.2 Easing Sibling Rivalry in Family Businesses

Family businesses can never realistically expect to be completely rid of problems created by sibling rivalries. However, family businesses can minimize such conflicts by following the seven simple tips given below:

- Seek more information and insights from those with whom you disagree—ask for information that will enable you to better understand other points of view.
- While disagreements on issues may be strong, do not forget that the family's values are a shared bond among siblings and represent a shared commitment to the common good.
- Establish a formal or informal forum for dialogue. Communication should be free and frank, and all issues should be discussed. In this way, any potential cause of conflict can be identified early and be dealt with.
- Establish time limits on discussions and debates—when that time limit is reached but closure is not attained, table the topic for further research and put it on the agenda for discussion at a future meeting.
- It is essential that siblings have clearly definded roles to avoid conflicts.

SNAPSHOT

- The succession plan in a family business should include the key goals for the succession process, a schedule of the transition stage, and a contingency plan.
- Succesion planning should be overseen by someone who is not a member of the family or an employee of the company.

DISCUSSION FORUM

- Explain the challenges faced by a family business.
- Discuss in small groups the importance of succession planning in a family business.

IMPROVING THE PERFORMANCE OF A FAMILY BUSINESS

Some family businesses are successful, having a long-term history of consistent profitability, while others are less successful. Let's discuss some common characteristics that professionally-managed successful family businesses share[8]:

- **Promoting family values across the organization:** The family's core business values are crucial to its performance. In a well-managed family business, family values are reflected in the way family-owned enterprises are run. These values are considered to be the foundation of major business decisions. The family should establish charitable foundations to promote the concretization of family values across generations.
- **Shared vision:** Conflicting visions about the direction of the business among family members involved in the business may lead to internal conflicts and adverse effects on the performance

of the business. On the other hand, a shared vision will lead to wholehearted participation of the family members in the business.

- **Professionalism:** Family firms should be run professionally. Family members should participate actively and serve the business. For that it is essential to train both family and non-family members in the organization. It is also essential to encourage family members involved in the business to work in a different company for some time in order to gain experience and exposure. The family firm should hire external talent and retain them as per requirements. There should be career development plans and management development plans for family and non-family members in the family business.
- **Good governance:** Family-owned businesses should develop an ownership structure that provides sufficient capital for growth while allowing the family to control key parts of the business. The top management in a family business comprises the family council, advisory board, board of directors, and management team. The board of directors and management team should develop the vision, mission, and strategy of the company and strive to implement it. The top management should stimulate, provoke, and challenge leaders. The advisory board should include outsiders and must focus on the company's long-term plans. There should be good governance by family members through the involvement of the family council.
- **Communication:** There should be formal and informal communication channels for the facilitation of free and frank communication among family members. All issues should be discussed so that any potential conflict may be identified. There should also be an established conflict resolution mechanism involving senior advisors. Clear documentation of rights, roles, and responsibilities of the members in the family business is essential to avoid conflicts. Documented strategic plans, the succession plan, and the will of the founder reduce the scope for conflict among family members.

BREAKTHROUGH ENTREPRENEURSHIP 4.3 Succession Planning in the Tata Group

The Tata Group is one of India's largest and most respected business conglomerates. Tata Sons was established as a trading enterprise by its founder Jamshedji Tata in 1868. It is the promoter of all companies of the Tata Group and holds the bulk of shareholding in these companies. The chairman of Tata Sons has traditionally been the chairman of the Tata Group. The trust and respect enjoyed by the Tata Group in our country is unparalleled. The Tatas enjoy this respect because they have found a way to manage their business while nurturing a highly principled value system within the family and without spilling the beans about internal disputes in public. Another reason for their continued success is their intelligent and timely succession planning.

When Jamshedji Tata named Ratan Tata as his successor, many doubted his choice. Yet, Ratan Tata disproved his critics. When he retired in December 2012, Ratan Tata left behind a group that was much bigger and more competitive than it was when he took over.

Cyrus Mistry, the younger son of Tata Sons's largest individual shareholder Pallonji Mistry, was appointed as the chairman of the Tata Group with effect from 28 December 2012.

DISCUSSION FORUM

- What are the strategies for improving the capability of a family-owned business?
- Discuss some of the sucessful family businesses in India in small groups.

SUMMARY

In India, family businesses give a lot of importance to family relationships and loyalty, involve family members in the board of directors, and are often male-dominated. As the fortunes of family members are often tied to that of the family business, family members show dedication in ensuring its continued survival and success. In the course of their development, family businesses go through various stages—entrepreneurial, functionally-specialized, process-driven, and market-driven. The Three-circle Model is a simple, powerful framework and a generally accepted model for family businesses.

Some challenges faced by family businesses are non-participating family members, negative emotion and rivalry among family members, partiality to family members over external talent, retention of human resources, undermining of the authority of younger family members by older family members, change management, decision-making, and succession planning. Succession is a highly emotional issue and involves preparing a succession plan, choosing a successor, and grooming the successor. The best-managed family businesses across the world promote family values in the running of the firm, have a shared vision, exhibit professionalism and good governance, and keep communication channels open to avoid conflict.

KEY TERMS

Family Assembly: A formal forum where family members can discuss about business and family issues.

Family Business: A firm owned, controlled, and operated by members of one or more families.

Family Council: A working governing body that is elected by the family assembly among its members to deliberate on family business issues.

Founder: In a family business, the founder is the person who identifies the business opportunity and establishes the business.

Succession: The process of change in a firm brought about when a new leader takes the rights and responsibilities of an existing one.

CASE STUDY

Sibling Rivalry in Family Business

Reliance Industries Limited (RIL) is India's largest private-sector company. The Reliance Group's annual revenue is in excess of USD 6,600 crore. However, the company has witnessed unprecedented rivalry between siblings Anil and Mukesh Ambani, sons of the late Dhirubhai Ambani, the group's founder.

Anil Ambani, born in 1959, joined RIL in 1983 as co-chief executive officer. He holds an MBA degree from the Wharton School of the University of Pennsylvania and is credited with having pioneered many financial innovations in the Indian capital markets. For this, he has been regarded as a financial wizard. He has steered the Reliance Group to its current status as India's leading textiles, petroleum, petrochemicals, power, and telecommunications company.

Mukesh Ambani, born in 1957, enrolled into the MBA programme at the Stanford Business School but dropped out after the first year to assist in his father's business. He joined RIL in 1981 and initiated its backward integration from textiles into polyester fibres and further into petrochemicals. In this process, he directed the creation of 60 new world-class manufacturing facilities involving diverse technologies.

The brothers fell out after the death of their father in 2002. Their father, Dhirubhai Ambani, had left no will. In 2006, the group was split between the brothers under terms suggested by their mother, Kokilaben. Mukesh kept the group's petrochemicals flagship, Reliance Industries (RIL), Indian Petrochemicals Corp. Limited, Reliance Petroleum and Reliance Industrial Infrastructure Ltd (RIIL) and kept the Reliance name. Anil formed the Anil Dhirubhai Ambani Group (ADAG) consisting of Reliance Communications (RCOM), Reliance Capital (RCL), Reliance Energy (REL), and Reliance Natural Resources Ltd (RNRL).

Almost eight years after they fought publicly, Mukesh and Anil signed a deal worth ₹1,200 crore that would allow Reliance Jio Infocomm, the telecom division of Mukesh's Reliance Industries, to roll out 4G services using the nationwide fibre network operated by Anil's Reliance Communications. This deal has sparked hopes of reconciliation between the brothers.

Questions:

1. What were the reasons for the split in Reliance Industries?
2. How could the ownership issues in this case have been sorted out?
3. Do you think the new deal entered into by the brothers marks the end of their rivalry?

Source: www.hindustantimes.com/Mukesh-Ambani-vs-Anil-Ambani; www.ril.com/html/aboutus/aboutus.html (last accessed in March 2013).

DISCUSSION QUESTIONS

1. What are the advantages and disadvantages of a family business compared to other businesses?
2. What are the important roles and responsibilities of the founder in a family-owned business?
3. "The older generation wants to leave a legacy and the new generation wants to make its mark. The main issue in managing a family business is to resolve this conflict." Comment.
4. In a family business, what can be done to attract and retain talented non-family managers?
5. What are the main challenges facing family firms? How do you see them evolving in the future?

ACTIVITY

1. Divide the class into groups comprising 4–5 students. Each group has to study the profile of one of the following family-owned businesses and prepare a PowerPoint presentation. Fifteen minutes should be allotted to each group in the class—ten minutes for presentation in the class followed by five minutes for interaction and discussion.
    1. The Godrej Group
    2. The Murugappa Group
    3. The Dabur Group
    4. The Kirloskar Group
    5. The Wadia Group

PROJECT

1. Visit any family-owned enterprise. Interview the family shareholders. Study the performance of the business and prepare a report containing the following information, not exceeding five A4 size pages with adequate margins and normal space between the paragraphs.
    1. Founder
    2. Family shareholders
    3. Type of business

4. Challenges the business is facing
5. Succession planning (if any)
6. Road ahead

ENDNOTES

1. Poza, Ernesto J. (2007). *Family Business*. Mason, OH: Thomson South-Western.
2. Siddiqui, Saif (2009). "Havells India: A Success Story." Centre for Management Studies, Central University, New Delhi, available at www.asiapacific.edu/vol.4_no.2/saif_siddiqui.html (last accessed in March 2013).
3. Ramachandran, K. (2009). "Indian Family Businesses: Their Survival Beyond Three Generations." Working Paper Series, ISB, Hyderabad.
4. Dutta, Sudipt (1997). *Family Business in India*. New Delhi: Response Books.
5. Barry, Bernard (1980), "The Development of Organization Structure in the Family Firm," *Family Business Review*, 2 (3): 293–315.
6. Sharma, Pramodita, James J. Chrisman, and Jess H. Chua (1997). "Strategic Management of the Family Business: Past Research and Future Challenges," *Family Business Review*, 10 (1): 1–35.
7. Bhattacharya, Ritu (2001). *Succession Process in Family-owned Business in India*. Pune University Ph.D. thesis.
8. Paisner, Marshall B. (1999). *Sustaining the Family Business: An Insider's Guide to Managing Across Generations*. Reading, MA: Perseus Books.

Entrepreneurial Perspectives

1. Entrepreneurship
2. Entrepreneurial Development and Training
3. Women Entrepreneurs
4. Family Business
5. **Micro, Small, and Medium Enterprises**

"Small opportunities are often the beginning of great enterprises."

—Demosthenes

Karsanbhai Khandidas Patel's is a legendary rags-to-riches journey, in the course of which the founder of the Indian detergent brand Nirma shattered and rewrote established business theories. Karsanbhai Patel is a befitting example of a self-made man. Coming from a humble family of farmers, he understood the need of the masses and decided to serve a segment that was neglected but at the same time highly profitable. Karsanbhai Patel started Nirma in 1969 and went on to create a whole new category in the Indian domestic lower-income-segment detergent market. During that time, the domestic detergent market had only the premium segment and there were very few companies, mainly the MNCs, which were into this business. Nirma started as a one-product, one-man outfit from a 100 sq. ft room. The company's mission to provide "Better Products, Better Value, and Better Living" contributed a great deal to its success.

Micro, Small, and Medium Enterprises

5

LEARNING OBJECTIVES

Upon completion of this chapter, you should be able to:

1. **Understand the role and importance of Micro, Small, and Medium Enterprises (MSME).**
2. **Introduce the concepts and definitions of MSME.**
3. **Explain the recent policy initiatives and other reforms with reference to MSME.**
4. **Trace the growth and performance of MSME in India.**
5. **Analyse the findings of the Fourth All-India Census of MSME.**
6. **Discuss the problems and prospects of MSME.**

INTRODUCTION

The role of MSME is becoming prominent for sustainable development and inclusive growth initiatives in most countries. The Micro, Small, and Medium Enterprises (MSME) is one of the most vibrant sectors of the Indian economy. MSME are a breeding ground of entrepreneurship at the grassroots level. The sector is credited with generating employment and accounts for a major share of industrial production and exports. It also plays a key role in the development of economies with its effective, efficient, flexible, and innovative entrepreneurial spirit. MSME provide ancillary support to large enterprises, promote balanced industrial growth, protect Indian handicraft and cultural products, provide local flexibilities, and promote regional and backward area development.

The Government of India supplements the development of the MSME sector through the Ministry of MSME. The Ministry is duly assisted in its effort by the Office of the Development Commissioner (MSME) and Agro and Rural Industry (ARI). The ARI division comprises the Khadi and Village Industries Commission (KVIC), the Coir Board, and the Mahatama Gandhi Institute for Rural Industrialization (MGIRI). The Government of India has laid special emphasis on the growth and progress of this sector through the enactment of the MSMED Act 2006. The enactment of the MSMED Act, 2006, has substantially revised the definition and coverage of the term by way of classification of the sector into micro, small, and medium segments and also extended coverage to wholly non-agricultural enterprises. A "Package for Promotion of Micro and Small Enterprises" was announced in February 2007. This includes measures for addressing concerns of credit, fiscal support, cluster-based development, infrastructure, technology, and marketing.

The Fourth All-India Census was launched by the Office of the Development Commissioner (MSME) in May 2008 with 2006–07 as the reference year. The broad objective of the Census was to strengthen the database for the MSME sector. The data was collected with respect to the number of units, women-owned enterprises, employment and rate of growth, share of GDP, value of production, extent of sickness/closure, exports, and all other relevant parameters of MSME. The study also included Khadi and Village Industry units set up under the Rural Employment Generation Programme and the Prime Minister's Rozgar Yojana, through annual sample surveys, and a quinquennial census.

ROLE AND IMPORTANCE OF MICRO, SMALL, AND MEDIUM ENTERPRISES

Some of the world's largest enterprises have started from the most humble beginnings, some having their origins even in garages.[1] It is simple and easy to start small enterprises as one needs less infrastructural facilities and capital. Stanford University classmates Bill Hewlett and Dave Packard founded Hewlett-Packard in 1939. HP has become one of the most popular electronics manufacturing companies in the world. Bill Gates and Paul Allen founded Microsoft in 1975. Today, Microsoft dominates the personal computing market. Apple was founded by Steve Wozniack and Steve Jobs in 1976 in Wozniack's garage in Cupertino, California. Today, Apple is the most valuable software and hardware technology company in the world. Jeff Bezos founded Amazon.com as an online bookstore in 1994 in his garage in Bellevue, Washington. Today, Amazon is the world's largest online retailer. Google was founded in 1998 by Larry Page and Sergey Brin in a rented garage belonging to Susan Wojcicki in Menlo Park, California. Today, Google is the most widely used and most popular search engine in the world.

Some of the world's largest companies began as small firms. Sony was born in a devastated shed after World War II in Tokyo, Japan; Volkswagen was a little car maker in Wolfsburg, Germany; Vodafone was a little spin-off from a company called Racal and was founded in Newbury, Berkshire, England. Subway and the Burger King Corporation started small, but today, they have chains of outlets all over the world. Apple, Inc., Whole Foods Market, Mattel, Inc., and Starbucks Corporation all had humble beginnings and yet have become *Fortune* 500 companies today. They are "rags to riches" stories of unique brands that have created wealth, generated employment, created their own niche, and possess vast market shares. In India, corporations like the Hero Group, Ranbaxy, Balaji Films, the Oberoi Group, Nirma, Infosys, the Reliance Group, Biocon India, Dr Reddy's Laboratories, HCL, and many others are large companies that started small.

MSME play a major role in the socioeconomic transformation as well as the sustainable growth of both emerging and developed countries. MSME create wealth, generate employment, need lower capital investment, and promote exports both in rural and urban areas, ensuring an equitable distribution of income and yielding balanced regional development.

MSME comprise a very heterogeneous group of businesses usually operating in the service, trade, agri-business, and manufacturing sectors. Some examples are artisans, village handicrafts, handlooms, small machine shops, entertainment, drugs and pharmaceutical, retail outlets, and high-tech software firms that possess a wide range of sophistication and skills in niche markets.

According to the United Nations Industrial Development Organization (UNIDO) estimates, small and medium enterprises around the world account for almost over 90 per cent of all enterprises and 50–60 per cent of total employment. In most European countries, such as Italy and Germany, SME have been engines of economic growth. In the USA, small and medium enterprises account for 99.9 per cent of the businesses, almost 50 per cent of total employment.[2]

MSME have been responsible for the industrial development and economic growth of most Asian countries. After World War II, industrial progress began in Japan with the development of small and medium enterprises. The sector accounts for about 74 per cent of employment in the manufacturing sector, 85 per cent of total employment in the finance and insurance sectors, and 95 per cent of employment in the real-estate services sector. Other Asian countries like South Korea, Taiwan, and China have been able to build their economy by promoting MSME. In China, for example, MSME have been instrumental in creating 75 per cent of the total employment, have contributed around 68 per cent of the total production output, and are accountable for 70 per cent of China's total exports. Again, in South Korea, MSME represent 99.8 per cent of total business enterprises, accounting for 86.5 per cent of total employment.[3]

The MSME sector constitutes an important segment of the Indian economy in terms of its contribution to the country's industrial production, exports, employment, and the creation of a broad entrepreneurial base. Naturally, it is rightly regarded as the backbone of the modern Indian economy.

According to the Economic Survey 2009–10, MSME contribute about eight per cent to the GDP of India, 45 per cent to the manufactured output, and about 40 per cent to exports. There are more than 8,000 products—ranging from traditional to high-tech—being manufactured by MSME in India. In 2008, MSME employed 600 lakh people, created 13 lakh jobs, and provided maximum opportunities, after the agricultural sector, for both self-employment and otherwise in India.[4]

As a developmental strategy, the MSME sector possesses key advantages in the Indian context of capital scarcity and high labour availability, including a relatively high labour–capital ratio, shorter gestation periods, lower investment requirements, and a focus on relatively smaller markets. These factors ensure a more equitable distribution of national income and employment generation and ensure a more effective mobilization of resources of capital and skills which might otherwise remain unutilized.

BREAKTHROUGH ENTREPRENEURSHIP 5.1 Small to Big—From Rags to Riches

This section provides information about first-generation entrepreneurs who started from scratch. Today, the small enterprises started by these entrepreneurs are very big business houses and global corporations. These are stories of rags to riches in which Indian entrepreneurs have made a big mark and created value and wealth. Some of these entrepreneurs are: Dhirubhai Ambani (Reliance); Karsanbhai Patel (Nirma); Dr K. Anji Reddy (Dr Reddy's Laboratory); Shiv Nadar (HCL): N. R. Narayana Murthy (Infosys); and M. S. Oberoi (The Oberoi Group).

Dhirubhai Ambani (Reliance): Armed with a matriculation certificate, Ambani went to Aden, a seaport city in southern Yemen, to work as a clerk in the French company A. Besse and Co. He returned to India in 1958 and started his own business in spices in Mumbai. He was responsible for starting the Reliance Group of Industries. In 1977, Reliance went public with an initial public offering. Dhirubhai Ambani introduced the equity cult, a new model of business leadership, in India, and is regarded as an icon for enterprise in India.

Karsanbhai Patel (Nirma): Karsanbhai Patel is an Indian industrialist—the founder of the Nirma group. He was born into a farmer's family in north Gujarat. He worked as a lab assistant, first in the New Cotton Mills, Ahmedabad, and then at the Geology and Mining Department of the Government of Gujarat. In 1980, he set up Nirma, a small-scale enterprise selling detergent powder, in the backyard of his house. He started door-to-door selling of the detergent powder, and priced it at ₹3 per kg. It was an instant success. Nirma revolutionized the detergent market, creating an entirely new segment for detergent powder in the economy.

Dr K. Anji Reddy (Dr Reddy's Laboratory): Dr Kallam Anji Reddy was born into a farmer's family and spent his early years in a village in the Nalgonda district of Andhra Pradesh. He started his career working for the State-owned Indian Drugs and Pharmaceuticals Limited. He founded Uniloids Ltd in 1976 and Standard Organics Limited in 1980. He established Dr Reddy's Laboratories Ltd in 1984. It was the first bulk drug company to become free from dependence on imports and to take up pharmaceutical research in India.

Shiv Nadar (HCL): Shiv Nadar is the founder and chairman of Hindustan Computers Limited (HCL) and the Shiv Nadar Foundation. Shiv Nadar began his career in 1967 at Walchand Group's Cooper Engineering in Pune. He started Microcomp to sell teledigital calculators in the Indian market under the brand name Televista. In 1976, Shiv Nadar led a team of eight to found HCL, which is now a global technology enterprise.

N. R. Narayana Murthy (Infosys): N. R. Narayana Murthy is an Indian software entrepreneur who co-founded Infosys Technologies Ltd. He started his career as the chief systems programmer at IIM Ahmedabad. In 1976 he started a company called Softronics and failed, after which he joined Patni Computer Systems in Pune. He, along with six other engineers, founded Infosys in 1981 in his house with an initial investment of ₹10,000 provided by his wife Sudha Murthy. Today, Infosys is an IT giant and a global corporation.

M. S. Oberoi (The Oberoi Group): M. S. Oberoi was a renowned Indian hotelier and is called the father of the Indian hotel industry. He started his career as a front desk clerk at The Cecil in Shimla on a salary of ₹50 per month. In 1934, he acquired his first property, The Clarkes Hotel, from his mentor Ernest Clarke by gathering all of the family resources. Later, he signed a lease to take over operations of the Grand Hotel in Calcutta and was able to convert this hotel into a highly profitable business venture. He became the first Indian to run one of the largest and finest hotel chains in the world.

WORLD OF ENTREPRENEURS 5.2 Small Is Beautiful

Dr Ernst Friedrich "Fritz' Schumacher was a Rhodes Scholar, a well-known economist, journalist, and progressive entrepreneur. He was the originator of the concept of "intermediate technology" (now called "appropriate technology") for developing countries. Schumacher first articulated his idea of "intermediate technology" in a 1962 report to the Indian Planning Commission, in which he called for an "intermediate industrial technology" to harness India's labour surplus. In 1973, he published *Small Is Beautiful,* a fabulous collection of essays that looks at the economic structure of the western world in a revolutionary way. Even today, it remains a visionary book and has been translated into many languages. It was named by *The Times Literary Supplement* as one of the 100 most influential books published since World War II.

In *Small is Beautiful*, Schumacher looks at man's current pursuit of profit and progress, which promotes giant organizations and greater specialization but has resulted in gross economic inefficiency and environmental degradation. Big corporations entail concentrations of economic power in fewer hands, resulting in unequal distribution of wealth.

Schumacher's theory of intermediate technology promotes decentralization, sustainability, and proposes a new orientation of science and technology towards organic, gentle, non-violent, and elegant solutions. Such solutions are simple and support the triple bottom line: "people" (social), "profit" (economic), and "planet" (environmental). Schumacher advocated "technology with a human face" that maximizes the well-being of people. For example, powerful Web-based information technology has made work from home possible for small, decentralized organizations that are often innovative and create many new jobs, focusing on achieving economies in scale and achieving big results. These small-scale operations are often more environment-friendly as well.

Schumacher identified Mahatma Gandhi as the people's economist. Schumacher and Gandhi both believed simplicity and non-violence to be closely related. The optimal pattern of consumption, producing a high degree of human satisfaction by means of a relatively low rate of consumption, allows people to live without great pressure and strain. Good work is essential for proper human development and production from local resources for local needs is the most rational way of economic life. In *Small Is Beautiful*, Mahatma Gandhi's words are quoted: "Earth provides enough to satisfy every man's need, but not every man's greed."

Source: Schumacher, E. F. (1993). *Small Is Beautiful: A Study of Economics as if People Mattered.* London: Vintage Books.

SNAPSHOT

- According to UNIDO, small and medium enterprises around the world account for almost over 90 per cent of all enterprises and 50–60 per cent of total employment.
- MSME contributed eight per cent to the GDP of India, 45 per cent to the manufactured output, 40 per cent to exports, and created employment for 600 lakh people and an average of 13 lakh jobs in 2008.

CONCEPTS AND DEFINITIONS OF MSME

Small and medium enterprises (SME) are defined in different ways across the world. In India, a standard definition of SME emerged when the Ministry of Micro, Small, and Medium Enterprises, Government of India, enforced the Micro, Small, and Medium Enterprises Development (MSMED) Act, 2006. In India, enterprises are broadly classified into two categories—manufacturing and services. According to the MSMED Act, MSME are defined differently in the manufacturing and services sectors.[5] Both categories of enterprises have been further classified into micro, small, medium, and large enterprises based on their investment in plant and machinery (for manufacturing enterprises) or in equipment (in case of enterprises providing or rendering services). In the estimation of this investment, the calculation of the original cost excludes the cost of land, building, and

Table 5.1 Definitions of MSME in India

Description	Indian Rupees (₹)	USD ($)
Manufacturing enterprises—investment in plant and machinery		
Microenterprises	Upto ₹25 lakh	Upto $62,500
Small enterprises	Above ₹25 lakh and upto ₹5 crore	Above $62,500 and upto $125 lakh
Medium enterprises	Above ₹5 crore and upto ₹10 crore	Above $125 lakh and upto $250 lakh
Service enterprises—investment in equipments		
Microenterprises	Upto ₹10 lakh	Upto $25,000
Small enterprises	Above ₹10 lakh and upto ₹2 crore	Above $25,000 and upto $5 lakh
Medium enterprises	Above ₹2 crore and upto ₹5 crore	Above $5 lakh and upto $15 lakh

Source: www.dcmsme.gov.in/ssiindia/defination_msme.htm (last accessed in March 2013).

the items specified by the Ministry of Small Scale Industries vide its notification SO 1722(E), dated 5 October 2006. The definitions of MSME in India are given in Table 5.1.

A manufacturing sector enterprise is defined as a business establishment engaged in production, processing, or preservation of goods for the list of eligible industries mentioned in the First Schedule of the Industries Development and Regulation Act, 1951. The MSMED Act of 2006 defines micro, small, and medium enterprises for the manufacturing (production, processing, or preservation) sector in the following way:

- A **microenterprise** is an enterprise where the investment in plant and machinery does not exceed ₹25 lakh.
- A **small enterprise** is an enterprise where the investment in plant and machinery is more than ₹25 lakh but does not exceed ₹5 crore.
- A **medium enterprise** is an enterprise where the investment in plant and machinery is more than ₹5 crore, but does not exceed ₹10 crore.

A service sector enterprise is defined as one engaged in the rendering of services. Such an enterprise can be established by professionally qualified medical practitioners setting up practice in semi-urban and rural areas, and professional and self-employed persons. The MSMED Act defines micro, small, and medium enterprises for the service sector in the following way:

- A **microenterprise** is an enterprise whose investment in equipment does not exceed ₹10 lakh.
- A **small enterprise** is an enterprise whose investment in equipment is more than ₹10 lakh, but does not exceed ₹2 crore.
- A **medium enterprise** is an enterprise whose investment in equipment is more than ₹2 crore, but does not exceed ₹5 crore.

THE MSMED ACT, 2006

The MSMED Act is a comprehensive legislation for the promotion, development, and enhancement of the competitiveness of the MSME sector. This Act came into effect from 2 October 2006 with the core purpose of strengthening the Indian MSME and making them globally competitive. The MSMED Act, 2006, is the first Act exclusively for micro, small, and medium enterprises in India. The salient features of the Act are the following:

- The Act, in response to the changing economic scenario, has established separate definitions for MSME in the manufacturing and service sector. The Act provides the first-ever legal framework for the proper classification of manufacturing and service-sector enterprises based on their original investment. The classification of companies engaged in production of goods and those engaged in rendering services was simplified by introducing the concept of enterprises as against industries which was used earlier.

- The Act has been responsible for bringing about some much-needed initiatives, such as the establishment of a statutory board for MSME called the National Board for Micro, Small, and Medium Enterprises, which replaced the non-statutory Small Scale Industries Board. The Act also has been responsible for the establishment of an advisory committee to assist the Board and the central and state governments to support MSME.
- The Act has simplified the process of registration as well as the closure of business in all the three categories of enterprises. The Act introduced schemes to facilitate such things as timely payments to MSME and credit and specific funds for the promotion, development, and enhancement of competitiveness of MSME.

WORLD OF ENTREPRENEURS 5.3 Definitions of SME in Other Countries

There is no single definition for small and medium enterprises (SME) either nationally or internationally. In India, the Ministry of Micro, Small, and Medium Enterprises, Government of India, sets the definition of SME. The definition of SME in India has changed with the passing of the Micro, Small, and Medium Enterprises Development Act, 2006. The Indian definition of MSME hinges around the investment in plant machinery/equipment. However, in most countries, SME are defined in terms of number of employees and turnover.

United States of America

In the United States, the U. S. Small Business Administration (SBA) sets the definition of small businesses. It defines SME by the number of employees. SME is a unit consisting of 1,500 employees or less with a turnover of $75 lakh to $2.9 crore, depending upon the type of business.

European Union

In the European Union, the definition of SME is based on the number of employees and the turnover of the enterprise. Microenterprises are companies with upto ten employees and turnover lesser or equal to ₹20 lakh; small enterprises employ upto 50 people and have a turnover lesser or equal to₹1 crore; and medium enterprises employ up to 250 personnel with a turnover lesser or equal to₹5 crore.

United Kingdom

In the United Kingdom, Sections 382 and 465 of the Companies Act, 2006, define an SME. A small company is one that has a turnover of not more than £65 lakh, a balance sheet total of not more than £32.6 lakh, and an employee count of not more than 50. A medium-sized company has a turnover of not more than £2.59 crore and a balance sheet total of not more than £1.29 crore, and an employee count of not more than 250.

Canada

Canada's definition of MSME, like that of the US, is based on the number of employees. This country defines a small business as one that has less than 100 employees for the manufacturing sector and less than 50 employees for the service sector. It defines a medium-sized enterprise as having less than 500 employees. A microenterprise is defined as a business with less than five employees.

Japan

In Japan, the definition of SME is based on capital investment and the number of employees. For the manufacturing sector, SMEs are those that employ less than 300 employees or have an invested capital of less than ¥10 crore. In wholesaling, SME are those that employ less than 100 employees or have an invested capital of less than ¥3 crore. In the service sector, SME are those that employ less than 50 employees or have an invested capital of less than ¥1 crore.

China

In China, the definition of SME depends on the industry category and is done on the basis of fixed assets and the number of employees. Companies are regarded as medium-sized enterprises if they employ 300 to 2,000 people, have annual sales of ¥3 crore to ¥30 crore, and own assets worth ¥4 crore to ¥40 crore. Companies that employ fewer than 300 people, earn less than ¥3 crore in annual sales, and have assets of less than ¥4 crore are classified as small sized.

Sources: Compiled from the Government Web sites of SME of the respective countries. USA: www.smeiift.com/sme/SME_Overseas.asp (last accessed in March 2013); Europe: http://*ec.europa.eu/enterprise/policies/sme/facts-figures-analysis/sme-definition.htm;* UK: www.lib.strath.ac.uk/busweb/guides/sme-define.htm (last accessed in March 2013); Canada: http://sbinfocanada.about.com/od/businessinfo/g/SME.htm,Japan:www.smeda.org.pk/main.php?id=2 (last accessed in March 2013); and China: www.china.org.cn/business/2010-10/27/content_21212569.htm (last accessed in March 2013).

DISCUSSION FORUM

- Discuss in small groups the role and importance of MSME in India.
- Define micro, small, and medium enterprises.
- Discuss the salient features of the MSMED Act, 2006.

GOVERNMENT POLICY INITIATIVES SINCE 1948

The history of SME in India can be traced back to the Gandhian model of economic self-reliance. The evolution of the policy framework and support measures of the Indian government for SME can be broadly grouped into the following four periods.

1948–1991 This period was characterized by the government protection given to the MSME sector through privileges like the reservation of items for exclusive manufacture in the MSME sector, access to bank credit through priority-sector lending, and excise exemption. Post-independence, India adopted the Industrial Policy Resolution of 1948 that defined the role of the State in industrial development for the first time.

During the First Five-Year Plan (1951–1956), top priority was given to agriculture, and as a result, village industries got a lot of government attention. In 1954, the Small Industries Development Organization (SIDO) was set up as an apex body for sustained and organized growth of small-scale industries. During 1955, the National Small Industries Corporation (NSIC), the Khadi and Village Industries Commission, and the Coir Board were also set up.

During the Second Five-Year Plan (1956–1961), the Government of India announced the Second Industrial Policy, in which the Karve Committee Report clearly placed the small-scale sector in an important position by giving it an official definition. The policy statement arranged for special legislation to recognize and protect self-employed people in cottage and home industries. Subsequently, the Small Industries Service Institutes (SISI) was set up all over India to promote entrepreneurship training among youth. District Industries Centres (DIC) were set up and made the focal point of small-scale industry (SSI) development all over the country.

During the Third Five-Year Plan (1961–1966) and Fourth Five-Year Plan (1969–1974), the Keynesian model was introduced to promote the SSI sector. This is a macroeconomic model based on principles of Keynesian economics that is used to identify the equilibrium level of and analyse disruptions to aggregate production and income. The foundation of the Keynesian model is built on aggregate expenditure by the four macroeconomic sectors: household, business, government, and foreign and net exports. This model is used to analyse several important topics and issues, including multipliers, business cycles, fiscal policy, and monetary policy.

In 1967, the manufacturing of 180 products was reserved for the small-scale industries by law in a move to give a boost to the sector. During the Fifth Five-Year Plan (1974–1979), the idea of the tiny sector was introduced. In 1977, the industrial policy for the protection of small-scale industries increased the number of products reserved for SSIs from 180 to 504. During the Sixth and Seventh Five-Year Plans (1980–1989) in a policy statement issued in 1980, the government recognized the importance of ancillary industries and promoted the development of rural and backward areas through the propagation of SSIs. The industrial policy statement of 1985 raised the investment ceiling limit from ₹20 lakh to ₹35 lakh for SSIs and ₹45 lakh for ancillary industries.

1991–1999 With the liberalization of the Indian economy in 1991, the protection policy of the Indian government for MSME was no longer relevant and there was an urgent need to make the SSI sector more competitive and resilient. The industrial policy measures announced in 1991 laid special emphasis on the promotion and strengthening of small, tiny, and village industries. The protection given to SSIs was replaced with a competitive approach to infuse more vibrancy and growth into SSIs. Liberalization also favoured foreign direct investment (FDI). Besides affecting changes in investment limits and allowing equity participation up to 24 per cent by other undertakings, a new scheme for integrated infrastructural development for SSIs with the participation of the state government and financial institutions was initiated. The policy also proposed to encourage and support industry associations to establish counselling and common testing facilities, and to pursue a reoriented programme of modernization and technological upgrading aimed at improving productivity, efficiency, and cost effectiveness in the small-scale sector.

During 1990, the Small Industries Development Bank of India (SIDBI) was set up to accelerate finance to the SSI sector. The Industrial Infrastructure Development (IID) scheme was launched to initiate mini industrial estates or small industries. The IID scheme was launched in 1994. The aim of the IID scheme is to provide developed sites with infrastructural facilities like a power distribution network, water, telecommunication, drainage and pollution control facilities, roads, banks, raw materials, storage, marketing outlets, and common service facilities.

The formation of the World Trade Organization (WTO) in 1995 forced the Government of India to drastically scale down quantitative restrictions on imports. In 1995, the government sanctioned modernization funds to accelerate the introduction of technological services to the SSI sector. Sub-contracting Exchanges were established. A sub-contracting exchange is a storehouse of data with regard to the capacities of the MSME in terms of products manufactured/services rendered and idle capacities available on particular processes/machines on one hand and storing data with regard to the requirements of the buyers on the other, which could be products/components/sub-assemblies/services. The exchange also stores data about the specifications, class of accuracy, and quantities. The DCSSI is assisting industrial associations/NGOs in setting up these sub-contracting exchanges throughout the country.

The Delayed Payment Act was enacted to facilitate prompt payment of dues to the SSI sector. This Act was promulgated on 1993 in order to protect SMEs from the problems of delayed payment from clients. The Act makes a provision for SMEs to charge a penal rate of interest on outstanding payments if the same are delayed beyond the agreed or stipulated period of time. The main objective of this act is to relieve SMEs from shortage of working capital arising from delayed payments against supplies made by them. This Act has been further amended from time to time to strengthen its efficacy.

In 1996, the Government of India set up a high-level committee, known as the Abid Hussain Committee, to review policies for small industries and recommend measures to help formulate a strong innovative policy package for rapid development of the SSI sector. During the Eighth Five-Year Plan (1992–1997) there was a vision to create employment for 500 lakh people.

1999–2006 This period focused on technology upgrading, investments in infrastructure, and quality improvement. In order to focus attention on the problems of the SSI sector, a new Ministry of Small-Scale Industries and Agro and Rural Industries (SSI & ARI) was created in 1999. The Ministry announced a new policy package in August 2000 with the intention of addressing the problems of the SSI industry relating to credit, infrastructure, technology, and marketing more effectively. The number of items reserved for manufacture by the SSI sector reduced substantially. The reduction of reserved items from the SSI sector is a result of the liberalization policy of the Government of India. In the Budget of 1999–2000, a new credit insurance scheme was announced to banks to improve the flow of investment credit to SSI units, particularly export-oriented and tiny units. A national programme to boost rural industrialization was also announced in the Budget of 1999–2000, with a mission to set up 100 rural clusters every year.

In 2005, the Indian government formulated the National Manufacturing Competitiveness Programme (NMCP) to support SSIs. The objective of the NMCP is to support SME to modernize and become competitive and strengthen their operations due to pressures caused by the liberalization policy of the government. The design of the scheme is worked out by the National Manufacturing Competitiveness Council (NMCC) in consultation with the industry. In the same year, a performance and credit rating scheme was introduced for the SSI sector. Between 1999 and 2006, the SSI sector saw a lot of support from the government sector. There was much entrepreneurial development and diversification of the industries in the SSI sector, along with ample employment opportunities for the youth.

2006 and Beyond A concerted effort to support and promote MSME in the context of the global economy began with the implementation of the Micro, Small, and Medium Enterprises Development (MSMED) Act, which was enacted in October 2006, and aims to remove several bottlenecks faced by the sector. The Act provided the first-ever legal framework for the recognition of the concept of "enterprise," which comprises both manufacturing and service enterprises. The Act defined medium enterprises for the first time.

In the Eleventh Five-Year Plan (2007–2012), there was a stress on enhancing the competitiveness of MSME. In 2007, a package for the promotion of MSME was announced once again. A "Package for Promotion of Micro and Small Enterprises" was announced in February 2007. This includes measures for addressing concerns of credit, fiscal support, cluster-based development, infrastructure, technology, and marketing.

Substantial higher-budget allocation has been made to a cluster development programme for micro and small enterprises in the Twelfth Five-Year Plan. The objective is to improve the performance and output from the clusters rather than the number of clusters and money spent. The cluster is a geographical concentration of MSME with close supply links, specialist suppliers, service providers, and related industries and institutions. The Government of India has approved the ₹600 crore Mega Leather Cluster development scheme for the Twelfth Five-Year Plan (2012–2017), to make the Indian leather industry globally competitive. The seven leather clusters seek to address the constraint of large infrastructure with integrated production chains in the country. The mega leather clusters will have, among others, core infrastructure, social infrastructure, and production infrastructure.

Report of the Task Force on MSME

The report of the Task Force on MSME[6] provides a roadmap for the development and promotion of MSME. The report was presented to the Prime Minister by the chairman of the task force, Shri T. K. A. Nair. The recommendations of the report cover six major thematic areas identified for development of the MSME sector. These are: credit; marketing; rehabilitation and exit policy; taxation matters; labour issues; and infrastructure/technology/skill development/institutional structures. The following points are the highlights of the MSME Task Force report (2010).

- Setting up of an independent body at the national level for the promotion and development of MSME with the integration of institutions like SIDBI, DC-MSME, NSIC, and others. The independent body could use the existing structures of these organizations with appropriate changes in their charter and mandate. This body may provide financial and managerial support for setting up of industrial estates/common facilities in partnership with the private sector, administer schemes for the unorganized sector, promote technology development, provide marketing support, and coordinate and disseminate information relevant to MSME.
- Stimulus packages should be extended for one more year to MSME. The establishment of the SME Exchange needs to be accelerated. MSME usually find it difficult to get listed on the Bombay Stock Exchange (BSE) main board. Therefore, the Government of India has created the SME Exchange, which is a dedicated stock exchange for MSME.
- A public procurement policy for MSME was introduced. The offset policy of the government, particularly in the defence and aviation sectors, should give priority to MSME. A development fund to the tune of ₹5,000–5,500 crore over the next three to five years needs to be earmarked for various schemes for benefitting MSME, specifically to remove deficiencies in the existing infrastructure and institutional set up. The concept of business incubators in educational institutions of repute should be encouraged by setting aside ₹1,000 crore within the overall package.
- A separate fund with SIDBI, named the "Special Fund for Micro Enterprises" may be created to facilitate lending to microenterprises. Suitable incentives, including tax concessions, should be extended to Micro-Finance Institutions (MFI) to finance microenterprises at reasonable rates. The government should ensure strict adherence to the stipulated targets by the commercial banks for microenterprises. Some modifications in the capital subsidy should be made.
- A Standing Review Committee under a member of the Planning Commission should be set up to monitor the flow of credit to the MSME sector. A new Direct Tax Code and Goods and Services Tax (GST) should be introduced. The implementation of GST will simplify and rationalize the tax structure in the country and also benefit the MSME. The Central Government proposes to unveil GST in India as a single tax thereby replacing direct/indirect levies such as Cenvat, Service Tax, and VAT.

- District Industries Centres (DIC) should be modernized with IT-enabled facilities and available resources. State governments may establish a mechanism at the district level, in the DIC, to re-examine the viability of sick units in coordination with the banks. New clusters for MSME should be created to meet the requirements of planned development growth.
- The government should consider earmarking funds to the tune of ₹1,500 crore to support clean technology initiatives of the different ministries involved with MSME growth.
- A separate sub-group was also constituted to look into the development of MSME in north-eastern India and in Jammu and Kashmir.
- Workable legal options should be developed for the securitization of trade credit receivables and for the promotion of factoring services. Labour laws should be simplified, especially those applicable to enterprises in the MSME sector.
- Wide publicity should be given to new formats like Limited Liability Partnerships and Single Person Companies.

GROWTH AND DEVELOPMENT OF MSME IN INDIA

The contribution of the MSME sector to production, employment, and exports is quite significant. As you probably know, a time series is a sequence of data points, measured typically at successive time instants spaced out evenly at uniform time intervals. The time-series data in respect of the MSME sector in various economic parameters is given in Tables 5.2 and 5.3.

The MSME sector registered a steady growth for the period 1992–2006 in the number of units, investment, production, employment, and exports as shown in Table 5.2. According to the data furnished in Table 5.2, the number of micro and small enterprises in India rose from 73.5 lakh in 1992–1993 to 123.2 lakh in 2005–2006 with an average growth rate of 4.07 per cent over the previous years. Investment in the MSME sector rose from ₹10,962,300 lakh in 1992–1993 to ₹18,811,300 lakh in 2005–2006. Fixed investment in 1992–1993 grew by 9.24 per cent over the previous year. There was an increase in production from ₹8,441,300 lakh in 1992–1993 to ₹49,784,200

Table 5.2 Trends in the Growth of Micro and Small Enterprises (MSE Sector)

Year	Total MSME (No. in Lakh)	Fixed Investment (₹ in Lakh)	Production (₹ in Lakh) Current Prices	Employment of Persons (in Lakh)	Exports (₹ in Lakh)
1992–1993	73.5 (4.07)	10,962,300 (9.24)	8,441,300 (4.71)	174.8 (5.33)	1,778,400 (28.10)
1993–1994	76.5 (4.07)	11,579,500 (5.63)	9,879,600 (17.04)	182.6 (4.46)	2,530,700 (42.30)
1994–1995	79.6 (4.07)	12,379,000 (6.9)	12,215,400 (23.64)	191.4 (4.79)	2,906,800 (14.86)
1995–1996	82.8 (4.07)	12,575,000 (1.58)	14,771,200 (20.92)	197.9 (3.42)	3,647,000 (25.46)
1996–1997	86.2 (4.07)	13,056,000 (3.82)	16,780,500 (13.60)	205.9 (4.00)	3,924,800 (7.62)
1997–1998	89.7 (4.07)	13,324,200 (2.05)	18,721,700 (11.57)	213.2 (3.55)	4,444,200 (13.23)
1998–1999	93.4 (4.07)	13,548,200 (1.68)	21,045,400 (12.41)	220.6 (3.46)	4,897,900 (10.21)
1999–2000	97.1 (4.07)	13,998,200 (3.32)	23,376,000 (11.07)	229.1 (3.88)	5,420,000 (10.66)
2000–2001	101.1 (4.07)	14,684,500 (4.90)	26,129,700 (11.78)	238.7 (4.21)	6,979,700 (28.78)
2001–2002	105.2 (4.07)	15,437,900 (5.11)	28,227,000 (8.03)	249.3 (4.44)	7,124,400 (20.07)
2002–2003	109.5 (4.07)	16,231,700 (5.16)	31,485,000 (11.54)	260.2 (4.36)	8,601,300 (20.73)
2003–2004	114.0 (4.07)	17,021,900 (4.87)	36,454,700 (15.78)	271.4 (4.31)	9,764,400 (13.52)
2004–2005	118.6 (4.07)	17,869,900 (4.98)	42,979,600 (17.90)	28.26 (4.11)	12,441,700 (27.42)
2005–2006	123.2 (4.07)	18,811,300 (5.27)	49,784,200 (15.83)	29.49 (4.37)	15,024,200 (20.76)

Source: http://msme.gov.in/MSME-Annual-Report-2010-11-English.pdf (last accessed in March 2013).
Note: The figures in brackets show the percentage growth over the previous year for SSI sector. The data for this period is for SSI.

lakh in 2005–2006. The total production by the MSME sector for 2008–2009 stood at ₹880,800 crore (at 2001–2002 prices). The total production of MSME between the period 2006–2007 and 2008–2009 grew at a CAGR of 11.4 per cent.

The employment opportunities provided by the MSME sector have an increasing trend. The sector provided employment to 174.8 lakh persons in India in 1992–1993. The numbers rose to 229.1 lakh persons in 1999–2000 and 294.9 lakh persons in 2005–2006. The role of the MSME sector in the country's exports is significant. The sector dominated in exporting leather, garments, processed foods, electronics and computer software, basic chemicals, pharmaceutical products, cosmetics, gems and jewels, handicrafts, and engineering goods. The exports were worth ₹1,778,400 lakh in 1992–1993 with 28.10 per cent growth over the previous years. It increased to ₹253,070 lakh in 1993–1994 with 42.30 per cent growth over the previous year. The export potential from this sector increased to ₹1,502,420 lakh in 2005–2006 with 20.76 per cent growth over the previous year.

According to the data furnished in Table 5.3, the number of MSME units rose from 123.4 lakh in 2005–2006 to 261.01 lakh in 2006–2007 (although part of this increase came from the inclusion of medium enterprises in the data for 2006–2007, in accordance with the MSMED Act 2006). Investment in the MSME sector has gone up considerably over the years as the sector shows steady increase in production and employment. The MSME sector has also seen a drastic improvement in productivity. This directly reflects the efforts made by the sector to integrate its workforce with technological enhancement to increase its productivity. The production per employee increased from ₹1.2 lakh in 2006–2007 to ₹1.3 lakh in 2008–2009 and to ₹1.4 lakh in 2009–2010.

As we can see from Table 5.4, the MSME sector has maintained a higher growth rate vis-a-vis the overall industrial growth rate. The average annual growth rates of MSME for a four-year period,

Table 5.3 Trends in the Growth of Micro, Small, and Medium Enterprises (MSME Sector)

Year	Total MSME (Lakh)	Fixed Investment (₹ Crore)	Production (₹ Crore) Current Prices	Employment of Persons (in Lakh)	Exports (₹ Crore)
2006–2007	261.01 (111.48)	5,007,580 (166.20)	709,398 (42.49)	594.61 (101.62)	182,538 (21.50)
2007–2008**	272.79 (4.51)	558,190 (11.47)	790,759 (11.47)	626.34 (5.34)	202,017 (10.67)
2008–2009**	285.16 (4.53)	621,753 (11.39)	880,805 (11.39)	659.35 (5.35)	–
2009–2010**	298.08 (4.53)	693,835 (11.59)	982,919 (11.59)	695.38 (5.47)	–

Source: http://msme.gov.in/MSME-Annual-Report-2010-11-English.pdf (last accessed in March 2013).

** Projected figures sourced from S&D Division—Office of the DC (MSME).

Note: The figures in brackets show the percentage growth over the previous year for the MSME sector. Here the data for medium enterprises is also included.

Table 5.4 Comparative Data on Growth Rates of the MSME Sector

Year	Growth Rates of 2001–02 Base IIP (%)	Overall Industrial Growth Rates of Sector (%)
2004–2005	10.88	8.40
2005–2006	12.32	8.00
2006–2007	12.60	11.90
2007–2008	13.00	8.70
2008–2009	Not available	3.20
2009–2010	Not available	10.50
2010–2011		7.80

Source: http://msme.gov.in/MSME-Annual-Report-2010-11-English.pdf (last accessed in March 2013).

Table 5.5 Contribution of Micro and Small Enterprises (MSE) to GDP—1999–2009

Year	Contribution	
	Total Industrial Production	Gross Domestic Product (GDP)
1999–2000	39.74	5.86
2000–2001	39.71	6.04
2001–2002	39.12	5.77
2002–2003	38.89	5.91
2003–2004	38.74	5.79
2004–2005	38.62	5.84
2005–2006	38.56	5.83
2006–2007	45.62	7.20
2007–2008	45.24	8.00
2008–2009	44.86	8.72

Source: http://msme.gov.in/MSME-Annual-Report-2010-11-English.pdf (last accessed in March 2013).
Note: The data for the period up to 2005–06 is for Small-Scale Industries (SSI).

from 2004–2008, was 12.2 per cent, outperforming overall industrial growth rates which recorded an average of 9.25 per cent for the same period.

The data furnished in Table 5.5 reveals that the contribution of total industrial production and GDP has increased over the years. The contribution of MSME to industrial production was 39.74 in 1999–2000 and increased to 44.86 in 2008–2009. The contribution of MSME to the GDP was 5.86 in 1999–2000 and increased to 8.72 in 2008–2009. The average contribution to the GDP by this sector for ten years (1999–2009) is 6.5 per cent and towards total industrial production is 40.91 per cent.

The contribution of MSME to economic development is highly significant. The SME sector generates opportunities for both direct and indirect employment. As per a Dun and Bradstreet (D&B) report *Emerging SMEs of India 2008,* in 2006–07, every ₹one crore invested by the MSME sector generated employment for over 150 people, while for the overall economy, the same amount of investment generated employment for 37.4 people.

DISCUSSION FORUM

- What are the salient features of the MSME Task Force Report (2010)?
- Analyse the performance of MSME in India in terms of:
  a. GDP
  b. Employment potential
  c. Production
  d. Exports

CURRENT SCHEMES FOR MSME

The objectives of the Ministry of Micro, Small, and Medium Enterprises include[7] supporting and developing existing MSME and creating new enterprises and providing support to Khadi, village, and coir industries. These objectives can be met by creating an ecosystem that supports entrepreneurship and skill development in MSME. The Ministry of Micro, Small, and Medium Enterprises offers attractive schemes, incentives, and subsidies for the development of MSME. Only registered MSME (having registration certificates or entrepreneur memorandum numbers) are eligible for these schemes. Let us discuss some of the major schemes offered by the Government of India.

Credit Guarantee Trust for Micro and Small Enterprises (CGTMSE)

This scheme provides collateral-free financing to the MSME sector for both existing and new enterprises. The Ministry as well as the Small Industries Development Bank of India (SIDBI) established the Credit Guarantee Trust scheme in 2000–2001 for micro and small enterprises. The coverage of the loan under CGTMSE shall ensure that the financial institution gets the guaranteed amount without any time lag at a minimal cost.

Technology Upgradation Schemes

SME need to gain competitive advantage in international markets by upgrading their technology. The various schemes provided by the government for technology upgrading are:

- **Credit Linked Capital Subsidy Scheme (CLCSS):** This scheme aims at facilitating technology upgradation by providing capital subsidy for the modernization of production equipment and techniques.
- **Technology Upgradation Fund Scheme (TUFS):** This scheme is provided by the Ministry of Textiles. It provides interest subsidy, capital subsidy, or margin money subsidy on the basic value of the machinery.

Marketing Assistance Scheme

The Ministry of MSME, through the National Small Industries Corporation (NSIC), provides marketing support to MSME under the marketing assistance scheme. MSME can get subsidies to organize and participate in domestic and foreign trade exhibitions and also buyer–seller meets. This would help MSME to develop contacts and venture into international markets.

Certification Scheme

In order to enhance the competitive strength of MSME, to improve quality, environment, and safety standards, certification is needed. To promote this, the government provides incentives to MSME obtaining ISO 9001, ISO 14001, and Hazard Analysis and Critical Control Point (HACCP) certifications. This scheme is administered by the development commissioner of MSME. The scheme envisages a one-time reimbursement of charges for acquiring ISO 9001/14001/HACCP certifications to the extent of 75 per cent of the expenditure, subject to a maximum of ₹75,000 in each case.

Credit Rating Scheme

The credit rating scheme for this sector has been formulated in consultation with the Indian Banks' Association and rating agencies. The NSIC has been appointed as the nodal agency for the implementation of this scheme through various empanelled agencies. Eligible enterprises get a subsidy of upto 75 per cent for getting themselves rated by a credit rating agency under the Performance and Credit Rating Scheme of NSIC.

It has been predicted that growth in the MSME sector would cross the double-digit mark in the next five years.[8] The key drivers would remain housing and infrastructure, white goods, and automobiles. The services would also continue to churn out employment in retail, transportation, education, telecommunications, entertainment, and recreation. MSME will continue to be an important link in India's long journey to becoming a developed nation. The sector has the potential to create millions of employment opportunities.

THE FOURTH ALL-INDIA CENSUS OF MSME

The Office of the Development Commissioner (MSME) assists the Ministry in formulating, coordinating, implementing, and monitoring different policies and programmes for the promotion and development of MSME in the country. In addition, it provides a comprehensive range of common facilities like technological support services and marketing assistance. The Development Commissioner of MSME—DC (MSME)—has so far conducted three censuses on micro and small enterprises. The latest quinquennial census conducted for the reference period of 2006–2007 was completed during 2009–2010. The findings of this census will be useful for planners, administrators, academicians, industrialists, entrepreneurs, and all other stakeholders in the promotion and development of MSME. Table 5.6 provides the summary results of the Fourth All-India Census of MSME

In the Fourth Census, the major change is the inclusion of medium enterprises in the census. All the enterprises permanently registered by 31 March 2007 at the District Industry Centres (DICs) of the State/UT were surveyed using the complete enumeration method. Compared to the Third All-India Census of Micro, Small, and Medium Enterprises, the Fourth Census brought out some structural changes in the registered MSME sector. The scope of the Fourth Census was expanded as compared to the Third Census by the inclusion of medium enterprises and the enlargement of services to include all non-agricultural service enterprises, in conformity with the new definition of the sector under the MSMED Act, 2006. The Fourth All-India Census of MSME covered the MSME registered with government agencies such as the District Industries Centres of the state/union territory; the Chief inspector/Inspector of factories of the state/union territory; the Karnataka Village Industries Commission (KVIC)/Karnataka Village Industries Board (KVIB); and the Coir Board.

All the 22.48 lakh MSME registered up to 31 March 2007 at District Industries Centres in the country were surveyed on an enumeration basis. Of the 22.48 lakh enterprises, only 15.64 enterprises were found working. During the survey, it was found that 4.96 lakh units were permanently closed and 1.88 lakh units were non-traceable. The data reveals that the number of working units has gone up by 9 per cent and closure among MSME has gone down by 17 per cent as compared to the Third All-India Census (2001–02).

Out of the 15.64 lakh total working enterprises, the percentage of microenterprises is 94.94, small enterprises is 4.89 per cent, and medium enterprises is 0.17 per cent. The data reveals that the number of microenterprises is more than small and medium enterprises. The percentage of rural enterprises is 45.23, which is less than half of the total number of working enterprises. The number of women enterprises is one-seventh of the total number of working enterprises. The number of enterprises found to be operating perennially was 15.14 lakh (96.81 per cent), whereas enterprises running seasonally were around three per cent. The data reveals that the number of enterprises running seasonally were found to be a minimum. The data also reveals that there was a domination of manufacturing units (67.10 per cent) compared to service enterprises (16.78 per cent) followed by repairing and maintenance enterprises (16.13 per cent). It was found that the main source of power used by these enterprises was electricity (67.07 per cent), whereas 24.25 per cent of the enterprises were not using any kind of fuel. The survey found that the most popular form of organization was proprietary (90.08 per cent), followed by partnership (4.01 per cent), and then private company (2.78 per cent).

Around 48.75 per cent of enterprises were found to be owned by socially backward groups. There was a domination of Hindu-owned enterprises (81.22 per cent) followed by Muslim (9.11 per cent), Christian (4.12 per cent), and Sikh (3.31 per cent), respectively. Per unit employment has gone up from 4.48 persons in the Third Census to 5.95 persons. The number of males employed by MSME (79.55 per cent) was more than the number of females (20.45 per cent). Small enterprises have built relatively more fixed assets (49.76 per cent) than microenterprises (37.75 per cent), followed by medium enterprises (12.49 per cent). The gross output from small enterprises is more than (45.06 per cent) microenterprises (44.24 per cent), followed by medium enterprises (10.71 per cent).

Table 5.6 Summary Results of the Fourth All-India Census of MSME

Sl No.	Attribute	No. in Lakh
1.	Total no. of enterprises	15.64
2.	No. of rural enterprises	7.07 (45.23%)
3.	No. of women enterprises	2.15 (13.72%)
4.	No. of enterprises by type:	
	a. Micro	14.85 (94.94%)
	b. Small	0.76 (4.89%)
	c. Medium	0.03 (0.17%)
5.	Enterprises by type of operation:	
	a. Perennial	15.14 (96.81%)
	b. Non-perennial	0.50 (3.19%)
6.	Enterprises by type of activity:	
	a. Manufacturing	10.49 (67.10%)
	b. Repair and maintenance	2.52 (16.13%)
	c. Services	2.62 (16.78%)
7.	Enterprises by main source of power:	
	a. No power	3.79 (24.25%)
	b. Coal	0.25 (1.59%)
	c. Oil	0.53 (3.40%)
	d. LPG/CNG	0.07 (0.42%)
	e. Electricity	10.49 (67.07%)
	f. Others	0.51 (3.28%)
8.	Enterprises by type of organization:	
	a. Proprietary	14.09 (90.08%)
	b. Partnership	0.63 (4.01%)
	c. Private Co.	0.43 (2.78%)
	d. Public Limited Co.	0.08 (0.54%)
	e. Cooperative	0.05 (0.30%)
	f. Others	0.36 (2.30%)
9.	Enterprises by type of social category:	
	a. SC	1.19 (7.60%)
	b. ST	0.45 (2.87%)
	c. OBC	5.99 (38.28%)
	d. Others	8.01 (51.26%)
10.	Employment:	
	a. Micro	65.34 (70.19%)
	b. Small	23.43 (25.17%)
	c. Medium	4.32 (4.64%)
11.	Employment by gender:	
	a. Male	74.05 (79.55%)
	b. Female	19.04 (20.45%)
12.	Fixed Assets:	44,913,800
	a. Micro	16,953,800
	b. Small	22,350,300
	c. Medium	5,609,700
13.	Gross output:	70,751,000
	a. Micro	31,297,300
	b. Small	31,879,400
	c. Medium	7,574,300
14.	Enterprises by source of finance:	
	a. Self-finance	13.64 (87.23%)
	b. Institutional finance	1.70 (10.87%)
	c. Non-institutional	0.16 (1.05%)
	d. Both (b. and c.)	0.13 (0.84%)
15.	Original value of plant and machinery	10,502,500
16.	Net worth	41,530,300
17.	No. of exporting units	0.47
18.	Total amount of exports	6,791,400

Source: www.dcmsme.gov.in/publications/FinalReport010711.pdf (last accessed in March 2013).

It was found that most of the MSME were self-financed (87.23 per cent). Data reveals that two lakh enterprises had taken loans worth ₹46,520 crore either from an institutional source or non-institutional sources or both. Out of the above, 1.17 lakh enterprises had loans of ₹32,922 crore as outstanding as on 31 March 2007. The original value of plant and machinery was ₹105,025 crore. The net worth of MSME was found to be ₹415,303 crore. Around 46,675 MSME were found to be exporting with the value of exports amounting to ₹67,914 crore.

SNAPSHOT

- Compared to the Third All-India Census, the Fourth All-India Census brought out some structural changes in the registered MSME sector.
- The survey found a domination of micro and manufacturing enterprises. The main source of power used by enterprises was electricity.
- The survey found that the most popular form of organization was proprietary and most MSME were self-financed.

PROBLEMS FACING THE MSME SECTOR

The MSME sector in India is highly heterogeneous in terms of the size of enterprises. The small and highly fragmented structure of MSME makes them vulnerable to the external business environment. The problems faced by MSME are quite unique to the nature of the sector. The common problems[9] that MSME face are high interest rates, the rising cost of raw materials, obsolescence of technology, restricted access to market, availability of skilled labour, and compliance with regulatory systems. Exports from the labour-intensive sector were also hit. The main problems faced by the MSME sector are briefly discussed below:

- **Lack of availability of adequate and timely credit:** Despite their dominant number, high growth potential, and importance in job creation, MSME face difficulty in obtaining adequate and timely equity capital on competitive terms. This is the most critical problem faced by this sector. The major reason for this problem is the high risk perception among the banks with regard to this sector and the high transaction costs for loan appraisal. The level of non-performing assets is also very high in this segment. Hence, banks are reluctant to provide credit to MSME. As MSME find it difficult to furnish collaterals, they have to pay higher interest rates. These companies face obstacles in raising funds for their expansion and meeting their working capital needs.
- **Inadequate infrastructural facilities:** MSME, along with the industry in general, suffer from an underdeveloped supply chain and the lack of logistical infrastructure in the country. MSME may be located in industrial estates, urban areas, or in an unorganized way in rural areas. The infrastructural facilities, including power, water, and roads, in such areas are often poor and unreliable, which can lead to problems like difficulties in reaching the target markets in an efficient and profitable manner. Poor physical infrastructure hurts the productivity and competitiveness of Indian MSME vis-à-vis imports. For example, the food processing industry in India has been facing non-availability of adequate critical infrastructural facilities like cold chains and packing and grading centres. Again, export-oriented segments such as garments, leather, and jewellery face a lack of connectivity to ports.
- **Technological backwardness and lack of product innovation:** In order to survive and to be competitive in the present global environment, it is critical to use the latest technology and invest in research and development (R&D) for product innovation. The knowledge gap of MSME will increase with the digital divide and rapid changes in technology. Due to their small scale of operation, MSME have limited access to R&D and cannot invest much in acquiring modern technologies. This is a major hindrance in scaling up their operations.

- **Lack of access to market:** MSME often do not have adequate resources to link to diverse markets beyond their immediate vicinity. The limited access to larger markets in terms of market linkages, transport, and information exchange seriously undermines the demand for their products. This is a limitation and a constraint to profitability and growth. Marketing efforts are required to increase demand for the products/services of MSME. Finding a differentiator for the product or service on offer, finding customers, and creating a brand are some challenges that MSME face. In the absence of large marketing budgets, most MSME cannot opt for television and media advertisements. They need to rely on innovative and cost-effective techniques to make their offerings popular.
- **Difficulty in finding and retaining human resources:** Although India has the advantage of a large pool of human resources, MSME continue to face a deficit in manpower with the right skill set for specific areas like manufacturing, service, and marketing. The human resource problem is further exacerbated by the low retention rate as MSME are generally unable to match large enterprises in terms of work environment and remuneration.

  MSME usually do not attract many experienced and talented workers due to their various limitations. They are left to hire young professionals, with little or no work experience, and need to provide on-the-job training. These employees take a fair amount of time to become productive. Once trained, many of them leave for better opportunities in bigger enterprises. Therefore, MSME typically become a training ground and stop-gap arrangement for employees.
- **Impact of WTO compliance and regulatory systems:** MSME are adversely impacted by complicated mechanisms of adapting to technical standards, approvals, and permits which imply additional costs. MSME are vulnerable to the impact of WTO regulations as they are now

CHECKLIST FOR ENTREPRENEURS 5.4 The Road to Success for MSME

1. **Make use of schemes favouring MSME:** The Ministry of Micro, Small, and Medium Enterprises offers attractive schemes, incentives, and subsidies for the development of MSME. Only the MSME having a Registration Certificate/Entrepreneur Memorandum Number are eligible for these schemes. MSME should be aware of these schemes and make use of them.
2. **Constant innovation in products and processes:** Carve a niche by investing in constant innovation in products and processes to achieve differentiation. Constant innovation in product and process give sustainability and make MSME globally competitive, thus enabling them to enter the global markets.
3. **Upgrade technology:** Technology and the Internet have already broken down information barriers. The Internet enables MSME to collaborate across organizations and reduce the disadvantages of scale. ICT applications enable process automation which, in turn, can lead to better reporting and performance measurement, informed decisions and analytics along with proper delegation of jobs and resources. Use SAP's portfolio of SME innovative solutions, which lower operating costs, improve operational excellence, and provide better business insight.
4. **Adopt credit rating from an external expert credit rating agency:** Rating from agencies like SME Rating Agency of India Ltd, (SMERA), ICRA, or CRISIL. This will help in benchmarking an MSME's strength and reliability of performance. Credit rating will provide an independent opinion of your business and help banks and investors make an accurate assessment on their investments or loans. Credit rating can also provide an important impetus in raising standards through better financial discipline, disclosure, and governance practices.
5. **List your enterprise in the SME Exchange:** This will offer a platform to MSME to raise funds from the primary and debt markets and reduce their cost of capital. A large group of investors could be interested in investing in MSME listed in the SME Exchange platform.

in direct competition with companies in Southeast Asian countries and China, which can manufacture goods at a lower cost. MSME will face greater competition from imports. Large companies in India have the option of procuring from overseas suppliers and this may put Indian MSME in a disadvantageous position. Tighter patent laws also put MSME at a disadvantage. Moreover, Indian MSME are unable to implement anti-dumping measures and counter other unfair practices such as moves by competitors to patent traditional Indian products. It has been observed that MSME in China, Malaysia, Thailand, Vietnam, and Korea dump several products in Indian markets.

ROLE OF CLUSTERS IN PROMOTING MSME

Today, MSME are facing fierce competition from each other within the nation and beyond. Therefore, MSME need to collaborate and cooperate with each other for their survival and growth. The term "business cluster" also known as "industry cluster" was popularized by Michael Porter in *The Competitive Edge of Nations.*[10] Clusters are sectoral and geographical concentrations of enterprises, in particular micro, small, and medium enterprises (MSME), faced with common opportunities and threats. According to Porter, the factors involved in creating these ecosystems are land, location, natural resources, labour, and size of local population. The United Nations Industrial Development Organization (UNIDO) is a main promoter of cluster-based economic development. The clusters are formed by groups of related businesses and associated subsidiaries and complementing entities using a particular geographic region of a unique nature. Clusters provide the economies of scale for firms for becoming competitive, which MSME cannot achieve individually. Clusters provide conducive eco-systems for the development of MSME by providing institutional support for promoting research and development, skill development, pooled resources, and logistics support. Clusters promote higher productivity, innovation, and competitiveness for MSME and build a strong community feeling in the region.

The cluster development process undergoes various phases such as the cluster initiation phase; the cluster analysis phase; the cluster planning phase; the cluster execution phase; and the cluster sustainability phase. The cluster initiation phase deals with the setting up of a joint task force by various organizations to conduct a preliminary analysis and identify a location and the appropriate industry sector for the cluster. The cluster analysis phase deals with conducting detailed analysis and justification for setting up an appropriate industrial cluster. The cluster planning phase deals with identifying stakeholders and the forming of groups of related businesses. The cluster execution phase deals with the actual setting up of business within the cluster. The cluster sustainability phase should ensure continuous nurturing by the management and deploying growth strategies to ensure the vibrancy of the cluster.

Some of the well known clusters in India are the power loom cluster located in Guntur (Andhra Pradesh); the diamond processing cluster in Surat (Gujarat); the auto components cluster in Faridabad (Haryana); the food processing cluster in Kullu (Himachal Pradesh); the electronics cluster in Bangalore (Karnataka); the silk cluster in Mysore (Karnataka); the sea food processing cluster in Kochi (Kerala); the diesel engine cluster in Kolhapur (Maharashtra); the sports goods and leather cluster in Jalandhar (Punjab); the foundry cluster in Howrah (West Bengal); the rice mills cluster in Puri (Orissa); the chemicals cluster in Noida (Uttar Pradesh); the marble slabs cluster in Udaipur (Rajasthan); and the hosiery cluster in Tirupur (Tamil Nadu).[11]

DISCUSSION FORUM

- Discuss the major findings of the Fourth All-India Census on MSME in small groups.
- Explain the problems and prospects of MSME in India.

SUMMARY

MSME are witnessing a paradigm shift from the comparative to the competitive era. The MSME sector, over the past seven decades, has acquired a prominent place in the socioeconomic transformation of the country. It is a well-known fact that the MSME sector provides the maximum opportunities for both self-employment and jobs after the agricultural sector. The contribution of the MSME sector to manufacturing output, employment, and exports of the country is quite significant. According to estimates, in terms of value, the sector accounts for about 45 per cent of the manufacturing output, 40 per cent of the total exports of India, and employs about 600 lakh people in over 13 million units throughout the country. The Micro, Small, and Medium Enterprises Development (MSMED) Act, 2006, seeks to facilitate the development of MSME and also to enhance their competitiveness. According to this Act, MSME are classified according to the level of investment in plant and machinery for the manufacturing and service sectors.

The Fourth All-India Census of MSME was conducted with the reference period 2006–2007. The findings of the census will have utility for planners, administrators, academicians, industrialists, entrepreneurs, and all other stakeholders in the promotion and development of MSME. The MSME sector in India is heterogeneous, dispersed, and mostly organized. The common problems faced by MSME are the absence of equity capital, infrastructural bottlenecks, inadequate capital, lack of financial support, delayed settlement of dues, technology upgradation problems, informational inefficiency, inadequate research and development support, procurement problems, problems related to marketing, and difficulty in competing in global markets. The institutional support for MSME pertains to: (i) development support institutions that include advisory set-ups and policy set-ups, (ii) financial support institutions, and (iii) clusters. The report of the Task Force–2010 on MSME provides a roadmap for the development and promotion of micro, small, and medium enterprises (MSME).

KEY TERMS

Cluster: The cluster is a geographical concentration of MSME with close supply links, specialist suppliers, service providers, and related industries and institutions, faced with common opportunities and threats.

General Agreement on Tariffs and Trade (GATT): It is a multilateral agreement regulating international trade. According to its preamble, its purpose is the "substantial reduction of tariffs and other trade barriers and the elimination of preferences, on a reciprocal and mutually advantageous basis."

Medium Enterprise (Manufacturing): An enterprise where the investment in plant and machinery is more than ₹5 crore, but does not exceed ₹10 crore.

Medium Enterprise (Services): An enterprise whose investment in equipment is more than ₹2 crore, but does not exceed ₹5 crore.

Microenterprise (Manufacturing): An enterprise where the investment in plant and machinery does not exceed ₹25 lakh.

Microenterprise (Services): An enterprise whose investment in equipment does not exceed ₹10 lakh.

Small Enterprise (Manufacturing): An enterprise where the investment in plant and machinery is more than ₹25 lakh, but does not exceed ₹5 crore.

Small Enterprise (Services): An enterprise whose investment in equipment is more than ₹5 lakh, but does not exceed ₹2 crore.

WTO: The World Trade Organization was formed on 1 January 1995, and now comprises 155 member nations. The WTO is a culmination of the rule-based GATT negotiation.

CASE STUDY

Tirupur Cluster

The Indian MSME sector has developed itself in the form of clusters, gaining the benefit of economies of scale, while at the same time working in a competitive environment. The United Nations Industrial Development Organization (UNIDO) defines a cluster as, "a sectoral and geographical group of enterprises and companies, small, and medium enterprises, who face similar opportunities and threats." Firms in one cluster usually produce similar or related goods and services. According to UNIDO, there are several factors that have facilitated the growth of clusters in India. The majority of clusters are market-based and are termed as natural clusters. A few of them have come up due to the infrastructure provided and are formed by government support; these are termed "induced clusters." These are mainly seen in the areas of software, electronics, biotechnology, and floriculture. The remaining clusters are resource-based and depend on the availability of raw material and skilled labour.

Tirupur Textiles: The internationally-known Tirupur cluster, located in Tamil Nadu, has emerged as the knitwear capital of India. The textile cluster at Tirupur is spread across the town and there are as many as 2,000 MSME engaged in some form or other of business related to textiles. After China, Tirupur has become the second choice for international buyers wanting to source cotton knitwear. Around 70 per cent of India's total cotton knitwear exports originate from here with annual exports of over ₹6,000 crore. The success story of Tirupur began in 1940, when small enterprises started producing a kind of innerwear known as the *banian* for the domestic market. The exporting of knitwear started in the early 1980s. In 1985, the turnover was just ₹1,500 lakh and touched ₹570,000 lakh in 2008–2009.

Tirupur Knitwear Cluster: Tirupur, popularly known as the "Banian City" of South India, is located 60 km away from Coimbatore city. It is the seventh-largest town in Tamil Nadu and is well connected by road and rail. The first unit in Tirupur started in 1937. Its size increased to 230 units by 1960. Till 1970 the cluster was catering to the domestic market. Merchant exports started during 1972. The turning point for the industry came in 1978, when Antony Verona from Italy came to Tirupur. Realising the potential of Tirupur, he supported manufacturers in their efforts to export to Europe in the subsequent years. Impressed with the quality of garment manufacturing, C&A, a major European retail chain, came to Tirupur in 1981 to buy garments. In 1987, the export revenue of Tirupur was ₹7,500 lakh. Since then, it has not looked back and the exports during 2004 touched a figure of more than ₹500,000 lakh, contributing almost 70–80 per cent of the country's exports in this sector.

The statistics disclosed by the Tirupur Exporters Association (TEA) states that exports from the Tirupur knitwear cluster had leapfrogged from ₹118,000 lakh in 2009–2010 to ₹125,000 lakh in 2010–2011. The cluster provides direct employment to 3,500 workers. However, the export-centric cluster is exposed to volatilities in foreign markets.

Tirupur's product category mainly comprises apparels such as knitted garments, polo t-shirts, and t-shirts. The manufacturers are specialized in the fabrication of knitted apparel, which are known world-wide for their unmatched designs. They also undertake customized orders as per the exact requirements of clients. A range of knitted readymade garments and knitted apparel are available at competitive prices. Polo t-shirts are made of 100 per cent pure cotton from superior quality fabric with matching thread and skillful stitching. The manufacturers also offer services such as fabric yarns and the printing of fabrics.

Tirupur Exporters' Association (TEA): The Tirupur Exporters' Association was established in 1990 exclusively for exporters of cotton knitwear with production facilities in the Tirupur cluster. From a modest beginning, the TEA has grown into a strong body of knitwear exporters. Presently, the TEA comprises 658 lifetime members and 155 associate members. The TEA mainly focuses on the development of infrastructural needs for Tirupur, the multilateral growth of the knitwear industry and exports, the implementation of schemes for the benefit of society, promoting participation in industrial trade fairs and exhibitions, upgrading of technology, and supporting research and development.

Issues: Despite the concerted efforts of the TEA to improve the infrastructure in the cluster, budgetary constraints did not result in any major investments. As a result, infrastructure services were below desired levels in terms of quality and reliability. Electricity is the major energy source for the units in the cluster. There is an acute power shortage with daily cuts of 30–45 minutes for two or three times a day. The majority of the units manufacturing grey fabric, which operate looms, do not have any power backup systems. Sourcing of labour is the major issue as the majority of the units operate on job-work basis. The current practice of water usage, effluent treatment, discharge and sludge storage, and disposal in the cluster are not sustainable and could cause irreparable damage to the ecosystem while threatening the livelihoods of the farmers in the vicinity of the textile units.

Questions:

1. Discuss the contribution of MSME to the Tirupur cluster.
2. What are the major issues found in the Tirupur cluster?
3. What are the possible solutions to solve these problems?

Source: Foundation for MSME Clusters (2006). *Working Together Works*. New Delhi: Foundation for MSME Clusters.

DISCUSSION QUESTIONS

1. Explain the significance of MSME in India.
2. Comment on the statement "small is beautiful."
3. Which are the five *Fortune* 500 companies that began as small enterprises? Explain.
4. Explain the process of cluster formation.
5. Discuss five strategies to promote the development of MSME in India.

ACTIVITY

1. Study the Fourth All-India Census on MSME and prepare a brief report containing the summary of the results and prepare a PowerPoint presentation for the class (20 minutes).

PROJECT

1. Conduct a SWOT analysis of MSME in India and prepare a brief report.
2. Your instructor will divide the class into small groups consisting of four to six members. Each group will visit a nearby micro/small/medium enterprise, study the problems of the enterprise, and under the supervision of their instructors, prepare a 15 minute PowerPoint presentation on the problems faced by the enterprise. Each group will then make their presentation in front of a panel consisting of three instructors. After all the presentations are over, the panel will announce the winning group and the first and second runners-up.

ENDNOTES

1. www.retireat21.com (last accessed in March 2013).
2. Luetkenhorst, Wilfried (2005). *Private Sector Development: The Support Programmes of the Small and Medium Enterprises Branch.* Working Paper No. 15, Private Sector Development: The Support Programmes of the Small and Medium Enterprises Branch, UNIDO.
3. Businessworld, 2010. *The SME Whitebook 2011–12: Essential Handbook for Small and Medium Enterprises.* New Delhi: Businessworld.
4. www.smechamberofindia.com/About_MSMEs.aspx (last accessed in March 2013).
5. http://dcmsme.gov.in (last accessed in March 2013).
6. Ministry of Law and Justice, Government of India (2006). "MSMED Act 2006 and Related Issues."
7. Businessworld, 2010. *The SME Whitebook 2011–12: Essential Handbook for Small and Medium Enterprises.* New Delhi: Businessworld.
8. Confederation of Indian Industry (2012). "Focus: Micro, Small, and Medium Enterprises," *Policy Watch*, December 2012, 1 (9).
9. The Government of India (2010), "Report of the Prime Minister's Task Force on Micro, Small, and Medium Enterprises," pp. 8–9.
10. Porter, M. E. (1990). *The Competitive Advantage of Nations*. New York: The Free Press.
11. Basu Guha, Ipshita (2012). "Sustainable Development and Inclusive Growth: Boosting Regional Economic Clusters," *SME World*, May.

New Venture Creation

6. Identification of Business Opportunities
7. Project Management and Financing
8. Business Plans
9. Institutions Supporting Business Enterprises
10. Business Organizations and Business Laws

Part 2

"We are all faced with a series of great opportunities brilliantly disguised as impossible situations."

—Charles R. Swindoll

Sanjeev Bikhchandani is the founder and executive vice-chairman of the job portal "naukri.com." The company is registered as Info Edge India Ltd, and became the first dot-com company to make an initial public offering on the Bombay Stock Exchange. Although Bikhchandani struggled for close to a decade in his initial days, he never gave up on his business idea and was successful ultimately.

Identification of Business Opportunities

6

LEARNING OBJECTIVES

Upon completion of this chapter, you should be able to:

1. **Identify the sources of business ideas.**
2. **Explain methods for generating new business ideas.**
3. **Understand the difference between a business idea and a business opportunity.**
4. **Identify various entrepreneurial opportunities.**
5. **Understand the nature of the occupational and geographical mobility of entrepreneurs.**
6. **Discuss business opportunities in India.**
7. **Explain the Ramp Model and Mullins's Seven-domain Framework for evaluating entrepreneurial opportunities.**

INTRODUCTION

A business opportunity may be defined as a set of favourable circumstances in which an entrepreneur can exploit a new business idea that has the potential to generate profits. Business opportunities have the following four fundamental features:

- They create or add significant value to the customer.
- They solve a significant problem by removing pain points or meeting a significant want or need for which someone is willing to pay a premium.
- They have a robust market, margin, and money making characteristics that will allow the entrepreneur to estimate and communicate sustainable value to potential stakeholders.
- They are a good fit with the founder(s) and management teams at the time and marketplace along with an attractive risk–reward balance.

What Defines a Good Business Opportunity?

An idea is a thought or a concept that comes into existence in the mind as a product of mental activity. A business idea is an idea that can be used for commercial purposes. There can be many sources of business ideas, including the following[1]:

- A resolved problem faced by an actual or potential entrepreneur.
- An unmet customer need discovered by an actual or potential entrepreneur at a place of employment.
- Changes in the business environment.

BREAKTHROUGH ENTREPRENEURSHIP 6.1 **Nano Ganesh**

In many parts of India, farmers have to walk several miles to switch on the pumps that water their fields. The idea of creating a device to remotely control irrigation pumps struck Pune-based entrepreneur Santosh Hiralal Ostwal while watching his grandfather use his walking stick to trudge multiple times each day to his fields, which were about a kilometer-and-a-half away, to start the motor in a village where the water and power supply were both erratic. His grandfather would sometimes make up to ten trips a day. One day, the motor burned out and he lost ₹22,000 in his orange orchards. This incident had a profound effect on his grandson Santosh Ostwal, an engineering student then, and inspired him to work to make farmers' lives easier.

After graduating as an electrical engineer, Santosh used his knowledge of electronics in the field of water management and established Ossian Agro Automation in 1996. In 2008, he introduced the Nano Ganesh, a unique electronic device that allowed farmers to use mobile phones to remotely switch irrigation pumps on and off.

The technology behind Nano Ganesh may seem simple, but developing the Nano Ganesh was no easy task. Among the problems that farmers face are power cuts, voltage fluctuations, frequent interruptions in the supply of electricity, shock hazards, open wiring, marshy terrain, trips to the field at night regardless of weather conditions, fear of scorpion and snake bites, and the danger of wild animals like leopards and wild boars. Moreover, there were obstacles such as R&D related difficulties, problems in conducting field tests for the products, depletion of funds, bureaucratic hurdles in obtaining permissions, educating farmers about the technology, and frequent requests for enhancement of the product based on market requirements.

In time, however, all these hurdles were overcome and a creative business idea was successfully made into a business opportunity and a success. Nano Ganesh works by acting as a mobile modem device that converts signals received on a mobile phone into commands for the switch of the pump set to switch on or off. It enables farmers to control the functioning of their motor pump sets from distant locations through a phone call.

Source: "About Us: Unveiling the Nano Ganesh: A Boon for Farmers," www.nanoganesh.com (last accessed in March 2013). Reproduced with permission.

Not all business ideas are found to be good business opportunities. This simple five-step framework helps screen ideas and find out whether a business idea truly represents a good business opportunity. An opportunity is characterized by the following:

- **Urgency of the market need**: The business idea should envision a product or service that satisfies a market need or a need of the customer. The market need has to be carefully assessed by consulting industry experts as well as potential customers. It is important to focus on the "need" of the customer rather than on the attributes of the offering and to evaluate the urgency of that need in order to gain the assurance that there are customers ready to purchase that product/service once it hits the market. The greater the market need, the greater the opportunity for a profitable business.
- **Adequate market size:** A business usually targets a particular market segment after assessing their demographic, geographical, and lifestyle factors. In order to make the business viable, a large number of potential customers should exist. There is a need to find out the potential market size for the product or service.
- **Sound business model:** In simple terms, a business model is a broad range of descriptions of various core aspects of business, such as purpose, strategies, infrastructure, organizational structures, marketing programmes, and operational processes and policies. In other words, a business model clearly gives the outline or the rationale of how the potential entrepreneur intends to satisfy a customer need and create value. A business model that presents a plan to generate profits within three to five years is considered to be relatively good.
- **Potential brand value:** The product/service being offered must be differentiated from those being offered by competitors to maintain a competitive advantage in the market. It is necessary

CHECKLIST FOR ENTREPRENEURS 6.2 Idea Generation

Here are a few tips to get you started in thinking up great business ideas:

- Define a problem.
- Brainstorm on possible solutions.
- Focus entirely on what you want.
- Have a genuine interest in what you are trying to solve.
- Look at parallel problems and solutions.
- Look at each task as a challenge.
- Turn the challenge/problem into a catchy expression.
- Daydream—let your creative subconscious work for you.
- Alter your routine regularly.
- Carry a notepad.

to assess the potential brand value of the product or service envisioned in order to ensure a fair chance of survival against competition by existing as well as future products.

- **An able management team:** The ability and passion of team members to use a business opportunity is important to success. The team should have contacts among suppliers, competitors, and customers. The number and quality of contacts up and down the value chain is an important determinant of eventual business success. On the whole, the business should be big enough to make it worthwhile and the team should be looking forward to being involved with it for a long time.

When Is an Idea an Opportunity?

A business opportunity is a set of favourable circumstances that creates a need for a new product or service. A business idea becomes a good business opportunity when it has the following four essential qualities[2]:

- Attractiveness.
- Timeliness.
- Durability.
- The quality of being anchored in a product or service that creates or adds value for its buyer or end user.

How to Generate Business Ideas

Having business ideas is central to the task of identifying business opportunities. Let's discuss some ways to generate business ideas.

Brainstorming Brainstorming is a technique used to quickly generate a large number of ideas and solutions to problems. The brainstorming session is conducted to generate ideas that might represent business opportunities. Brainstorming works well individually as well as with a varied group of people. A group brainstorming session requires a facilitator, white board, and space to accommodate the participating people. Brainstorming works well with 8–12 people and should be performed in a relaxed environment. Participants are encouraged to share every idea that enters their mind with the assurance that there is no right or wrong answer. The brainstorming session usually starts with the facilitator broadly stating the problem and setting the time limit (such as, say, 30 minutes) for the session. The facilitator clearly sets down the rules, discouraging criticism of any kind and encouraging a freewheeling approach, the voicing of as many ideas as possible, and a collective and constructive

BREAKTHROUGH ENTREPRENEURSHIP 6.3 Sacred Moments

Sacred Moments, founded in 2006 by Mumbai-based entrepreneur Prakash Mundhra, is a company that pioneered and implemented the business idea of selling designer festival kits containing religious items customized for various Indian festivals. Their portfolio includes kits for Diwali, Durga Puja, Holi, Satyanarayana Puja, Ganapati Puja, general Puja, Griha Pravesh Pooja, and a kit called the "Muslim kit." Having targeted a niche market by leveraging Indian traditions, Mundhra is hopeful of becoming a leader in providing religious and spiritual solutions for all religions across the world. At present, Sacred Moments's client base comprises religious organizations, gifting portals, corporate organizations (festival gifts), retails chains, and exporters.

Idea

After acquiring his master's degree in human resource development from the Symbiosis Centre for Management and Human Resource Development (SCMHRD), Pune, Mundhra chose to start his own business. After a detailed study of the market, Mundhra came upon the idea of Puja kits that were delivered straight to the customer. Mundhra's business idea of Puja kits won several business plan competitions. At each competition, he further refined the idea to reach the final stage.

Opportunity

During his market study, Mundhra found a growing need in the market. He found that people today are often unaware of the items that go into a particular Puja as well as about where to find products of good quality and how to use them. This presented a good business opportunity for customized, well-packaged, and meticulously-labelled Puja kits to address that gap. Additionally, Mundhra saw an opportunity in the corporate gifting sector.

Today, Mundhra's Puja kits are available at several stores in Mumbai and he is looking to expand both within the country and globally. Mundhra's Puja kits are a classic example of the identification of a business opportunity.

Source: www.nenonline.org/startup-profile/sacred-moments (last accessed in March 2013).

SNAPSHOT

- An idea is a thought, an impression, or a notion. A business idea is a concept which can be used for commercial purposes.
- Business ideas can be generated by environmental analysis, industry analysis, and SWOT analysis.

effort towards the improvement of ideas. Once the session starts, participants can informally present their ideas for possible solutions. The facilitator writes each idea down for everyone to see. Once time is up, the best ideas are selected, based on a few criteria decided upon in advance (such as, say, cost-effectiveness). The selection must be made on the basis of a consensus from everyone in the group. Next, a score (say, zero to ten points) is given to each idea depending on how well it meets the criteria. The idea with the highest score may be used to solve the problem. However, it is advisable for the facilitator to keep a record of the best ideas in case the chosen best idea does not work. The facilitator should make the session fun for everybody, with no one dominating or inhibiting the discussion.

Survey Method The survey method is used to collect information by direct observation of a phenomenon or systematic gathering of data from a set of people. The survey method involves gathering information from a representative sample population, that is, a fraction of the whole population under study that presents an accurate proportional representation of that population. Surveys generate new products, services, and business ideas because they ask specific questions and get specific answers. For example, Hindustan Unilever Limited undertook a market survey to explore the possibility of penetrating rural markets in India, and this helped the market research team to identify the idea of introducing shampoo sachets, which became an instant hit with people who would not buy an entire bottle of shampoo. Surveys may be of different types, such as general and specific surveys, regular and ad hoc surveys, preliminary and final surveys, and census and sample surveys.

Reverse Brainstorming This is a method that is similar to brainstorming, with the exception that criticism is allowed. It is, therefore, also called "negative brainstorming." In this technique, the focus is on the negative aspects of every idea that has been generated through brainstorming. Also called the "sifting" process, this process most often involves the identification of everything that is wrong with an idea, followed by a discussion of ways to overcome these problems.

The Gordon Method This is a creative technique developed by A. F. Osborn in his book *L'arte della Creativity* to develop new ideas. This method is similar to brainstorming. Collective discussion addresses every aspect of the planned product in an uninhibited solution-oriented way. For example, to devise a new pen-holder, the group discusses the "holding" theme and examines all possible meanings of this word and all possible examples of "holding" (such as items, nature, etc.). The group will later sit and study each idea to see if any of them may be useful for the planning of a new pen-holder. This discussion encourages a fresh, creative, and unusual approach to developing a new product.

What Leads to the Creation of Opportunities

Entrepreneurial opportunities often come into being because of certain external changes, such as technological change, regulatory and political change, social and demographic change, and economic change.[3]

Technological Changes Technological changes lead to entrepreneurial opportunities because they make it possible for people to do things in new and more productive ways. Technological changes can take the form of five forms of business opportunity—new products and services, new methods of production, new markets, new ways of organizing, and new raw material. Some examples are given in Table 6.1.

Table 6.1 Forms of Business Opportunity

Technological Change	Form of the Opportunity	Example of a Business Idea in Response to the Opportunity	Reasoning
Internal combustion engine	New product or service	Automobile	Used to power automobiles
Internet	New way of marketing	Online shopping	Allows people to buy and sell products without the help of retail outlets
Cold storage	New market	Fruits	Allows one to export fruits
Computer	New method of production	Computer-aided design	Allows one to design products without building physical prototypes
Sensor	New material	Security	Used in shopping malls, theatres, and public halls

WORLD OF ENTREPRENEURS 6.4 **Edward de Bono's Six Thinking Hats**

The six thinking hats method is a creative technique, which can be used by entrepreneurs to arrive at decisions. Dr Edward de Bono invented this method in the early 1980s. The six coloured hats represent six different modes of thinking. Thinkers can put on different hats to indicate exactly the type of thinking that they are using. When using this technique, it is essential never to categorize individuals according to the hats they choose to wear. The six thinking hats method is a good technique for looking at the effects of a decision from different points of view. It allows necessary emotion and skepticism to be brought into what would otherwise be purely rational decisions and opens up the opportunity for creativity within decision making. The six hats are briefly explained below:

1. **White hat thinking**: A white hat represents factual or data analysis. The white hat indicates that a thinker is looking at facts, figures, information needs, and gaps.
2. **Red hat thinking**: A red hat represents feelings and intuition. With this hat on, a thinker may voice intuition, feelings, and emotions without having to justify them.
3. **Black hat thinking**: A black hat represents judgement and caution. With this hat on, a thinker may logically point out why a suggestion does not fit the available facts or the system in use.
4. **Yellow hat thinking**: A yellow hat represents optimism. With this hat on, a thinker may emphasize the positive aspects of an idea.
5. **Green hat thinking**: A green hat represents creativity and innovation. With this hat on, a thinker may present an alternative way of looking at the situation, proposals, interesting aspects, provocations, and changes.
6. **Blue hat thinking**: A blue hat represents process control. With this hat on, a thinker may decide which hat is to be put on at a given point of time.

Source: Roberts, Rohan (2011). "Six Thinking Hats," www.sites.google.com/site/winchestercpd/assignments/sixthinkinghats (last accessed on 8 March 2013) and Labelle, Sylvie (2005). "Six Thinking Hats: A Summary," http://members.optusnet.com.au/charles57/Creative/Techniques/sixhats.htm (last accessed on 8 March 2013).

SNAPSHOT

The various methods that can be used for generating business ideas are:

- Brainstorming
- Survey method
- Reverse brainstorming
- The Gordon method

DISCUSSION FORUM

- Differentiate between an idea and an opportunity.
- Use one of the methods mentioned in this chapter and generate a business idea.
- What are the various methods for generating new ideas?
- What are the various sources of business opportunity?

Political and Regulatory Changes Political and regulatory changes lead to business opportunities by paving the way for new, more productive use of resources or a redistribution of wealth from one person to another. Statutory and regulatory requirements create opportunities for entrepreneurs to start firms that help other firms and the community to comply with the requirements.

When the use of helmets was made compulsory by the government, helmets were reintroduced into the market with new features and the demand for helmets improved substantially. Similarly, political suppport for the country's infrastructural development, such as in the case of the construction of the Golden Quadrilateral, led to many business opportunities in the construction sector. Again, many firms were started just to help companies comply with the ISO 9000 Quality Management System, the ISO 14000 Environmental Management System and the Sarbanes–Oxley Act of 2002.

Social and Demographic Changes Social and demographic changes, such as changes in family and work patterns, the ageing of the population, increasing diversity at the workplace, increasing focus on health and fitness, the increase in the number of cell phone and Internet users, and new forms of entertainment, lead to the creation of business opportunities because they alter people's preferences or demand for products and services, and consequently make it possible to generate new ideas to meet new demands. For example, the ageing of the Indian population over the last 25 years generated business opportunities for entrepreneurs to make products and services for the elderly.

Economic Changes Economic forces affect business opportunities by determining who has money to spend.[4] An increase in the number of women in the workforce over the last few decades and their related increase in disposable income is largely responsible for the number of boutique clothing stores targeting professional women that have opened in the past few years.

SNAPSHOT

A business opportunity has four essential qualities:

- Attractive
- Timely
- Durable
- Anchored in a product, service, or business that creates or adds value for its buyer or end user.

How to Identify a Business Opportunity

Several studies have shown that previous experience in an industry helps entrepreneurs to recognize business opportunities. In addition, the extent and depth of an individual's social network also affects the identification of opportunity. People who build a substantial network of social and professional contacts will be exposed to more opportunities and ideas than people with sparse networks. Studies have demonstrated that the identification of a business opportunity may also be a cognitive process or an innate skill. Some people believe that entrepreneurs have an intuition or a "sixth sense" that allows them to see opportunities that others miss. Creativity is the process of generating a novel or useful idea. Opportunity recognition may be, at least in part, a creative process as well.

It is important for entrepreneurs to grab a business opportunity before the market becomes saturated with competitors and the window of opportunity is closed to them. There are three general approaches entrepreneurs use to identify an opportunity. They are:

1. **Observing trends**: Entrepreneurs can identify business opportunities by carefully observing trends. The most important trends to follow are economic, social, technological, and political trends. For example, the development of the Internet and the miniaturization of electronics goods led to the development of e-commerce and laptop computers, respectively.
2. **Solving a problem**: Another approach to identifying business opportunities is to recognize and solve a pressing problem that customers are facing today. From an entrepreneur's point of view, every problem is a disguised opportunity. For example, one of the most pressing problems facing countries round the globe is finding alternatives for fossil fuels. As a result, a number of entrepreneurial firms have been (and are still being) launched to take on this challenge.

3. **Finding gaps in the marketplace**: A third approach to identifying business opportunities is to find a gap between what is needed by the customer and what is actually provided to the customer. Finding such gaps can help entrepreneurs develop new products and improve existing ones. For example, over three decades ago, the lack of toy stores focusing on a child's intellectual development resulted in the development of Discovery Toys, a California-based company specializing in educational toys.

DISCUSSION FORUM

- Identify a business opportunity and discuss its essential qualities.
- Explain the term "window of opportunity" with an example.

MOBILITY OF ENTREPRENEURS

Entrepreneurial mobility is the movement of entrepreneurs from one location to another (geographical mobility) or from one occupation to another (occupational mobility) based on business opportunities. Entrepreneurial mobility is usually caused by political, economic, cultural, and social factors. The various factors that influence entrepreneurial mobility are listed below:

- **Political conditions:** Entrepreneurial mobility is influenced by political factors. For example, Tata Motors's shifting of the Tata Nano project from Singur, West Bengal, to Gujarat clearly demonstrated that political conditions are more congenial to business in Gujarat than in West Bengal.
- **Education:** Education imparts knowledge and hones one's analytical thought process. In general, an educated entrepreneur will be able to scan and understand the business environment—whether domestic or global—better in order to exploit both domestic and international business opportunities. An educated entrepreneur will also usually be able to communicate, interact, and network more effectively. A number of institutes have set up successful entrepreneurship centres, which provide support to potential entrepreneurs by conducting formal training and mentorship. This may cause brain drain to more favourable environments, resulting in the mobility of entrepreneurs.
- **Experience:** Entrepreneurs with experience in business and industry are quick to exploit opportunities. Their past experiences enable entrepreneurs to take up various types of ventures in distant places, leading to entrepreneurial mobility.
- **Size of enterprise:** The larger the size of the business, the greater is the entrepreneur's mobility. Large business houses want to grow organically and inorganically through diversification, expansion, mergers, acquisitions, and joint ventures.
- **Availability of facilities:** Availability of labour, land, water and power, and proximity to market, transport, suppliers, clusters, and communication increases the mobility of entrepreneurs. We can see more IT industries located in cities such as Bangalore and Chennai due to the availability of knowledgeable workers and other infrastructural facilities.

Geographical Mobility of Entrepreneurs

As mentioned earlier, geographical or locational mobility refers to the movement of entrepreneurs from one location to other locations in search of better business opportunities. The factors responsible for geographical mobility of entrepreneurs are the availability of raw material, new and emerging markets, skilled labour, government incentives, better infrastructural facilities, and access to resources. When the dot-com bubble began forming during 1995–2000, many entrepreneurs moved to Bangalore—the Silicon Valley of India—to start their ventures.

There are three stages in the mobility of entrepreneurs. In the initial stages, an entrepreneur sets up a venture at one place and sticks to one place of working. In the next stage, as the business grows,

BREAKTHROUGH ENTREPRENEURSHIP 6.5 Info Edge (India) Ltd

Sanjeev Bikhchandani is the founder and executive vice-chairman of Info Edge, popularly known by the name of its Web site, www.naukri.com. After completing his MBA from IIM Ahmedabad, he worked in several companies. While working for GlaxoSmithKline, Sanjeev noticed that people often picked up and read magazines carrying job advertisements. He found that even people who already had jobs wanted to know the current job scenario—to know what else was out there. This observation led Sanjeev to the business idea of creating a database of vacancies and job requirements.

In 1990, Sanjeev started operations of Info Edge (India) Ltd from his house. In 1996, Sanjeev was exposed to the "World Wide Web" and he launched naukri.com, a pioneer in its field, in 1997. Later, he started the matrimonial Web site, Jeevansathi.com (Jeevansathi Internet Services), and 99acres.com (Info Edge Ltd), a real-estate Web site. As of 31 March 2011, naukri.com had a database of about 25 million job seekers.

Sanjeev's advice to young entrepreneurs is to be an early bird, not to exaggerate the business plan, and to base the business on deep customer insights.

Source: Bansal, Rashmi (2008). *Stay Hungry Stay Foolish*. New Delhi: Westland.

entrepreneurs start moving out within a limited area of business development. In the third stage, as the business expands and there is an increase in the entrepreneurs' resources and network size, there will be a greater degree of mobility as they cross boundaries and start working in the global arena.

Occupational Mobility

As mentioned earlier, occupational mobility denotes movement or change in occupation. The occupation chosen by an entrepreneur is not always the same as that of his/her family. Studies have revealed that though business communities still constitute the dominant source of entrepreneurship, people from technical backgrounds, and those working in corporate and government jobs, are also swelling the ranks of entrepreneurs. This emerging class of entrepreneurs is characterized by better education and technical knowledge.

Liberalization, privatization, and globalization of the Indian economy have brought about drastic changes in the occupation of people. Earlier, most people followed one vocation throughout their lives. Today, the rapid changes happening in the economy demand that people learn, unlearn, and relearn, leading to a higher level of occupational mobility. The major factors influencing occupational mobility are one's personal preference, motivation, opportunities, and skill set. Occupational mobility takes place from farming (primary occupation) to profession and then to industry in the case of intergenerational occupational mobility, and from profession to industry in the case of intragenerational occupational mobility. Occupational mobility may also occur when someone changes their occupation due to the spouse getting transferred elsewhere. This is called "intergenerational occupational movement." The other type may be a change in one's own occupation during one's own occupational career. This is called "intragenerational occupational movement." Occupational mobility is termed as "horizontal" when it happens between occupations of equal rank and "vertical" when it happens between occupations of unequal rank, perhaps due to promotion or demotion.

BUSINESS OPPORTUNITIES IN INDIA

Being the seventh-largest country in the world by area and the second-largest by population, India has a growing market and is a land of opportunities. The opportunities for importing, exporting, trading, investing, and franchising are immense. A potential entrepreneur needs to take into account the economy, the consumer, and business trends. One should also understand that what may be a good business opportunity for one entrepreneur may not be a good opportunity for another. It is essential for entrepreneurs to pick opportunities that they are passionate about.

There are several factors that create favourable business opportunities in India:

- India is a well-established democratic country with a free and fair judicial system.
- The country also has a well-established banking system consisting of public and private banks and other financial institutions.
- The country has a huge middle-class with enhanced purchasing power. Coupled with a high-growth economy, this creates the potential for a huge growth in manufacturing, services, and the retail sector.
- India has vibrant trade links with the South Asian Association for Regional Cooperation (SAARC) nations such as Sri Lanka, Pakistan, Nepal, Bhutan, Bangladesh, and the Maldives.
- India has a competitive advantage in the global market with the availability of a huge pool of cheaper labour and knowledgeable workers to enhance industrial productivity.
- Economic reforms and policy changes have created an investment-friendly environment.
- The capital markets in India are one of the fastest-growing markets in the world, attracting huge foreign investments. A lot of international companies have started outsourcing and setting up international operations in the country.
- The country is self-sufficient in agriculture and rich in natural resources.
- India is a part of the BRICS group of nations comprising Brazil, Russia, China, and South Africa. India has developed vibrant trade links with these nations.

MODELS FOR OPPORTUNITY EVALUATION

Business opportunity evaluation is the process of evaluating a business opportunity and developing it into an effective business model. The following section discusses two models to evaluate business opportunity. They are the RAMP Model and the Seven-domain Framework by John Mullins.

WORLD OF ENTREPRENEURS 6.6 Agri-tourism—Opportunities for Enterprising Farmers in Rural India

Agri-tourism (short for agricultural tourism) embraces the concept of attracting visitors or travellers to an area used primarily for agricultural purposes. Visitors' purpose may be enjoyment, education, or active involvement in the activities of the farm or its operation. It not only provides additional income to farmers but also helps to generate more jobs in rural areas, thus reducing large-scale migration of the village youth to cities. Agri-tourism can be developed with little investment, full family involvement, and full utilization of agricultural resources. In short, agri-tourism is an enterprise that combines the primary elements of agriculture and tourism and is a great business opportunity for farmers.

India is a suitable destination for agri-tourism as the country is primarily agrarian and farmers are simple and hospitable here. Agri-tourism allows tourists to see the realities of famers' lives and the crops they grow as well as experience the local food, dress, music, language, festivals, and art by involving themselves in the activities of farming. Tourists usually help milk cows and goats, take bullock-cart rides, participate in village sports, pick fresh fruits and vegetables from the farm, and enjoy being a part of various festivals. In this way, farmers can increase their income while providing entertainment, education, and fun-filled experiences to visitors.

The Agriculture Tourism Development Corporation (ATDC) is a nodal agency, which helps farmers market their farms and also provides training to them to help them start agri-tourism units on a revenue-sharing basis. The ATDC has also roped in several banks to finance agri-tourism projects.

Sources: www.agritourism.in (last accessed in March 2013) and Shaikh, A. (2010). "Agri-tourism—An Indian Experience," paper presented at the 4th International Conference on "Responsible Tourism in Destinations," 10–12 October.

The RAMP Model

While analysing your business idea, it can be passed through the RAMP test to see if it is truly a valid business opportunity. RAMP is an acronym for four factors—return, advantage, market, and potential. Let us look at each factor.

Return on Investment Ask the following questions:

- Will your revenues be higher than your expenses? Is the business profitable?
- How much time will the business take to break even?
- How much investment is needed to start the business? How are you going to raise this investment?
- What is the exit strategy?

Advantages Ask the following questions:

- What are the barriers to entry?
- What will be your distribution channel for selling your product?
- Do you have a proprietary advantage such as a patent or exclusive license on what you will be selling?
- What is the cost structure taking into account things like suppliers and sourcing?

Market Ask the following questions:

- Is there a value proposition? What is the need you will fill or problem you will solve?
- How do you define the targeted market? Are you selling to consumers? Businesses? What are the demographic features of your targeted market?
- What per cent of the market do you believe you could gain? How fast is the market for your product growing?
- How is the competition? What will be the price of your product?

Potential Ask the following questions:

- Does the team have the potential to successfully launch and sustain the business? What will be the nature of the business entity (e.g., sole proprietorship, partnership, cooperative, etc.)?
- Is the business concept compatible with the business mission of the team?
- What is the risk involved? What is the reward for the founders and investors if the company succeeds?
- How will you differentiate your company from what is already out there?

Mullins's Seven-domain Framework

Successful entrepreneurship comprises three critical elements—market, industry, and the key people that make up the entrepreneurial team. John Mullins of the London Business School has developed a seven-domain model for evaluating entrepreneurial opportunity. The domains are[5]:

- Market domain—macro level
- Market domain—micro level
- Industry domain—macro level
- Industry domain—micro level
- Team domain—aspirations
- Team domain—capability of execution
- Team domain—connections or networks

These seven domains address the following central elements in the assessment of any entrepreneurial opportunity:

- Are the market and the industry attractive?
- Does the opportunity offer compelling customer benefits as well as a sustainable advantage over other solutions to the customer's needs?
- Can the team deliver the results they seek and promise to others?

Market Domain—Macro Level This domain requires an analysis of the attractiveness of the overall market based on certain factors. Some of these factors are:

- The number of customers in the market.
- The amount of money spent by customers on the relevant class of goods or services.
- The number of relevant products or usage occasions for services bought annually.

Market Domain—Micro Level This domain requires an analysis of the benefits and attractiveness of the targeted market segment. Some of the factors on the basis of which the analysis is made are:

- Identifying the target market and the market segment where customers are ready to pay premium prices.
- Product/service differentiation.
- The size of the market segment and the phase of growth.
- Future growth potential and the future plan of the business.

Industry Domain—Macro Level This domain requires an analysis of the attractiveness of the industry, based on certain factors. Some of these factors are:

- The threat of displacement by competitors.
- The bargaining power of suppliers and buyers.
- Competitive rivalry and the threat of substitutes.

Industry Domain—Micro Level This domain requires an analysis of the sustainable advantages of the industry. Ask yourselves the following questions:

- Does the venture have proprietary elements—patents, trade secrets, and so on— that other firms are unable to duplicate or imitate?
- What will be the likely presence of superior organizational processes, capabilities, or resources that others would have difficulty duplicating or imitating?
- Is there an economically viable business model?

Team Domain—Aspiration This domain requires an analysis of the team's mission, aspirations, and propensity for risk taking. A question that this analysis will answer is:

- Does the opportunity fit the team's business mission, personal aspirations, and risk propensity?

Team Domain—Capability of Execution This domain requires the ability of the team to execute tasks on the basis of the identified critical success factors. One question that needs to be addressed is:

- Does the team have what it takes, in a human sense—in terms of experience and industry know-how—to deliver a superior performance for this particular opportunity, given its critical success factors?

Team Domain—Connections or Networks This domain requires an analysis of the team members' connectedness—up, down, and across the value chain. A question you may ask yourself is:

- Is the team connected well enough to notice any opportunity or need to change its approach if conditions warrant?

Look for ideas that will change the way people live and work. High-potential opportunities invariably solve an important problem, want, or need that someone is willing to pay for now.

SNAPSHOT

- Entrepreneurs can identify a business opportunity by observing trends, solving a problem, and finding gaps in the marketplace.
- The two models commonly used for evaluating business opportunities are the RAMP Model and Mullins's Seven-domain Framework.

DISCUSSION FORUM

- Discuss three business opportunities available in rural India and evaluate them in small groups.
- Explain the RAMP Model and Mullins's Seven-domain Framework.

SUMMARY

A business idea, which is a concept that can be used for a commercial purpose, typically involves the introduction of new products and services or entry into new markets. Some of the methods used to generate business ideas are brainstorming, survey method, reverse brainstorming, and the Gordon method. An entrepreneurial opportunity is a situation in which a person can exploit a new business idea that has the potential to generate a profit. Entrepreneurial opportunities exist because of external sources of change, particularly technological change, regulatory and political change, and social and demographic change. Business opportunities can be identified by observing trends, recognizing and solving a problem, and finding a gap between what the customer wants and what the customer gets. Entrepreneurial mobility occurs as entrepreneurs move from one place to another or one occupation to another in search of better business opportunities. This mobility may be caused by social, economic, political, and cultural factors. Two models for opportunity evaluation are the RAMP Model and Mullins' Seven-domain Framework.

KEY TERMS

Brainstorming: This is a technique used to quickly generate a large number of ideas in which a group creativity exercise is designed to come up with a number of solutions to a problem.

Business Idea: A business idea is a concept that can be used for commercial purposes.

Entrepreneurial Opportunity: An entrepreneurial opportunity is a situation in which a person can exploit a new business idea that has the potential to generate a profit.

The Gordon method: This is an idea generation technique using collective discussion to address every aspect of the planned product in an uninhibited solution-oriented manner for developing new ideas when the individuals are unaware of the problem.

Idea: A thought or concept existing in the mind as a result of mental activity.

Locational/Geographical Mobility: This is the movement of entrepreneurs from one location to other locations in search of better business opportunities.

Occupational Mobility: Occupation mobility denotes movement or change in the occupation of entrepreneurs in search of better opportunities.

Reverse Brainstorming: This is an idea generation method that is similar to brainstorming, with the exception that criticism is allowed. The focus is on identifying the negative sides of every idea that has been generated through brainstorming.

Survey Method: This is an idea generation technique used to collect information by direct observation of a phenomenon or systematic gathering of data from a set of people.

Window of Opportunity: The term "window of opportunity" is a metaphor describing the time period in which a firm can realistically enter a new market.

CASE STUDY

Chinese Restaurants: A Good Business Opportunity

Deepak and Nandan both want to start their own businesses. On conducting an environment and industry analysis and a market study, they found that there is a demand for Chinese food and the market seems quite large. The market study revealed that customers are looking for restaurants that offer fun family dining at a reasonable price in key locations. Presently, there is no competition in the low-to-medium price range in those locations. Now Deepak and Nandan both want to start a chain of mid-priced Chinese food restaurants in key locations.

Nandan is a successful investment banker with an experience of 6 years. He conducted the environment and industry analysis of the project, but he has no background in hospitality and no particular passion for food.

Deepak started his career in a junior position in the hospitality industry and is now the operations manager at a well-known, high-end Chinese restaurant. He has a successful track record of managing restaurants and a strong networking capability with suppliers, chefs, marketing people, and other related individuals. He is very passionate about food and well-informed about the hospitality industry.

Both Deepak and Nandan have the same business idea—to start a chain of mid-priced, family-oriented Chinese restaurants. But is it an equally valid business opportunity for both of them?

Questions:

1. Is starting a Chinese restaurant an equally valid business opportunity for both Deepak and Nandan?
2. What type of business do you suggest for Deepak and Nandan and why?

Opportunity Identification by Sanjeev Bikhchandani

Sanjeev Bikhchandani, the founder of Info Edge (India) Ltd and the CEO of Naukri, is one of India's most successful Internet entrepreneurs. He has been serving as a director on the board of directors of Info Edge since 2010. Indo Edge was the first Indian Internet company to list on Indian stock exchanges and is a premier online classifieds company dealing with recruitment, matrimony, real estate, education, and related services. Naukri, the brand name of the leading job Web site, www.naukri.com, is the flagship business of Info Edge. The company employs over 2,100 people and had a market capitalization of over ₹300,000 lakh in 2012. The vision of the company is to create world-class platforms that transform lives.

The Info Edge recruitment division comprises the classifieds portals; www.naukri.com; www.naukrigulf.com; www.quadranglesearch.com; www.brijj.com; and www.firstnaukri.com. The matrimonial division includes www.jeevansathi.com and 14 offline Jeevansathi match points. The real-estate division comprises www.99acres.com and www.allcheckdeals.com. The education division comprises the online education classifieds portal, www.shiksha.com. The company invests in early-stage companies to tap into the growing Indian Internet market.

Background: Sanjeev's family does not have a background in business. His father was a doctor in the government service and his mother was a homemaker. His brother is a management graduate from the Indian Institute of Management Ahmedabad (IIMA) and a Ph.D. from Stanford

University, California. After completing his bachelor's degree in economics from St. Stephens, Delhi, Sanjeev joined Lintas and worked as an executive trainee for three years. He then wrote the Common Admission Test (CAT) and joined IIMA in 1989. The courses he took at IIMA sparked his interest in entrepreneurship. After completing his post-graduate programme in management at IIMA, he joined GlaxoSmithKline (then Hindustan Milkfood Manufacturers) as a marketing executive. He also worked in a senior management position at CMYK Printech Private Limited.

Though Sanjeev did not have a business background, he had a strong urge to be an entrepreneur. He wanted the independence that he could only get by being part of a business. Sanjeev wanted to be his own boss—doing his own things and fixing his own priorities.

Business Idea to Business Opportunity: During his tenure at GlaxoSmithKline, Sanjeev noticed that his colleagues read the *Business India* back to front instead of front to back. At that time, *Business India* carried the maximum recruitment advertisements for managers. The magazine usually carried over 40 pages of advertisments. Sanjeev realised that people were always looking for better job opportunities. A number of recruiters would keep calling employees at GlaxoSmithKline from time to time to convince them to change jobs. These jobs were never advertised in newspapers and magazines. Sanjeev felt that if the huge fragmented database of jobs with recruiters and HR managers were aggregated and kept current, it could prove to be a very valuable resource.

Sanjeev struggled hard for almost a decade to convert his idea into a business opportunity. He faced lots of hurdles during his entrepreneurial journey—from being unable to pay his employees for almost six years and to taking a second job to support his family. He also struggled to obtain funding for his business. However, he did not give up in spite of these hurdles.

Business Model: Sanjeev figured out that that the recruitment advertisements featured in the print media were simply the tip of the iceberg. The presence of thousands of recruiters, each with four or five clients and armed with 10 to 15 jobs, emphasized the massive fragmented database of jobs in the market. Conversations with headhunters also led to the realisation that there were a lot of unadvertised jobs in the marketplace.

The business model of www.naukri.com is almost a cross between a brokerage model and advertising model. It is a medium where corporate employers and potential employees come together. Sanjeev had a clear revenue model from the beginning. There was a direct inflow of revenue for the services rendered by the customers. Only a few services were offered free of cost to job seekers and job providers.

Entrepreneurial Journey: Sanjeev quit his job at GlaxoSmithKline and started Info Edge Ltd in 1990. At the beginning, Info Edge was not an online recruitment service but was in the business of generating and selling databases, reports, and feasibility studies. Info Edge operated from the servants' quarters above the garage at Sanjeev's home. The company carried out entry-level salary surveys and a few sundry consulting assignments for the first seven years.

In October 1996, Sanjeev attended the annual Information Technology Asia exhibition in Delhi and came across a stall with "www" written on it. On further enquiries, he learnt that "www" stood for the World Wide Web and it could be used to share information on the Internet. Sanjeev figured out that he could upload a database of job vacancies on a Web site using the Internet. At that time, India had a total 14,000 Internet users and all the servers were based in the United States. Sanjeev's brother, a professor at the UCLA business school, hired a server in the United States in 1997 and received a 5 per cent stake in the company

The naukri portal was set up and started operating in March 1997 as a division of Info Edge Private Limited. Anil Lall, Sanjeev's friend and an expert programmer, wrote the initial software code and enabled it to go commercial in October 1997. Anil Lall is now a member of the board of directors of Info Edge. The other co-founder of naukri.com was Saroja, a 1990 alumnus of IIMA. She looked after operations till 2003 and left to become an independent management consultant.

Info Edge got funding from ICICI Ventures in April 2000. In the quarter ending December 2010, Info Edge raked in ₹7,500 lakh in net sales with a net profit of ₹2,100 lakh. The flagship business naukri.com contributed handsomely to this revenue. The company had the first-mover advantage, a clear value proposition, constant innovation, a great team, and a buoyant market. It is a forum where employers, placement agencies, and job seekers can exchange information, quickly, effectively, and inexpensively.

Accolades and Awards: Sanjeev Bikhchandani is a pioneering entrepreneur in the Indian Internet services space. Sanjeev, along with his partner, Hitesh Oberoi, won the "Ernst and Young—Entrepreneur of the Year" Award in 2008 for business transformation. He also won the Dataquest Pathbreaker Award and the Teacher's Achievement Award for business in 2008. Sanjeev is a frequent and popular speaker on entrepreneurship at conferences and business schools.

Sanjeev's Advice to Young Entrepreneurs: Sanjeev believes that an entrepreneur should understand the risks in the creation of a new venture and focus on reducing it. An entrepreneur should not start a business only for making money. The chances of failure are pretty high and hard times might test an entrepreneur's resolve. However, if an entrepreneur strives towards a goal other than money, the chances of success are high.

Questions:

1. How did Sanjeev convert his idea into a business opportunity?
2. Analyse the business model of naukri.com.

Sources: www.infoedge.in/corporate-contactus.asp (last accessed in March 2013); Bansal, Rashmi (2010). *Connect the Dots.* New Delhi: Think Ink Media, Inc.; and www.thesmartceo.in/sanjeev-bikhchandanis-search-for-a-naukri.html (last accessed in March 2013).

DISCUSSION QUESTIONS

1. What is the difference between an idea and an entrepreneurial opportunity? What defines a good opportunity?
2. What are the things to be taken into consideration for generating business ideas?
3. Classify business opportunities based on origin, application, user or source, and external sources of change.
4. Explain how "solving a problem" can create a business opportunity.
5. Identify major changes that create opportunities for entrepreneurs.
6. Explain John Mullins's seven-domain framework.

ACTIVITY

Brainstorming and Idea Generation

Introduction: This method is based on the fact that people can be stimulated to greater creativity by meeting others and participating in organized group exercises. Brainstorming works well with a varied group of people.

Learning Objective: To generate as many ideas as possible without assessing their value in a team.

Guidelines:

- Keep the session relaxed and fun.
- Generate as many ideas as possible without discussion or evaluation.
- Encourage everyone to contribute.
- Write down every idea.
- Do not allow anyone to dominate.

The Exercise: A brainstorming session requires a facilitator, white board, flip chart, and space to accommodate 8–12 people. Brainstorming works well with a small group and should be performed in a relaxed environment. Participants are encouraged to share each and every idea that enters their mind. There is no right or wrong answer. Usually the brainstorming session starts with a broad problem statement.

Running the Exercise:

- Ask the students to come up with one problem that their college is facing and one problem that their city is facing.
- Students share their problems and the faculty (facilitator) lists the problems on the board.
- Students vote on the problems that they feel are the most important.
- Divide the number of students enrolled in the class by five and select the number of problems. (For example, for a class of 50 students select the 10 problems that received the most votes.)
- Students are put into groups of five and each group is assigned a problem.
- Each student brainstorms individually about possible solutions to the problem (a minimum of five minutes of brainstorming).
- Students share their solutions with their group members and determine which solution or combination of solutions is the best. The students will work throughout the semester to develop this solution into a business venture.

Time: 30–45 minutes.

Follow-up Activity: Help the students to work throughout the semester to develop this solution into a business venture.

PROJECT

1. You will need to identify an entrepreneurial opportunity to start your business. To do so, please follow these steps:

   Step 1: Make a list of recent changes in: (a) technology, (b) demographics, (c) lifestyle, (d) markets, and (e) government policies.

   Step 2: Now try to identify the following: (a) new products or services that these changes make possible, (b) new production processes that they allow firms to use, (3) new markets that they open up, (4) new ways of organizing that these changes would lead to, and (5) new raw materials that they make possible.

   If you have completed these two steps, congratulations! You have just accomplished the first stage in the entrepreneurial process—identifying an entrepreneurial opportunity.
2. Identify different business opportunities under the following circumstances.
   - Growing number of MBA institutes in the city
   - Growing number of health-conscious people
   - Stressful life
3. Write five different but new features you can add to:
   - A mobile phone
   - A pen
   - A table lamp
   - A wristwatch
   - A ceiling fan

ENDNOTES

1. Timmons, Jeffrey A. and Stephen Spinelli Jr (2009). *New Venture Creation: Entrepreneurship for the 21st Century*. McGraw-Hill International Edition.
2. Christensen, P. S., O. O. Madsen, and R. Peterson (1994) "Conceptualizing Entrepreneurial Opportunity Recognition" in G. E. Hills (ed.) *Marketing and Entrepreneurship: Research Ideas and Opportunities*. Westport, CT: Quorum Books, pp. 61–75.

3. Ramesh, N. (2006). "How to Identify Business Opportunities," *Science Tech Entrepreneur*, July.
4. Casson, Mark (2003). *The Entrepreneur: An Economic Theory*. UK: Edward Elgar Publishing.
5. Mullins, John (2003). *New Business Road Test: What Entrepreneurs and Executives Should do Before Writing a Business Plan*. Financial Times Press.

New Venture Creation

6. Identification of Business Opportunities
7. Project Management and Financing
8. Business Plans
9. Institutions Supporting Business Enterprises
10. Business Organizations and Business Laws

"A project is complete when it starts working for you, rather than you working for it."
—Scott Allen

redBus is the brand name of www.redBus.in, a bus ticketing Web site owned by Bangalore-based Pilani Soft Labs Pvt. Ltd. The company was founded in 2006 and was self-funded by Phanindra Sama and his two classmates from BITS Pilani. The founders who held jobs at top IT MNCs in Bangalore quit their jobs to start redBus. The promoters initially raised project financing from Seedfund Advisors in 2007. The second influx of capital came in 2009 from Seedfund, Helion, and Inventus Capital. redBus today has 400 employees and 18 offices spread across India.

Project Management and Financing

7

LEARNING OBJECTIVES

Upon completion of this chapter, you should be able to:

1. **Introduce the concept of project management.**
2. **Discuss the capital budgeting process.**
3. **Explain project feasibility study and project appraisal.**
4. **Understand project financing.**
5. **Study the process of scheduling in a project.**
6. **Prepare project reports.**

INTRODUCTION

Entrepreneurial ventures use project management to accomplish outcomes under conditions of limited resources with critical time constraints. Project management is one of the basic approaches followed by entrepreneurs to accomplish the things that they undertake. A project is initiated to achieve a mission.

A project is a one-shot, time-limited, goal-directed major undertaking, requiring the commitment of varied skills and resources. It is a combination of human and non-human resources pooled together in a temporary organization to achieve a specific purpose. The Project Management Institute (PMI)[1] defines a project as "a temporary endeavour undertaken to create a unique product or service." The PMI defines project management as "the application of knowledge, skills, tools, and techniques to project activities to meet project requirements."

A project has a fixed set of objectives and is unique and sees many changes throught its lifespan. It is a single entity and has a life cycle reflected by growth, maturity, and decay. Every project has risk and uncertainty associated with it. All projects have to pass through the following five phases:

1. Conception phase
2. Definition phase
3. Planning and organizing phase
4. Implementation phase
5. Project clean-up phase

The main activities undertaken in each of these stages are as follows:

1. **Conception phase:** This is the idea generation phase. An idea may be generated when the entrepreneur scans the environment. A well-conceived idea should be implemented only when it is a business opportunity. The concepts of business idea and business opportunity are explained in Chapter 6.

2. **Definition phase**: During this phase, the project manager should prepare a document explaining the project in detail covering all aspects required by the customer and the financial institution. The document is the blueprint of the project and explains all details such as raw material requirement; plant capacity; plant location; project layout; plant and machinery; utilities required; organizational structure; manpower requirement; project feasibility: and implementation schedule.
3. **Planning and organizing phase**: This phase focuses on the preparation for the project to take off smoothly. Major decisions such as budget allocation, project scheduling, and resource allocation are made during this phase. The objectives and goals are set. The authority, responsibility, and accountability of people involved in the project are clearly defined.
4. **Implementation phase**: This phase requires implementing the project and is a period of hectic activity. During this phase, the project manager allocates budgets and resources for various activities. The project manager is ultimately responsible for the completion of the project as per the techno-economic stipulations made in the feasibility report.
5. **Project clean-up phase**: This is the final phase wherein the project is completed. During this phase, the completion certificate is given by the customer to the project manager. The success of the project is also evaluated at this phase. Project management is successful if it is completed within the time and budget and satisfies the customer.

PROJECT MANAGER

The selection of the project manager is one of the most important decisions concerning the project. The project manager is the person in charge of the project. If the firm is engaged in only one or two projects, the entrepreneur can be the project manager. However, as the firm evolves, it will be necessary for the role of the project manager to be delegated to other able individuals. Project managers are change agents; they make project goals their own and use their skills and expertise to inspire a sense of shared purpose within the project team. The project manager is responsible for the effective

BREAKTHROUGH ENTREPRENEURSHIP 7.1 Project Management Institute (PMI)

The PMI is the world's leading not-for-profit membership association for the project management profession, with more than half a million members and credential holders in more than 185 countries. The services offered by the PMI are the basis of greater recognition and acceptance of project management's successful role in governments, organizations, academia, and industries. The PMI headquarters is located in Newtown Square, PA, United States, and its operations are guided by the Executive Management Group and professional staff.

The PMI has recruited volunteers to create industry standards targeted at projects, programmes, people, organizations, and the profession. One such standard is "A Guide to the Project Management Body of Knowledge," which has been recognized by the American National Standards Institute (ANSI). The PMI offers a wide range of professional development opportunities to project management professionals. These comprise the development of standards, research and publication, education, the hosting of conferences, training and seminars, and networking opportunities in the local chapter.

The Institute offers various career development credentials to project management professionals. They are Certified Associate in Project Management (CAPM); Project Management Professional (PMP); PMI Agile Certified Practitioner (PMI-ACP); PMI Scheduling Professional (PMI-SP); PMI Risk Management Professional (PMI-RMP), and Program Management Professional (PgMP). In addition to career development credentials, PMI offers one more certification, the Organizational Project Management Maturity Model Certified Consultant (OPM3-CC).

Source: www.pmi.org.in (last accessed in March 2013).

management of work, human resources, communications, quality, time, and cost. The following is a list of attributes generally sought in a project manager:

- The project manager should be a generalist, having worked in several functional departments with varied responsibilities.
- People with experience are generally chosen for the job.
- The project manager should have good skills such as interpersonal skills, communication skills, and team-building skills.
- People with technical knowledge are preferred as they are able to understand the technical requirements of the project.
- The project manager should have leadership qualities to lead the team and achieve the goals.

PROJECT LIFE CYCLE

The life cycle of a project consists of five stages—the concept stage, analysis stage, planning stage, execution stage, and completion stage.[2] These stages of the project life cycle are depicted in Figure 7.1. The five stages of the project life cycle are explained below.

1. **Concept stage**: The first stage in project management is the concept stage. This includes two activities, namely, idea generation and the screening of ideas.
2. **Analysis stage**: After a project proposal is conceptually cleared, it enters into the analysis stage. At the time of preparation of the detailed project report, all costs and benefits are projected based on studied assumptions. The cost–benefit analysis involves three primary analyses, namely, market analysis, technical analysis, financial analysis, and additionally social-cost benefit analysis and risk analysis.
3. **Planning stage**: The projects that are successful at all the stages of analysis are found to be "acceptable" from financial and strategic perspectives. However, at any given time, there could be several projects claiming funds that are limited. Therefore, in the planning stage, the project must first win budgetary allocation before resource planning, contract negotiation, and the

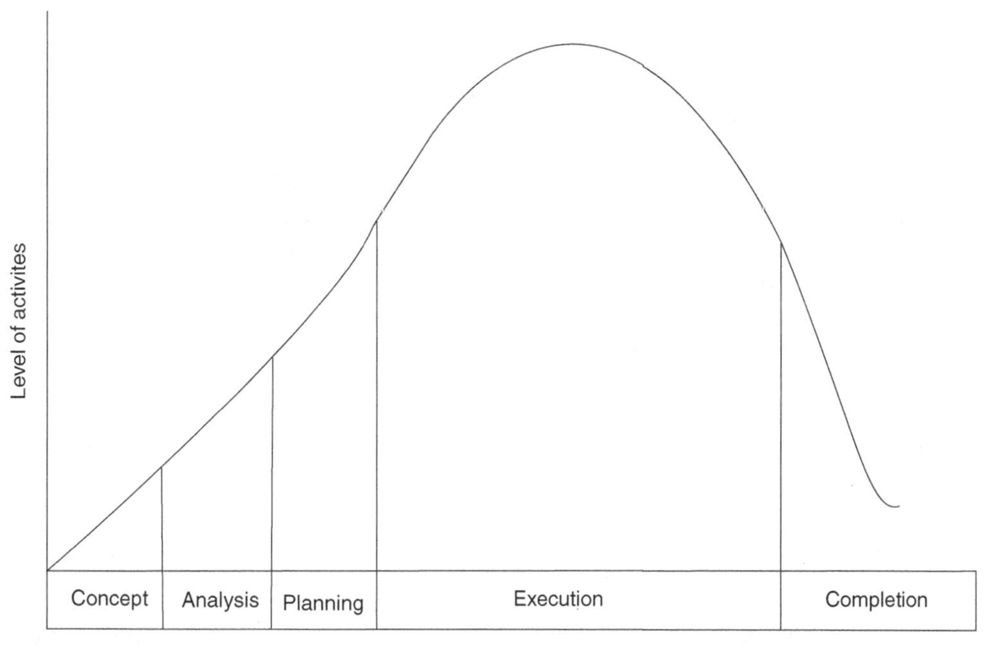

Figure 7.1 Stages in the Project Life Cycle

preparation of a detailed project report are done. During this phase, a detailed project definition known as the work breakdown structure (WBS) is examined. A WBS is similar to a bill of materials and divides the work into packages. The planning stage involves capital budget allocation, resource planning, contracting, and preparation of the detailed project report (DPR).

4. **Execution stage**: During the planning stage, sub-contracts are given, teams and sub-teams are formed, team leaders are appointed, coordination is established, documentation is designed, and the reporting system is developed. Now, it is the time to execute the project. Project execution is a very active stage in project management. It involves activities such as action, coordination, monitoring, and control.
5. **Completion stage**: At the end of the project execution stage, the last work package is constructed and the project is ready for running. In this stage, the constructed project must be transferred to the operating team, and the learning exercises must begin. It involves activities such as project transfer, project completion report, and post-completion audit.

SNAPSHOT

- A project is "a temporary endeavour undertaken to create a unique product or service."
- Project management is "the application of knowledge, skills, tools, and techniques to project activities to meet project requirements."
- The life cycle of a project consists of the concept stage, analysis stage, planning stage, execution stage, and completion stage.

DISCUSSION FORUM

- Define the term project management.
- Discuss the qualities required for a project manager.
- Explain the stages in the project life cycle.

PROJECT SCHEDULING

Project scheduling establishes the time and sequence of the various phases of the project. A project consists of interrelated activities, which are to be executed in a certain order before the entire task is completed. The activities, in a project are interrelated in a logical sequence, which is known as a precedence relationship. An activity of a project cannot be started until all its immediate preceding activities are completed. In project scheduling, the project manager considers the various activities of an overall project and the tasks that must be accomplished and relates them coherently to one another over the project's time horizon.

Techniques for project scheduling include Gantt charts and network techniques. Financial institutions and the Government of India insist that a network plan should accompany project reports. There are two basic types of network techniques: program evaluation and review technique (PERT) and critical path method (CPM). PERT is used for probabilistic projects where the time required for completing various activities can be highly variable. CPM is used for realistic or deterministic projects that employ a fairly stable technology and are relatively risk free.

Gantt Charts

A Gantt chart is also known as a project chart. It is a simple bar chart developed by Henry Gantt. It is commonly used for scheduling small projects that fit on a single sheet or screen. It consists of two coordinate axes, one representing activities and the other representing time. Each activity has a bar extending across the time columns, representing the duration of the task. The length of a bar indicates the duration of the activity required for completion. The Gantt chart is not feasible for project scheduling, when the project is complex in nature and involves a number of activities.

In a Gantt chart, every activity should have a start date and a finish date. These charts are easy to understand and to modify and are of low cost. They cannot show the interdependencies among various activities and do not reflect the uncertainties or tolerances in the duration times estimated for various activities. Table 7.1 provides the data and Figure 7.2 illustrates the Gantt chart for the construction of a house.

Network Techniques

Network techniques have been found useful for proper planning, scheduling, and control of the activities of a project. They provide interrelationships and constraints on the availability of resources.

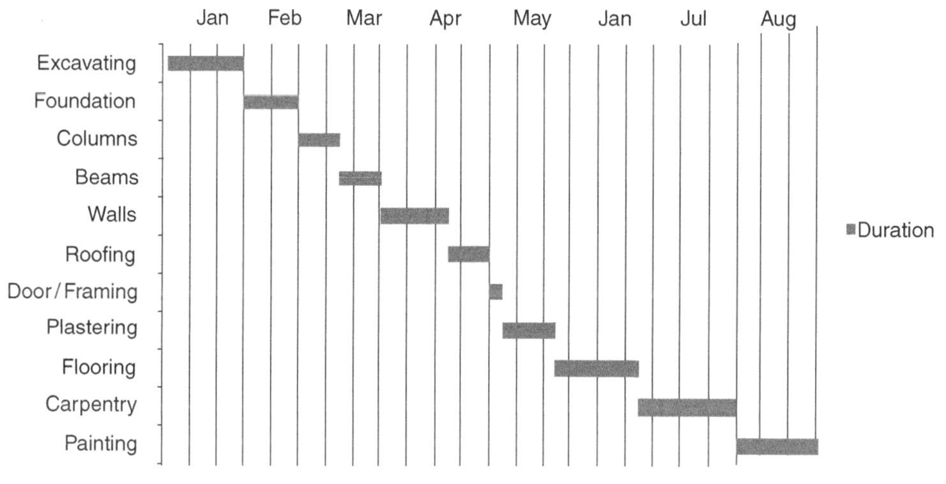

Figure 7.2 Gantt Chart for the Construction of a House

Table 7.1 Schedule for the Construction of a House

Tasks	Start Date	Duration	End Date
Excavating	1 Jan	28	29 Jan
Foundation	29 Jan	20	18 Feb
Columns	18 Feb	15	4 Mar
Beams	4 Mar	15	19 Mar
Walls	19 Mar	25	13 Apr
Roofing	13 Apr	15	28 Apr
Door/framing	28 Apr	5	3 May
Plastering	3 May	20	23 May
Flooring	23 May	30	22 Jun
Carpentry	22 Jun	36	28 Jul
Painting	28 Jul	30	27 Aug

The two basic types of network techniques are PERT and CPM. The main benefits of scheduling using network techniques are that it establishes a common framework for evaluating the progress of activities in relation to the project; it demonstrates the interdependence of all activities in the project; it identifies any slack that can have a cushioning effect and the critical activities that can delay the project; and it helps to predict the project completion time.

PERT was first developed in the mid-1950s for the Polaris submarine project. CPM was developed by E. I. du Pont de Nemours and Company as a way to schedule the start up and shut down of major plants. PERT is mainly used for probabilistic projects characterized by uncertainty. CPM is used for realistic and deterministic projects that are risk free. CPM is activity-oriented and PERT is event-oriented. CPM places dual emphasis on time and cost, and evaluates the tradeoff between project cost and project time. PERT is primarily concerned with project time. CPM is generally used for those projects which are repetitive in nature. PERT is generally used for those projects which are not repetitive in nature. The main difference between PERT and CPM networks are whether the time estimates are probabilistic or deterministic.

Rules for Network Construction The network diagram is constructed in terms of activities and events. An activity is a definite task to be performed in a project. An event is a specific point of time indicating the beginning or end of one or more activities. Each activity is uniquely numbered and represented by an arrow and must have a preceding and succeeding event. Not more than one activity can have the same preceding and succeeding events. Each event is represented by a circle with a distinct number inside it. There should be no loops in the project network. A dummy activity is an imaginary activity, which can be accomplished in zero time and does not consume resources used to represent proper relationship between the activities.

Once the network is constructed, time estimates may be assigned to each activity. There are three time values assigned for each activity: optimistic time (t_o), most likely time (t_m), and pessimistic time (t_p). The optimistic time, t_o, is the time required if no hurdles or complications arise, the pessimistic time, t_p, is the time required if unusual complications arise. The most likely time, t_m, is the time in which the activity is most likely to be completed. The average time (t_e) is obtained by using the following formula:

$$t_e = \frac{t_o + 4t_m + t_p}{6}$$

Calculate the activity variance and project variance. Activity variance is the square of 1/6th of the difference between the pessimistic and optimistic time estimates. Project variance is the variance of the critical path duration which, in turn, is the sum of variances of the activities on it. The standard deviation is the square root of project variance and is calculated using the formula:

$$\text{Variance} = \sigma^2 = \left(\frac{t_p - t_o}{6}\right)^2$$

Calculate the earliest occurrence time for each event. The early start schedule refers to the schedule in which all activities start as early as possible. Calculate the latest occurrence time for each event. The late start schedule reflects a desire to commit resources as late as possible. Figure 7.3 illustrates a PERT chart.

Determine the critical path, event slacks, and activity floats. The chain of critical activities is called the critical path of the project. Some projects may have more than one critical path. Each critical activity will not have any cushion time to either postpone or advance its original starting time. The critical path is the longest path from the beginning event to the end event. The critical path starts with the beginning event, terminates with the end event, and is marked by events that have zero slack. The minimum time required for completing the project is the duration on the critical path.

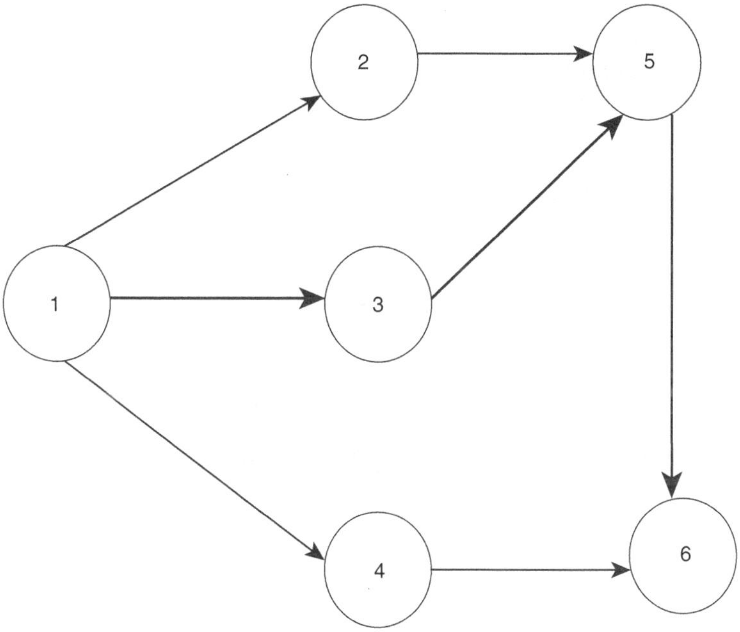

Figure 7.3
PERT Chart

EXAMPLE

A project has the following activities and characteristics:

Activity	Estimated Duration in Days		
	Optimistic (t_0)	Most Likely (t_m)	Pessimistic (t_p)
1–2	3	6	9
1–3	5	11	17
1–4	2	8	14
2–5	6	9	12
3–5	3	9	15
4–6	7	10	13
5–6	5	8	11

1. Find the expected duration of each activity.
2. Draw the project network and expected duration of the project.
3. Find variances of activities on the critical path and its standard deviation.

Solution:
The variance can be calculated as follows.

Activity	Expected Duration $t_e = \dfrac{t_0 + 4t_m + t_p}{6}$	*Variance* $= \sigma^2 = \left(\dfrac{t_p - t_o}{6}\right)^2$
1–2	6	1
1–3	11	4
1–4	8	4
2–5	9	1
3–5	9	4
4–6	10	1
5–6	8	1

Various Paths	Duration of Paths
1-2-5-6	6 + 9 + 8 = 23
1-3-5-6	11+ 9 + 8 = 28
1-4-6	8 + 10 = 18

Hence, the critical path is 1-3-5-6 with an expected project duration of 28 days. The activities lying on the critical path are 1-3, 3-5, and 5-6.

$$\text{Variance} = 4 + 4 + 1 = 9$$
$$\text{Standard deviation} = \sqrt{\text{Variance}} = \sqrt{9} = 3.$$

PROJECT MANAGEMENT SOFTWARE

Project management software programs are used in the case of complex and large projects as they are difficult to handle manually. These software programs help in a number of functions such as scheduling, cost control, budgeting, resource allocation, documentation, communication, quality management, and administration. There are various project management software programs available in the market. The most prominent among them are Microsoft Project, InstaPlan III, Yojana, Prism, and Primavera.

Microsoft Project

Microsoft Project is a popular project management software program developed and sold by Microsoft. The software delivers a project management system with powerful, visually enhanced ways to effectively manage a wide range of projects and programs. It assists project management professionals in developing plans, assigning resources to tasks, tracking progress, managing budgets, and analysing workloads. The software recognizes different classes of users. These different classes of users can have differing access levels of projects, views, and other data. The program allows users to understand and control project schedule and finances, organize work and people to make sure that projects are completed on schedule, and communicate and present project information.

Microsoft Project has several different editions or versions, based on the needs of the users and the organization. These are Project Standard 2010, Project Professional 2010, and Project Server. Microsoft Project Standard 2010 is a single-user edition of the software and is targeted toward the desktop user. Microsoft Project Professional 2010 includes all the capabilities in Project Standard 2010 as well as collaborative features that allow users to work together when the organization is also using Microsoft Project Server 2010. Microsoft Project Server 2010 maintains the project plan information and data on a server. Project Server allows multiple users to access that data through their client applications, Microsoft Project Professional and Microsoft Project Web Access.

InstaPlan

InstaPlan is an innovative project planning software package developed and marketed by the General Electric Company, which helps project managers to plan, manage, and communicate efficiently and effectively. It is a fast and natural way of using techniques like PERT and CPM without going through a whole learning process. The software provides a multi-project outlining feature that allows the project manager to define activity lists for the different projects which use the common resources of the organization into a single plan. The software enables planning, scheduling, resource allocation, forecasting, tracking, and reporting.

InstaPlan allows three different options for planning or a combination of these, within the same plan. They are normal planning, deadline planning, and open-ended planning. Normal planning follows the standard critical path method. InstaPlan assumes that all activities lead to one objective, showing the earliest possible start date and slack for each activity. Deadline planning works backwards from the fixed end date of the project and shows the latest possible start date for each activity. The critical path and slack are computed based on the planning option. Open-ended planning can be used when several activities are to be scheduled, assigned, and managed and also when there is no single final objective to be met.

Yojana

The Yojana software program provides advanced project management functions. It uses the graphical user interface Microsoft Windows to support multiple windows. Yojana provides many functions such as scheduling by Gantt chart or PERT and CPM network, time and cost analysis, resource allocation, and S-curve to indicate the progress of the project. The software provides a flexible reporting system with various views, graphs, and reports for effective project monitoring and control.

PRISM Project Manager

The PRISM Project Manager, developed and sold by the Ares Corporation, is a collection of integrated project management software applications designed to help project managers. This is suitable for all types and sizes of projects in all industries. This software provides various benefits such as reducing project risk by providing necessary critical project information, reducing project costs by providing single source data entry and data integrity, achieving time/cost integration with project planning data, and providing the kind of good reporting system required by government agencies. The PRISM Project Manager was developed using a modular approach. The ten modules are grouped into four functional areas. They are:

- **Cost management:** 1. Baseline estimate, 2. Schedule interface, 3. Cost and progress
- **Engineering management:** 4. Engineering progress, 5. Document control
- **Contracts management:** 6. Contract administration, 7. Site reports
- **Procurement management:** 8. Capital equipment, 9. Procurement, and 10. Materials management.

PRIMAVERA

PRIMAVERA P6 is a professional project management software designed to handle large-scale, highly sophisticated, and multifaceted projects. It is an integrated project management product developed by Oracle Corporation and is created for globally prioritizing, planning, managing, and executing projects, programs, and portfolios. The software has the ability to organize mega projects containing up to 100,000 activities. The software provides a single solution for managing projects of any size and adapts to various levels of complexities within a project. It intelligently scales to meet the needs of various roles, functions, or skill levels in the project.

PRIMAVERA offers various useful functions to project managers. Some of its prominent features are the ability to plan, schedule, and control complex projects; balance resource capacity; allocate best resources and track progress; monitor and visualize project performance versus plan; conduct what-if analysis; and analyse alternative project plans. PRIMAVERA has developed different software programs based on the specific requirements of the project manager. The different software programs of PRIMAVERA are ProSight, Contract Manager, Pertmaster, and Cost Manager.

SNAPSHOT

- PERT and CPM are two network techniques used for project planning, scheduling, and control.
- Project management software programs such as Microsoft Project, InstaPlan, Yojana, and PRISM Project Manager help in project scheduling and execution.

DISCUSSION FORUM

- Distinguish between PERT and CPM.
- Evaluate various project management software programs.

CAPITAL BUDGETING

Capital budgeting is the process of evaluating and selecting long-term investments that are consistent with the goal of shareholders' wealth maximization. The capital budgeting process deals with identifying and selecting investment projects whose returns are expected to extend beyond one year. Capital budgeting decisions are of paramount importance in financial decision making because such decisions are long term, not easily reversible, involve cost, and affect the profitability of an enterprise. The decisions are made at three levels: operating decisions, administrative decisions, and strategic decisions. Capital budgeting relates to fixed assets and enables the enterprise to generate finished goods that can ultimately be sold for profit. Capital budgeting involves:

- Generating investment project proposals consistent with the firm's strategic objectives.
- Project analysis or project feasibility study.
- Evaluating and selecting projects based on a value maximizing acceptance criteria.
- Project financing.
- Implementing investment projects continually.

GENERATING AN INVESTMENT PROJECT PROPOSAL

The enterprise may allocate budget to new products/services or expansion of existing products/services, replacement of equipment or buildings, and research and development. The enterprise may be confronted with three types of capital budgeting decisions: (i) the accept–reject decision, (ii) the mutually exclusive choice decision, and (iii) the capital rationing decision.

The accept–reject decision is the evaluation of the capital expenditure proposal to determine whether it meets the minimum acceptance criteria. If the proposal is accepted, the firm would invest in it; if the proposal is rejected, the firm does not invest in it. In general, proposals which yield a rate of return greater than the cost of capital are accepted and the rest are rejected. Mutually exclusive projects are projects that compete with one another; the acceptance of one eliminates the others from further consideration. The alternatives are mutually exclusive and only one may be chosen. Capital rationing decision is a situation where the firm has unlimited funds. All the independent investment proposals yielding return greater than some predetermined level are accepted. Capital rationing is the financial situation in which a firm has only a fixed amount to allocate among competing capital expenditures. The benefits received from the project are expressed in terms of cash flows and cash flows should be measured on an incremental, after-tax basis.

PROJECT ANALYSIS

This is also known as project feasibility study. Once a project proposal is identified and if the project seems worthwhile, detailed analysis of the marketing, technical, economic, and ecological aspects are undertaken. Based on the information developed in the analysis, the stream of costs and benefits associated with the project can be defined. The important facets of project analysis are market analysis, technical analysis, financial analysis, economic analysis, and ecological analysis. A schematic diagram of the project feasibility study is shown in Figure 7.4.

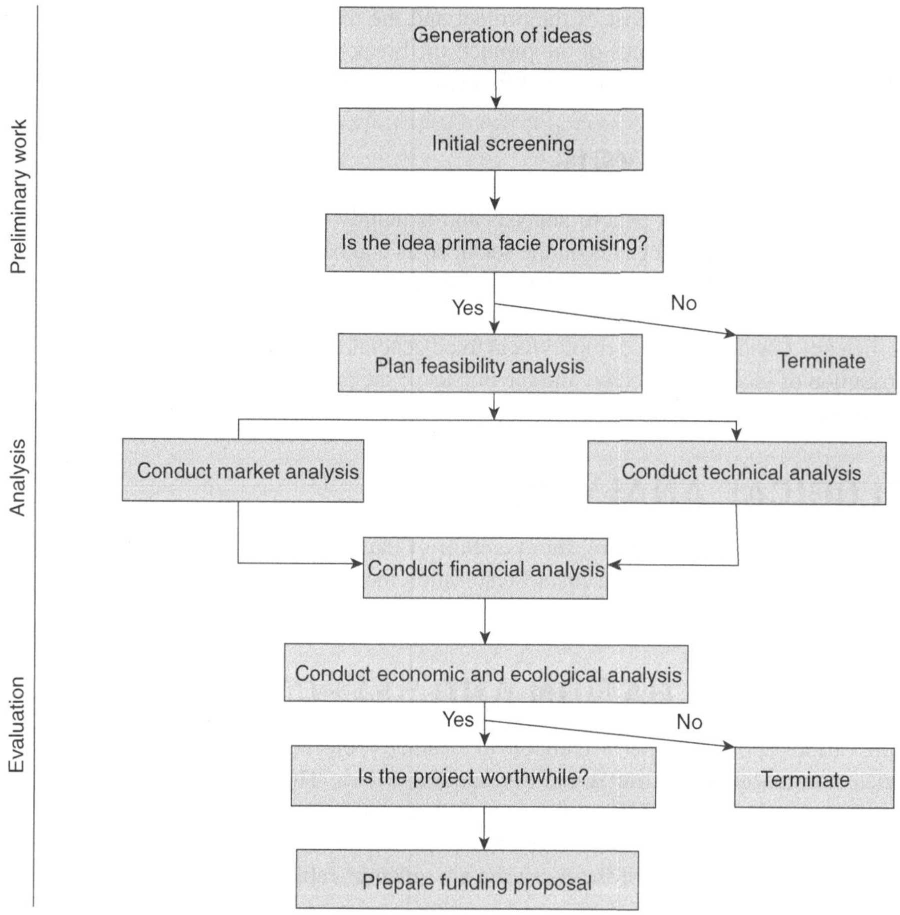

Figure 7.4 Project Feasibility Study: A Schematic Diagram

Source: Chandra, Prasanna (2010). *Projects: Planning, Analysis, Selection, Financing, Implementation and Review.* New Delhi: Tata McGraw-Hill. Reproduced with permission.

MARKET ANALYSIS

This mainly deals with determining the potential market and the market share for the proposed project. Market analysis is concerned with forecasting the demand for the product/service under consideration. It requires finding a variety of information on consumption trends, cost structures, structures of the competition, the elasticity of demand, consumer behaviour, and exports and imports.

TECHNICAL ANALYSIS

This principally deals with determining the technical viability for successful commissioning of the proposed project and for ascertaining whether sensible choices have been made with respect to location, size, process, etc. Technical analysis requires finding a variety of information on the availability of raw material and various other inputs; the type of technology to be adopted; choosing a suitable layout for the site, building and plant; and choosing the appropriate plant, machinery, and process.

FINANCIAL ANALYSIS

This mainly deals with determining the risk and return for the proposed project. Financial analysis seeks to ascertain whether the proposed project will be financially viable. It requires finding a variety of information on the cost of the project and the means of finance; the cost of capital; the projected profitability; cash flows of the project; the break-even point; the level of risk; the investment outlay and worthiness; and projected financial position.

ECONOMIC ANALYSIS

This is also called social-cost benefit analysis and is mainly concerned with judging a project from the social point of view. The focus is on the social costs and benefits of the proposed project. It deals with determining benefits and costs in terms of shadow prices and other social impacts. Economic analysis requires finding a variety of information on economic costs and benefits measured in terms of the efficiency (shadow) prices; employment to be generated by the project; impact of the project on the distribution of income in society; and the impact of the project on the level of savings and investment in society.

ECOLOGICAL ANALYSIS

This mainly deals with determining the quantum of damage likely to be caused by the proposed project to the environment, and the cost of restoration measures required to be undertaken to ensure that the damage to the environment is within acceptable limits.

PROJECT EVALUATION AND SELECTION

There are various appraisal criteria available to evaluate projects. These are broadly divided into two categories: non-discounting criteria and discounting criteria. The various types of non-discounting criteria are payback period (PBP) and accounting rate of return (ARR). The various types of discounting criteria are net present value (NPV), the internal rate of return (IRR), and benefit–cost ratio (BCR). The rules for selection of these criteria are given in Table 7.4.

The Payback Period

The payback period represents the amount of time that it takes to recover the cost of investment made in a project. All other things remaining equal, the better investment is the one with the shorter payback period. This method ignores the time value of money. Benefits occur after the payback period and do not measure profitability. The method of calculating the payback period is shown below:

$$\text{Payback period (PBP)} = \text{Cost of project/Annual cash inflows}$$

For example, If a project costs ₹100,000 and is expected to return ₹20,000 annually, the payback period is 5 years.

$$\text{Payback period} = 100{,}000/20{,}000 = 5 \text{ years}$$

Accounting Rate of Return (ARR)

This is also referred to as the average rate of return on investment. It is a measure of profitability which relates income to investment, both measured in accounting terms. It is an accounting method used for purposes of comparison. It provides a quick estimate of a project's worth over its useful

Table 7.4 The Appraisal Criteria

Criteria	Accept	Reject
Payback period (PBP)	PBP < Target period	PBP > Target period
Accounting rate of return (ARR)	ARR > Target rate	ARR < Target rate
Net present value (NPV)	NPV > 0	NPV < 0
Internal rate of return (IRR)	IRR > Cost of capital	IRR < Cost of capital
Benefit–cost ratio (BCR)	BCR > 1	BCR < 1

life. ARR is used internally when selecting projects and can be associated with the simple concept of return on investments. It can also be used to measure the performance of projects and subsidiaries within an organization. The higher the accounting rate of return, the better the project. The ARR can be calculated using the formula:

ARR = Average annual profit after taxes/Average investment over the life of the project

The ARR ratio is primarily used in capital budgeting where a lot of planning is done to determine whether long-term investments made in the project are worth pursuing or not. ARR is derived by finding profits before taxes and interest. The limitation of the ARR method is that it uses profit rather than cash flows and it does not account for the time value of money.

EXAMPLE

Shakti Construction Company has an option of two projects, A and B, with the same initial capital investment of ₹100,000. The profits for both the projects are given below. The estimated resale value of both projects at the end of the third year is ₹22,000. Calculate the ARR for each project and advise the company.

Project	Year 1	Year 2	Year 3
A	₹10,000	₹5,000	₹15,000
B	₹12,000	₹11,000	₹4,000

Solution:

ARR for Project A

Average profit = (10,000 + 5,000 + 15,000)/3 = ₹10,000
Average investment = (100,000 + 22,000)/2 = ₹61,000
Accounting rate of return = 10,000/61,000 = 16.39%

ARR for Project B

Average profit = (12,000 + 11,000 + 4,000) /3 = ₹9,000
Average investment = (100,000 + 22,000)/2 = ₹61,000
Accounting rate of return = 9,000/61,000 = 14.75%
Since Project A has higher ARR, it should be chosen.

Net Present Value (NPV)

The difference between the discounted value of the cash flows and the initial outlay is taken as the net present value of the project. Every project involves initial outlay irrespective of the means of financing. NPV is one of the two discounted cash flow techniques (the other one is the internal rate of return) used in comparative appraisal of investment proposals where the flow of income varies over time.

For example, an investment of ₹10,000 today at 10 per cent will yield ₹10,100 at the end of the year; therefore, the present value of 10,100 at the desired rate of return is 10,000. The amount of investment of ₹10,000 is deducted from this figure to arrive at the net present value, which is zero. A zero net present value signifies that the project repays the original investment plus the required rate of return. For a project to be viable, the net present value of the project has to be positive. A negative net present value indicates that the project is not viable. When choosing among mutually exclusive projects, the project with the largest (positive) NPV should be selected. The NPV is calculated as the present value of the project's cash inflows minus the present value of the project's cash outflows. This relationship is expressed by the following formula:

$$NPV = \sum_{t=0}^{n} \frac{CF_t}{(1+r)^t} = \frac{CF_0}{(1+r)^0} + \frac{CF_1}{(1+r)^1} + \cdots + \frac{CF_n}{(1+r)^n}$$

where CF_t is the cash flow at time t ($t = 0 \ldots n$), n is the life of the project, and r the cost of capital.

EXAMPLE

Consider capital budgeting projects A and B, which yield the following cash flows over a period of five years. Calculate the NPV of A and B and suggest which of the two projects should be accepted. The cost of capital for the project is 10 per cent.

Year	Project A: Cash Flow in ₹	Project B: Cash Flow in ₹
0	−1,000	−1,000
1	500	100
2	400	200
3	200	200
4	200	400
5	100	700

Solution:

NPV for Project A

$NPV = -1{,}000 + 500/(1+0.10)^1 + 400/(1+0.10)^2 + 200/(1+0.10)^3 + 200/(1+0.10)^4 + 100/(1+0.10)^5 = ₹134.08$

NPV for Project B

$NPV = -1{,}000 + 100/(1+0.10)^1 + 200/(1+0.10)^2 + 200/(1+0.10)^3 + 400/(1+0.10)^4 + 700/(1+0.10)^5 = ₹114.31$

Thus, if Projects A and B are independent projects, then both the projects should be accepted. On the other hand, if they are mutually exclusive projects then Project A should be chosen since it has a larger NPV.

Internal Rate of Return (IRR)

IRR is sometimes referred to as the "economic rate of return." IRR is the rate of return on an investment. It finds the discount rate that makes the NPV equal to zero. IRR is the rate of growth that a project is expected to generate. The higher a project's internal rate of return, the more desirable it is to undertake that project. Therefore, IRR can be used to rank several prospective projects that a firm is considering. It can be used to compare one investment with another.

The internal rate of return by definition is the rate of return at which the net present value of a stream of payments/incomes is equal to zero. It is the discount rate which equates the present value of future cash flows with the initial investment. It is the value of r in the following equation:

$$\text{Investment} = \sum_{t=1}^{n} \frac{C_t}{(1+r)^t}$$

where C_t is the cash flow at the end of year t, r is the internal rate of return, and n is the life of the project. However, when using the IRR, you should make sure that the calculated IRR is not very different from a realistic reinvestment rate.

In NPV calculation, it is assumed that the cost of capital is known to determine the NPV. In IRR calculation, the NPV is set equal to zero and then the value of the discount rate that satisfies this condition is determined. For example, consider the cash flows of a project being considered by Techno-Systems Private Limited.

Year	0	1	2	3	4
Cash Flow	100,000	30,000	30,000	40,000	45,000

The IRR is the value of r that satisfies the following equation:

$$100{,}000 = 30{,}000/(1+r)^1 + 30{,}000/(1+r)^2 + 40{,}000/(1+r)^3 + 45{,}000/(1+r)^4$$

The calculation of r involves a process of trial and error and r =15.37% in this case. The project can be accepted if the IRR is greater than the cost of capital.

EXAMPLE

Find the IRR of the following investment proposals. The initial investment is ₹70,000 and the expected annual cash inflow is ₹24,000. The economic life of the project is four years. The present value of ₹1 for 4 years at 10% is 3.17, at 12% is 3.037, and at 14% is 2.914.

Solution:

At 12%,

$$\text{PV of total cash inflow} = 3.037 \times 24{,}000 = 72{,}880$$

At 14%,

$$\text{PV of total cash inflow} = 2.914 \times 24{,}000 = 69{,}936$$

$$\text{IRR} = 12 + \left(\frac{72{,}880 - 70{,}000}{72{,}880 - 69{,}936}\right) \times 2$$

$$= 13.6\ \%$$

Benefit–Cost Ratio (BCR)

The BCR is also referred to as the "profitability index." It is an investment appraisal technique. Profitability index is actually a modification of the net present value method. While NPV is an absolute measure as it gives the total value in Indian rupees for a project, the profitability index is a relative measure as it gives the value in the form of a ratio. It defines the value of a project versus the money that will be spent in doing the project in the overall assessment of a cost–benefit analysis. This ratio provides a value of benefits and costs that is represented by actual Indian rupees spent and gained. The benefit–cost ratio is an important formula to be used in the decision-making process for selecting a project. A project is accepted for investment if the benefit–cost ratio is greater than or equal to one, and rejected otherwise. There are two ways of defining the relationship between benefits and costs.

$$\text{BCR} = \text{BCR} = \text{PVB/I}$$

$$\text{Net Benefit–Cost Ratio (NBCR)} = \text{BCR} - 1$$

where PVB is the present value of benefits and I is the initial investment.

The following decision rules are associated with them:

When BCR	or	NBCR	Rule is
>1		> 0	Accept
=1		= 0	Indifferent
<1		< 0	Reject

If the profitability index is equal to or more than one, the proposal is accepted. If there are more than one investment proposals, the one with the highest profitability index will be preferred. As the value of the profitability index increases, so does the financial attractiveness of the proposed project. This method is more useful in comparing projects with different cash outlays. Hence, it is superior to the NPV method. The profitability index is the ratio of the PV of the future cash inflow to the PV of cash outflow, i.e. initial cost of the project. Therefore, profitability index = PV of cash inflow/PV of cash outflow.

$$\text{Profitability index} = 1 + (\text{NPV/Initial investment required})$$

EXAMPLE

Alliance Solar Company is undertaking a project at a cost of ₹50 crore, which is expected to generate future net cash flows with a present value of ₹65 crore. Calculate the profitability index.

Solution:

$$\text{Profitability index} = \frac{\text{PV of cash inflow}}{\text{PV of cash outflow}} = 65/50 = 1.3$$

It can also be calculated as below:

Profitability Index = 1 + (NPV/Initial investment required)

NPV = Present value of net future cash flows – Initial investment required

NPV = 65 – 50 = 15

Profitability Index = 1 + 15/50 = 1.3

WORLD OF ENTREPRENEURS 7.2 Capital Budgeting and Evaluation Practices

A survey of capital budgeting practices in India by U. Rao Cherukuri reveals that firms use multiple evaluation methods for capital budgeting. The maximum number of investments undertaken is of the type "expansion of productive capacity," followed by "replacement of assets" and then "new projects." It was found that more than 90 per cent of the companies have been using capital budgeting methods. Firms also use the discounted cash flow techniques, with IRR being the most widely used. Accounting rate of return and the payback period are widely employed as supplementary evaluation methods. The NPV method produces an amount that is the expected value added from investing in a project. The profitability index, on the other hand, produces an indexed value that is useful for ranking projects.

A survey of corporate finance practices in India published in the October–December 2002 issue of *Vikalpa*, revealed that 85 per cent of companies use IRR, 67.5 per cent use PBP, 66.30 per cent use NPV, and 35.10 per cent use BCR. Risk assessment and adjustment techniques have gained in popularity. The most popular risk assessment technique is sensitivity analysis and the most common risk adjustment techniques are shortening of the payback period and increasing the required rate of return.

The most popular methods for evaluating small-sized projects are the payback method and accounting rate of return. For larger projects, IRR appears to be the most commonly used method. In the United States, IRR, NPV, ARR, and PBP are the most popular methods of project appraisal. Japanese firms mainly use a one year return on investment analysis and a residual investment analysis.

Source: Anand, Manoj (2002). "Corporate Finance Practices in India: A Survey," *Vikalpa*, October–December, 27 (4): 29–56 and Cherukuri, U. Rao, (1996), "Capital Budgeting Practices: A Comparative Study of India and Select South East Asian Countries," *ASCI Journal of Management*, pp. 30–46.

SNAPSHOT

- A wide range of criteria has been suggested to judge the worthwhileness of investment projects. They fall into two broad categories: the discounting criteria and the non-discounting criteria.
- The important discounting criteria are NPV, BCR, and IRR. The important non-discounting criteria are PBP and ARR.

DISCUSSION FORUM

- Discuss various appraisal criteria on the basis of certain theoretical and practical considerations in small groups.

PROJECT FINANCING

Funds can be raised from a variety of sources for financing a project. The two broad sources of finance available to a firm are equity financing and debt financing. The key factors in determining the debt–equity ratio for a project are the cost, nature of assets, business risk, norms of lenders, control considerations, and market conditions. Equity and debt come in a variety of forms and are raised in different ways.[3]

Equity Financing

This is a shareholder's fund and it may be in the form of equity capital, preference, internal accrual venture capital, and angel investing. Equity financing means exchanging partial ownership in a firm for funding. Equity shareholders enjoy the rewards as well as bear the risk of ownership. However, their liability, unlike the liability of the owner in a proprietary firm and the partners in a partnership concern, is limited to their capital contributions. The rights of equity shareholders consist of the right to residual income; the right to control; the pre-emptive right to purchase additional equity shares issued by the firm; and the residual claim over assets in the event of liquidation.

Equity Capital This represents ownership capital as equity shareholders collectively own the firm. When a company is formed, it first issues equity shares to promoters and also, in most cases, raises loans from banks, financial institutions, and other sources. As the need for financing increases, the company may issue shares and debentures privately to promoters' relatives, friends, business partners, employees, financial institutions, banks, mutual funds, venture capital funds, and others. Venture capital funds are likely to be an important source of finance for a nascent venture. Such investors are specific and small in number. As the company grows, it may raise capital from the public. The first issue of equity shares to the public by an unlisted company is called the initial public offering (IPO). Subsequent offerings are called seasoned offerings. Apart from equity shares, a firm may issue preference shares and debentures to the general investing public through a public issue.

Preference Capital This represents a hybrid form of financing. It has some characteristics of equity and some attributes of debentures. It is a special class of a company's shares, on which dividends are paid before the dividends on ordinary shares, and whose holders are repaid before others if the company goes bankrupt.

Internal Accruals The internal accruals of a firm consist of depreciation charges and retained earnings. Depreciation represents the allocation of capital expenditure to various periods over which the capital expenditure is expected to benefit the firm. Even though the amount that may be available by way of internal accruals may be limited and the opportunity cost of retained earnings quite high, internal accruals are viewed favourably by most corporate management because internal accruals are readily available; the use of internal accruals in contrast to external equity eliminates issue costs and losses on account of under pricing; there is no dilution of control when a firm relies on internal accruals; and the stock market views internal accruals with a pessimistic approach.

Venture Capital (VC) It is finance invested by professionals, called venture capitalists, in start-ups with growth potential. A venture capitalist provides guidance to the company and is a business partner sharing both risk and rewards. Venture capital is an important source of equity for start-up companies. Venture capital injects equity finance with a solid capital base for future growth. Venture capital firms provide equity for business and expect 20 to 40 per cent equity stake in a company and high returns on their investments within three to five years.

Venture capital firms in India invest the shareholders' money in start-ups. The Indian Venture Capital and Private Equity Association (IVCA) is the national-level organization for venture capital firms in India. The organization promotes and encourages the venture capital industry in the country and encourages members to invest in high-growth companies. A few well-known venture capital firms in India are Sequoia Capital India, Ventureast, Intel Capital, Helion Venture Partners, DFL

India, Nexus India Capital, IndoUS Ventures, DG India Ventures, Kleiner Perkins, Norwest Venture Partners, Canaan Partners, and Inventus Capital Partners.

Stages of Venture Capital Financing The requirements of funds vary with the life cycle stage of the enterprise. Depending upon the stage they finance, venture capitalists are called angel investors, venture capitalists, or private equity suppliers/investors. The venture capital investment process is different from normal project financing. In 1984, A. V. Bruno and T. T. Tyebjee of the School of Business, University of Santa Clara, California, formulated a model of venture capital investment activity which with some variations is commonly used today.[4] As per this model, this activity is a five-step process as follows:

1. Deal organization.
2. Screening.
3. Evaluation or due diligence.
4. Deal structuring.
5. Post-investment activity and exit.

Tyebjee and Bruno identified six stages of venture capital financing, which are given below:

1. **The seed money stage:** A small sum of money required to prove a concept or develop a product.
2. **Start-up:** Financing of firms that are less than one year old. The funds are primarily meant for marketing and product development.
3. **First-round financing:** Additional money needed to begin sales and manufacturing after the start-up funds are exhausted.
4. **Second-round financing:** Funds required for working capital for a firm that is selling its product but still losing money.
5. **Third-round financing:** Financing of a firm that has broken even and is planning an expansion. This is also called mezzanine financing.
6. **Fourth-round financing:** Financing of a firm that is expected to go public within six months. This is also called bridge financing.

Angel Investing

Angel investors are wealthy individuals who invest in entrepreneurial firms, usually during start-up. They provide cash to young investors and take equity in return. Angels are usually entrepreneurs who have successfully built companies, or have spent a part of their professional career in mentoring start-ups. Angels invest their own money and actively mentor the company. Angels usually expect a lower return on investment than venture capital firms.

Business angels are high-net-worth individuals, usually successful people or professionals, who provide early stage capital to start up businesses in the form of either debt, equity capital, or both. They are often self-made millionaires and are accustomed to taking calculated risks with their own money. They provide financing for start-up and early-stage firms that are too small to get the attention of VC firms, often too limited in their revenue potential at maturity to interest VC firms, and too risky for bank loans and for most VC appetites.

An angel network is a unique concept, which brings together highly successful CEOs and entrepreneurs from India and around the world interested in investing in start-ups and have a potential of creating high-growth companies. The network provides equity finance along with high-quality mentoring. Some of the well-known angel investing networks in India are Chennai Funds, the Indian Angel Network, the Mumbai Angels, and the TiE Entrepreneurship Acceleration Programme.

Debt Financing

Debt financing is basically money that is borrowed to run the business. Debt financing refers to borrowing money from a source outside the company under certain terms and conditions relating to interest rates and the period of return of the principal amount. Most entrepreneurs prefer to start their operations with money borrowed from banks and financial institutions. When a firm raises money for working capital or capital expenditures by selling bonds, bills, or notes to individual and/or institutional investors, this money is called a debt fund. In return for lending the money, the individuals or institutions become creditors and receive a promise that the principal and interest on the debt will be repaid. Term loans and debentures are two important ways of raising long-term debt.

Term Loans Financial institutions and banks have traditionally been the primary source of long-term debt for public and private firms. Term loans represent a source of debt finance, which is generally repayable in less than ten years. They are typically employed to finance the acquisition of fixed assets. Financial institutions give Indian rupee term loans as well as foreign currency term loans. Term loans represent secured borrowing. Usually assets, which are financed with the term loan, provide the prime security. In order to protect their interests, financial institutions impose restrictive covenants on the borrowers. Financial institutions such as SIDBI, IDBI, and ICICI fund entrepreneurial ventures.

Debentures For large firms, debentures are a viable alternative to term loans. Debentures are instruments for raising debt finance. Debentures often provide more flexibility than term loans as they offer greater choice with respect to maturity, interest rate, security, repayment, and special features.

Miscellaneous Sources

Working capital advance by commercial banks represents the most important source for financing current assets. Apart from principal sources like equity, internal accruals, venture capital, term loans, debentures, and working capital advance, there are several other ways in which finance may be obtained. These include deferred credit, lease finance, hire purchase, unsecured loans and deposits, special schemes of institutions, subsidies, sales tax deferments and exemptions, commercial paper, factoring, and securitization.

PROJECT IMPLEMENTATION PHASE

The implementation phase for a project involves the setting up of facilities. For project planning and control, two basic network techniques are available: program evaluation and review technique (PERT) and critical path method (CPM). These techniques help in monitoring the project. Once the project is commissioned, performance review is done periodically to compare the actual performance with projected performance.

CAPITAL STRUCTURE AND COST OF CAPITAL

The term "capital structure" denotes the composition of the types and ratios of funding from different sources availed of in a business.[5] In finance, capital structure refers to the way a corporation finances its assets through some combination of equity, debt, or hybrid securities. The cost of capital is a central concept in financial management. It is used for evaluating investment projects, for determining the capital structure, for assessing leasing proposals, and for setting the rates that regulated organizations like electric utilities can charge to their customers.

A firm's cost of capital is the weighted average cost of various sources of finance used by it such as equity, debt, and preference. It will be the overall or average required rate of return on the aggregate of the investment projects. The cost of capital is the rate of return that a firm must earn on its project investments to maintain its market value and attract funds.

The overall cost of capital is computed by calculating the weighted average cost of capital (WACC). WACC is calculated taking into account the relative weights of each component of the capital structure, debt and equity, and is used to see if the investment is worthwhile. The computation of the overall cost of capital involves three steps: assigning weights to specific costs, multiplying the cost of each of the sources by the appropriate weights, and dividing the total weighted cost by the total weights. The WACC tends to rise as the firm seeks more and more capital. The method of computation of a WACC is as follows:

Sources	Amount in ₹	Cost of Capital (%)	Total Cost in ₹
Debt	300,000	8	24,000
Preference capital	200,000	14	28,000
Equity capital	500,000	17	85,000
Total	1,000,000		137,000

WACC = (137,000/1000,000) $\times$ 100 = 13.7%

SNAPSHOT

- The two broad sources of finance for a project are equity and debt.
- A firm's cost of capital is the weighted average cost of various sources of finance used by it such as equity, debt, and preference.

DISCUSSION FORUM

- Discuss in small groups the cost of project and the means of finance.
- Explain the term "cost of capital."

DETAILED PROJECT REPORT

The project report is the blueprint of a project. It is a very important document and is the summary of the varied activities of a project. The report strives to accomplish the vital task of providing an overall view of project activity. The project report must contain the detailed information which ultimately helps in the decision-making process of whether or not to encourage the project conceived.[6]

A detailed project report (DPR) is drawn up based on the data and results obtained from varied detailed studies. The preparation of a detailed project report is a further step in firming up the proposal. When an investment proposal has been approved on the basis of a functional report and the proposal is a major proposal, it would be necessary for a detailed project report to strengthen the proposal for the capital cost as well as the various facilities. The DPR includes a project feasibility report and has the following components:

- Introduction of the proposed project, objective, and scope of the report.
- Product characteristics: Specifications, product uses and application, standards, and quality.
- Market position and trends: Installed capacity, production and anticipated demand, export prospects and information on import and export, price structure, and trends.
- Raw materials: Requirement of raw materials, prices, sources, and properties of raw materials.
- Manufacturing: Processes of manufacture, selection of process, production schedule, and production technique.
- Plant and machinery: Equipment and machinery, instruments, laboratory equipment, electricity and water supply, and the essential infrastructure.
- Land and building: Requirement of land area, building, and construction schedule.
- Financial implications: Fixed and working capital investment, project cost, and profitability.
- Marketing channels: Trading practices and marketing strategy.
- Management and personnel: Promoters' background, requirements of staff, labour, and expense on wage payment.

CHECKLIST FOR ENTREPRENEURS 7.3 ✓ Guidelines for Project Financing

- Use project management software to deal with large projects. These software programs help in a number of activities including scheduling, cost control, budgeting, resource allocation, documentation, communication, quality management, and administration. The various project management software available are Microsoft Project, Planisware, Project.net, Eventum, Open Workbench, and Gantt Project.
- Follow the guidelines of the planning commission to prepare a project report to obtain finance from financial institutions.
- Always have a short, medium, and long-term goal for control and required capital while raising equity.
- Use more equity when the tax rate applicable is negligible; the business risk exposure is high; the dilution of control is not an important issue; the assets of the project are mostly intangible, and the project has many valuable growth options.
- Use more debt when the tax rate applicable is high; the business risk exposure is low; the dilution of control is an issue; the assets of the project are mostly tangible; and the project has few growth options.
- Tap the banks, financial development corporations, and non-banking finance corporations for debt financing.
- Use the WACC taking into account the relative weights of each component of the capital structure, debt and equity, to see if the Investment is a worthwhile undertaking.

The above documents should be prepared before investment is made in a project. Thus, the formulation of investment is based on the various studies conducted by the entrepreneur. These can be considered as part of the pre-investment decision. A detailed project report is prepared not only for the investment decision-making approval, but also for the execution of the project and the preparation of the plan. The Planning Commission of India provides guidelines for preparing the project report.

The detailed project report is a complete document for investment decision making, approval, and planning whereas the feasibility study report is a base document for investment decision making. A detailed project report is the base document for planning and implementing the project. The project report is prepared for submission to the financial institutions for getting a loan, a grant of land, and other financial concessions. Financial institutions insist upon such a project report in order to be sure about the feasibility of the project. Since the financial commitments would be huge in many cases, it becomes necessary that precautionary measures be taken before money is sanctioned or else it would result in a huge loss in case an unprofitable project is financed. The sanctioning body also wants to ascertain from the report the possibility of the generation of substantial funds by the project itself to repay the amount within a stipulated period.

Project Profile A project profile is a simplified description of a project. It is a "snapshot" of the project report. It is required for MSME to get a provisional registration certificate from the District Industries Centre (DIC). It is also required for getting infrastructural facilities and utilities from government agencies. A project profile format is given in Annexure 7.1. A project profile usually contains the following principal elements:

- Common information about the project.
- Details of product, plant and machinery, utilities, raw material, and manpower.
- Details of market survey.
- Cost of project.
- Working capital requirement.
- Means of finance.
- Profitability.

SUMMARY

Entrepreneurial ventures use project management to accomplish outcomes under conditions of limited resources with typical time constraints. Project management is the science (and art) of organizing the components of a project, whether the project involves the development of a new product, the launch of a new service, a marketing campaign, or a wedding. Capital budgeting is a complex process, which may be divided into six broad phases: planning, analysis, selection, financing, implementation, and review. The important facets of project analysis are market analysis, technical analysis, financial analysis, economic analysis, and ecological analysis.

A wide range of criteria has been suggested to judge the appraisal of investment projects. They fall into two broad categories: discounting criteria and non-discounting criteria. The important discounting criteria are net present value, benefit–cost ratio, and internal rate of return. The major non-discounting criteria are payback period and accounting rate of return. The two broad sources of finance available to a firm are equity (shareholders' funds) and loan funds (debt funds). Equity and debt come in a variety of forms and are raised in different ways.

The two basic network techniques used for project planning, scheduling, and control are PERT and CPM. PERT is used for probabilistic projects and CPM is used for realistic projects. A detailed project report is a complete document for investment decision-making, approval, and planning whereas a feasibility study report is a base document for investment decision-making. The project report is prepared for submission to financial institutions for getting loans, grants of land, and other financial concessions.

KEY TERMS

Accounting Rate of Return: It is a measure of profitability that relates income to investment, both measured in accounting terms. This is also referred to as the average rate of return on investment.

Benefit–Cost Ratio: This ratio provides a value of benefits and costs that are represented by actual Indian rupees spent and gained. BCR is also referred to as the "profitability index." It is an investment appraisal technique.

Capital Budgeting: The capital budgeting process deals with identifying and selecting investment projects whose returns are expected to extend beyond one year. It is the process of making investment decisions in capital expenditures. These are otherwise called long-term investment decisions. It is the process of deciding whether or not to invest in a particular project.

Cost of Capital: A firm's cost of capital is the weighted average cost of various sources of finance used by it such as equity, debt, and preference. It will be the overall or average required rate of return on the aggregate of the investment projects.

Debt: This refers to borrowing money from a source outside the company under certain terms and conditions relating to interest rates and the period of return of the principal amount. It represents loan funds such as bonds, term loans, and working capital advances.

Detailed Project Report: This is the blueprint of the project and is prepared for submission to financial institutions for getting loans, grants of land, and other financial concessions.

Ecological Analysis: This mainly deals with determining the quantum of damage likely to be caused by the proposed project to the environment and the cost of restoration measures required to be undertaken to ensure that the damage to the environment is within acceptable limits.

Economic Analysis: This is also called social-cost benefit analysis and is mainly concerned with judging a project from the social point of view. The focus is on social costs and benefits of the proposed project.

Equity: It represents ownership capital such as shares and internal accruals. This is a shareholder's fund and it may be in the form of equity capital, preference, internal accrual, venture capital, and angel investing. Equity financing means exchanging partial ownership in a firm for funding.

Financial Analysis: This mainly deals with determining the risk and return for the proposed project. Financial analysis seeks to ascertain whether the proposed project will be financially viable.

Internal Rate of Return: IRR is the rate of return on investment. IRR finds the discount rate that makes the NPV equal to zero.

Market Analysis: Market analysis is concerned with forecasting the demand for the product/service under consideration. It analyses the potential market and market share.

Net Present Value: It is the difference between the discounted value of the cash flows and the initial outlay of the project.

Payback Period: The payback period represents the amount of time that it takes to recover the cost of investment made in a project.

Project Management: The Project Management Institute (PMI) defines a project as "a temporary endeavour undertaken to create a unique product or service."

Project Profile: A project profile is a simplified description of an eventual project.

Technical Analysis: This principally deals with determining the technical viability for successful commissioning of the proposed project and for ascertaining whether sensible choices have been made with respect to location, size, process, etc.

Venture Capital (VC): It is finance invested by professionals, called venture capitalists, in start-ups with growth potential. It is an important source of finance for enterprises that have very few avenues for raising funds.

CASE STUDY

The Story of redBus

I booked my bus ticket to Pune through your Web site. It was a wonderful experience. When we have the facility to book train and air tickets online, I was wondering why no was offering the same facility for bus tickets. Thank you providing such a large number of options for customers. You guys are doing a great job. I would like to thank Mr Ali from the Bangalore office who guided me through the reservation process. Thanks and cheers!

—*Ajay, Bangalore*

redBus is India's largest online bus ticket booking system and positioned as a platform for a centralized reservation system in India. redBus offers bus ticket reservation through its Web site and over the phone. Customers can also get bus tickets delivered to their home and pay through a range of payment options. The company offers a ticket inventory for over 1.8 lakh bus routes across India, operated by more than 700 bus operators. The company sold around 40–50 lakh tickets during the financial year 2012. It sold more than 100 lakh seats and has recorded a registered consumer base of 20 lakh, reporting an average growth rate of 250 per cent during the last five years.

The company was founded in 2006 by Phanindra Sama, Charan Padmaraju, and Sudhakar Pasupunuri, who were classmates from BITS Pilani. All the three founders who used to work in Bangalore with top IT MNCs such as IBM, Texas Instruments, and Honeywell quit their well-paying, secure jobs to found redBus. During the *Diwali* season of 2005, Phanindra Sama wanted to spend the festival in his home town but was not able to buy a ticket. He never made it home and that was the beginning of redBus. Phanindra realised the need for a system, which could be used by bus operators to display their seats and remove middlemen from the ticket reservation process. He decided to bring to those traveling by buses the same convenience that consumers enjoy while booking air tickets online.

Once Phanindra and his two co-founders felt that they understood the business, they developed a plan and submitted it to the TiE, Bangalore chapter (the Indus Entrepreneurs) mentorship competition. They were among the three winners. The initial seed funding and mentoring was provided by TiE and the founders also made personal investments to launch their portal and service. redBus has raised more than $75 lakh from three rounds of funding. In 2007, the company raised 1000,000 USD in angel funding from Seedfund, an early-stage investor. In 2009, the company received an undisclosed second round funding from Inventus Capital Partners and Seedfund. Again, during May 2011, redBus raised $65 lakh from Helion Venture Partners, Inventus Capital Partners, and Seedfund in its Series C funding.

Today, customers can book return tickets, get standard fares, and comprehensive information from a single source. Travel agents can bill more by offering return tickets and get access to all bus operators instead of only a handful. Bus operators realise their payments on the day the customer travels unlike the 3–4 weeks it took earlier. Updates are available on extra buses during festive occasions. redBus is looking for business expansion and is in talks with a few offline bus ticketing companies in Singapore and Malaysia. Can you help redBus prepare a project report on business expansion?

Questions:

1. How could redBus attract funding from investors in the initial stages?
2. What was the value proposition for investors?
3. According to you, how should redBus raise finance from the market for business expansion?

Source: www.redBus.in (last accessed in March 2013); www.boss.travel/Landing.html (last accessed in March 2013); and www.seatseller.in (last accessed in March 2013).

DISCUSSION QUESTIONS

1. Why are capital budgeting decisions often the most important decisions taken by a firm?
2. Discuss the six broad phases of capital budgeting.
3. Present a schematic diagram of the project feasibility study.
4. What is the internal rate of return of an investment, which involves a current outlay of ₹300,000 and results in an annual cash inflow of ₹60,000 for seven years?
5. A project costs ₹500,000 and yields a profit of ₹80,000 annually after depreciation at the rate of 12 per cent per annum but before a tax deduction of 50 per cent. Calculate the payback period.
6. Project X requires an investment of ₹50,000 and has a scrap value of ₹2,000 after five years. It is expected to yield profits after depreciation and taxes during the five years amounting to ₹4,000, ₹6,000, ₹7,000, ₹5,000, and ₹2,000. Calculate the average rate of return.
7. Rank the following investment proposals in order of their profitability according to: (a) payback method, (b) internal rate of return method, and (c) benefit–cost ratio method. The cost of capital is 10 per cent.

Project	Initial Outlay	Annual Cash Flow	Life in Years
A	25,000	3,000	10
B	3,000	1,000	5
C	12,000	2,000	8
D	20,000	4,000	10
E	40,000	8,000	12

8. Draw a schematic diagram depicting the formalities for setting up a business enterprise.
9. What are the benefits of a DPR?
10. A project has the following activities and time duration. Draw the project network and find variances of activities on the critical path and its standard deviation.

Activity	Optimistic Time	Most Likely Time	Pessimistic Time
1–2	3	6	9
1–3	7	7	7
1–4	2	8	14
2–5	4	10	16
3–5	3	9	15
4–6	7	10	13
5–6	5	8	11

ACTIVITY

Project Feasibility Study

Introduction: This activity enables participants to understand the practical approach to project feasibility study/project appraisal. The participants should refer to Figure 7.4 on Page 141 before conducting the project feasibility study. The participants may use secondary data for doing the study.

Objective: To help the participants understand the various facets of project analysis such as market, technical, financial, economic, and ecological analysis.

Time: 1 hour 30 minutes

Instructions: Divide the class into groups comprising 5–6 students. Each group should identify a project, conduct a project feasibility study, and present it in the class. These instructions should be given in advance so that participants can prepare well and present it in the class.

PROJECT

1. Refer to the project profile format given in the annexure below and prepare a project report of your choice, not exceeding two pages of A4 size with adequate margins and normal space between the paragraphs.

ENDNOTES

1. Chandra, Prasanna (2009). *Projects: Planning, Analysis, Selection, Financing, Implementation and Review*. New Delhi: Tata McGraw-Hill.
2. Choudhury, S. (2008). *Project Management*. New Delhi: Tata McGraw-Hill.
3. Chandra, Prasanna (2010). *Financial Management: Theory and Practice*. New Delhi: Tata McGraw-Hill.
4. Verma, J. C. (1997). *Venture Capital Financing In India*. New Delhi: Response Books.
5. Panneerselvam, R. and P. Senthilkumar (2009). *Project Management*. New Delhi: PHI Learning.
6. Pahwa, H. P. S. (2000). *Project Reports and Appraisals*. New Delhi: Bharat Law House.

ANNEXURE

Project Profile Format

1. **Common Information**
   a. Name of the unit and address:
   b. Product:

c. Constitution of the unit:
d. Name of the promoter:
e. Educational qualification:
f. Technical training and experience:

2. **Details of Project**

a. Product details

Sl No.	Details	Monthly Capacity	Value (₹)	Total (₹)
1.				
2.				

b. Details of machinery

Sl No.	Details	Nos.	Value (₹)	Total (₹)	Name and Address of Suppliers
1.					
2.					

c. Details of raw materials (monthly)

Sl No.	Details	PGR (₹)	Quantity (₹)	Value (₹)	Source of Suppliers
1.					
2.					

d. Utility (monthly)

Sl No.	Details	Rate (₹)	Quantity	Total (₹)
1.				
2.				

e. Manpower (monthly)

Sl. No	Details	Salary (₹)	Nos.	Total (₹)
1.				
2.				

3. **Market Survey**

Market survey has to be conducted by an entrepreneur before he/she embarks upon their selected project to prepare the SWOT analysis.

4. **Cost of Project**

a. Fixed capital

Sl No.	Details	Value (₹)
1.	Land/building	
2.	Machinery	
3.	Office equipment	
4.	Miscellaneous items	
	Total	

b. Working capital

Sl No.	Details	Value (₹)
1.	Stock in raw material	
2.	Semi-finished goods	
3.	Finished goods	
4.	Balance (bills receivable)	
5.	Working expenses	
	Total	

c. Total investment

Sl No.	Details	Value (₹)
1.	Fixed capital	
2.	Working capital	
3.	Preliminary and preoperative expenses	
4.	Interest during implementation	
5.	Contingency	
	Total	

d. Means of finance

Sl. No	Details	Value (₹)
1.	Term loan	
2.	Working capital loan	
3.	Own investment (with incentives)	
	Total	

e. Profitability

Sl No.	Details	Value (₹)
1.	Revenue	
2.	Production cost (Raw material + Manpower – Utilities)	
3.	Depreciation	
4.	Administrative expenses	
5.	Interest	
6.	Maintenance	
7.	Sales and advertisement	
8.	Profit [1–(2+3+4+5+6+7)]	
9.	Annual income (before tax)	
10.	Taxes	
11.	Net profit (9 – 10)	

New Venture Creation

6. Identification of Business Opportunities
7. Project Management and Financing
8. Business Plans
9. Institutions Supporting Business Enterprises
10. Business Organizations and Business Laws

"A good plan is like a roadmap—it shows the final destination and usually the best way to get there."

—H. Stanley Judd

Rasika Kadolkar, an entrepreneur from Belgaum, launched Fragrance House in 2005. The unit manufactures a customized range of hand-blended perfumes, designer candles, colognes, and other products sold in India and abroad. Rasika received advanced training in the preparation and execution of business plans under the "10,000 Women Entrepreneurs Goldman Sachs-ISB Programme." Rasika is shown in the photograph accepting an award for her business plan, which was selected as one among the top ten business plans in her batch. Rasika believes that a business plan reflects the conviction and can-do spirit of the entrepreneur. Her award-winning business plan is included at the end of this chapter.

Business Plans

8

LEARNING OBJECTIVES

Upon completion of this chapter, you should be able to:

1. **Understand the importance of a business plan.**
2. **Explain the contents of a business plan.**
3. **Discuss the significance of an executive summary in a business plan.**
4. **Prepare, write, and present a business plan.**
5. **Describe the procedure for setting up an enterprise.**
6. **Understand a sample business plan.**

INTRODUCTION

A business plan is a roadmap and blueprint of the project. A business plan is a written document that describes in detail how a business is going to achieve its goals. It is a document that explains a business opportunity, identifies the market to be served, and provides details about how the entrepreneurial organization plans to pursue it.[1] Ideally, the business plan describes the unique qualifications that the management team brings to the effort, explains the resources required for success, and provides a forecast of results over a reasonable time horizon. A business plan is based on estimates. This chapter explains the importance and purpose of a business plan, provides the contents of a business plan, and gives the process of preparing and presenting a business plan. It includes two sample business plans and gives a step-by-step procedure for starting a business enterprise.

PURPOSE OF A BUSINESS PLAN

A business plan is the written representation of an entrepreneur's vision for his/her business. A business plan is a written document between 20–40 pages in length that describes where a business is heading and how it hopes to achieve its goals and objectives. A workable business plan should determine the direction of the company; highlight the challenges in the path of the business; and formulate strategies and contingencies to keep the business on track in order to reach predetermined goals and objectives.

A business plan is not just for a start-up company but also for those which are growing. It prepares for a spin-off from a parent firm, or even for a project within an established organization. It can be used to establish realistic goals or targets to achieve, and to determine the current position. A business plan is used to help make crucial start-up decisions, to reassure investors, to measure operational progress, to test planning and assumptions, to adjust forecasts, and to set the standard for good operational management.[2]

The reasons for preparing a business plan are given below:

- Entrepreneurs reap benefits from the planning activity itself.
- A business plan is used to get finance from banks or to get equity funding from angel investors or venture capitalists.
- It can also be used to attract business partners and key employees or to make business alliances.
- If the business plan is prepared within a large organization, then it enables the board of directors to make capital investment decisions.
- The act of writing the plan will force the entrepreneur and his team to think through all the key elements of the business.
- The plan provides a basis for measuring actual performance against expected performance.
- The plan's financial projections can be used as a budget. Actual results that fall short of planned results will prompt the entrepreneur to investigate and take corrective action.
- The plan acts as a vehicle for communicating to others what the business is trying to accomplish.

CONTENTS OF A BUSINESS PLAN

Business plans follow a broadly similar structure. The key sections in a business plan along with the average number of pages to be included in each section are given in Table 8.1. Most business plans contain the following components.

Cover Page and Table of Contents

Every business plan should have a cover page. The cover page presents the first impression of your business plan to readers. This is just like a newspaper headline that gives quick information to readers, which helps the reader to decide whether to read the complete article. The cover page should have a clean and professional appearance and should contain the following information:

- Name of the business or project.
- The company's name, logo, address, telephone and fax numbers, Web site address, e-mail address.
- The name and designation of the contact person.

The table of contents is usually on the second page of the business plan and gives at a glance the topics covered in the business plan. The table of contents should be written for easy navigation to the rest of the plan by numbering each topic.

Table 8.1 Contents of a Business Plan

Sl No.	Contents	Pages
1.	Cover page and table of contents	2
2.	Executive summary	2
3.	Business concept	4
4.	Management summary	4
5.	Business strategy	2
6.	Operations plan	4
7.	Marketing plan	4
8.	Financial plan	4
9.	Appendices	10

Executive Summary

The executive summary is a standalone document two or three pages long and is probably the most important section of the business plan. It is designed to be a complete yet concise business plan by itself. It is a snapshot of the entire business plan and usually written last. The executive summary is a concise presentation of the main points of the business plan and gives a brief overview of the business venture. The purpose of the executive summary is to give the reader a quick understanding of the business proposal and provide the whole picture.[3]

Bankers and venture capitalists generally do not read through the entire business plan when it is presented to them. They go through the executive summary. In a number of business plan competitions around the world, the finalists are shortlisted on the basis of their executive summary. A full business plan is required to be submitted only by the shortlisted finalists. The main objective of the executive summary is to entice the reader to go through the entire plan. The executive summary is a formal statement and should include the following information:

- A brief description of the industry and market environment in which the business opportunity will develop and flourish.
- The uniqueness of the business opportunity and the key strategies for success.
- Profiles of the company's management team.
- Financial requirements and budget allocation.
- The anticipated risk and reward of the business.

Business Concept

This is another summary and gives the history of the business, the basic nature, and the purpose of the business. It clearly states the business objectives. There is no point in starting or expanding a business unless the entrepreneur has identified a lucrative opportunity. This section describes the business opportunity. It analyses the economics underlying the opportunity and the key factors that will drive its success, such as market penetration and product innovation. This section is used to describe the company and to explain how it is organized. It gives the usage, description, and specifications of the products and services to be offered. If the product/service prototype is ready, high-quality photographs are included.

Business Strategy

This section provides the SWOT analysis of the firm and analysis of the business environment. It provides information on the nature of the industry, competition within the industry, anticipating barriers to entry, the market, and the customers within the market. The industry background provides information to understand the shape, size, trends, and key features of the industry and to understand how the company's product or service will fit into that industry. The goals of the company and the business strategy are explained in this section. Strategy is the game plan of the business. It is about differentiation and competitive advantage. This section should give the mission, vision, future plan, and exit strategy of the business.

Management Summary

The management team is very important in any business. The success of the business mainly depends on the quality of the management team. Investors are also keen to know about the people behind the business who they see as key assets. It is a well-known fact that without the right team, none of the other parts really matter. This section should be able to answer the following questions. In this section, information regarding the description of the form of organization and ownership is explained. This section will answer questions such as:

- What is the profile of the founders, the team's management philosophy, and their reputation in the business community?
- Who are the current owners, and what percentages do they control?
- How is ownership evidenced—for example, in terms of common and preferred stock?
- Have any options, warrants, or convertible bonds that could expand ownership been issued?
- Which owners are involved in the day-to-day working of the business?

Marketing Plan

The term "market" is often used to describe the various elements of the total business environment. The market is where the company's product or service will be sold. The marketing plan is written after conducting a market analysis. This section provides information on assessing the market's size and growth, defining the target market, and articulating the value proposition. The value proposition gives the unique set of benefits that the customers will get if they choose to purchase the company's offerings over its competitor's offerings.

Stakeholders know that marketing is the activity most associated with success or failure. A company that is not able to connect with its customers will fail even if it offers attractive products or services. A sound and realistic marketing plan is the best guarantee that a solid customer connection will be made. The marketing plan should be supported with a solid market intelligence report for the plan to be credible. The plan should be clear about all aspects of marketing, including price, position, promotion, place, and customer value proposition. The marketing plan provides strategies to sell the company's product or service. The marketing plan should be a dynamic plan used to monitor the progress of the business.

Operations Plan

Operations deals with the transformation of ideas or raw materials into products or services to be sold to the customer. It gives an overview of the flow of the daily activities of the business operation and the strategies to support them. The operations plan should focus on the critical operating factors that will make the proposed business a success.

The operations plan section of a business plan describes the physical necessities of the business's operation, such as the business's physical location, raw materials, technology, human resource, facilities, and equipment. Information about inventory requirements, suppliers, and employees may be included depending on the kind of business. An operations plan provides a description of the break-even analysis, quality control measures, and the manufacturing process.

Financial Plan

The financial plan is a critical section of the business plan as it translates all the other parts of the business into anticipated financial results. The financial plan section is the section that determines whether or not your business idea is viable, and is a key component in determining whether or not your business plan is going to be able to attract any investment in your business idea. Basically, the financial plan section of the business plan consists of an analysis of financial statements such as the income statement, the cash flow projection, projected balance sheet, break-even charts, cost of the project, sources, and uses of funds.

Appendix

This section contains document attachments and the milestones of the project. This comes at the end of the business plan. It contains the market survey report, financial projections, product and technological specifications, process flow charts, photographs of the existing or proposed firm, lists of plants and machinery, organizational charts, and résumés of each member of the management team. The milestones plan lists the major events in the business's development such as prototype development, installation of plant and equipment, market test and penetration, recruitment of key personnel, funding from investors, and the break-even point. It includes only major events and the schedule of the project that the entrepreneur can meet. This may impress investors and improve the reputation of the company.

SNAPSHOT

- A business plan is a roadmap and the blueprint of the project.
- An executive summary is a standalone document two or three pages long and is the most important section of the business plan.
- The section on business strategy provides the SWOT analysis and analysis of the business environment.

DISCUSSION FORUM

- What is the purpose of a business plan?
- What are the contents of a business plan?
- Discuss the significance of the executive summary in a business plan.

PRESENTING A BUSINESS PLAN

A business plan should be well-written in crisp and to the point language and should not contain irrelevant information. It should be written in a professional manner. The contents of the plan are critical; the document should be attractive, impressive, and easy to read. The writing style should be clear and concise. The business plan should be printed on plain white bond paper of A4 size using a good quality printer. Each page should follow a standard layout with clear headings. Each new section should begin on a fresh page. Information such as document title, date, page number, and file name should be included either in the header or in the footer. Dividers can be used to make the contents of the document more accessible.

The business plan should be written by one or two key people from the management team (entrepreneur). However, individual sections should be written by those responsible for implementing the plan. The services of professional consultants may be taken while preparing the document. The business plan is a dynamic document and each version of the document should be clearly labelled and old versions of the document should be maintained as back-ups. It is appropriate to routinely monitor it and update it to help track the progress of your business. The contact details of the people responsible for the business plan should be easily accessible. It is generally advisable to use generic dates such as months rather than actual dates in the milestones portion of the business plan.

A good business plan can be the most important factor in the success of the business. It should be brief, clear, and properly organized. Before writing your business plan, it is necessary to know for whom it is written. Business plans usually take from one week to three months to write. A business plan is not only a tool for raising money; it also helps the entrepreneur to identify and define business goals and to determine the best methods for achieving those goals. A business plan should highlight the points that can attract investors. The assumptions made in preparing the business plan should be realistic.

The executive summary should be a concise presentation of the major points of a business plan and is written once the rest of the business plan is complete.[4] The executive summary is the first section to be read and must engage readers and excite them about the potential business idea. It should be the most carefully written of all the sections. An executive summary is a written version of what is sometimes referred to as an elevator pitch. It should be able to explain the key ideas and features of the business concept in two or three minutes.

Oral and Visual Presentation

It is necessary to prepare for an oral presentation of a business plan. The oral presentation is required in cases such as when the entrepreneur is participating in a B-plan competition; in front of potential partners and investors; for potential customers and other stake holders in the business. The presentation should be carefully structured and a script can be prepared. A good set of slides should be prepared to support the oral presentation.[5] The visual presentation enables the presentation of visual information such as product images, charts, graphs, and numerical tables.

DISCUSSION FORUM

- What are the points to be considered while writing a business plan?
- What are the points to be considered while presenting a business plan?

WHY DO SOME BUSINESS PLANS FAIL?

Like any other project, writing a business plan needs careful planning and systematic execution. Some business plans fail because of the following reasons.[6]

BREAKTHROUGH ENTREPRENEURSHIP 8.1 — Business Plan Competitions

A number of business plan competitions are conducted by technical institutions and business schools around the world. Some of these give very good prize money to the winners. Some well-known business competitions conducted at the national and international level are discussed here.

Business plan competitions have become an important part of the curriculum at the Harvard Business School. The competition has two tracks: business venture track and social venture track. This competition is conducted under the Harvard Business School's Arthur Rock Center for Entrepreneurship and the Social Enterprise Initiative. The competition is funded by the Rock Center, which was created through the generosity of the prominent venture capitalist Arthur Rock. Many of the past participants of the contest have executed their plans after graduation. Some examples include MyHappyPlanet, Bluesolid, Bang Networks, Chemdex, Ventro Corporation, www.suppliermarket.com, and Modulo among others.

TiE Global, in association with Rice University (USA), conducts the All-Asia Business Plan Competition, which provides a mentoring platform by TiE members (senior entrepreneurs) and venture capitalists from TiE. Other well-known international B-plan competitions are: the Berkeley Business Plan Competition, the DFJ Venture Challenge, and HKUST MBA International Business Plan Competition.

Eureka is an international business plan competition organized by the e-cell at IIT Bombay. This competition aims at encouraging people from across the globe to form international enterprises that combine vision, business acumen, and technology. The e-cell of NIT Trichy organizes Ventura, a B-plan competition where the top three business plans are successfully converted into start-ups. The Department of Science and Technology (Government of India) and Intel in partnership with NSRCEL@IIM Bangalore conduct a B-plan competition called the Next Big Idea. IIT Madras conducts Breakthrough, a B-plan competition which focuses on initiating innovations. The S. P. Jain Institute of Management and Research conducts Uddayam, an annual B-plan competition. Some well-known B-plan competitions in India are: Empresario, conducted by IIT Kharagpur; Vishishth, conducted by the entrepreneurship cell of IIT Delhi; Conquest, conducted by BITS Pilani; and Eximius conducted by IIM Bangalore.

Sources: www.hbs.edu/entrepreneurship/bplan/ (last accessed in March 2013); www.tie.org/initiative/TiE-International-Business-plan-competition (last accessed in March 2013); ecell.in/eureka11/ (last accessed in March 2013); www.twenty19.com/opportunities/organiser/nit trichy/ventura-12 (last accessed in March 2013); and www.nextbigidea.in/Champion.php (last accessed in March 2013).

WORLD OF ENTREPRENEURS 8.2 B-plan Software Programs

It often takes several days to prepare a business plan. Writing the business plan manually is also a cumbersome process. A number of software programs are available for pre-paring a business plan. The advantage of a business plan software program is that it helps in preparing the business plan in less time and is able to put all the information needed into a professionally presentable format. While choosing the B-plan software program, it is necessary to evaluate the software on certain criteria given below.

Business plan software programs should be user friendly. The software should be easy to handle and allow the user to shift from section to section quickly without any ambiguity. The software should have research tools for allowing access to business publications, articles, data for developing the market, and financial analysis. It should also have forecasting tools to feed the data and estimate future demand and future projections. It should have import options to import financial data into a business plan. The software program should have the ability to print and publish a professional type of document. It should have help and support options for beginners and advanced users. It should also have sample B-plans from similar business types and support features such as recommendations for wording and phrases. Special features such as tutorials, videos, Internet help, and telephone technical support should be incorporated.

Business Plan Pro by Palo Alto Software is a popular B-plan software program developed by Tim Berry. Berry and his team also provide consultancy services for developing B-plans using the Business Plan Pro software program. There are two primary versions of this software program, Standard and Premier. This product offers the ability to print and publish professional charts, graphs, and reports. It has the ability to import data from other applications such as MS Excel and MS Word files as well as Adobe PDF files. Two other popular business plan software programs are BizPlan Builder and BizPlan.com. BizPlan Builder has multi-user capabilities and is a fully-encompassing business tool. BizPlan.com, launched by the Go BIG Network, provides online collaboration, integration, and can be easily submitted to several funding providers on the Go Big Network.

Sources: www.paloalto.com/ (last accessed in March 2013); push2check.com/bizplan.com (last accessed in March 2013); and www.businessplanpro.com/ (last accessed in March 2013).

SNAPSHOT

Why do some business plans fail?

- Failure to address the customer's problems and needs
- Unrealistic goals set by the promoters
- Lack of commitment to the business by the promoters
- Lack of experience of the promoters
- Lack of professionalism

- **Failure to address the customer's problems and needs:** The business plan should address the customer's problems/needs/wants. It should clearly state how big the business opportunity is. The entrepreneur should document customer pain points before preparing the plan. Customer needs can be identified from direct experience, letters from customers, or from market research.
- **Unrealistic goals set by the promoters:** Setting goals requires the entrepreneur to be well informed about the type of business and the business environment. The goals set by the entrepreneur are based on data and the business plan is no good if it does not include a lot of data. The goals set by the entrepreneur should be Specific, Measurable, Achievable, Realistic, and Time-bound (SMART). The financial and market projections should be realistic, logical, and reasonable.
- **Lack of commitment to the business by the promoters**: The promoters must make a total commitment to the business in order to be able to meet the demands of a new venture. Investors will not be interested in a venture that does not have committed promoters. Investors also expect the promoter to make a significant commitment to the business. It is also required to have complete

CHECKLIST FOR ENTREPRENEURS 8.3 **Essentials of a Good Business Plan**

- **A business plan should have all the relevant sections:** Ensure that your business plan has a professional outlook and contains all the sections such as the cover page and table of contents; executive summary; business concept; business strategy; management summary; marketing plan; operations plan; financial plan and the appendix. You may also use a B-plan software program for preparing your plan.
- **Describe the opportunity:** Every business plan should start with the problem you are solving. The bigger the problem, the bigger the business opportunity. You should also explain how you are going to solve the problem. Clearly define the customer, channel, and revenue model associated with this solution.
- **Explain the business model:** Start with the industry, market, and competition in which you are operating and the market size. Explain how your business will make money; provide the financial forecast, and your profit margins. Explain the revenue, profit, and volume growth clearly.
- **Team:** Include key industry people as advisory members. Investors invest in people. Describe their experience and leadership qualities. Describe the organizational plan supported by an organizational chart.
- **Strategy:** Explain the uniqueness of your business and how it is going to be a differentiator and provide competitive advantage. State the vision, mission, and values of the business. Identify your preferred exit strategy. Explain how your rate of return would be attractive to investors.

focus on the business especially if it is a new venture and promoters should not be over enthusiastic in trying to do all things at once.

- **Lack of experience of the promoters:** A lack of experience will result in failure unless the entrepreneur can either attain the necessary knowledge or team up with others who already have experience in this area.
- **Lack of professionalism:** The business plan should be brief, clear, and nicely organized. It should highlight those points that can attract investors. The assumptions made in preparing the business plan should be realistic.

PROCEDURE FOR SETTING UP AN ENTERPRISE

The formalities for setting up of a business enterprise are shown in Figure 8.1 and discussed below.

Selection of a Project

A strong entrepreneur is the most vital aspect of every successful project. In order to set up a business enterprise, a suitable project has to be decided upon. This involves selecting a product or service, and a location for the unit. Based on these selections, a project feasibility study has to be conducted and then a brief profile has to be prepared for the proposed project. Then an entrepreneur has to prepare a business plan. Depending on the type of project, location, investment involved, and so on, the entrepreneur has to proceed to take further steps in establishing the unit.

Project selection is the initial decision that an entrepreneur has to make. Project selection and preliminary activities involve the following:

- Product or service selection.
- Location selection.
- Project feasibility study.
- Business plan preparation.
- Preparation of a project profile.

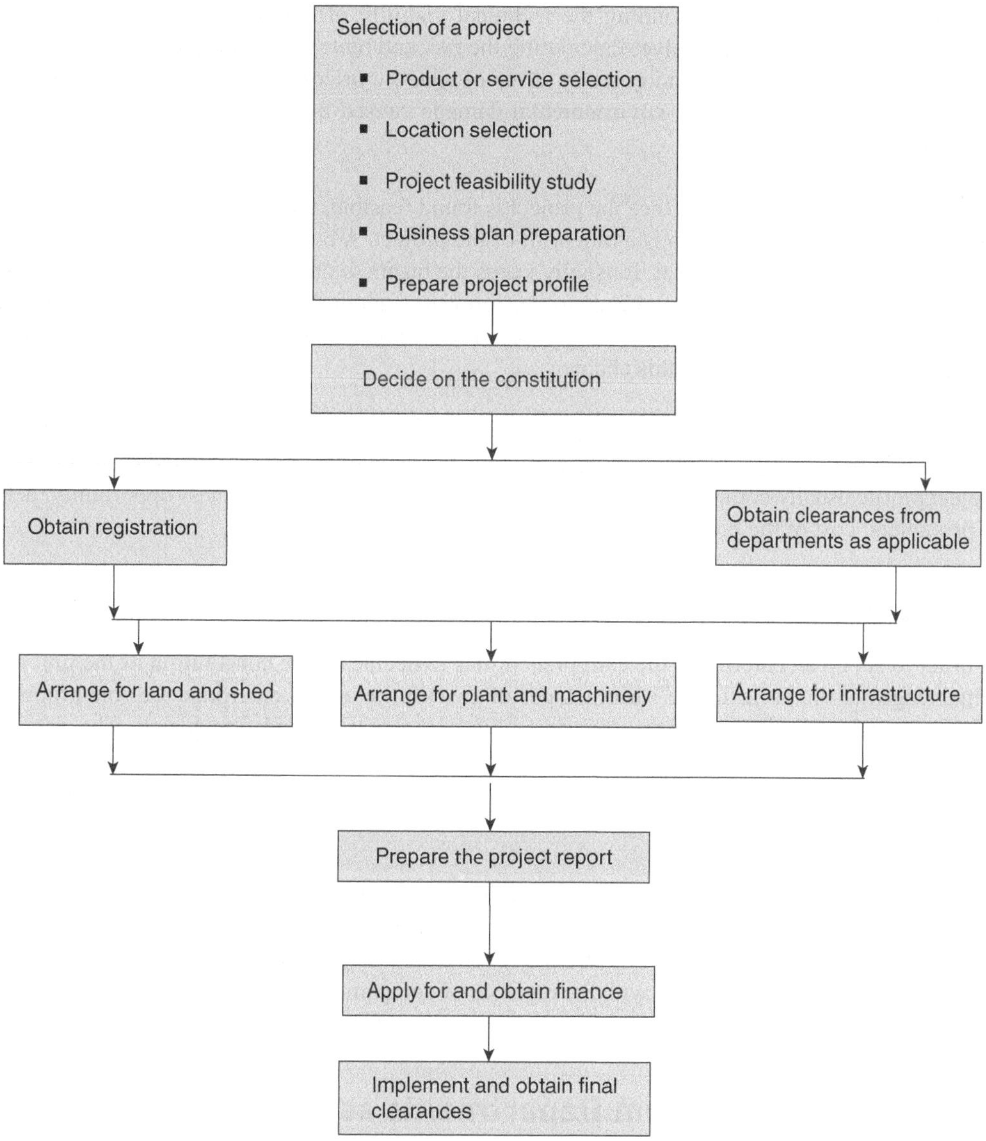

Figure 8.1 Formalities for Setting Up a Business Enterprise

Product or Service Selection The product or service is selected by the entrepreneur depending on the existing business opportunity. The entrepreneur has to make a careful analysis in choosing the product/service. While choosing the product or service, the entrepreneur has to consider factors such as experience of the promoters, marketability of the product or service, availability of raw material, availability of technology, investment capacity, and availability of infrastructural facilities.

Location Selection While selecting the location for the project, the entrepreneur has to consider factors such as proximity to the market; government policy; incentives and subsidies; the availability of suitable infrastructural facilities for the project; the availability of raw material and labour, and the availability of transportation and communication facilities.

Project Feasibility Study A project feasibility study is an analysis that involves finding and documenting potential solutions to a particular business opportunity. The project feasibility study involves market analysis, technical analysis, financial analysis, economic analysis, and ecological analysis. Market analysis deals with understanding the potential market and market share.

Technical analysis deals with finding the technical viability of the project and making sensible choices. Financial analysis involves calculating the risk and return of the project. Economic analysis involves finding benefits and costs in terms of shadow prices and other impacts. Ecological analysis involves assessing the environmental damage caused by the project and the restoration measures to be carried out.

Business Plan Preparation Once the project is found feasible, the next step is the preparation of a business plan. A business plan is a blueprint of the project. A business plan is a document which provides a roadmap to the project. It usually keeps the business on track to reach its planned goals. It determines where the company needs to go; forewarns about the possible roadblocks along the way, and formulates responses to contingencies. The details of the preparation of a business plan have already been explained in this chapter.

Preparation of Project Profile A project profile is a summary of a detailed project report. It is a "snapshot of the project." It is the first step towards the development of a detailed project report. A project profile usually comprises five parts: introduction to the project; business opportunity; details of promoters; cost of the project and means of finance; and risk and return.

Decide on the Constitution

In order to set up an enterprise, the entrepreneur has to decide on the constitution of the unit at the initial stages of the project. The various types of constitution of the enterprise are sole proprietorship, partnership, limited company (private/public), cooperative, and franchising. The details of these constitutions are explained in Chapter 10.

Obtain Registration

The sole proprietor has no legal formalities. Usually MSME choose to register with the District Industries Centre for obtaining various facilities and incentives. Partnership firms are governed by the Indian Partnership Act, 1932. The terms and conditions of partnership are contained in the partnership deed. Companies register with the registrar of companies and cooperatives register with the registrar of cooperatives. The details of registration are explained in Chapter 10.

Obtain Clearances from Departments as Applicable

For setting up a new enterprise in India, a number of clearances and approvals are required from concerned authorities depending on the type of enterprise. The approvals and clearances that may be required from various departments are given in Table 8.2.

Arrange for Land/Shed

For any industrial project, a suitable industrial site or a ready industrial shed is required. The promoters of the unit could consider taking an industrial site and constructing a shed as per their requirements. Alternatively, they could consider taking a ready industrial shed on ownership basis.

Industrial Land Once the location of the unit is decided, the land for the project could be conveniently taken from the State Industrial Areas Development Board. However, private land could also be purchased, but it has to be converted for industrial purpose and other necessary legal/formalities will have to be completed.

Industrial Shed For setting up an enterprise, the promoters could consider using a ready industrial shed. This could be on rent or on ownership basis. Rental sheds have to be arranged from private

Table 8.2 Approvals and Clearances Required from Various Departments

Approvals/Clearances Required	Department to be Approached and Consulted
Incorporation of company	Registrar of Companies
Registration/IEM/ Industrial license	DIC for MSME/SIA for large and medium industries
Allotment of land	State DI/SIDC/Infrastructure Corporation /SSIDC
Permission for land use (in case industry is located outside an industrial area)	▪ State Directorate of Industries ▪ Dept. of Town and Country Planning Local Authority/District Collector
NoC and consent under Water and Air Pollution Control Acts	State Pollution Control Board
Approval of construction activity and building plan	▪ Town and country planning ▪ Municipal and local authorities ▪ Chief Inspector of Factories ▪ Pollution Control Board ▪ Electricity Board
Sanction of power	State Electricity Board
Use and storage of explosives	Chief Controller of Explosives
Boiler Inspection Certificate	Chief Inspector of Boilers
Finance	▪ SFC/SIDC for term loans ▪ For loans higher than ₹150 lakh, financial institutions like IDBI, ICICI, IFCI, etc.
Registration under States Sales Tax Act and Central and State Excise Act	▪ Sales Tax Department ▪ Central and State Excise Departments
Extraction of minerals	State Director of Mines and Geology
ISI Certificate	Regional Office of the Bureau of Indian Standards (BIS)
Quality Marking Certificate	Quality Marking Centre of the State Government
Weights and measures	Inspector of Weights and Measures
Code number for export and import	Regional Office of the Director General of Foreign Trade

Source: http://dcmsme.gov.in/publications (last accessed in March 2013).

owners. The purchase of industrial sheds has to be arranged from private owners. This is possible under an outright purchase or a hire purchase scheme.

Application Formalities Application in the prescribed form is to be submitted along with the following documents:

- A copy of the Provisional Registration Certificate (PRC).
- A detailed project report.
- Certified copies in support of educational qualification, experience, and other categories as may be applicable.
- Applicable earnest money deposit.

Arrange for Plant and Machinery

The plant and machinery required for the project could be purchased from recognized manufacturers/dealers. The plant and machinery could be taken on a direct or hire purchase scheme.

Direct Purchase The entrepreneur has to select and buy the required plant and machinery from recognized and approved manufacturers or dealers. Banks and the State Financial Corporations maintain a list of approved machinery suppliers. The entrepreneur is advised to refer to such a list before deciding on the supplier.

The entrepreneur should compare the quality, performance, and service terms, price, and other details of the alternate plant and machinery that may be available in the market. Then they should decide on an appropriate plant and machinery for their proposed project. Detailed quotations should be taken for preparing the project report and also for submission to State Financial Corporations along with the loan application. Some items of plant and machinery may have to be fabricated against orders. For such items, the entrepreneur should seek quotations from reputed and experienced fabricators and get their equipment fabricated as per the required specifications. Entrepreneurs have to take steps to order their plant and machinery from the selected suppliers/fabricators after the State Financial Corporations and banks sanction the loans.

NSIC Hire Purchase Scheme In the hire purchase scheme offered by NSIC, the required plant and machinery will be the asset of NSIC and they will lease it to the promoters of the industrial unit. As per the NSIC scheme agreement, once the required lease installment is paid, the assets (plant and machinery) will become the property of the industrial unit. The hire purchase scheme requires earnest money deposit to be brought in by the promoters of the unit.

Arrange for Infrastructure

The main infrastructure facilities required for an enterprise are land or shed for the project, power connection, water supply, and telephone facility. Single Window Agencies (SWA) are set up at the district level for the benefit of MSME. The SWA provide clearances for various infrastructure and other facilities for MSME. The assistance provided by the SWA is given below:

- Grant of land in industrial areas and allotment of sheds in the industrial estates for all MSME.
- Grant of power up to the limit prescribed by the state government.
- Review and recommendation of sanction of term loans and working capital loans by the State Financial Corporation and commercial banks within the district for the new and existing MSME.
- Grant and disbursement of all incentives and concessions for MSME.
- General review of the position regarding problems faced by entrepreneurs and existing MSME within the district and doing such other work as may help promotion of the enterprises.

Land and Construction of Building After deciding the location and site, three important factors have to be kept in mind before purchasing/leasing the land.

- Availability of basic amenities like power and water.
- Connectivity to nearest rail, road, or port.
- Price of the land.

The purchase or lease of land must be done after careful analysis because of the long-term nature of the commitment. After an industrial plot for the unit is secured, the next step is to find a suitable architect to design the outlay of the area and factory. The design of the factory building has to be in consonance with the type of industry. An appropriate plant layout must be selected. If a home business is being set up, the area which is to be used as the production centre or office should be selected carefully. The services of a professional may be used to ensure that the area is utilized optimally. An architect's estimate of building construction is essential for loan applications. An architect's certificate for money spent on the building is also needed for the disbursement of the loan. The entrepreneur also has to apply to concerned authorities for getting utilities connections such as water, power, and telephone connections.

In order to encourage entrepreneurship, the government offers several incentives such as land and building tax concessions, and providing land at cheaper rates through its agencies. This is to promote the growth of entrepreneurship.

Prepare Project Report

The project report is an important document and should be prepared carefully. Banks and other financial institutions decide whether a loan should be granted, and if granted, the amount that should be sanctioned on the basis of this report. The project report is generally prepared to cover the following broad segments:

- **General information:** The following information should be provided.
  - Name of the unit and address.
  - Name of product/service.
  - Constitution of the unit.
  - Name of the promoter.
  - Educational qualification.
  - Experience.
- **Details of the project:** The following information should be provided.
  - Product/service details.
  - Details of machinery.
  - Details of raw material.
  - Utility.
  - Manpower requirement.
  - SWOT analysis.
- **Market survey:** The market survey report should be enclosed.
- **Cost of project:** The following details should be provided.
  - Fixed cost: Land/building, machinery, office equipment, miscellaneous items.
  - Working capital: Stock in raw material, semi-finished goods, finished goods, bills receivable, working expenses.
  - Total investment: Fixed capital, working capital, preliminary and preoperative expenses, interest during implementation, contingency.
  - Means of finance: Term loan, working capital loan, own investment (with incentives).
  - Profitability: Revenue, production cost, depreciation, administrative expenses, interest, maintenance, sales and advertisement, profit, annual income before tax, taxes, net profit.
- **Annexure:** Promoter's biodata, organizational chart, details of group units if any, statutory sanctions/approvals, project feasibility study report, project schedule, arrangement of land and building, statement of cost of plant, machinery and other equipment, details of orders and enquiries, process chart, financials for project and its analysis, financials of the company and its analysis, manpower planning, and financial statements.

SNAPSHOT

- A project feasibility study is an analysis that involves finding and documenting potential solutions to a particular business opportunity.
- A project profile is a summary of a detailed project report. It is a "snapshot of the project."
- The project report is an important document on the basis of which banks and other financial institutions decide whether a loan should be granted, and if granted, the amount that should be sanctioned.

Apply for and Obtain Finance

A formal application needs to be made for loans from financial institutions and commercial banks. The details of documentation that need to be provided with the loan application are given below:

- Balance sheet and profit and loss statement for the previous three consecutive years of firms held by promoters.
- Income tax assessment certificates of partners/directors, proof of possession of land/building.
- Architect's estimate for construction cost.
- Partnership deed/memorandum and articles of association of the company.
- Project report.
- Budgetary quotations of plant and machinery.

A bank issues a sanction or rejection letter after it completes an assessment of the application for funding. If the loan is approved, the bank sends a sanction letter to the applicant. Applicants need to indicate in writing their acceptance of the terms and conditions laid down by the financial institutions/banks after receiving the sanction letter. The loan is disbursed according to the phased implementation of the project. Apart from commercial banks and government-owned financial institutions, entrepreneurs can also approach venture capital funds and non-governmental finance companies for funding.

Implement the Project and Obtain Final Clearances

Entrepreneurs will have to take necessary steps to physically implement the project after obtaining the various licenses, clearances, infrastructure facilities and so on. The following are the major activities that entrepreneurs have to undertake for implementing the project:

- Construct shed.
- Order machinery.
- Recruit personnel.
- Arrange for raw materials.
- Generate a marketing plan.

Erection and Commissioning Once the building is ready and the necessary plant and machinery have arrived, entrepreneurs have to take steps to erect the machinery. The various items of plant and machinery should be erected as per the prepared plan. Sometimes sophisticated machinery is supplied along with the service of erection. In such cases, the erection and commissioning will be undertaken and completed by the machinery suppliers. Alternatively, the entrepreneurs have to take the necessary steps to erect the plant and machinery. After the plant and machinery is erected, the entrepreneurs should proceed to commission the plant. Initially, during the trial-run period, entrepreneurs will have to make necessary adjustments and changes in production and processes to obtain the desired quality of the products. Once the production/process of the unit is standardized, they can proceed with commercial production.

Obtain Final Clearances Entrepreneurs are required to take several final clearances when the unit is ready for commissioning or as soon as it goes into production. Accordingly, entrepreneurs are advised to refer to the various preliminary clearances they have obtained from different departments /organizations and take necessary steps to obtain final clearances or approvals as required.

DISCUSSION FORUM

- Discuss the procedure for setting up an enterprise in small groups.
- What are the uses of a project report?
- What is the difference between direct purchase and hire purchase?

SUMMARY

A business plan is the blueprint of a project. It is a document that explains a business opportunity, identifies the market to be served, and provides details about how the entrepreneurial organization plans to pursue it. A business plan is the written representation of an entrepreneur's vision for his/her business. Every business, whether it is a start-up company, an expansion of an existing business, a spin-off from a parent organization, or a project within an established corporation, needs a business plan as a roadmap.

A business plan should have a professional outlook and contain all the relevant sections such as the cover page and table of contents, the executive summary, the business concept, the business strategy, the management summary, the marketing plan, the operations plan, the financial plan, and an appendix. There are a number of B-plan software programs available for preparing a business plan. The executive summary is a standalone document two or three pages long and is probably the most important section of the business plan. It is designed to be a complete yet concise business plan by itself. It is a snapshot of the entire business plan and is usually written last.

The procedure for setting up a business enterprise involves various phases such as selection of a project, decision about the constitution, obtaining registration, obtaining clearances from departments as applicable, arranging for land and shed, arranging for plant and machinery, arranging for infrastructure, preparing a project report, applying for and obtaining finance, proceeding towards implementation, and obtaining final clearances.

KEY TERMS

Break-even Point: The number of units of the product or service that must be sold in order to have revenues equal to the operating costs for producing that product or service.

Business Concept: The section of the business plan that summarizes the basic nature and the purpose of the business and states the business objectives.

Business Opportunity: The terms "industry" and "market" describe parts of the total business environment. The area of interaction between industry and market represents business opportunity—the space in which customer needs and the product or service meet.

Business Plan: A written document of an entrepreneur's vision for his business.

Business Strategy: The section of a business plan which provides the SWOT analysis of the firm and the analysis of the business environment.

Executive Summary: A complete yet concise business plan by itself; often preceding the rest of the business plan.

Financial Plan: It is a critical section of the business plan, which translates all the other parts of the business into anticipated financial results and determines the viability of the business idea.

Industry: The industry is the group of companies that produce and sell products or services to a particular market; it includes both colleagues and competitors.

Management Team: The management team consists of people that make a business work.

Market: The various elements of the total business environment where products or services will be sold determines the opportunity and customers.

Marketing Plan: The marketing plan includes all that the enterprise proposes to do to promote and sell its products or service.

Milestones: The list of the major events in the business's development.

Operations Plan: The section of a business plan that describes the physical necessities of the business's operation, such as the business's physical location, raw materials, technology, human resource, facilities, and equipment. It gives an overview of the flow of the daily activities of the business operation and the strategies to support them.

Organizational Chart: A chart representing the structure of an organization in terms of ranks, roles, and reporting relationships.

Value Proposition: The unique set of benefits your customers will get if they choose to purchase your offering over competitors' offerings.

CASE STUDY

Effective Paperless Administration in Educational Institutions

Introduction: The executive summary of a business plan on effective paperless administration in educational institutions is discussed in this case study. This executive summary is a hypothetical business plan prepared for effective paperless administration and is designed to be a complete yet concise business plan by itself at Belgaum.

Need and Social Cause: Since educational institutions create future citizens of the country, it is very essential for them to function efficiently and effectively. The twenty-first century demands that citizens be environmentally conscious. Tapping these two necessities, we can use the latest technology, i.e. use a new concept called cloud computing and design a cost-effective software program that will ensure lean administration of an educational institution and also cut down on the usage of paper to the maximum extent.

Product Description: The software (application) will be used in the overall administration of an educational institution. The sample process for the administration of an institution offering an MBA course is shown in Figure 8.01.

Benefits: The software eliminates repetitive processes, ensures better time management, creates a paperless office, and improves human resource utilization, which results in cost reduction.

Advantages and Strengths of Cloud Computing: In the ordinary course, an investment of ₹1 lakh is required for hardware and ₹30,000 to ₹300,000 is required for software licensing. However, the use of cloud computing will relieve us of these costs as costs do not have to be incurred for purchasing hardware or software. The product can be provided to any customer who has a computer, with Internet facility being the only requirement, which is a *de facto* standard in any school or college. This implies that the investment for the customer, other than buying the product, is nil.

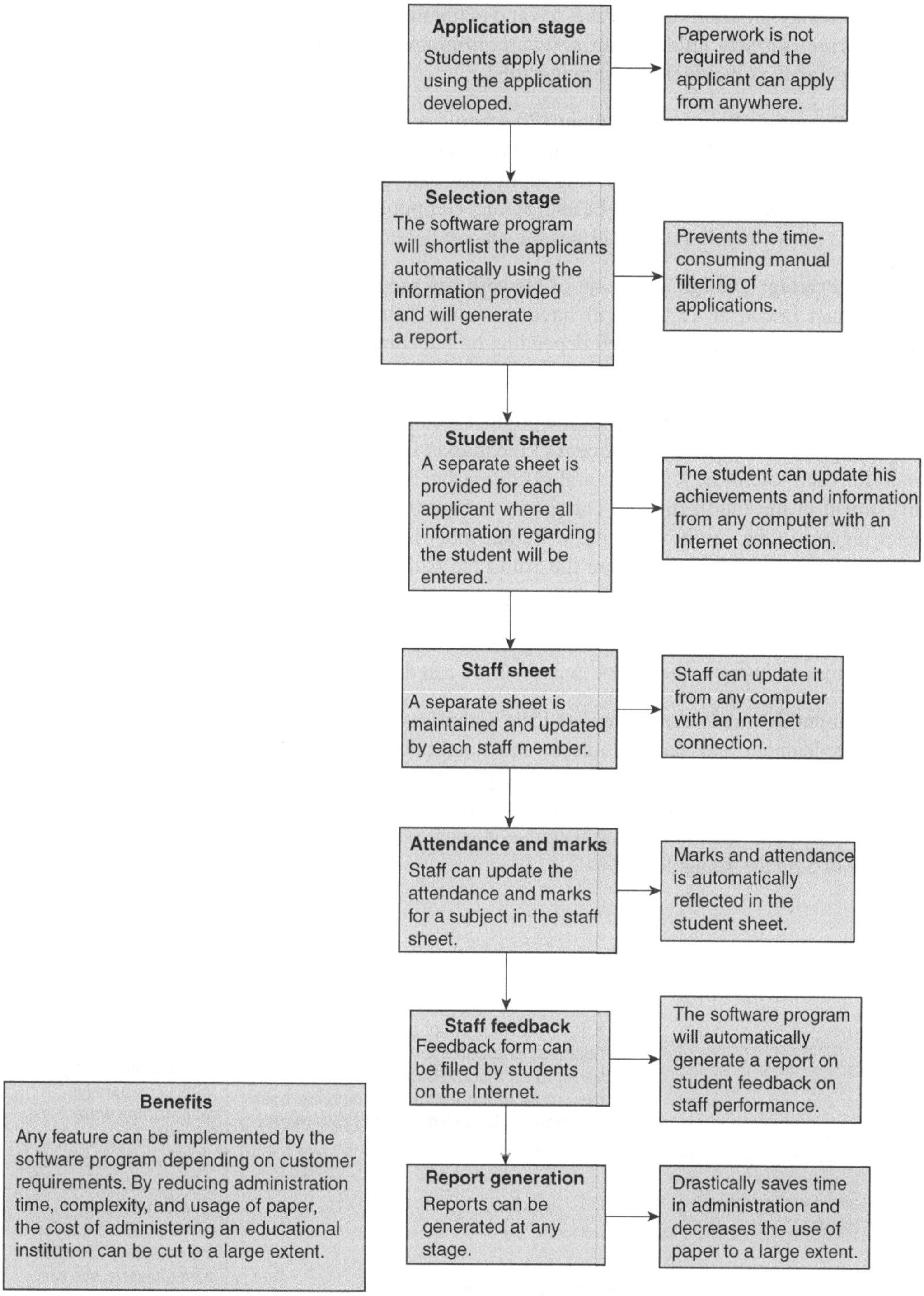

Figure 8.01 Sample Process for Administration

The product can be easily upscaled with no additional investment for hardware; other software programs in the market require a server for upscaling, which would be expensive. Upscaling is easily achievable with the use of cloud computing. Google offers cloud computing for developers; it is free for some amount of resources. If it exceeds the resources, a monthly bill similar to a phone bill is generated which is very marginal.

The software program can be accessed and maintained from anywhere in the world where there is an Internet service, unlike other software programs that have to be accessed and fixed from specific computers in which they are installed.

Market Potential: Belgaum has about 120 schools and colleges still using paper in the process of administration. The entire sandbox region has schools and colleges constituting a potential market for this software program. Further, this application can replace other school or college administration software programs as we will be using cloud computing. This may be extended to other regions in the next phase. Figure 8.02 describes the market potential of the business in detail.

Product Pricing: The initial pricing of the software program will range from ₹5,000 to ₹50,000. The product priced at ₹5,000 will have minimum features. If any client customization is required, that feature will be charged depending on the complexity of the requirement from ₹10,000 onwards.

Product Launch: The marketing of the product would start from Belgaum, covering 120 schools and colleges. If we capture 10 per cent of the market in the first six months, assuming the average price for each sale to be ₹10,000, and assuming linear growth, we will break even for the initial investment in the fourth month. The graph in Figure 8.02 shows growth in INR. We will enter other regions in the sandbox starting with the Hubli–Dharwad region from the 7th month and will be expecting a similar growth from the 7th to the 12th month. At the end of a year, we will have approximate cash reserves of ₹267,400.

Upscaling: After 15 months of operations, we can market the product in different domains such as small offices, industries, and banks, for which we can design ERP software using cloud computing.

Management Team: The management team comprises software engineers Amit M. Charantimath, Chetan Doddamani, and Manoj Bableshwar. All hold Bachelor of Engineering degrees from RVCE. Amit is pursuing a diploma in entrepreneurship from the Entrepreneurship Development Institute of India and Manoj is doing his masters in business law from the National Law School of India University, Bangalore. Chetan is doing a course in cryptography and network security from the Indian Institute of Science, Bangalore.

Figure 8.02 Market Potential for the Business

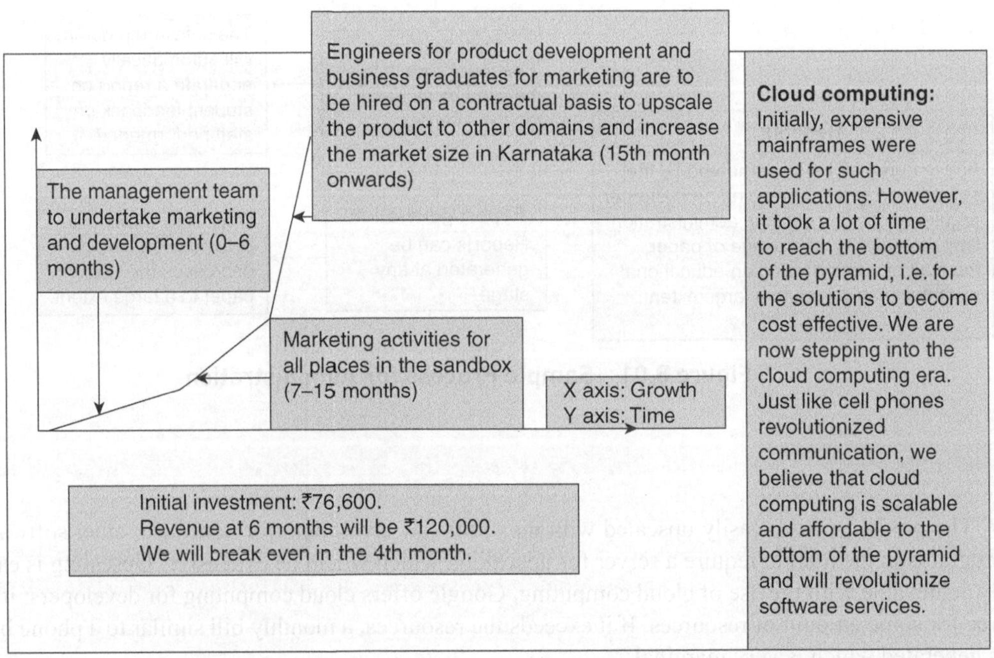

Questions:

1. What are the main strengths and weakness of the proposed business?
2. What are the questions raised by the executive summary, which can be answered by a full business plan?
3. Is there any additional information you would have added in the executive summary?

DISCUSSION QUESTIONS

1. What is a business plan? What does the reader expect to learn from a business plan?
2. Outline a structure for a business plan.
3. What are the uses of a business plan?
4. Why is the executive summary considered to be the most important part of a business plan?
5. While discussing the management team, what information should be included in the business plan?
6. Discuss the various B-plan software programs available in the market. Which one will you choose and why?
7. Explain the procedure for setting up a business enterprise with the help of a schematic diagram.
8. Explain the significance of a project report.

ACTIVITY

1. Invite a bank manager from a local bank and request him to address your class to find out what they look for in a business plan. Find out whether they have a prescribed format for the business plan.
2. Download a business plan from the business plan archive and critically evaluate the business plan.

PROJECT

1. Follow the guidelines given in the chapter and prepare a business plan for your intended business.
2. Organize a B-plan competition in your class. Ask your professors to lend help.

ENDNOTES

1. Covello, Joseph and Brian Hazelgren (1998). *Your First Business Plan*. Naperville, IL: Source Books.
2. DeThomas, Arthur and William B. Fredenberger (1995). *Writing a Convincing Business Plan*. Hauppauge, NY: Barrons.
3. Gumpert, David E. (1999). *How to Really Create a Successful Business Plan: Step-by-Step Guide*. Boston: Inc. Publishing.
4. HBS Toolkit, available at www.alumni.hbs.edu/new_alumni/toolkit/ (last accessed in March 2013).
5. Sahlman, William A. (1997). "How to Write a Great Business Plan," *Harvard Business Review*. July–August.
6. Harvard Business School Press (2007). *Creating a Business Plan*. Harvard Business School Press (Pocket Mentor series).

ANNEXURE

BUSINESS PLAN I: MICRO, SMALL, AND MEDIUM ENTERPRISES (MSME) CLINIC

TABLE OF CONTENTS

Sl No.	Contents
1.	Executive summary
2.	Business concept
3.	Management summary
4.	Operations plan
5.	Marketing plan
6.	Strategic plan
7.	Financial plan
8.	Appendices

EXECUTIVE SUMMARY

The Firm Micro, Small, and Medium Enterprises Clinic is a Belgaum-based partnership firm offering training and business solutions under one roof to MSME located in the Belgaum district. The market is untapped and there is an urgent need for a single-window business solution provider in this region.

Target Market The firm has already started its operations in Belgaum district and during upscaling will penetrate other districts such as Dharwad, Haveri, Gadag, and Uttara Kannada districts of the North Karnataka region.

Vision The firm's vision is to be the preferred total business solution providers in the Northern Karnataka region by 2020.

Mission The firm's mission is to provide need-based, cost-effective, total business solutions for nurturing the growth of MSME in the North Karnataka region.

Identification of Business Opportunity and Customer Pain Points An essential problem confronting MSME in a developing country like India is that they are unable to hire consultancy services from big consulting houses unlike the large units. They need training and consultancy services to nurture them throughout the entire life cycle of the unit. Presently, MSME in this region are availing consultancy services on an *ad hoc* basis from some consultancy agencies at a higher cost.

There is a need for a single-window approach for providing complete business solutions. Most of the consultancy firms are from Pune, Mumbai, and Bangalore. The services are at the convenience of service providers and not at the convenience of customers. Moreover, it is not a cost-effective solution. The dissatisfaction faced by customers from the existing service providers supplies a window of opportunity for the MSME Clinic to provide total business solutions under one roof.

Solution The MSME Clinic offers a solution in the form of consultancy and training services to nurture the growth of MSME in this region. The services may be in areas such as the preparation of a business plan for start-ups, quality management, strategic management, and training.

Table 8.01 Team Members and Responsibilities

Sl No.	Name	Location	Designation	Experience
1.	Milind Oak	Belgaum	Director, Strategy	Teaching, training, and consultancy
2.	Nitish Suntankar	Belgaum	CEO	Marketing, training, and consultancy
3.	Dilip Chitnis	Hubli	Director, Finance	Finance and accounting
4.	Nandan Murthy	Bangalore	Director, Marketing	Software development

Team The entrepreneurial team consists of Nitish Suntankar, CEO, who has 15 years of industrial experience, Milind Oak, Director of Strategy, Dilip Chitnis, Director of Finance, and Nandan Murthy, Director of Marketing and Business Development. Table 8.01 lists the team members and their responsibilities. The team members know each other and are also aware of the market conditions in the existing area.

Marketing The firm has already tested its services and received a good response in this area. It will also host promotional campaigns at local industrial exhibitions. The pricing is based on mutual agreement between the industry association and the team.

Company and Operations The team has tried out pilot projects in this area. It will be completely operational by May 2009. The operations will start from the existing office of the CEO who is presently providing consultancy services on ISO 9000 certification. Wherever there is a need for specialized knowledge, the firm may take the help of agencies from outside Belgaum on a one-to-one basis.

To begin with, the operations will start from Belgaum district and will be extended to other districts of North Karnataka such as Dharwad, Haveri, Gadag, and Uttar Kannada.

Finance Each member of the team will invest ₹100,000 from personal savings. Considering the ready market and good response from potential customers, revenues are expected to pick up once the project is launched.

Risks Similar solutions may spring up creating direct competition. But the firm will always have the advantage of being an early bird. Moreover, since all the members of the management team are from this area, there is good rapport and mutual trust between the local industries and members of the team.

Genesis India has a vibrant micro- and small-enterprises sector, which plays an important role in sustaining the economic growth. It has contributed around 39 per cent to the manufacturing output and 34 per cent to exports in 2004–05. It is the second-largest employer of human resources after agriculture, providing employment to around 2.95 crore people (2005–06) in the rural and urban areas of the country. Their significance in terms of fostering new entrepreneurship is well recognized. This is because most entrepreneurs start their business from a small unit, which provides them an opportunity to harness their skills and talents, to experiment, to innovate, and transform their ideas into goods and services, and finally nurture it into a larger unit.

As on 31 March 2008, Belgaum had 30,027 MSME registered with an investment of ₹500 crore and generating direct employment of 90,000. The district also has a foundry cluster. These units need consultancy and training services to nurture them at each stage of their entrepreneurial life cycle.

BUSINESS CONCEPT

What Is an MSME Clinic?

An MSME Clinic is the process of helping MSME to improve the overall performance of the units by identifying and analysing specific business problems that the organization is facing, to develop plans and strategies to overcome that problem, and to implement the strategies planned in these companies. The MSME Clinic covers a wide spectrum of areas including implementation of best practices, benchmarking, using analytical and statistical techniques for problem solving, the management of change, new technology implementation, and development of plans and strategies. An MSME Clinic suggests a more effective and efficient method for performing specific tasks in the business by introducing a framework or a methodology for identifying and analysing specific business problems. Clients can avail of the services of the MSME Clinic on account of the following reasons:

- The credibility of the team.
- The consulting approach—general and specific approach.
- The nature of the assignment contract—for a period or for a particular project.
- Client references.
- The competence of the organization.
- The competitive consulting fee.

The Future of the MSME Clinic An MSME Clinic is essentially helpful for business and non-business organizations that do not have an adequate knowledge pool in specific technology or domains. The organization helps in enhancing the business performance of the clients by closely studying the different business processes of an organization, thereby streamlining them, and helping to gain leverage on the resources of an organization. The role of the MSME Clinic has changed from being a mere advisor to an active participant in the implementation of the suggested plan by the consulting organization to achieve the desired results.

MANAGEMENT SUMMARY

Nitish Suntankar

Nitish Suntankar is a first-generation entrepreneur and the chief executive officer of this MSME Clinic. Nitish holds an industrial engineering degree from NITIE, Mumbai and a master's degree in management science from Pune University.

He has a rich experience of 15 years in the engineering industry. He started his career in Larsen & Toubro Limited (L&T), India's largest engineering and construction conglomerate, with additional interests in electrical, electronics, and IT. He worked at the Ahmednagar unit for four years and then was promoted to work at their Mumbai office for another four years.

He later joined Kirloskar Copeland, a joint venture by Kirloskar Brothers Limited and the Copeland Corporation of USA at Karad, Maharashtra. He worked at Kirloskar Copeland for four more years at various departments. He then joined Reva Electric Car Company. REVA is a battery operated electric vehicle designed for low speed, congested urban conditions, and is classified as a quadricycle (category L7e) under UK and European law. At REVA, Nitish worked with international teams for more than two years.

Later, due to family pressures, Suntankar came back to Belgaum and joined Ashoka Iron Works (AIW), a QS 9000 company at Belgaum, which is one of India's finest and most integrated jobbing foundries. Located 500 km south of Mumbai, and 150 km from Goa, the AIW Group has foundries and machine shops that add value, by machining over 60 per cent of the castings manufactured to a fully finished condition. Here he worked in the export marketing division for three years by virtue of his earlier international exposure.

Nitish Suntankar had always wanted to start something on his own. After 15 years of industrial experience in various departments such as quality, international business, manufacturing, marketing, purchasing, vendor development, logistics, and supply chain management, he decided to start his own consultancy firm at Belgaum. In 2005, he founded NVST–TQM Consultants at Belgaum as the sole proprietor. After three years, he felt the need to build a team as the business started growing.

In 2007, Suntankar came in contact with Milind Oak, a professor from a local business school, where he was teaching as a part-time faculty member. He, along with Milind Oak, Dilip Chitnis, a chartered accountant, and Nandan Murthy, a software engineer from Bangalore, founded the MSME Clinic in 2008 as a partnership firm. Nitish Suntankar will be working full-time for the firm.

Milind Oak

Milind Oak is a professor at a management institute located at Belgaum and has 25 years of experience in industry, consultancy, teaching, and administration. He has a bachelor's degree in engineering with a post-graduate degree in management from the University of Pune. He has conducted training, workshop, and consultancy assignments for several organizations such as TATA Motors, Pune, the Aditya Birla group of industries, Hindustan Latex Limited, and G-5 Solutions in the area of total quality management (TQM) and strategic management.

He is a fellow of the Institution of Engineers (India). He is the assessor for the CII-EXIM Bank Award for Business Excellence and the Ramkrishna Bajaj National Quality Award for Business Excellence of the Indian Merchants' Chamber. He is a recipient of the Association of Overseas Technical Scholarship (AOTS) and has visited Japan for workshops on TQM and strategic management.

Dilip Chitnis

Dilip Chitnis is an eminent academician and a chartered accountant having 25 years of experience in industry. He is a graduate in commerce, and a fellow of the Institute of Chartered Accountants of India. He holds a Ph.D. in the area of corporate governance. He will be working part-time for the firm.

Nandan Murthy

Nandan Murthy is a software development engineer with an experience of five years in the industry. He will be working part-time for the firm. Apart from the promoters, the firm also has an advisory board. The details of the members of the advisory board are furnished in Table 8.02.

Table 8.02 Advisory Board of MSME Clinic

Sl No.	Name	Organization	Experience
1.	Satya Narayana Chetty	Business Excellence Champion, Confederation of Indian Industries (CII) Bangalore.	30 years' experience in industry, retired as an Executive Director, BEL.
2.	Suresh Lulla	QIMPRO, Mumbai.	35 years' experience in industry. Associated with ASQ, advisor to Ramkrishna Bajaj Award Committee for business excellence.
3.	Naveen Jha	Director, Deshpande Foundation, Hubli.	10 years' experience with international exposure.
4.	Santosh Hurlikoppi	CEO, Infotech, USA.	10 years' industry experience in international business, Chairman of The Indus Entrepreneurs (TiE), Hubli Chapter.

BUSINESS STRATEGY

Strategy and Implementation Summary

Our strategy is simple—we intend to succeed by giving MSME differential business solutions. The strategy is to have a three-tier approach:

1. **Microenterprises:** To begin with, we had a meeting with the microenterprises association in Belgaum, which has a membership of 250. After a discussion with the office bearers, it was decided to have four days of training in a year, i.e. one day training per quarter in the area of kaizen, 5-S, quality, and productivity. Each enterprise will pay ₹250 per training programme excluding expenses. Presently, 50 units have agreed to pay ₹1,000 per annum for the training programme.
2. **Small enterprises:** The market survey conducted to identify the requirements of small enterprises reveal that there is a need for consultancy in various areas but mostly in the areas of kaizen, 5-S, quality certification, and business development. Business solutions may be offerred for a group of industries, for example, foundries, valves, textiles, and food processing among others.
3. **Medium enterprises**: The market surveys conducted to identify the requirements are diversified and are specific to the organization.

We have established a strong network with the Confederation of Indian Industry (CII), the foundry clusters, and the Chamber of Commerce and Industry. We have already provided services to the Aditya Birla Group, Harihar, Tata Motors, Pune, HLL, Sankeshwar, and many more. We receive business through existing customer referrals as well. We will host promotional campaigns at local industrial exhibitions and training programmes.

Sales and Pricing Strategy

As Tables 8.03–8.05 show, we intend to deliver sales of about ₹400,000 in the first year, and to increase it by four times in the second year of the plan. Unit rates are worked out based on the market survey in this area and mutual agreement between the industry association and the team.

Roll-out Plan

The MSME Clinic will be a part-time option with minimum fixed overheads in the first year. During the first year, we will be offering our services in Belgaum district. Once it becomes viable,

Table 8.03 Unit Sales Forecast

	2009	2010	2011	2012
Microenterprises	50	100	200	400
Small enterprises	50	100	200	400
Medium enterprises	10	20	35	50
Total unit sales	110	220	435	850

Table 8.04 Unit Prices

	2009 (PMD/Unit)	2010 (PMD/Unit)	2011 (PMD/Unit)	2012 (PMD/Unit)
Microenterprises	1,000	2,000	4,000	5,000
Small enterprises	5,000	10,000	15,000	20,000
Medium enterprises	10,000	20,000	30,000	40,000

Note: PMD/Unit: Per man days per unit.

Table 8.05 Total Sales

	2009	2010	2011	2012
Microenterprises	50 × 1,000 = 50,000	100 × 2,000 = 200,000	200 × 4,000 = 800,000	400 × 5,000 = 2,000,000
Small enterprises	50 × 5,000 = 250,000	100 × 10,000 = 1,000,000	200 × 15,000 = 3,000,000	400 × 20,000 = 8,000,000
Medium enterprises	10 × 10,000 = 100,000	20 × 20,000 = 400,000	35 × 15,000 = 525,000	50 × 20,000 = 1,000,000
Total sales	₹400,000	₹1,600,000	₹4,325,000	₹11,000,000

we will penetrate other districts, principally Dharwad. We are developing different tool kits to standardize our services. We have already tested our services and have received a good response in this area.

Key Success Factors

The MSME Clinic has identified the following key success factors:

- Establishing an efficient networking system with industry associations (CII, TiE, and the Chamber of Commerce and Industry).
- Developing innovative training tool kits.
- Offering cost-effective business solutions because of price-sensitive customers.
- Service differentiation.
- Identifying and inviting resource persons based on the need.

Competitive Strategy

Our service is differentiated by the value proposition that it offers to our customers. The MSME Clinic would follow a "Service Differentiation" strategy, portraying it as a service with value additions.

Competitive Advantage

We offer the following competitive advantages to our clients:

- Single-window approach.
- Cost-effective business solution.
- Client references.
- Service differentiation.
- Innovative training tool kit.

OPERATIONS PLAN

Operational Requirements

The consultancy services demand value-added services and differentiation. The demand for consultancy services ranges from preparing business plans for start-ups to business excellence (CII-EXIM Bank, Ramkrishna Bajaj National Quality Award), quality, productivity management, technology upgradation, kaizen, innovation, marketing, and training. The team has tried pilot projects in this area. It may have to be a part-time option, with minimum fixed overheads, before we can confirm the full-time potential.

Company Location and Facilities

The consultancy service demands high variety and service differentiation. The operations will start from the existing office of the CEO who is presently providing consultancy services on quality management systems. The office is strategically located in Bhagyanagar, which is near many industrial estates. Wherever there is a need for specialized knowledge, the company may take the help of some of the agencies from outside Belgaum on a one-to-one basis. Consulting is sold and purchased mainly by word-of-mouth, with relationships and previous experience being by far the most important factors.

The most important component of the operational plan is business solutions. A detailed list of services provided is given in Appendix A on Page 190. Apart from the services mentioned in Appendix A, external experts may be hired on a project-to-project basis depending on the requirement.

Manpower Planning

MSME Clinic is managed by working partners. To begin with, two business graduates have been hired and trained for promoting the MSME Clinic. As we upscale the business to different geographic areas, we will be increasing the manpower by one employee each year till 2011. The office will have a receptionist cum secretary to look after the day-to-day operations of the CEO's office. Table 8.06 shows the human resource plan for the business.

Upscaling To begin with, the operations will start from Belgaum district and will be extended to other districts of North Karnataka such as Dharwad, Haveri, Gadag, and Uttar Kannada.

MARKETING PLAN

Current Business Consulting Industry

The fortune of the business consulting industry is linked to the overall business and economic scenario. This industry has been growing at a rapid pace. There are three types of consulting organizations. Firstly, there are large and diversified consulting organizations that offer a wide variety of services to address business issues in various domains. Secondly, there are consulting organizations, which offer only general management consulting without any specialization in any specific industry. The third type consists of small firms, which address a specific industry or a technology.

In addition to the above, there are organizations that have internal consulting groups to address the consulting needs of the organization internally. This will help the organization to save paying hefty amounts of money to business consulting organizations as consulting fees, and to keep the corporate information contained in the privacy of the organization. These internal consulting groups are also helpful in closely working with and monitoring workgroups in the client organization.

Market Analysis

Belgaum district, the second largest in Karnataka in terms of geographical area, is growing into a vibrant economy. Its strategic location, connectivity, salubrious climate, huge natural resources, vast pool of human talent, cheap and skilled labour, educational facilities, and recreation facilities have lead the district towards phenomenal growth in the social, economical, industrial, and trade sectors.

Table 8.06 Human Resource Plan

	2009 (₹)	2010 (₹)	2011 (₹)
Receptionist cum secretary	12 × 5,000 = 60,000	12 × 6,000 = 72,000	12 × 7,000 = 84,000
Marketing executive	1 × 12 × 8,000 = 96,000	2 × 12 × 9,000 = 216,000	3 × 12 × 10,000 = 360,000
Marketing assistant	1 × 12 × 5,000 = 60,000	2 × 12 × 6,000 = 144,000	3 × 12 × 7,000 = 252,000

Belgaum has a high potential in terms of available resources and infrastructural facilities. The Government of Karnataka has conceived a new industrial promotional policy through which many incentives and concessions are offered to prospective entrepreneurs. The district has well-developed industrial areas and estates both in the government sector as well as in the cooperative sector.

Foundries

Belgaum has developed as an important centre for the manufacture of heavy machine tools. Foundries and units producing auto components are today flooding the international markets. Autonagar houses 1,200 auto-related industrial units, which manufacture auto components, crankshafts, and machine tools that act as ancillary units to large-scale enterprises. The Government of India recently approved a foundry cluster project costing ₹24.7 crore to improve the infrastructure and promote research and development. The booming automobile industry also accounts for a great leap in the foundry sector of Belgaum.

Sugar

Belgaum is popularly known as the "Sugar Bowl" of Karnataka with over 150,000 hectares of land being utilized for commercial production. The annual production of sugar amounts to 120,000 quintals with only 95 lakh tonnes being crushed annually out of the 140 lakh tonnes being grown. There is one mega unit supported by 14 medium and large industries with co-generation and distilleries. Many more projects are in the pipeline.

Textiles

Belgaum has established itself as an indigenous axis of the textile sector. Yarn processing, fabric processing, calendaring, silk reeling, twisting, hosiery, knitted garments, and t-shirts form Belgaum's export forte. With over 13,610 power looms and 4,546 handlooms, the sector employs 54,440 individuals. For more than five decades now, Belgaum has been known the world over for its distinctive Shahpur sarees. An enormous scope for investments distinguishes the textile sector in Belgaum.

Mineral Processing

Belgaum has a strong base of mineral resources with over 120,000 metric tonnes of aluminium nitrate, over 40,000 metric tonnes of dolomite, and over 45,000 metric tonnes of limestone supported by minor mineral stakes like silica, bauxite, china clay, and manganese ore. These huge resources are yet to be explored.

Agro and Food Processing

Belgaum produces over 40,000 tonnes of mango and over 43,000 tonnes of bananas every year. More than 13,100 tonnes of grapes are cultivated annually in a cumulative area of 714 hectares. Over 5,600 tonnes of citrus fruits are cultivated every year from a bed of over 245 acres. There is a wide scope for units engaged in pulp extraction, food processing, and wine packaging.

Dharwad District

Hubli is an important industrial centre in Dharwad district, with more than 1,000 established small and medium industries. There are machine tools industries, electrical industries, steel furniture, food products, rubber and leather industries, and tanning industries. Dharwad has gathered momentum with the establishment of K. E. C., Bhoruka Textile Mill, Universal Group of Industries, Microfinish Group, N. G. E. F., K. M. F., and the BDK Group of Industries known for the export of hydraulic valves.

The popular group of hotels, the Kamat Group, started off in this city. The IT Park is situated in the heart of the city and is promoted by the Government of Karnataka. The IT Department and KEONICS act as the nodal agency for maintaining and marketing the IT Park in Hubli. Sankalp

Semiconductor and Alpha Information Systems India Pvt. Ltd are well-known companies in the fields of software, semiconductors, and chip design currently operational in the BVB Engineering College campus. Software Technology Parks of India (Organization under the Dept of IT, Govt of India) has been operational from May 2001 and is located on the fourth floor of the IT Park, and provides data communication, industry promotion, and incubation services to the IT/ITES industry. The industry matrix of the North Karnataka region is given in Appendix B. The number of registered units are mentioned in the matrix.

Market Analysis

We have identified three market segments—microenterprises, small enterprises, and medium enterprises. We will be providing training only to microenterprises. The training will be provided in association with the local Chamber of Commerce and Industry, who will be facilitating the training programmes. Consultancy services will be provided for small and medium enterprises.

FINANCIAL PLAN

Start-up Costs and Sources of Funds

The start-up expenses are met by an initial investment of ₹200,000 by each of the promoters. The start-up expenses are given in Table 8.07.

The initial investment of ₹400,000 will be spent on setting up the office. The remaining amount of ₹400,000 will be used as working capital till the firm starts generating profits.

Operating Expenses

The operating expenses comprise salaries and wages; maintenance; telephone and postage; miscellaneous administrative overheads; marketing and advertising; conveyance; and rent.

Salaries and Wages This includes the salaries of the receptionist cum secretary, marketing executive, and the marketing assistant. All the staff will be on probation for a period of one year. Provident fund and other benefits will be provided to employees after they complete the probationary period. The details for 2009 are given in the following table.

Manpower	Total
Receptionist cum secretary	12 × 5,000 = ₹60,000
Marketing executive	1 × 12 × 8,000 = ₹96,000
Marketing assistant	1×12 × 5,000 = ₹60,000

Maintenance Maintenance includes expenses for cleaning, security, and housekeeping. This is estimated at ₹5,000 per month.

Table 8.07 Start-up Expenses

Item	Amount in ₹	Timing	Source of Funds
Purchase of office furniture	₹100,000	Start of business in March 2009	Promoter's source
Printing of brochure	₹100,000	April 2009	Promoter's source
Web site design and maintenance	₹50,000	May 2009	Promoter's source
Stationery and equipment	₹50,000	May 2009	Promoter's source
Printing of manuals	₹50,000	May 2009	Promoter's source
Miscellaneous expenses	₹25,000		Promoter's source
Pre-opening marketing costs	₹25,000	June 2009	Promoter's source
Total	₹400,000		

Telephone and Postage Telephone and postage expenses are estimated at ₹2,500 for the first month and ₹1,500 per month, subsequently.

Administrative Overheads Miscellaneous administrative expenses are estimated at ₹3,500 per month.

Marketing and Advertising Besides a start-up allocation of ₹25,000 for initial promotion, a provision of ₹2,000 per month is made from June 2009 to December 2009.

Travel and Conveyance A provision of ₹5,000 per month is made for travel and conveyance.

Rent The rent for the premises would be ₹7,000 per month.

Expansion as a Business Goal

Our overall goal is to sustain the MSME Clinic in Belgaum district and later expand our business to neighbouring districts such as Dharwad, Gadag, Haveri, and Uttar Kannada of the North Karnataka region.

Payback and Break-even Point

The payback and creation of surplus is one of the main attractions in this business. With low investment and quick assured revenue inflows given the membership nature of the business, the investment is paid back within a few months and cash surplus increases every month. It will take only four to five months to recover the investments.

Computation of Break-even Point The monthly fixed expenses are given in Table 8.08. The figures have been taken from the operational costs.

Projected sales for 2010: ₹1,600,000
Therefore, average monthly sales: –1,600,000/12 = ₹133,333
Costs of services for the first year: ₹160,000
Therefore, average monthly product costs: 160,000/12 = ₹13,333
Contribution: Sales – Product costs: 133,333 – 13,333 = ₹120,000
Contribution margin: 120,000/133,333 = 90%
Monthly break-even point: Monthly fixed cost/Contribution margin = 50,000/0.90 = ₹55,555
Break even as a percentage of sales: 55,555/133,333 = 41.66%
In the present scenario, the firm would be able to break even at revenues of ₹55,555.

Computation of Payback Period Payback period can be computed using the following formula:
Payback period = Initial investment including working capital/Cash flow
The cash flow can be calculated as shown in Table 8.09.
Initial investment including working capital: ₹800,000
Payback Period = 800,000/598,000
= 1.33 years

Table 8.08 Monthly Fixed Expenses

Monthly Fixed Expenses	Amount in ₹
Manpower	18,000
Maintenance	5,000
Telephone	1,500
Administration overheads	3,500
Marketing	2,000
Travel	5,000
Rent	7,000
Miscellaneous	8,000
Total	**50,000**

Table 8.09 Computation of Cash Flow

Income	1,600,000
Expenses	
Product costs	160,000
Other costs (50,000 × 12)	600,000
Profit before tax	**840,000**
Tax (30%)	252,000
Profit after tax	588,000
+Depreciation	10,000
Cash flow	598,000

The payback period of initial investment in capital (excluding working capital) can be calculated as follows:

Payback period = Initial investment/Cash flow
= 400,000/598,000
= Approximately 7 months

Tables 8.10–8.12 show the pro forma profit and loss statement, pro forma balance sheet, and pro forma cash flow statement from 2009 to 2012.

Table 8.10 Pro Forma Profit and Loss Statement

Sales	FY 2009	FY 2010	FY 2011	FY 2012
	400,000	1,600,000	4,325,000	11,000,000
Expenses				
Payroll	216,000	252,000	288,000	324,000
Marketing and other expenses	25,000	27,500	30,250	33,275
Stationary and equipment	50,000	55,000	60,500	66,550
Printing of brochure	100,000	75,000	50,000	30,000
Printing of manuals	50,000	55,000	60,500	66,550
Miscellaneous expenses	96,000	105,600	116,160	127,776
Telephone	18,000	19,800	21,780	23,958
Administration Overheads	42,000	46,200	50,820	55,902
Rent	84,000	92,400	101,640	111,804
Travel	60,000	66,000	72,600	79,860
Web site design and maintenance	50,000	30,000	30,000	30,000
Total operating expenses	791,000	824,500	1,927,250	949,675
Profit before interest and taxes	(391,000)	775,500	2,397,750	10,050,325
Taxes incurred	–	255,915	791,257	3,316,607
Net profit/Profit after tax	**(391,000)**	**519,585**	**1,606,492.5**	**6,733,717.75**

Table 8.11 Pro Forma Balance Sheet

	FY 2009	FY 2010	FY 2011	FY 2012
Assets				
Current assets				
Cash	172,700	458,412	1,181,100	2,510,628
Accounts receivable	200,000	946,173	1,415,392	4,217,344
Bank balance	518,100	515,000	610,000	1,705,745.75
Total current assets	890,800	1,919,585	3,206,492	8,433,717
Fixed assets	600,000	600,000	600,000	600,000
Total assets	1,490,800	2,519,585	3,806,492	9,033,717.75
Liabilities and capital				
Current liabilities				
Accounts payable	500,000	500,000	500,000	500,000
Subtotal current liabilities	500,000	500,000	500,000	500,000
Long-term liabilities	581,800	700,000	900,000	1,000,000
Total liabilities	1,081,800	1,200,000	1,400,000	1,500,000
Capital	800,000	800,000	800,000	800,000
Earnings	−391,000	519,585	1,606,492.5	6,733,717.75
Total capital	409,000	1,319,585	2,406,492.5	7,533,717.75
Total liabilities and capital	1,490,800	2,519,585	3,806,492.50	9,033,717.75

Table 8.12 Pro Forma Cash Flow Statement

	2009	2010	2011
Cash received			
Cash from operations			
Cash sales	400,000	1,600,000	4,325,000
Cash from receivables	200,000	946,173	1,415,392
Subtotal: cash from operations	600,000	2,546,173	5,740,392
Expenditures	**2009**	**2010**	**2011**
Expenditures from operations			
Bill payments	500,000	500,000	500,000
Subtotal: spend on operations	500,000	500,000	500,000
Additional cash spent			
Purchase other current assets	890,800	1,919,585	3,206,492
Purchase long-term assets	600,000	0	0
Subtotal: cash spent	1,490,800	1,919,585	3,206,492
Cash balance	172,700	458,412	1,181,100
Net cash flow	**−1,218,100**	**585,000**	**3,215,000**

APPENDICES

Appendix A: Particulars of Consultancy Services

Sl No.	Particulars of Consultancy Services
1.	Need-based training
2.	Strategic management
3.	Quality management
4.	Technology management
5.	Productivity management
6.	Financial management
7.	Company law
8.	Preparation of business plan
9.	Corporate governance
10.	Supplier management
11.	Human resource management
12.	Logistics and supply chain management

Appendix B: Number of Registered Units in the North Karnataka Region

Market Segment	Foundries	Sugar	Textiles	Mineral Processing	Agro and Food Processing	IT/ITES	Engineering
Micro	23,000		25,000	22,500	22,000	20,000	28,000
Small	25,000	1,800	24,000	24,500	24,000	14,250	25,000
Medium	1,000	1,500	15,000	12,000	18,000	20,000	30,000
Total	49,000	3,300	64,000	59,000	64,000	54,250	83,000

BUSINESS PLAN II: FRAGRANCE HOUSE

The following award-winning business plan was prepared by Rasika B. Kadolkar in 2012 on her venture, Fragrance House, as part of the Goldman Sachs "10,000 Women" programme. The initiative by Goldman Sachs and its academic partner, Indian School of Business, Hyderabad, is based on the premise that partnerships between education, development, and business experts can help bring about significant changes through improved business education for women. Over the last four years (2009–2013), more than 600 women entrepreneurs have successfully completed the 19-day free training programme across Bangalore, Delhi, Hyderabad, Mumbai, and Pune. The training is spread across various modules required to prepare a business plan. The modules include Finance, Marketing, Strategy, Human Resource, Operations, Administration, etc. The participants have access to business advisors, mentors, and representatives from financial institutions as they work to create actionable business plans.

TABLE OF CONTENTS

Sl No.	Contents
1.	Executive summary
2.	Introduction to the business
3.	Industry analysis
4.	Production strategy
5.	Marketing strategy
6.	Financial plan
7.	Organizational structure
8.	Competitive business strategy
9.	The path ahead

EXECUTIVE SUMMARY

Fragrance House manufactures and exports an enchanting range of perfumes and designer candles to an exhaustive clientele. Our product range is highly acclaimed in the national and international markets and have gained good acceptance among customers of diverse tastes and liking.

We consistently participate in nationwide exhibitions to gain client feedback and demonstrate the quality of our products. The quality of our products has led to our company receiving exposure in the country's renowned newspapers, magazines, and TV channels. We are committed to maintaining high standards of quality.

Our high business principles have helped us in catering to our clients' needs with augmented products and in reaching the desired heights of our output. We are catering to a diverse clientele; hence, we offer a spectrum of products that encompasses various types of designer candles and hand-blended perfumes.

Apart from this, we also offer gift sets/hampers of both the products in customized packaging as well. We offer customized perfumes and designer candles as per the client's requirements at reasonable prices.

Our enticing range has enabled us to cater to the demand of households, showrooms, shops, malls, clubs, restaurants, hotels, offices, associations, and corporate undertakings. We ensure that utmost client satisfaction is generated by our quality products. Customer satisfaction is our ultimate goal.

INTRODUCTION TO THE BUSINESS

Hand-blended Perfumes

We are a renowned manufacturer of hand-blended perfumes. Our hand-blended perfumes are a mixture of a natural blend of perfumes, essential oils, and resinous and aromatic chemicals along with absolute alcohol.

Our perfumes are unique. They are eco-friendly and blended with natural essential oils. They are long lasting, mild, refreshing, fashionable, and elegant. The distinctive feature of our perfumes is that they are exclusively prepared from natural raw materials and do not contain any chemicals. The perfumes are packaged in attractive packs and are available at very affordable prices. We also provide the facility of customization of packaging to the clients.

We create the perfect perfume for you, the perfect gift for your friends and for yourself. The one thing that we can't do, on paper or online, is to let you smell and feel the products. We can describe them as best as our limited imagination can manage. We can tell you all about the effects they have, what we put into them, and how much we love them, but you are always going to be missing a couple of sensory experiences.

Please believe us when we say that it is a wonderful experience and you are bound to be delighted. You will be happy to find yourself in a calming haze of essential oils. We are always there to help you to choose only the perfumes that will suit you the best. We want you to choose just what's good for you, and to come back as often as you like. We always do our very best to make you feel welcome with our range of products.

We believe in making our own fresh fragrances by hand, and printing and designing our packaging ourselves. We believe that our products should provide good value, that we should make a profit, and that the customer is always right.

Designer Candles

We excel in the manufacture of designer candles. These come in various shapes, designs, and colours. Whether you are looking for pillar, votive, or floating candles, our candles will definitely satisfy your taste and liking. Being one of the country's leading candle manufacturers, we can make different kinds of candles and meet wholesale requirements. We are also renowned for the customization of candles, since we provide designer candles according to client requirements. The special feature of our designer candles is the superior quality refined wax used in the manufacturing process. As a result, our candles are dripless, smokeless, have a long burning capacity, come in attractive colours, and are perfumed with aromatic oils. Our products are available in exquisite designs in a number of sizes with prompt delivery and at affordable prices.

The Process

We use 85 per cent ethanol, i.e. 100 per cent absolute alcohol as the main ingredient in the production process. The other ingredients that we add are fixenol, biscuit powder, and essence. These ingredients are processed as follows:

1. The ethanol is pumped with the help of stroke pumps through a tank (with a capacity of 10,000 litres) into a blending tank.
2. The other ingredients are also added into a blending tank, which has a capacity of 100 litres. The mixing process is done in the blending tank with the help of an agitator for six hours till the flavour matures. The finished product is then filtered and scanned through the inspection lab, which then flows automatically into the filling machine.
3. At this point, the product is poured into bottles of various sizes and the caps are sealed. The labelling and final packing completes the process.

The process flow is shown in Figure 8.03.

Entrepreneur's Background

Rasika Kadolkar was brought up in the city of Belgaum in Karnataka. Her father, a businessman, was her role model while she was growing up. She learnt from him never to give up and to be ready and open to new opportunities. Rasika completed her graduation in business management from G.C.C., Belgaum. Highly ambitious, she had always dreamed of starting her own independent business. At

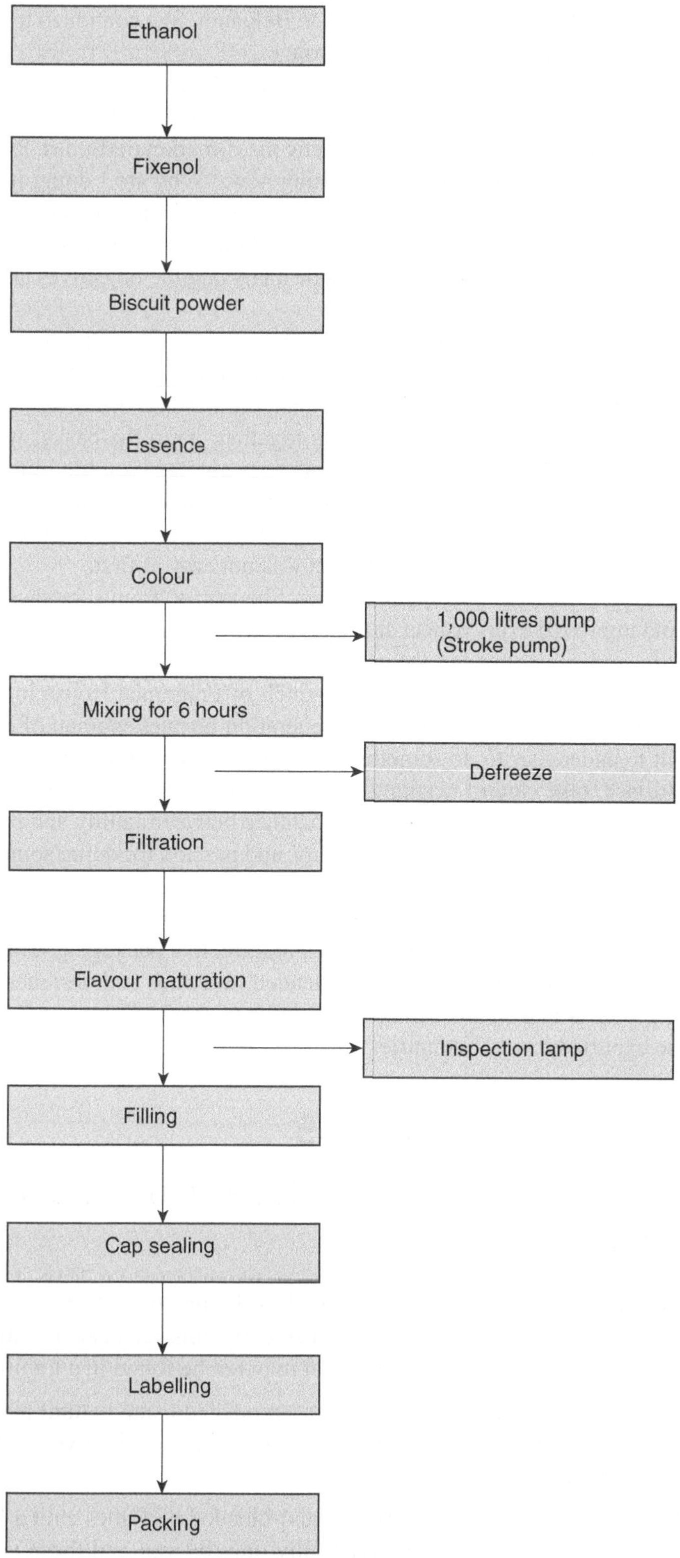

Figure 8.03 Process Flow Chart

21, Rasika got married to a businessman in Belgaum. She continued to pursue her interest in making candles and perfumes even after her marriage.

Later, due to certain personal circumstances, she had to convert her hobby into a business. She started making designer candles and handmade perfumes, which was her passion. She was not interested in making normal candles or synthetic mass-market perfumes. Rasika believes that one should ask three questions before starting anything new, "Why am I doing it, what will the results be and will I be successful? Only when you think deeply and find satisfactory answers to these questions, go ahead." More often, projects are started with huge investments without a clear idea of their feasibility and success rate. Rasika spent time analysing the objectives and scope of the project clearly before proceeding towards execution.

Rasika was very aware of changes in the market trend. She believed that "greeting cards and frames are old gifting options. They have their own significance, but the newest trend is aromatic designer candles and perfumes that suit many moods and occasions. Grab a basket, club perfumes, sparkling candles, and other accessories together, wrap the basket with a ribbon and your gift is ready to impress anyone. Besides, the gift does not cost you too much." Having a keen interest in perfumery, Rasika learnt the art of making and manufacturing hand-blended perfumes and designer candles, and underwent training for setting up a business. She then set up her manufacturing unit in Udyambag. However, selling the product was not easy at first.

This new world was a challenge to her. She started from scratch, studied the basics, and developed and improved every aspect at each step. Once you start working on something, don't be afraid of failure, and don't abandon the project. People who work sincerely will reach their goal. Rasika's love for aroma and art resulted in the launch of Fragrance House in 2005. Taking immense pride in her maiden venture, Rasika, a first-generation businesswoman of her family, recalls, "It is very difficult to endeavour to do something new and risky. Initially, I faced a lot of difficulties as I had to multi-task, take care of accounts, source materials, monitor the manufacturing process, and the marketing efforts. Trying to maintain a balance between family and business was a great challenge for me. But my confidence, creative ability, and passion for doing something independently kept me growing. Thankfully, my family was very supportive."

Rasika continues, "I learnt that candles are good luck charms and very popular as gifts. This encouraged me to develop designer candles in attractive packaging. Fragrance House today prepares a wide and customized range of hand-blended perfumes and designer candles, colognes, and other related products like air fresheners and fragrance beads. These products are not only sold here, but are also exported to other countries."

INDUSTRIAL ANALYSIS

A Comparison: Hand-blended Perfumes and Traditional Perfumes

- Hand-blended essential oils are rooted in the practice of aroma therapy. This means that surrounding yourself with hand-blended essential oils can heal your mind and body, and give you a feeling of comfort and tranquility that may not be found in a traditional perfume.
- Since most hand-blended perfumes are produced using natural materials, they are 100 per cent free of synthetic oil fragrances. They also do not contain dyes and other chemicals that can be potentially dangerous to the skin.
- The smell is rarely overpowering. Hand-blended perfumes emit a fragrance that others are only slightly aware of, and are enjoyed fully only by you and those you choose to have extremely close to you.
- Since hand-blended oils are considered to be fairly high in ion concentration, they need to be used only in small amounts.

Why Hand-blended Perfumes?

Our perfumes are preferred over synthetic perfumes because:

- They do not contain skin-drying alcohol.
- They are very long lasting on your skin and in the bottle.
- They are very concentrated—you need only a little for maximum impact.
- They do not burn or irritate normal skin. They are made for body use.
- They contain natural perfumes. These are a great bargain when compared to store-bought perfumes, which are mostly alcohol. Why pay big for cheap alcohol when all you really want is the perfume essence?
- They are a fun way to have an extensive fragrance wardrobe for very little money compared to store bought perfumes or colognes.
- They contain pure fragrance oils that are hand-blended with moisturizing, odourless base oils. So the scent is not compromised in any way.
- They are packaged in the perfect size for purses, travel, and for use on the go.

Why Designer Candles?

Our candles are popular because:

- They come in various shapes, designs, and colours.
- They are made of superior quality refilled wax.
- They are dripless, smokeless, and have a long burning capacity.
- They are infused with aroma oils, which also act as a mosquito repellent.

The Venture

Industry Overview The size and growth rate of this industry at present is 30 per cent. This industry will continue to grow robustly as there are immense opportunities for growth. Our goal is to grow and focus on developing products that provide complete customer satisfaction.

Vision Our vision is to manufacture innovative products without losing sight of our values. We aspire to do business in a transparent and ethical manner.

Mission Our mission is to grow in the industry by developing innovative products that satisfy customers.

Objectives We work towards achieving the following objectives:

- Increasing monthly sales steadily throughout.
- Building trust and a strong brand image.
- Expanding services/production.
- Achieving a gross margin higher than 50 per cent on the products.
- Improving the profit margin by 50–60 per cent.
- Manufacturing creative and innovative products.
- Doing better than the competitors.
- Sustaining the venture by following competitive strategies.

PRODUCTION STRATEGY

Our production plant is located in the industrial estate in Belgaum. The location has been sanctioned as the most suitable for the plant after an on-site inspection by various officials and experts from various departments such as the DIC and MSME, fire fighting, pollution, and excise. Many safety measures have been undertaken as our product is a hazardous product. We have also obtained certifications from various government departments that our processes comply with all specified regulations.

The Plant

The plant consists of a storage tank, a blending tank, and a volumetric bottle-filling machine. The total space required for the plant is approximately 200 sq. ft, which includes the open space for a storage tank with a capacity of 3,000 litres. The other sections include:

1. The security enquiry booth.
2. Front office—receiving centre for customers and delivery office for finished products.
3. Office for finished products.
4. Office rooms—proprietors' office, R&D section, formulation, and testing.
5. Blending room—space for mixing and blending.
6. The cold storage room—space for maturing the perfume after blending.
7. Workshop—space where bottles are filled, labelled, and packaged in a completely air-conditioned environment.
8. Warehouse—used to store the finished and packed goods/products.
9. Fire equipment blocks at specified places.

Labour Requirements

A total of five labourers have been hired at present. Of these, two are skilled labourers who have been trained to handle the machinery and manage the process. The other three semi-skilled labourers assist in the manufacturing process. More labourers will be hired/outsourced if there is an increase in the demand.

Inventory Management

The capacity required is fixed and approved by the Excise Department. Inventory is stored in the storage tank (capacity of 3,000 litres) in an open space with security. The Excise Department maintains the key. The quantity of inventory utilized is measured every month by officials of the department. The orders have to be taken and adjusted accordingly. The finished goods are stored in the warehouse and have to be dispatched immediately according to the orders received.

MARKETING STRATEGY

Target Customers

The customers we target are evaluated in terms of age, gender, educational qualification, income level, ambition, and aspiration in life. Among our target customers are consumers, distributors, retailers, superstockists, shops, direct sellers (exhibitions), hotels, malls, organizations, social media (online) wholesalers, clubs, schools/colleges, students, churches, corporation, and marketing representatives.

Need Fulfillment We practise two methods of need fulfillment, i.e. identifying the need and creating the need.

- We carried out a survey to identify the need. We got to know that customers are aware of the different brands of perfumes and candles available in the market.
- We created a need, i.e. we represented our products as exceptional, unique, and different. We disseminated information about hand-blended perfumes and designer candles to create a need.
- We listened to people by taking feedback. The resultant material was analysed with empathy. Feasible changes were incorporated according to the desire of the consumer and delivered.
- We cater to a varied customer base through the following marketing channels:
    - **Word-of-mouth publicity:** Demand was generated through word-of-mouth publicity.
    - **Small social groups:** Friends, students, and customers selling to customers.
    - **Networking:** Various associations, clubs, organizations, churches, vendors, hotel boutiques.
    - **Direct selling through exhibitions:** The immediate feedback was received, implemented, and improvised.
    - **Sales executives:** Marketing representatives collected orders and delivery was made in the stipulated time in Karnataka.
    - **Superstockists:** They approached us.
    - **Direct distributors:** Selling the product directly in different regions.
    - **Retailing:** Various shops and malls approached us.
    - **Social media**: We created our own Web site, and registered in portals like Alibaba, Indiamart, and Yellow Pages.

Our marketing strategy is a simple one: Satisfied customers are our best marketing tool. Our purpose is achieved when customers are happy and have got what they want.

Pricing Strategy

The pricing strategy is based on market surveys. It is different for different areas, locations, states, and countries. The terms and conditions described are different and the products are liable to accrue taxes and excise.

The firm has built its reputation by focusing on quality and its pricing reflects this professional image. The general strategy is to tailor the pricing to the "Cream of the Crop."

Promotional Strategy

As it is a new product, customer awareness about hand-blended perfumes is low. Therefore, live demonstrations have to be performed and aspects of quality, pricing, and differentitaion need to be explained.

Our promotional strategy comprises the following areas:

- Direct selling by word of mouth.
- Selling through exhibitions, showing live demonstrations, taking feedback, implementing, and improvising.
- Introducing pouch strategy—packing in 10 ml and 3 ml bottles.
- Introducing one-day perfumes in hotels.
- Selling through social groups and marketing persons.

- Samples sent to various superstockist distributors.
- Sponsoring events.
- Advertising in newspapers, social media, and television.
- Encouraging customer-to-customer selling.
- Distributing brochures and pamphlets to customers.
- Microfinancing and giving commissions.

Packaging

Packaging plays a very important role in our business. Presentation adds a lot of value in the case of luxury products such as perfumes and candles. We provide customized packaging as per customer needs.

FINANCIAL PLAN

Fixed Capital

The fixed capital requirements are given in Table 8.13.

Table 8.13 Fixed Capital

Particulars	Amount
Fixed capital	
1. Land and building	Rented
2. Machinery	372,900
3. Preoperative expenses (Interior security arrangements)	50,000
Working capital	577,100
Means of finance	1,000,000
Margin money (proprietor's share: 25%)	250,000
Loan from bank (75%)	750,000
Total	**1,000,000**

Break-even Analysis

The break-even analysis is shown in Table 8.14.

Daily Production Schedule/Sales and Inventory Forecast

The daily production schedule and the sales and inventory forecast is shown in Table 8.15.

Financial Policy

The highlights of the financial policy are:

- Taxes: Extra as applicable.
- Payment mode: 50 per cent in advance and 50 per cent against delivery.

Table 8.14 Break-even Analysis

	2007	2008	2009	2010
Sales	2,010,000.00	2,060,000.00	2,121,800.00	2,391,800.00
Less: Variable expenses				
Materials	320,000.00	329,600.00	339,488.00	389,088.00
labour	500,000.00	515,000.00	530,450.00	545,450.00
Variable overheads	125,000.00	128,750.00	132,612.50	186,362.50
Others	0.00	0.00	0.00	
Contribution margin	**1,065,000**	**1,086,650**	**1,119,250**	**1,120,900.5**
Contribution margin ratio	**52.99%**	**52.75%**	**52.75%**	**46.86%**
Fixed expenses				
Salaries and wages	190,000.00	190,000.00	190,000.00	190,000.00
Employee benefits	50,000.00	51,500.00	53,045.00	54,545.00
Payroll taxes	30,000.00	30,900.00	31,827.00	32,727.00
Rent	5,000.00	5,150.00	5,304.50	5,454.50
Utilities	3,000.00	3,090.00	3,182.70	3,272.70
Repairs and maintenance	1,000.00	1,030.00	1,060.90	1,060.90
Insurance	1,000.00	1,030.00	1,060.90	1,060.90
Travel	2,133.00	2,196.99	2,262.90	2,262.90
Telephone	11,000.00	11,330.00	11,669.90	12,669.90
Postage	4,000.00	4,120.00	4,243.60	4,243.60
Office supplies	6,000.00	6,180.00	6,365.40	6,365.40
Advertising	1,000.00	1,030.00	1,060.90	1,060.90
Marketing/promotion	3,000.00	3,090.00	3,182.70	3,182.70
Professional fees	1,000.00	1,030.00	1,060.90	1,060.90
Training and development	1,000.00	1,030.00	1,060.90	1,060.90
Bank charges	1,000.00	1,030.00	1,060.90	1,060.90
Depreciation	1,000.00	1,030.00	1,060.90	1,060.90
Interest expense	6,000.00	6,000.00	6,000.00	6,000.00
Other	0.00	0.00	0.00	0.00
Total fixed expenses	**317,133**	**320,767**	**324,510**	**328,150**
Total fixed expenses ratio	**15.78%**	**15.57%**	**15.29%**	**13.72%**
Break-even sales	**598,533**	**608,089**	**615,185**	**700,213**
Break-even percentage	**29.78%**	**29.52%**	**28.99%**	**29.27%**
Operating profit	**747,867**	**765,883**	**794,740**	**792,750**

Table 8.15 Sales and Inventory Forecast

Sl No.	Daily Production Schedule				Sales and Inventory Forecast				
	Product Description	Qty in Units	Base Material in Litres	Other Material in Litres	Sale in Units Per Day	Qty in Stock Per Day	Sale in Units Per Month	Qty in Stock Per Month	Sale in Units Per Year
1.	10 ml	600	6	0.9	500	100	15,000	3,000	180,000
2.	15 ml	700	10.5	1.575	650	50	19,500	1,500	234,000
3.	20 ml	200	4	0.6	150	50	4,500	1,500	54,000
4.	30 ml	500	15	2.25	400	100	12,000	3,000	144,000
5.	60 ml	500	30	4.5	450	50	13,500	1,500	162,000
6.	100 ml	350	35	5.25	300	50	9,000	1,500	108,000
7.	150 ml	0	0	0	0	0	0	0	0
8.	200 ml	0	0	0	0	0	0	0	0
9.	Wastage (3% of usage)		3.015						
10.	Evaporation per day (0.25% of stock; Stock 500 litres)		1.25						
11.	Non-usable quantity (20 litres)		20						
Total requirement/Per day			124.765	15.075	2,450	400	73,500	12,000	882,000
Total requirement/Per month			3119.125	376.875					
Total requirement/Per quarter			9357.375	1130.625					
Total requirement/Per annum			37429.5	4522.5					

- F.O.R. with 25–30 days.
- No claim for shortage, damage, or leakage will be entertained after the goods leave our premises.
- Interest will be charged at 24 per cent per annum if the bill is not paid on presentation.
- Goods once sold will not be taken back.

ORGANIZATIONAL STRUCTURE

The organizational structure is shown in Figure 8.04.

Legal Requirements

The following legal requirements are to be fulfilled before starting this business:

- Licensing from the Karnataka Directorate of Industries and Commerce to be acquired.
- License from the Government of Karnataka Fire and Emergency Service Academy, Bangalore, to be taken.

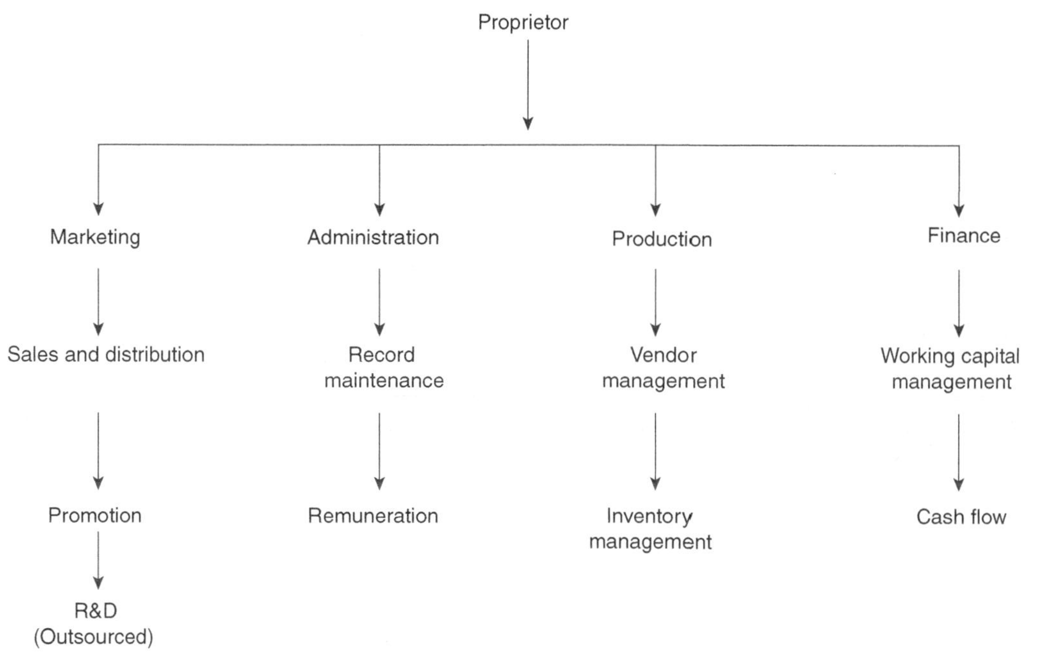

Figure 8.04 Organizational Structure

- License for the possession and use of ethanol (including 100 per cent absolute alcohol) for industrial purposes, according to the provisions of the Karnataka Excise Act, 1965, to be taken from the deputy commissioner.
- License from the Karnataka State Pollution Control Board to be acquired.
- Joint inspection certificate from the DIC and MSME for the allotment of ethanol (100 per cent absolute) to be acquired.
- Certificate to be acquired from the Ministry of MSME on attending training-cum-workshop in essential oil perfumery and aromatherapy.

COMPETITIVE BUSINESS STRATEGY

Analysis of Industry Structure (Porter's Five Forces)

- **Threat of new entrants:** The threat is minimal in the case of hand-blended perfumes as it is a unique product and formulated with unique ingredients. But the concept can be adopted. Since license facility is available, this product can be adopted and developed.
- **Threat of substitute products:** In case of perfumes, substitute products can be marketed using attractive packaging. For candles, the designs can be copied and reproduced in low quality wax.
- **Power of supplies:** The design is not delivered if the quantity is low. Once the purpose/design is set, the demand from suppliers increases.
- **Power of buyers:** Different terms and conditions for different regions make it difficult to set a price but there is always scope for bargaining power with buyers.
- **Rivalry among existing players:** There are no competitors as of now but there may be in the future. Such a situation will lead to revisions in price, concept, and design.

SWOT Analysis

Table 8.16 gives the SWOT analysis for the venture.

Table 8.16 SWOT Analysis for Fragrance House

Strengths	Opportunities
Highly unique and innovative product. Bulk production is possible. Customization, gift hampers, giving value, variety. Resources—modern equipment, latest technology, good communication skills, manpower, innovation. Brand enjoys a good reputation in the market. Support from the government.	Little/no competition. Existence of a global market. Scope to diversify into more innovative products. Large varied market. We can apply our strength to packaging/productivity. Customer needs are changing. Time saving availability of labour.
Weaknesses	**Threats**
Presentation of product difficult due to the variety of products. Competitors have introduced better product designs. Enquiry feedback is slow.	Customers want the product they have always used. Thus, alternative products are preferred. Obsolescence of technology. Government regulations.

THE PATH AHEAD

There are a lot of opportunities for growth in the rapidly expanding national and international markets. We need to focus on marketing through the social media, expand the production capacity for both candles and perfumes, and focus on product development. Our goal is to just grow and continue growing.

New Venture Creation

6. Identification of Business Opportunities
7. Project Management and Financing
8. Business Plans
9. Institutions Supporting Business Enterprises
10. Business Organizations and Business Laws

"There is always plenty of capital for those who can create practical plans for using it."

—Napoleon Hill

The Wadhwani Centre for Entrepreneurship Development is a Centre of Excellence at the Indian School of Business, Hyderabad. The WCED was funded in 2001 by the Wadhwani Foundation (a philanthropic institution) founded by Ramesh Wadhwani, the Silicon Valley-based entrepreneur. The Centre directs its energy and resources towards creating an effective entrepreneurial ecosystem that facilitates entrepreneurs to become an integral part of the global economy. Under the able leadership of its Executive Director, Krishna Tanuku, the WCED focuses on creating an effective and holistic ecosystem for broad-based entrepreneurial development in India. Dr Tanuku's mission is to promote purposeful entrepreneurship that fosters equitable socioeconomic growth in the country.

Institutions Supporting Business Enterprises

9

LEARNING OBJECTIVES

Upon completion of this chapter, you should be able to:

1. **Identify the central-level institutions/agencies supporting business enterprises.**
2. **Discuss the state-level institutions/agencies supporting business enterprises.**
3. **Explain various other agencies supporting business enterprises.**

INTRODUCTION

Many enterprises start small and many entrepreneurs in MSME need an institutional support system for guidance, support, and mentoring at different stages of business development. Most of the enterprises need support at the pre-start up, start-up, development, and growth phase. An entrepreneur should be aware of governmental and non-governmental support systems available for his enterprise. This chapter deals with these organizations, which play a supportive role for the development of enterprises in India.

A number of support institutions set up by the central and state governments and various other agencies help entrepreneurial development in various ways. The activities of support institutions cover a wide range of services such as financing, equipment support, technical assistance, training, marketing, and providing subsidy and grants. The various institutions supporting entrepreneurial activities in India (also shown in Figure 9.1) are given below:

1. **Central-level institutions**: Central-level institutions for supporting entrepreneurial activities are set up by the Central Government. These are: National Board for Micro, Small, and Medium Enterprises (NBMSME); Khadi and Village Industries Commission (KVIC); Coir Board; Micro Small Medium Enterprises Development Organisation (MSME–DO); National Small Industries Corporation (NSIC); National Science and Technology Entrepreneurship Development Board (NSTEDB); National Productivity Council (NPC); Entrepreneurship Development Institutes (EDI); National Research Development Corporation of India (NRDCI); and National Entrepreneurship Development Institutes.
2. **State-level institutions:** The state-level institutions for supporting entrepreneurial activities are set up by the various state governments in India. These are: State Directorate of Industries; District Industries Centres (DIC); State Financial Corporations (SFC); State Industrial Development Corporation (SIDC); and State Industrial Area Development Board (SIADB)
3. **Other institutions**: Apart from central and state-level institutions, there are various other institutions supporting entrepreneurial activities in India. These are: National Bank for Agriculture and Rural Development (NABARD); Housing and Urban Development Corporation (HUDCO);

Figure 9.1 Institutional Support for Enterprises

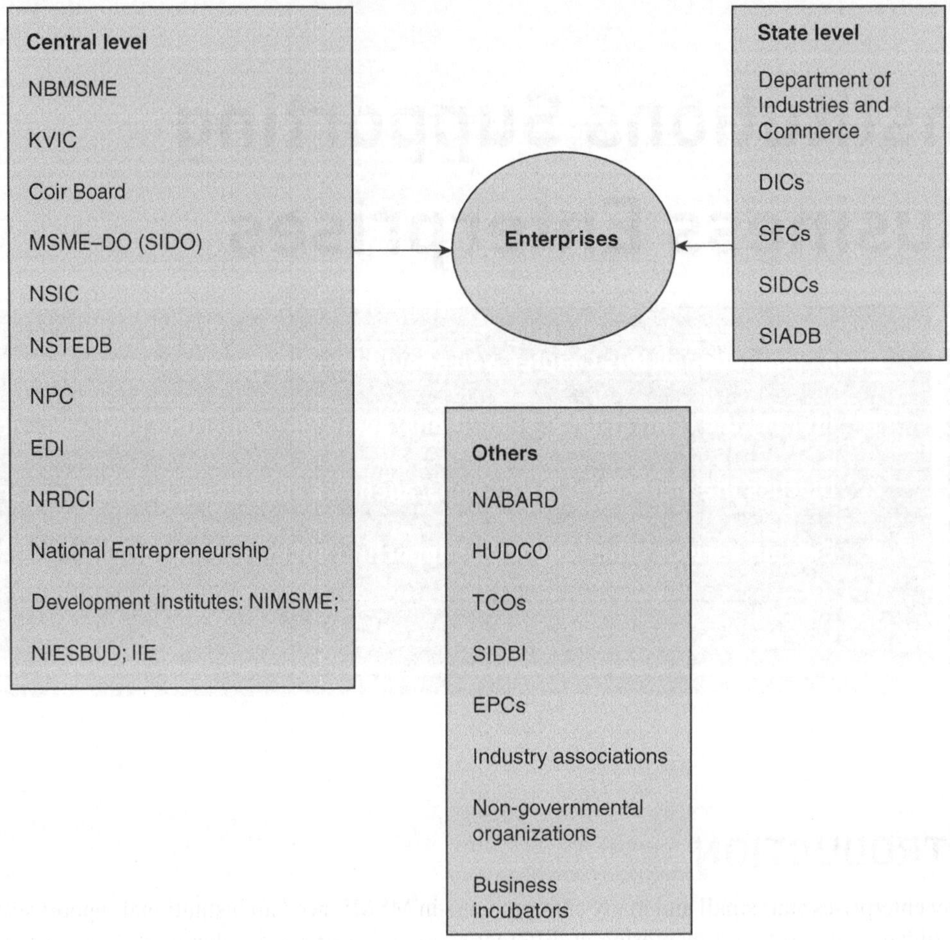

Technical Consultancy Organizations (TCOs); Small Industries Development Bank of India (SIDBI), Export Promotion Council (EPC); Industry Associations; Non-Governmental Organizations (NGOs); and Business Incubators.

CENTRAL-LEVEL INSTITUTIONS

National Board for Micro, Small, and Medium Enterprises (NBMSME)

The National Board for Micro, Small, and Medium Enterprises (NBMSME)[1] was constituted in 2007 in pursuance of the MSME Development Act, 2006, to facilitate the coordination and inter-institutional linkages for the development of MSME. The Board has a statutory backing and is an apex advisory body constituted to render advice to the government on all issues pertaining to the MSME sector.

The Office of the Development Commissioner (MSME) serves as the secretariat for the Board. The Union Minister of Commerce and Industry is the chairman of the Board. The NBMSME comprises 50 members including state industry ministers; select members of Parliament; secretaries of various departments of the Central Government; financial institutions; public-sector undertakings; industry associations; and eminent experts in the field as members.

The Board examines the factors affecting the promotion and development of MSME and advises the Central Government to facilitate their promotion and development in order to enhance competitiveness. The Board broadly operates in areas such as policies and programmes; the development of industries in a specific region such as the North East; ancillary development; quality improvement and marketing assistance; credit facilities, taxation and modernization; and industrial sickness.

The Khadi and Village Industries Commission (KVIC)

The Khadi and Village Industries Commission (KVIC)[2] is a statutory body established by an Act of Parliament (No. 61 of 1956). KVIC functions under the administrative control of the Ministry of Micro, Small, and Medium Enterprises, Government of India. The primary objective of KVIC is to provide employment to rural artisans through production of saleable products and to create self-reliance in order to build a strong rural community spirit.

Mahatma Gandhi started khadi and village industries to rejuvenate the rural economy as part of the freedom struggle. Khadi products are hand-spun and hand-woven. The spinning and weaving process creates opportunities for employment for a large number of spinners and weavers in rural India. More than 80 per cent among them are women. KVIC has been promoting the use of eco-friendly organic cotton and natural dyes. It deals with traditional rural industries such as pottery, leather, hand-made paper, non-edible oil, soap, and the processing of cereals and soaps. Due to the rigorous efforts of KVIC, *khadi*, which was seen as a cloth worn by the common man, has become glamorous.

The KVIC is entrusted with the task of planning, organizing, implementing, and promoting various programmes for the development of *khadi* and other village industries in rural areas. The Commission provides financial assistance to institutions and individuals for the development of these industries and for guiding them through the supply of designs, prototypes, and other technical information. It also creates common service facilities for the processing of raw materials and facilitates the marketing of the products through cooperative efforts.

The Government of India has taken a number of steps to promote exports of khadi and village industries products. The designs are being improved upon in collaboration with premier institutions like the National Institute of Design (NID) and the National Institute of Fashion Technology (NIFT). In September 2010, KVIC received a funding of $1,500 lakh from the Asian Development Bank (ADB) under a three-year ADB programme. Under this programme, 300 institutions will be provided ₹1.19 crore each to undertake reforms at all levels. KVIC has promoted cluster development to meet market demands and the taste of all classes of consumers within and outside the country. During the Eleventh Five-Year Plan, ending 31 March 2012, KVIC has granted funds to selected clusters for the regeneration of village industries.

KVIC has embarked on various initiatives to promote khadi and village industries in rural India. Some of these are the Prime Minister's Employment Generation Programme (PMEGP); Rural Employment Generation Programme (REGP); Scheme of Fund for Regeneration of Traditional Industries (SFURTI), Rural Industry Service Centres (RISC); the export incentive scheme; and the interest subsidy scheme. KVIC also has taken various steps towards the welfare of artisans. The Khadi Karigar Janashree Bima Yojana (JBY), a group insurance scheme, aims at enhancing the productivity and competitiveness of the khadi industry and artisans. The Workshed Scheme for Khadi Artisans is an attempt to facilitate the development of khadi artisans by providing them financial assistance on a pilot basis for the construction of worksheds.

The Coir Board

The Coir Board is a statutory body established by the Government of India for the promotion and development of the coir industry under the Coir Industry Act[3], 1953, enacted by the Parliament. This is one of the oldest traditional industries. It generates value out of waste by providing eco-friendly products that generate large-scale employment and contribute to around ₹600 crore worth of exports annually. The Coir Board has constituted various committees for implementing various functions such as the executive committee; the research and development committee; the export promotion committee; the marketing and publicity committee; the brown fibre development committee; and the Hindustan advisory committee.

The Central Coir Research Institute, established in 1959, is the prime research centre of the Coir Board. It is recognized by the Department of Science and Technology, Government of India. The Central Institute of Coir Technology is a research institute of the Coir Board established in 1979. It is an autonomous body, which undertakes research in the utilization of brown coir fibre. These research institutes formulate Indian standards for coir products and provide extension services and technical assistance to coir entrepreneurs. The Coir Board established the National Coir Training and Design Centre in 1965 for developing skilled manpower for the coir industry. The Coir Board also established Hindustan Coir in 1968. Hindustan Coir promotes the mechanization of the coir industry on modern lines.

The Government of India has embarked upon various initiatives for the rejuvenation, modernization, and technological upgradation of the coir industry. These are: Scheme of Fund for Regeneration of Traditional Industries (SFURTI); skill upgradation and quality improvement scheme; science and technology scheme; export market promotion scheme; domestic market promotion scheme; trade and industry related functional support services scheme; and welfare measures scheme. In order to promote market development and the welfare of coir artisans, the Coir Board has promoted schemes such as the marketing development assistance scheme and personal accident insurance scheme for coir workers.

MSME–DO

The Office of the Development Commissioner, Ministry of Micro, Small, and Medium Enterprises,[4] Government of India (DC–MSME) is a nodal agency for formulating, coordinating, and monitoring the policies and programmes for the promotion and development of MSME in the country. Micro, Small, and Medium Enterprises–Development Organization (MSME–DO) is the apex body for assisting the government in formulating, coordinating, implementing, and monitoring policies and programmes for the promotion and development of MSME in the country. MSMEDO provides a comprehensive range of common facilities, technology and support services, marketing assistance, and entrepreneurial development support to MSME.

MSME–DO has over 60 offices and 21 autonomous bodies under its management. The autonomous bodies include tool rooms, training institutions, and project-cum-process development centres. The MSME–DO offers advice to the Central Government in policy formulation and provides liaison services between different institutions for the promotion and development of the MSME sector.

MSME–DO has a network of 30 MSME development institutes, 28 branch MSME development institutes, four MSME testing centres, and seven MSME field-testing stations. There are also two MSME departmental training institutes and one departmental MSME hand-tools development centre. These institutes conduct consultancy, training, and provide common facility services to MSME.

MSME has initiated various schemes for the promotion of the MSME sector in India. These are: Small Enterprise Information and Resource Network; entrepreneurship development programmes; management training programmes; WTO cells; motivation campaigns; skill-development programmes; and initiatives for environmental control. MSME–DO has a library at its headquarters at Nirman Bhawan, New Delhi, and at all its field institutes in the country. These libraries are valuable repositories of information and are maintained with the objective of providing information for entrepreneurs so that they might get to know about new developments taking place in the industrial and business environment.

National Small Industries Corporation (NSIC)

This is a Government of India enterprise under the Ministry of Micro, Small, and Medium Enterprises (MSME). The NSIC[5] work towards the growth of micro, small, and medium enterprises in the country. The NSIC has obtained ISO 9001–2008 certification and operates through a countrywide network of offices and technical centres. In order to manage its operations in African countries it has set up an office at Johannesburg in South Africa. The NSIC provides a package of services and various schemes to support MSME in the country. These schemes comprise facilitating market support, credit support, technology support, and other support services.

The NSIC has devised a number of schemes such as consortia and tender marketing; single-point registration for government purchase; B2B web portal for marketing; marketing intelligence; exhibition and technology fairs; export; and buyer–seller meets to support MSME in their marketing efforts. The NSIC facilitates the credit requirements of MSME by providing financial assistance for the procurement of raw materials for up to 90 days; finance through syndication with banks; and facilitating import of scarce raw materials. In order to evaluate the strengths and weaknesses of existing operations and to take corrective and preventive actions, the NSIC has started operating a performance and credit rating scheme through empanelled agencies such as ICRA, ONICRA, CRISIL, Fitch, CARE, Brickwork Ratings, and SMERA. The NSIC offers various support services through its technical services centres and extension centres located at various places in India.

Due to its consistent good performance, the NSIC has received various accolades and awards. The Government of India has accorded it the "Mini Ratna" status, which will give the NSIC a higher degree of autonomy to provide greater service through its innovative schemes for the growth and development of the MSME sector in the country. Other awards received by the NSIC are Icon of the Year, Meri Dilli, Small Business Mentor of the Year, and the FSIA–V. B. Gulati Award.

National Science and Technology Entrepreneurship Development Board (NSTEDB)

This is a Government of India enterprise under the Ministry of the Department of Science and Technology. The NSTEDB[6] was established in the year 1982 with the primary objective of promoting self-employment among the science and technology (S&T) manpower in the country and to set up knowledge-based and innovation-driven enterprises. The NSTEDB has representation from socioeconomic and scientific departments, ministries, premier entrepreneurship development institutions, and all-India financial institutions.

The NSTEDB promotes and develops technology entrepreneurs, and facilitates and conducts various informational services relating to the promotion of entrepreneurship. The NSTEDB networks with various central and state government agencies for S&T-based entrepreneurship development. The Board acts as a policy advisory body with regard to entrepreneurship. The NSTEDB aims to convert "job-seekers" into "job-creators" and "job-providers" through S&T interventions.

The NSTEDB has instituted various initiatives to promote knowledge-based and innovation-driven enterprises. It generates employment through technical skill development using the science and technology infrastructure. Some of the main initiatives are the institutional mechanism for promoting entrepreneurship, training programmes, and information dissemination. Institutional support is provided through the Innovation and Entrepreneurship Development Centre (IEDC); the Science and Technology Entrepreneurship Development (STED) project; the Science and Technology Entrepreneurs Park (STEP); and the Technology Business Incubator (TBI).

The NSTEDB conducts various training programmes through Entrepreneurship Development Cells. The various training programmes conducted by the Board are Entrepreneurship Awareness Camp (EAC), Entrepreneurship Development Programme (EDP), and Faculty Development Programme (FDP) focusing on the entrepreneurship domain, and the Technology-based Entrepreneurship Development Programme (TEDP). The Board publishes a magazine titled *Science Tech Entrepreneur* and has hosted a Web portal named "TIME IS" for the dissemination of information for promoting entrepreneurs. Some of the major activities undertaken by NSTEDB are elaborated on this Web portal.

National Productivity Council (NPC)

The National Productivity Council (NPC) is a national-level organization established as a registered society in 1958 by the Government of India. NPC[7] is an autonomous, tri-partite, non-profit organization, which aims to promote a culture of productivity in India. The NPC has equal representation from the government, employers, workers' organizations, and technical and professional institutions. The NPC provides training, consultancy services, and undertakes research in the area of productivity. The NPC also implements productivity promotion plans and programmes of the Asian Productivity Organization (APO) based in Tokyo, Japan.

The NPC acts as a change agent to assist the central and state governments, local bodies, and other organizations in improving the quality and efficiency of public services. The NPC aims at promoting productivity as an evolving concept, which includes paying attention to special issues, quality, environment, energy, women workers, and integrated rural and community development. The NPC's head office is based in New Delhi and regional offices are spread acros India at Chandigarh, Kanpur, Gandhinagar, Bhopal, Mumbai, Patna, Kolkata, Guwahati, Hyderabad, Bangalore, Chennai, Jaipur, and Bhubaneshwar.

The NPC has its own training institute, the Dr Ambedkar Institute of Productivity (AIP) in Chennai. The Institute is situated in an industrial environment in the industrial estate of Small Industry Development Corporation (SIDCO) of Tamil Nadu, Ambattur, Chennai. The Institute prepares and develops consultants in managerial and technical areas to cater to the needs of the NPC. It trains consultants for absorption into the NPC and also the industry on a sponsored or self-financing basis.

The AIP conducts a two-year post-graduate diploma programme in industrial engineering, plant engineering, industrial pollution prevention and control, energy management, human resources management, productivity research, inter-firm comparison, total quality management, total productivity management, and agricultural productivity.

The NPC provides consultancy services to enhance the quality and productivity of Indian industries such as agri-business services, economic services, energy management, environment management, human resource management, information technology, process management, and technology management. *Productivity* is the principal journal published quarterly by the NPC in India. The journal disseminates information on concepts, techniques, and data in the area of productivity and its growth in India and abroad. The articles in the journal are written and the issues addressed by top-level and senior-management technologists, policy makers, educationists, and researchers.

Entrepreneurship Development Institute of India (EDI)

The Entrepreneurship Development Institute of India (EDI) is an autonomous and not-for-profit institute established in 1983. The Institute is registered under the Societies Registration Act, 1860 and the Public Trust Act, 1950. The Institute is sponsored by apex financial institutions such as the Industrial Development Bank of India (IDBI), the Industrial Finance Corporation of India (IFCI), the Industrial Credit and Investment Corporation of India (ICICI) Ltd, and the State Bank of India (SBI).

The EDI[8] has been spearheading the entrepreneurship movement throughout the nation and developing entrepreneurs through well-conceived and well-directed activities. The EDI is committed to entrepreneurship education, training, and research. The Institute strives to provide innovative training techniques, competent faculty support, consultancy and quality teaching, and training material. The EDI aims to inculcate the spirit of entrepreneurship in the youth, create a multiplier effect on opportunities for self-employment, and sensitize the support system to facilitate potential and existing entrepreneurs to establish and manage their enterprises and develop and disseminate new knowledge and insights in entrepreneurial theory and practice through research.

The EDI campus is located in a rural area amidst verdant surroundings spread over 23 acres of land in Gandhinagar district, Gujarat, India. It is one of the best maintained educational campuses in the world and the campus has state-of-the-art conference halls, seminar halls, and lecture halls. Hostel and dining facilities are provided to students and residential blocks to faculty members. The recreation facilities in the campus include a music room, satellite television, and a range of competitive sporting activities. The campus has an inviting environment for work, interaction, and repose. The campus was awarded the prestigious "Aga Khan Award for the Best Architecture" in 1992.

The EDI has been selected as a member of the Economic and Social Commission for Asia and the Pacific (ESCAP) network of centres of excellence for HRD research and training. As a member of the network, the EDI will have interactive access to information on the other 123 member institutions via the Internet. In order to address the need for developing new committed entrepreneurs on a large scale, the EDI has launched several programmes. Some of them are the Post Graduate Diploma in Management–Business Entrepreneurship (PGDM–BE); the Post Graduate Diploma in Management–Development Studies (PGDM–DS); and the Diploma in Entrepreneurship and Business Management. The Institute also conducts international programmes sponsored by the Ministry of External Affairs, Government of India.

The Open Learning Programme in Entrepreneurship (OLPE) cell of the EDI conducts open learning programmes through correspondence and personal counselling. The programmes offered are Diploma in Entrepreneurship and Business Management and Diploma in Social Entrepreneurship. The Diploma in Entrepreneurship and Business Management is an online course and is recognized by the Distance Education Council, IGNOU, New Delhi. The Diploma in Social Entrepreneurship is a six-month programme providing a unique opportunity to learn about and start a social enterprise and to contribute towards the social development of our country.

In order to promote entrepreneurship at the school and college level, the EDI conducts summer camps and entrepreneurship awareness programmes for children and the youth. To promote entrepreneurial education and training in India, the EDI conducts a faculty development programme in entrepreneurship. The Institute organizes national seminars on approaches to entrepreneurship education and deliberates on the establishment of entrepreneurship and business development centres (EBDCs) in educational institutions.

SNAPSHOT

- The NBMSME is an apex advisory body constituted to advise the government on all issues pertaining to the MSME sector.
- The primary objective of KVIC is to provide employment to rural artisans through the production of saleable products and to create self-reliance in order to build a strong rural community spirit.
- The Coir Board is a statutory body established by the Government of India for the promotion and development of the coir industry in the country.
- MSME-DO is the apex body for assisting the government in formulating, coordinating, implementing, and monitoring policies and programmes for the promotion and development of MSME in the country.
- The NSIC provides a package of services and various schemes to support MSME in the country.
- The NSTEDB was established with the primary objective of promoting self-employment among the Science and Technology (S&T) manpower in the country and to set up knowledge-based and innovation-driven enterprises.
- NPC is an autonomous, tri-partite, non-profit organization, which aims to promote a culture of productivity in India.
- The EDI has been spearheading the entrepreneurship movement throughout the nation and developing entrepreneurs through well-conceived and well-directed activities. The EDI is committed to entrepreneurship education, training, and research.

National Research Development Corporation of India (NRDCI)

The National Research Development Corporation of India (NRDCI) was established in 1953 as a Government of India enterprise. It is presently working under the Department of Scientific and Industrial Research, Ministry of Science and Technology. The Corporation aims to develop, promote, and transfer technologies emanating from various national research and development institutions. The Institute has facilitated the supply of technologies and services to entrepreneurs both in the developing and developed countries. The Corporation has exported technologies to countries such as the United States, Germany, Malaysia, Brazil, Bangladesh, Burma, Nepal, Senegal, Madagascar, Indonesia, the Philippines, Vietnam, Sri Lanka, Kenya, and Egypt.

The vision of the NRDCI[9] is to be a provider of world-class business services that nurture technological ideas in Indian minds, to ensure their propagation in world markets, and to satisfy human needs. The Corporation makes a profit by enabling new technologies to transit smoothly from their source points, through the corporate world into global businesses. The NRDCI also acts on behalf of large enterprises that develop technologies in their R&D laboratories and chooses to license them out for commercialization. The main programmes of the NRDCI are invention promotion, technology promotion, and the commercialization of invention. The NRDCI has strong networking links with scientific and industrial agencies in India and abroad for the commercialization of the know-how developed in their laboratories.

The NRDCI, on behalf of the Department of Scientific and Industrial Research (DSIR), provides tax-free cash awards to stimulate the spirit of inventiveness among technicians, artisans, craftsmen, and students in order to recognize the creative talent which could be harnessed to benefit enterprises. The cash awards are given in three categories: the NRDC Innovation Award (maximum two awards of ₹5 lakh each); the NRDC Societal Innovation Award in the agriculture, environment, and rural energy sectors (maximum three awards of ₹3 lakh each); the NRDC Budding Innovators Award for students registered for bachelors or masters courses in academic or research institutions, and universities or affiliated colleges with a maximum age limit of 28 years at the time of applying (maximum five awards of ₹1 lakh each).

An important activity of the Corporation is to disseminate information on new processes to enterprises for the promotion and commercialization of technologies. There are many Indian technologies commercialized by the industry under license from the NRDC. These are, to name a few: infant food, Swaraj Tractor, indelible ink for election purposes, Cinema ARC Carbon, soft ferrite, titanium substrate insoluble anodes, silver impregnated graphite (SIG) contacts, beta naphthol, phosphamidon, mini cement plants, water filter candles, artificial heart valves, fly ash bricks, thrombinase, invert sugar, spirulina algae, liquid biofertilizers, high draught continuous kilns, FRC manhole covers, mini climbing cranes, spice oleo resins, gene delivery systems, glycol-based antifreeze coolants, rice husk particle board, 777 oil, and anti-corrosive treatments of steel reinforcing rods in RCC construction.

National Entrepreneurship Development Institutes

There are three national-level institutes for promoting entrepreneurship set up by the Ministry of Industry. These are:

- National Institute for Micro, Small, and Medium Enterprises (NI-MSME), Hyderabad
- National Institute of Entrepreneurship and Small Business Development (NIESBUD), New Delhi
- Indian Institute of Entrepreneurship (IIE), Guwahati

National Institute for Micro, Small, and Medium Enterprises (NI-MSME) The Institute was formerly known as the National Institute for Small Industry Extension and Training (NISIET). The NI-MSME was registered under the Public Societies Registration Act effective from 1 July 1962 and is located at Hyderabad in Andhra Pradesh. It is a premier institute in India for the promotion, development, and modernization of the MSME sector. It is an autonomous institute, which functions under the Ministry of Micro, Small, and Medium Enterprises. The Institute is managed by a governing council constituted by the Government of India. The secretary to the Government of India, the Ministry of MSME, is the chairman of the governing council.

The NI-MSME[10] was conferred the status of a National Institute by the Government of India with a charter of assisting in the promotion of MSME by creating a pro-business environment. The UNIDO recognized the NI-MSME as an institute of meritorious performance under its Centres of Excellence scheme in 1984. The Institute is providing support to MSME in the area of research, consultancy, information, training, and extension. The Institute has extended its expertise and services to other developing and developed nations. The *Small Enterprises Development, Management, Extension* (*SEDME*) is a quarterly journal published by the Institute. The contributors to *SEDME* include policy makers, researchers, academicians, financiers, executives, and other officials associated with MSME activities from India and other developing as well as developed countries.

The infrastructure and facilities at the NI-MSME campus are at par with international standards. The Institute is now being recognized as among the best training, research, and extension facilities in the world. The NI-MSME has an interface with several international agencies such as the Commonwealth Fund for Technical Cooperation (CFTC), the United Nations Educational Scientific and Cultural Organization (UNESCO), the United Nations Development Programme (UNDP), the United States Agency for International Development (USAID), the International Labour Organization (ILO), the Ford Foundation, and GTZ of Germany.

National Institute for Entrepreneurship and Small Business Development (NIESBUD) The NIESBUD was founded in 1983 by the Ministry of MSME, Government of India. The Institute was registered as a society under the Government of India Societies Registration Act, 1860. The Institute is presently functioning from its integrated campus in Noida, Delhi. It is an apex body for coordinating and overseeing the activities of various institutions and agencies engaged in the development of entrepreneurship in the MSME sector. The NIESBUD[11] serves as the secretariat for the National Entrepreneurship Development Board (NEDB), the apex body which determines policy for entrepreneurship development in the country.

The Institute is managed by a governing council, constituted by the Government of India. The chairman of the governing council is the honourable minister of MSME and the vice-chairman is the Secretary of MSME to the Government of India. The executive committee consists of nine members and includes the Secretary (MSME) as chairman, the Additional Secretary and Development Commissioner (MSME) as its vice-chairman, and the executive director of the Institute as its member secretary. The policies and decisions of the governing council are executed through the executive committee. The NIESBUD has joined hands and signed a Memorandum of Understanding (MoU) with the International Finance Corporation (IFC), a member of the World Bank group, for jointly undertaking different projects relating to entrepreneurship development in India. The NIESBUD will collaborate with the IFC in conducting the training of trainers (TOT) programme for reinforcing the training skills of MSME trainers. The objective is to create a cadre of master trainers who would, in turn, replicate the model to impart training for the MSME sector in a much bigger way.

The NIESBUD mission is to promote, support, and sustain entrepreneurship and MSME through training, education, research, consultancy, and other interventions throughout the globe. The Institute offers information and support to trainers, promoters, and entrepreneurs by providing research, consultancy, and documentary services relevant to entrepreneurship development. The major activities of the Institute include evolving model syllabi for training various target groups; providing effective training strategies, methodology, manuals, and tools; facilitating and supporting central/state government institutions and other agencies in executing programmes for entrepreneurship development; maximizing benefits and accelerating the process of entrepreneurship development; conducting programmes for motivators; and training entrepreneurs and organizing activities.

Indian Institute of Entrepreneurship (IIE) The Indian Institute of Entrepreneurship (IIE) was established in 1993 as an autonomous national institute by the Ministry of MSME with its headquarters at Guwahati. The aim of the Institute is to undertake training, research, and consultancy services for entrepreneurship development with a focus on the MSME sector. The Institute has a board of management whose chairman is the secretary to the Government of India, Ministry of MSME. The board provides the policy framework and guidance for its functioning. The Institute has a governing council headed by the chairman of the North East Council (NEC) and the executive committee is headed by the Secretary, Ministry of MSME, Government of India.

The IIE[12] was specially developed to address the needs of the north-eastern hill states with a view to market and develop traditional and handicraft industries. The Institute acts as a catalyst for entrepreneurship development by creating an eco-system. It undertakes research on entrepreneurship development, documenting, and disseminating information for policy formulation and implementation of entrepreneurship and self-employment. The Institute promotes entrepreneurship education and training by evolving strategies and methodologies for different target groups and locations and conducts field tests. It organizes seminars, workshops, and conferences for providing a forum for interaction and exchange of views by various agencies and entrepreneurs.

SNAPSHOT

- The NRDCI facilitates the supply of technologies and services to entrepreneurs in both developing and developed countries.
- There are three national entrepreneurship development institutes set up by the Ministry of Industries. These are NI-MSME at Hyderabad, NIESBUD at New Delhi, and IIE at Guwahati.

BREAKTHROUGH ENTREPRENEURSHIP 9.1 Innovation at NRDCI

The NRDCI promotes and finances research and development on a selective basis in both laboratories and industry. The Corporation has continued to maintain good overall performance in all areas of its operations, the principal source of revenue being the lump-sum premium and the royalty received on licensing of technologies to industry. The details of major projects financed by the corporation commercialized by the industry under license from the NRDCI are discussed in this section.

Infant Food

The Central Food Technological Research Institute (CFTRI) developed a process for the production of infant food from buffalo milk and established that buffalo milk could be processed into excellent baby food. Earlier, India met its entire requirement of infant food by importing foreign brands like Glaxo, Demex, and Lactogen. NRDCI licensed this process to the Kaira District Milk Producers Union, which produced infant food under the brand name "Amul Spray" and became very popular in Indian households.

Swaraj Tractors

These are extensively used to promote mechanized farming and promote agricultural production in India. In the early 1970s, the Central Mechanical Engineering Research Institute, Durgapur, undertook the development of a small tractor to facilitate mechanized farming. The Corporation licensed know-how to Punjab Tractors Limited to manufacture "Swaraj Tractors" in India. This was the first tractor developed and manufactured with indigenous technology and also the first to be exported to a number of developing countries. Swaraj Tractors have contributed significantly to the green revolution in India.

Water Filter Candles

These are ceramic bowls developed by the Central Glass and Ceramics Research Institute, Calcutta and Regional Research Laboratory, Jorhat. They filter water instantaneously and are simple, easy to use, remove impurities and bacteria, and make water safe for drinking. The Corporation has licensed manufacturing to a large number of parties in the country. The water filter candle caters to the needs of the common people. It has become an essential item in Indian households.

Invert Sugar

This is an equimolecular mixture of glucose and fructose. It is extensively used as a sweetener in the food and pharmaceutical industries. The technology for the production of invert sugar from sugar cane was developed by the Bhabha Atomic Research Centre, Mumbai. The technology has been licensed by the NRDCI to several companies.

In order to promote entrepreneurship education, the Institute offers post-graduate diploma courses in the area of entrepreneurship and management. Prominent among them are the post-graduate diploma in management and entrepreneurship with agri-business management; the post-graduate diploma in management and entrepreneurship with service-sector management, and the post-graduate diploma in management and entrepreneurship with small and medium enterprises management. The IIE has been working in association with the South Asia Enterprise Development Facility, an organization of the World Bank group based in Dhaka, Bangladesh, for increasing the availability of need-based services useful for the MSME sector of the north-east region.

DISCUSSION FORUM

- Which are the central-level institutions supporting business enterprises in India?
- Explain the primary objectives of NBMSME, KVIC, Coir Board, MSME-DO, NSIC, NSTEDB, NPC, EDI, NRDCI and National Entrepreneurship Development Institutes' in promoting entrepreneurship in the country.

STATE-LEVEL INSTITUTIONS

The state-level institutions for supporting entrepreneurial activities are set up by the various state governments in India. They are State Directorate of Industries and Commerce; District Industries Centres (DIC); State Financial Corporations (SFC); State Industrial Development Corporations (SIDC); and State Industrial Area Development Boards (SIADB). This section provides information on state-level institutions supporting entrepreneurial activities, which have been set up by the various state governments in India.

State Directorate of Industries and Commerce

At the state level, the State Directorate of Industries and Commerce acts as a catalyst for the overall development of the industrial sector through effective implementation of policies. The policies developed by the Central Government serve as guidelines but each state evolves its own policy and package schemes. The Directorate develops growth centres, industrial parks, export zones, special economic zones, industrial clusters, and infrastructure required for industrial development.

The main function of the Directorate is to carry out industrial development in the state. It also implements policies and schemes of the Government of India and the state government. The Commissioner/Director of Industries and Commerce is the head of the institution and is assisted by additional directors, joint directors, deputy directors, assistant directors, and other support staff. In all the states and union territories the Directorate oversees the industrial activities of the state and the District Industries Centres (DIC) at the district level.

District Industries Centres (DIC)

The concept of DIC was announced by the Government of India during the new industrial policy formulated on 23 December 1977. DIC are the main focus agencies for promoting MSME at the district level. DIC were established with the aim of generating greater employment opportunities especially in the rural and backward areas of the country. The functions and activities of DIC are monitored by the Directorate of Industries and Commerce.

DIC are district-level institutions set up by the government, which provide all services and facilities to entrepreneurs in one place to set up MSME. These services and facilities include identification of a suitable scheme, preparation of a project feasibility report, arrangements for the supply of plant, machinery, and equipment, provision of raw materials, credit facilities and input for marketing and extension services, quality control, and research and entrepreneurial training.

DIC are headed by a joint director. The joint director is assisted by the deputy director/assistant director, industrial promotion officer, and industrial extension officer at the *taluk* level. The functions of DIC are registration of MSME; providing infrastructure assistance to entrepreneurs; formulating employment generation programmes; implementing incentive schemes; and conducting entrepreneurship development and awareness programmes at village, *taluk*, and district levels. The functions also include arranging buyer–seller meets; organizing industrial exhibitions; creating cluster development and sensitizing programmes; recovering departmental loans; and following up industrial approvals.

SNAPSHOT

- The state-level institutions for supporting entrepreneurial activities are set up by the various state governments in India. They are State Directorate of Industries and Commerce; District Industries Centres (DIC); State Financial Corporation (SFC); State Industrial Development Corporation (SIDC); and State Industrial Area Development Board (SIADB).
- DIC are district-level institutions set up by the government, which provide all services and facilities to entrepreneurs in one place to set up MSME.

State Financial Corporation (SFC)

The State Financial Corporation is established in each state under the State Financial Corporations Act, 1951. The SFC plays an important role in the development of MSME at the state level. They aim to finance and promote MSME in their respective states for achieving balanced industrial growth. They act as catalysts to generate employment and widen the industrial base. SFCs promote the development of MSME by providing various services. The important services provided by SFCs are infrastructure development, financial services, and term loans.

SFCs are managed by a board of directors, an executive committee, an audit committee, and principal officers. Branch managers manage operations at the district level. SFCs have a decentralized system of working. SFCs operate through a wide network with branch offices, circle offices, field offices, and internal audit cell. Financial services to MSME are provided by term loans, direct subscription to equity/debentures, guarantees, discounting of bills of exchange, and seed capital assistance. SFCs operate a number of schemes for refinance of IDBI and SIDBI. SFCs have tailor-made schemes for women, artisans, ex-servicemen, disabled people, and special target groups such as the SC/ST.

State Industrial Development Corporation (SIDC)

SIDCs are wholly-owned undertakings of the state governments set up under The Companies Act, 1956. SIDCs act as catalysts for industrial development in their respective states. They develop land for providing industrial infrastructural facilities in the form of industrial estates by developing industrial land and readymade industrial sheds. They also provide facilities such as roads, power, water supply, drainage, and other amenities required for industrial development.

State Industrial Area Development Board (SIADB)

The SIADB is a statutory board constituted under the Industrial Areas Development Act, of the respective state governments in India, for example, the Karnataka Industrial Areas Development Act,

1966, in Karnataka. The SIADB's primary objective is to promote and assist in the rapid growth and development of enterprises in industrial areas. The SIADB acquires and provides developed land suited for industries. It prepares industrial plots of various sizes to suit different industries along with the requisite infrastructural facilities.

The basic facilities developed by the SIADB in industrial areas include roads, drainage, water supply, and power supply. The SIADB also provides various common amenities in industrial areas such as banks, post offices, telephone exchanges, telecommunications, fire stations, police outposts, canteens, ESI dispensaries, bus depots, and petrol bunks. It also makes provision for technical training centres, research and development centres, and common effluent treatment plants.

SNAPSHOT

- The important services provided by SFC to MSME are infrastructure development, financial services, and term loans.
- SIDC provide infrastructural facilities to MSME in the form of industrial land, industrial shed, roads, power, water supply, drainage, and other amenities required for industrial development.
- The SIADB acquires and provides developed land suited for industries.

DISCUSSION FORUM

- Explain the main function of the State Directorate of Industries and Commerce in brief.
- Which are the various state-level institutions set up by the state governments for promoting MSME in India?
- Explain the procedure for acquiring industrial sheds/plots.
- Discuss in small groups the primary objectives of DIC, SFC, SIDC, and SIADB.

OTHER INSTITUTIONS

Apart from central and state-level institutions, there are various other institutions supporting entrepreneurial activities in India. These are the National Bank for Agriculture and Rural Development (NABARD); the Housing and Urban Development Corporation (HUDCO); Technical Consultancy Organizations (TCOs); the Small Industries Development Bank of India (SIDBI); the Export Promotion Council (EPC); Industry Associations; Non-Governmental Organizations (NGOs); and Business Incubators.

National Bank for Agriculture and Rural Development (NABARD)

NABARD was established by an Act of Parliament in July 1982 to provide focused attention to the development of rural India by facilitating credit flow for the promotion of agriculture and the rural non-farming sector. It provides refinance assistance to State Cooperative Banks, Regional Rural Banks, and other approved institutions for all kinds of production and investment credit to industries, artisans, cottage and village industries, handicrafts, and other allied activities. NABARD also helps entrepreneurs to procure loans for setting up industries in any part of the country.

NABARD's primary goal is to promote sustainable and equitable agriculture and rural prosperity through effective credit support, related services, institution development, and other innovative initiatives.[13] NABARD's functions can be classified into four major categories: credit planning; financial services; promotion and development; and supervision. NABARD has effectively brought in a number of innovations in the rural credit domain. Some of them are the formation and linkage of self-help groups; farmers' clubs; rural infrastructure development funds; watershed development; the Kisan Credit Card; the district rural industries project; women and development; the Rural Entrepreneurship Development Programme (REDP); rural marketing; NABARD Consultancy Services (NABCONS); co-financing; cluster development programmes; and the Rural Innovation Fund.

NABARD is governed by a board of directors and assisted by approximately 25 departments working for the improvement of the rural economy. It has regional offices, training establishments, and district development offices for implementing policies and various initiatives. NABARD extends assistance to the government, the Reserve Bank of India (RBI), and other organizations in matters relating to rural development. It acts as a regulator for cooperative banks and Regional Rural Banks (RRB). It is a refinancing agency for financial institutions, offering production credit and investment credit for promoting agriculture and developmental activities in rural areas.

NABARD recorded high levels of performance in purveying rural credit during 2011–12. The aggregate assets held by NABARD rose to ₹182,300 crore as on 31 March 2012, an increase of ₹235,000 crore compared to the position as on 31 March 2011. NABARD is implementing subsidy schemes for various sectors on behalf of the Government of India. The subsidy schemes cover sectors such as animal husbandry and poultry development including poultry venture capital fund; cold storages; rural godowns; and solar lighting and photovoltaic cells schemes. In 2011–12, NABARD released an amount of ₹486.55 crore as subsidy to the beneficiaries of various banks.

SNAPSHOT

- NABARD's primary goal is to promote sustainable and equitable agriculture and rural prosperity through effective credit support, related services, institution development, and other innovative initiatives.
- NABARD's functions can be classified into four major categories: credit planning; financial services; promotion and development; and supervision.

Housing and Urban Development Corporation (HUDCO)

HUDCO is a public-sector company wholly owned by the Government of India. It was incorporated in April 1970 as a private-limited company and, subsequently, converted into a public-limited company in 1986. HUDCO's primary focus is to provide assistance for urban, social-sector infrastructure, and the creation of housing facilities. Of late, the Corporation has also undertaken activities to create infrastructure for the industrial sector. HUDCO also extends assistance to the promotion of building material industries, besides imparting consultancy, training, and technical assistance in related matters.

HUDCO[14] aims to promote sustainable habitat development to enhance the quality of life. It is governed by a board of directors and has established regional offices at the operations level. HUDCO was established with an equity base of ₹2 crore. Over the years, the government has expanded the equity base. The net worth of HUDCO as on 31 March 2011 is ₹5,520.97 crore. HUDCO's services and product portfolio can be classified into five main categories: housing, urban infrastructure, building technology promotion, research and training, and consultancy.

HUDCO is an ISO 9001:2008 certified institution and has received many accolades and awards for its sustained performance. In 1991, HUDCO received the Habitat Council of Honour Award in recognition of its innovation in the development, and promotion of building materials; design and construction of affordable housing for the poor and training in construction skills. In 1998–99, HUDCO received the prime minister's MoU Award for Excellence in Performance for being among the top ten public-sector institutions in performance.

HUDCO was awarded the status of Mini Ratna in 2004–05 by the Central Government for its sustained outstanding performance and profitability. It received the Enterprise Excellence Award by the Indian Institute of Industrial Engineering in 2007. The Building Industry Leadership Award was conferred on HUDCO by the building information bureau in 2008.

Technical Consultancy Organization (TCO)

A TCO is a premier professional, industrial, technical, and management consultancy organization. A network of Technical Consultancy Organizations (TCOs) was established by the all-India financial institutions in the seventies and the eighties in collaboration with state-level financial/development institutions and commercial banks to cater to the consultancy needs of MSME and new entrepreneurs. At present, there are 18 TCOs operating in various states, some of them covering more than one state. These 18 TCOs are listed in Table 9.1.

TCOs provide a total package of consultancy services to enterprises, government departments, commercial banks, and other institutions for activities relating to industrial development and financing. Initially, the functions of TCOs were focused on pre-investment studies for enterprises. Over the years, they have diversified their functions to include the following:

- To prepare project profiles and feasibility profiles.
- To undertake industrial potential surveys.
- To identify potential entrepreneurs and provide them with technical and management assistance.
- To undertake market research and surveys for specific products.
- To supervise the project and where necessary, render technical and administrative assistance.
- To undertake export consultancy for export-oriented projects based on modern technology.
- To conduct entrepreneurship development programmes.
- To offer merchant banking services.

Table 9.1. Technical Consultancy Organizations in India

1. Andhra Pradesh Industrial and Technical Consultancy Organization Ltd (APITCO).
2. Bihar Industrial and Technical Consultancy Organization Ltd (BITCO).
3. Gujarat Industrial and Technical Consultancy Organization Ltd (GITCO).
4. Haryana–Delhi Industrial Consultants Ltd (HARDICON).
5. Himachal Consultancy Organization Ltd (HIMCO).
6. Industrial and Technical Consultancy Organization of Tamil Nadu Ltd (ITCOT).
7. Jammu and Kashmir Industrial and Technical Consultancy Organization Ltd (J&KITCO).
8. Technical Consultancy Services Organization of Karnataka (TECSOK).
9. Maharashtra Industrial and Technical Consultancy Organization Ltd (MITCON).
10. Madhya Pradesh Consultancy Organization Ltd (MPCON).
11. North-Eastern Industrial Consultants Ltd (NECON).
12. North-Eastern Industrial and Technical Consultancy Organization Ltd (NEITCO).
13. North-India Technical Consultancy Organization Ltd (NITCON).
14. Orissa Industrial and Technical Consultancy Organization Ltd (ORITCON).
15. Rajasthan Consultancy Organization Ltd (RAJCON).
16. U.P. Industrial Consultants Ltd (UPICO).
17. Kerala Industrial and Technical Consultancy Organization Ltd (KITCO).
18. West Bengal Consultancy Organization Ltd (WEBCO).

Small Industries Development Bank of India (SIDBI)

SIDBI was founded in 1990 under an Act of Parliament. It is the principal financial institution for the promotion, financing, and development of the MSME sector and other institutions engaged in similar activities. SIDBI facilitates the timely flow of credit for term loans and working capital to MSME in collaboration with commercial banks. In addition to refinancing and discounting of bills, SIDBI participates in equity loans, term loans, working capital, venture capital support, and various forms of resource support to banks and other institutions.

SIDBI[15] seeks to empower the MSME sector with a view to contribute to the process of economic growth, employment generation, and balanced regional development. The four main functions set by SIDBI for the development of MSME sector are financing, promotion, development, and coordination. SIDBI finances technology transfer and upgradation, quality improvement programmes, export promotion, environmental care, and rural industrialization. It uses the services of consultants and NGOs at national and international levels for various improvement programmes on a need basis.

SIDBI as an apex institution makes use of the existing network of banks and state-level financial institutions to convey financial assistance to the MSME sector. It has entered into a memorandum of understanding with many banks, governmental agencies, international agencies, research and development institutions, and industry agencies in India and abroad to reach out to and facilitate the development of the MSME sector in the country.

Export Promotion Councils (EPCs)

In order to overcome problems in the marketing of MSME products in the overseas markets, it is considered desirable to adopt a consortium approach. The export promotion councils for different industries make efforts to promote the exports of their member units through direct marketing, developing vendor relations, opening respective sales outlets abroad, and so on, as a collective export marketing strategy. The activities of different councils are targeted to increase the exports from the sector.

MSME get access to export-related services from the councils. Some of the councils obtain bulk purchase orders from foreign buyers and distribute these among member units for supply to the council for onward export. This process ensures export orders to every member unit and thereby facilitates the timely delivery of goods abroad. For such a service, the councils charge a nominal fee from member units. EPCs also offer a package of other services to existing as well as new members by providing information about the developments taking place in the international arena. They keep the members informed of the changes with regard to export–import policies and procedures, customs and excise duty rules, and so on. Besides trade enquiries, tender notices are circulated among members in order to assist them to avail the business opportunities for augmenting overall exports.

SNAPSHOT

- NABARD's primary goal is to promote sustainable and equitable agriculture and rural prosperity through effective credit support, related services, institution development, and other innovative initiatives.
- HUDCO's primary objective is to provide assistance for urban, social-sector infrastructure, creation of housing facilities, and infrastructure for the industrial sector.
- A TCO is a premier professional, industrial, technical, and management consultancy organization. TCOs provide a total package of consultancy services to enterprises, government departments, commercial banks, and other institutions for activities relating to industrial development and financing.
- The four main functions set by SIDBI for the development of the MSME sector are financing, promotion, development, and coordination.
- EPCs make efforts to promote exports for MSME.

Industry Associations

In addition to the central and state government agencies, industry associations also impart institutional support to the MSME sector. Industry associations provide MSME with a common platform to raise industry-related issues and to initiate cooperative efforts for promoting the sector. The government's policies, in recent years, have stressed the increasing role of industry associations in setting up common facilities and other cooperative ventures in the areas of technology, marketing, and other support services. Some of the major associations and the services provided by them are given below:

Confederation of Indian Industry (CII) In 1895, five British engineering firms formed the Engineering and Iron Trade Association (EITA). EITA was renamed the Indian Engineering Association (IEA) in 1912. With the *swadeshi* movement gaining momentum, the Engineering Association of India (EAI) was formed in 1942 by a group of indigenous entrepreneurs. IEA and EAI were merged in 1974 to form the Association of Indian Engineering Industry (AIEI). The 1980s ushered in an era of competiveness and liberalization, and the AIEI was renamed the Confederation of Engineering Industry (CEI). In 1992, the name was again changed to the Confederation of Indian Industry (CII), which reflected the extension of the confederation's coverage.

The main objectives of the CII are to provide information, advisory, consultative, and representative services to industry and the government. The CII is represented on major policy-making bodies concerned with the industry. It also organizes industry exhibitions, specialized sectoral trade fairs, and the India Engineering Trade Fair. Apart from these, the CII also plays an important role in promoting international industrial cooperation.

The CII has taken up the agenda of "Business for Livelihood" for the year 2011–12. This conflates the fundamental themes of spreading growth to disadvantaged sections of society, building skills for meeting emerging economic compulsions, and fostering a climate of good governance. In line with this, the CII is placing increased focus on affirmative action, skills development, and governance during the year.

World Association for Small and Medium Enterprises (WASME) The World Association for Small and Medium Enterprises (WASME), founded in 1980, has emerged as the largest professionally-managed global non-governmental organization with members and associates including national governments, chambers of commerce and industry, small business authorities and associations, banks and financial institutions, and training and consultancy agencies in 120 countries serving micro, small, and medium enterprises.

It has a governing body comprising representatives drawn from chambers of commerce, banks and financial institutions, small business development corporations, the Department of Small Industries in various governments, and so on. WASME organizes the international MSME convention annually. Among other activities, WASME's focus is on ensuring business cooperation among enterprises of the developing countries by facilitating technology transfer, training, and marketing. The facilities provided by WASME include (i) information on promotion of SME in member countries, (ii) providing opportunities for the marketing of products, (iii) facilitating contacts with sources offering latest technologies, equipment, and services for MSME, and (iv) identification of facilities for the training of entrepreneurs, managers, and production personnel.

Some of the thrust areas of WASME activities include technology transfer, training, maintaining a roster of expert consultants, organizing or sponsoring seminars/ workshops/ conferences, acting as a clearing house of information relating to MSME, undertaking special studies and research on areas of relevance to MSME, and strengthening or assisting in the setting up of associations of MSME and/or women entrepreneurs.

Federation of Associations of Small Industries of India (FASII) The Federation of Associations of Small Industries of India, set up in 1959, represents associations of small industries and individual SSI units. The main objectives of FASII are: (i) to promote the development of MSME and cottage industries; (ii) to cooperate with industrial, business, educational, and research institutions in collecting and exchanging information pertaining to MSME; (iii) to undertake professional, technical, and management consultation services; (iv) to undertake studies, surveys, and research assignments; (v) to further the cause of MSME by interacting with union and state governments and other bodies; (vi) to establish and operate trade centres, display centres, sub-contract exchanges, and other promotional institutions for the benefit of the MSME sector; and (vii) to establish test centres, laboratories, and common facility centres for the MSME sector.

In this direction, the federation offers services such as organizing meetings/conferences, liaising with policy makers, analysing and interpreting policies, and taking up members' difficulties with the concerned department/organization for redressal.

Laghu Udyog Bharati (LUB) Laghu Udyog Bharati was established in 1995. The main objective of the organization is to promote and safeguard the interests of the small-scale industry. Entrepreneurial training, support for technology upgradation, and marketing are within the extended scope of its activities. Laghu Udyog Bharati has its representation in the national and state-level government bodies connected with MSME.

Indian Council of Small Industries (ICSI) The Indian Council of Small Industries, founded in 1979, represents around 1,500 associations of the decentralized sector. The major objectives of the council include extending help to MSME, cottage enterprises, and artisans. In the process, the ICSI aims at enhancing the contribution of the MSME sector in the overall growth of the Indian economy. The major functions of the ICSI are consultancy, information dissemination, entrepreneurship development, training, research, and so on. The ICSI represents the cause of its member enterprises by giving suggestions for appropriate policy making. The council follows the consortium approach to provide market-related services and extends facilities relating to testing centres and quality control outlets.

Council of Scientific and Industrial Research (CSIR) The CSIR has set up a large number of Regional Research Laboratories all over the country, which are developing new processes for the manufacture of industrial products on a commercial scale. These agencies act as pillars of support for the promotion and growth of MSME in India.

Non-Governmental Organizations (NGOs)

Besides the central and state governments and autonomous bodies, there has been an emergence of NGOs in different states to provide financial assistance, information, training, marketing support, legal advice, and so on to MSME. The 1991 SSI policy of the Government of India favoured assistance to MSME through NGOs. A few training programmes for unemployed youth to help set up industries under the PMRY have been assigned by state governments to some NGOs. In the present scenario, the role of NGOs is assuming increasing importance for assistance to entrepreneurs, particularly under microfinancing activities. Many NGOs have set up Sub-Contracting Exchanges (SCXs) to promote entrepreneurship by developing and strengthening linkages between buyers and sellers.

DISCUSSION FORUM

- Discuss the role of SIDBI in supporting MSME in India.
- Explain the various functions of NABARD.
- Discuss the role of HUDCO, TCO, and EPC in promoting MSME in India.
- Name the industry associations that promote MSME in India.

SNAPSHOT

- Industry associations provide MSME a common platform to raise industry-related issues and to initiate cooperative efforts for promoting the sector.
- The main objectives of CII are to provide information, advisory, consultative, and representative services to the industry and the government.

BREAKTHROUGH ENTREPRENEURSHIP 9.2 Sub-Contracting Exchanges (SCXs)

Sub-Contracting Exchanges, also called Sub-Contracting and Partnership Exchanges, are centres for technical information, promotion, and matchmaking for industrial subcontracting between large and small enterprises. They aim to optimize the utilization of the manufacturing capacities and capabilities of the affiliated enterprises. Sub-Contracting Exchanges help local firms in developing countries identify the opportunities for supplying components to large company clients.

The United Nations Industrial Development Organization (UNIDO) established the Industrial SCX in India in 2007. UNIDO provides technical assistance to developing countries for establishing and operating SCXs. It assists in setting up a roster of buyer and suppliers. UNIDO also advises governments of developing countries to create the eco-system required to set up SCXs. It also helps to develop policies and programmes for the promotion of industrial sub-contracting using industrial legislation. UNIDO has developed a software called OUTSOURCING 2007 to promote industrial subcontracting.

SCXs act as meeting points for and instruments of regulation between the supply and demand of industrial sub-contracting orders. They also provide assistance to both the partners, particularly MSME. The primary function of SCXs is the collection, analysis, storage, and organization of data for rapid retrieval of existing production capacities and capabilities of enterprises, especially MSME. They also assist in identifying sub-contracting supply and partnership inquiries and negotiation in India and abroad.

The Confederation of Indian Industry (CII) is partnering with UNIDO's consolidated project for the development of MSME in India. The project is funded by the Italian government and implemented by UNIDO in partnership with the Ministry of MSME. As part of this project, CII has set up SCXs in India as part of a national network. This serves as a national outsourcing agency and provides a "One-Stop Shop" for information on the existing sub-contracting capacity and capabilities of the Indian industry. It provides linkages between the Indian Industry, four regional SCXs, and 45 international SCXs in 30 countries, thereby being part of the Global Sourcing Network.

Source: www.unido.org (last accessed in March 2013).

Business Incubators

A business incubator is an organization designed to accelerate the growth and success of entrepreneurial companies through an array of business support resources and services that could include physical space, capital, coaching, common services, and networking connections. It plays the role of an accelerator to start-up ventures. Business incubators are shared office-space facilities that incubate with a strategic, value-adding intervention system through mentoring, business assistance, and monitoring. Thus, new venture development processes are facilitated while simultaneously making ventures aware of major risks and minimizing the cost of potential failures.

Business incubators play a key role in providing assistance to nascent entrepreneurs, particularly in the initial phases of their life cycle. University-based incubators are a special type of business incubators that are located in universities. These business incubators are useful not only in developed countries but also in emerging economies. They play a significant role in job creation and economic development. They provide a unique opportunity to nascent entrepreneurs to benefit from the talent and resources located in the university.

WORLD OF ENTREPRENEURS 9.3 SEZ and EPZ

A Special Economic Zone or SEZ is a geographical region that has economic laws that are more liberal than a country's typical economic laws. An Export Processing Zone or EPZ is one or more special areas of a country where some normal trade barriers such as tariffs and quotas are eliminated and bureaucratic requirements are lowered in the hopes of attracting new business and foreign investments. The approved special economic zones in India are:

- Santacruz Electronics Export Procesing Zone (SEEPZ) SEZ in Mumbai: Chiefly houses electronic hardware manufacturing companies, software companies, and jewellery.
- Kandla SEZ, Gujarat: Multi-product zone
- Cochin SEZ, Cochin: Multi-product zone
- Visakhapatnam SEZ: Ship building
- Falta SEZ: Multi-product zone
- Noida EPZ: Apparel
- Surat SEZ: Apparel
- Salt Lake SEZ, West Bengal: Gems and jewellery
- Indore SEZ: Multi-product zone
- Jaipur SEZ: Gems and jewellery
- Mahindra City SEZ, Chennai, Tamil Nadu: Houses information technology, auto ancillaries, apparel, and fashion accessories
- Salt Lake Electronic City, Kolkata, West Bengal: Software development and IT-enabled services
- Moradabad SEZ: Handicrafts
- Jodhpur SEZ: Handicrafts
- Nokia India Pvt. Ltd, Sriperumbudur, Tamil Nadu: Houses telecom equipment and telecom services

Source: www.indianindustry.com (last accessed in March 2013).

A non-business-organization incubator or an academic institution incubator is not for profit. They have an objective of promoting an enterprise and facilitating the implementation of the process of creating an enterprise. The role of these incubators has been to create some kind of a forum whereby science and technology researchers as well as students and entrepreneurs come together to create an enterprise or create value out of their own efforts.

The other model of incubators comprises those supported by organizations such as Microsoft, Infosys, Wipro, and Intel. They promote their own employees to spin-off an idea, do the proofing, and go and attack the market. If the idea is successful, the company goes ahead and acquires it, giving the founders a return on their innovation. There are certain venture capitalists that run incubators themselves. The major benefit of being a part of an incubator is that it insulates the entrepreneur from the impact of the macro and micro business environment.

DISCUSSION FORUM

- Name some of the prominent NGOs in the country set up to promote entrepreneurial development in the country.
- Explain the role of SCXs in promoting entrepreneurship development.
- Name at least five business incubators in India.

WORLD OF ENTREPRENEURS 9.4 Business Incubators in India

India has over 50 business incubators as per the 2010 figures compiled by the National Entrepreneurship Network (NEN). There are different models of incubators. Some of the well-known incubators in India are given below:

1. N. S. Raghavan Centre for Entrepreneurship Learning (NSRCEL), IIM Bangalore
2. Technology Business Incubator, Birla Institute of Technology, Pilani
3. Centre for Innovation Incubation and Entrepreneurship, IIM Ahmedabad
4. Entrepreneurship Cell, IIT Kharagpur
5. Center for Entrepreneurship, S. P. Jain Institute of Management & Research
6. C-TIDES, IIT Madras
7. The Telecommunications and Computer Networking Group, IIT Madras
8. Society for Innovation and Entrepreneurship, IIT Bombay
9. Nirma Labs
10. SIDBI Innovation and Incubation Centre, IIT Kanpur
11. Entrepreneurial Development Cell, IIT Guwahati
12. Entrepreneurship Development Cell, IIT Delhi
13. Entrepreneurship Cell, FMS Delhi
14. Abhiyan, IIM Lucknow
15. E-Cell, IIM Kozhikode
16. Centre for Entrepreneurship and Innovation, IIM Calcutta
17. Entrepreneurship Development Institute of India, Ahmedabad
18. ICFAI Center for Entrepreneurship Development, Hyderabad
19. MICA Entrepreneurship Development Centre, Ahmedabad
20. Wadhwani Centre for Entrepreneurship Development, Hyderabad
21. Technology Innovation Management & Entrepreneurship Information Service, Delhi
22. Science & Technology Entrepreneurs Park, JSS Academy of Technical Education, Noida
23. National Institute of Industrial Engineering, Mumbai
24. Entrepreneurship Development Cell, IIT Roorke

Source: www.indianwebstartups.com/Incubators.html (last accessed in March 2013).

CHECKLIST FOR ENTREPRENEURS 9.5 Know Your Institutional Support System

- You should be aware of the institutional support systems and schemes provided by various agencies at national and international levels for nurturing your enterprise.
- It is essential to participate in select industrial exhibitions and technology fairs to showcase your competencies for marketing your products/services. Participation in these events exposes you to international business practices and enhances your business prowess.
- Prepare a comprehensive list of various agencies, which would provide support to your business.
- In order to solve problems in respect of delayed payment for the sale of products/services, SIDBI has set up factoring services. Under this facility, delayed payments on the sales of MSME will be handled by SIDBI who would undertake to make the payment on behalf of the purchasers.
- It is better to set up your enterprise in an industrial estate even though it appears a little costly. As all infrastructural facilities are readily available in industrial estates, hassles are fewer. Think twice before establishing your enterprise outside an industrial estate, even though land may be cheaper, as this involves hidden costs.
- You should participate in selected training programmes conducted by various institutions in India and abroad to understand the business environment.

SNAPSHOT

- NGOs provide assistance to entrepreneurs under microfinancing activities. Many NGOs have set up SCXs to promote entrepreneurship by developing and strengthening linkages between buyers and sellers.
- Business incubators play a key role in providing assistance to nascent entrepreneurs, particularly in the initial phases of their life cycle.

SUMMARY

A number of support institutions set up by the central and state governments of the country and various other agencies help entrepreneurial development in various ways. The activities of support institutions cover a wide range of services such as financing, equipment support, technical assistance, training, marketing, and providing subsidy and grants. The various institutions supporting entrepreneurial activities in India are divided into central level, state level and other institutions.

The central-level institutions for supporting entrepreneurial activities are set up by the Central Government. They are: National Board for Micro, Small, and Medium Enterprises (NBMSME); Khadi and Village Industries Commission (KVIC); Coir Board; Micro, Small, and Medium Enterprises Development Organization (MSME–DO); National Small Industries Corporation (NSIC); National Science and Technology Entrepreneurship Development Board (NSTEDB); National Productivity Council (NPC); Entrepreneurship Development Institutes of India (EDI); National Research Development Corporation of India (NRDCI); and National Entrepreneurship Development Institutes.

The state-level institutions for supporting entrepreneurial activities are set up by the various state governments in India. They are: State Directorate of Industries; District Industries Centres (DIC); State Financial Corporations (SFC); State Industrial Development Corporation (SIDC); and State Industrial Area Development Board (SIADB).

Apart from central- and state-level institutions, there are various other institutions supporting entrepreneurial activities in India. They are: National Bank for Agriculture and Rural Development (NABARD); Housing and Urban Development Corporation (HUDCO); Technical Consultancy Organizations (TCOs); Small Industries Development Bank of India (SIDBI), Export Promotion Council (EPC); Industry Associations; Non-Governmental Organizations (NGOs); and Business Incubators.

KEY TERMS

Business Incubator: A business incubator is an organization designed to accelerate the growth and success of entrepreneurial companies through an array of business support resources and services that could include physical space, capital, coaching, common services, and networking connections.

Export Promotion Zone/Export Processing Zone (EPZ): An EPZ or Export Processing Zone is one or more special areas of a country where some normal trade barriers such as tariffs and quotas are eliminated and bureaucratic requirements are lowered in the hopes of attracting new business and foreign investments. It is an industrial estate that specializes in manufacturing for export and offers firms free trade conditions and a liberal regulatory environment.

Industrial Estate: An industrial estate can be defined as a method of organizing, housing, and servicing industry, a planned clustering of industrial enterprises offering standard factory building erected in advance of demand and providing a variety of services and facilities to the occupants.

Special Economic Zone (SEZ): An SEZ or Special Economic Zone is a geographical region, which has economic laws that are more liberal than a country's typical economic laws. Moreover, these regulations tend to contain measures that are conducive to foreign direct investment. Conducting business in a SEZ usually means that a company will receive tax incentives and the opportunity to pay lower tariffs.

Sub-Contracting Exchanges (SCX): Subcontracting Exchanges, also called Sub-contracting and Partnership Exchanges, are centres for technical information, promotion, and matchmaking for industrial subcontracting between large and small enterprises.

Venture Capital: The money provided by investors to start firms and small businesses with perceived long-term growth potential is termed as venture captial. This is a very important source of funding for start-ups that do not have access to capital markets. It typically involves a high risk for the investor, but it has the potential for above-average returns.

CASE STUDY

IndiaCo: A Business Incubator with a Difference

IndiaCo is an investment management firm listed on the Bombay Stock Exchange. The promoters of IndiaCo have a long history in India. It was the first company in India to launch a private incubator in 2000. In 2002, this incubator was recognized by the World Bank group and also received support from the Department of Science and Technology, Government of India.

Business incubation is a business support process that facilitates in the successful development of start-ups and early growth stage companies by providing entrepreneurs with an array of resources and services through its network of contacts. A business incubator's main goal is to produce successful firms that will leave the project financially viable and self-sustaining.

The promoters of IndiaCo aim to provide transparency and regularize a new model for private equity markets. They invest the capital required to frame the new business model of the acquired company. IndiaCo has had the experience of working with incubators across different geographical locations. Based on its experience, the most common problems that business incubators face in developing countries are the lack of innovative high-growth projects; non-availability of capital; lack of basic operating infrastructure; and problems of self-sustenance. Institutional marketing for incubators is a major challenge in most developing countries.

Since its inception, IndiaCo has been active in the area of incubation and technology transfer. The key success factors of IndiaCo are the entrepreneurial experience of the founder; visionary leadership; strategic positioning in the domestic and international markets; good management teams; and milestone-based e-mentoring. IndiaCo functions as a "venture creation engine" for high-tech start-ups and early-stage companies. It provides the infrastructure and network to translate research into innovative products to support entrepreneurs. The international network at IndiaCo is made available to the companies even before they graduate from the incubator.

The traditional model of business incubators consists of a group of start-up firms that are located in a common physical space sharing various resources and mentorship. IndiaCo follows an equity model unlike most incubators. It deploys its funds and investments directly through the holding company into the portfolio companies. This structure provides the flexibility to invest in the holding company, a sector of choice, or just the company of choice.

Questions:

1. Analyse the business model of IndiaCo.
2. List the key success factors for the success of IndiaCo.
3. Critically examine how IndiaCo enables new venture creation.
4. Why is IndiaCo a business incubator with a difference?

DISCUSSION QUESTIONS

1. Describe the institutional set up for entrepreneurial development in India.
2. Discuss the need for institutional support for MSME.
3. What are District Industries Centres (DIC)? Explain the functions of DIC.
4. Explain the various schemes offered by SIDBI for supporting enterprises.
5. Critically examine the role played by the Export Promotion Council in promoting exports from India.
6. Explain the role of national-level training institutes in conducting EDPs.

ACTIVITY

1. In a small group visit the local District Industries Centre (DIC) in your area and invite the joint director to your institution. Request him to address the class regarding the role of the DIC in promoting enterprises. Make the session interactive. Request your professor to lend his support to this activity.
2. Visit an entrepreneur in your area and collect details of the institutions from which he has received support.

PROJECT

1. Visit any one of the incubation centres listed in Box 9.4. This should hopefully help to give you a starting point if you intend to start your own company. Prepare a brief report of the business model of an incubator not exceeding four A4 size pages with adequate margins and normal space between the paragraphs.
2. Divide your class into small groups (say five) with four to six members in each group. Each group has to visit the Web site of the following institutions of your state (in this case Karnataka is given) and study the schemes available for supporting entrepreneurs. Each group has to prepare a brief report of four pages of A4 size and make a ten-minute presentation (each group) in the class. Request your professor to lend his support.
   - Karnataka Industries Area Development Board (KIADB). Web address: www.kiadb.in.
   - Karnataka Council for Technological Upgradation (KCTU). Web address: www.kctu.kar.nic.in.
   - Technical Consultancy Services Organization of Karnataka (TECSOK). Web address: www.tecsok.com.
   - Centre for Entrepreneurship Development of Karnataka (CEDOK). Web address: www.cedok.kar.nic.in.
   - Karnataka State Financial Corporation (KFC). Web address: www.ksfc.in.

ENDNOTES

1. http://dcmsme.gov.in (last accessed in March 2013).
2. www.kvic.org.in (last accessed in March 2013).
3. www.coirboard.gov.in (last accessed in March 2013).

4. www.dcmsme.gov.in/sido (last accessed in March 2013).
5. www.nsic.co.in (last accessed in March 2013).
6. www.nstedb.com (last accessed in March 2013).
7. www.npcindia.org (last accessed in March 2013).
8. www.ediindia.org (last accessed in March 2013).
9. www.nrdcindia.com (last accessed in March 2013).
10. www.nimsme.org (last accessed in March 2013).
11. www.niesbud.nic.in (last accessed in March 2013).
12. www.iie.nic.in (last accessed in March 2013).
13. www.nabard.org (last accessed in March 2013).
14. www.hudco.org (last accessed in March 2013).
15. www.sidbi.com (last accessed in March 2013).

New Venture Creation

6. Identification of Business Opportunities
7. Project Management and Financing
8. Business Plans
9. Institutions Supporting Business Enterprises
10. **Business Organizations and Business Laws**

"It is an immutable law in business that words are words, explanations are explanations, promises are promises but only performance is reality."

—Harold S. Geneen

The Gujarat Cooperative Milk Marketing Federation (GCMMF), a cooperative society based in Anand, is the apex organization of the dairy cooperatives of Gujarat. The GCMMF markets its products under the brand name Amul. The cooperative is India's largest marketer of food products and achieved a turnover of ₹12,975 crore in 2011–12. It procures approximately 1.3 crore litres of milk per day from 16,117 village milk cooperative societies and 17 member unions covering 24 districts, and 31.8 lakh milk-producer members. Dr Verghese Kurien, widely acclaimed as the father of the White Revolution in India, was the founder chairman of the GCMMF. The Amul advertisements featuring the smiling Amul moppet and witty one-liners have ensured phenomenal brand recall for this brand.

Business Organizations and Business Laws

10

LEARNING OBJECTIVES

Upon completion of this chapter, you should be able to:

1. **Explain the different forms of organizations.**
2. **Analyse the various factors that determine the choice of the form of buisness.**
3. **Discuss the business laws that are prevalent in India.**

INTRODUCTION

A business enterprise can be owned and organized in various forms. Every entrepreneur has to decide on the form of business organization. Business organization refers to all necessary arrangements required to conduct a business. Each form has its own advantages and disadvantages. The choice of the form of business is governed by several interrelated and independent factors such as the nature of the business, scale of operations, area of operation, liability, the degree of control desired by the promoter(s), the cost of the project, risk and return, and comparative tax liability.

The choice of the form of enterprise not only helps in the initial phase but also during the growth of the enterprise. To start an enterprise, the promoters have to decide on the constitution of the unit. The constitution of the unit has to be decided at the initial stages of the project and the necessary formalities should be completed. There are six major types of business organizations.[1]

1. Sole proprietorship.
2. Joint Hindu family business.
3. Partnership.
4. Joint stock company.
5. Cooperative society.
6. Franchising.

Sole Proprietorship

Sole proprietorship is the most common and simple form of business organization as it does not have any legal formalities. In a sole proprietorship, a single person owns and controls the enterprise. The enterprise does not have any separate entity from the owner. The promoter and business is one in the eyes of law. In this form of organization, the proprietor has unlimited liability. The sole proprietor enjoys all the profits made by the enterprise alone. In the same way, all losses are also entirely borne by him. He alone reaps the return and is subject to the risk of the business. Sole proprietorship is suitable only for micro and small business enterprises. In order to avail facilities from the government, the registration of the firm may be done with a District Industries Centre.

The sole proprietorship form of business organization refers to a business enterprise exclusively owned, managed, and controlled by a single person with all authority, responsibility and risk. A sole proprietor contributes and organizes the resources in a systematic way and controls all activities with the objective of earning profit.

The main features of the sole proprietorship form of organization are single ownership, no separation of ownership and management, less legal formalities, no separate entity from proprietor thus no sharing of profit and loss with others, one-man control on business, and unlimited liability.

The sole proprietorship form of business organization is advantageous because it is easy to form and wind up the organization, take quick decisions and prompt action, enjoy all the profits made by the enterprise, possess flexibility in business operations, maintain control of business secrets from outsider, and give a personal touch to the organization. It also promotes entrepreneurial skills in individuals.

The limitations of the sole proprietorship form of business organization are unlimited liability, limited resources, not suitable for large operations, limited managerial expertise, and uncertainty of the continuity of business operations.

Joint Hindu Family Business

The joint Hindu family business came into existence as per the Hindu inheritance laws[2] of India. It is a distinct type of organization, which is unique to India. In this form of business organization, all members of an undivided Hindu family do business jointly under the control of the head of the family who is known as the *karta*. The members of the family are known as "co-parceners." There is no membership other than the members of the joint family. All co-parceners have equal shares in the profit of the business. The liability of the *karta* is unlimited. The liability of each member of the joint Hindu family business is limited to the extent of their share in the business.

The Joint Hindu Family (JHF) is a jointly-owned business and is governed by the Hindu Succession Act, 1956. For forming the JHF business there must be at least two members in the family and the family should have some ancestral property. The firm enjoys continuity of operations as its existence is not subject to death or insolvency of a co-parcener or even of the *karta* himself. A joint family business can be dissolved at any time, either through mutual agreement between the members or by partition.

The joint Hindu family mode of business has many advantages The *karta* enjoys full freedom in conducting the family business. The decision making in this case is very fast. Every member is assured a share in the profits irrespective of his/her contribution to the successful running of the business. There is a sharing of knowledge, experience, and grooming from elder to younger members. There is continuity in business operations.

The JHF also has some limitations. There are limited financial and managerial resources. There is scope for misuse of power by the *karta*. There is scope for conflict among the members. There may be a split in the family business. This type of family business is losing its ground with the gradual decline in the joint Hindu family system.

Partnership

The partnership firm is the most common form of business organization in India. Partnership firms are governed by the Indian Partnership Act, 1932. Section 4 of the Indian Partnership Act defines partnership as the relation between persons who have agreed to share the profits of the business carried on by all or any of them acting for all.[3] In a partnership form of organization two or more persons are associated to run a business with a view to earn profit. The partnership form of business organization is suitable for medium sized businesses that require limited capital and face moderate risks.

Each individual member in a partnership firm is known as a partner. Partners can be classified into various categories:

- Based on the extent of participation, the partners can be classified as active partners and sleeping partners. The working or active partners participate in day-to-day business operations. The partners who do not do so are kn.own as sleeping partners or dormant partners. These partners contribute to capital and share the profits and losses.
- Based on sharing of profits the partners may be classified as partners in profit and nominal partners. Nominal partners allow the firm to use their name as partner. They do not invest nor participate in everyday business operations. They are not entitled to share the profits of the firm and are liable to a third party for all the acts of the firm.
- Based on liability the partners can be classified as general partners and limited partners. Every partner who is not a limited partner is a general partner. The partners having unlimited liability are called general partners. The liability of limited partners is limited to the extent of their capital contribution.
- Based on the behaviour and conduct exhibited there are two types of partners: Partner by estoppels (liable to false representation) and partner by holding out (liable to the firm's debt). Such partners are not entitled to the firm's profits but are liable to false representation and the firm's debt.

A minimum of two persons are required to start a partnership business. The maximum number of partners is limited to ten in the case of a banking business and 20 in the case of any other business. The terms and conditions of partnership are contained in the partnership agreement known as the "Partnership Deed." The partners have unlimited liability. Partners are not allowed to transfer or sell their interest in the firm to anyone without the consent of other partners. The partnership firm may be registered. Dissolution of partnership implies complete closure and termination of the partnership business.

The partnership deed generally contains particulars regarding the name of the firm, the nature of the business to be carried out, the names of the partners, the place where the business will be carried out from, the amount of capital to be contributed by each partner, the salaries and withdrawals of the partners and the interest payable on them, the role and responsibilities of each partner, the profit and loss sharing ratio, the duration of partnership, the procedure for accounting and auditing, the procedure for dissolution of the firm, and the procedure for settlement of disputes.

According to the Indian Partnership Act, 1932, the registration of the firm is not compulsory, but desirable. This is so because an unregistered firm suffers from certain limitations. For registration, the firm should apply to the registrar of firms of the respective state government in a prescribed application form. The form should be duly signed by all the partners. The prescribed application form contains particulars such as the firm's name, the location of the business, the date of commencement of business, the date when each partner joined the firm, the full names and permanent addresses of all the partners, and the duration of the firm, if any. The completed form along with the prescribed registration fee must be deposited in the office of the registrar of firms. The registrar will scrutinize the application form and issue the certificate of registration if found satisfactory. The partnership firm may be dissolved by an agreement or as per compulsory order of a court of law.

The advantages of partnership firms are that they are easy to form without many legal formalities. Since two or more partners are involved, it is easy to pool the resources and the collective wisdom of partners enable a better decision-making process. The partnership firm is a flexible organization and there is a sharing of risk and responsibility.

The limitations of a partnership firm are as follows. The liability of partners is unlimited; every partnership firm has uncertain life, the dissolution of the firm leads to the dissolution of partnership. The difference of opinion among partners may lead to conflict among the partners and may give rise to dissolution of the firm. With the dissolution of partnership the business of the firm does not come to an end but there is a new agreement between the remaining partners. As the number of partners is restricted to 20, the capacity to raise funds is limited and the share of interest of one partner cannot be transferred to another partner or to an outsider.

Limited Liability Partnership (LLP)

An LLP is a widely accepted form of business organization worldwide. This is midway between a partnership firm and a company form of business organization. An LLP is a new corporate firm that would provide an alternative to the traditional form of the partnership firm, with unlimited personal liability on the one hand and the statute-based governance structure of the limited liability company on the other, in order to enable professional expertise and entrepreneurial initiative to combine, organize, and operate in a flexible, innovative, and efficient manner.

The law governing an LLP is the Limited Liability Partnership Act, 2008[4] which received the assent of the president of India on 7 January 2009. This form of business organization comprises two or more persons associated for carrying on a lawful business with a profit motive. The LLP shall be a corporate body and a legal entity, separated from its partners and registered with the registrar of firms. There are distinct features of an LLP, especially in terms of simplicity, flexibility, and cost effectiveness.

The members of an LLP have limited liability and they are protected against being held liable in case of the dissolution of the partnership. The LLP shall be under the obligation to maintain annual accounts reflecting a true and fair view of its state of affairs. A statement of accounts and solvency shall be filed by every LLP with the registrar every year. The accounts of LLPs shall also be audited, subject to any class of LLPs being exempted from this requirement by the Central Government.

The LLP has a number of advantages over a partnership firm and a company. The greatest advantage in a LLP is non-applicability of minimum alternate tax on the book profits of the partnership. There is no limit to the maximum number of members and thus the business can be expanded according to requirements. The liability of the partners of an LLP is limited to their contribution. The personal assets of partners are free from the liabilities of the partnership, unless it has committed a fraud or a wilful misconduct. Table 10.1 provides the key differences in terms of features between a company, a partnership, and an LLP.

Joint Stock Company

Companies are governed by the Indian Companies Act,[5] 1956. According to this Act, a company is an artificial person created by law, having separate entity, with perpetual succession and a common seal. The essential characteristic features of a company are:

- **Incorporation entity:** A company must be registered under the Companies Act. A company is formed by the initiative of a group of persons known as promoters.

Table 10.1 Differences Between Company, Partnership, and LLP

Sl No.	Particulars	Company	Partnership	LLP
1.	Governing law	Companies Act, 1956.	The Indian Partnership Act, 1932.	The Limited Liability Partnership Act, 2008.
2.	Registration	Compulsory	Optional	Compulsory
3.	Legal entity	Separate legal entity.	Not separate legal entity from partners.	Separate legal entity.
4.	Legal liability	Liability of shareholders is limited to the value of shares taken in the company.	Joint and several liabilities attached to all partners, irrespective of profit sharing ratio.	Liability of partners limited to their contribution.
5.	Succession	Company will continue and shares will be transmitted to legal heirs.	Partnership continues with other partners, subject to the deed.	LLP will continue with other partners.
6.	Ease of formation	Created by law. Procedure of formation is still rigid, time consuming, and more expensive.	Created by contract. Simplified procedure of registration and less expensive.	Created by law. Moderate procedure and expenses.

- **Artificial person**: A company is designated as an artificial person, created by law and does not possess the physical attributes of a natural person.
- **Separate legal entity**: A company is a corporate body and is known by a name mentioned in the memorandum of association. A company has an existence independent of its members. It has a distinct legal status apart from the subscribers to the memorandum of association. A shareholder cannot be held responsible for the acts of the company.
- **Separate property**: A company can own property, enter into a contract, and conduct any lawful business in its own name. Members are not owners of company property. They can only be shareholders in a company. A company can sue and can be sued in a court of law.
- **Common seal**: A company has a common seal by which it is represented while dealing with outsiders. The common seal is like the official signature of a company.
- **Limited liability**: The liability of a member is limited to the value of shares taken in the company.
- **Share certificates:** Share certificates are generally issued to members on completing shares issue formalities and when the same are fully paid up. The shareholders of the company are free to transfer the shares held by them to anyone else. SEBI regulates the transferability of shares held by the promoters or core directors in the case of listed companies in India.
- **Perpetual succession:** The company continues perpetually, irrespective of the ill-health, retirement, insolvency, or death of any of its members. In such circumstances, the company will continue and shares will be transmitted to legal heirs. The company as a legal entity continues to exist till it is officially winded up.
- **Capital:** A joint stock company generally raises a large amount of capital through the issue of shares.
- **Management:** A joint stock company has democratic management and control. The shareholders are the owners of the company. The company is managed by the elected representatives of the shareholders known as directors.
- **Membership:** A company may be a private limited or a public limited one. The members of a joint stock company are known as its shareholders. A company having a minimum membership of two persons and a maximum of fifty is called a private limited company. In case of a public limited company, the minimum number of members is seven and maximum membership is unlimited.

A joint stock company is suitable where the volume of business is quite large, there is a need for huge financial and manpower resources, the areas of operation is spread wide, and the risk involved in the business is heavy. It is suitable when there is a need for flexibility of operations and professional management. Banking and insurance businesses are chiefly joint stock companies.

A joint stock company has many advantages. The company not only helps in overcoming the limitations of sole proprietorship and partnership but also enables the entrepreneur to procure a huge amount of capital with limited liability. A joint stock company can provide the capital for large-scale operations and opens up scope for future expansion. Perpetual existence enables the management of a company more professionally because of the financial strength. It also creates employment op portunities for a large number of people and promotes research and development.

The disadvantages of a joint stock company are as follows. The formation of the company is not easy as it involves a number of legal formalities and documentation under the Companies Act. The time and cost involved is relatively high and it is also difficult to wind up a company. A company is subject to elaborate statutory and regulatory requirements in its day-to-day operations. It is managed and controlled by a small number of people called directors; therefore, the democratic virtues of a company do not really exist in practice. The levels in management and formalities delay the decision-making process. In a joint stock company there is a concentration of economic power, which may influence the government, politicians, and exploit workers and investors

Companies can be classified on the basis of the mode of incorporation into statutory and registered companies. The statutory company is created by a special act and examples are Life Insurance Corporation, State Bank of India, Unit Trust of India, and Reserve Bank of India. Registered companies are formed and registered under the Companies Act, 1956. On the basis of the liability of members, companies are classified into companies limited by shares, limited by guarantee, and unlimited. Based on the number of members, they are classified into the private limited company (minimum two and maximum 50) and the public limited company (minimum seven and maximum unlimited).

Private Limited Company A private limited company[6] is a voluntary association having a minimum membership of two persons and a maximum of 50. It has a separate legal entity; the liability of members is limited; it enjoys continuity of the existence of business and maintains the privacy of business. A private limited company is a compromise between a partnership and a public limited company. It is free from excessive government regulation and progressive income tax liability. Compared to the public limited company, the private limited company is less cumbersome to organize and operate. A limited company is preferred to take advantage of limited liability and at the same time to keep control over the business within a limited group and to maintain the privacy of business.

Public Limited Company A public limited company[7] is a voluntary association of individuals with a minimum of seven members and with the maximum membership unlimited. The company has a separate legal existence apart from its members who compose it. The formation, working, and winding up of the company are strictly governed by laws, rules, and regulations by its memorandum of association and articles of association and as per the general provision of the Companies Act, 1956. In the case of a public limited company, in addition to a certificate of incorporation; a certificate to commence business is also fundamental.

The company collects its share capital from the sale of share certificates by the members who are called shareholders. As the maximum number of members is unlimited, a large amount of capital can be collected from shareholders. The liability of the members is limited and the continuity of the existence of the business is assured. The shareholders of a company do not have the right to participate in the day-to-day management of its business. This ensures separation of ownership from management. The power of decision making in a company is vested in the Board of Directors, and all policy decisions are taken at the Board level by the majority rule. The advantages of a public limited company include the availability of a large amount of capital, the continuity of business operations, limited liability, employment generation, unity of direction, and professional management. The disadvantages of a public limited company include scope for frauds, concentration of power in a few hands, strict rules and regulations, and the cumbersome formation of the Corporation. Table 10.2 provides the differences between a private limited company and a public limited company.

Formation of a Company The entire process of the formation of a company may be divided into four stages: promotion, registration, floatation, and commencement of business. Promotion denotes the preliminary steps taken for the registration of the company by the promoters. The promoters of the company prepare a memorandum of association (MOU), articles of association, and other necessary documents. The MOU of a company is an important document as it defines and confines the powers of the company. A company can only act as per the objects given in the MOU.[7] The articles of association of a company are its by-laws or rules and regulations. It controls the internal management of the company and defines the powers of its office.

The articles contain provisions relating to share capital, the rights of shareholders, shares and stock, meetings, and directors. A public company normally invites the public to subscribe to its share capital by issuing a prospectus. A prospectus is a document described or issued and includes any notice, circular, advertisement, or other documents inviting deposits from the public. The prospectus must be dated, signed, and registered with the registrar.

The winding up of a company is a process whereby its life is ended and its assets are administered for the benefit of its creditors and members. The winding up is overseen by an administrator called the liquidator. The liquidator is appointed to take control of the company, collect its assets, pay its debts, and finally distribute any surplus among members in accordance with their rights. Winding up may be of two kinds—a compulsory winding up under the orders of the National Company Law Tribunal (NCLT) or a voluntary winding up.

Table 10.2 Differences Between Private Limited and Public Limited Companies

Sl No.	Particulars	Private Limited Company	Public Limited Company
1.	Number of members required to form a company	Minimum number is two and maximum is 50.	Minimum number is seven and maximum is unlimited.
2.	Managerial remuneration	No restrictions on managerial remuneration.	Total managerial remuneration cannot exceed 11% of the net profits, and in case of inadequate profits a maximum of ₹87,500 can be paid.
3.	Compliance requirements	Reasonable compliance requirements with adequate record keeping and audit are required.	Strict and extensive record keeping, audit, and more stringent compliances are required.
4.	Corporate governance	Regulations exist in relation to transactions which could substantially affect shareholders.	In addition to the procedures prescribed for private limited companies, more exhaustive procedures exist for public limited companies, especially when listed.
5.	Access to capital markets for fund raising	Given restrictions on number of shareholders and transfer of ownership, conversion into a public limited company is required for accessing the capital market for fund raising.	Can be listed on one or more stock exchanges by complying with the respective listing requirements and have access to capital markets for fund raising.
6.	Transfer of shares	The right to transfer shares is restricted.	Shares are freely transferable.
7.	Issue of prospectus	Prospectus cannot be issued.	The general public is invited to subscribe for shares, debentures, or deposits through a prospectus.
8.	Commencement of business	Business can be immediately started after acquiring the certificate of incorporation.	Business can only start after receiving the certificate to commence the business from the Registrar of Companies.
9.	Directors	The number of directors must be at least two and it may be increased to any number. Directors can be approved by a single resolution. Directors are not required to retire by rotation.	The number of directors must be at least three and the number should not exceed 12 without the approval of the Central Government. Each director's appointment requires a separate resolution. At least two-third of directors must retire by rotation.
10.	Public deposits	Cannot accept deposits from the public.	Can accept deposits from public.
11.	Filing of various returns	Exempted from filing of various returns.	Not exempted.
12.	Statutory meeting	Need not hold a statutory meeting or file a statutory report.	Needs to conduct a statutory meeting and file a statutory report.

Corporate Governance

The persons through whom a company acts and does its business are termed as directors. Before a person is appointed as a director, his prior written consent with signature is required to be filed with the registrar and the company. The board of directors of a company shall be entitled to exercise all such powers, and do all such acts and things, as the company is authorized to exercise and do. All decisions of the company are taken in board meetings by passing resolutions. There are three kinds of meetings: statutory meetings, annual general meetings, and extraordinary meetings. The shareholders have the option to remove the directors by passing an ordinary resolution. The Central Government has the power to make reference to the Tribunal (NCLT) against managerial personnel if deemed unfit. The Tribunal may order the termination of the agreement of the company with the director. A director has the right to make representations.

Good governance is integral for the existence of a company. Corporate governance is required to promote a healthy environment for long-term sustenance and growth of the company. Corporate governance can be evaluated by rating agencies like CRISIL or ICRA. Minimal corporate governance can be achieved by following statutory and regulatory requirements enforced by law. For better governance the management has to be professional but best corporate governance is achieved by following the fundamental principles of corporate governance, which are as follows:

- A company must observe ethical standards.
- It must be transparent in all business transactions.
- The board of directors must be accountable to shareholders.
- There must be a principle of trusteeship of the board of directors to protect and enhance stakeholders' value.
- There must be empowerment of people at various levels in the organizational hierarchy.
- There should be fairness and equitable treatment for all stakeholders.
- The company must prevent misuse of power by developing a system of check points and control points.
- External audit must be conducted by an independent professional body.
- The company should adopt a whistle-blowers policy. There must be an appropriate regulatory regime to back these obligations.

Cooperative Society

A cooperative society is a voluntary association of ten or more members who work together to promote their economic interests. The primary objective of all cooperative societies is to provide service to its members. Section 4 of the Indian Cooperative Societies Act, 1912 defines a cooperative society as "a society which has its objectives for the promotion of economic interests of its members in accordance with the cooperative principles."[8] The Cooperative Societies Act is a central act. This Act has been specifically repealed in almost all the states and those states have their own Cooperative Societies Acts. The state government appoints a registrar of cooperative societies. A society which has as its objective the promotion of the economic interests of its members in accordance with cooperative principles can be registered as a cooperative society. A cooperative society operating in more than one state is known as a multi-state cooperative society. These are registered under the Multi-State Cooperative Societies Act, 2001.

A society can be registered with limited or unlimited liability. A society can be formed with at least ten members above 18 years of age. Membership is open to all those having a common economic interest irrespective of one's caste, creed, religion, colour, or sex. Any amendment to its by-laws shall be registered with the registrar. Each society will be managed by a committee. A committee is a governing body of a registered society to whom the management of its affairs is entrusted. A registered cooperative society is a corporate body with perpetual succession and a common seal. It can hold property, enter into contracts, institute and defend legal proceedings, and do all things necessary for the purpose of its constitution.

The capital of a cooperative society is contributed by its members. A registered society can give loans only to its members. The members get returns on their capital invested in the form of dividends. After giving a limited dividend to the members of the society, the surplus profit is distributed in the form of a bonus, keeping aside a certain percentage as reserve and for the general welfare of the society. The various types of cooperative societies are given below:

- **Credit cooperative society:** These accept deposits from members and grant them loans at a reasonable rate of interest and are started in order to give credit to members.
- **Consumers' cooperative society:** These make available consumer goods of high quality at a reasonable price in order to protect the interests of consumers.
- **Farming cooperative society:** These are formed by small farmers in order to get the benefits of large-scale farming.
- **Producers' cooperative society:** These are formed to protect the interests of small-scale producers and artisans by making available items needed for their production such as raw materials, tools, and equipments.
- **Housing cooperative society:** These are formed to provide residential houses to members.
- **Marketing cooperative society:** These are formed by small producers who join together to market their products.

A cooperative society can be formed as per the provisions of the Cooperative Societies Act, 1912. It can also be formed under the Cooperative Societies Acts of respective states. The following guidelines should be followed for the formation of a cooperative society.

- The number of members required for the formation of cooperative society is ten. They should have common economic interests and should be able to enter into a contract. For multi-state cooperative societies, there should be a representation of 50 members at least from each state.
- A draft of the by-laws of the society should be prepared.
- A suitable name should be proposed for the society and the society should be registered with the registrar of cooperative societies of the state.
- The application for registration must be signed by each member of the society and be accompanied by four copies of the proposed by-laws of the society.
- The society can start its operation after receiving the certificate of registration from the registrar of cooperative societies of the state.

The cooperative society is the only form of business organization that gives utmost importance to the service of its members rather than to maximizing its own profits. It promotes mutual help among the members in place of competition, self-help in place of dependence, and moral solidarity in place of unethical business practices.

The main advantages of cooperative society type of organization are the ease of formation, limited liability, membership open to all, ability to get assistance from the Central and State Government in the form of grants, loans, subsidies, and tax concessions. It enjoys a democratic type of management and the benefit of perpetual succession. Most of the cooperative societies suffer from a lack of capital, managerial expertise, and motivation of members due to the lesser rate of return on the capital invested. This form of organization is mainly suitable for small and medium operations.

If an entrepreneur carries out the existing business successfully over a period of time the chances of expanding the business is high. During that phase they will have to review the existing form of business organization and analyse the possibility of changing over to another format to carry out their business operations. The various alternatives available to an entrepreneur to change the existing form of an organization are as follows:

- A sole proprietor may change over to a partnership.
- A partnership firm may change over to a private limited company.
- A private limited company may change over to a public limited company.

Franchising

Franchising is the practice of using the model adopted by another successful entity. In this model, the franchisor provides a licensed privilege to the franchisee to carry out business and offers assistance in organizing, training, merchandising, marketing, and managing in return for monetary consideration.

A franchise is a system of distribution that enables the supplier (called the franchisor) to arrange for a dealer (called the franchisee) to handle a specific product or service under certain mutually agreed upon conditions. The franchisor is a company which has developed and thoroughly tested its business methods and has decided to increase the size of its business by offering individuals, the franchisees, the right to trade under its business name. The individuals concerned pay a fee, not only for the right to trade under the name of the franchisor, but also in order to benefit from its expertise. The franchisee can be a sole proprietorship, partnership or, a private company.

Major Factors Influencing Franchising According to experts, five major factors influence the growth and expansion of franchising. These are:

- A leveling off of sales growth among franchise outlets in traditional fields such as fast food, hotels, bakeries, greeting cards, and gift shops.
- Continuing rapid growth and expansion of service type businesses, for example, childcare, business aids, and services.
- Conversion of independent businesses to franchises—like shirt brands.
- Globalization of franchising—franchise companies in the United States continue to expand overseas, for example, McDonald's, Pizza Hut, and Kentucky Fried Chicken in India.
- An increasingly mature and diversified franchise company.

Types of Franchising Arrangement There are two types:

1. **Franchising of a product or service:** In this type of franchising, the franchisee receives a product from the franchisor and sells it through a wholesale or retail outlet. If it is a service, he/she

BREAKTHROUGH ENTREPRENEURSHIP 10.1 Milkman of India

Dr Verghese Kurien, whose name is synonymous with the Amul brand, was the founder chairman of the Gujarat Cooperative Milk Marketing Federation (GCMMF). He was the pioneer in the development of the Amul model. Dr Kurien was born on 26 November 1921 in Kozhikode, Kerala. After graduating from Tata Steel Technical Institute, Jamshedpur, in 1946, Kurien completed his M.Sc. in metallurgical engineering from Michigan State University. After his return from the United States in 1948, he came to Anand, Gujarat, on government service. Dr Verghese Kurien left his government job and assumed leadership of the cooperative movement in 1949. He then built the dairy development cooperative model, Amul, into one of the largest and most successful institutions in India.

The National Dairy Development Board (NDDB) was founded in 1965 under the leadership of Dr Kurien. He is credited with being the architect of "Operation Flood," the largest dairy development programme in the world. The programme heralded the beginning of the White Revolution in India that brought substantial profits to milk farmers and made a dramatic change in their lives. He also founded the GCMMF in 1973 to market the products produced by its dairies. Dr Kurien and his team were pioneers in inventing the process of making milk powder and condensed milk from buffalo's milk instead of cow's milk.

Dr Kurien was responsible for successfully leading India to become the largest milk producer in the world. Dr Kurien is known as the "Father of the White Revolution" and the "Milkman of India." He has won many accolades and awards and served as a role model to many others. He is the recipient of the Lifetime Achievement Award (CNN-IBN 2011), the Padma Vibhushan (1999), the World Food Prize (United States 1986), the Krishi Ratna Award (1986), the Padma Bhushan (1966), the Padma Shri (1965), and the Ramon Magsaysay Award (1963).

Sources: www.amul.com and www.gcmmf.coop (last accessed in March 2013).

agrees to provide the service from his own premises with a license from the franchisor for using the trade name.

2. **Franchising of an entire business enterprise:** Here the franchisee operates under the trade name of the franchisor in a particular area mutually agreed upon, for example, McDonald's in Delhi, Mumbai, Bangalore, and other cities. In this case, the business operation, appearance of the establishment, merchandise, and even operating procedures and service are standardized to a high degree.

SNAPSHOT

- The various forms of business organization are sole proprietorship, joint Hindu family business, partnership, joint stock company, cooperative society, and franchising.
- Sole proprietorship is the most common and simple form of business organization as it does not have any legal formalities.
- The joint Hindu family business is a distinct type of organization, which is unique to India.
- Partnership firm is the most common form of business organization in India in which two or more persons are associated to run a business with a view to earn profit.
- Joint stock companies are governed by the Indian Companies Act, 1956. Based on the number of members, they are classified into private limited company and the public limited company.
- A cooperative society is a voluntary association of ten or more members who work together to promote their economic interests. The primary objective of all cooperative societies is to provide service to its members.
- Franchising is a form of business by which the owner (franchisor) of a product, service, or method obtains distribution through affiliated dealers (franchisees).

DISCUSSION FORUM

- Explain the suitability of the sole proprietorship form of business organization.
- What is a joint Hindu family business?
- Distinguish between a partnership and an LLP.
- Distinguish between a private and a public limited company.
- Name any five types of cooperatives.
- Discuss different types of franchising agreements.

BUSINESS LAWS

A knowledge of law as applicable to business is essential for the owners of businesses, managerial teams, and all the stakeholders in a business. Business professionals and management graduates are also required to have a current awareness of business or commercial laws, as this helps the individuals to possess better information and be accurate in matters of business transactions. Business law is that branch of law which comprises laws concerning trade, industry, and commerce. Table 10.3 provides information on various business laws, their nature, purpose of enactment, effective date of operation of the laws in India, and the authorities governing them in India.

Table 10.3 Business Laws Prevalent in India

Sl No.	Name of the Law	Purpose of Enactment	Effective Date of Operation of the Law	Authorities Governing the Law
1.	The Indian Contract Act	To regulate contracts or agreements or the relations of parties.	1872	Authorities designated or courts of law.
2.	The Sale of Goods Act	To regulate and deal with laws relating to the sale of goods in India.	1930	Courts of law/ arbitration authorities.
3.	The Indian Partnership Act	To regulate the relationship of partners, firms, and the commencement, management, and dissolution of a firm.	1932	The District Registrar of Firms/ Societies and courts of law or arbitrators.
4.	The Limited Liability Partnership Act	To promote a simplified and flexible form of business organization and smoothen business transactions involving multi-disciplinary professionals across the world.	2008	Courts of law.
5.	The Indian Companies Act	To consolidate and amend the laws relating to companies and other associations.	1956	The Registrar of Firms/ Societies and courts of law or arbitrators
6.	The Negotiable Instruments Act	To define and amend the laws relating to promissory notes, bills of exchange, and cheques.	1881	Courts of law.
7.	The Information Technology Act	To provide legal recognition for transactions carried out by means of electronic data interchange.	2000	Registering authority, cyber courts.
8.	Intellectual Property Rights	To regulate intangible property which includes patents, trademarks, copyrights, and design rights.		Courts of law.
9.	The Consumer Protection Act	To protect the interests of consumers.	1986	Consumer disputes redressal agencies, courts of law.
10.	The Right to Information Act	To provide a right to information for citizens to secure information under the control of public authorities.	2005	Central Information Commission and State Information Commission, courts of law.
11.	The Competition Act	To prevent practices having adverse effect on competition, to promote and sustain competition in markets, to protect the interests of consumers, and to ensure the freedom of trade carried on by other participants.	2002	Courts of law, regulating authorities.
12.	The Foreign Exchange Management Act	To facilitate external trade and payments and promote the orderly development and maintenance of the foreign exchange market in India.	1999	Financial regulators like the RBI, Ministry of Finance, courts of law.

The Indian Contract Act, 1872

The law of contracts is the oldest law in India. The law of contract is applicable not only to business but also to other transactions. A contract is an agreement made between two parties and enforceable by law. It consists of a proposal by one party and its acceptance by the other party. In order to be a contract, an agreement must give rise to legal consequences and remedies in a court of law in case of its breach. It extends to the whole of India except the state of Jammu and Kashmir and came into existence on 1 September 1872.

The law of contract is the foundation upon which the superstructure of modern business, trade, and commerce is built. The parties to a contract should be competent to enter into valid contracts. A person who is a major, with sound mind, and is not disqualified from contracting by law is always considered to be competent to enter into a valid contract. A person may be male or female. The capacity to enter into a contract is always influenced by the mental or physical condition of a person and his/her status in society.

Every business transaction must be founded on the principles of a valid contract. The essential elements of a valid contract are[9]:

- An agreement i.e. proposal and acceptances
- An intention to create a legal relationship
- Parties competent to contract
- Lawful consideration
- Free consent
- Not expressly declared void
- Possibility of performance
- Certainty
- A lawful object
- Legal formalities

Contracts could be classified into various types according to the categories given below:

- **Enforceability:** Valid contracts, void contracts, void agreements, voidable contracts, unenforceable contracts, and illegal contracts.
- **Mode of creation:** Express contracts, implied contracts, and quasi contracts.
- **Extent of execution:** Executed contracts and executory contracts.
- **Form of the contract:** Formal contracts and simple contracts.

The Indemnity and Guarantee Law, 1872, protects the promisor against the anticipated laws in courts of law. Indemnity is a contract by which one party promises to save the other from loss to him/her through the conduct of the promisor himself, or through the conduct of any other person. A contract of guarantee is a contract to perform the promise or discharge the liability of a third person in case of his default. A bailment is the delivery of goods by one person to another for some purpose, upon a contract that they shall, when the purpose is accomplished, be returned or otherwise disposed of, according to the direction of the person delivering them. The person delivering the goods is called the bailor. The person to whom the goods are delivered is called the bailee.

The bailment of goods as security for the payment of a debt or the performance of a promise is called a pledge. The pledge is a kind of bailment. The Bailment and Pledge Law, 1872, regulates and controls the purpose of the contract made for the delivery of goods. It also regulates the payment of a debt or performance of a promise and may be enforced in a court of law.

The Law of Agency, 1872, regulates the relationship between an agent and his principal and may be enforced in the court of law. An agent is a person employed to do any act for another or to represent another in dealings with third persons. When the rights and obligations arising out of a contract are executed, the contract is said to be discharged or terminated by performance (actual or attempted), mutual consent or agreement, subsequent or supervening impossibility or illegality, lapse of time, operation of law, and breach of contract. In case of breach of a contract, the injured party may have one or more of the following remedies: rescission, damages, and compensation for loss or damage caused by breach of contract.

The Sale of Goods Act, 1930

The Sale of Goods Act, 1930, deals with the laws relating to the sale of goods in India. The Act contains 66 sections, came into force from 1 July 1930, and extends throughout India except the state of Jammu and Kashmir. The sale of goods is the most common of all commercial contracts. This Act is considered to be fundamental in nature, next only to the Indian Contract Act, 1872, as most business transactions are governed under this law.

According to the Act, "a contract of sale of goods is a contract whereby the seller transfers or agrees to transfer the property in goods to the buyer for a price. There may be a contract of sale between one part-owner and another." Goods are movable goods only and price must be expressed in money. A sale by auction is a public sale where different intending buyers try to outbid each other. The goods are ultimately sold to the highest bidder. The essential elements of a contract of sale of goods are given below:

- There must be two distinct parties, buyer and seller to a contract of sale of goods.
- There must be either a transfer of ownership of goods or an agreement to transfer the ownership of goods.
- Goods of any kind except immovable property may be transferred. It does not include actionable claims and money. Goods may be of three types: existing goods, future goods, and contingent goods.
- There must be money consideration for the sale of goods. However, the consideration may also be partly in money and partly in goods. When the consideration is only goods, it amounts to "barter" and is not sale.
- The term "contract of sale" is a generic term and includes both a "sale" and an "agreement to sell."
- A contract of sale of goods can be made by mere offer and acceptance by the seller or the buyer. Neither payment nor delivery is necessary at the time of making the contract of sale.
- The seller's duty is to deliver the goods and the buyer's duty is to accept and pay for the goods as per the terms of the contract of sale.

In a sale, the property in the goods is transferred from the seller to the buyer. In an agreement to sell, the transfer of property in the goods is to take place at a future time or subject to some condition thereafter to be fulfilled. It is an executor contract and refers to a conditional sale. In hire purchase, property does not pass when the agreement is made out but only passes when the option is finally exercised after complying with all the terms of the agreement. A hire purchase agreement is regulated by the Hire Purchase Act, 1972. The distinction between sale, agreement to sell, and hire purchase is given in Table 10.4.

A contract of sale of goods must possess all the essentials of an ordinary contract. It may be in writing or orally or partly in writing and partly orally or may be implied from the conduct of the parties. There must be an offer to buy or sell existing or future goods for a price and acceptance of such an offer. The contract may provide for immediate payment of the price or payment by installment or payment may be postponed. There may be immediate delivery of the goods or delivery by installment or delivery at a future date.

The Indian Partnership Act, 1932

The partnership firm is the most common form of business organization in India. The Indian Partnership Act, 1932, defines and amends the law relating to partnerships. Section 4 of the Indian Partnership Act defines partnership as "the relation between persons who have agreed to share the profits of the business carried on by all or any of them acting for all." The Indian Partnership Act is administered by state governments through the registrar of firms to regulate the legal aspects of a firm including the procedural aspects of the firm's functioning.[10]

The persons who have entered into the partnership agreement or deed are individually called partners and collectively a firm. The name under which partners carry on their business is called "firm name" or "trade name." A partnership deed is the contract, in writing, of partnership entered into by the partners with agreed clauses or the terms and conditions of their relation in the firm.

Table 10.4 Distinction Between Sale, Agreement to Sell, and Hire Purchase

Sl No.	Points of Distinction	Sale	Agreement to Sell	Hire Purchase
1.	Nature of contract.	It is an executed contract.	It is an executor contract.	It is a bailment plus an agreement to sell.
2.	Risk of loss.	Loss will be borne by the buyer even if the goods are in possession of the seller.	Loss will be borne by the seller since the ownership of goods has not passed to the buyer.	If the hirer fails to pay an installment, the owner takes back the goods.
3.	Transfer of property in goods.	Property in goods is transferred to the buyer immediately at the time of contract.	Conveyance of goods may take place subsequently.	Property in goods passes to the hirer upon payment of installment.
4.	Rights of ownership.	The position of the buyer is that of the owner of the goods.	The buyer can sell or pledge the goods.	The buyer cannot exercise any ownership rights; hence, cannot sell or pledge the goods.
5.	Law applicable.	Sale of Goods Act, 1930	Sale of Goods Act, 1930	Hire Purchase Act, 1972

The essential elements of partnership are the association of two or more persons, agreement between persons to carry on a business, agreement to share profits, and a binding contract of mutual agency between the partners. The registration of a firm under the Partnership Act is not compulsory, but is desirable.

The Limited Liability Partnership Act, 2008

The Limited Liability Partnership (LLP) Act, 2008, is an enactment introduced for the first time extending to the whole of India. An LLP is to have at least two designated partners and at least one shall be a resident of India. Every LLP shall have a registered office to which all communication and notices may be addressed and shall be received.

An LLP is a corporate business vehicle[11] that enables the integration of professional expertise and entrepreneurial initiative. It operates in a flexible, innovative, and efficient manner by providing benefits of limited liability. It provides flexibility in the organizational structure among the partners. Since an LLP is a separate legal entity, its existence is not affected by the entry and exit of its partners. The LLP does not require a memorandum or article of association. The LLP structure is found useful for venture capital and technology-based enterprises.

The procedure for the establishment of an LLP is:

- Decide upon the partners and the designated partners.
- Obtain designated partner identification number and a digital signature certificate.
- Decide upon the name of the LLP to be incorporated (not identical with company or an LLP already registered in India).
- Draft the LLP agreement.
- File the LLP agreement and incorporation documents.
- Obtain the certificate of incorporation with the registrar of companies.

The Indian Companies Act, 1956

The law relating to companies in India is contained in the Companies Act, 1956. The latest amendment to the Act was made in 2006 by the Companies (Amendment) Act, 2006. A company in a broad sense means a voluntary association of persons grouped together for the attainment of a common end, social or economic. A promoter is a person who does the necessary preliminary work incidental to the formation of a company. The promoter of a company decides its name and ascertains that it will be accepted by the registrar of companies. He is responsible for bringing the company into existence by the nomination of directors, solicitors, bankers, auditors, secretary, and selection of the registered office of the company. Companies may be classified into various kinds on the following basis:

- Classification on the basis of incorporation: Statutory companies and registered companies.
- Classification on the basis of liability: Companies with limited liability (limited by shares or by guarantee) and companies with unlimited liability.
- Classification on the basis of the number of members: Private company and public company.
- Classification on the basis of control: Holding company and subsidiary company.
- Classification on the basis of ownership: Government company and non-governmental company.

The Ministry of Corporate Affairs (MCA) has launched a project named MCA–21.[12] The project is designed to fully automate all processes related to the enforcement and compliance of legal requirements under the Companies Act, 1956. The following nine matters have been covered under the MCA-21 project since 15 September 2006:

1. Registration and incorporation of new companies.
2. Filing of annual returns and balance sheets.
3. Filing of forms for change of name/address/director's details.
4. Registration, modification, and verification of charges.
5. Inspection of documents.
6. Issue of certified copies.
7. Application for permissions required under various provisions of the company law.
8. Approval from the Central Government, the regional director, and the registrar of companies.
9. Investor grievance redressal.

The Negotiable Instruments Act, 1881

The law relating to negotiable instruments is contained in the Negotiable Instruments Act, 1881.[13] It deals with promissory notes, bills of exchange, and cheques. The Act extends to the whole of India. According to Section 13 (1), "A negotiable instrument means a promissory note, bill of exchange, or cheque payable either to order or to bearer." The term negotiable signifies transferability from one person to another. Instrument implies a written document, which creates a right in favour of the other person.

A promissory note is an instrument in writing containing an unconditional undertaking signed by the maker to pay a certain sum of money only to, or to the order of, a certain person or to the bearer of the instrument. A bill of exchange is an instrument in writing containing an unconditional order signed by the maker directing a certain person to pay a certain sum of money only to, or to the order of, a certain person or to the bearer of the instrument. A cheque is a bill of exchange drawn on a specified banker, not expressed to be payable on demand, and it includes the electronic image of a truncated cheque and a cheque in the electronic form.

A negotiable instrument is a piece of paper, which entitles a person to a sum of money and which is transferable from one person to another by mere delivery or by endorsement and delivery. There are two types of negotiable instruments: (a) Recognized by statute: promissory notes, bill of exchange, and cheques and (b) Recognized by usage: *hundi*, bill of lading, share warrant, dividend warrant, railway receipts, and delivery orders.

An instrument in order to be treated as negotiable must be in writing, signed by the maker/drawer, a promise or order to pay, unconditional, paid in money for a certain sum, payable at a time of arrival, and the drawee must be named or described with reasonable security. The characteristic features of a negotiable instrument are: (a) It is freely transferable from one person to another by delivery or endorsement and delivery, (b) The title of the holder is free from all defects, (c) The holder in due course can sue upon a negotiable instrument in his own name for the recovery of the amount, (d) It should have presumptions such as consideration, date, time of transfer, stamp, proof of protest, order of endorsement, and time of acceptance, and (e) It can be transferred any number of times till it is matured.

The holder of a negotiable instrument is a person entitled to the possession of the instrument in his own name and to recover the amount due thereon from the parties thereto. The holder of a negotiable instrument enjoys certain privileges and can endorse the negotiable instrument with his signature. The negotiable instrument may be dishonoured due to non-acceptance, by non-payment, by intensity of notice, and when the party receiving the notice is dead.

SNAPSHOT

- The Indian Contract Act of 1872 regulates contracts or agreements or the relations of parties.
- The Sale of Goods Act of 1930 regulates and deals with laws relating to the sale of goods in India.
- The Indian Partnership Act of 1932 regulates the relationship of partners, firms and commencement, management and dissolution of a firm.
- The Limited Liability Partnership Act of 2008 is a corporate business vehicle that enables the integration of professional expertise and entrepreneurial initiative.
- The Indian Companies Act of 1956 consolidates and amends the laws relating to companies and other associations.
- The Negotiable Instruments Act of 1881 defines and amends the laws relating to promissory notes, bills of exchange, and cheques.

DISCUSSION FORUM

- Discuss the essential elements of a valid contract.
- Briefly explain the Indemnity and Guarantee Law, 1872, and the Law of Agency, 1872.
- Which are the essential elements of the Sale of Goods Act?
- Discuss the essential elements of partnership.
- Explain the relevance of the Limited Liability Partnership Act, 2008.
- Name the two types of negotiable instruments.

The Information Technology Act, 2000

India enacted the Information Technology Act, 2000, on 17 October 2000. The Information Technology Act, 2000, was amended by the Information Technology (Amendment) Act, 2008, which was notified in the official government gazette in February 2009. There have been numerous amendments in various sections of the Information Technology Act.

This Act provides for the legal recognition for transactions carried out by means of electronic communication, commonly referred to as "electronic commerce," which eliminates the need for paper-based transactions. The Act also provides for digital signature certificates, penalties, adjudication, the Cyber Appellate Tribunal, and the liability of the network service provider. E-governance is provided by means of the legal recognition of electronic records, of digital signatures, retention of electronic records, and publication of rules and regulations in an electronic gazette.

In India the laws relating to information technology are based on this model law and contained in the Information Technology Act, 2000. The objectives of this Act are e-commerce and e-governance. The Act extends to India but it also has extra-territorial applications outside India. The Act is not applicable to certain documents like negotiable instruments, wills, trusts, power of attorney, and any conveyance of immovable property. The authentication of electronic records is done by digital signature, which is based on the concept of private and public key. The Government of India has launched the national e-governance portal with the intent to support the growth of e-governance within the country.

Cyber law is the law governing cyber space. Cyber laws[14] are contained in the Information Technology (IT) Act, 2000. Cyber law encompasses laws relating to cyber crimes; electronic and digital signatures; intellectual property; and data protection and privacy. Cyber laws[15] provide legal recognition to electronic documents and a framework to support e-filing and e-commerce transactions and also provides a legal framework to mitigate and check cyber crimes.

A cyber crime is an unlawful act wherein the computer is either a tool or a target or both. A cyber crime may be committed against a person, property, and/or the government. The abuse of computers has also given birth to a gamut of new-age crimes that are addressed by the Information Technology Act, 2000. Cyber crime is regulated by cyber laws or Internet laws. Cyber crimes may be of two categories:

1. **The computer as a target:** Using a computer to attack other computers. For example: hacking, virus attack.
2. **The computer as a weapon:** Using a computer to commit real-world crimes. For example: cyber terrorism, IPR violations, credit card frauds, pornography.

Electronic signatures are used to validate electronic records. Digital signatures are electronic signatures that satisfy three major legal requirements: signer authentication, message integrity, and message authentication. Intellectual property refers to original creations of the human mind, for example, design, fiction, music, and painting[16]. The various facets of intellectual property related to cyber law include copyright law, semiconductor law, trademark law, patent law (computer hardware and software), and software and source code licenses. Data protection and privacy laws aim to achieve a balance between the privacy rights of the individual and the interests of data controllers such as hospitals, banks, and Internet service providers.

WORLD OF ENTREPRENEURS 10.2 / E-governance Initiatives in India

The Government of India has implemented a comprehensive programme to accelerate e-governance at all levels of the government to improve efficiency, transparency, and accountability. The IT Act was enacted in 2000 to provide legal status to the information available on and transactions carried out in the Internet. Several significant initiatives taken in India are given below:

Projects

e-Choupal: A quiet revolution spearheaded by the Indian Tobacco Corporation (ITC) is reshaping the lives of farmers in remote Indian villages. In these villages farmers are largely illiterate and have never seen a computer. But farmers in these villages are conducting e-business through a unique Web-based initiative called e-*Choupal* created by ITC. e-*Choupal* is a cost-effective supply chain system for dealing directly with the farmer to buy crops for exports. The e-*Choupal* initiative has been specially cited in the Government of India's Economic Survey of 2006–07 for its transformational impact on rural lives.

Dairy Information Services Kiosk (DISK): This project is an initiative of the Indian Institute of Management Ahemdabad's e-governance centre. The project has been developed with an objective of empowering dairy farmers through extensive collaboration with the cooperative dairy unions of Gujarat. The project consists of two basic components: an application running at the rural milk collection society that could be provided Internet connectivity and a portal at the district level serving the transactional and information needs of all members. Software called AkashGanga has been developed with special features to enable speedier collection of milk and faster disbursement of payment to dairy farmers.

Vidya Vahini: This is a portal developed by Shiksha India, a non-profit organization. It is an initiative of the Government of India under the Ministry of Information Technology and the Ministry of Human Resources under the CLASS scheme. Project Vidya Vahini equips schools with the 5Cs—computers, connectivity, coaching, content, and models of commercial sustainability. This portal provides an opportunity for schools, teachers, and students across the country, to express and share their creative and academic potential through the Internet.

Sources: www.itcportal.com; www.iimahd.ernet.in/egov/documents/disk-and-dairy-portal.pdf (last accessed in March 2013); and www.vidyavahini.ernet.in (last accessed in March 2013).

INTELLECTUAL PROPERTY RIGHTS

Intellectual property is the property derived by an individual for his intellectual efforts. Under the World Trade Organization, the Trade Related Intellectual Property Rights (TRIPS)[17] are:

- Patents
- Copyrights
- Trademarks
- Geographical indications
- Industrial designs
- Integrated circuits
- Trade secrets or confidential information.

In 1974, the World Intellectual Property Organization (WIPO)[18] became a specialized agency of the United Nations system of organizations, with a mandate to administer intellectual property matters recognized by the member states of the United Nations. WIPO expanded its role by entering into a cooperation agreement with the WTO in 1996.

The Patents Act, 1970

The law relating to patents is contained in the Patents Act, 1970. The Act extends to the whole of India. The fundamental principle of patent law is that a patent is granted only for an invention, which must be new and useful. The Patents Act, 1970, is an Act to amend and consolidate the law relating to patents. "Patent" is a grant made by the government to an inventor, conveying and securing to him the exclusive right to make, use, and sell his invention for a term of years. Patents are a powerful tool for stimulating the creation of new technologies and industries. The patent is a protection given to a patentee for his invention for a limited term by the government in consideration for his disclosing the invention.

The process for the registration of a patent includes:

- Filing of application
- Meeting procedural objections
- Publication of the application
- Request for examination
- Pre-grant opposition
- First examination report
- Meeting official objections
- Grant of the patent
- Post-grant opposition

The headquarters of the patent office is at Kolkata and branch offices are at Mumbai, Chennai, and New Delhi. The Controller General supervises the administration of the Patents Act, Designs Act, and Trade Marks Act, and also advises the government on matters relating to these subjects. Various amendments were made to the Act, in 1999, 2002, 2005, and 2006 on account of India's obligations towards TRIPS.

A patent application can be made by the true and first investor, his assignee or their legal representative. Every application shall be made for one invention and accompanied by complete specifications. It should be published and sent to an examiner for a report. The term of a patent shall be 20 years from the date of filing of the application for the patent. For any infringement of patent, the court may grant injunction, seizure of goods, or damages.

The Copyright Act, 1957

The law relating to copyright is contained in the Copyright Act, 1957. The Act is in conformity with international conventions and treaties. This Act has been amended five times: 1983, 1984, 1992, 1994, and 1999. Copyright is a bundle of rights, which grants protection to the expression of ideas in a material medium that is the subject matter of copyright protection. The Copyright Act secures the interest of authors, artists, architects, composers, music production companies, producers, computer programmers, and designers. The Act provides motivation and incentives for the creation of original works.

Section 9 of the Copyright Act requires the establishment of a copyright office. The copyright office is to be under the immediate control of a registrar of copyright, appointed by the Central Government. In India, the copyright office is located at New Delhi. Section 11 of the Copyright Act requires the Central Government to constitute a copyright board headed by a chairman with not less than two and not more than 14 other members. The registrar of copyrights is to be the secretary of the copyright board. The copyright board supervises the office of the registrar of copyright. Section 12 of the Copyright Act lays down the powers of the copyright board.

Copyright signifies exclusive rights in all the works in which the copyright subsists. The copyright subsists in original literary, dramatic, musical, artistic works, cinematograph films, and sound recordings. The author of the work is the first owner of the copyright. The owner of the copyright may assign to any person the copyright, either wholly or partly. The term of the copyright in any literary, dramatic, musical or artistic work is 60 years. The term of broadcasting reproduction right is 25 years and of performers' right is 50 years. The Act provides for international copyright and for optional registration of copyright.

The Trade Marks Act, 1999

The law relating to trademarks is contained in the Trade Marks Act, 1999. A trademark serves the purpose of identifying the source of goods or service. It is a visual symbol in the form of a word, figure, numeral design, device, label, or a combination of any of these applied to articles of commerce. The functions of a trademark are to create an image of the product, to identify the product, to advertise the product/service, and to guarantee the quality of product/service. The objective of the Trade Marks Act, 1999, is to register trademarks applied in the country. The Act provides for better protection of trademarks for goods and services and also to prevent fraudulent use of the mark. Some examples of trademarks are:

- Symbols such as the logos of Apple Computers or Mercedes Benz
- Letters such as 3M, IBM, NIIT
- Numbers can be trademarks as in the case of 501 Tea and 555 Cigarettes
- Colour can be part of the trademark. In the case of Orange cell phone, the company has included the colour, orange in the trademark.
- Sound can be a trademark as in the case of MGM's "roar of the lion."

The Trade Marks Act, 1999, which has been in force since 15 September 2003, has made certain improvements over the Trade and Merchandise Marks Act, 1958. These are:

- Expanded the definition of the trademark so that it includes the shape of goods, packaging, and combination of colours.
- Inclusion of service mark.
- Simplified procedure for registration of trademarks.
- Introduction of a collective mark.
- Increase in the period of registration and renewal from 7 to 10 years.
- Establishment of an intellectual property appellate board for speedy disposal of appeals from the registrar's orders and decision.
- Inclusion of the certification mark.
- Stringent requirements for registration.
- Broadening the concept of criminality.
- Transfer of the final authority for registration of certification of trademarks to the registrar.

The trademarks registry, established in India in 1940, administers the Trade Marks Act, 1999. It acts as a resource and information centre and is a facilitator in matters relating to trademarks in the country. The main function of the registry is to register trademarks, which qualify for registration under the Act and rules. The controller general of patents, designs, and trademarks is the registrar of trademarks and the office is located in Mumbai. The registration of a trademark shall be for 10 years but may be renewed from time to time on payment of a renewal fee. The registered trademark is recognized as an asset having commercial value.

The New Designs Act, 2000

The term design has been defined as "the features of shape, configuration, pattern, ornament, or composition of lines or colours applied to any article." Industrial designs are an element of intellectual property. Under the TRIPS agreement, minimum standards of protection of industrial designs have been provided in the Act. The existing legislation on industrial designs in India is contained in the New Designs Act, 2000. The Act is aimed to perform a more detailed classification of design to conform to the international system and to take care of the proliferation of design-related activities. The present legislation is aligned with the changed technical and commercial scenario to conform to international trends in design administration. The geographical indication identifies a product as originating from a place that has quality, reputation, or any other characteristic attributable to its place of origin.

THE CONSUMER PROTECTION ACT, 1986

The law relating to consumer protection is contained in the Consumer Protection Act, 1986. The Act has been amended by the Consumer Protection (Amendment) Act, 2002. Its objectives are the protection of the interests of consumers, protection of the rights of consumers, providing consumer protection councils, and providing quasi-judicial machinery for speedy redressal of consumer disputes.

The Consumer Protection Act[19] requires the establishment of consumer protection councils at the central, state, and district levels for the purpose of spreading consumer awareness. The objectives of the councils are to promote and protect the rights of consumers in the following matters:

- The consumer is protected against the marketing of goods and services that are hazardous to life and property.
- The consumer is informed about the quality, quantity, potency, purity, standard, and price of goods or services.

CHECKLIST FOR ENTREPRENEURS 10.3 What Every Entrepreneur Should Know About IPR

Intellectual property rights or IPR is a valuable resource in the modern knowledge economy. Here are key things that every entrepreneur should know and do about your IPR:

- Monitor patents in your industry. A patent confers monopoly rights on the inventor for a limited period of time. Obtain patent clearances searches for your key products.
- In case you do not have the financial strength or the organizational reach to do justice to your invention, it is a good idea to license it to another company.
- Select a trademark that should be distinctive and appealing to the customers. Protect the trademark by regularly scanning the market for imitations. Scan the TradeMarks Journal to ensure that similar or identical trademarks do not get registered.
- Guard against improper use of your Web site content and potential liability in connection with the Web site. This is important for e-commerce Web sites and Web sites that link to other sites.
- Make sure your employees realise their responsibility to protect confidential material such as product formulae, business process documents, customer lists, financial documents, and banking information.
- Use non-disclosure agreements to ensure protection of confidential information. Enter into non-disclosure agreements regarding trade secrets with employees, suppliers, customers, and potential financiers.

- The consumer is protected against unfair trade practices.
- The consumer is assured access to a variety of goods and services at competitive prices.
- It is assured that the consumer's voice is heard and his/her interest protected in appropriate forums. Access to consumer education is provided.
- The consumer is assured that he/she is entitled to seek redressal against unfair trade practices and exploitation.

The Consumer Protection Act, 1986, provides for the establishment of the following consumer disputes redressal agencies for the settlement of consumer disputes. They are:

- **District forum:** A consumer disputes redressal forum established by the state government in each district of the state. A consumer can file his/her claim if it is less than ₹20 lakh.
- **State commission:** A consumer disputes redressal commission established by the state government. Appeal from the decision of the district forum is to be filed within 30 days of its order to the state commission. A consumer can file his/her claim if the claim is more than ₹20 lakh but less than ₹1 crore.
- **National commission:** A consumer disputes redressal commission established by the Central Government. Appeal from the decision of the state commission is to be filed within 30 days of its order to the national commission. A consumer can file his/her claim if it is more than ₹1 crore. The national commission also has appellate and revisional jurisdiction.

THE RIGHT TO INFORMATION ACT, 2005

The Right to Information Act (RTI) 2005 is a revolutionary law in the democratic republic of India.[20] The right to information and its relevance is very useful for businessmen for protecting their business from the clutches of acute competition. The right to information has been recognized as a fundamental human right. It is essential to ensure accountability and good governance.

The RTI Act is viewed as one of the tools for sensitizing the governance mechanism comprising political power, bureaucratic power, and administrative power under various laws of land administered by state, central, and other delegated bodies or agencies. In order to make the wheels of a democratic country work it has become a necessary task of every responsible citizen to acquire information by taking shelter in the Right to Information Act, 2005.

Through this Act, information may be collected from various government officers entrusted with the task of giving such information. By submitting a simple form with a nominal fee, significant information could be obtained by citizens for their knowledge and application elsewhere.

The RTI Act, 2005, mandates a timely response to citizen requests for government information. The RTI portal has been set up by the Government of India for citizens to facilitate a quick search of information. The portal also provides access to RTI-related disclosures on the Internet by various public authorities under the central and state governments.

Even electronic information could be obtained on par with hard data. Controlled information including documents, extracts, and reports could be taken from various authorities. An obligation is set on the information officer to forward the required information in a time-bound manner, failing which there may be enforcement against the defaulting officer as per law. As India is emerging as a knowledge hub of the world with a vast pool of talent, the passing of the Right to Information Act has given citizens of India the legal right to seek justice through the fundamental right to information.

THE COMPETITION ACT, 2002

The Competition Act was passed by the Parliament in 2002. It was subsequently amended in 2007. The law relating to competition is contained in the Competition Act, 2002. It extends to the whole of India except Jammu and Kashmir. The Act states that a businessman in India must not engage in any activity for promoting monopoly. The Act prohibits anti-competition agreements, abuse of a dominant position, and regulates the operation and activities of combinations by laying down monetary limits for acquisitions, mergers, or amalgamations outside India.

The Act also provides for the establishment of the Competition Commission of India (CCI) under this law. In accordance with the provisions of the amendment act, the CCI and the competition appellate tribunal have been established. The CCI has a chairperson and six members. The function of the CCI is to stop any activity and practice that promotes monopoly, to encourage competition, to protect the interests of consumers, and to ensure that the freedom of trade carried on by other participants in markets in India is protected. The provisions of the Competition Act relating to anti-competitive agreements and the abuse of a dominant position were notified on 20 May 2009.

THE FOREIGN EXCHANGE MANAGEMENT ACT (FEMA), 1999

FEMA extends to the whole of India and applies to all branches, offices, and agencies outside India owned and controlled by a person resident in India. FEMA replaces the Foreign Exchange Regulation Act, 1949. FEMA permits only an authorized person to deal in foreign exchange or foreign security.

The Act regulates two types of foreign exchange transactions: capital account transactions and current account transactions. An Indian company may receive foreign direct investments under two routes: the automatic route and/or the government route. A non-resident Indian (NRI) is authorized to maintain accounts in India. These are non-resident ordinary rupee accounts, non-resident external rupee accounts, and foreign currency non-resident accounts.

The objectives of FEMA are to facilitate external trade and payments and to promote the orderly development and maintenance of the foreign exchange market in India. The Act has assigned an important role to the Reserve Bank of India (RBI) in the administration of FEMA. The Central Government from time to time may give to the RBI some general or special directions. The RBI shall comply with such directions. The RBI appoints in writing any person as an authorized dealer to deal in foreign exchange or in foreign security. The RBI has powers to issue directions to and inspect the authorized person.

SNAPSHOT

- The Information Technology Act, 2000, provides legal recognition for transactions carried out by means of electronic data interchange.
- Intellectual property rights regulate intangible property, which includes patents, trademarks, copyrights, and design rights.
- The Consumer Protection Act, 1986, protects the interest of consumers.
- The Right to Information Act, 2005, provides a right to information for citizens to secure information under the control of public authorities.
- The Competition Act, 2002, prevent practices having adverse effect on competition in markets to protect the interests of consumers.
- The Foreign Exchange Management Act ,1999, facilitates external trade and payments and promotes the orderly development and maintenance of the foreign exchange market in India.

DISCUSSION FORUM

- What is a cyber crime? Give one example.
- Which are the different types of trade-related intellectual property rights?
- What are the main objectives of the Consumer Protection Act, 1986?
- Discuss the relevance of the Right to Information Act, 2005.
- What are the primary objectives of the Competition Act, 2002?
- Explain the relevance of the Foreign Exchange Management Act, 1999.

SUMMARY

The choice of the form of business is governed by several interrelated and independent factors such as the nature of the business, the scale of operations, the area of operation, liability, the degree of control desired by the promoter, the cost of the project, risk and return, and comparative tax liability. The choice of the form of enterprise not only helps in the initial phase but also during the growth of the enterprise. To start an enterprise, the promoters have to decide on the constitution of the unit. The various forms of business organization are sole proprietorship, joint Hindu family business, partnership, joint stock company, cooperative society, and franchising.

The terms "business," "commercial," and "mercantile" are used alternatively in relation to law. Business law is the branch of law that comprises laws concerning trade, industry, and commerce. The Indian Contract Act, 1872, regulates contracts or agreements or relations of parties. The special type of contracts refer to the contract of indemnity and the contract of guarantee. Bailment and pledge is a special type of law contained in the Indian Contract Act, 1872. The Indian Contract Act also governs the law of agency and the relationship between an agent and the principal. The Sale of Goods Act, 1930, deals with the law relating to the sale of goods in India. The Indian Partnership Act, 1932, deals with the law relating to partnerships in India. The relationship between partners and the firm is generally covered in this law. The partnership firm is the most common form of business organization in India. The Limited Liability Partnership (LLP) Act, 2008, has distinct advantages over conventional limited liability companies. The Indian Companies Act, 1956, deals with the laws relating to companies in India.

The law relating to negotiable instruments is contained in the Negotiable Instruments Act, 1881, which deals with promissory notes, bills of exchange, and cheques. The Information Technology Act, 2000, provides legal recognition for transactions carried out by means of electronic data interchange. Intellectual property is the property possessed by an individual by virtue of his/her intellectual efforts. Under the World Trade Organization, The trade-related intellectual property rights (TRIPS) are: (1) patents, (2) copyrights, (3) trademarks, (4) geographical indications, (5) industrial designs, (6) integrated circuits, and (7) trade secrets or confidential information. The law relating to consumer protection is contained in the Consumer Protection Act, 1986. The Central Government enacted the Right to Information (RTI) Act in 2005. The law regarding competition is contained in the Competition Act, 2002. The Foreign Exchange Management Act, 1999, is related to foreign exchange with the objective of facilitating external trade and payments and for promoting the orderly development and maintenance of the foreign exchange market in India.

KEY TERMS

Bailment: A bailment is the delivery of goods by one person to another for some purpose, upon a contract that they shall, when the purpose is accomplished, be returned or otherwise disposed of, according to the direction of the person delivering them.

Company: A voluntary association of persons recognized by law and registered under the Companies Act, 1956.

Contract: A contract is an agreement made between two parties that is enforceable by law.

Cooperative Company: It is an enterprise governed by the State Cooperative Societies Act and the Multi-state Cooperative Societies Act, 2002.

Corporation: An entity that has a legal personality. It is capable of enjoying and being subject to legal rights and duties and possesses the capacity for succession.

Franchising: Franchising is a form of business by which the owner (franchisor) of a product, service, or method obtains distribution through affiliated dealers (franchisees).

Indemnity: It is a contract by which one party promises to save the other from loss to him/her through the conduct of the promisor himself, or through the conduct of any other person.

Intellectual Property: An umbrella term for various legal entitlements that attach to property resulting from original creative thought, such as patents, copyright material, and trademarks.

Listed Public Companies: A public company that has listed any of its securities in any recognized stock exchange.

Memorandum of Understanding (MOU): The MOU of a company is an important document as it defines and confines the powers of the company. A company can only act as per the objects given in the MOU.

Partnership Deed: It is an agreement entered into between partners to carry on business.

Partnership: The relationship between persons who have agreed to share profits of a business carried on by all or any of them acting for all.

Pledge: A pledge is a special kind of bailment.

Sole Proprietorship: The enterprise is owned and controlled by one person.

CASE STUDY

Amul—The Taste of India

The Gujarat Cooperative Milk Marketing Federation (GCMMF) is a farmers' cooperative in India marketing dairy products in the state of Gujarat. GCMMF was established in 1973 and is India's largest marketer of food products. It is a state-level apex body of milk cooperatives in Gujarat. The Federation aspires to provide competitive returns to the farmers and also to serve the interest of consumers by providing quality products at reasonable prices. Its flagship brand Amul (Anand Milk Union Ltd) has become one of the best recognized brand names in India.

GCMMF is India's largest food products marketing organization with an annual turnover of USD 250 crore (2011–12). Its milk procurement is approximately 130 lakh litres per day from 16,117 village milk cooperative societies, 17 member unions covering 24 districts, and 31.8 lakh milk producer members. The GCMMF is also India's largest exporter of dairy products and has been accorded "trading house" status. The establishment of Amul heralded the White Revolution in India.

The Amul model of dairy development has a three-tier cooperative structure. The dairy cooperative societies at the village level are affiliated to a milk union at the district level, which in turn are grouped under a milk federation at the state level. Milk collection is carried out at the village dairy society, milk procurement and processing at the district milk union, and the marketing of milk and milk products at the state milk federation. The entire institutional infrastructure set up at the village level, the district level, and the state level is owned and operated by farmers. Amul's mission is the development of farmers, nutrition to the nation, and the real development of India.

The Amul model is also known as the Anand pattern of dairy cooperatives. This model eliminated middlemen and brought the producers in direct contact with the consumers. It also gives a fair price to the farmer and good quality milk and milk products to the consumer. The assured market for milk has improved the quality of life of farmers. Milk producers (farmers) control procurement, processing, and marketing. The hallmark of the Amul model is the maximization of profit and productivity by cooperative efforts and by utilizing resources in the most profitable manner by professional management at the grassroots level. The spread of the cooperative movement in the villages contributed to positive social changes in the community. The Amul brand is a movement representing the economic freedom of farmers. It has given farmers the courage to dream, hope, and live.

The GCMMF is the recipient of many awards and accolades for its consistent adherence to quality, customer focus, and dependability. It bagged India's Most Respected Company Award instituted by *Businessworld* in 2002. It was awarded the IMC Ramkrishna Bajaj National Quality Award in 2003. The GCMMF is the first and only Indian organization to win the topmost International Dairy Federation Marketing Award for the launch of probiotic ice cream in 2007. The GCMMF has been awarded the "Golden Trophy" for its outstanding export performance and contribution in the dairy products sector by APEDA for 2009–10.

Questions:

1. What are the key success factors of the Amul model?
2. Is it possible to replicate the Amul model across India?
3. Comment on the statement "the cooperative movement has given farmers the courage to dream, hope, and live."

Source: www.amul.com (last accessed in March 2013).

The Pain of Partnership

Mahesh and Raja met while working at a compact disc production company. Mahesh was in charge of editorial and production, and Raja ran the sales force. Mahesh decided to start his own company and invited Raja to join him. Raja would handle sales and administration, while Mahesh managed the clients and directed production.

MR Communications seemed like a perfect partnership. Things seemed to be going well, and they even landed a major project. As time went by, Raja decided that he wanted a "creative" job too. He spent most of his time producing compact discs rather than looking for new business. Mahesh's loyalty to Raja made him blind to many things that were obvious to others. Because of their friendship, he trusted that Raja was taking care of his side of the business. As it turned out, Raja was not very good at the tasks he had taken on. He made mistakes that reduced expected profits. He was not making new sales contracts, which was supposed to be the main part of his job. If that were not enough, the feeling that he was letting his friend down made Raja feel even worse. Raja began to avoid talking to Mahesh. He stopped coming to the office. Finally, he stopped returning phone calls.

By the time Mahesh realised what was happening to the business, it was too late. There were no new sales. What Mahesh thought were profits was the result of Raja not paying their bills. Mahesh was left with more than ₹750,000 in unpaid bills and a tearful message on the answering machine from Raja, "I'm moving out to Chennai for a while. Sorry it didn't work out."

It took Mahesh three years to dig out of the financial mess and get his new company up and running successfully.

Questions:

1. How could Mahesh and Raja have avoided the problems that led to the end of their partnership?
2. Why is this situation a good example of the difficulty in maintaining partnerships between friends?

DISCUSSION QUESTIONS

1. What are the different ownership forms available to entrepreneurs? Discuss each form in brief.
2. Explain the advantages and disadvantages of the different forms of business organization.
3. "Control should remain with one man if the man is big enough to control everything." Do you agree? Give reasons.
4. What are the various problems that a firm is likely to face as it expands? How can these be solved by changing the form of ownership?

5. Explain the advantages and disadvantages of incorporation of a company.
6. Explain the various business laws prevalent in India as discussed in this chapter.

ACTIVITY

1. Two situations are given below. Divide the class into groups of five students each. Each situation should be discussed in these small groups and a decision should be taken on each situation.
   - Ajay Choubey, the secretary of a company, issues a share certificate in favour of Rohit Bhatnagar by forging the signatures of two directors. He also affixes the seal of the company on the certificate without authority. Can Rohit Bhatnagar hold the company liable for the shares covered by the share certificate?
   - The directors of a company are prosecuted for default in filing the balance sheet and the profit and loss account with the Registrar of Companies (RoC). Their defence is that the annual meeting for the relevant year was not held for some reason and, therefore, since the occasion for placing the same before the general meeting did not arise, they are not guilty of contravention of the Company Law (Section 220). The RoC contends that the directors cannot take advantage of their own default in holding the annual general meeting and should therefore be held guilty.
2. Divide the class into groups of five students each. Fill up the following table in your small groups.

Types of Cooperative Societies	Who Forms the Society	Objectives of the Society	Functions of the Society	Examples from India
Consumers' cooperative society				
Producers' cooperative society				
Marketing cooperative society				
Housing cooperative society				
Farming cooperative society				
Credit cooperative society				

3. Make a list of products in the market that have been developed and patented in India.

PROJECT

1. You plan to start a small business enterprise. How would you choose the appropriate form of ownership pattern for your enterprise? Explain the step-by-step procedure explaining the constitution of the unit.
2. You and your two friends decide to start a partnership firm. Prepare a Deed of Partnership.

ENDNOTES

1. Gupta, C. B. (2011–12). *Business Studies*. New Delhi: Tata McGraw-Hill.
2. Singla, R. K. (2009–10). *Business Organization and Management*. New Delhi: V. K. India Enterprises.
3. *The Indian Partnership Act* (2011). New Delhi: Universal Law Publishing Company (Universal Law series).
4. Naik, S. A. (2010). *Law Relating to Limited Liability Partnership in India*. Nagpur: Butterworths Wadhwa.
5. Singh, Avatar (2009). *Company Law*. Lucknow: Eastern Book Company.
6. Ravindranath, Sushila (ed.) (2010). *The CII Entrepreneur's Handbook*. Chennai: Westland.
7. Tyagi, Madhu and Arun Kumar (2003). *Company Law*. New Delhi: Atlantic Publishers and Distributors.
8. *Societies Registration Act* (2012). Law Publishers (India) Pvt. Ltd, 8th ed.
9. Bangia, R. K. (1990). *The Indian Contract Act*. Allahabad Law Agency.
10. Mulla, Sir Dineshah Fardunji and Justice K. Kannan (2002). *The Sale of Goods Act and The Indian Partnership Act*. Nagpur: Butterworths Wadhwa, 10th ed.
11. www.llp.gov.in (last accessed in March 2013).
12. www.mca.gov.in/MCA21 (last accessed in March 2013).
13. India Legislative Department (2010). *The Negotiable Instruments Act 1881*. Whitefish, MT: Kessinger Publishing House.
14. Singh, Justice Yatindra (2011). *Cyber Laws*. New Delhi: Universal Law Publishing Company 4th ed.
15. Nagpal, Rohas (2010). *IPR and Cyberspace—The Indian Perspective.* Leicester, UK: ASCL Publications.
16. Nagpal Rohas (2010). *IPR and Cyberspace—The Indian Perspective,* Leicester, UK: ASCL Publications.
17. www.ipindia.nic.in/ (last accessed in March 2013).
18. Vaver, David (1997). *Intellectual Property Law: Copyright, Patents, Trademarks*. Toronto, ON: Irwin Law.
19. Bakshi, P. M. (2005). *Consumer Protection Laws*. New Delhi: Jain Book Deport
20. Yashwantrao Chavan Academy of Development Administration (2008). *Right to Information Act, 2005*. New Delhi: Tata McGraw-Hill.

Management of Enterprises

11. Preventing Sickness in Enterprises
12. Financial Management in Enterprises
13. Operations and Human Resource Management in Enterprises
14. Managing Marketing and Growth in Enterprises

Part 3

"So many fail because they don't get started; they don't go. They don't overcome inertia."

—W. Clement Stone

Lakshmi Niwas Mittal is the chairman and CEO of ArcelorMittal, which is the world's largest steel manufacturing company. He started business operations in 1976 by buying and turning around a defunct steel manufacturing company in Indonesia. Over the next two decades, the company has grown through a series of acquisitions in North America, Europe, Africa, and Asia. Popularly known as the Turnaround Man, Lakshmi Niwas Mittal's Midas touch has been responsible for turning around the fortunes of many sick steel manufacturing plants.

Preventing Sickness in Enterprises

11

LEARNING OBJECTIVES

Upon completion of this chapter, you should be able to:

1. **Identify problems faced by entrepreneurs.**
2. **Understand the effects of industrial sickness.**
3. **Explain the Sick Industrial Companies Act (SICA).**
4. **Identify the causes of sickness and explain the remedies to avoid sickness.**
5. **Explain the rehabilitation packages available to enterprises.**

INTRODUCTION

Entrepreneurs face a number of problems in the promotion of units and during production, marketing, distribution, procurement of raw material, and availing of incentives offered by the government.[1] Let us broadly study the general problems faced by entrepreneurs and the specific problems faced by their units.

The problems of entrepreneurs may be divided into two groups—external and internal. External problems are those that result from factors beyond the control of the entrepreneur, while internal problems are those that are under the control of the entrepreneur and not influenced by external factors.

Although the small-scale sector and the large and organized sector face similar problems, organized industries can face their problems more effectively as they are financially very strong and have large resources. Owing to their weak financial structure, the resources of small-scale sector enterprises are limited. While the large and organized sector can employ trained and experienced managers; in a small-scale sector enterprise, its proprietor or partners; or if the unit is a company, its director or directors themselves have to take care of all the problems. The large and organized sector can influence its raw material suppliers, its customers, and at times even the government in framing its policies, but the small entrepreneur is helpless in this respect. Some of the problems faced by the entrepreneur are given below:

1. **Political instability:** This does not encourage an investor to invest in the economy. Even if he has already invested, he might decide to fold up due to the prevailing hostile economic climate.
2. **Presence of inflation:** Inflation is an economic condition characterized by a general and continuous rise in the price level coupled with a fall in the value of money. Inflation is economically harmful to suppliers as it leads to unstable quoted market prices.

3. **Inadequacy of information:** The collation and analysis of relatively dependable, reliable, and authentic data may facilitate and enhance forecasting and planning. It is pertinent to point out that the entrepreneur may not be conscious of the existing forces of the law of demand and supply that directly or indirectly affects consumers' behaviour.
4. **Capital:** The entrepreneur may not find the required initial capital for the take-off of the business.
5. **Inadequate infrastructural facilities:** This may hamper or hinder the development of entrepreneurial activities.
6. **Inadequate government support or motivation:** Lack of government support or motivation may hinder a business through lack of free consultancy services and soft loans.
7. **Type of business to establish:** At the onset, it may be a Herculean task for new entrepreneurs to choose a type of business to establish, as they may lack experience in setting and managing the enterprise.

SPECIFIC MANAGEMENT PROBLEMS

Besides the internal and external problems of entrepreneurs, some specific problems faced by the entrepreneurs are discussed in this section.

Management Deficiency

It is a well-known fact that management deficiency is one of the main reasons for the poor performance and sickness of small enterprises. New entrants in the field of small industries in general do not have any prior training or background in the management of their units. With growing sophistication and modernization of market requirements for their products, it is very important for entrepreneurs to employ modern methods of management. Entrepreneurial ability can be honed through application and training. Various colleges and universities in advanced countries offer courses in starting and managing small enterprises.

Finance

Financial inadequacy is also reported to be one of the most important causes leading to sickness of small-scale units. The Fourth All-India Census of MSME reveals that 70 per cent of the units have considered finance as a stumbling block in setting up and diversification of industrial units.

Critical issues in financial management require to be constantly borne in mind to ensure that a business enterprise remains healthy. Planning for profits must be ensured at all times by resorting to periodical performance evaluation. The proper utilization of various assets is critical to profit maximization. Along with credibility, solvency, and liquidity are essential for enterprise growth. During emergencies, liability management can be helpful. But all this would be possible only if proper books of accounts are maintained. An accountant ensures the smooth functioning of financial planning and management and takes care of the timely provision of financial information. All aspects of financial management contribute in a small or big measure towards maintaining business survival and growth.

Manufacturing and Technical Problems

Most units face production problems due to lack of raw material availability, skilled labour shortage, under-utilization of capacity, and time and cost overrun. Manufacturing and technical problems arise right at the stages of project planning and feasibility report preparation. Problem areas are product pricing; selection of right equipment, plant and machinery; selection of personnel and their training; technical know-how; technology transfer; industrial engineering; production engineering; use of standard quality control, and use of high-tech equipment.

Product Planning

The selection of a product depends on technical know-how, the infrastructural facilities available, and the technical and managerial abilities of entrepreneurs to complete a project successfully. Product planning is the ongoing process of identifying market requirements that define a product's feature set, promotion, distribution, and price. Most small-scale business enterprises don't do any product planning.

Selection of Equipment, Plant, and Machinery

Most entrepreneurs ignore the importance of making a detailed scrutiny before selecting equipment, plant, and machinery. However, entrepreneurs should give importance to production capacity, process capability, accuracy requirements, and other supporting facilities before buying their equipment. They are required to look for alternative and appropriate high-tech equipment if it is techno-economically feasible as technically superior equipment will lead to higher quality, quantity, reliability, and productivity. Such things increase productivity and lower the cost of production.

Human Resource Development

Selecting the right person for the right job would contribute to the smooth and efficient working of the enterprise. After selecting the right personnel on scientific lines, it is very essential to train them at appropriate organizations so that they have both theoretical and on-the-job training in improving the productivity of the enterprise. Entrepreneurs should know that it is not machines alone that work, but the people behind the machines who make it work. Organizations like the North India Technical Consultancy Organization Ltd (NITCON) and various training institutes are coming forward in a big way to help small business houses train their personnel.

Technical Know-how

While there are numerous ways of doing a job, there is only one way of doing it in a manner that is most effective, efficient, and highly productive. Many entrepreneurs do not realise this and their trial-and-error method wastes time, money, energy, and other resources.

Preparation of Project Report

A project report is usually not prepared on scientific lines. Very often project feasibility reports are prepared for availing loans. A project report, also referred to as pre-investment feasibility study, or business plan, is a detailed description of the business. It is the roadmap showing how and when the business will achieve its goals. It is an operating document—the description of a project indicating what products are to be manufactured or what services are to be offered and to whom. It is essential that the promoter of a business venture have conceptual clarity on what business he is in. Details of the infrastructure required for the business; manpower, material, and the financial resources needed to reach the envisaged activity level; how such resources would be mobilized and managed and with what financial resources; how the business will achieve the stated goals; the time frame within which a project will be implemented; when it will produce the envisaged output; and when the business would reach optimal activity level and generate financial surplus would constitute a business plan.

INDUSTRIAL SICKNESS

Companies become sick at some stage of their existence if they are not managed well. If early signs of impending sickness are ignored, the sickness grows over a period of time. A well-managed company picks up the signals at the appropriate time and becomes healthy. If a management team is unable to revive a sick unit, the stakeholder has limited choices: to bring in a new management team to revive the unit, to close down the unit and cut losses, or to sell it off if there is a buyer.

Sickness in industrial units is universal and not a new phenomenon in developing economies. An industrial unit may face a number of problems during the implementation and operation stage because of a number of factors in the macro and microenvironment. The problem of sickness in industries is very grave and adversely affects production and employment in the country besides producing other socioeconomic repercussions. The following are the ill effects of industrial sickness:

- Sick industries are unable to utilize the production capacity of goods and services. There is an under utilization of capital assets.
- It leads to substantial loss of government revenue and enhances public expenditure.
- Increase in industrial sickness discourages the development of entrepreneurship in the country.
- Industrial sickness results in large-scale unemployment and industrial unrest.
- It locks up necessary resources and funds in the sick unit. This also increases the non-performing assets of banks and financial institutions.
- The profitability of banks and financial institutions gets adversely affected as the return on investments on projects is reduced. Since their funds get blocked in sick units, it results in problems of project financing.
- The confidence of investors goes down. The rate of project financing also comes down.

Therefore, the prevention of sickness and rehabilitation of sick units assumes greater importance.

DEFINITION OF SICKNESS

The Sick Industrial Companies (Special Provisions) Act, 1985, as amended in 1993, defines a non-SSI sick industrial company as follows:

> A sick industrial unit is defined as a unit or a company (having been in existence for not less than five years) which is found at the end of any financial year to have incurred accumulated losses equal to or exceeding its entire net worth.
>
> According to Section 3 (1) (ga) of the Amendment Act, 1993, "net worth" is calculated as the sum total of the paid up capital and free reserves of a company less the provision and expenses, as may be prescribed. While the term "free reserves" means all reserves credited out of the profits and share premium account, but does not include reserves out of revaluation of assets, write back of depreciation provisions, and reserves created out of amalgamations.
>
> An industrial unit is also regarded as a potentially sick or weak unit if, at the end of any financial year, it has accumulated losses equal to or exceeding 50 per cent of its average net worth in the immediately preceding four financial years and had failed to repay debts to its creditor(s) in three consecutive quarters on demand made in writing for such repayment.
>
> A company should be engaged in any scheduled industry, i.e. any industry specified in the First Schedule to the Industries (Development and Regulation) Act, 1951. Scheduled industries include metallurgical industries, telecommunication, transportation, chemicals, textiles but not financial services, and software technology.

Government companies having state or central shareholdings of 51 per cent or more are kept outside the purview of the Act. Also small and medium enterprises and ancillary units are kept outside the purview of the Act.

Definition of Sick Enterprises—Micro and Small Enterprises

A micro or small enterprise (as defined in the MSMED Act, 2006) may be said to have become "Sick" if

- Any of the borrowal accounts of the enterprise remains a non-performing asset for three months or more, or
- There is erosion in the net worth due to accumulated cash losses to the extent of 50 per cent of its net worth.

A micro or small unit may be treated as having reached the stage of incipient sickness/potential sickness if any of the following events are triggered:

- There is a delay in commencement of commercial production by more than six months for reasons beyond the control of the promoters and entailing cost overrun.
- The company incurs losses for two years or cash loss for one year, beyond the accepted timeframe on account of change in economic and fiscal policies affecting the working of micro and small enterprises or otherwise.
- The capacity utilization is less than 50 per cent of the projected level in terms of quantity or the sales are less than 50 per cent of the projected level in terms of value during a year.

SNAPSHOT

- A unit is considered sick (non-SME) if it has accumulated losses equal to or exceeding its entire net worth as at the end of the latest financial year.
- A micro or small enterprise (as defined in the MSMED Act, 2006) is said to have become sick, if any of the borrowal accounts of the enterprise remains a non-performing asset for three months or more or there is erosion in the net worth due to accumulated losses to the extent of 50 per cent of its net worth.

SICK INDUSTRIAL COMPANIES ACT, 1985

Sick Industrial Companies (Special Provisions) Act,[2] 1985, commonly known as SICA, was a special legislation enacted in the public interest with the main objectives of:

- Securing the timely detection of sick and potentially sick companies,
- Speedy determination by a body of experts of the preventive, ameliorative, remedial, and other measures which need to be taken with respect to such companies, and
- Expediting the revival of potentially viable units and affecting the closure of unviable units.

The Board of Industrial and Financial Reconstruction (BIFR) and the Appellate Authority for Industrial and Financial Reconstruction (AAIFR) were also established in 1987 to look after the matters covered under the purview of SICA. The Act was further amended in 1991 to bring government companies under its purview. Again, in 1993, certain changes were brought out in the Act for the determination of industrial sickness. Some companies perceived SICA as an official exit route, resulting in losses to creditors, and increased non-performing assets in the banking sector. Therefore, SICA, 1985, was repealed and replaced by the Sick Industrial Companies (Special Provisions) Repeal Act, 2003.

SICA, 2003, diluted some of the provisions of the 1985 Act and plugged certain loopholes. It aimed not only to combat industrial sickness but also to reduce the same by ensuring that the companies did not view the declaration of sickness as an escape route from legal provisions after the failure of the project or similar other reasons and thereby gain access to various benefits or concessions from financial institutions. Under it, the Board for Industrial and Financial Reconstruction (BIFR) and the Appellate Authority for Industrial and Financial Reconstruction (AAIFR) were dissolved and replaced by the National Company Law Tribunal (NCLT) and the National Company Law Appellate Tribunal (NCLAT), respectively.

The comprehensive revision of the Companies Act, 1956, was taken up by the Ministry and the Companies Bill was introduced. The Companies Bill, 2009, seeks to enable the corporate sector in India to operate in a regulatory environment comprising best international practices that foster entrepreneurship, investment, and growth.[3] The details of the Act are given below:

- A revised framework for regulations of insolvency, including rehabilitation, liquidation, and winding up of companies, and the process to be completed in a time-bound manner.

- Consolidation of fora for dealing with the rehabilitation of companies, their liquidation, and winding up in the single forum of the National Company Law Tribunal with appeal to the National Company Law Appellate Tribunal with suitable transitional provisions. The nature of the Rehabilitation and Revival Fund proposed in the Companies (Second Amendment) Act, 2002, to be replaced by the Rehabilitation and Insolvency Fund with voluntary contributions linked to entitlements to draw money in a situation of insolvency.
- A more effective regime for inspections and investigations of companies while laying down the maximum as well as minimum quantum of penalty for each offence with suitable deterrents for repeated defaults. A company is identified as a separate entity for the imposition of monetary penalties from the officers in default. In case of fraudulent activities, provisions for recovery and disgorgement have been included.
- Levy of additional fee in a non-discretionary manner for procedural non-compliance, such as late filing of statutory documents, to be enabled through rules. Defaults of a procedural nature to be penalized by levy of monetary penalties by the adjudicating officers not below the level of registrars. The appeals against orders of adjudicating officers to lie with suitably designated higher authorities.
- Special courts to deal with offences under the Bill, company matters such as mergers and amalgamations, reduction of capital, insolvency including rehabilitation, liquidation, and winding up are proposed to be dealt with by the National Company Law Tribunal.

National Company Law Tribunal (NCLT)

The Central Government constituted a committee under the chairmanship of Justice V. Balakrishna Eradi, a retired Supreme Court Judge, to review the law relating to insolvency and winding up of companies and the Sick Industrial Companies (Special Provisions) Act, 1985 (SICA). The government established the NCLT based on the recommendations of the committee. The main objective of the NCLT is to expedite the revival/rehabilitation of a sick company and to protect the worker's interest.[4] With the setting up of the NCLT, all the matters relating to companies that were earlier handled by various high courts, Company Law Board (CLB), BIFR, and AAIFR were to be handled by the NCLT.

The members of the NCLT are to be appointed by the Central Government. The NCLT will be headed by its president, who has been a judge of the high court or is eligible to be appointed as a judge of a high court and such number of judicial and technical members but not exceeding 62. The tenure of the president and of the members of the tribunal is three years, subject to reappointment, or removal, before the completion of the term. The tribunal will be functioning through its various benches all over the country. These benches would expedite the disposal of the cases and, at the same time, make available the mechanism at the companies' doorsteps, reducing the cost and efforts involved.

National Company Law Appellate Tribunal (NCLAT)

Any appeal against the order of the NCLT will now be made to the NCLAT instead of the AAIFR. The NCLAT is constituted by the Central Government and will consist of a chairperson and not more than two members. The chairperson shall be an individual who has been a judge of the Supreme Court or chief justice of a high court. Members of the NCLAT should be persons of ability, integrity, and possessing professional experience of not less than 25 years, which would be, in the opinion of the Central Government, useful to the Appellate Tribunal.

DISCUSSION FORUM

- Define a sick unit.
- Explain the Sick Industrial Companies Act (SICA).
- Prepare a note on the NCLT and the NCLAT.

INDUSTRIAL SICKNESS IN INDIA

Industrial sickness is one of the most complex problems of the Indian economy.[5] Table 11.1 furnishes data on industrial sickness in India. Among the non-SSI units, the number of sick units increased from 1,455 in 1990 to 2,880 in 2002. Thus, the increase in the incidence of industrial sickness in the non-SSI sector during the period 1990–2002 was almost 100 per cent. Outstanding bank credit in the case of these sick units increased from ₹453,900 lakh in 1990 to ₹1,759,100 lakh by 2002. The bank credit locked up in non-SSI units increased by four times during this period.

The total of sick units, taking into account both small-scale and non-SSI sectors, increased from 220,283 in 1990 to 264,332 in 1996 and declined to 236,980 units in 1997 and 224,012 units in 1998. The number of sick units increased to 308,578 in 1999 and again showed a declining trend with 180,216 units in 2002. The bank credit locked up in sick units of the two sectors, increased from ₹853,900 lakh in 1990 to ₹2,241,100 lakh in 2002. The bank credit locked up in sick units increased by two and a half times during this period.

Sickness in Micro, Small, and Medium Enterprises

The Fourth All-India Census of Micro, Small, and Medium Enterprises for the reference period 2006–07 had found that a total of 4.81 lakh enterprises were closed at the end of March 2007.

As for the sickness in the small-scale industrial sector, the number of sick units increased from 218,828 in 1990 to 304,235 in 2000 and showed a downward trend from 2000 to 2007. The number of sick units decreased from 304,235 in 2000 to 114,132 in 2007. The percentage decrease in the number of sick SSI units during this period was almost 60 per cent. The bank credit locked up in

Table 11.1 Total Incidence of Industrial Sickness in India

Year (As at the End of March)	No. of Sick SSI Units	Outstanding Bank Credit in INR lakh	No. of Sick Non-SSI Units	Outstanding Bank Credit in INR lakh	Total No. of Sick Units	Total Outstanding Bank Credit in INR lakh
1990	218,828	242,700	1,455	453,900	220,283	853,900
1991	221,472	279,200	1,461	510,600	222,933	789,800
1992	245,575	310,100	1,536	578,700	247,111	888,700
1993	238,176	344,300	1,867	790,100	240,043	1,134,400
1994	256,452	368,000	1,909	815,100	258,361	1,183,200
1995	268,815	354,700	1,915	874,000	270,730	1,228,700
1996	262,379	372,200	1,956	882,300	264,332	1,254,500
1997	235,032	360,900	1,948	861,400	236,980	1,222,300
1998	221,536	385,700	2,030	986,200	224,012	1,568,200
1999	306,221	431,300	2,357	1,311,400	308,578	1,742,700
2000	304,235	460,800	2,742	1,674,800	306,977	2,135,700
2001	249,630	450,500	2,928	1,847,800	252,558	2,298,300
2002	177,336	481,900	2,880	1,759,100	180,216	2,241,100
2003	167,980	570,600	-	-	-	-
2004	143,366	577,300	-	-	-	-
2005	138,041	538,000	-	-	-	-
2006	126,824	498,100	-	-	-	-
2007	114,132	526,700	-	-	-	-

Source: Compiled from reports of the Reserve Bank of India from 1990–2007.

sick units of the small-scale sector increased from ₹242,700 lakh in 1990 to ₹526,700 lakh in 2007, showing an increase of 117 per cent. It was found that the unavailability of capital and the lack of managerial expertise are the two biggest reasons for falling sick.

The data compiled by the Reserve Bank of India on sickness in small and medium enterprises as on 31 March 2006 and 31 March 2007 are given in Table 11.2 and Table 11.3. These data reveal that:

- The number of sick small enterprises decreased from 126,824 in 2006 to 114,132 in 2007 showing a perceptible decline of ten per cent in 2007. But the amount outstanding in the banks against them went up from ₹498,100 lakh to ₹526,670 lakh, which was almost a six per cent increase as compared with 2006.
- In the small enterprises sector in 2006, out of 126,824 sick units, only 3.63 per cent units were found viable by the banks. Out of the same, only 0.72 per cent sick units were placed under nursing.
- In the small enterprises sector in 2007, out of 114,132 sick units, only 3.76 per cent units were found viable by the banks. Out of the same, only 0.52 per cent sick units were put into nursing.
- The number of sick medium enterprises increased from 13,513 in 2006 to 17,949 in 2007 showing an increase of 33 per cent. But the amount outstanding in the banks against them

Table 11.2 Bank-wise Viability Position of Sick Small Enterprises (INR Lakh)

	As at the End of March 2006						As at the End of March 2007					
	Total Sick Units		Potentially Viable		Units Under Nursing		Total Sick Units		Potentially Viable		Units Under Nursing	
	Units	O/s	Units	O/s	Units	O/s	Units	O/s	Units	O/s	Units	O/s
Public sector	124,530	459,300	4,565	47,400	903	23,000	112,305	501,400	4,240	40,410	581	26,220
Private sector	2,291	37,700	28	1,820	12	430	1,824	23,850	45	1,570	7	670
Foreign	3	1,130	1	600	0	0	3	1,420	2	770	0	0
Total	126,824	498,130	4,594	49,820	915	23,430	114,132	526,670	4,287	42,750	588	26,890

Source: Compiled from the reports of the Reserve Bank of India.

Table 11.3 Bank-wise Viability Position of Sick Medium Enterprises (INR Lakh)

	As at the End of March 2006						As at the End of March 2007					
	Total Sick Units		Potentially Viable		Units Under Nursing		Total Sick Units		Potentially Viable		Units Under Nursing	
	Units	O/s	Units	O/s	Units	O/s	Units	O/s	Units	O/s	Units	O/s
Public sector	12,856	298,590	133	31,160	56	19,560	17,902	210,160	1,925	28,830	117	18,210
Private sector	657	30,520	74	6,090	32	220	47	10,370	9	570	0	0
Foreign	0	0	0	0	0	0	0	0	0	0	0	0
Total	13,513	329,110	207	37,250	88	19,780	17,949	220,530	1,934	29,400	117	18,210

Source: Compiled from the reports of the Reserve Bank of India.

decreased from ₹329,110 lakh in 2006 to ₹220,530 lakh in 2007, which was almost by 33 per cent.

- Among the sick medium enterprises, in 2006, out of 13,513 sick units, only 1.5 per cent units were found viable by the banks, and out of the same, only 0.65 per cent sick units were put into nursing.
- Among the sick medium enterprises, in 2007, out of 17,949 sick units, only 10.77 per cent units were found viable by the banks, and out of the same, only 0.65 per cent units were placed under nursing.
- For the SME sector as a whole, in 2006, out of 140,337 sick units, the total number of units found viable was only 3.4 per cent, of which 0.71 per cent units were placed under nursing.
- For the SME sector as a whole, in 2007, out of 132,081 sick units, the total number of units found viable was 4.7 per cent only, of which only 0.53 per cent units were put under nursing.

Causes of Industrial Sickness

The causes of industrial sickness in India may vary from one unit to another. In India, the Tiwari Committee report outlines the causes of industrial sickness and divides them into several factors.[6] These causes can be classified into two categories: internal causes and external causes.

Internal Causes These are the factors that are internal to the organization and over which the management has control. Sickness due to internal causes can be avoided if the management is proactive enough to identify the causes and eliminate them at the initial stage itself. The internal factors that cause industrial sickness are the following:

- **Project formulation:** Some industries are born sick. Some industrial concerns are sick from the very inception. This is attributed to ill-conceived projects, poor planning, poor appraisal, uneconomic size of the project, outdated production process, and high input costs.
- **Project implementation:** Delayed implementation gives a project a difficult start. This will lead to time overrun and cost overrun, affecting the financial viability of the project. This may be due to inadequate mobilization of finance.
- **Project management:** The problems of project management can be discussed under four broad headings—poor management of production, marketing, finance, and general and personnel administration.
- **Constraints of production:** The problems may be due to wrong selection of site; inappropriate technology; lack of maintenance system; absence of research and development for innovation; and poor quality and productivity.
- **Constraints of marketing:** The problems may be due to lack of market research, a poor and inadequate distribution system, absence of a costing and pricing system for the products, and the dependence on a limited number of customers.
- **Constraints of finance:** Problems may be due to poor resource management, lack of financial planning and budgeting, weak equity base, and inadequate working capital.
- **Problems due to general and personnel administration**: Poor industrial relations leading to labour unrest, lack of motivation and coordination, lack of manpower planning, poor talent management, lack of professionalism, lack of control systems, excessive expenditure, and incompetent and dishonest management.

External Causes External causes are those that are external to the organization and over which the management of the organization has no control. Sickness due to external causes can be minimized if the management plans suitable strategies and takes on the external factors to reduce their impact. The external factors that cause industrial sickness are the following:

- **Infrastructural and technology management:** Irregular supply of raw material, non-availability of technology, shortage of power, water, and other resources, transport bottlenecks.

- **Government policy:** Delays in disbursement of loans from financial institutions, delay in getting approvals from government authorities, import–export restrictions.
- **Marketing constraints:** The sickness could be due to liberal licensing policies, restraint on purchase by bulk purchasers, changes in the global marketing scenario, excessive tax policies by the government, and market recession.
- **Extraneous factors:** Natural calamities, political climate, non-availability of skilled labour, and required talent.

SNAPSHOT

- Industrial sickness is one of the most complex problems facing the Indian economy.
- The causes of industrial sickness can be classified into two categories: internal causes and external causes.
- Internal causes are due to the factors that are internal to the organization, over which the management of the organization has control.
- External causes are those that are external to the organization, over which the management of the organization has no control.

DISCUSSION FORUM

- Discuss the magnitude of industrial sickness in India.
- Explain the causes of industrial sickness in India.

SYMPTOMS OF INDUSTRIAL SICKNESS

It is essential to identify sickness in advance to prevent its widespread ill effects on society as a whole on the one hand and, on the other hand, to save the limited resources of banks, financial institutions, and investors for more productive use elsewhere. Thus, it becomes imperative to predict and monitor industrial sickness in advance so that the interests of all concerned could be safeguarded. An early warning signal of probable failure will enable both the management team and the investor to take preventive measures, make policy changes, reorganize the financial structure, upgrade infrastructure, and even undertake voluntary liquidation. This usually shortens the length of time for which losses are incurred and thereby improves both private and social resource allocation.

The symptoms of industrial sickness may be in the form of financial distress starting with short-term liquidity problems, revenue losses, operating losses, and moving in the direction of overuse of external credit until it reaches a stage where it is overburdened with debt and is not able to generate sufficient funds to meet its obligations.[7] In case of large units whose shares are quoted in stock exchanges, a signal of sickness is sent when dividends are skipped and share price sharply declines. This measure, therefore, will have to be used very cautiously with other identifiable symptoms to judge whether skipping dividends indicates sickness or represents a temporary downward slide in financial performance. The existence of symptoms and signals provides grounds for suspecting that the industrial unit concerned is prone to sickness.

The symptoms of industrial sickness act as leading indicators of sickness, and if immediate remedial actions are not taken, the sickness will grow to the extent that the organization will face its natural death. Just as diseases are identified by certain symptoms, industrial sickness can be identified by the following symptoms:

- Continuous reduction in turnover.
- Continuous reduction of the net profit to sales ratio.
- Lack of movement of stocks and rising level of inventories.
- Default in payment of interest on borrowings and default in repayment of term loan installments.
- Short-term borrowings at high interest rates.

- Continuous cash losses leading to erosion of tangible net worth.
- Approaching the banker for temporary overdraft at frequent intervals.
- The "sundry debtors" as well as the "sundry creditors" keep growing and reaching a disproportionately high level.
- High turnover of personnel.
- Change in accounting procedure with a view to window dressing.
- Delay in finalization of accounts.
- Poor current ratio.
- Low capacity utilization.
- Frequent return of cheques deposited/bills drawn by the party.
- Non-submission/delayed submission of stock statements/financial statements.

Prediction of Sickness

The symptoms of industrial sickness can be observed from the leading indicators, which suggest that the unit is potentially sick. In order to identify measurable parameters that can be used for predicting sickness, the following methods[8] are generally used. They are:

- Univariate analysis.
- Multivariate analysis: Altman's Model and Dr L. C. Gupta's Sickness Prediction Model.

Univariate Analysis The main objective of univariate analysis is to predict industrial sickness on the basis of a single financial ratio. Though many financial ratios were used by analysts for predicting sickness, there was no consensus on the most appropriate ratio for the prediction of sickness. According to William H. Beaver's study on univariate analysis conducted in 1966, the "ratio of cash flow to total debt" is the most useful ratio in predicting impending sickness. Beaver selected this ratio because it showed minimum error in the prediction of industrial sickness.

Multivariate analysis The main limitation of univariate analysis is that the joint effect of more than one financial ratio in predicting industrial sickness is not taken into consideration. However, multivariate analysis can be used to study the combined influence of several financial ratios. Two important models developed for multivariate analysis are discussed below:

- **Altman's Sickness Prediction Model:** Edward I. Altman presented his model of multivariate analysis for predicting industrial sickness in 1966. His model was based on a statistical procedure known as "multiple discriminant analysis." He examined 22 financial ratios to identify their combined influence on sickness and selected five ratios. These five ratios jointly possessed the maximum power to predict bankruptcy. In his model, Altman combined several financial ratios into a single index. He named this index as the "Z-score." Altman derived a discriminant function 'Z' that contains five financial ratios.

  A cut-off point for the "Z" score was determined by Altman in such a way that it minimized the overlap between bankrupt and non-bankrupt groups. His research found that a cut-off value of 2.675 for "Z"' minimized the possibility of misclassification. The firms with "Z" score less than 2.675 are prone to become bankrupt and firms with "Z" score more than 2.675 are free from the threat of bankruptcy. The discriminant function derived by Altman is

$$Z = 1.20x_1 + 1.40x_2 + 3.30x_3 + 0.60x_4 + 0.999x_5$$

  where,

  Z = Discriminant score
  x_1 = Working capital/Total assets
  x_2 = Retained earnings/Total assets

x_3 = Earnings before interest and tax/Total assets
x_4 = Market value of equity/Book value of total debt
x_5 = Sales/Total assets

The limitation of Altman's model is that it could only predict bankruptcy one year before the firm becomes bankrupt. But one year is too short a period to take any remedial action. The model also predicts only "bankruptcy." But a firm becomes sick well before it becomes bankrupt. Therefore, a sickness prediction model is useful only when it predicts the starting symptoms of sickness so that suitable remedial measures can be taken before the unit really becomes sick.

- **Dr L. C. Gupta's Sickness Prediction Model:** This model attempts to distinguish between sick and non-sick companies on the basis of financial ratios. A simple non-parametric test was used to measure the relative predicting power of different financial ratios. Dr Gupta studied the predictive power of 63 financial ratios and observed that the following two ratios have comparatively better predictive power.

1. Earnings before interest and taxes/Sales
2. Operating cash flow/Sales

where,
Operating cash flow = Profit after tax + Depreciation

PROCESS OF INDUSTRIAL SICKNESS

An industrial unit passes through various stages before it becomes sick and gets closed. The various stages in the process of industrial sickness from healthy (normal) to sick are shown in Figure 11.1. The various stages of sickness are healthy, tending towards sickness, incipient sickness, sick, and total sickness.

Normal or Healthy

A unit is called normal when all its functional areas such as production, marketing, finance, and personnel are functioning efficiently. The indicators of a healthy unit are cash profit and positive values of net working capital and net worth. A healthy unit may have the following features:

- Generation of cash profit.
- All functional areas such as production, marketing, finance, and personnel are functioning effectively and efficiently.

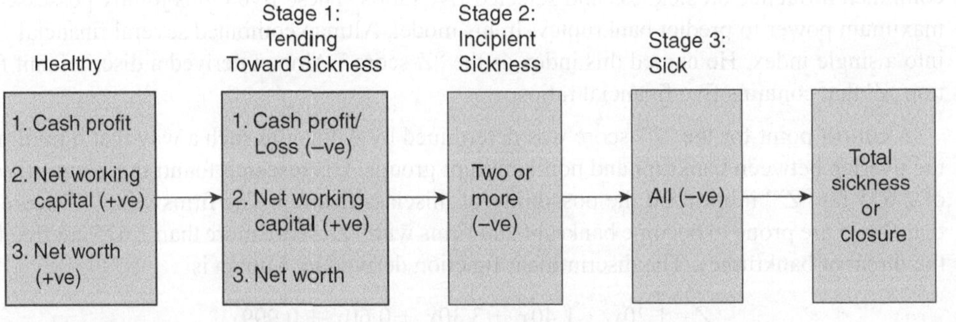

Figure 11.1 Process of Industrial Sickness

Source: Satyanarayan, A. and P. V. Purna Kumari (2009). "Industrial Sickness in India: Causes Consequences and Cures," *The IUP Journal of Entrepreneurship Development*, June 2011, Vol. VIII, No. 2. Reproduced with permission.

- Positive value of net worth.
- Positive values of net working capital or the current ratio is more than one.
- Required debt equity ratio (2:1).

Tending Towards Sickness

This stage indicates the first warning signals of sickness. In this stage (tending towards sickness), units have to face initial aberrations in functional areas or external constraints. As a result, the cash profit begins to decline in comparison to the previous year and the unit may even suffer cash loss in the current year. This might happen even though the unit may have positive values of net working capital and net worth and may not be declared a defaulter in the list of banks and financial institutions. Sickness at this stage can be averted, if some preventive measures with follow-up actions are taken by the management team. When the industrial unit enters this stage it may have the following features:

- Negative value of cash profit showing cash loss.
- Positive values of net working capital or the current ratio is more than one.
- Positive value of net worth.

Incipient Sickness

The incipient sickness stage indicates the second warning signal of sickness. As the industrial unit reaches the incipient stage of sickness, two or more financial indicators may become negative. At this stage, the management team, along with financing agencies and consultants, should collectively review the overall performance of the unit. In order to prevent the industrial unit from becoming completely sick, a turnaround strategy and suitable remedial measures should be taken.

Complete Sickness

If the suitable measures have not been taken at the incipient stage of sickness, the unit finally becomes sick. At this stage, all the functional areas become inefficient and all the financial indicators such as cash profit, net working capital, and net worth show negative values. Such a unit will require a comprehensive rehabilitation programme for revival and intensive care for a certain period of time in case it might still be potentially viable. If the unit is potentially not viable for reviving, it becomes a costly and expensive affair to revive and the unit may finally need to be closed.

DISCUSSION FORUM

- What are the symptoms of industrial sickness?
- Explain the stages of industrial sickness.
- Discuss the methods used for the prediction of industrial sickness.

SNAPSHOT

- The symptoms of industrial sickness act as leading indicators of sickness, and if immediate remedial actions are not taken, the sickness will grow to the extent that the organization will face its natural death.
- The methods used for predication of industrial sickness are univariate analysis and multivariate analysis.
- The process of industrial sickness comprises four stages—tending towards sickness, incipient sickness, sickness, and closure.

REHABILITATION OF SICK UNITS

The revival and rehabilitation of sick units is implemented based on a detailed and thorough viability study to ensure that the revival programme will really bear fruit. The viability study should be completed within three months of the unit becoming sick. The banks and financial institutions that support a revival programme for the sick unit should be convinced about the viability of the project in order to get investments for revival. The viability study should be conducted taking into account the following aspects[9]:

- Causes for sickness.
- Future market for products/services.
- The managerial competence of the borrowers to implement the rehabilitation.
- Technical appraisal—to examine the requirements of technology upgradation.
- Commercial appraisal—to study the market, competition, product development, and product diversification.
- Management appraisal—to examine the management team and the organizational structure.
- Financial appraisal—whether the projections are acceptable.
- Subsidies and concessions—concessions and subsidies available from the government and the ability of the borrowers to bring in their own contributions.

Technical Appraisal

Technical appraisal involves the study of the overall operations management of the unit. As part of technical appraisal:

- Study the manufacturing process used by the unit. Explore the possibility of switching over to the latest manufacturing process and study the cost and benefit of such a switchover.
- Study the production capacity of different production sections and check for balancing the production line. Discover any possibility of increasing the overall plant capacity by balancing the production line.
- Explore the possibility of changing the product mix so that it is in tune with market requirements. Examine the possibilities of adding extra features to the product that will add a competitive edge to the product.
- Improve the plant efficiency by a major overhaul.
- Examine the existing plant layout and study the required modifications in order to improve the efficiency of operations and improve the output.
- Study the plant location and examine the possibility of shifting the location to an advantageous place by conducting a cost–benefit analysis.
- Conduct a make or buy study, which may result in cost reduction.

Commercial Appraisal

This study involves a market study and a study of competitors. The inputs from this study are used for product development and product diversification. Every product follows a life cycle which passes through four stages: introduction, rapid expansion, maturity, and decline. The profit margins shrink when the product reaches the decline stage. Product innovation may sustain the product at this stage. In case there is no possibility of product innovation, product diversification may prove to be a feasible solution. At this stage, the feasibility of switching over to diversified products making use of existing production facilities may be examined. The cost–benefit analysis of additional investments needed for product diversification and the additional benefits that may be realised may be analysed.

Management Appraisal

The management team is very important for the success of any project. The management appraisal entails examining the organizational structure. The managerial appraisal shall suggest required changes in the organizational structure, possible reduction in manpower that can be achieved, and the likely compensation payable for retrenchment.

Financial Appraisal

The financial appraisal consists of finding ways to ease the burden of debt. This necessitates the restructuring of debts. Banks and financial institutions offer the following concessions in their package for a rehabilitation programme:

- Offer of a revised schedule of repayment for the principal components of the term loan.
- Conversion of short-term loans into long-term loans and part of long-term loans into equity.
- Reduction in the interest rate of existing loans.
- Sanction of an additional loan to meet the required additional investment.
- Enhancement of working capital limits and the regularization of the irregular portion of the working capital finance already availed.
- Funding of the overdue interest and making it repayable in easy installments. At times the funded amount may carry a concessional rate of interest or even at times bear no interest.

Turnaround Strategy

The term turnaround strategy[10] is applied to the strategy used to revive a sick unit. The turnaround brings a rapid change that is needed to deal with issues such as falling profitability, lower return on investment, or loss of market share.[11] These issues result from sudden changes in demands from the external marketplace, be it competitors, suppliers, or customers. There are three stages of a turnaround strategy:

- The revival and rehabilitation of sick units is implemented based on a detailed and thorough viability study to ensure that the revival programme will really bear fruit.
- The various steps in a turnaround strategy are: changing the leadership, redefining the strategic focus, selling or divesting of unnecessary assets, improving profitability, and making careful acquisitions.

SNAPSHOT

BREAKTHROUGH ENTREPRENEURSHIP 11.1 Lakshmi Nivas Mittal—The Turnaround Man

Lakshmi Niwas Mittal, the CEO and chairman of ArcelorMittal, was born on 15 June 1950 in Sadulpur, Rajasthan, India. He was listed in the *Forbes* list of billionaires in 2006 as the richest Indian and the fifth-richest man in the world with an estimated wealth around $2,500 crore.

Lakshmi Niwas Mittal (LNM) founded Mittal Steel in 1976, which soon became a global steel producer with operations in 14 countries. His success mantra lies in the identification, acquisition, and turnaround of many loss-making steel companies across the world.

In 1994, he took over the international operations of his family's steel business. His company, ArcelorMittal, is presently the world's largest producer of low and mild grade steels, with operations in Romania, Bosnia-Herzegovina, South Africa, Poland, the Czech Republic, Indonesia, Kazakhstan and many other countries. Over the years, Mittal has bought 21 steel mills in 17 countries, from Trinidad to France, and turned them around.

LNM, with his vision of consolidation in the steel industry, focused on geographical reach and product-line expansion for success in the twenty-first century. He was able to identify the right plants for acquisition and invest the right amount of money and people in it and turn them around into profitable ventures. LNM used vertical integration strategies to enjoy the cost advantage. Most of Mittal's major acquisitions were considered very risky by industry experts. Mittal's takeover of Arcelor in 2006 resulted in the creation of the world's largest steel company.

Source: Bouquet, Tim and Byron Ousey (2008). *Cold Steel*. Little Brown and www.arcelormittal.com (last accessed in March 2013).

BREAKTHROUGH ENTREPRENEURSHIP 11.2 Sugar King Narendra Murkumbi

Narendra Murkumbi is the vice-chairman and managing director of the ₹2,822 crore Shree Renuka Sugars, the leading manufacturer of sugar in India. The company operates 11 integrated sugar mills globally and two port-based refineries in India.

Murkumbi started Shree Renuka Sugars in Belgaum in northern Karnataka soon after his graduation from the Indian Institute of Management Ahmedabad. The foundation of the company was laid in 1998 with the acquisition of Nizam Sugars Ltd in Andhra Pradesh. Murkumbi undertook a capacity building exercise by buying or leasing a number of distressed sugar mills across the country.

Murkumbi's strategy of acquiring sick units and turning them around paid good dividends for Shree Renuka Sugars. Between 1999 and 2008, he acquired six sick units and fine-tuned processes to make the units profitable. Narendra never focused on setting up his own plants as the gestation periods are large in the case of greenfield projects.

In 2010, Murkumbi went global with a vengeance, acquiring two companies in the world's largest sugar producing nation, Brazil. Shree Renuka paid ₹350 crore to buy Vale Do Ilvai SA Acucar E Alcool (VDI), a loss-making sugar mill in Brazil. Murkumbi also acquired another stuttering sugar company, Equipav SA, for ₹1,500 crore. Today, Shree Renuka is India's largest sugar company.

Narendra Murkumbi shares a seat with steel baron L. N. Mittal on the board of ICICI Bank. He also shares Mittal's penchant for building a business by turning around distressed assets. That's why Murkumbi is also referred to as the L. N. Mittal of the sugar industry.

Source: Nayak, Mahesh (2010). "The Turnaround Man," *Outlook Business*, 03 April 2010 and www.renukasugars.com (last accessed in March 2013).

- **Stage 1—Pre-turnaround:** The first stage is the period just before the profitability begins to decline. The company is still considered profitable at this point, but losing ground.
- **Stage 2—Period of crisis:** The second stage, marked by a decline in profits, a fall in market share, and the company's poor cash situation, is known as the period of crisis. The company needs a turnaround at this point.
- **Stage 3—Period of recovery:** The third stage is the period of recovery or the turning point. This is the stage where serious action is taken to turn the company around. Important decisions like scaling back production or returning to an aggressive growth stage are taken. This is the longest period and may last for years.

WINDING UP OF A COMPANY

"Failure" is the termination of a business that has closed operations with a loss to creditors. A sick unit is not necessarily a failed unit; although prolonged sickness may lead to failure. Failure denotes the result of a series of reversals in the fortunes of a company.

"Closure" denotes the ceasing of operations voluntarily or involuntarily. The desire or need to close a business does not mean failure.

The two terms "insolvency" and "bankruptcy," though generally used together, are not synonymous. Insolvency is a term used to describe the "state" of a company or a person that is unable to pay their creditors. It is a financial condition when assets no longer exceed liabilities, (commonly referred to as "balance sheet" insolvency), or when the person or entity can no longer meet debt obligations (commonly referred to as "cash flow" insolvency).

"Bankruptcy," on the other hand, is a "status" granted by law. It is a legally declared inability or impairment of the ability of an individual or an organization to pay creditors. Bankruptcy is the "legal" state of insolvency.[12] The warning signs of bankruptcy are:

- The management of finances becomes lax, so that no one can explain how money is being spent.
- Increase in customers' complaints regarding service and product quality.
- Suppliers demand payment in cash.
- Payroll taxes are not paid.
- Directors cannot document major transactions.
- Lack of materials to meet orders.
- Key personnel leave company.
- Bank requests the subordination of its loans.
- Customers are given large discounts to enhance payments because of poor cash flow.
- Contracts are accepted below standard amounts to generate cash.

The two terms "winding up" and "liquidation" are used interchangeably. The winding up or liquidation represents the proceedings by which a company is dissolved. During the winding up stage, the assets of the company are disposed of and the debts are paid off out of the realised assets (or from contribution from its members). The surplus if any is then distributed among the members in proportion to their holdings in the company.

The right to "exit" refers to the right of the promoter to close or sell off a business after settling his liabilities without affecting his future prospects. In India, "exit" is a right sought by large corporations for the closure of business without mandatory approval from the government beyond a certain limit of the number of employees.

The winding up of a company is a process whereby its life is ended and its property administered for the benefits of its creditors and its members. An administrator, called liquidator, is appointed and he takes control of the company, collects its assets, pays its debts, and finally distributes any surplus among the members in accordance with their rights. There are three modes of winding up a company:

1. Winding up by the tribunal.
2. Voluntary winding up:
    - Members' voluntary winding up.
    - Creditors' voluntary winding up.
3. Winding up subject to supervision of the tribunal.

A company may be wound up by the tribunal in the following cases:

- If the company has, by special resolution, resolved that the company be wound up by the tribunal.
- If a default is made in delivering the statutory report to the registrar or in holding the statutory meeting.
- If the company does not commence its business within a year from its incorporation, or suspends its business for a whole year.
- If the number of members is reduced, in the case of a public company, below seven, and in the case of a private company, below two.
- If the company is unable to pay its debts. A creditor can file a winding up petition if the company is indebted for a sum exceeding ₹1 lakh.
- If the tribunal is of the opinion that it is just and equitable that the company should be wound up.
- If the company has made a default in filing its balance sheet, profit and loss account, or annual return with the registrar for any five consecutive financial years.
- If the company has acted against the interests of the sovereignty and integrity of India, the security of the state, friendly relations with foreign states, public order, decency, or mortality.
- If the tribunal is of the opinion that the company should be wound up under the circumstances specified in Section 424G.

Practising chartered accountants, company secretaries, and cost accountants can appear before the tribunal on behalf of the creditor, contributory, or official liquidator.

Exit Strategy

An exit strategy[12] can be termed as the planning behind terminating one's ownership of a company. The exit strategy is a way of "cashing out" an investment. Examples include an initial public offering (IPO) or being bought out by a larger player in the industry. Exit strategy is also referred as a "harvest strategy" or "liquidity event." There are several reasons for an entrepreneur to exit his venture. Some of the more common reasons are: lack of profits, loss of interest, lack of future prospects, dissolved partnership, lack of willingness of the entrepreneur to take future risks, other exciting opportunities, personal reasons, and favourable economic conditions.

Initial Public Offering

Instead of selling the enterprise or taking on additional partners, the entrepreneur may decide to list it at a stock exchange. This is done through an initial public offering (IPO). An IPO is the first sale of the stock of a company through the public. IPOs are often issued by smaller, younger companies seeking the capital to expand, but can also be done by large privately-owned companies looking to become publicly traded. It is also referred to as a "public offering."

When a company goes public, it transforms from a closely-held corporation to one where the general public has proprietary interest. Before going public, an entrepreneur must carefully analyse the advantages and the disadvantages and also check whether the enterprise is ready to go public. The entrepreneur must take into account factors such as the size of the company, earnings and performance, market conditions, the urgency of monetary need, and the desires of the current owners.

WORLD OF ENTREPRENEURS 11.3 *Chakravyuha*

Abhimanyu perished in the battle of Kurukshetra (*Mahabharata*) for the lack of an exit strategy. In Indian folklore, Abhimanyu was the son of warrior Arjuna (one of the *Pandavas*) and Subhadra. He had learnt a deadly military technique called the *chakravyuha* that involved trapping enemy soldiers in an enclosed lotus-like formation.

The thirteenth day of the *Mahabharata* is memorable for the construction of the *chakravyuha* by Dronacharya. The formation was used in the battle of Kurukshetra by Dronacharya, who became the commander-in-chief of the *Kaurava* army after the fall of Bhishma *Pitamaha*. The *chakravyuha* is a multi-tier defensive formation that looks like a blooming lotus when viewed from above. The warriors at each interleaving position would be in an increasingly tough position to fight.

When this technique was applied, enemy soldiers could not escape the layered maze formation of opposing army soldiers and they would be slaughtered. Abhimanyu learnt this technique as an unborn baby, when he was in the womb of his mother Subhadra, listening to his father, Arjuna, discussing this technique with his mother. Unfortunately, the conversation was not completed. Arjuna did not finish explaining to Subhadra how to escape from the *chakravyuha*. Abhimanyu was able to get into the *chakravyuha* but did not learn how to escape and was subsequently killed in it.

Arjuna was the only person who knew how to enter and also to exit the *chakravyuha*. Knowing this, Susharma, a *Kaurava* warrior lured Arjuna far away while Dronacharya formed the *chakravyuha* so that he would be able to trap the very important head of the *Pandavas*, Yudhisthhira. This led to Abhimanyu getting trapped inside the maze. Susharma was slain by Arjuna. However, it was too late as Abhimanyu fell inside the *chakravyuha* and was attacked by seven warriors simultaneously in his attempt to exit.

But what is the implication of the *chakravyuha*? The implication is that entrepreneurs should be like Arjuna and not like Abhimanyu. Most entrepreneurs are modern-day Abhimanyus. They know how to start a company, and how to create the initial momentum and velocity. However, like Abhimanyu, most of them do not have an exit strategy.

Source: www.funtrivia.com/en/subtopics/The-Great-War-The-Mahabharatha-II-150304.html (last accessed in March 2013).

CHECKLIST FOR ENTREPRENEURS 11.4 ✓ Check the Health of Your Enterprise

- Think about an exit strategy while starting a business.
- When you are selling your business, get a realistic valuation of your business from a reliable, outside expert.
- Check the health of the company on a regular basis.
- While reviving a sick unit, utilize the commitment of managers and employees of the organization.
- Provide a leadership role in reviving a sick unit. This would generate confidence in the employees that the organization can and will be revived.
- Use the turnaround strategy to revive sick units. While reviving a sick unit, remember profits are a legitimate goal towards which the sick unit's revival efforts may be usefully directed.
- When you revive a sick unit, you will not only become a turnaround expert but also will get professional satisfaction and respect. You will also save hundreds of jobs and huge amounts of public finance invested in valuable assets.

DISCUSSION FORUM

- Discuss the phases of turnaround strategy.
- Which are the factors usually taken into consideration for conducting the viability study for reviving a sick unit?
- How do you revive a sick unit?
- Explain exit strategy.

Going public is often the best way to obtain needed capital on the best possible terms. Going public also provides a mechanism for valuing the company and allowing this value to be easily transferred among parties. There are three primary advantages of going public: obtaining new equity capital, obtaining value and transferability of the organization's assets, and enhancing the company's ability to obtain future funds. There are three primary disadvantages of going public: disclosure of information, loss of control, and pressure to maintain growth.

The steps involved while filing an IPO depends on the exchange that the entrepreneur is planning to get the company listed in. In India, Companies that want to be listed need to conform to the guidelines specified by the Securities and Exchange Board of India (SEBI). The main stock exchanges in India are the Bombay Stock Exchange (BSE) and the National Stock Exchange (NSE). Filing an IPO is also possible in any of the international exchanges popular with entrepreneurial companies, such as NASDAQ in the USA and AIM in the UK. The steps involved in listing include choosing an investment banker and underwriter, coming out with a red herring prospectus, and organizing a roadshow.

SUMMARY

A unit is considered sick (non-SME) if it has accumulated losses equal to or exceeding its entire net worth as at the end of the latest financial year. A micro or small enterprise (as defined in the MSMED Act, 2006) may be said to have become sick, if any of the borrowal accounts of the enterprise remains a non-performing asset for three months or more or there is erosion in the net worth due to accumulated losses to the extent of 50 per cent of the net worth. The Sick Industrial Companies Act (SICA) 1985, after being amended twice, was replaced by the Sick Industrial Companies (Special Provisions) Repeal Act, 2003. The work of revival and rehabilitation was entrusted to the National Company Law Tribunal (NCLT) constituted under the Companies Act, 1956. Any appeal against the order of the NCLT will now be made to the National Company Law Appellate Tribunal (NCLAT). In India, the Tiwari Committee report categorizes the causes of industrial sickness into several factors. These causes can be broadly classified into two categories: internal causes and external causes.

The symptoms of industrial sickness may be in the form of financial distress starting with short-term liquidity problems, revenue losses, operating losses, and moving in the direction of over use of external credit until it reaches a stage where the industry is overburdened with debt and is unable to generate sufficient funds to meet its obligations. In case of large units whose shares are quoted in stock exchanges, a signal of sickness is sent when dividends are skipped and share price sharply declines. The symptoms of industrial sickness act as leading indicators of sickness, and if immediate remedial actions are not taken, the sickness will grow to the extent that the organization will face its natural death. The symptoms of industrial sickness can be observed from the leading indicators, which suggest that the unit is a potentially sick unit. In order to identify measurable parameters that can be used for predicting sickness, the methods that are generally used are univariate analysis and multivariate analysis.

The industrial unit passes through various stages before it becomes sick and gets closed. The various stages of sickness are: tending towards sickness, incipient sickness, sick, and total sickness. The revival and rehabilitation of a sick unit is implemented based on a detailed and thorough viability study to ensure that the revival programme will really bear fruit. The viability study comprises a technical appraisal, a commercial appraisal, a financial appraisal, and a management appraisal.

KEY TERMS

Bankruptcy: It is the "legal" state of insolvency.

Exit Strategy: The planning behind terminating one's ownership of a company or the operation of some part of the company.

Failure: Termination of a business that has closed operations with a loss to creditors.

Initial Public Offering (IPO): The first sale of the stock of a company to the public; takes place when the entrepreneur decides to list the company in a stock exchange.

Investment Bank: A financial institution which is in the business of raising capital for private companies and other entities.

Liquidation: The process of converting assets into cash, usually through a partial or complete sale. It represents the last stage in the life of a company.

Red Herring: A tentative prospectus circulated by the underwriters of a new issue of stocks or bonds that is pending approval.

Stock Exchange: An association or group of people organized to provide an auction market for the purchase and sale of listed securities.

Turnaround Strategy: The strategy used to revive a sick unit.

Underwriter: An entity who assumes the risk and responsibility of distributing a securities issue to the public.

Valuation: The process of appraising the current worth of an asset or a company.

CASE STUDY

Turnaround of Indian Railways

"Indian Railways has staged a dramatic turnaround with the same employees and assets. The turnaround strategy has been based on simple principles—have higher freight volumes, improve occupancy in passenger trains, control costs, and most importantly reduce tariffs."

— Prime Minister Manmohan Singh, 27 September 2006

According to the Expert Group report submitted to the Government of India in July 2001, the Indian Railways (IR) was on the verge of a financial crisis in 2001. The report forecast that the government would be saddled with a financial liability of over ₹61,000 crore by 2017. The IR staged a turnaround in 2005–2006 under the leadership of the new railways minister.

The Indian Railways, a legacy from the British rule, has a monopoly on the country's rail transport. It constitutes the lifeline and the mainstay of the country's transport infrastructure with its route network of 63,221 km. It is the world's largest commercial utility employer with more than 16 lakh employees.

The policies of the railways became obsolete with the liberalization of the Indian economy in 1991. The IR battled challenges posed by other low-cost means of transport, stiff competition from roads in the lucrative finished goods market, safety issues, and an under-trained employee base. By 2001, the consensus was that the IR had failed to utilize its capacity and achieve its profit goals by obliging political and social agendas.

In 2003–2004, IR staged a remarkable turnaround under the leadership of Lalu Prasad Yadav, a political leader from Bihar. He proved to be a dark horse, as under his leadership, IR adopted and implemented cost-effective strategies to raise revenues. Some of the key strategies that the Indian Railways adopted were downsizing, outsourcing, product innovation, and rise in demand. These are discussed below.

Downsizing: The employee strength was brought down to 14.72 lakh by 2003 and to 14.12 lakh by 2006 from a high of 16.52 lakh in 1991. The IR followed the approach of not filling up vacancies created due to retirement or other reasons.

Outsourcing: Catering, parcel service activity, and advertising activity was outsourced. IR adopted the strategy of outsourcing through public–private partnership and wholesaling rather than retailing. The retrenchment strategy for outsourcing helped IR to contain costs.

Product Innovation: The introduction of double-stack container trains on some diesel routes led to savings of about seven per cent on capital cost and 25 per cent on operating expenses. These containers increased the carrying capacity of each train to 2,500 tonnes against 1,500 tonnes, and also reduced line capacity constraints by half. Safety features were improved with a new design of wagons with higher carrying capacity and lower weight.

Rise in Demand: IR also used the high international demand for iron ore to raise the freight on iron ore by 17 per cent.

The product-innovation and cost-cutting strategy combined with a "value for customer" philosophy were the main factors in bringing about the turnaround of the Indian Railways. The essence of the "turnaround" was in the fact that total revenues increased by a significant percentage and the net revenues continued in a robust upward trend.

Questions:

1. Analyse the situation of the Indian Railways in 2001.
2. What was the turnaround strategy adopted by the Indian Railways?

3. Analyse the benefits derived from the turnaround strategy.

Source: www.infrastructure.gov.in/pdf/brochure_railway.pdf (last accessed in March 2013) and www.crawford.anu.edu (last accessed in March 2013).

DISCUSSION QUESTIONS

1. Discuss the symptoms that can be used to identify industrial sickness?
2. Explain the causes of industrial sickness.
3. "Thinking about an exit strategy while starting a business is too early to be doing it." Comment.
4. Discuss turnaround strategy with an example.
5. Name the circumstances responsible for the winding up of a company.

ACTIVITY

1. Visit a local sick enterprise. Identify the causes of sickness and prepare a brief report on the cost of rehabilitation and the means of finance, not exceeding four A4 size pages with suitable margins.
2. Invite a local entrepreneur to your institute and ask him to address the class about the problems faced by his enterprise.

PROJECT

1. Make a list of all public-sector undertakings in India. Identify any one of the sick units, find out the reasons of industrial sickness, and prepare a report not exceeding five pages of A4 size.
2. Make a list of all recent IPOs by entrepreneurial firms. How are the stocks performing in the market?

ENDNOTES

1. Kent, Calvin A., Donald L. Sexton, and Karl H. Vesper (eds.) (1982). *Encyclopedia of Entrepreneurship*. New Jersey: Prentice Hall.
2. Section 4 (2) and 4 (3) of SICA, 1985.
3. Section 229 (1) and 237 (2) of the Companies Bill, 2009.
4. Dokania, Gopal Pd. (2003). "National Company Law Tribunal and Appellate Tribunal," *Chartered Accountant*, August.
5. Balan, K. (1996). *Managing Industrial Sickness.* Mittal Publications.
6. Goyal, Alok and Mridula Goyal (2010–11). *Business Environment*. New Delhi: V. K. (India) Enterprises.
7. Kumar, S. Anil, S. C. Poornima, M. K. Abraham, and K. Jayashree (2003). *Entrepreneurship Development*. New Delhi: New Age International Publishers.
8. Nagarajan, K. (2005). *Project Management*. New Delhi: New Age International Publishers.
9. Prahalad, C. K. and P. S. Thomas (1977). "Turnaround Strategy: Lessons from HPF's Experience," *Vikalpa,* April, 2 (2).

10. Pandia, Rajeev (2010). "Case Study: Turnaround: A Challenge and Opportunity," *Business and Management Chronicle*, July.
11. Hisrich, Robert D., Michael Peters, and Dean Shepherd (1998). *Entrepreneurship*. Burr Ridge, IL: Irwin/McGraw-Hill Publishing Company, pp. 588–603.
12. Roy, Rajeev (2009). *Entrepreneurship.* New Delhi: Oxford University Press.

Management of Enterprises

11. Preventing Sickness in Enterprises
12. Financial Management in Enterprises
13. Operations and Human Resource Management in Enterprises
14. Managing Marketing and Growth in Enterprises

"You need to have enough immediate profits that you can finance the long-range growth without diluting the stock."

—Paul Cook

S. Mahalingam, the chief financial officer of Tata Consultancy Services, was nominated as the best CFO with commitment towards triple bottom line by Business Today *in 2012. S. Mahalingam joined TCS in 1968 and has been involved in myriad aspects of the company's operations and growth. A chartered accountant by qualification, he has played a key role in helping TCS become a USD 600 crore global company with over 160,000 employees.*

Financial Management in Enterprises

12

LEARNING OBJECTIVES

Upon completion of this chapter, you should be able to:

1. Understand the importance of financial management in enterprises.
2. Describe accounting and bookkeeping.
3. Discuss financial statements.
4. Understand the relevance of working capital management.
5. Explain break-even analysis.
6. Identify various financial ratios that impact business decisions.

INTRODUCTION

Finance is the lifeblood of a business. Financial management is a managerial activity concerning the finances of the firm. It deals with planning, control, and management of the financial resources of the firm. It is not only enough to raise the finance for industrial activity; it is necessary to manage it properly as well. Financial management is assuming increased importance in the modern context because some of the most crucial decisions of a firm are those that relate to finance. An enterprise has to undertake five important management functions as a part of its business: (1) finance, (2) operations and production, (3) human resource management, (4) marketing, and (5) strategy.

Chapter 12 explains financial management in business enterprises. Chapter 13 explains operations and human resource management in business enterprises. Chapter 14 explains marketing and strategic management in business enterprises. There exists an inseparable relationship between the finance function and the production, marketing, and human resource management functions. Finance is at the root of any business activity. Therefore, there is a need to properly manage it. Financial management is the process of the procurement and judicious use of financial resources with a view to maximizing the value of the enterprise.

FUNCTIONS OF FINANCIAL MANAGEMENT

Financial management involves two types of functions[1]: (1) managerial finance functions and (2) routine finance functions. Managerial finance functions require skilful planning, control, and execution of financial activities. Routine finance functions, on the other hand, do not require any great managerial ability to be carried out. They are clerical in nature and incidental to the effective handling of the managerial finance functions. Managerial finance functions are mainly: (1) estimating financial requirements; (2) identifying sources of finance; (3) raising of finance; (4) proper use of finance; and (5) control of finance.

1. **Estimating financial requirements:** Before starting an industrial unit, it is necessary that an entrepreneur estimate its financial requirements. There is a need to scientifically calculate the fixed capital and working capital requirements. The project report must be prepared with the help of a finance expert or a consultant.
2. **Identifying sources of finance:** Once the total financial requirement is known, the entrepreneur should identify the sources from which finance can be raised. There are many sources open to a small industrial unit. These are: (1) personal funds, (2) funds from friends, (3) banks, (4) financial institutions, and (5) public deposits. After a careful analysis, the entrepreneur should decide from which source he can raise funds.
3. **Raising of finance:** Raising of finance does not mean the mere collection of funds. It has four important dimensions: (1) right source, (2) time schedule, (3) cost, and (4) adequacy. The raising of finance should be adequate, at the right time, from a powerful source, and at the right price or cost. The finance raised should be adequate and sufficient. This helps in the smooth running of business.

   An entrepreneur should select the right type of source to raise finance. This requires a lot of thought. The projection of time, that is, when the finance is needed, at what stage, and so on should also be given consideration. All the finance is not required on the first day. One can phase out the time for collecting funds. Funds should be collected as and when required. This will reduce the cost (interest charges). Finance should be so arranged that it becomes available at the proper time, neither too early nor too late. The cost aspect should also be considered while raising funds.
4. **Proper use of finance:** Finance raised for the purpose of any business activity should be carefully used. The project report prepared by the entrepreneur with the help of experts indicates clearly how the finance collected should be used. Financial discipline has to be observed to keep the enterprise in good health. Money should not be used for any purpose other than purely business activity. Many units become sick due to a lack of proper use of finance.
5. **Control of finance:** Control relates to establishing proper procedures and systems to check the financial activity of the business enterprise. A business should be carried out as planned in the project report. Income and expenditure should be kept under control. A review should be made periodically to know whether the business is being carried out along the proper lines or not.

Routine finance is incidental to the effective execution of the managerial finance functions. They involve a lot of paperwork and time. They deal with procedural aspects. The most important routine finance functions are: (1) supervision of cash receipts and payments; (2) safeguarding cash balances; (3) record keeping (accounting); (4) custody and safeguarding of securities, insurance policies, and other important documents; (5) taking care of the mechanical details of outside finances; and (6) regular return of borrowed funds.

Financial management at the firm level also requires proper management of fixed assets, working capital, and costs. Fixed assets themselves cannot generate profits. Idle fixed assets do not generate profits. They should be properly used and managed. Repairs, maintenance, replacement, and revaluation of assets need skilful management.

ACCOUNTING AND BOOKKEEPING

Accounting is the language of business as it communicates the results of business operations to various stakeholders in the business. Accounting is the process of identifying, measuring, and communicating economic information to permit informed judgements and decisions by users of the information.[2] The main function of accounting is to provide quantitative information of a financial nature about the economic entities, which is useful in making economic decisions. Bookkeeping is mainly concerned with the recording of financial data relating to business transactions in a systematic and chronological manner. The objectives of bookkeeping and accounting are to maintain a systematic record; to ascertain the financial position of the business; to facilitate rational decision making; to have knowledge of debtors, creditors, purchase, sales, cash, bank balance, and closing stock; and to know the amount of taxes to be paid to the government.

Process of Accounting

Accounting helps to know the financial position of a business during the accounting period. The financial position of a business can be analysed by preparing trading accounts, profit and loss accounts, and balance sheets at the end of the accounting period. If the books of accounts are maintained properly, an entrepreneur will know how much he has to pay to the government in taxes. The accounting cycle comprises the following phases:

- **Documentation** of business transactions that are capable of being expressed in terms of money, by way of what is known as a voucher. Activities carried out by a business enterprise related to purchase, sales receipts, payments, etc. are recorded using vouchers.
- **Recording** of vouchers in a daybook called a journal. The journal is also known as the daybook because all the transactions are recorded daily on a chronological basis.
- **Classifying** the transactions so recorded by their nature, for example, putting all purchase transactions in one place chronologically so as to enable an understanding of the total, and build an understanding of the effect of that particular activity. This is done through a book called a ledger.
- **Summarizing** the transactions so classified to understand and appreciate the total build up and effect of various activities. This is done through a statement called the trial balance. This document provides the net effect of all transactions, by their nature, carried out by the enterprise during a particular period. From the trial balance, the entrepreneur can prepare a profit and loss account and the balance sheet in order to measure the financial position of the enterprise.
- **Analysis and interpretation** of the accounting information by ratio analysis in order to judge the past and present performance of the company in order to make future plans.
- **Communicating** the results of analysis and interpretation to stakeholders in the form of financial statements such as profit and loss account, balance sheet, and cash flow statements. The annual report is usually prepared comprising financial statements, ratios, graphs, and diagrams for taking appropriate decisions.

Accounting and bookkeeping are not different from each other. The accounting cycle includes various phases such as documentation, recording, classifying, summarizing, analysis, and interpretation and communication. Bookkeeping involves the recording of financial transactions in a systematic manner. The differences between bookkeeping and accounting are given in Table 12.1.

Table 12.1 Differences Between Bookkeeping and Accounting

Sl No.	Criteria	Bookkeeping	Accounting
1.	Objective	Recording financial transactions in a systematic manner.	Documentation, recording, classifying, summarizing, analysis, and interpretation and communication.
2.	Origin	First stage of accounting.	This stage starts where bookkeeping ends.
3.	Scope	Limited scope.	Wider in scope.
4.	Level of work	Clerical work and is carried out by employees at a lower level.	It is carried out by accountants with higher responsibility.
5.	Knowledge required	Simple	Higher level
6.	Type of document	Data	Information

Types of Accounting

Accounting can be classified as follows:

- **Financial accounting:** Financial accounting aims at preparing financial statements of an enterprise such as balance sheet, profit and loss account, and cash flow statements in order to ascertain the financial position of an enterprise.
- **Cost accounting:** Cost accounting aims to ascertain the cost per unit of a product or process and to control the cost.
- **Management accounting:** Management accounting aims to provide necessary information for discharging various management functions such as planning, controlling, decision making, and evaluating the performance of the enterprise.

Generally Accepted Accounting Principles

Generally Accepted Accounting Principles[3] (GAAP) constitute the foundation of the accounting structure. GAAP is an acronym for a set of generally accepted accounting principles that are used during the preparation of financial records, reports, and statements. These accounting practices and procedures are authorized by the accounting profession's rule-setting body, the Financial Accounting Standard Board (FASB). These broad guidelines are accounting standards that bring about uniformity in recording, classifying, summarizing, interpreting, reporting, and the presentation of the accounting information. Publicly-owned corporations must provide an annual report to stockholders, which summarizes and documents the firm's financial activities during the past year. The letter to stockholders is the first element of the annual stockholders' report and is the primary communication from the management.

Accounting standards are the rules that ensure a uniform framework of preparation, presentation, and reporting of accounting information imposed by law or a professional body. The international Financial Reporting Standards are issued by the International Accounting Standards Board (IASB)

Types of Books of Accounts

The different types of books of accounts are:

- **Journal:** The accounting process starts with the recording of transactions in the basic book of accounting called the journal. The journal is a book of prime entry and is used to record, classify, or sort out transactions in a convenient form to record their subsequent entry in the ledger. The journal is a chronological record of business transactions.
- **Ledger:** A ledger is an analytical record and is the book of secondary entry. It is the most important book of accounts and is also called the book of final entry. The transactions recorded in the journal are finally carried to the ledger. This is a permanent record of various accounts. It is the basis for preparing final accounts.
- **Purchase book:** It records all purchases of goods on credit. The purchase book is prepared on the basis of invoices. It has columns for date of purchase, invoice number, name of the party, ledger folio, and amount.

SNAPSHOT

- Financial management involves two types of functions—managerial finance functions and routine finance functions.
- The users of accounting and bookkeeping are internal users such as owners, management, and employees. External users are creditors, investors, the government, customers, researchers, and foreign companies.
- The different types of accounting are financial accounting, cost accounting, and management accounting.
- Some examples of books of accounts are journal, ledger, purchase book, sales book, and cash book.

- **Sales book:** It records all sales of goods on credit. Cash sales are never recorded in the sales book. It has columns for date of sale, invoice number, name of the party, ledger folio, and amount.
- **Cash book:** It is a principal book in which all cash transactions, whether receipts or payments, are recorded. It is used for recording the receipts and payments of money in coins, notes, cheques, postal orders, and bank drafts.

DISCUSSION FORUM

- Discuss the significance of financial management in enterprises in small groups.
- Describe the different types of books of accounts.
- Explain the difference between bookkeeping and accounting.

WORLD OF ENTREPRENEURS 12.1 Tata Motors's C. Ramakrishnan Is India's Best CFO

The changes in the environment over the last decade have transformed the way the chief financial officer (CFO) operates. CFOs have transitioned from being accountants to decision makers in an increasingly competitive business environment. Today, CFOs take centre stage and play a strategic role in the organization. An effective CFO is critical to the success of any organization.

The top 10 qualities of an effective CFO are financial foresight, integrity and ethical standards, strategic vision and leadership skills, a deep understanding of business, accounting and financial competence, excellent communication skills, a perspective on risk, a result-oriented mindset, self-confidence, and reliability.

In order to recognize and acknowledge the exemplary achievements of CFOs in India, *Business Today* and YES Bank instituted awards for Best CFOs in 2010. This initiative has been designed based on parameters such as outstanding contribution of the CFO in building the institution; adding value to shareholder's wealth; raising capital; treasury management; controlling the business while partnering; and being dynamic in conceptualizing, structuring, and executing important deals.

All "*Business Today* 500" companies were eligible to participate in the process. The selection process was a robust three-step approach based on a detailed quantitative analysis in the first phase, an independent market survey, followed by an eminent panel of jury meeting. There were 10 award categories—exemplary all-round performance, sustained wealth creation, remarkable leverage management, consistent liquidity management, best transformation agent, enhancing competitiveness through mergers and acquisitions, best CFO of a public-sector undertaking (PSU), commitment towards triple bottom line (CSR), best CFO of an MNC, and best female CFO.

The CFO of Tata Motors, C. Ramakrishnan, was selected as India's best CFO for 2012. The panel of jury members felt that Ramakrishnan's exemplary handling of Tata Motors's Jaguar Rover acquisition, introduction of innovative products, efficiencies in working capital management, cost reduction, and improved channel management along with CSR initiatives, gave him the edge in the race.

Source: Bhattacharya, Alokesh (2012). "India's Best CFOs," *Business Today*, 29 April.

FINANCIAL STATEMENTS

Financial statements are the most important part of financial reporting. They are recorded in the company's annual report for the benefit of all the stakeholders of an enterprise. Based on this financial information, a business formulates its strategies for revenue enhancement, cost economies, efficiency, and improvements. It may be used for corporate restructuring and further expansion/diversification for creating and enhancing the wealth of its stakeholders. A complete set of financial statements normally consists of:

- A balance sheet.
- A profit and loss account or income statement.
- A cash flow statement.

Balance Sheet

It is a significant financial statement of an enterprise and is called a fundamental accounting report. A balance sheet shows the financial status of an enterprise at any given moment in time. The balance sheet will always balance. The balance sheet contains information in respect of assets, liabilities, and shareholder's equity. The features of a balance sheet are given below:

- Prepared as on a given date.
- Comparative position.
- Vertically drawn.
- Grouping and sub-grouping of assets and liabilities.
- Details in schedules and notes to the accounts.
- Matching of assets and liabilities.
- Signed by person who prepared it and the auditors.

Contents of Balance Sheet: The contents of the balance sheet consist of the assets of the enterprise and the means by which they have been financed, i.e. liabilities and owners' equity:

- **Assets (application of funds):** Assets are valuable resources owned by an enterprise that are acquired at a measurable cost. All assets are grouped into various categories. The standard classification of assets is fixed assets, current assets, investments, and other assets. The asset which is the most permanent appears first in the balance sheet and the asset which is closer to being turned into cash comes last in the balance sheet.
- **Fixed assets:** These are long-term resources to be retained in the enterprise to produce goods and services and are not for sale. They are held for longer than one accounting period and are also known as long-term assets. Fixed assets may be tangible and intangible. These include land and buildings; plant, machinery and equipment; fixtures and fittings; motor vehicles; patents; copyrights; trademarks; and goodwill.
- **Current assets:** These are short-term resources either held in the form of cash or expected to be realised in cash within the accounting period. Current assets include inventory, accounts receivable (debtors), cash, and marketable securities. Investments are long-term assets outside the business of the enterprise. They represent the investment of funds in the securities of another enterprise. Other assets are deferred charges (pre-payments) for services for periods exceeding the accounting period.
- **Liabilities (sources of funds):** Liabilities are sources of funds to buy the enterprise's assets and represent the obligation of an enterprise payable after the accounting period. Depending on the periodicity of the funds, liabilities can be classified into long-term liabilities and current liabilities. Long-term liabilities are the sources of finance, which are not due for repayment in less than one year but have to be repaid either as a lump sum at the maturity of the loan or in installments over the life of the loan. The sources of long-term borrowings are debentures, bonds, mortgages, and secured loans from financial institutions and commercial banks.

In contrast to long-term liabilities, current liabilities are obligations to outsiders and intended to be repayable within the accounting period. They are usually paid out of current assets. Current liabilities include accounts payable, bills/notes payable, tax payable, accrued expenses, deferred income, and short-term bank credit.

Owner's equity is the third major component of a balance sheet. It is that part of the resources of a firm supplied by its owners also known as shareholders. The consolidated balance sheet of Tata Consultancy Services for 2011–2012 is provided in Table 12.2.

Table 12.2 Balance Sheet of Tata Consultancy Services Ltd for 2011–2012

Year	March 2012 (₹ in Crore)
Sources of funds:	
Share capital+	295.72
Reserves total+	29,283.51
Equity share warrants	0.00
Equity application money	0.00
Total shareholders' funds	**29,579.23**
Minority interest	558.77
Secured loans+	112.61
Unsecured loans+	**13.94**
Total debt	**126.55**
Policy holders' funds	0.00
Other liabilities	502.66
Total liabilities	**30,767.21**
Application of funds:	
Cross block+	12,991.29
Less: Accumulated depreciation+	4,329.23
Less: Impairment of assets	0.00
Net block+	8,662.06
Lease adjustment	0.00
Capital work in progress+	1,446.37
Investments+	1,350.33
Current assets, loans, and advances	
Inventories+	17.77
Sundry debtors+	11,520.35
Cash and bank+	6,003.47
Loans and advances+	4,960.82
Total current assets	22,502.41
Less: Current liabilities and provisions	
Current liabilities+	5,659.78
Provisions+	4,794.05
Total current liabilities	10,453.83
Net current assets	12,048.58
Miscellaneous expenses not written off+	0.00
Deferred tax assets	256.04
Deferred tax liabilities	173.45
Net deferred tax	82.59
Other assets	7,177.28
Total assets	**30,767.21**
Contingent liabilities+	2,636.73

Source: Annual report of Tata Consultancy Services Ltd. Reproduced with permission.

Profit and Loss Account

This is also known as income statement, statement of earnings, statement of operations, and profit and loss statement. The profit and loss account of an enterprise reports the results of operations in terms of income/net profit in a year. The statement of profit and loss depicts the total income of the company, the expenditure incurred in deriving that income, the income tax payable to the government, the net profit earned, the dividend paid to the shareholders, and the profit retained and ploughed back into the company. The salient features of a profit and loss account are:

- Prepared for a given period.
- Comparative position.
- Vertically drawn.
- Grouping on income and expenditure.
- Details in schedules and notes to the accounts.
- Appropriation of profit and transfer to the balance sheet.
- Signed by person who prepared it and the auditors.

The profit and loss account represents the scoreboard of the performance of the enterprise in terms of the profitability of operations. The main contents of a profit and loss account are revenues, sales income, and net income/profit/loss. Revenue is the income the enterprise generates by sale of goods/services/assets or by supply of the firm's resources to others. The revenue is also the value that an enterprise receives from its customers. The sales income equals net sales. The difference between the revenues and expenses is net profit. The gross profit is the difference between the cost of goods that have been sold and the proceeds of their sales, without any deduction for distribution expenses and general establishment charges. Gross profit less operating expenses will give the net profit. A company's total revenues less total expenses for a set period are its net profits. The consolidated profit and loss account of Tata Consultancy Services Ltd for 2011–2012 is given in Table 12.3.

Cash Flow Statements

The cash generated and utilized by a company is depicted in the cash flow statement. This statement completes the set of financial statements. The cash flow statement is derived from the balance sheet, profit and loss account, and cash equivalents of an enterprise by classifying cash flows during the period from operating, investing, and financing activities. Cash has been defined as comprising cash on hand and demand deposits with banks. Cash equivalents refer to short term, highly liquid investments that are readily convertible into known amounts of cash. These investments are subject to an insignificant risk of change in value. Cash flows refer to inflows and outflows of cash and cash equivalents. The cash flow statement of Tata Consultancy Services is given in Table 12.4. The salient features of a cash flow statement are:

- Prepared for a given period.
- A derived statement.
- Comparative position.
- Vertically drawn.
- Cash flows from operating, investing, and financing activities.
- Reconciliation with the opening and closing balances of cash and cash equivalents.
- Indirect method for cash flows from operating activities.
- Signed by the person who prepared it and the auditors.

When a cash flow statement is used in relation with other financial statements, it provides the following benefits:

- It enables users to analyse the changes in the net assets of an enterprise, its financial structure including its liquidity and solvency, and its ability to affect the amount and timing of cash flows in order to adapt to changing circumstances and opportunities.

Table 12.3 Profit and Loss Account of Tata Consultancy Services Ltd

Year	March 2012 (₹ in Crore)
Income:	
Operating income +	48,894.08
Excise duty	0.25
Net operating income	48,893.83
Other income +	428.17
Stock adjustments +	0.00
Total income	**49,322.00**
Expenditure:	
Cost of traded software packages	0.00
Operating expenses +	5,259.10
Employee cost +	24,703.99
Power/electricity charges +	366.32
Selling and administration expenses +	3,584.98
Miscellaneous expenses +	544.13
Less: Pre-operative expenses capitalized +	0.00
Total expenditure	34,458.52
Operating profit	14,863.48
Interest +	22.23
Gross profit	14,841.25
Depreciation+	917.94
Minority interest (before tax)	0.00
Profit before tax	13,923.31
Tax+	3,431.03
Fringe benefit tax +	0.13
Deferred tax+	-31.30
Net profit	10,523.45
Minority interest (after tax)	109.96
Profit/loss of associate company	0.00
Net profit after minority interest and P/L Asso.Co.	10,413.49
Extraordinary items +	22.68
Adjusted net profit	10,390.81
Adjustment below net profit +	0.00
P&L balance brought forward	18,635.05
Appropriations +	6,888.00
P&L balance carried down	22,160.54
Dividend	4,893.04
Preference dividend	22.00
Equity dividend (%)	2,500.00
EPS before minority interest (unit curr.)	49.53
EPS before minority interest (adj.) (unit curr.)	0.00
EPS after minority interest (unit curr.)	48.97
EPS after minority interest (adj.) (unit curr.)	0.00
Book value (unit curr.)	150.62

Source: Annual report of Tata Consultancy Services Ltd. Reproduced with permission.

Table 12.4 Cash Flow Statement of Tata Consultancy Services Ltd

Year	March 2012 (₹ in Crore)
Cash flow summary	
Cash and cash equivalents at the beginning of the year	1,548.59
Net cash from operating activities	7,008.35
Net cash used in investing activities	-2,608.36
Net cash used in financing activities	-3,955.09
Net inc/(dec) in cash and cash equivalent	444.9
Cash and cash equivalents at the end of the year	1,993.49

Source: Annual report of Tata Consultancy Services Ltd. Reproduced with permission.

- The information can be used to assess the ability of an enterprise to generate cash and cash equivalents and enables users to develop models to evaluate and compare the present value of the future cash flows of different enterprises.
- It enhances the comparability of the reporting of operating performance by different enterprises because it eliminates the effects of using different accounting treatments for the same transactions.
- Historical cash flow information is often used as an indicator of the amount, timing, and certainty of future cash flows.
- It is useful in checking the accuracy of the past assessments of future cash flows.
- It helps in examining the relationship between profitability and net cash flow.

SNAPSHOT

- Financial statements are the most important part of financial reporting. They are recorded in the company's annual report for the benefit of all the stakeholders of an enterprise.
- A complete set of financial statements normally consists of balance sheet, profit and loss account or income statement, and cash flow statement.
- The balance sheet contains information in respect of assets, liabilities, and shareholder's equity.
- The profit and loss account of an enterprise reports the results of operations in terms of income/net profit in a year.
- A cash flow statement depicts the cash generated and utilized by a company.

WORKING CAPITAL MANAGEMENT

Working capital refers to the funds that a company must possess to finance its day-to-day operations. It is a short-term fund needed to meet operating expenses. The management of working capital is important for the smooth functioning of enterprises. Working capital is the net of current assets minus current liabilities. It is equal to the value of raw materials, work in progress, finished goods inventories, and accounts receivable less accounts payable.

There are two concepts of working capital. These are gross working capital and net working capital. Gross working capital is the sum of all current assets that appear in the balance sheet. Net working capital is the excess of current assets over current liabilities. It can be positive or negative. Net working capital helps decide the extent of long-term capital in financing current assets. Current assets are the short-term assets, which can be converted into cash within the normal financial year without much loss. These include: cash and bank balances, receivables, inventory, prepaid expenses, short-term advances, and temporary investments. Current liabilities are the debts of the enterprise intended to be paid in the current accounting period or within a year out of the current assets. These include creditors for goods purchased, outstanding expenses, short-term borrowings, advances received against sales, taxes and dividends payable, and other liabilities maturing within a year.

Working capital can be classified into permanent and temporary working capital taking the time period as the basis of classification. Assets that are required on a continuing basis over the entire year comprise permanent working capital. Temporary working capital represents additional assets required at different times during the year.

The requirement of working capital differs depending on the nature of the industry that a company operates in. The company's operating cycle (working capital cycle) also determines the level of working capital. The working capital cycle is the length of time between the company's outflow on raw materials, wages, and other expenditures and the inflow of cash from the sale of goods. The working capital cycle refers to the time it takes to purchase inventory or components to making the sale and receiving the cash and is shown in Figure 12.1. Working capital is made up of the following three core components in the cycle:

- Inventory and work in progress (work in progress generally applies to manufacturers)
- Accounts payable (payments due to suppliers; creditor payments)
- Accounts receivable (cash due from customers; debtor collection)

Calculation of Working Capital Cycle

The working captial cycle can be calculated by using the following formula:

Working capital cycle = Inventory days + Receivable days – Payable days

where,

Inventory days = Inventory/Cost of sales × 360 days
Receivable days = Receivables/Sales × 360 days
Payable days = Payables/Cost of sales × 360 days

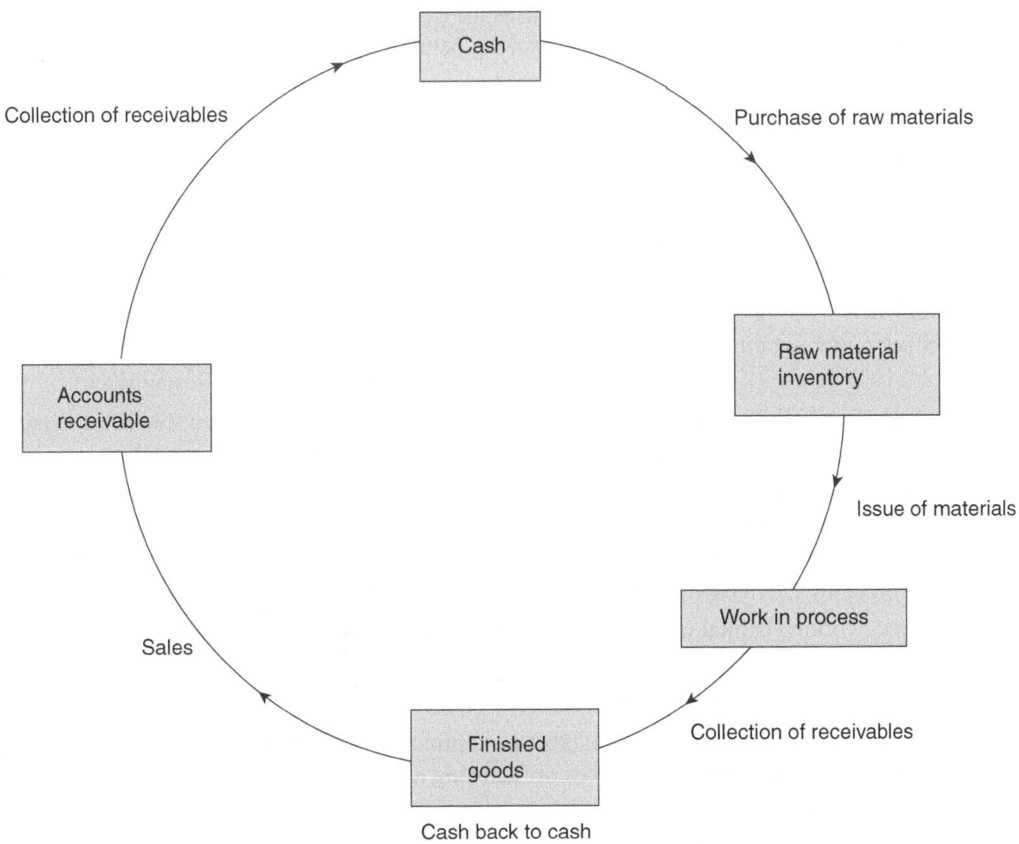

Figure 12.1 Working Capital Cycle

Ratio Analysis for Working Capital Management

The following ratios can be used for measuring the efficiency in managing working capital. Most of these ratios have been standardized in terms of normative values based on historical experience. Any deviation from such values indicates inefficient management of funds.

- **Current ratio (CR):** This ratio indicates the ability of an enterprise to manage its current affairs. The ratio shows the funds available with the enterprise in terms of current assets to meet the current liabilities. The ratio can be computed by using the formula:

  CR = Current assets/Current liabilities

  Though a current ratio of 2:1 is considered ideal, the composition of current assets is equally important. If the majority of current assets are in the form of stock, which is not easily realisable, even with a 2:1 current ratio, the enterprise will face severe liquidity problems. Therefore, it is not only the quantum of current ratio that is important but also its quality, that is, the extent to which assets and liabilities are really current.
- **Quick ratio (QR):** The quick ratio measures the ability of a company to meet its short-term obligations with its most liquid assets. The ratio can be computed by using the formula:

  QR = Liquid assets/ Current liabilities

  A ratio of 1:1 between liquid assets and current liabilities is considered to be ideal. However, the quick ratio varies across industries depending on the prevalent conditions. In this ratio, liquid assets can be computed by subtracting assets that are not quickly realisable from the current assets.
- **Debtors' turnover ratio:** The debtors' turnover ratio reveals how many days credit is outstanding by debtors. This ratio can be calculated using the formula:

  Debtors' turnover ratio = (Debtors + Bills receivable)/(Net credit sales) × 360 days

  When credit is allowed to buyers, they are expected to pay the money within the specified time limit allotted to them. Cash is blocked for debtors during this period. This ratio shows the time taken for the recovery of money from buyers. It can be compared with the standard time allotted and any deviation reveals the excess or deficit, as the case may be, in terms of the time needed for recovering blocked funds. The fewer the days, the better it is for the enterprise.
- **Creditors' velocity ratio:** The creditors' velocity ratio specifies the rate at which a payment is to be made. This helps in identifying the net cash flow. This ratio can be calculated using the formula:

  Creditors' velocity ratio = (Creditors + Bills payable)/(Net credit purchases) × 360 days

  As in the case of credit sales, while purchasing raw materials, a supplier allows a credit period to the buyer who made the payment within a specified time.
- **Stock turnover ratio:** This ratio specifies the rate at which the stock is turned over. The ratio can be calculated using the formula:

  Stock turnover ratio = (Cost of goods sold + Average stock holding)
  = (Selling price – Gross profit)/(Opening stock + Closing stock)

  This ratio indicates the marketability of a product. The rate at which stocks are sold helps to analyse the profitability position of a concern and aids in formulating the production policy.
- **Stock–working capital ratio:** This ratio is worked out to know the position of working capital vis-à-vis raw materials, inventories, work-in-progress, and so on. Normally, the raw material cost constitutes around 60 per cent of the total cost of production. This brings forth sufficient liquidity to invest in the purchases and finished goods. The ratio can be calculated using the formula:

  Stock–working capital ratio = Closing stock/(Current assets – Current liabilities)

Sources of Working Capital

Working capital should be financed by a suitable and optimal mix of short-term source of funds and long-term source of funds. The main sources of financing are:

- **Long-term financing:** Long-term finance is raised for a period of above five years. Long-term finance includes ordinary share capital, preference share capital, debentures, long-term loans from bankers, and surpluses. An enterprise that needs to finance net current assets may go for any of these sources.

- **Short-term financing:** Short-term finance is obtained for a period of less than one year. The various sources of short-term finance may include trade credits, accruals, commercial banks, short-term public deposits, deferred incomes, commercial papers, factoring of receivables, bills discounting, retention of profits, and others.
- **Spontaneous financing:** It refers to automatic sources of short-term funds. Spontaneous sources of finance are available usually free of cost. The source includes trade credit and outstanding expenses.

EXAMPLE

Determine the working capital required to finance a level of activity of 180,000 units of output for a year. The cost structure is given below:

Particulars	Cost Per Unit (₹)
Raw materials	20
Direct labour	5
Overheads (including depreciation of ₹5)	15
Total cost	40
Profit	10
Selling price	50

Additional Information:

1. Minimum desired cash balance is ₹20,000.
2. Raw materials are held in stock, on an average, for two months.
3. Work-in-progress (assume 50 per cent completion stage) will approximate to half a month's production.
4. Finished goods remain in the warehouse, on an average, for a month.
5. Suppliers for materials extend a month's credit and debtors are provided two months' credit. The cash sales are 25 per cent of total sales.
6. There is a time lag in payment of wages for a month and half a month in the case of overheads.

Solution:

The estimation of working capital is shown in the following table.

Particulars	Amount in ₹
A. Estimation of current assets	
Raw materials: (180,000 × 20 × 2)/12	600,000
Work-in-process: (180,000 × 35 × 0.5)/12 × 0.5	131,250
Finished goods: (180,000 × 35 × 1)/12	525,000
Debtors (75% of total units produced): (135,000 × 35 × 2)/12	787,500
Cash balance	20,000
Total current assets	**2,063,750**
B. Estimation of current liabilities	
Suppliers: (180,000 × 20 × 1)/12	300,000
Wages: (180,000 × 5 × 1)/12	75,000
Overheads: (180,000 × 10)10.5)/12	75,000
Total current liabilities	**450,000**
C. Working capital (A–B)	**1,613,750**

SNAPSHOT

- Working capital is the money needed to fund the normal, day-to-day operations of the enterprise. It is needed for the smooth operation of an enterprise.
- The working capital cycle is the length of time between the company's outflow on raw materials, wages, and other expenditures and the inflow of cash from the sale of goods.
- Working capital = Current assets - Current liabilities
- The various ratios used for measuring the efficiency in managing working capital are the quick ratio, the debtors' turnover ratio, the creditors' velocity ratio, the stock turnover ratio, the current ratio, and the stock–working capital ratio.

DISCUSSION FORUM

- Write a note on the various types of financial statements of an enterprise.
- Discuss the working capital cycle.
- Explain the sources of working capital financing.
- Name the various ratios used for measuring the efficiency of management of the working capital.

BREAK-EVEN ANALYSIS

Break-even analysis[4] is a technique widely used by accountants. The break-even analysis is a calculation that forecasts the point at which a company's total revenues are equal to its total expenses. The break-even point is the point of business operations when the business neither earns any profit nor incurs any loss. If the sales volume exceeds this point, profit starts picking up. It is important to estimate for what volume of sales the business will be earning a profit. Break-even analysis focuses on the relationship between fixed cost, variable cost, and selling price.

A break-even chart is a strategic tool used to plot the financial revenue of a business unit against time or sales to determine the break-even point when sales output is equal to revenue generated. In its simplest form, the break-even chart is a graphical representation of costs at various levels of activity shown on the same chart as the variation of income with the same variation in activity. The point at which neither profit nor loss is made is known as the "break-even point" and is represented on the chart shown in Figure 12.2 by the interaction of the two lines. The break-even point is calculated by using the following formula:

$$\text{Break-even point} = \frac{\text{Fixed costs}}{\text{Selling price per unit} - \text{Variable costs}}$$

Fixed costs are costs that do not vary in relation to the level of sales output, for example, rent and rates, depreciation, research and development, marketing costs, and administration costs. Variable costs are costs that vary in proportion to the level of sales output, for example, raw materials, direct labour, fuel, and revenue-related costs such as commission. The price that a unit is sold for is referred to as the selling price per unit.

EXAMPLE

The data regarding the fixed costs and variable costs of a company are given below. If the company has to break even, how many units should it sell?

Fixed costs:

Monthly rent: ₹1,000

Insurance: ₹500

Total monthly fixed costs: ₹1,500

Variable costs:
Materials: ₹30
Labour: ₹40
Total variable cost: ₹70
Selling price: ₹100

Solution:

$$\text{Break-even point} = \frac{\text{Fixed costs}}{\text{Selling price per unit} - \text{Variable costs}}$$

$$\text{Break-even point} = \frac{1{,}500}{100-70} = \frac{1{,}500}{30} = 50$$

The company should sell 50 units per month to break even.

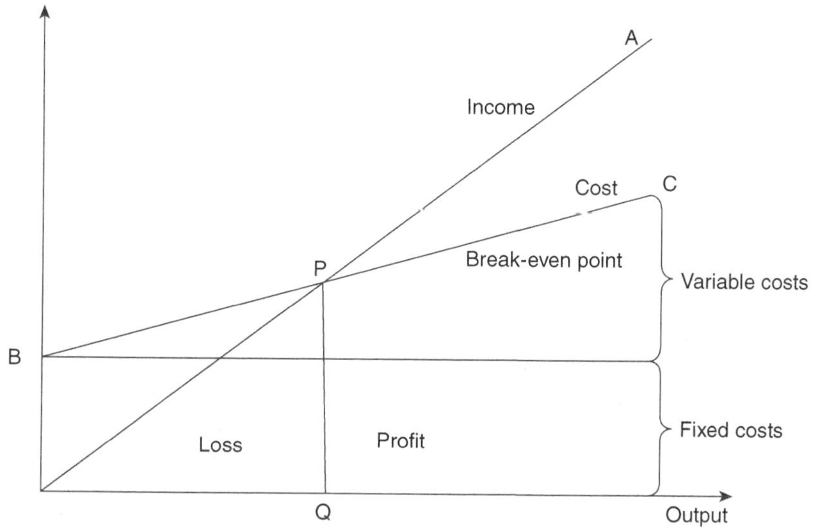

Figure 12.2 The Break-even Chart

SNAPSHOT

- Break-even analysis is used to forecast the point at which a company's total revenues are equal to its total expenses.
- Break-even point is the point of business operation when the business neither earns any profit nor incurs any loss.

FINANCIAL RATIO ANALYSIS

Ratio analysis seeks to measure and establish cause-and-effect relationships between either two items of a balance sheet or of a profit and loss account, or both the balance sheet and the profit and loss account. Thus, ratio analysis is a more focused analysis of financial statements. It involves methods of calculating and interpreting financial ratios to analyse and monitor the firm's performance. The firm's balance sheet and income statement are the basic inputs needed for ratio analysis. Ratio analysis does not merely involve the calculation of a given ratio. The interpretation of results for decision making is the most critical part of ratio analysis. Two types of ratio comparisons can be made: time-series analysis and cross-sectional analysis. Ratio analysis is of particular significance in the following cases:

- Comparison against industry benchmarks.
- Inter-firm comparison because absolute figure comparison will not be conclusive.

- Intra-firm comparison.
- Analysis of chronological performance over a long period.

Financial ratios can be divided for convenience into five basic categories: liquidity, activity, debt, profitability, and market ratios. Liquidity, activity, and debt ratios measure risk. Profitability ratios measure return. Market ratios capture both risk and return. The DuPont system of analysis is used to dissect the firm's financial statements and to assess its financial condition. Financial analysts wish to take an overall look at the firm's financial performance and status.

The two popular approaches to a complete ratio analysis are summarizing all the five basic categories of ratios and the DuPont system of analysis. The summary analysis approach tends to view all aspects of the firm's financial activities to isolate key areas of responsibility. The DuPont system acts as a search technique aimed at finding the key areas responsible for the firms' financial condition. Ratios are classified[5] according to their functions and objectives as given below:

- Liquidity ratios
- Activity/turnover ratios
- Debt/solvency ratios
- Profitability ratios
- Capital market ratios
- DuPont analysis

Liquidity Ratios

The liquidity of a firm is measured by its ability to satisfy its short-term obligations as they come due. The capacity of an enterprise to discharge its suppliers and service providers and to meet its day-to-day expenses indicates its liquidity and ensures the smooth continuity of operations, which in turn, has a strong bearing on the long-term survival of the company. These are particularly useful for the suppliers, employees, providers of services, and lenders to assess the short-term financial default risk attached to a company. The two basic measures of liquidity are the current ratio and the quick (acid-test) ratio. The five major ratios here are:

- Current ratio = Current assets/Current liabilities
- Quick ratio (acid-test) ratio = Current assets – (Inventory/Current liabilities)
- Collection period to customers (days) = Receivables × (365/Credit sales)
- Suppliers' credit (days) = Payables × (365/Credit purchases)
- Inventory-holding period = Inventory × (365/Cost of goods sold)

Activity/Turnover Ratios

Activity ratios measure the speed with which various accounts are converted into sales or cash inflows or outflows. The efficiency with which the assets and resources of a company are utilized in generating operational revenue has a direct bearing on the top line. It is, therefore, important to study the turnover ratios. The four major ratios are:

- **Inventory turnover ratio:** The inventory turnover measures the activity or liquidity of a firm's inventory. It can be calculated using the following formula:

  Inventory turnover = Cost of goods sold/Inventory

- **Average collection period:** The average collection period measures the average amount of time needed to collect accounts receivable. It can be calculated using the following formula:

  Average collection period = Accounts receivable/Average sales per day

- **Average payment period:** The average payment period measures the amount of time needed to pay the accounts payable. It can be calculated using the following formula:

  Average payment period = Accounts payable/Average purchases per day

- **Total asset turnover:** The total asset turnover indicates the efficiency with which the firm uses its assets to generate sales. It can be calculated using the following formula:

  Total asset turnover = Sales/Total assets

Debt/Solvency Ratios

The capacity of an enterprise to discharge its obligations towards long-term lenders indicates its financial strength and ensures its long-term survival. The debt position of a firm indicates the amount of other people's money being used to generate profits. It is important to analyse the capacity of an enterprise to raise further capital borrowings. These are particularly useful for financial institutions, banks, and other lenders to assess the creditworthiness of a company and the attendant financial default risk. The various solvency ratios are:

- **Debt ratio:** The debt ratio measures the proportion of total assets financed by the firm's creditors. It can be calculated by using the formula:

  Debt ratio = Total liabilities/Total assets
- **Net asset value (NAV):** This ratio measures the net worth or net asset value per equity share. It seeks to assess to what extent the value of an equity share of a company contributed at par or at a premium has grown or the value/wealth that has been created for the shareholders. It can be calculated by using the formula:

  NAV = Equity shareholders' funds/No. of equity shares
- **Debt equity (D/E) ratio:** This ratio measures the proportion of debt and capital. It can be calculated by using the formula:

  Debt equity ratio = Long-term debt/Total net worth
- **Interest cover ratio:** This ratio measures the capacity of a company to pay the interest liability it has incurred on its long-term borrowings out of its cash profits. It can be calculated by using the formula:

  Interest cover = PAT interest on long-term debt + (Non-cash charges/Interest on long-term debt)
- **Debt-coverage service (DSCR) ratio:** The ratio measures the capacity of a company to pay the installments of the principal due and the interest liability it has incurred on its long-term borrowings out of its cash profits. It can be calculated by using the formula:

  DSCR ratio = PAT + Interest on long-term debt + (Non-cash charges/Interest on long-term debt) + Installments of principal due

Profitability Ratios

Profitability ratios enable the analyst to evaluate the firm's profits with respect to a given level of sales, a certain level of assets, or the owner's investment. These ratios analyse the profitability of an enterprise at different steps or at intermediate levels of business activities. The major profit margin ratios are:

- **Gross profit margin:** The gross profit margin measures the percentage of sales rupees remaining after the firm has paid for its goods. It can be calculated using the formula:

  Gross profit margin = Gross profits/sales
- **Operating profit margin:** The operating profit margin measures the percentage of sales rupees remaining after all costs and expenses, other than interest, taxes, and preferred stock dividends, are deducted. It represents the "pure profits" earned on each sales rupee. It can be calculated using the formula:

  Operating profit margin = Operating profits/sales
- **Net profit margin:** The net profit margin measures the percentage of sales rupees remaining after all costs and expenses, including interest, taxes, and preferred stock dividends, have been deducted.

Net profit margin = Earnings available for common stockholders/Sales

- **Earnings per share (EPS):** The earnings per share represent the amount in rupees earned on behalf of each share, not the amount of earnings actually distributed to shareholders.

$$\text{Earnings per share (EPS)} = \frac{\text{Earnings available for common stockholders}}{\text{Number of shares of common stock outstanding}}$$

- **Return on total assets (RoA):** The return on total assets measures the overall effectiveness of the management in generating profits with its available assets; also called return on investment (RoI).

$$\text{Return on total assets (RoA)} = \frac{\text{Earnings available for common stockholders}}{\text{Total assets}}$$

- **Return on common equity (RoE):** The return on common equity (RoE) measures the return earned on the common stockholders' investment in the firm.

$$\text{Return on common equity (RoE)} = \frac{\text{Earnings available for common stockholders}}{\text{Common stock equity}}$$

The maximization of RoI is the ultimate objective of an enterprise and it is the ultimate measure of the efficiency of performance of a management. It is the expectation of a high return that motivates equity shareholders to continue with the company and new investors to put in their money in the company's equity. The three major RoI ratios are:

- **Return on net worth (RoNW):** This ratio measures the net profit earned on the equity shareholders' funds. It is the measure of the overall profitability of a company after discharging the cost of borrowed capital and the income tax payable to the government. It can be calculated using the formula:

RoNW = (PAT – Preference dividend/Equity shareholder's funds or net worth) × 100

- **Earnings per share (EPS):** This ratio measures the overall profitability in terms of per equity share of capital contributed by the owners. It can be calculated using the formula:

EPS = PAT – Preferences dividend/Weighted average no. of equity shares outstanding

- **Cash earnings per share (CEPS):** This ratio measures the overall cash profitability in terms of per equity share of capital contributed by the owners. It is a refinement of EPS in that it takes into account the cash earning, and not accrual-based earnings. It can be calculated using the formula:

CEPS = PAT – Preference dividend + (Non-cash charges/Weighted average no. of equity shares)

Capital Market Ratios

The capital market has become a major source of capital, both for equity as well as bonds and debentures for the industry. Market ratios relate a firm's market value, as measured by its current share price, to certain accounting values. It is necessary for the entrepreneur to have a knowledge of these ratios. The two important market ratios are:

- **Price-earnings (P/E) ratio:** The P/E ratio measures the amount that investors are willing to pay for each rupee of a firm's earnings; the higher the P/E ratio, the greater is investor confidence. This ratio can be calculated by using the following formula:

$$\text{Price/earnings (P/E) ratio} = \frac{\text{Market price per share of common stock}}{\text{Earnings per share}}$$

- **Market-book (M/B) ratio:** The M/B ratio provides an assessment of how investors view the firms' performance. Firms are expected to earn high returns relative to their risk typically to sell at higher M/B multiples. This ratio can be calculated using the formula:

$$\text{Market/book (M/B) ratio} = \frac{\text{Market price per share of common stock}}{\text{Common stock equity}}$$

DuPont Analysis

The DuPont model is a technique that can be used to analyse the profitability of a company using traditional performance management tools. The DuPont model integrates elements of the income statement with that of the balance sheet. The DuPont analysis seeks to measure the relationship between net profit margin and net worth turnover, which is the ultimate overall profitability ratio. Key financial ratios and the DuPont Model for five years (2011–2007) for Tata Consultancy Services are given in Tables 12.5 and 12.6.

$$\frac{\text{Net profit}}{\text{Total assets}} = \frac{\text{Net profit}}{\text{Net sales}} \times \frac{\text{Net sales}}{\text{Total assets}}$$

Table 12.5 Key Financial Ratios for Tata Consultancy Services

Key Financial Ratios	March 2012
Debt-equity ratio	0.00
Long-term debt-equity ratio	0.00
Current ratio	1.74
Turnover ratios	
Fixed assets	5.84
Inventory	8,172.20
Debtors	5.59
Interest cover ratio	816.02
PBIDTM (%)	36.21
PBITM (%)	34.44
PBDTM (%)	36.17
CPM (%)	30.02
APATM (%)	28.25
ROCE (%)	59.29
RONW (%)	49.53

Source: Annual report of Tata Consultancy Services Ltd. Reproduced with permission.

Table 12.6 DuPont Model for Tata Consultancy Services

DuPont Model	March 2012
PBIDT/Sales (%)	36.21
Sales/Net assets	1.54
PBDIT/Net assets	0.56
PAT/PBIDT (%)	78.00
Net assets/Net worth	1.02
RoE (%)	49.53

Source: Annual report of Tata Consultancy Services Ltd. Reproduced with permission.

CHECKLIST FOR ENTREPRENEURS 12.2 Five Commandments for Financial Planning and Analysis

- Remember financial reporting is no longer the primary responsibility of the CFO. The role of today's CFO has broadened to include strategic planning and information management.
- Understand GAAP, the practice and procedure guidelines used to prepare and maintain financial records and authorized by the Financial Accounting Standards Board (FASB).
- Prepare the annual report, which is the report that publicly-owned corporations must provide to stockholders. It summarizes and documents the firm's financial activities during the past year.
- Use a summary of financial ratios and the DuPont system of analysis to perform a complete ratio analysis. The ratio analysis of your firm's financial statement is of interest to shareholders, creditors, and the firm's own management. The basic inputs to ratio analysis are the firm's income statement and balance sheet. Use audited financial statements for ratio analysis.
- Use time-series analyses for evaluating the performance of your firm over a period of time using financial ratio analysis. Conduct cross-sectional analysis for comparing your firm's ratios with a key competitor or group of competitors that you wish to benchmark against.

BREAKTHROUGH ENTREPRENEURSHIP 12.3 Regulatory Institutions

The financial system in India is regulated by the Government of India. The five regulatory institutes of the Government of India are the Reserve Bank of India (RBI), the Securities and Exchange Board of India (SEBI), the Insurance Regulatory and Development Authority (IRDA), the Industrial Development Bank of India (IDBI), and the Small Industries Development Bank of India (SIDBI). The three major regulatory institutes are the RBI, SEBI, and IRDA.

The RBI was set up in 1935 and was nationalized in 1949. It is the apex institution and the central bank in the banking and financial system of the country. The RBI acts as the banker to the banks and shoulders the responsibility for the management of the Indian economy to a certain extent. The main objectives of the RBI are to maintain the internal value of the nation's currency, preserve the external value of the currency, secure reasonable price stability, and promote economic growth.

SEBI was established in 1988 with a view to regulating and developing the capital market in India. The SEBI has been entrusted with both regulatory and developmental functions. The objective of SEBI is to protect the interest of the investors by ensuring fair practices by fund raisers.

The IRDA was established in 2000 by the Government of India in compliance with the suggestions of the Malhotra Committee. The objectives of the IRDA are to regulate and ensure the orderly growth of the insurance industry and to protect the interests of policy holders.

Sources: www.rbi.org.in (last accessed in March 2013); www.sebi.gov.in (last accessed in March 2013); and www.irda.gov.in (last accessed in March 2013).

SUMMARY

Finance is the lifeblood of a business. The main objective of financial management is to maximize shareholders' wealth. The financial management function covers decision making in three interrelated areas, namely, working capital management, financing, and dividend policy. The financial system helps the economic development of a country by acting as a bridge between savers and investors.

Generally Accepted Accounting Principles (GAAPs) are the basic foundation of the accounting structure authorized by the Financial Accounting Standards Board (FASB). Accounting is the process of identifying, measuring, and communicating economic information to permit informed judgements and decisions by users of the information. The main function of accounting is to provide quantitative information of a financial nature about economic entities, which is useful in making economic decisions. Bookkeeping is mainly concerned with the recording of financial data relating to business transactions in a systematic and chronological manner. The important types of books of accounts are purchase book, sales book, cash book, journal, and ledger.

Financial statements are a critical part of financial reporting. The complete set of financial statements normally includes a balance sheet, a profit and loss account or income statement, and a cash flow statement. Financial statements present a summary of the financial position of the company at a given point of time. Financial analysis gives a comprehensive understanding of business operations and their impact on financial health. Ratio analysis is a tool used for the financial analysis of an enterprise. It is the systematic use of ratios to interpret the financial statements so that the strengths and weaknesses of an enterprise, as well as its past and current financial performance, are determined for taking appropriate financial decisions. The most common types of ratios used in ratio analysis are return on investment (ROI) ratios, solvency ratios, liquidity ratios, turnover ratios, profitability ratios, DuPont analysis, and capital market ratios.

Working capital is defined as the excess of current assets over current liabilities. Working capital requirements are financed by a combination of long-term and short-term sources. The working capital cycle creates the need for working capital and its length in terms of the time span required to complete the cycle is the major determinant of the working capital cycle. The working capital cycle consists of conversion of cash into inventory, inventory into receivables, and receivables into cash. The various ratios used for measuring the efficiency in managing working capital are quick ratio, debtors' turnover ratio, creditors' velocity ratio, stock turnover ratio, current ratio, and stock-working capital ratio. Break-even analysis is undertaken through graphical charts or mathematical formulae. The break-even point is the level of activity at which there is neither profit nor loss.

KEY TERMS

Accounting Cycle: It is a complete sequence starting with the recording of transactions and ending with presenting and communicating financial accounts.

Accounting: The process of recording, classifying, summarizing, analysing, interpreting, and communicating economic information to all the stakeholders of a business.

Balance Sheet: It presents the assets and liabilities of a firm at a given moment in time.

Bookkeeping: It refers to the recording of financial data relating to business.

Break-even Point: It is the level of activity at which there is neither profit nor loss.

Cash Book: It records cash and bank transactions.

Cash Flow Statement: It depicts the cash generated and utilized by a firm.

Current Ratio: It is a measure of liquidity calculated by dividing the current assets by the current liabilities.

Financial Statement: It is an organized collation of data arranged according to logical and consistent accounting principles.

Journal: It is a book of original or prime entry.

Ledger: It is a book of secondary entry.

Liquidity Ratio: It gives the ability of a firm to satisfy its short-term obligations as they become due.

Net Working Capital: It is a measure of liquidity calculated by subtracting current liabilities from current assets.

Net Worth: It is calculated by subtracting the liabilities from the assets. Profits increase the net worth and losses reduce the net worth of a business.

Profit and Loss Account/Income Statement: It shows the profit and loss of the business at a given moment in time.

Purchase Book: It records all purchases of goods on credit.

Quick Ratio: It is a measure of liquidity calculated by dividing current assets minus inventory and prepaid expenses by current liabilities.

Ratio Analysis: It is a systematic use of ratios to interpret/assess the performance and status of the firm.

Return on Investment (RoI): It is a measure of the overall effectiveness of management in generating profits with its available assets.

Sales Book: It records all sales of goods on credit.

Trial Balance: It provides the net effect of all transactions carried out by the enterprise during a particular period.

Working Capital = Current assets – Current liabilities

CASE STUDY

Tata Consultancy Services Ltd

Tata Consultancy Services Limited (TCS), headquartered in Mumbai, Maharashtra, was founded in 1968. TCS is a subsidiary of the Tata Group and is a leading information technology (IT) services, business solutions, and outsourcing services multinational company. It is listed on the Bombay Stock Exchange (BSE) and the National Stock Exchange (NSE) of India and is the largest India-based IT services company by 2012 revenues.

TCS has over 254,000 trained consultants operating in 44 countries and has more than 142 offices across 21 countries. The company generated consolidated revenues of $1,017 crore for the year ending on 31 March 2012. Strong leadership and effective corporate governance inherited from the Tata culture are the company's hallmark strengths.

TCS had a total of 58 subsidiary companies, which provide a range of information technology-related products and services including application development; capacity planning; business process outsourcing; consulting; enterprise software; payment processing; software management; and technology education services.

TCS is unique because of its customer-centric engagement model; global network delivery model; full services portfolio; innovation labs; and co-innovation network. TCS has collaborated with SAP on the development of SAP@Retail execution 3.0 mobile applications. The company is in compliance with the requirements stipulated under Clause 49 of the listing agreements entered into with the stock exchanges with regard to corporate governance.

The company has constituted effective corporate governance practices. Its corporate governance philosophy has been strengthened through the Tata Business Excellence Model, the Tata Code of Conduct for Prevention of Insider Trading, and the Code of Corporate Disclosure Practices. TCS has also developed an Information Security Policy that ensures proper utilization of IT resources.

As of 30 September 2012, TCS has applied for 1,017 patents and the company has been granted 74 patents. TCS was recognized as one of the "Big Four" of IT service providers by *Brand Finance India* in 2012. It was rated as the top ICT employer of the year by the Government of the Netherlands for 2012. TCS won the SAP Customer Award of Excellence for 2012. It was recognized as one of the 50 most engaged workplaces in the US for 2012.

TCS BPO won eight awards at Asia's Best Employer Brands Awards for 2012. It was ranked as one of South Africa's top employers for 2012. It won three awards at the Best CIO awards for 2012. It was ranked as the world's seventh-greenest company in *Newsweek*'s Green Rankings 2011. TCS was the highest ranked Asia-based company and the second-highest ranked globally in the information technology and services company category. Tables 12.01–12.03 provide the consolidated balance sheet, the consolidated profit and loss account, and the consolidated cash flow statements of the company for FY 2008–2012.

Table 12.01 Consolidated Balance Sheet of Tata Consultancy Services Ltd

Year	March 2012	March 2011	March 2010	March 2009	March 2008
Sources of funds:					
Share capital+	295.72	295.72	295.72	197.86	197.86
Reserves total+	29,283.51	24,209.09	18,171.00	15,502.15	12,102.26
Equity share warrants	0.00	0.00	0.00	0.00	0.00
Equity application money	0.00	0.03	0.03	0.05	0.05
Total shareholders funds	29,579.23	24,504.84	18,466.75	15,700.06	12,300.17
Minority interest	558.77	458.17	361.71	277.16	212.73
Secured loans+	112.61	34.16	31.21	37.89	18.07
Unsecured loans+	13.94	40.64	72.04	525.99	436.95
Total debt	126.55	74.80	103.25	563.88	455.02
Policy holders fund	0.00	0.00	0.00	0.00	0.00
Other liabilities	502.66	324.84	0.00	0.00	0.00
Total liabilities	30,767.21	25,362.65	18,931.71	16,541.10	12,967.92
Application of funds:					
Gross block+	12,991.29	11,024.24	9,635.50	9,105.26	5,556.75
Less: Accumulated depreciation+	4,329.23	3,545.15	2,897.47	2,359.72	1,622.20
Less: Impairment of assets	0.00	0.00	0.00	0.00	0.00
Net block+	8,662.06	7,479.09	6,738.03	6,745.54	3,934.55
Lease adjustment	0.00	0.00	0.00	0.00	0.00
Capital work in progress+	1,446.37	1,193.89	1,017.37	705.49	906.87
Investments+	1,350.33	1,762.67	3,682.08	1,614.41	2,606.16
Current assets, loans and advances					
Inventories+	17.77	22.82	17.79	36.60	42.43
Sundry debtors+	11,520.35	8,194.97	5,855.41	6,134.02	5,379.93
Cash and bank+	6,003.47	4,700.85	4,718.59	2,698.14	1,223.40
Loans and advances+	4,960.82	3,433.78	5,197.09	4,643.10	3,386.60
Total current assets	22,502.41	16,352.42	15,788.88	13,511.86	10,032.36
Less: Current liabilities and provisions					
Current liabilities+	5,659.78	4,489.97	4,093.76	4,340.39	3,192.38
Provisions+	4,794.05	2,718.93	4,300.07	1,627.30	1,286.61
Total current liabilities	10,453.83	7,208.90	8,393.83	5,967.69	4,478.99
Net current assets	12,048.58	9,143.52	7,395.05	7,544.17	5,553.37
Miscellaneous expenses not written off+	0.00	0.00	0.00	0.00	0.00
Deferred tax assets	256.04	160.18	167.86	60.04	103.02
Deferred tax liabilities	173.45	109.49	68.68	128.55	136.05
Net deferred tax	82.59	50.69	99.18	-68.51	-33.03
Other assets	7,177.28	5,732.79	0.00	0.00	0.00
Total assets	30,767.21	25,362.65	18,931.71	16,541.10	12,967.92
Contingent liabilities+	2,636.73	1,777.40	2,631.17	2,678.58	2,273.01

Source: Annual report of Tata Consultancy Services Ltd. Reproduced with permission.

Table 12.02 Consolidated Profit and Loss Account of Tata Consultancy Services Ltd

Year	March 2012	March 2011	March 2010	March 2009	March 2008
Income:					
Operating income+	48,894.08	37,324.78	30,029.31	27,814.96	22,622.35
Excise duty	0.25	0.27	0.39	2.08	2.83
Net operating income	48,893.83	37,324.51	30,028.92	27,812.88	22,619.52
Other income+	428.17	604.00	272.07	354.37	729.74
Stock adjustments+	0.00	0.00	0.00	0.00	0.00
Total income	49,322.00	37,928.51	30,300.99	28,167.25	23,349.26
Expenditure:					
Cost of traded software packages	0.00	0.00	0.00	0.00	0.00
Operating expenses+	5,259.10	3,928.10	3,197.55	3,023.02	2,867.85
Employee cost+	24,703.99	18,805.70	15,065.75	14,483.20	11,411.05
Power/electricity charges+	366.32	302.08	250.59	196.23	158.22
Selling and administration expenses	3,584.98	2,739.31	2,169.31	2,315.94	1,883.10
Miscellaneous expenses+	544.13	370.96	651.17	1,406.05	589.37
Less: Pre-operative expenses Capitalized+	0.00	0.00	0.00	0.00	0.00
Total expenditure	34,458.52	26,146.15	21,334.37	21,424.44	16,909.59
Operating profit	14,863.48	11,782.36	8,966.62	6,742.81	6,439.67
Interest+	22.23	26.48	16.10	28.66	30.01
Gross profit	14,841.25	11,755.88	8,950.52	6,714.15	6,409.66
Depreciation+	917.94	735.26	660.89	564.08	563.71
Minority interest (before tax)	0.00	0.00	0.00	0.00	0.00
Profit before tax	13,923.31	11,020.62	8,289.63	6,150.07	5,845.95
Tax+	3,431.03	1,813.71	1,389.25	773.80	739.01
Fringe benefit tax+	0.13	-0.03	-4.57	26.44	26.20
Deferred tax+	-31.30	17.15	-187.71	38.71	21.10
Net profit	10,523.45	9,189.79	7,092.66	5,311.12	5,059.64
Minority interest (after tax)	109.96	121.45	90.99	54.00	34.42
Profit/loss of associate company	0.00	-0.30	-1.03	-0.70	0.80
Net profit after minority interest and P/L Asso. Co.	10,413.49	9,068.04	7,000.64	5,256.42	5,026.02
Extraordinary items+	22.68	65.87	120.81	45.15	15.37
Adjusted net profit	10,390.81	9,002.17	6,879.83	5,211.27	5,010.65
Adjustment below net profit+	0.00	0.00	0.00	0.00	0.00
P&L balance brought forward	18,635.05	13,604.84	11,835.03	8,688.21	5,721.12
Appropriations+	6,888.00	4,037.83	5,230.83	2,109.60	2,058.93
P&L balance carried down	22,160.54	18,635.05	13,604.84	11,835.03	8,688.21
Dividend	4,893.04	2,740.10	3,914.43	1,370.05	1,370.05
Preference dividend	22.00	11.00	17.00	7.00	0.08
Equity dividend (%)	2,500.00	1,400.00	2,000.00	1,400.00	1,400.00
EPS before minority interest (unit curr.)	49.53	44.55	32.76	51.79	49.31
EPS before minority interest (adj) (Unit curr.)	0.00				
EPS after minority interest (unit curr.)	48.97	43.93	32.29	51.23	48.96
EPS after minority interest (adj) (Unit curr.)	0.00				
Book value (unit curr.)	150.62	124.69	93.84	159.41	124.67

Source: Annual report of Tata Consultancy Services Ltd. Reproduced with permission.

Table 12.03 Consolidated Cash Flow Statement of Tata Consultancy Services Ltd

Year	March 2012	March 2011	March 2010	March 2009	March 2008
Cash flow summary					
Cash and cash equivalents at beginning of the year	1,548.59	1,024.37	1,459.54	1,067.4	1,147.76
Net cash from operating activities	7,008.35	6,614.38	7,359.4	5,498.35	3,880.72
Net cash used in investing activities	-2,608.36	-1,431.26	-5,413.22	-3,434.54	-2,363.38
Net cash used in financing activities	-3,955.09	-4,658.9	-2,381.35	-1,671.67	-1,441.7
Net inc/(dec) in cash and cash equivalents	444.9	524.22	-435.17	392.14	75.64
Cash and cash equivalents at the end of the year	1,993.49	1,548.59	1,024.37	1,459.54	1,223.4

Source: Annual report of Tata Consultancy Services Ltd. Reproduced with permission.

Questions:

1. Evaluate the performance of the company from 2008–2012 using time-series analysis.
2. Summarize the findings of the time-series analysis.
3. What suggestions would you like to give to the CFO of TCS?

Source: www.tcs.com (last accessed in March 2013).

DISCUSSION QUESTIONS

1. Explain the accounting cycle.
2. What do you mean by "Generally Accepted Accounting Principles"? Discuss its need and its essential features as well.
3. Write a note on: (a) RBI (b) SEBI, and (c) IRDA.
4. The fixed costs of a company for a year are ₹80,000. The variable cost per unit for a single product made is ₹4. The estimated sales for the period are valued at ₹200,000. The number of units involved coincides with the expected volume of output. Each unit sells at ₹20. Calculate the break-even point.
5. Explain the "working capital cycle" with a schematic diagram.

ACTIVITY

1. Visit a local manufacturing company. Study the working capital management of the enterprise and analyse the present working capital cycle using suitable ratios. Provide suggestions to improve the efficiency of working capital management and present them in the class.
2. Invite the CFO of a local enterprise and request him to address the class on financial management in his enterprise.

PROJECT

1. Collect the annual reports of Tata Motors and Maruti Udyog Limited for the current financial year. Study their financial statements and conduct a cross-sectional analysis. Prepare a brief report, not exceeding four A4-size pages with adequate margin and normal space between the paragraphs summarizing your findings and recommendations.

2. Collect the annual report of Nestlé India Limited. Examine and analyse the key indicators and evaluate the performance and financial position of the company for the last five years.

ENDNOTES

1. Reddy, G. Sudarsana (2010). *Financial Management: Principles and Practice*. Mumbai: Himalaya Publishing House.
2. Sofat, Rajni and Preeti Hiro (2010). *Basic Accounting*. New Delhi: Prentice Hall of India.
3. Gupta, Ambrish (2005). *Financial Accounting Management: An Analytical Perspective*. New Delhi: Pearson Education.
4. Thomas, Andrew (2002). *Introduction to Financial Accounting*. McGraw-Hill.
5. Gitman, Lawrence J. (2005). *Principles of Managerial Finance*. Pearson Education.

Management of Enterprises

11. Preventing Sickness in Enterprises
12. Financial Management in Enterprises
13. Operations and Human Resource Management in Enterprises
14. Managing Marketing and Growth in Enterprises

"Perfection is not attainable, but if we chase perfection we can catch excellence."

—Vince Lombardi

Mother Dairy, a wholly-owned company of the National Dairy Development Board (NDDB), was founded in 1974 under the Operation Flood programme. The company provides quality food and beverages to consumers at affordable prices while ensuring fair returns to the producers. Mother Dairy is committed to delivering products that meet all regulatory, industrial, consumer quality, and food safety requirements. It is focused on building a sustainable "Quality and Food Safety Programme" across the food chain using state-of-the-art processes and innovative technologies.

Operations and Human Resource Management in Enterprises

13

LEARNING OBJECTIVES

Upon completion of this chapter, you should be able to:

1. **Understand the importance of operations, production, and technology management in enterprises.**
2. **Explain operations strategy and forecasting methods.**
3. **Describe the concept of supply chain management and materials management.**
4. **Identify the importance of productivity, quality, maintenance, and safety management.**
5. **Understand the importance of human resource management and industrial relations in enterprises.**
6. **Explain labour laws relevant to enterprises.**

INTRODUCTION

This chapter deals with two important functions of business enterprises. One is operations management in business enterprises and the other is human resource management in business enterprises. The first section explains operations strategy and forecasting models and discusses the importance of operations management in business enterprises. The concept of supply chain and materials management in business enterprises and the importance of productivity, quality, maintenance, and safety management in enterprises are discussed in detail. The second section deals with the importance of HRM and industrial relations in enterprises and explains labour laws relevant to enterprises.

OPERATIONS MANAGEMENT

Operations management is the business function, which manages business activities that transform raw materials and human inputs into goods and services of higher value. Operations management helps the firm to develop products/services that possess the capability to satisfy the customer's functional need with the desired level of design, quality, and cost. It must also design and manage the supply chain needed to create, deliver, and service the products sold.

Operations management is a systematic approach to address issues in the transformation process that converts inputs into useful, revenue generating outputs. Operations management is the key to achieving competitive advantage for organizations. Its processes address the questions that an organization faces in its choice of products, manufacturing technology, utilization of capacity, maintenance of quality, costing and sourcing of materials, and customer handling policies.

Globally, India is emerging as an important manufacturing base and recent studies[1] point to emerging opportunities for Indian manufacturing to grow and attain a global presence. But there are some challenges faced by operations firms which include the need to address increased competition due to economic liberalization and globalization, the growing aspirations of customers, rapid technological changes, and emerging environmental concerns. A CII–McKinsey study projected that the export of auto components from India will grow to USD 2,500 crore by 2015. The automobile sector is poised to become a global manufacturing base on account of better management practices followed in the sector.

There are several important similarities between products and services from an operations management perspective. The similarities are:

- Both have to make an estimate of demand.
- Both products and services must balance capacity with demand by a careful choice of resources.
- Both must make choices about capacity, location, and layout.
- Both are concerned with quality, productivity, and timely response to customers.
- Both have suppliers to deal with.
- Both have to plan operations schedules and resources.

Services differ from manufacturing with respect to tangibility, heterogeneity, and perishability. Table 13.1 shows a comparison between products and services.

OPERATIONS STRATEGY

Operations strategy[2] is the process of making appropriate decisions in the operations function on the basis of inputs from the corporate strategy. Operations strategy is the process of making key operations decisions that are consistent with the overall strategic objectives of the organization. It comprises six components. They are: positioning the control system, focus on factories and service

Table 13.1 A Comparison of Products and Services

Operations Factor	Products	Services
Value	Value is provided by physical processing during manufacturing.	Value is provided by the availability of the service, leading to sensory or psychological satisfaction.
Tangibility	Goods are tangible.	Services are intangible.
Process design	Manufacturing can be isolated from the customer and designed for efficiency.	The service process must be designed to occur in the presence of the customer.
Inventory	Products can be stored for later consumption.	Services are consumed as they are created.
Capacity	Manufacturing capacity can be designed for average demand.	Capacity must be designed for maximum demand.
Quality	Manufacturing processes can achieve a high level of precision and repeatability. Quality is easily measured.	Consistency of human performance is more difficult to maintain; customer perceptions are subjective. Quality is not easily measured.
Location	Facilities can be located to minimize operations and transportation costs.	Service facilities must be located near the customer
Customer Contact	Low customer contact.	High customer contact.

systems, product/service design and development, technology selection and process development, allocation of resources to strategic alternatives, facility planning, capacity, location, and layout.

Translating corporate strategy to operations strategy requires making appropriate choices with respect to product portfolio, processes, technology, capacity, and the supply chain. The main part of operations strategy is the determination of how products/services will be produced. Four generic performance measures are found to be useful in any operations strategy exercise— quality, cost, delivery, and flexibility. World-class organizations feature five basic elements of operational excellence. These include: just-in-time (JIT), total quality management (TQM), total productive maintenance (TPM), employee involvement, and simplicity.

DEMAND FORECASTING

A forecast is a statement about the future. Forecasts are estimates of the timing and magnitude of the occurrence of future events. Forecasting is the estimation of the future demand for products/services and the resources necessary to produce these outputs. It is the first step in planning. Demand forecasting deals with projections of demand for a company's products or services throughout a predetermined future period. Forecasting the demand for products and services is needed for new facility planning, production planning and control, workforce scheduling, and financial planning. A forecast is usually classified by the future time horizon it covers. Accordingly, the three categories of forecasts are: short-range forecast, medium-range forecast, and long-range forecast.

Short-range forecast has a time span of up to one year, but usually less than three months. Medium-range forecast has a time span from three months to three years. Long-range forecast has a time span of three years or more. Short-range objectives of demand forecasting deals with formulation of production strategy and policy; formulation of pricing policy; planning and control of sales; and financial planning. Medium or long-range objectives of demand forecasting deal with long-range planning for production capacity, labour requirements, and restructuring the capital structure. The forecast should be timely, accurate, reliable, and simple to understand and use. The seven basic steps involved in forecasting are: determine the objectives of the forecast; select the items for which forecasts are needed; determine the time horizon for the forecast; select the forecasting method or technique (model); gather and analyse the data needed for the forecast; prepare the forecast; and monitor the forecast.

Forecasting Models

Forecasting models[3] are broadly classified into two types: quantitative models and qualitative models. Quantitative models involve projection of historical data or development of associative models. Quantitative models are broadly classified into two types:

1. **Time-series models** use a series of past data to make a forecast for the future. A time series is a time-ordered sequence of observations taken at regular intervals over a period of time. The data may be a measurement of demand, earnings, profits, outputs, productivity, and consumer price index. There are three techniques of time-series forecasting. They are: (i) naïve approach (ii) moving averages (simple and weighted), and (iii) exponential smoothing.

   Naïve approach is a simple way to forecast in which the forecast of demand for the next period is assumed to be equal to the actual demand in the current period. Moving average is a forecasting method that uses a number of most recent historical actual data values to generate a forecast. Exponential smoothing is a weighted moving average method in which data points are weighted by an exponential function.

2. **Causal models** may be of two types. They are: (i) trend projection and (ii) linear regression analysis. Trend refers to gradual, long term, upward, or downward movement in the data over time. Regression analysis is a method of predicting the value of one variable based on the value of other variables used to forecast both time series and cross-sectional data.

   Causal models such as linear regression incorporate the variables or factors that might influence the quantity being forecast. The demand forecast is a dependent variable and other factors that affect demand are independent variables. In linear regression the dependent variable is related to one or more independent variables by a linear equation. Correlation analysis measures the degree of relationship between normally distributed dependent and independent variables and is signified by the correlation coefficient "r."

SNAPSHOT

- Forecasting involves the projection of the past into the future.
- The factors to be considered in the selection of a forecasting method are cost and accuracy, data available, time span, nature of products and services, impulse response, and noise dampening.

DISCUSSION FORUM

- Discuss the importance of operations management.
- Define the term forecasting and mention the uses of forecasts.
- Discuss the factors to be considered in the selection of a forecasting method.

TECHNOLOGY MANAGEMENT

Technology is defined to be the know-how, physical objects, and procedures used to produce products and services. Advanced technology refers to the application of the latest scientific or engineering discoveries to the design of production and operations processes. Technology can be classified as: manual technology, mechanized technology, automated technology, current technology, appropriate technology, state-of-the-art technology, advanced technology, capital-intensive technology, and labour-intensive technology. The three primary areas of technology are product technology, process technology, and information technology.

The recent developments in the technology of product design comprises certain tools provided by the information sciences that contribute to the better, cheaper, and faster design of products. They are computer-aided design (CAD), computer-aided manufacturing (CAM), standard for the exchange of product data (STEP), and virtual reality technology.

CAD is an electronic system using computers for designing new parts or products or for modifying existing ones. CAM uses computer software programs to direct and control manufacturing equipments. STEP provides a format allowing the electronic transmittal of three-dimensional data to be exchanged internationally, allowing geographically dispersed manufacturers to integrate design, manufacture, and support processes. Virtual reality technology is a visual form of communication in which images substitute for the real thing, but still allow the user to respond interactively. STEP and virtual reality technology are used to speed up product development, reduce design lead time, reduce costs, and improve products.

Many machines such as lathes, boring machines, drilling and milling machines are designed for electronic control called numerical control (NC). NC machines have control systems to read instructions and translate them into machine operations. Computer numerically controlled (CNC) machines are programmed through their own computers and have memories to store these programs or instructions.

Robotics is a rapidly developing field of technology in which human-like machines perform production tasks. Robots are designed to move materials, parts, tools, or specialized devices through variable programmed motions for the performance of a variety of tasks. Robots are reprogrammable and can perform multiple functions.

A flexible manufacturing system (FMS) is a flexible automation system that builds on the programmable automation of NC and CNC machines. In an FMS, a group of production machines are connected by automated material handling and transferring machines and integrated by a computer system. The computer system is equipped to provide instructions to produce different parts based on the order specified.

PRODUCTION MANAGEMENT

Production management[4] refers to the application of planning, organizing, and directing to the production process. Production can be defined as the "process through which goods and services are created." Therefore, we include both manufacturing and service organizations within the purview of production management. The essential features of the production function are to bring together people, machines, and materials to provide goods and services thereby satisfying the wants of people at large. The production function or operations function is the primary function of an industrial enterprise. It is also known as a conversion process or a transformation process, which transforms some of the inputs into outputs that are useful for the consumers. A simple production system is shown in Figure 13.1.

The basic techniques of analysis for improving the manufacturing and service organizations are the same. However, since service organizations have some special features, the management of such systems is slightly more difficult. Some of these special features are: output from the service organization cannot be stocked; demand for the service is variable; operation may be labour intensive; and location of service operation is dictated by the location of users.

Production Planning and Control (PPC)

No work can be done without planning. There are those who plan when the actual work is to be executed. They run about to collect all that is required, thus extending the period of working. There are others who plan well in advance and arrange for all that is required before starting work. The advantages of the latter approach have led to the development of production planning and control. The production planning and control function focuses on planning production in a manufacturing organization before actual production activities start and exercising control activities to ensure that the planned production is undertaken successfully after taking into account the quantity, quality, delivery schedule, and cost of production. The main functions or elements of PPC are given in Figure 13.2.

Phases in PPC Function The various phases in PPC are discussed below:

1. **Planning phase:** This includes preplanning and active planning.
   - Preplanning: This activity involves product planning and development, demand forecasting, resource planning, facilities planning, plant planning, plant location, and plant layout.
   - Active planning: This involves planning for quantity, determination of product mix, routing, scheduling, material planning, process planning, capacity planning, and tool planning.

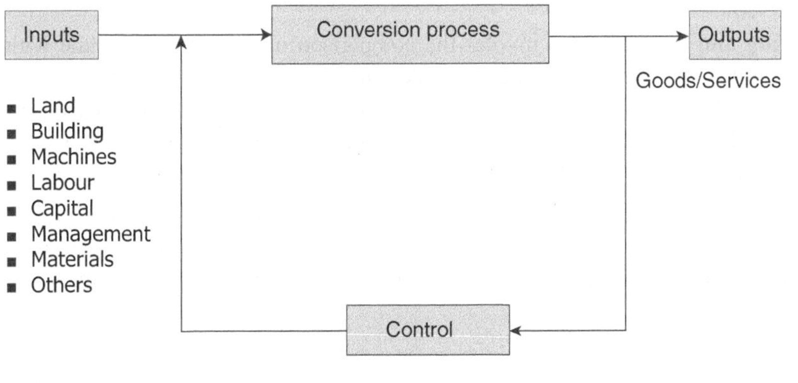

Figure 13.1 Simple Production System

Figure 13.2 Elements of PPC

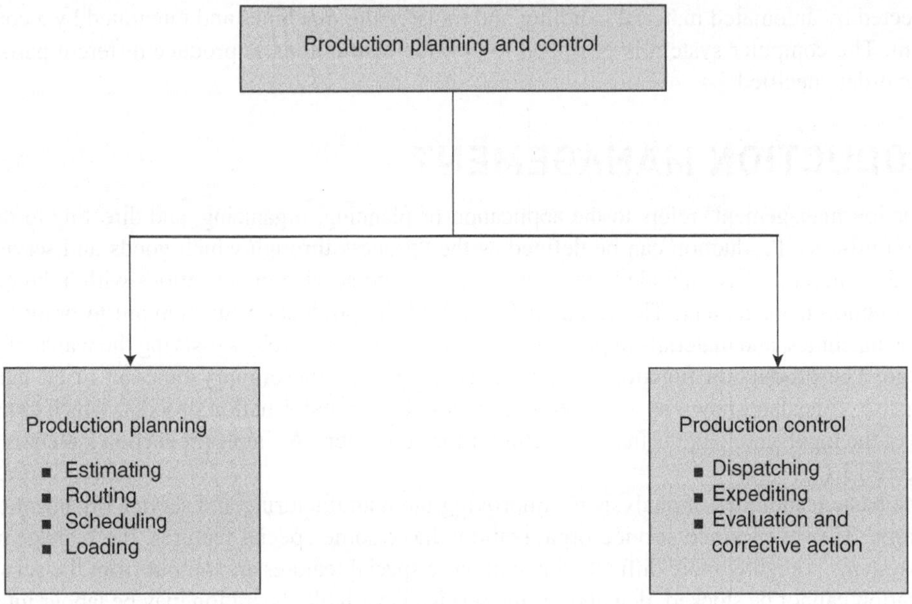

2. **Action phase:** Execution or implementation phase—includes dispatching and progressing functions.
3. **Control phase:** This includes status reporting, material control, tool control, inventory control, labour output control, and cost control.

Work Content and Capacity Determination[5]

The steps in work content and capacity determination are as follows:

- **Estimating:** Using simple methods of work measurement, determine the work content of various operations and capacities of various workstations.
- **Loading and routing**: With the help of work content and capacities, decide the machines on which each operation is to be carried out or, in other words, plan the route for the product. Once we know the standard capacity of each machine/facility (85 per cent utilization of a machine/facility capacity in a shift is considered a fair average), we can decide on how much load is to be put on each machine. The use of a Gantt loading chart will help in loading and routing.
- **Scheduling:** Here we decide the exact time of starting and finishing each operation.
- **Dispatch:** This is the green signal to commence work. This can be done either by a work order or a job card.
- **Monitoring and control:** This involes the comparison of the actual schedule with the planned schedule so that appropriate action can be taken if necessary. Most of the time, some jobs will be running behind schedule while others will be ahead of schedule. A careful analysis of the situation would show that some of the work can be brought back on schedule by making a few changes or by using the spare capacity of those machines/facilities that are ahead of schedule.

The planning and programming phase is relatively simple since the problem of a reliable measure of work content has been solved. But even a crude plan is useless if the people concerned are not given clear instructions. This means having a simple system of paperwork to convey all the necessary information.

SNAPSHOT

- Technology is defined as the know-how, physical objects, and procedures used to produce products and services.
- Production management refers to the application of planning, organizing, and directing to the production process.
- Production can be defined as the "process through which goods and services are created."
- Plant layout refers to the arrangement of machinery, equipment, and other industrial facilities—such as the receiving and shipping departments, tool rooms, maintenance rooms, and employee amenities—for the purpose of achieving the quickest and smoothest production at the least cost.
- The production planning and control function essentially consists of planning production in a manufacturing organization before actual production activities start and exercising control activities to ensure that the planned production is realised in terms of quantity, quality, delivery schedule, and cost of production.

DISCUSSION FORUM

- Discuss the characteristics of modern production function in small groups.
- Explain the relevance of technology management. Explain the role of PPC in the engineering industry.

SUPPLY CHAIN MANAGEMENT

Supply chain management (SCM)[6] has gained considerable importance in recent years in the manufacturing and services sector. Good supply chain management helps organizations to procure the right quantity and quality of material at the right price at the right place. It also enables organizations to respond to customer orders quickly, reduce costs, and add value to the supply chain. The supply chain consists of organizations that are connected through three key flows across their boundaries—the flow of information, product/materials, and funds between the different stages. The objectives of a supply chain are to maximize the overall value generated, to achieve maximum supply chain profitability, and to reduce the supply chain costs to the minimum possible level.

The supply chain integrates the organization to the environment around itself. It also reflects the competitiveness of business organizations. Supply chain management invoIes integration-oriented skills required for providing a competitive advantage to the organization. There are four generic processes involved in any supply chain: planning, procurement, production, and distribution of goods and services. A typical supply chain may involve various intermediaries such as customers, retailers, wholesalers/distributors, manufacturers, and component/raw materials suppliers.

The supply chain is made of three distinctive entities, the inbound supply chain, the in-house supply chain, and the outbound supply chain. The inbound supply chain pertains mainly to providing raw materials and components to an organization. The in-house component of the supply chain relates to the physical configuration of the conversion process. The outbound supply chain pertains to the distribution of goods and services to the end customers. Due to an increase in the use of the Internet and information technology infrastructure, third-party logistics providers play an important role in the outbound supply chain of many firms. The supply chain structure addresses issues pertaining to the number of layers that make up a supply chain, the composition of each layer, the type of information flow across the layers, and the nature of integration achieved between the layers.

WORLD OF ENTREPRENEURS 13.1 SAP Enterprise Resource Planning

SAP is an enterprise resource planning (ERP) software program. In German, SAP stands for Systeme, Anwendungen, Produkte, and in English it stands for "Systems Applications and Products in data processing." SAP was developed by five former IBM employees of the German software company SAP AG in Mannheim, Germany, in 1972. The initial version was called SAP R/1. In 1979, SAP launched SAP R/2 and in 1981, SAP R/3 was launched.

Enterprises can effectively manage their resources, people, money, machines, etc. using SAP's application programming. SAP modules are classified into three types: (1) SAP functional modules, (2) SAP technical modules, and (3) SAP new modules. SAP focuses on six industry sectors: process industries, discrete industries, consumer industries, service industries, financial services, and public services.

SAP ERP is one of five enterprise applications in SAP's business suite. The other four applications are: Customer Relationship Management (CRM), Product Lifecycle Management (PLM), Supply Chain Management (SCM), and Supplier Relationship Management (SRM).

SAP Labs is the research and development organization of the parent company. Each SAP Lab has a prominent area of expertise and focus. SAP Labs India is the largest development unit in terms of the number of employees outside the SAP headquarters located in Waldorf, Germany. SAP Pinnacle awards are presented annually to the top SAP partners that have excelled in developing and growing their partnership with SAP, delivering unparalleled technology, services, and solutions to mutual customers.

Source: www.sap.com (last accessed in March 2013).

MATERIALS MANAGEMENT

Every business organization stocks a number of materials depending on the business it is in, for its own use (input), and also for selling (output). Stock is held in various stores/warehouses and shop floors. Capital, which is a scarce resource for a business is blocked in stock. Hence, there is a need for efficient management of materials. This helps to reduce the cost of production. Materials management is the process which coordinates, supervises, and executes the tasks associated with the flow of materials to, through, and out of an organization in an integrated approach.

Materials management[7] involves organizing and coordinating all management functions that are responsible for every aspect of materials, storage, and transformation. The three basic objectives of materials management are: buying, storage, and movement of materials. It refers to the movement of production materials from the stage of their acquisition to the stage of their consumption. The basic objective of materials management is to obtain materials at the optimum cost, in the right quantity and quality, ensuring the continuity of supply and to maintain minimum inventory of materials, so as to free the working capital for other useful purposes. The detailed objectives of materials management are: purchasing materials and equipment at optimum price; faster inventory turnover; continuous supply of materials; reduced lead time; reduced transportation cost; zero obsolescence; better supplier relationships and management of inventories

Materials planning determines the requirement of all kinds of materials to meet the production needs economically. Materials budgeting is the process of preparing the materials budget or the purchase budget in terms of quantity and the monetary value of materials to be procured for a given period of time. The material control function deals with maintaining constant availability of all kinds of materials required for the manufacture of products.

The purchasing function provides materials to the enterprise without which the wheels of machines cannot move. "Purchasing" is a managerial activity which goes beyond the simple act of buying and includes planning and policy activities covering a wide range of related complementary activities. The five basic principles of purchasing are buying the right quality of materials at the right price from a right source and at the right time and place. The purchasing function can be explained by a purchase cycle, the steps in which are: recognition of need; description of need; selection of a suitable source for the supply but also sometimes development of a source; determination of price and availability;

preparation of a purchase order and sending it to the supplier; obtaining the acceptance of the purchase order from the supplier; following up to ensure the timely delivery of the material; receiving the material; checking the invoice and approving it for making payment to the supplier; and making the payment to the supplier.

The make or buy decision relates to deciding whether a part should be purchased or manufactured. This is the most basic supply chain management decision pertaining to whether to make a given product in-house or to buy it from a supplier. A make or buy decision[8] is normally taken by a committee comprising representatives from different departments. The considerations that favour making the part are:

- Cost
- Desire to integrate plant operations
- Utilization of excess plant capacity to help absorb fixed overheads
- Need to have direct control over production and/or quantity
- Unreliable suppliers
- Desire to maintain a stable workforce

The considerations that favour buying the part are:

- Supplier's research and specialized know-how
- Cost consideration
- Small volume requirements
- Limited production capacity
- Desire to maintain a stable workforce
- Desire to maintain multiple sources of supply and indirect material control

Vendor development is the ability to select reliable vendors and develop them. It is a mark of a successful purchasing action. Vendor rating is the process of rating a supplier based on some rating technique. It is a valuable tool for the purchasing manager in making purchase decisions and providing objective feedback to the vendors. There are several rating techniques available for vendor rating:

- **Categorical plan method**: Personnel from various divisions such as purchasing, engineering, and quality control maintain informal evaluation records based on the performance factors which are important to her/him. At a monthly meeting, each supplier is evaluated based on the evaluator's list of factors. Based on evaluation, each suppler is assigned an overall group evaluation and categorized as "Preferred," "Neutral," or "Unsatisfactory."
- **The weighted point plan**: The performance factors are evaluated by assigning weights. The rating may be done using parameters such as quality, delivery, quantity, and price. Vendor performance on each factor must be expressed in quantitative terms. To determine a vendor's rating, each factor weight is multiplied by the vendor's corresponding performance parameter. To get the overall rating, the total score of the performance parameter is calculated for that period. The final evaluation will depend on judgement, which is substantiated by facts. The rating may be done as per the following parameters.
    - Quality performance: (Number of lots accepted/Number of lots supplied) × Weightage
    - Delivery performance: (Number of deliveries made in time/Total number of scheduled delivery) × Weightage
    - Quantity performance: (Quantity supplied/Scheduled delivery) × Weightage
    - Price performance: (Minimum price offered/Vendor's price) × Weightage
- **Critical incidents method:** This method is based on the buyer–vendor relationship. This method requires that a record of events and occurrences related to the buyer–vendor relationship be maintained in each vendor's file. This method is usually used in small organizations where the number of suppliers is less.

INVENTORY MANAGEMENT

The term inventory includes materials—raw, in process, finished, packaged, spares, and others—stocked in order to meet an unexpected demand or distribution in the near future. Inventory includes the following categories of items:

- **Production inventories:** Raw materials, parts, and components which are consumed in the production process and become part of the product.
- **Maintenance, repair, and operating supplies (MRO) inventories:** These are consumed in the production process, but do not become part of the product (for example, lubricating oil, soap, machine repair parts).
- **In-process inventories:** These are semi-finished products found at various stages of the production operation.
- **Finished goods inventories:** These are completed products ready for shipment.

Inventory Costs

Inventory costs are of three types — ordering costs, carrying costs, and finacial costs.

- Ordering costs are the expenses of placing an order with a vendor of materials. These include: preparing a purchase order; processing payments; receiving and inspecting the material; and ordering from the plant
- Carrying costs are costs connected directly with materials and include obsolescence, deterioration, and pilferage.
- Financial costs include taxes, insurance, storage, and interest.

Inventory Control Techniques

Several techniques of inventory control are in use and it depends on the convenience of the firm to adopt any of them. What should be stressed, however, is the need to cover all items of inventory and all stages, that is, from the stage of receipt from suppliers to the stage of their use. The following points should be kept in mind while managing the inventory.

- **Shortage of inventory:** This gives rise to stockout cost. This includes: cost of customer dissatisfaction; downtime cost; changeover cost; and opportunity cost.
- **Excess inventory carrying cost:** If large inventories are carried as an insurance against stockouts, a large amount of capital is blocked. This results in a high inventory carrying cost.

Inventory Control Techniques The following techniques are most commonly used for inventory control:

- Always better control (ABC)
- High, medium, and low (HML)
- Vital, essential, and desirable (VED)
- Scarce, difficult, and easy to obtain (SDE)
- Fast moving, slow moving, and non-moving (FSN)
- Economic order quantity (EOQ)
- Maximum–minimum system
- Two-bin systems
- Materials requirement planning (MRP)
- Just-in-time (JIT)

These tcchniques are explained in detail below:

- **ABC analysis**: Inventory in an organization can be classified into three categories— A, B, and C. On the basis of the annual consumption in monetary value, "A" items will be of high value, "B" items will be of medium value, and "C" items will be of low value. There is no hard and fast limit for these categories, and they will vary from organization to organization and even from product to product. However, we can have the following categorization:

Category	Value	No. of Items
A	70%	10%
B	20%	20%
C	10%	70%

Having once determined the categories, the intensity of control in each case can be different. This classification is also referred to as the Pareto analysis (after the Italian philosopher and economist Vilfredo Pareto).

- **High, medium, and low (HML):** The high, medium, and low (HML) classification is based on the unit value of the item. The classification follows the same procedure as is adopted in the ABC classification. The items of inventory should be listed in the descending order of unit value and it is up to the management to fix the limits for three categories. If a part is high value, it is given the "H" classification; if it is of medium value, it is given the "M" classification; and if it is of low value, it is given the "L" classification.
- **Vital, essential, and desirable (VED):** In the ABC classification, inventories are classified on the basis of their consumption value. In the HML classification, the unit value is the basis, whereas the criticality of inventories is the basis for the vital, essential, and desirable classification. VED classification is done to determine the criticality of an item and its effect on production and other services. If a part is vital, it is given the "V" classification; if it is essential, then it is given the "E" classification; and if it is not so essential, the part is given the "D" classification. For "V" items, a large stock of inventory is generally maintained, while for "D" items, minimum stock is enough. VED classification is specially used for the classification of spare parts.
- **Scarce, difficult, and easy to obtain (SDE):** The SDE classification is based upon the availability of items and is very useful in the context of scarcity of supply. The SDE classification is based on problems faced in procurement. It is vital in lead-time analysis and in deciding on purchasing strategies. In this classification, "S" refers to "scarce" items, which are generally imported and are in short supply. "D" refers to difficult items, which are available indigenously but are difficult to procure. "E" refers to items that are easy to acquire and are easily available in the local market.
- **Fast moving, slow moving, and non-moving (FSN):** The FSN classification is based on the pattern of issues from stores and useful in controlling obsolescence. It is useful in identifying active items, which need to be reviewed regularly and surplus items, which have to be examined further. Non-moving items may be examined further and their disposal can be considered.
- **Economic order quantity (EOQ):** EQO technique answers the question of how much to order and establishes the frequency with which orders are placed. EOQ is the order size at which the total cost, comprising ordering cost plus carrying cost, is the least. EOQ is applicable both to single items and to any group of stock items with similar holding and procurement costs.
- **Maximum–minimum system**: This system is often used in connection with manual inventory control systems. The minimum quantity is established in the same way as any reorder point. The maximum is the minimum quantity plus the optimum lot size.
- **Two-bin system**: In the two-bin system, the stock of each item is separated into two bins. One bin contains just enough stock to last from the date a new order is placed until it is received in inventory. The other bin contains a quantity of stock, which is enough to satisfy probable demand during the period of replenishment. To start with, the stock is issued from the first bin. When the first bin is empty, an order for replenishment is placed, and the stock in the second is utilized until the ordered material is received.
- **Materials requirement planning (MRP)**: MRP is most useful to firms with finished goods or end products, which are made from a number of components and are also subject to uneven or

lumpy demand. The technique separates the various components and coordinates purchasing and delivery with production. This results in materials arriving exactly when needed for production and, at the same time, reduces the length of time when materials are held in stock. MRP plans and controls goods on order and generates data for determining what specific materials will be needed to meet the previously planned production schedule and when.

- **Just-in-time (JIT):** The JIT concept originated from the Motomachi plant of Toyota in Japan. As a concept, JIT means that virtually no inventories are held at any stage of production and that the exact number of units is brought to each successive stage of production at the right time.

EXAMPLE

The consumption of 12 items in a company in the previous year was as below. Classify the items using ABC analysis.

Item Code No.	Annual Consumption in ₹	Item Code No.	Annual Consumption in ₹
1.	20,000	7	2,500
2.	200	8	2,400
3.	15,000	9	300
4.	4,000	10	25
5.	3,000	11	30
6.	2,000	12	50

Solution:
An ABC analysis can be done by ranking the items in the descending order of their annual consumption value and determining the cumulative per cent as shown below:

Rank	Item Max%	Item Code No.	Annual Consumption in ₹	Percentage of Total Value	Cumulative Percentage Value	Category
1	8.3	1	20,000	40.00	40.00	A
2	16.6	3	15,000	70.00	30.00	A
3	25.0	4	4,000	8.70	78.70	B
4	33.3	5	3,000	6.00	84.70	B
5	41.6	7	2,500	5.00	89.70	B
6	50.0	8	2,400	4.80	94.50	B
7	58.3	6	2,000	4.00	98.50	B
8	66.6	9	300	0.60	99.10	C
9	75.0	2	200	0.45	99.55	C
10	83.3	12	50	0.30	99.85	C
11	91.6	11	30	0.10	99.95	C
12	100	10	25	0.05	100.00	
		Total	49,505	100.00		

Benefits of Inventory Control

The major benefits that accrue from inventory control are as follows:

- Stock control ensures adequate supply of materials, stores, spares, minimizes stockouts and shortages, and avoids costly interruptions in operations.
- It keeps investment in inventories, inventory carrying costs, and obsolescence losses to the minimum.
- It facilitates ecnomic purchasing through the measurement of requirements on the basis of recorded experience.
- It facilitates cost accounting activities by providing a means for allocating materials costs to products, departments, or other operating accounts.
- Perpetual inventory values provide a consistent and reliable basis for preparing financial statements.

SNAPSHOT

- Good supply chain management helps organizations to procure the right quantity and quality of material at the right price at the right place.
- Materials management refers to the movement of materials from the stage of their acquisition to the stage of their consumption.
- Vendor rating is the process of rating a supplier based on some rating techniques.
- Inventory includes materials—raw, in process, finished, packaged, spares, and others—stocked in order to meet an unexpected demand or distribution in the near future.

DISCUSSION FORUM

- Discuss the importance of supply chain management in enterprises.
- Explain lean management.
- Define materials management. Bring out its scope and importance.
- Discuss the factors influencing make or buy decisions.
- Explain vendor rating.
- Discuss the various inventory control techniques.

PRODUCTIVITY

The more the output from one worker or one machine (or piece of equipment) per day per shift, the higher the productivity. High productivity is never a question of higher workloads or faster machines alone. It is always because of the elimination of waste of all types of labour (time and skill), machine, time, capital, materials management, and so on. The widely used productivity improvement techniques are just-in-time, lean manufacturing, visual management, waste reduction, inventory control, value engineering, quality circles, training, etc. Mathematically, productivity is defined as:

$$\text{Productivity} = \text{Output per unit of input}$$

TOTAL QUALITY MANAGEMENT

Total quality management (TQM)[9] is an approach to business that looks critically not only at the products and services a company provides in relation to the process it employs to create them, but also at the workforce to ensure that outputs fully satisfy customer requirements. This approach is called "total" because it encompasses everything the company does—all its processes and employees at every level in the company at all times. TQM is a management philosophy that seeks to integrate all organizational functions (marketing, finance, design, engineering, production, and customer service) to focus on meeting customer needs and organizational objectives. It is a totally integrated effort for gaining a competitive advantage by continuously improving every facet of an organization's activities.

BREAKTHROUGH ENTREPRENEURSHIP 13.2 "Total Quality" at Mother Dairy

Mother Dairy is a wholly-owned company of the National Dairy Development Board (NDDB). Mother Dairy's heritage is intrinsically linked to the cooperative movement in India. It provides quality food and beverages to consumers at affordable prices while ensuring fair returns to the producers. Mother Dairy manufactures, markets, and sells its products in India as well as abroad. Milk and dairy products are marketed under the Mother Dairy brand, fresh fruits and vegetables, purees, pulp, concentrates, and frozen vegetables under the Safal brand, and packaged edible oil under the Dhara brand.

The key strength of Mother Dairy is its supply chain. Fruits and vegetables are procured from different states of India and delivered straight to outlets using an efficient delivery mechanism. Mother Dairy has used technology to effectively streamline its supply chain management system. The SAP ERP application has been used to link and monitor the movement of products between its 11 plants, 45 distributors, and 16 packaging locations. Its fleet is equipped with radio frequency identification (RFID) tags. The company received the SAP Ace Award in 2010 for achieving customer satisfaction and business excellence through the implementation of SAP.

Mother Dairy is committed to deliver products that meet all regulatory, industrial, consumer quality, and food safety requirements to consumers. The company's Innovation Centre is the first of its kind in India's organized dairy and food sector. The Centre has a dedicated team of scientists who constantly collaborate to develop novel products, innovating packaging systems, and best practices for quality and food safety.

Mother Dairy maintains stringent measures to ensure product quality and safety. It is an ISO 9001:2008 (QMS), ISO 22000:2005 (Food Safety Management System), and ISO 14001:2004 (EMS) company. The company has a Certificate of Approval from the Export Inspection Council of India. Its Quality Assurance Laboratory is certified by the National Accreditation Board for Testing and Calibration Laboratory of the Government of India. The company has gained recognition at international and national levels by receiving several prestigious accolades and awards. Mother Dairy's endeavour is to create a culture of "total quality" where continuous improvement of people, processes, and products becomes a way of life.

Source: www.motherdairy.com (last accessed in March 2013).

Prerequisites for TQM

The following points should be kept in mind while implementing TQM:

- The management must establish TQM as an objective and accept responsibility.
- Top management must be able to overcome obstacles, most of which would emanate from the management itself.
- It must be understood that TQM cannot be accomplished with the participation of only a few. All employees in the organization must pursue this end.
- Resources, i.e. people, time, money, and effort, must be dedicated over a long period of time.
- Employees will need to be continually assured of the management's commitment in the form of actions and not mere words.
- As it will require cultural change, managers must change their style and methods from one of controlling employees in a bureaucratic manner to encouraging employee initiative and involvement. Their role must change from that of controller to coach.
- It will require a high level of effort for the top management to create a quality environment by launching behavioural changes, building skills through training and communication, and ensuring timely actions to sustain the effort.

Benefits of TQM

There are many advantages of TQM. Essentially, it refers to the total quality in fulfilling the needs of the customers, the quality of the products, and the quality of life (both in the workplace and also at home). Having these focuses lead to better business results and also benefit businesses in several different ways. Here are some of the benefits of total quality management:

- **Creates a good corporate culture:** Total quality management is an approach where the focus of the business is customer-centric and not department-centric and transforms quality from a production department issue to a strategic business entity to meet global challenges. Since the TQM philosophy revolves around developing a culture that advocates total commitment to customer satisfaction through continuous improvement, it is embedded in the organizational culture and creates a corporate culture for perfection.
- **Better reviews from customers:** Another benefit of total quality management is that customers and clients become better satisfied with the performance. Because of the quality assurance testing, the products manufactured will constantly meet the requirements and needs of clients and customers. Therefore, customers stay with the company longer, deepen their relationship with the company, demonstrate less price sensitivity, and recommend the company's products or services to others. This customer satisfaction and high performance results can also possibly lead to good reviews in various publications and newspapers, which will further augment the image of the company and in turn increase business.
- **Better performance from employees:** There is often more attention placed on meeting the needs of the employees or internal customers within the company through total quality management. The training given to the employee as part of the programme can boost employee morale at the workplace and this can cause employees to work harder to help achieve the goals of total quality management.

QUALITY MANAGEMENT SYSTEM (QMS)

QMS should be a strategic decision of an organization. Quality management focuses on activities carried out by the organization to fulfill customers' quality requirements and applicable regulatory requirements, aiming to enhance customer satisfaction, and achieving continual improvement in performance. ISO 9001:2008 was officially released on 13 November 2008 and provides a set of standardized requirements for a quality management system, regardless of what the user organization does, its size, or whether it is in the private or public sector.

The ISO 9000 is a series of standards in a quality management system, which can be adopted by all types of organizations belonging to the government, public, private, or joint sectors. These standards are generic and not specific to any particular product. The ISO 9001:2008 provides a tried and tested framework for using a systematic approach for managing an organization's processes so that it consistently turns out products that satisfy customer expectations. The standard consists of eight clauses. Clauses 1 to 3 are basic clauses and Clauses 4 to 8 are main clauses. The requirements to be met for ISO 9001:2008 QMS certification are given in Table 13.2.

MAINTENANCE

Maintenance[10] is a fundamental requirement for the upkeep and running of any system. A good maintenance management programme enables the organization to maintain high levels of efficiency, resulting in superior products that meet the aspirations of today's customers. Maintenance management is a systematic approach to the planning of maintenance activities using decision-making tools to improve the overall efficiency and effectiveness of the operating system. A good maintenance function has a favourable impact on quality. Maintenance management is closely linked to other operations management functions such as quality management, scheduling, and aggregate production planning. A good maintenance programme enables better planning in these functional areas.

Maintenance in manufacturing management is concerned with the day-to-day need of keeping the physical plant in good operating condition. It is an essential activity in every manufacturing establishment because it ensures the availability of the machines, buildings, and services needed by other parts of the organization for the performance of their functions. The objectives of maintenance

Table 13.2 QMS Requirements for ISO 9001:2008

Clause No.	Contents	Clause No.	Contents
	Basic clauses		**Main clauses**
1.	Scope	6.3.	Infrastructure
1.1.	General	6.4.	Work environment
1.2.	Application	7.	Product realisation
2.	Normative reference	7.1.	Planning of product realisation
3.	Terms and definitions	7.2.	Customer related processes
	Main clauses	7.3.	Design and development
4.	Quality management systems	7.4	Purchasing
		7.5.	Production and service provision
4.1.	General requirements	7.6.	Control of monitoring and measuring equipment
4.2.	Documentation requirements		
5.	Management responsibility	8.	Measurement, analysis, and improvement
5.1.	Management Commitment		
5.2.	Customer focus	8.1.	General
5.3.	Quality policy	8.2.	Monitoring and measurement
5.4.	Planning	8.3.	Control of non-conforming products
5.5.	Responsibility, authority, and communication	8.4.	Analysis of data
		8.5.	Improvement
5.6.	Management review		
6.	Resource management	Annexure A	Correspondence between ISO 9001:2008 and ISO 14001:2004
6.1	Provision of resources	Annexure B	Changes between ISO 9001:2000 and ISO 9001:2008
6.2	Human resources		

Source: www.iso.org (last accessed in March 2013). Reproduced with permission. Copyright remains with ISO.

management are: minimizing the loss of productive time because of equipment failure; minimizing repair time and repair cost; minimizing loss due to production stoppages; ensuring efficient use of maintenance personnel and equipment; prolonging the life of capital assets by minimizing the rate of wear and tear; keeping all assets of the enterprise in good working condition; maximizing efficiency and economy in production through optimum use of facilities; minimizing accidents through regular inspection and repair of safety devices; minimizing the total maintenance cost; and improving quality and productivity

Machine maintenance means looking after machines and equipment, including vehicles, by oiling, greasing, checking calibration, replacing worn-out parts before they break, and checking electrical parts and wiring. If a machine has to work well, maintenance must be done regularly, oiling and greasing must be carried out about once a week, and electric motors must be checked every three months. The more a machine costs, the more important becomes its maintenance. If you must stop a machine for a long time, plan to stop it when you think it is most suitable. It is better to stop a machine when you want to rather than have it break down and stop when it is doing important work. Effective maintenance requires the use of troubleshooting mechanisms, fault-tree analyses, and a good maintenance management information system.

Several performance measures are available to assess maintenance management. These include availability, mean time between failures (MTBF), mean time to repair (MTTR), and overall equipment effectiveness (OEE). Availability refers to the fraction of the time for which the equipment is available for productive use. MTBF is the expected time of the arrival of a failure. MTTR is the expected time for restoring the equipment back to working condition. The various types of maintenance are: breakdown maintenance, routine maintenance, preventive maintenance, predictive maintenance, and total productive maintenance (TPM).

Breakdown Maintenance This is a frequent method of maintenance in several organizations that do not have a robust maintenance set up. In breakdown maintenance some repair is carried out to restore the equipment to working condition. Breakdown maintenance is both expensive and undesirable and is rather reactive. The simplest form of maintenance is routine maintenance, which involves routine inspection of the equipment. These include checking the lubrication of the moving components, looking for loosened fasteners, and dusting and cleaning of surfaces with high-precision requirements and moving components. Often, routine maintenance results in keeping the plant in good operating condition.

Planned Maintenance This is a maintenance activity for which a pre-determined job procedure has been documented and all labour, materials, tools, and equipment required to carry out the task have been estimated and their availability assured. Preventive maintenance is a conscious decision on the part of the maintenance management team to perform some maintenance on the equipment even when it is in working condition. Predictive maintenance is a method in which the condition of the equipment is constantly monitored and the decision to carry out maintenance is taken based on the analysis of the equipment behaviour. Total productive maintenance (TPM) is an alternative approach to equipment maintenance that seeks to achieve zero breakdowns and zero defects. It is based on the premise that production operators play a crucial role in maintenance. Overall equipment effectiveness (OEE) is used to assess the performance of TPM. OEE essentially captures six big losses that occur in any organization, which result in reduced effectiveness of using the equipment. The six big losses are: loss due to breakdown, loss due to setup and adjustment (downtime losses); loss due to idling and minor stoppage, loss due to reduced speed (speed losses); loss due to rejections and rework and loss due to start-up (quality losses). By eliminating the "six big losses," the OEE of equipment could be improved.

SNAPSHOT

- TQM is an integrated effort designed to improve the quality of performance at every level of the organization.
- Maintenance is that function of manufacturing management, which is concerned with the day-to-day need of keeping the physical plant in good operating condition.
- ISO 9000 is a series of standards in quality management system, which can be adopted by all types of organizations belonging to the government, public, private, or joint sectors. These standards are generic and not specific to any particular product.
- ISO 9001 is a QMS that provides a tried and tested framework for using a systematic approach for managing an organization's processes so that it consistently turns out products that satisfy customer expectations.

DISCUSSION FORUM

- Discuss various productivity improvement techniques in small groups.
- Explain different types of maintenance systems.
- Identify the clauses of ISO 9001 QMS.

OCCUPATIONAL HEALTH AND SAFETY ADVISORY SERVICES

Every day, workplace injuries, illnesses, and fatalities cause immeasurable pain and suffering to employees and their families. Many of the world's foremost companies accept that, quite apart from employees' well-being, the impact of poor occupational health and safety on a company's bottom line may include higher absenteeism and more downtime leading to loss of productivity;

CHECKLIST FOR ENTREPRENEURS 13.3 — Occupational Health and Safety Management Systems

The critical elements of an effective Occupational Health and Safety Management System are: a. management commitment and employee involvement, b. worksite analysis, c. hazard prevention and control, and d. training for employees.

Management Commitment and Employee Involvement

- Develop and communicate an occupational health and safety policy to all employees.
- Demonstrate management commitment by providing resources, practising safety rules, reviewing accident reports, and instilling accountability for occupational health and safety. Conduct regular occupational health and safety meetings involving all employees.
- Identify and authorize responsible employees to coordinate occupational health and safety activities and make them accountable.
- Integrate occupational health and safety into business functions.
- Involve employees in occupational health and safety-related activities.
- In order to encourage occupational health and safety, recognize and reward employees for developing and maintaining safe and healthy work practices.

Worksite Analysis

- Evaluate workplace processes and activities for hazards.
- Reevaluate workplace processes and activities when there are changes in materials, machinery, and processes.
- Develop a hazard reporting system for employees to report unsafe and unhealthy conditions.
- Conduct onsite inspections, identify hazards, and take corrective and preventive actions.
- Investigate all accidents and determine the root causes.

Hazard Prevention and Control

- Establish a preventive maintenance programme.
- Eliminate and control workplace hazards and plan and prepare for emergencies.
- Keep employees informed of occupational health activities and conditions.
- Record and analyse occupational injuries, illnesses, and fatalities.

Training for Employees

- Provide training on occupational health and safe work practices before the employee joins work.
- Create an evacuation plan, train employees, and conduct mock drills.
- Provide refresher training on a routine basis.

Source: www.osha.gov (last accessed in March 2013).

low employee morale leading to loss of productivity; payment of compensation and associated legal costs; higher insurance premiums; damage to equipment and premises due to accidents; disputes with trade unions and local authorities; and loss of image.

Occupational Health and Safety Advisory Services (OHSAS) is a cross-disciplinary area concerned with protecting the safety, health, and welfare of employees in a company. The main focus in OHSAS is on the maintenance and promotion of workers' health and working capacity, the improvement of the working environment and the development of working cultures to improve productivity at the workplace. Effective OHSAS have proven to be a decisive factor in reducing the extent and severity of work-related injuries, illnesses, fatalities, and injury-related costs. Savings that arise due to an effective OHSAS if properly administered will exceed the cost of a workplace OHSAS.

OHSAS require the adoption of a structured approach for the identification of hazards, their evaluation, and control of risks in the workplace. OHSAS 18000 is an internationally recognized assessment specification for occupational health and safety management systems. It comprises two parts, 18001 and 18002, and embraces a number of other publications. OHSAS 18000 is maintained by the International Organization for Standardization (ISO) and is administered by accreditation and certification bodies. The standards are revised often to keep them up-to-date. The main objectives of OHSAS 18000 are to reduce risks by improving the management of health and safety; provide a competitive advantage of commitment to health and safety; improve operational efficiency and performance; and reduce insurance premiums and compensation for breached legislations.

OHSAS 18000 is the generic name given to a family of international standards developed to provide a framework around which an occupational health and safety management system can effectively be implemented. The OHSAS 18000 series of standards has been designed to be compatible with other management systems, such as those for quality (ISO 9000 series) and environmental responsibility (ISO 14000 series). OHSAS operates on the basis of policy planning, implementation and operation, checking and corrective action, management review, and continual improvement. It comprises two parts:

1. **OHSAS 18001**—Occupational health and safety assessment series for health and safety management systems.
2. **OHSAS 18002**—Guidelines for the implementation of OHSAS 18001.

OHSAS 18001 was first published in 1999. OHSAS 18001:2007 supersedes OHSAS 18001:1999. There have been a number of significant changes to the document since it was first published in 1999. The statutes relating to OHSAS are broadly divided into three: statutes for safety at workplaces, statutes for safety substances, and statutes for safety activities. The requirements of OHSAS 18001:2007 are given in Table 13.3.

Benefits of OHSAS 18001 Registration

- **Customer satisfaction**—through the delivery of products and services that consistently meet customer requirements while safeguarding their health and property.
- **Reduced operating costs**—by decreasing downtime through fatal incidents and ill health and reducing costs associated with legal fees and compensation.
- **Improved stakeholder relationships**—by safeguarding the health and property of staff, customers, and suppliers.
- **Legal compliance**—by understanding how statutory and regulatory requirements impact the organization and its customers.
- **Improved risk management**—through clear identification of potential incidents and implementation of controls and measures.
- **Proven business credentials**—through independent verification against recognized OHSAS 18001 standards.
- **Ability to win more business**—particularly where procurement specifications require certification as a condition to supply.

Table 13.3. OHSAS Requirements

4.1. General requirements
4.2. OH&S policy requirements
4.3. Planning requirements
4.3.1. Hazard identification, risk assessment, etc.
4.3.2. Legal and other requirements
4.3.3. Objectives and programmes
4.4. Implementation requirements
4.4.1. Resources, roles, responsibility, accountability, and authority
4.4.2. Competence, training, and awareness
4.4.3. Communication, participation, and consultation
4.4.3.1. Establish OH&S communication procedures
4.4.3.2. Establish OH&S participation and consultation
4.4.4. Documentation
4.4.5. Control of documents
4.4.6. Operational control
4.4.7. Emergency preparedness and response
4.5. Checking requirements
4.5.1. Performance measurement and monitoring
4.5.2. Evaluation of compliance
4.5.2.1. Evaluate compliance with legal requirements
4.5.2.2. Evaluate compliance with non-legal requirements
4.5.3. Incident investigation, non-conformity, corrective action, and preventive action
4.5.4. Control of records
4.5.5. Internal audit
4.6. Management review

Source: www.ohsas.org (last accessed in March 2013).

The Ministry of Labour, Government of India and labour departments of the states and union territories are responsible for the occupational health and safety of workers. The major legislations are the Factories Act, 1948; Mines Act, 1952; Plantation Labour Act, 1951; Explosives Act, 1884; Petroleum Act, 1934; Insecticides Act, 1968; Indian Electricity Act, 1910; Indian Boiler Act, 1923; Indian Atomic Energy Act, 1962; Building and Construction Workers Act, 1996; and Beedi and Cigar Workers' Act, 1966.

National Safety Council of India (NSCI)

The NSCI was set up by the Government of India to promote safety consciousness among workers to prevent accidents, minimize dangers and mitigate human suffering, and arrange programmes, lectures, and conferences on safety. NSCI conducts educational campaigns to arouse consciousness among employers and workers and collects educational and information data. The National Safety Awards are given in three categories: manufacturing sector, construction sector, and MSME sector.

At the international level, the NSCI has developed close collaborative associations with the International Labour Organization, the World Bank, and the United Nations Environment Programmes. In order to promote and encourage OH&S, the Government of India has instituted the following awards.

- The National Safety Awards for Factories and Docks (1965) to recognize industrial undertakings at the national level for good safety performance.

- The National Safety Awards for Mines (1983) to recognize mines at the national level for outstanding safety performance.
- The Shram Vir Awards (Vishwakarma Rashtriya Puraskar—1965) for recognizing workers for their meritorious performance at the national level.

ENVIRONMENTAL MANAGEMENT SYSTEM

The ISO 14000 is a series of international standards on environmental management that provide a framework for the development of an environmental management system and a supporting audit programme. The ISO 14001 is the cornerstone standard for the ISO 14000 series. This standard specifies a framework of control for an environmental management system against which an organization can be certified by a third party. Other standards in the series are actually guidelines. ISO 14001 is the principal management system standard that specifies the requirements for the formulation and maintenance of an EMS. If an organization wants to ensure that its environmental policy confirms to ISO 14001, it needs to commit to prevention of pollution, compliance with legislation, and continual improvement of the EMS.

The ISO 14001 is accompanied by ISO 14004, the Environmental Management Systems—General guidelines on principles, systems, and support techniques. These guidelines are applicable to organizations of all types, sectors, and sizes that seek to improve their environmental performance through the implementation of this standard. Organizations need to register by completing the EMS questionnaire. After registration, the assessment for ISO 14001 is undertaken. This includes two mandatory visits that form part of the initial certification audit by an external certification authority. Registration is granted and maintained by the client. Maintenance is confirmed through a programme of annual surveillance visits and a three-yearly re-certification audit. The requirements of ISO 14001–2004 are given in Table 13.4.

Benefits of Environmental Management System

The major benefits of an environmental management system are as follows:

- Improved environmental performance led by top management commitment.
- Cost savings can be achieved through improved efficiencies in energy, water usage, and through waste minimization.
- Conservation of resources.
- Compliance with legislation through the identification of new legislation in adequate time to address appropriate issues.
- Improved profitability, brand image, and customer satisfaction.
- Maintaining good public and community relations.

SNAPSHOT

- Occupational Health and Safety (OHS) is a cross-disciplinary area concerned with protecting the safety, health, and welfare of workers in employment.
- OHSAS 18000 is the generic name given to a family of international standards developed to provide a framework around which an occupational health and safety management system can effectively be implemented.
- The OHSAS 18000 series of standards has been designed to be compatible with other management systems, such as those for quality (ISO 9000 series) and environmental responsibility (ISO 14000 series).
- ISO 14000 is a series of international standards on environmental management. It provides a framework for the development of an environmental management system and a supporting audit programme.

Table 13.4 Environmental Management System Requirements: ISO 14001-2004

1.0. Scope
2.0. Normative references
3.0. Definitions
4.0. EMS requirements
4.1. General requirements
4.2. Environmental policy
4.3. Planning
4.3.1. Environmental aspects
4.3.2. Environmental and other requirements
4.3.3. Objectives, targets, and programmes
4.4. Implementation and operation
4.4.1. Roles, resources, responsibilities, and authority
4.4.2. Training, awareness, and competence
4.4.3. Communication
4.4.4. System documentation
4.4.5. Document control
4.4.6. Operational control
4.4.7. Emergency preparedness and response
4.5. Checking
4.5.1. Monitoring and measurement
4.5.2. Evaluation of compliance
4.5.3. Non-conformity, corrective action, and preventive action
4.5.4. Control of records
4.5.5. System audit
4.6. Environmental management review

Source: www.iso.org (last accessed in March 2013). Reproduced with permission.

DISCUSSION FORUM

- Explain how safety and maintenance are interconnected.
- Discuss ISO 14001 QMS in small groups.
- Discuss OHSAS 18001 in small groups.

HUMAN RESOURCE MANAGEMENT

Human resource management (HRM) is that part of the management process, which is concerned with the management of human resources in an organization. HRM is a process of bringing people and the organization together with a common purpose. HRM is mainly concerned with effective management of human resources, which is the most important asset of an organization. All aspects of enterprise activities are determined by the competence, motivation, and general effectiveness of its workforce. Of all the tasks of management, managing the human resource is the central and most important task because all depends on how well it is done.

The dynamic business environment poses lots of challenges to HR managers. The challenges arise due to globalization, development in technology, demographic changes, and continuous change in the business environment. The challenge of HR managers today is to recognize talent and nurture it carefully to achieve significant productivity gains over a period of time. Cross-cultural and cross-border mingling has resulted in the creation of a new class of people—global citizens with global attitudes, tastes, and networks. It is in managing these human assets that the HR manager's capabilities are tested because of the following reasons:

- **Diversity in workforce:** Human resources are highly diversified as they consist of individuals from a borderless world with many and varied personalities, genders, races, ethnicities, emotions, values, attitudes, motives, and modes of thought.
- **Managing knowledgeable workers:** Knowledge has become a direct competitive advantage for technology-driven companies and professional-service companies. Such companies will become successful if they can attract, nurture, compensate, and retain talent.
- **Women workforce:** Women employees today constitute a major share of the workforce. The rights of working women need to be considered by providing a safe and secure environment where women can work with dignity.
- **Change management:** HR mangers are required to have a thorough knowledge of organizational intricacies and complexities. They need to impart continuous education to employees regarding the changes and challenges facing the macro and microenvironments through small booklets, video films, and lectures. The ultimate goal of every HR manager is to develop a strong linkage between the employee and the enterprise to promote employee engagement at the workplace.
- **Improve quality of life:** The basic approach to HRM is to perceive the enterprise in its totality. It has to support the work–life balance of employees working in the enterprise and improve the quality of life of human resources in the enterprise.

With businesses going global, competition becoming intense, and rapid advancement in technology, HRM has emerged as a major function in an organization. The HR role has changed from a supportive to a strategic one. Therefore, HRM has received tremendous attention in recent years. The HR role has undergone substantial change from traditional personnel management to a human resource approach. HR professionals need to perceive the organization in its totality. The HR manager needs to convert organizational strategy into results and build organizations to create value, manage talent, and play the key role of a change agent to make things happen better, faster, and cheaper through an adroit handling of human resources.

HRM Policy

HRM policies are systems of codified decisions, established by an organization, to support HR functions. HRM policy is defined as, "a set of proposals and actions that act as a reference point for managers in their dealings with employees." The establishment of a HRM policy enables an organization to be clear with employees regarding: the nature of the organization; what the organization expects from them; what they should expect from the organization; how policies and procedures work; what are acceptable and unacceptable behaviour; and the consequences of unacceptable behaviour. HRM policies can also be very effective at supporting and building the desired organizational culture.

Functions of HRM

The basic objective of HRM is to ensure the availability of competent employees to work positively towards the realisation of organizational objectives. The success of an organization depends on the accomplishment of organizational objectives. The functions of HRM can be broadly classified into two categories: managerial functions and operative functions

- **Managerial functions:** The five important managerial functions of HRM in an organization are planning, organizing, staffing, directing, and controlling. Planning is a course of action required to achieve organizational objectives. For an HR manager, planning involves forecasting the quantity and quality of the workforce required. An HR manager needs to formulate plans to fill job vacancies by recruitment and selection and conduct training. Organizing refers to developing an organizational structure, defining and allocating roles and responsibilities, delegating authority, and making the workforce accountable as and when required.

Staffing involves filling up the existing vacancies with the right quantity and the right quality of people at the right time. Directing function refers to leading, guiding, and motivating the employees of the organization for accomplishing organizational objectives. Controlling helps an HR manager to evaluate the performance of the HR department. The controlling function refers to reviewing organizational plans to identify deviations and to take corrective and preventive measures to overcome deviations. Some examples of controlling are: auditing training programmes, analysing labour turnover records, and conducting exit interviews.

- **Operative functions:** The operative functions of HRM are: human resource planning (HRP), recruitment and selection, placement and induction, training and development, compensation, performance appraisal, health and safety, industrial relations, and managing exit. HRP refers to the process of determining the present and future staffing requirements of the organization. HRP is the process of analysing and identifying the need and availability of human resources in order to meet enterprise objectives. It is the process by which the management determines how an organization should move from its current manpower position to its desired manpower position. The various steps involved in the HRP process are: organizational environment scanning, formulation of organizational objectives and policies, demand forecasting, supply forecasting, human resource programming and implementation, and HR controlling. Recruitment is the process of searching for and inviting applications from prospective employees. Selection involves choosing the best candidate and appointing them for the required job. It mainly deals with the matching of employee specifications with job requirements. New employees in the organization are also given induction and orientation to make then acquainted with the new environment. Training and development deals with providing training to new employees based on present and future job requirements. It also deals with employees' career planning, retention, and development.

WORLD OF ENTREPRENEURS 13.4 Google—A Great Place to Work

According to Robert Levering, co-founder, the Great Place to Work® Institute, "A great place to work is one in which you trust the people you work for, have pride in what you do, and enjoy the people you work with." Great workplaces are built through the day-to-day relationships that employees experience and not from a checklist of programmes and benefits. A great place to work adopts a "giftwork" approach that doesn't change the way an organization conducts business. The giftwork framework includes nine key action areas that contribute to creating a great workplace. These key action areas have been identified as inspiring, speaking, listening, thanking, developing, caring, hiring, celebrating, and sharing in the workplace.

The *Economic Times* and the Great Place to Work Institute® collaborated to find the best workplaces in India for 2012. The study was carried out as per the methodology followed by the Great Place to Work Institute® in 49 countries. More than 600 companies signed up for the survey of which 514 companies met the eligibility criteria. More than 80,000 employees participated in the survey. Google India was selected as the "Best Company to Work for" in 2012. The top 10 companies in the order of ranking are Google India, Intel Technology India, NTPC, MakeMyTrip India, Forbes Marshall, American Express India, Marriott Hotels India, Intuit Technologies Services, Qualcomm India, and NIIT. As per the survey, 75 per cent of employees in the companies surveyed are below 35 years of age and their views about the workplace culture are significantly less positive than employees above 45 years of age. Only 20 per cent of employees, on an average, have worked in the same organization for more than five years. There is a slow but gradual improvement in employee perception as one stays longer in an organization.

Sources: wwwgreatplacetowork.in (last accessed in March 2013) and http://economictimes.indiatimes.com/best-companies-to-work-for-2012-how-they-stack-up/articleshow/14803879.cms (last accessed in March 2013).

Compensation is the process of providing adequate, equitable, and fair remuneration to employees. It deals with job evaluation, wage and salary administration, incentives, bonus, fringe benefits, and social security measures among others. Performance appraisal mainly aims at evaluating the performance of employees and developing them. The results of the evaluation are used for identifying training and development needs and taking decisions regarding promotions and compensation. Health and safety refers to providing a safe and healthy working environment to the workforce to maintain efficiency and effectiveness at the workplace. It also includes motivating the workforce by providing various welfare services such as a cafeteria, group insurance, a fitness centre, and infrastructure for recreational facilities at the workplace. Industrial relations mainly aim at maintaining peace and harmony in the workplace. This deals with avoiding industrial conflicts and improving workers' participation in management by addressing the problems and grievances of employees. Managing exit deals with conducting exit interviews with retired employees and employees leaving the enterprise. This helps in identifying causes and taking corrective measures, if required, to decrease the employee turnover. This responsibility also deals with ensuring that the employees leaving the organization get their benefits on time.

CHECKLIST FOR ENTREPRENEURS 13.5 ✓ Best Workplace Practices

The following best practices improve profitability and productivity and lower attrition:

- Arrange an induction programme for new employees to provide them with information about the organization. Create a culture where you clearly state the vision, mission, values, policy, and standards, and state exactly what is expected from employees. Encourage the employee to ask questions to clarify doubts.
- Find the right people possessing the required skill and pay them appropriately. Recognize talent and provide the opportunity to use it. Involve people by asking their opinion and listening to their advice and feedback, and provide an environment that is open for innovation and improvements.
- Design good appraisal systems and give positive and constructive feedback. Establish a reward and recognition system. Develop promotional opportunities for all the employees.
- Institute training and development programmes. Allocate sufficient funds for training and development.
- Implement positive work environment policies, such as flexible working arrangements, fun at work, systematic career development, and work-life balance. Ensure that the employee takes ownership of the task assigned and feels pride in their contribution.

SNAPSHOT

- Human resources are one of the most vital resources for any organization to support its various critical functions.
- The functions of HRM can be broadly classified into two categories: managerial functions and operative functions.

DISCUSSION FORUM

- "People are an organization's most valuable asset." Comment.
- Discuss the importance of human resource policies in an organization.

WORLD OF ENTREPRENEURS 13.6 Employees First, Customers Second

Employees First, Customers Second is a bestselling business book written by Vineet Nayar, the CEO of HCL Technologies. In the book published in 2010, Nayar describes his revolutionary philosophy of configuring and managing an enterprise by focusing on its value creators (frontline employees) to achieve remarkable growth and profits.

HCL Technologies Ltd (HCLT) is one of India's fastest-growing global information technology services companies. Vineet Nayar joined HCL in 1985 and became the CEO in 2007. He led a remarkable turnaround in the company over the next five years.

The book discusses Nayar's experiences leading HCL Technologies, and its turnaround from a $70 crore company that was losing market share to a $200 crore company at the forefront of its business. Nayar provides a clear and frank discussion of the issues he faced, his personal thought processes, and his learning journey during the transformation. The main factor behind the turnaround was Nayar's belief that employees are the biggest assets of an organization. Therefore, companies should strive for both employee satisfaction as well as customer satisfaction.

Nayar recognized that the asset base of an organization is increasingly coming to reside in the talent and creativity of its employees. He provides a new configuration of approaches putting employees first to create a new style of organization. He provides tried and tested tools that are helpful for understanding what you can do to change your enterprise. The main tools included in the book are value zone, mirror/mirror, transparent zone, zero tickets, and true 360-degree evaluation and feedback.

HCL Technologies has been recognized around the world for its innovative and transformative management practices. In 2009, HCLT was named the best employer in India and one of the top twenty-five best employers in Asia by Hewitt Associates. *BusinessWeek* has also listed HCLT as one of the five emerging companies in the world to watch out for.

Source: Nayar, Vineet (2010). *Employees First, Customers Second: Turning Conventional Management Upside Down.* Boston, Massachusetts: HBP.

INDUSTRIAL RELATIONS

Industrial relations constitute one of the most delicate and complex problems of modern industrial society. The term "industrial relations" commonly denotes "employee–employer relations." According to J. T. Dunlop, "Industrial relations is the complex interrelations among managers, workers, and agencies of the government." According to Dale Yoder, "Industrial relations is the process of management dealing with one or more unions with a view to negotiate and subsequently administer collective bargaining agreements or labour contracts."

The scope of industrial relations includes all aspects of relationships such as bringing about cordial and healthy labour–management relations, creating industrial peace, and developing industrial democracy. Healthy industrial relations are vital for the survival and growth of the business enterprise. Harmonious industrial relations are a key to the progress and success of the enterprise as this establishes industrial democracy, contributes to economic growth and development, improves the morale of the workforce, ensures optimum use of scarce resources, discourages unfair practices on the part of both management and unions, prompts enactment of sound labour legislation, and helps the workforce to adjust themselves to change easily and quickly.

Industrial progress is not possible without the cooperation of the workforce. Therefore, it is necessary to create and maintain good relations between employees (workforce) and employers (management). The HR manager directs the organization's employee-relations function. They develop employee-relations policies and ensure consistent application of company policies and procedures. They are also responsible for employee dispute resolution procedures and taking appropriate action to correct any employee-relations issues. Successful industrial relations involve striking a balance of interests. From the employer's point of view, it is about the ability to plan for the future, to make profits for its shareholders, and to keep its employees engaged. From the employee's point of view, it is about securing a better quality of work and life.

The objectives of industrial relations are to bring better understanding and cooperation between employers and employees; to establish an effective communication channel between employer and employee; to avoid industrial conflicts and to maintain harmonious relations; to safeguard the interests of both employer and employee and to ensure constructive contribution of trade unions; to ensure employees' participation in decision making; to ensure a better working environment, living conditions, reasonable wages, and to increase the morale and discipline of the workforce; to work for employee development; and to establish and maintain industrial democracy.

EMPLOYEE ENGAGEMENT

Employee engagement is the level of commitment and involvement that employees have towards their organization and its values. An engaged employee works with colleagues to improve performance within the job for the benefit of the organization. According to the consulting organization Gallup[11], there are three different categories of employee engagement: (1) "Engaged" employees are builders. They use their talents and strengths effectively at work every day to deliver high levels of performance consistently. (2) "Not Engaged" employees tend to concentrate on tasks rather than the goals. (3) "Actively Disengaged" employees sow seeds of negativity in the organization and can cause great damage to the functioning of the enterprise.

Employee engagement is critical to any organization that seeks to retain valued employees. Employee engagement levels have a direct impact on an employee's performance and on the company's bottom line. Engaged employees will stay with the company, create a sense of loyalty, and contribute to the business results. They provide a high-energy working environment, build passion, commitment, and align with the organization's strategies and goals. Engaged employees are much more likely to be satisfied in their positions, remain with the company, be promoted, and strive for higher levels of performance. A highly engaged employee will consistently deliver beyond expectations. Therefore, it is necessary to know the level of employee engagement. Gallup provides an approach to measure current level of employee engagement and improve employee engagement in enterprises. The approach is a continuous process of measuring, analysing, defining, and implementing and comprises four steps.

- **Step 1**—deals with listening to employees on a continuous basis to understand them.
- **Step 2**— deals with measuring current level of employee engagement. Gallup has developed a twelve-question survey that identifies strong feelings of employee engagement.
- **Step 3**—identifies the problem areas which lead to disengaged employees.
- **Step 4**— deals with taking action to improve employee engagement by acting upon the problem areas. Employee engagement should be a continuous process of learning, improvement, measurement, and action. Raising and maintaining employee engagement requires a good blend of time, effort, commitment, and investment at the enterprise level.

The factors that lead to employee engagements are: career development, respectful treatment of employees, effective communication, employee empowerment, equal opportunities and fair treatment, performance appraisal, proper pay system, benefits and compensation, health, safety, and welfare measures, job satisfaction, and the quality of life.

An engaged employee is aware of the business context, and works with associates to improve performance within the job for the benefit of the enterprise. This requires a two-way relationship between employer and employee. The organization should construct a sincere and structured approach for developing and nurturing employee engagement. Thus, employee engagement is a measure that determines the employer–employee relationship.

DISCUSSION FORUM

- What do you mean by industrial relations?
- Discuss the step-by-step approach used for measuring employee engagement using the "Gallup survey" method in small groups.

SNAPSHOT

- The term industrial relations commonly denote employer–employee relations.
- Employee engagement is the level of commitment and involvement an employee has towards the organization and its values. It is critical to any organization that seeks to retain valuable employees.

LABOUR LAWS

Ignorance of law cannot be given as an excuse in a court of law. Therefore, every human resource manager should have a thorough knowledge of labour laws. Many human resource functions are based on labour laws and should be implemented in accordance with them. The HR manager's knowledge of labour laws can resolve conflicts in the organization and can save time and money by preventing the disgruntled employee from approaching the labour courts. Knowledge of labour laws is very important and supportive in improving employer–employee relations in enterprises. The various labour laws[12] which are in force in India are mentioned below:

- Indian Factories Act, 1948
- Payment of Wages Act, 1936
- Minimum Wages Act, 1948
- Payment of Bonus Act, 1965
- Industrial Employment Act, 1946
- Industrial Disputes Act,1947 (82 and 84)
- Trade Unions Act, 1926
- Child Labour Act, 1986
- The Equal Remuneration Act, 1976
- Sexual Harassment of Women at Their Work Place (Prevention) Act, 2003

CHECKLIST FOR ENTREPRENEURS 13.7 — Activites to Improve Employee Engagement

- Conduct an induction programme for new employees.
- Have a daily column, written by the CEO, on the intranet with company announcements, programmes, etc.
- Establish employee suggestion systems and quality circles to improve employee participation in decision making.
- Provide online real-time tracking of company progress. Employees can view company progress towards established goals.
- Circulate an internal magazine/newsletter on the intranet recognizing employees for significant business achievements.
- Establish monthly and annual awards for employees.
- Conduct leadership development and team-building activities.
- Establish problem-solving committees.
- Celebrate every employee's birthday and arrange to show a movie at intervals of two to three months.
- Conduct social activities like family get-togethers, celebrations of festivals, and arrange picnics at regular intervals.
- Conduct soft-skills training programmes and outbound training programmes as well as management development programmes.
- Appoint emergency management and disaster management teams.
- Provide indoor games as well as outdoor games facilities.

- Laws relating to environment and pollution control—Water Act, 1974; Air Act, 1981; and Environment Act, 1986.

The various social security laws are as follows:

- Workmen's Compensation Act, 1923
- Employees' State Insurance (ESI) Act, 1948
- Employees' Provident Fund (EPF) Act and Family Pension Fund Act, 1952
- Payment of Gratuity Act, 1972
- Maternity Benefit Act, 1961
- Miscellaneous legislation—The Mines Act, 1952; The Plantations Labour Act, 1951; The Contract Labour Act, 1970

Indian Factories Act, 1948

This law regulates the conditions of work in factories and establishments and extends to the whole of India and applies to every factory. The aim and object of the Act is to safeguard the interests of workers and protect them from exploitation. A factory is a premise employing 10 or more workers engaged in a manufacturing process with the aid of power, and where 20 or more workers work without the aid of power. The Act prescribes certain standards with regard to safety, health, welfare, and working hours, apart from other provisions.

The enterprise covered by this Act must have the approval of the chief inspector of factories. Registration and licensing is also required on payment of the prescribed fees. According to the Act, a worker (adult) should not be allowed to work in a factory for more than 48 hours in any week and not more than nine hours in any day. The period of work for workers in a factory each day shall be so fixed that no period shall exceed five hours. The worker should have one holiday for a whole day in a week. In case of overtime work, the worker is entitled to wages at the rate of twice his ordinary rate of wages. Workers should be given annual leave with wages if they work for 240 days or more in a year, to be calculated at the rate of one day for every 20 days of work. Women are allowed to work between 6 a.m and 7 p.m and not allowed to work during the night hours from between 10 p.m. and 5 a.m.

The Act makes detailed provisions with regard to various matters relating to the health, safety, and welfare of the workers. The provisions require HR managers to maintain inspection staff and to make provision for maintenance of health, cleanliness, prevention of accidents, and overcrowding and to provide amenities such as lighting, ventilation, drinking water, latrine, urinals, and spittoons to workers. The Act was amended in 1987.

Payment of Wages Act, 1936

The Act extends to the whole of India and is applicable only to "certain classes" of persons engaged in factories and industries drawing an average wage of not more than ₹1,600 per month. It applies to the payment of wages to persons employed in any factory, railways, or industrial establishments and was enacted for the purpose of safeguarding the wages of employees under certain conditions laid down in the Act.

The Act ensures regularity of payment, payment in legal tender, prevention of arbitrary deductions, restrictions of employers to impose fines, and provides remedy to the workers. According to the Act, every employer is responsible for the payment of wages to persons employed by him. The person responsible for the payment of wages shall fix the wage periods in respect of which wages shall be payable. Such period shall not exceed one month. The Act requires that all wages shall be paid in current currency. After obtaining a written authorization of the employee, wages may be paid by cheque or by crediting his/her wages to a bank account.

The Act requires the employer to display an abstract of the Act and rules made in a prominent place in the establishment. The employer shall pay workmen their wages regularly and in time as required under the Act. The employer shall not make any unauthorized deductions and impose fines only for permissible acts and omissions. The employer has to maintain a register with the personnel responsible for the payment of wages, furnishing details about persons employed, the work performed by them, the wages paid to them, fines imposed, and realisations made. Every employer who contravenes any provision of this Act shall be punishable with a fine extending up to ₹500.

Minimum Wages Act, 1948

The Minimum Wages Act extends to the whole of India. The minimum wage, as the name itself implies, is a prescribed wage by the government in respect of scheduled employments. It represents the level below which wages cannot be allowed to drop. The Act prescribes a minimum time rate; a minimum piece rate; a guaranteed time rate; and an overtime rate for the fixation of wages. The minimum rate of wages fixed or revised may consist of basic rate and cost of living allowance, or a basic rate with or without the cost of living allowances, and the cash value of the concession in respect of essential commodities supplied at a concessional rate or an all-inclusive rate.

All establishments covered by the Act are required to maintain a register of wages and muster roll in the prescribed manner. It shall give particulars of employees; the work performed by them; the wages paid to them; overtime work; the minimum rates of wages; gross wages; deductions made and wages actually paid; and the receipt given by them. The Act authorizes the government to appoint inspectors and other authorities to hear and decide claims related to wages. The Act also provides the procedures for dealing with the violation of provisions of the Act and for imposing penalties for offences committed under this Act.

Payment of Bonus Act, 1965

The Payment of Bonus Act, 1965, is the principal Act for the payment of bonus to employees, which was enacted with the objective of rewarding employees for their good performance. The bonus is payment made to employees out of the profits earned by the employers, over and above the remuneration that they get. The Act is a step forward to share prosperity reflected by the profits earned by the establishment. This Act also extends to whole of India. Every employee shall be entitled to a bonus in a given accounting year by the provisions of the Act, provided he/she has worked in the establishment for not less than thirty days in that year.

Bonus is not an ex-gratia payment but the statutory right of the employee. The Act prescribes the formula for calculating bonus; payment of minimum and maximum bonus; time-limit for payment of bonus; eligibility of employee for bonus payments; penalty for offences; and the redressal mechanism. It is a statutory obligation on the part of the employer to maintain a register in the prescribed form showing respectively the computation of the allocable surplus and the disbursement of the bonus to the employees and other accounts as prescribed under the Act. Any employer who contravenes the provision of the Act shall be liable for punishment.

Industrial Employment Act, 1946

This is a Central Act and extends to the whole of India. The Act is applicable to every industrial establishment wherein 100 or more employees are employed; or wherein 100 or more employees were employed on any day of the preceding 12 months; and the establishment of a contractor who employs workmen in order to fulfill a contract with the owner of an industrial establishment. The Act provides uniformity of the terms of employment in respect of all employees belonging to the same category and discharging the same or similar work in an industrial establishment.

The Act clearly states that the standing orders shall deal with the conditions of employment of workers in an industrial establishment. The standing orders are the rules relating to the terms and conditions of employment with respect to the employer and the employee. The Act makes provision for the certification of standing orders from the competent authority, which constitutes the statutory terms and conditions of employment in industrial undertakings. The purpose of the standing orders is to create an attitude among both the parties to maintain proper discipline and harmony, and achieve higher productivity by providing satisfactory employment and working conditions.

It is the obligation of all employers covered by this Act to define precisely the conditions of employment under them, which will govern relations between the employer and the employees and to make the said conditions known to all the employees. This Act requires the employers to define the conditions of service in their establishments and to reduce them to writing and to get them compulsorily certified with a view to avoiding unnecessary industrial disputes. If an employer acts in contravention of the standing orders certified, he is punishable with a fine as specified in the Act.

The objectives of the Act are to define, with sufficient precision, the principal conditions of employment in industrial establishments and to make the conditions known to the workforce employed by them; to specify the rights, duties, and responsibilities of both the employers and the employees; and to regulate the code of conduct of the employers and employees in order to maintain and improve good relations.

Industrial Disputes Act, 1947 (82 and 84)

The law relating to industrial relations in India is contained in the Industrial Disputes Act of 1947. This is an Act to make provision for the investigation and settlement of industrial disputes and for certain other purposes. This is a special legislation, which applies to workmen drawing wages not exceeding a specified amount per month and which governs the service conditions of such persons. The purpose of this Act is to harmonize the relations between the employer and the workmen; to provide a suitable machinery for investigation and settlement of industrial disputes between employers and employees; to prevent illegal strikes and lockouts; to give the workmen the right to collective bargaining; and to provide relief to workmen in cases of wrongful dismissals.

An "industrial dispute" means any dispute or difference between employers and employees; between employers and workmen; or between workmen and workmen with a right of representation by a registered trade union or by an association of employers. The disputes may be connected with the employment or non-employment, or terms of employment, or the conditions of labour of any person. The Act provides the mechanics of dispute resolution and sets up the necessary structure so as to create a congenial climate.

The Act contains 40 sections, which have been grouped into seven chapters. Chapter I deals with title, extent, commencement, and definitions. Chapter II provides the details of the various authorities under the Act and how they are constituted. Chapter III relates the reference of disputes to the various authorities, their cancellation, amendment, or modification, and voluntary reference by parties of disputes to arbitration. Chapter IV deals with the procedures, powers, and duties of authorities and the procedure to be adopted in dealing with industrial disputes. Chapter V and V-A deal with strikes, lockouts, their prohibition, layoffs, compensation, retrenchment, and re-employment of retrenched workers. Chapter V-B deals with closing down of establishments and V-C deals with unfair labour practices. Chapter VI deals with penalties for illegal strikes and lockouts, instigation, breach of settlement, and other offences. Chapter VII deals with miscellaneous provisions.

The Act contains five schedules. Schedule I specifies the industries which may be declared to be public utility services; Schedule II deals with matters within the jurisdiction of labour courts; Schedule III deals with matters within the jurisdiction of industrial tribunals; Schedule IV mentions the conditions of service for change of which notice is to be given; and Schedule V deals with unfair labour practices.

The International Labour Organization (ILO) is an institution which deals with international labour problems. It is a tripartite body consisting of representatives of employers, labour, and the government. The ILO consists of three principal organs, namely, the international conference, the governing body, and the international labour office. The three constituents are; namely, the government that finances it, the workers for whose benefit it is created, and the employers who share responsibility for the welfare of the workers. The main objective of the ILO is to promote worldwide respect for the freedom and dignity of the working person and to create conditions in which that freedom and dignity can be more fully and effectively enjoyed.

Trade Unions Act, 1926

Trade unions in India are governed by the Trade Unions Act, 1926, which extends to whole of India. A trade union is an organization of workers acting collectively who seek to protect and promote their mutual interests through collective bargaining. A trade union is an association of either employees or employers or of independent workers. It is formed for the purpose of maintaining and improving the conditions of their working lives such as wages and salaries, working conditions, discipline, personnel policies, welfare, and harmonious relations between the employees and employer for industrial peace.

The Trade Unions Act, 1926, legalizes the formation of trade unions by allowing employees to form trade unions and get them registered. Registration provides legal status to the trade union and it becomes a corporate body. The Act lays down the obligations of a registered trade union and fixes the rights and liabilities of registered trade unions. Trade unions can hold moveable and immoveable property and can enter into contracts. They can sue and can be sued.

The Employers' Organization (EO) is a formal group of employers set up to defend, represent, or advise affiliated employers and to strengthen their position in society at large with respect to labour matters as distinct from economic matters. The EO is formed with the following main objectives: to develop healthy and stable industrial relations; to promote collective bargaining at different levels; to bring a unified employers' viewpoint to bear upon the issues of industrial relations to the government in a concerted manner; and to represent in the meetings of the Indian Labour conference (ILC) and the Standing Labour Committee (SLC) boards. Both ILC and SLC play a vital role in shaping the industrial relation system in India. The All-India Organization of Employers (AIOE) was set up in 1953. The International Organization of Employers (IOE) founded in 1920 with headquarters in Geneva has a membership of employers' associations from over 100 countries.

Child Labour Act, 1986

The Child Labour (Prohibition and Regulation) Act, 1986, extends to the whole of India and was amended in 1988. The Act outlines where and how children can work and where they cannot. The Act defines a child as any person who has not completed his fourteenth year of age. The Act is applicable to all establishments such as workshops, farms, residential hotels, restaurants, eating houses, theatres, or other places of public amusement where child labour is largely employed. The Act calls for the establishment of a Child Labour Technical Advisory Committee (CLTAC).

The Act is divided into four parts. Part I is preliminary and it gives the title and definitions. Part II gives the prohibition of employment of children in certain occupations and processes. Part II of the Act prohibits children from working in any occupation listed in Part A of the schedule; for example, construction works on the railway or anywhere near the track and plastic factories. The Act also prohibits children from working in places where certain processes are being undertaken, as listed in Part B of the schedule; for example, beedi making, tanning, brick kilns, and soap manufacture.

Part III regulates the conditions of work of children. It outlines the conditions in which children may work in occupation/processes not listed in the schedule. Children are not permitted to work for more than six-hour stretches including their break interval and cannot work between 7 p.m and 8 a.m. Children are not allowed to work overtime or work in more than one place in a given day. A child is entitled to a holiday from work every week. The employer is required to keep a register of all children and send a notification to an inspector about a child working in their establishment. The rules and working environment of the establishment where the child is working shall be set by the appropriate government. Part IV provides miscellaneous conditions such as penalties and procedures relating to offences.

The Equal Remuneration Act, 1976

The objective of the Act is to provide for the payment of equal remuneration to men and women workers and for the prevention of discrimination, on grounds of sex, against women in employment. It also seeks to provide for increasing opportunities for women in specified employments. It is the duty of the employer to pay equal remuneration to men and women workers for the same work or work of a similar nature. The Act prohibits discrimination against women not only in recruitment but also in relation to the conditions of service subsequent to employment, such as promotions, training, and transfers. The Act provides guidelines relating to penalties for the violation of its provisions.

Sexual Harassment of Women at Their Workplace (Prevention) Act, 2003

Sexual harassment is a legal term, created for the purpose of ending harassment and discrimination against women in the workplace. The Act extends to the whole of India. Sexual harassment includes such unwelcome sexually determined behaviour (whether directly or by implication) as physical contact and advances; a demand or request for sexual favours; sexually coloured remarks; showing pornography; and any other unwelcome physical, verbal, or non-verbal conduct of a sexual nature. Here the workplace shall include an employed woman visiting premises in connection with work. The Act is applicable to all government offices, the private sector, and the unorganized sector. Every woman, who draws a regular salary, receives an honorarium, or works in a voluntary capacity is covered under this Act.

A working woman has the right to work with dignity in a safe and secure environment. The employer should prioritize the prevention of sexual harassment and formulate a policy to demonstrate zero tolerance towards sexual harassment and deter all such acts. The employer shall provide procedures for resolution, settlement, and prosecution of instances of sexual harassment. All workplaces shall have a complaints committee for prevention and redressal of sexual harassment. The complaints committee shall have a woman as the chairperson, fifty per cent women members, and an NGO or external expert familiar with and oriented towards sexual harassment as an issue. The complaints committee members shall be accessible, approachable, committed, sensitive, and understanding.

Laws Relating to Environment and Pollution Control

Water Act, 1974 The objective of the Water (Prevention and Control of Pollution) Act, 1974, is to prevent and control water pollution and to maintain the wholesomeness of water. The Act requires the establishment of a Central Pollution Control Board and State Pollution Control Boards to monitor and enforce the regulations. Sections 3–12 of the Act provide information on the Board such as its composition and terms and conditions of service of members. The Board advises the government on matters related to the prevention and control of water pollution. The Board develops the policy and sets the standards and penalties for non-compliance for polluting bodies.

Air Act, 1981 The objective of the Air (Prevention and Control of Pollution) Act, 1981, is to provide for the prevention, control, and abatement of air pollution for the establishment. The Act requires the establishment of central and state boards to monitor and enforce regulations. The Act extends to the whole of India. The Act comprises 54 sections grouped into seven chapters. Chapter I is preliminary and provides a short title, extent, and commencement of the Act with definitions. Chapter II provides general powers and guidelines for the Central Government for the establishment of central and state boards for the prevention and control of air pollution. Chapter III outlines the powers and functions of the boards. Chapter IV provides guidelines for the prevention and control of air pollution. Chapter V provides the method of governance of the board, for example, the funding to be provided to the board and accounts and audit of the board. Chapter VI provides the penalties to be levied on establishments for the non-compliance of the standards set by the board. Chapter VII provides miscellaneous provisions.

The Environment Act, 1986 The Environment (Protection) Act, 1986, extends to the whole of India. The environment includes water, air, land (soil), and the inter-relationship which exists among water, air, land, human beings, other living creatures, plants, and microorganisms. No industrial project can be set up or expanded unless it has been accorded environmental clearance by the Central or State Government (pollution control board). The Act comprises 26 sections and has been divided into four chapters: preliminary; general powers of the Central Government; prevention, control, and abatement of environmental pollution; and miscellaneous provisions.

The Act empowers the Central Government to take all appropriate measures to prevent and control pollution and to establish effective machinery for the purpose of protecting and improving the quality of the environment and preventing, controlling, and abating environmental pollution. The Central Government is empowered to collect samples of air, water, soil, or other substances as evidence of the offences under the Environment Protection Act, 1986. The concerned person has to handle the hazardous substances according to the procedure of the Act. The Central Government is empowered to enter and inspect any establishment. The Act also authorizes the pollution control boards to issue directions for the operation or process, prohibition, closure, or regulation of any industry. The Act consists of and deals with more stringent penal provisions.

Social Security Laws

Workmen's Compensation Act, 1923 The passing of the Workmen's Compensation Act, 1923, was the first step towards ensuring the social security of workmen. The objective of this Act is to impose an obligation upon employers to pay compensation for workmen in cases of industrial accidents incurred in the course of employment. The Act enables a worker to get compensation irrespective of his/her negligence. It provides guidelines on the various amounts payable in case of an accident depending upon the type and extent of injury. An injured worker may either file a civil suit for damages against the employer or claim compensation under the Workmen's Compensation Act, 1923.

The Act comprises 32 sections. The main outline of the Act consists of the scope and coverage of the Act; definitions; rules regarding workmen's compensation and employer's liability for compensation; defenses available to employers; guidelines for calculation of the amount of compensation; mode of distribution of compensation; notice and claim of compensation; enforcement of the Act by appointment of commissioners by the state government and their powers; and the rule-making powers of state governments and the Central Government.

Employees' State Insurance (ESI) Act, 1948 The Employees' State Insurance (ESI) Act was enacted with the objective of introducing a scheme of health insurance for industrial workers. The Act confers benefits on employees against sickness, maternity, and employment injury. Under the Act, employees will receive medical relief, cash benefits, maternity benefits, pension to dependents of deceased workers, and compensation for fatal or other injuries and diseases. The scope of coverage and the benefits provided under the Employees' State Insurance Act, 1948, are much more liberal than those available to a workman under the Workmen's Compensation Act, 1923.

The Act extends to the whole of India. It applies to all the factories including government factories (excluding seasonal factories), which employ ten or more employees and carry on a manufacturing process with the aid of power and 20 employees where manufacturing process is carried out without the aid of power. The Act also applies to shops and establishments. The provisions of the Act are administered by the Employees State Insurance Corporation (ESIC). It comprises members representing employees, employers, the central and state governments, and representatives of Parliament and the medical profession.

The employer should get his factory or establishments registered with the ESIC within 15 days after the Act becomes applicable to it and also obtain the employer's code number. An employee is required to file a declaration form upon employment in the factory or establishment to show that he is covered under the Act. Contributions are raised from covered employees and their employers as a fixed percentage of wages. The contribution is deposited by the employer in cash or by cheque at designated branches of any nationalized bank. The responsibility for payment of all contributions is that of the employer. He also has the right to deduct the employees' share of contribution from employees' wages relating to the period in respect of which the contribution is payable.

Employees covered under the scheme are entitled to various benefits for self and dependants. The various benefits are: medical benefit; sickness benefit; extended sickness benefit; enhanced sickness benefit; maternity benefit; disablement benefit; and dependants benefit. Other benefits covered under the Act are: funeral expenses; vocational rehabilitation; free supply of physical aids and appliances; preventive health care; and medical bonus. The Act also stipulates various obligations of employers and the records to be maintained by him/her for inspection by ESI authorities. Any dispute arising under the ESI Act will be decided by the Employees Insurance Court constituted by the State Government for local areas.

Employees' Provident Fund and Miscellaneous Provisions Act, 1952

This Act is enacted to provide a kind of social security to industrial workers. The social security provided in this Act, however, differs from the security provided to them under the Workmen's Compensation Act or the Employees' State Insurance Act. The objective of the Employees' Provident Fund and Miscellaneous Provisions Act, 1952, is to provide for the institution of provident fund, family pension, and Employees' Deposit Linked Insurance (EDLI) schemes for employees in factories and other establishments.

The Employees' Provident Fund and Miscellaneous Provisions Act mainly provides retirement or old age benefits, such as provident fund, superannuation pension, invalidation pension, family pension, and deposit linked insurance. The Act is applicable to every establishment which is engaged in any one or more of the industries specified in Schedule I of the Act or any activity notified by the Central Government in the Official Gazette and employing 20 or more persons. In case of cinema theatres, the number of employees is five or more. Any person who is employed for work in an establishment or employed through a contractor in or in connection with the work of an establishment is eligible for the benefit. Employees eligible for these schemes are those whose maximum pay limit is ₹6,500 per month.

The employer shall pay the contribution payable to the EPF, EDLI, and the Employees' Pension Fund in respect of the member of the Employees' Pension Fund employed by him directly or through a contractor. The principal employer is responsible to pay the contribution payable to the EPF, EDLI, and the Employees' Pension Fund by himself in respect of the employees directly employed by him and also in respect of the employees employed by or through a contractor.

Payment of Gratuity Act, 1972

The main purpose and concept of gratuity is to help workers after retirement, whether the retirement is a result of the rules of superannuation, or physical disability, or impairment of a vital part of the body. Gratuity is an amount given freely to recognize the service that the employee has rendered to the organization for more than five years.

The Act is applicable to every factory (as defined in the Factories Act), mine, oilfield, plantation, port, and railway; every shop or establishment to which the Shops and Establishment Act of a state applies in which ten or more persons are employed at any time during the year end; and any establishment employing ten or more persons and may be notified by the Central Government. Any employee shall be said to be in continuous service even if his/her service in interrupted by way of sickness, accident, leave, absence from duty without leave, leave with full wage, temporary disablement, laid-off period, and maternity leave for 12 weeks (in case of females). The latest amendment to the Act was made in 1984.

The appropriate government may, by notification, appoint any officer to be a controlling authority, who shall be responsible for the administration of this Act and different controlling authorities may be appointed for different areas. Gratuity shall be payable to an employee on the termination of his employment after he has rendered continuous service for not less than five years on his superannuation; on his retirement or resignation; and on his death or disablement due to accident or disease. The completion of service is not necessary where the termination of the employment of any employee is due to death or disablement. In case of death of an employee, gratuity is payable to his/her nominee or to his/her heirs as may be prescribed. The calculation of gratuity is given below:

$$\text{Gratuity} = \frac{\text{Monthly salary} \times 15 \times \text{Number of years of service}}{26}$$

where,

Monthly salary = Last monthly salary drawn by the employee
26 = Total number of working days in a month
15 = Number of days in half a month

Maternity Benefit Act, 1961

The Act was passed to regulate the employment of women in certain establishments for certain periods before and after childbirth and to provide for maternity benefit and certain other benefits. The latest amendment to the Act was made in 1988. It extends to the whole of India and applies to: every factory, mine, plantation, establishment for the exhibition of equestrian, acrobatic, and other performances and to every shop or establishment defined under any law applicable to such establishments in a state in which persons are employed on any day of the preceding twelve months.

A woman shall be entitled to maternity benefit only if she has actually worked in the establishment of the employer for a period of not less than eighty days in the twelve months immediately preceding the date of her expected delivery. The employment of women or work by women is prohibited in any establishment during the six weeks immediately following the day of her delivery or her miscarriage. Every employer shall be liable for the payment of maternity benefit at the rate of the average daily wage for the period of her actual absence, and any period of her actual absence, and any period immediately following the date of delivery and including the actual day of her delivery. In addition to the maternity benefit, every woman shall also be entitled to receive a medical bonus of ₹250 if there is no prenatal confinement, and post-natal care is provided free of charge.

Every employer shall prepare and maintain a muster roll of women entitled for maternity leave in Form A specified in the Act. The maximum period of maternity benefit is 12 weeks of which not more than six weeks shall precede the date of her expected delivery. The Act also provides provisions for leave for miscarriage, leave for illness arising out of pregnancy or delivery, premature birth of the child or miscarriage, and nursing breaks for nursing the child until the child attains the age of 15 months. Any claim due under this Act may be filed to the inspector appointed under Section 14 of the Act. Any appeal against the decision of the Inspector may be made within 30 days to the Deputy Labour Commissioner, who is the appellate authority.

Miscellaneous Legislation

The Mines Act, 1952 This Act applies to all types of mines, including mines of atomic minerals and oil fields. The Act extends to the whole of India, and prescribes safe and satisfactory conditions of work in the mines. The Act was amended in the year 1983. The Act provides that the hours of work of all adult workers, both surface and underground, should not exceed 48 hours a week, and further that no worker will be required or allowed to work for more than nine hours a day above ground, with a time spread of 12 hours. A worker employed above ground is also not allowed to work continuously for more than five hours, unless he/she is given a rest interval of at least half an hour. For workers employed to work underground, their hours of work shall not exceed eight hours a day. The Act also provides provisions for overtime work, employment of adolescents, employment of women, maintenance of a register, leave with wages, health and safety provisions, and penalties.

The Plantations Labour Act, 1951 This Act provides for the welfare of labour and regulates the conditions of service in plantations. The Act applies to any land used or intended to be used for growing tea, coffee, rubber, or cinchona which measures 10.117 hectares or more and on which 15 or more persons are employed on any day of the preceding 12 months. The Act provides for the compulsory registration of plantations and has been amended in 1981. Workers drawing ₹750 per month are covered under the Act. The Act provides provisions for the appointment of a chief inspector and an inspector for its regulation.

The Contract Labour (Regulation and Abolition) Act, 1970 This Act applies to every establishment in which 20 or more workers are employed and to every contractor who employs more than 20 workmen. Though the Act is a central legislation, it is administered both by the central and state governments. The Act has provisions for setting up of advisory boards; registration of establishments; prohibition of employment of contract labour; licensing of contractors; the welfare and health of contract labour; the contractor's obligations and responsibility for payment of wages; the appointment of inspectors; penalties for offences and contraventions; the rights of contract labour; and the rights of principal employers and contractors.

SUMMARY

Operations management is a systematic approach for addressing issues in the transformation process that converts input into useful, revenue-genetrating output. From an operations perspective, there are several important differences and similarities between goods and services. Operations strategy is the process of making appropriate decisions in the operations function on the basis of inputs from the corporate strategy. TQM is an integrated effort designed to improve the quality of performance at every level of the organization. Forecasting is an important planning tool, which helps to estimate future demand. The production system is a system whose function is to convert a set of inputs into a set of desired outputs. Production management refers to the application of management principles to the production function in an enterprise.

The ISO 9000 is a generic set of standards, which enables organizations to build a quality management and assurance system. ISO 14001 provides organizations with the elements for an environmental management system, which can be integrated into other management systems to help enterprises to achieve environmental and economic goals. OHSAS 18000 is the generic name given to a family of international standards developed to provide the framework around which an occupational health and safety management system can effectively be implemented. All these three systems may be integrated in an enterprise in order to achieve goals related to quality, environment, and safety.

Materials management is the process of management which coordinates, supervises, and executes the tasks associated with the flow of materials to, through, and out of an organization in an integrated fashion. It is a systematic approach for the control of materials to, through, and out of an organization throughout its flow cycle. A supply chain includes the chain of entities involved in the planning, procurement, production, and distribution of products and services. A good maintenance programmme enables better planning in these functional areas.

With businesses going global, competition becoming intense, and rapid advancements in technology, HRM has emerged as a major function in any organization. The HR role has changed from a supportive to a strategic one. Human resource management is the process of acquiring, training, appraising, and compensating employees and attending to their labour relations, safety, and fairness concerns. Human resource development (HRD) is the process of improving, moulding, and changing skills, knowledge, creative ability, aptitude, attitude, values, and commitment, based on present and future job and organizational requirements. The basic objective of HRM is to ensure the availability of competent employees to work positively towards the realisation of organizational objectives. The success of an organization depends on the accomplishment of organizational objectives. The functions of HRM can be broadly classified into two categories: managerial functions and operative functions.

The knowledge of labour laws is very important and supportive for improving employer–employee relations in enterprises. The important labour laws are: Indian Factories Act, 1948; Payment of Wages Act, 1936; Minimum Wages Act, 1948; Payment of Bonus Act, 1965; Industrial Employment Act, 1946; Industrial Disputes Act, 1947 (82 and 84); Trade Unions Act, 1926; Child Labour Act, 1986; The Equal Remuneration Act, 1976; Sexual Harassment of Women at Their Workplace (Prevention) Act, 2003. The laws relating to environment and pollution control are: Water Act, 1974; Air Act, 1981; and Environment Act, 1986. The various social security laws are: Workmen's Compensation Act, 1923; Employees' State Insurance (ESI) Act, 1948; Employees' Provident Fund and Miscellaneous Provisions Act, 1952; Payment of Gratuity Act, 1972; Maternity Benefit Act, 1961. Miscellaneous legislation include: The Mines Act, 1952; The Plantations Labour Act, 1951; and The Contract Labour Act, 1970.

KEY TERMS

HR Policy: A set of proposals and actions that act as a reference point for HR managers in their dealings with employees.

HR Strategy: Strategies specific to HR functions form part of the HR strategy.

Human Capital: This refers to the gathered stock of knowledge, skills, expertise, and talent of the workforce that provides long-term advantages to the organization.

Industrial Relations: It is the interrelations among managers, workers, and agencies of the government.

Inventory Control: Finding the optimal combination of products to stock for production or sale in a warehouse or store.

ISO 14000: The series provides organizations with the elements for an environmental management system.

ISO 9000: It is a generic set of standards that enable organizations to build a quality management and assurance system.

Materials Management: It is a systematic approach for the control of materials to, through, and out of an organization throughout its flow cycle.

Occupational Health and Safety (OH&S): It is a cross-disciplinary area concerned with protecting the safety, health, and welfare of employees.

OHSAS 18000: It is the generic name given to a family of international standards developed to provide the framework around which an occupational health and safety management system can effectively be implemented.

Operations Management: It is a systematic approach to addressing issues in the transformation process that converts inputs into useful, revenue-generating outputs.

Overall Equipment Effectiveness (OEE): This is used to assess the performance of TPM. OEE essentially captures six big losses that occur in any organization, which result in reduced effectiveness of equipment use.

Production Management: It refers to the application of management principles to the production function in an enterprise.

Production System: It is a system whose function is to convert a set of inputs into a set of desired outputs.

Productivity: It is the ratio of the output achieved from an activity to the inputs consumed to make that output.

Supply Chain: A supply chain includes the chain of entities involved in the planning, procurement, production, and distribution of products and services.

Total Productive Maintenance (TPM): A company-wide equipment management programme, which emphasizes production operator involvement in equipment maintenance and continuous improvement.

CASE STUDY

HRM at the Aditya Birla Group

The Aditya Birla Group is a USD 3,500 crore conglomerate with operations in 36 countries. The group is anchored by a workforce of over 133,000 employees belonging to 42 different countries. The group's businesses are spread across a swath of industries. Under the leadership of Kumar Mangalam Birla, the group has made 22 acquisitions in 17 years in India and globally.

The broad philosophy of the company is to focus on employee empowerment by promoting organizational trust and meritocracy and providing ample growth opportunities for employees within the group. The Group Human Resources' (Group HR) role is focused on creating stakeholder value through organizational and people capability, in line with the strategy of the group. Group HR is the key process owner, which develops HR policy and provides specialist services and partners with businesses and other functions to realise the group people vision.

The HR policies established at the Aditya Birla Group have helped the organization to demonstrate that it meets the requirements of diversity, ethics, and training. Policies are common at the group level, while execution is tailored to meet the needs of individual businesses. The Group has a multi-pronged recruitment approach. All openings are offered to existing employees via the group intranet. Employees who apply for the openings compete with external candidates for suitability in terms of competency and qualifications. Particular emphasis is made on honouring commitments made during the recruitment process. With mergers and acquisitions becoming commonplace, Group HR often has to deal with the challenges arising out of quick turnaround on turnkey projects and hiring in key positions arising out of acquisitions.

HR managers of the Aditya Birla Group play a significant role in the mergers and acquisition strategy. They assess the HR strengths of both the organizations and strengthen them further. They help top management to assess pension and provident fund, improve the employee morale, manage and unify cultural diversity, and counsel employees. The HR team is also responsible for organizational restructuring, integrating structures, benefit programmes, and seniority. The team establishes career and succession plans, clarifies leadership styles, and cultural issues.

The HR policies of the Aditya Birla Group broadly comprise human resource development (HRD), HR initiatives, and nurturing talent.

HRD: Group HR provides specialist services in the areas of staffing, learning, leadership development, reward and benefits, job analysis and evaluation, performance management, organizational development, and the human resource management system. It also provides desired standards of professional conduct.

HR Initiatives: The HR initiatives are aimed at developing human capital in order to retain and groom talent. The various initiatives are discussed below.

- **Group growth policy:** The organization helps to further build on leadership positions and provide opportunities for employees to charter their career path of choice across businesses spread in the countries where the Aditya Birla Group has a presence.
- **Drug-free workplace:** The possession, use, or sale of illegal drugs is prohibited. Any employee under the influence of drug or alcohol that may impair judgement, performance, or the safety of the employee or others while on company property, business, or during working hours, is subject to discipline including termination.
- **Opportunities for learning:** The Aditya Birla Group has developed and deployed various learning channels to transform into a learning organization. Gyanodaya is a managerial and strategy programme, conducted by leading academics from Indian and overseas business schools like the London Business School, Harvard Business School, and the Indian Institute of Management Calcutta. Over the years, more than 10,000 managers across a range of businesses have participated in managerial and strategy programmes. The group's Knowledge Integration Programme (KIP) provides a platform for the sharing of best practices within and across the group's businesses and fosters learning.

  Continued Learning is a mid-career education programme that offers an online MBA programme. The programme facilitates the continuing education of management staff in collaboration with Universitas 21, a Singapore-based e-university. Pratibimb (e-360-degree instrument) is an online 360-degree feedback tool to heighten self-awareness. Managers receive feedback on group values, global leadership competency, and career stage competency. Gyandhara (Knowledge @ desktop) is a knowledge portal that offers three unique services: (a) a research assistance facility that guarantees less than 72 hours' response time; (b) e-books to help managers stay at the cutting-edge of thought leadership; and (c) a bi-monthly e-newsletter focusing on industry updates, latest industry news, and management updates.

  Adityadisha is the group intranet, which serves as the repository of organizational information and the channel for organizational communication. It is the information gateway for businesses and the corporate world and hosts features like a career helpdesk, management circulars, and access for multiple learning microsites. Anubhav captures the tacit learning of managers across various businesses of the group. It is a knowledge repository of organizational case studies documenting success stories as well as learning from practical problems. The managers of the group participating in this programme learn issues from real-life experiences and find solutions. The company has also created favourable ecosystems for the growth of women employees.

- **Nurturing talent:** The Aditya Birla Group has developed a "talent management framework." This encompasses eight career stages and 17 career-stage-specific behavioural competencies. The key steps in the process are: development assessment centres (DACs), talent reviews, talent engagement, career moves, and succession plans. DACs have been designed to support managers in assessing and developing their capabilities. Talent reviews, done annually, encompass a three-tier talent review process, held at the unit level, business level, and group level. The reviews provide inputs into the career and succession planning process.

The Aditya Birla Group was ranked number one in India and among the best in Asia by Hewitt–*Economic Times* and the *Wall Street Journal* in their Best Employers' Survey 2007. The group's HR processes are replicated across businesses spread over different countries. Aligning employee needs and business interests, a clear focus on employee engagement, a strong orientation towards continuous personal and professional growth, and a values-driven work culture and quality of life are some of the elements that catapulted the group to the top employer position in 2007.

Questions:

1. What are the challenges faced by HR managers due to mergers and acquisitions at the Aditya Birla Group?
2. Comment on the statement "managing global human resource is a challenge" with reference to this case study.
3. How has HR policy helped the Aditya Birla Group?

Source: www.adityabirla.com (last accessed in March 2013).

DISCUSSION QUESTIONS

1. Discuss the role of operations management in strategic management.
2. Discuss the need for forecasting.
3. Explain the various phases of production planning and control.
4. What are the requirements of ISO 9001:2008 quality management system?
5. What are the requirements of the safety management system?
6. What are the requirements of the environmental management system?
7. What is "lean production"? What is its relevance to JIT?
8. "TQM and JIT are complementary to each other." Comment.
9. Calculate the vendor rating for the following. The item under consideration is the same from all suppliers.

Supplier's Data	A	B	C
Quantity supplied	90	80	75
Quantity accepted	78	80	70
Price of each item (₹)	4	4.2	3.9
Delivery promised (in weeks)	6	6	6
Actual deliveries made (in weeks)	8	6.2	7

10. The following data is available on the consumption pattern of certain materials in an organization. Find out A, B, and C items when "A" items account for 85% of consumption value, "B" items account for 10% of consumption value, and "C" items account for 5% of consumption value.

Group	No. of Items	Monthly Consumption (Units)	Price item (₹)
I	40	3,000	9
II	20	270	100
III	100	1,700	5
IV	200	1,500	4
V	60	340	50
VI	300	2,500	1
VII	250	2,000	2
VIII	30	170	500

11. Outline the various types of maintenance.
12. State the need for supply chain management and its potential benefits.
13. Explain the changing role of HR managers.
14. Discuss the essentials of a sound HR policy in an enterprise.
15. Bring out the significance of industrial relations.
16. Give an overall view of labour laws in India.

ACTIVITY

1. Divide the class into groups of four students. Each group is required to collect the quality policy, safety policy, environmental policy, and HR policy of an organization of their choice and discuss it in class.
2. Invite a labour officer in your area and ask him to give a talk on labour laws in India. Request your professor to lend his support.

PROJECT

1. Visit a local manufacturing organization. Study their existing supply chain. Suggest areas for improvement in the existing supply chain. Prepare a report and present it in the class.
2. Visit a service enterprise in your area and study its existing operations management. Suggest areas for improvement. Prepare a report and present it in the class.

ENDNOTES

1. Jayakar, R. (2005). "Manufacturing's Next Export Wave," *Business Today*, 24 April, pp. 66–72.
2. Mahadevan, B. (2010). *Operations Management: Theory and Practice*. New Delhi: Pearson Education, 2nd ed.
3. Aswathappa, K. and K. Shridhara Bhat (2010). *Production and Operations Management*. Mumbai: Himalaya Publishing House.

4. Kachru, Upendra (2001). *Production and Operations Management: Text and Cases*. New Delhi: Excel Books.
5. Elion, Samuel (1994). *Elements of Production Planning and Control*. Bombay: Universal Publishing Corporation.
6. Handfield, R. B. and E. L. Nichols, Jr (1999). *Introduction to Supply Chain Management*. Upper Saddle River, New Jersey: Prentice Hall.
7. Datta, A. K. (1998). *Materials Management Procedures: Text and Cases*. New Delhi: PHI Learning.
8. Aljian, G. W. (ed.) (1966). *Purchasing Handbook*. New York: McGraw-Hill.
9. Charantimath, Poornima M. (2011). *Total Quality Management*. New Delhi: Pearson Education, 2nd ed.
10. Levitt, J. (1997). *Handbook of Maintenance Management*. New York: Industrial Press.
11. www.gallup.com/consulting/52/employee-engagement.aspx (last accessed in March 2013).
12. Sinha, P. R. N., Indu Bala Sinha, and Seema Priyadarshini Shekhar (2006). *Industrial Relations, Trade Unions, and Labour Legislation*. New Delhi: Pearson Education.

Management of Enterprises

11. Preventing Sickness in Enterprises
12. Financial Management in Enterprises
13. Operations and Human Resource Management in Enterprises
14. Managing Marketing and Growth in Enterprises

"A customer is the most important visitor on our premises. He is not dependent on us. We are dependent on him. We are not doing him a favour by serving him. He is doing us a favour by giving us the opportunity to do so."

—Mahatma Gandhi

Kumar Mangalam Birla is an Indian entrepreneur and the chairman of the Aditya Birla Group. The Aditya Birla Group has a presence in 20 countries operating in different cultural environments and is India's third-largest business house. Under Kumar Mangalam Birla's leadership, the group has consolidated its businesses through mergers and acquisitions. He has set the ambitious target of doubling the group's revenue to USD 6,500 crore by 2015 using the acquisition strategy.

Managing Marketing and Growth in Enterprises

14

LEARNING OBJECTIVES

Upon completion of this chapter, you should be able to:

1. Understand the concept and importance of marketing in enterprises.
2. Discuss the marketing process of an enterprise.
3. Explain new techniques of marketing.
4. Describe the export marketing and EXIM policy.
5. Understand the phases in an enterprise's life cycle.
6. Discuss the growth strategies for enterprises.
7. Understand the essence of business ethics and corporate social responsibility.

INTRODUCTION

India today has become a lucrative hub for enterprises. The role of marketing forms the backbone of any form of enterprise. Marketing makes or breaks an enterprise. There are cases of success and failures of enterprises, which are the repercussions of marketing activities carried out by the enterprises. Hindustan Unilever Limited is a marketing success story. However, there are many examples of enterprises which have failed in the same field. Even a highly efficient production unit may be rendered useless if the product cannot find a market.

INDIA'S GROWING SERVICES SECTOR

In line with the global trend, the services sector in India is growing rapidly. According to the Economic Survey 2011–2012, the service sector grew by 9.4 per cent and continues to remain a growth engine for the economy.

The entertainment industry is one of the most popular segments of India's services sector. Indian films are popular across West Asia, Afghanistan, Central Asia, Russia, South Africa, and Southeast Asia. They are now penetrating the Western world, thanks both to the uniqueness of the entertainment offered by them, which transcends cultural barriers, and also due to the global Indian diaspora.

Even though the service sector is more than twice the size of the manufacturing sector in most highly industrialized economies, both the study and the practice of marketing have focused on manufacturing industries much more than on the services sector. The growing competitive market for services means that a marketing orientation has become essential for the competitive survival for service industries too.

Marketing can be defined as a process which identifies, anticipates, and satisfies customer needs efficiently and profitably in keeping with the objectives of the enterprise.[1] Marketing is a specialized and dynamic area. It requires appropriate actions in response to market demands by developing suitable products and effective strategies.

COMMON MARKETING PROBLEMS FACED BY ENTERPRISES

Some of the common marketing problems faced by enterprises are as follows:

- **Lack of brand image:** Consumers may be guided by brand image. Large-scale units formulate their strategy and create and monitor the market with the help of the media. In such an environment, enterprises with limited propaganda and advertising will find it difficult to penetrate the market.
- **Product quality:** Enterprises in the initial stages have a serious limitation in terms of product quality. It is costly and difficult for an enterprise to have quality testing and evaluating equipment. The stipulation of minimum wages on the one hand, and low labour productivity on the other, makes it difficult for enterprises to compete in terms of prices. They may, therefore, be compelled to reduce the profit margin or use low-priced inputs or zero-wage family labour.
- **Credit sales:** The enterprise is invariably called upon to sell on credit. However, when it comes to purchasing inputs, they are denied liberal credit facilities. With the result that enterprises often have to borrow excessive working capital compared to what is legitimately needed. The effective interest cost increases the general cost of production and prices, making it non-competitive. In a way, the enterprise faces a buyer's market while marketing its products and a seller's market while buying raw materials.
- **Low prices:** Price determination in an enterprise is generally non-institutional. The prices quoted by large enterprises are accepted together with the predetermined terms of sale. In case of enterprises, the prices are "bargained" on a one-to-one basis and brought down to the lowest level possible.
- **Local and limited market:** Enterprises generally cater to the needs of the local and limited market due to the prohibitive cost of creating a wider distribution network. This is a blessing as well as a curse for the enterprise. The addition of transport cost will make the product non-competitive in upcountry markets.

SNAPSHOT

- Marketing can be defined as a process that identifies, anticipates, and satisfies customer needs efficiently and profitably in keeping with the objectives of the enterprise.
- The common marketing problems faced by enterprises are the lack of brand image; poor product quality; credit sales; low prices; and local and limited market.

DIFFERENCES BETWEEN PRODUCT AND SERVICES MARKETING

Although there are some tools, concepts, and strategies that can be generalized to all marketing situations, it is important to understand that marketing management tasks in the services sector differ from those in the manufacturing sector in several respects.[2] However, it should be recognized that each of the distinguishing characteristics discussed here is only a generalization and does not apply equally to all types of services.

Intangible Nature of the Service Product

While goods are tangible, services are intangible. A manufactured good can be wrapped up and taken home, becoming the property of the purchaser. It is different in the case of services, for example, motor repairing, supplying information, offering an insurance policy, maintenance and rental services, catering, running a creche, beauty parlour, laundry, hair-cutting salon, school, or hospital, and so on.

Trust Aligned with the Product

When a product is sold, the enterprise should have sufficient trust in the ability of the product to perform the service described in its specifications. However, while marketing a service, the enterprise must have complete trust in the ability of the employees providing the service. In the case of a service, customers must receive the assured result instead of a tangible product. This could be best explained with an example of tailors catering to each of their customers differently as per set requirements.

Product Positioning

Positioning is the vital strategy of marketing, which helps an enterprise to institute a distinct position for its brand in the minds of the target customer. While marketing a product, companies try to position it when it is introduced in the market taking into account its features such as low cost and added value. In services, the product is only positioned in the minds of the customer if it matches their expectation and persuades them that it is the best on offer.

More Contacts Between Customers and Service Personnel

Few consumer goods involve contact between customers and the manufacturer's employees. Customer contact tasks are usually delegated to independent retail intermediaries such as stores, dealerships, and approved service suppliers (all of which are, of course, service businesses). There is more contact in the case of industrial goods since these are often sold directly rather than through intermediaries.

In contrast, almost all services entail direct contact with the service supplier, usually in person or by mail or telephone. Frequently, the demeanour and behaviour of service personnel play an important role in determining whether or not customers are satisfied.

Customer Involvement in Production

Service operations can be divided into "front office" and "back office" components. Customers are usually exposed to the former and not to the latter. In high contact services that are delivered directly to the customer—such as passenger transportation, health care, and restaurants—the front office represents a relatively large proportion of the total service operation.

Interactions Among Marketing, Operations, and Human Resources

A distinction needs to be made between the marketing function and the marketing department in a service firm. The former embraces all activities experienced by customers. The department, by contrast, is simply an organizational unit that is responsible for some (but not necessarily all) of the marketing activities performed by the firm.

Problems in Controlling Product Quality and Consistency

Since many services are consumed as they are produced, the final "assembly" and delivery of product elements must take place under real-time conditions. Mistakes and shoddy work in the front office are likely to be noticed by the customer before they can be caught and corrected by a quality-control inspector. In contrast, there is a better chance of catching such problems in the back office or in a manufacturing plant.

Absence of Inventories

Since a service is a deed or performance rather than a tangible item that the purchaser gets to keep, it cannot be inventoried. Unused capacity in a service business is like having a running tap in a sink with no stopper. The flow is wasted unless customers are present to receive it. When demand exceeds capacity, customers are likely to be sent away disappointed, since no inventory is available for backup. Therefore, one of the key tasks for marketers in capacity-constrained service firms is to find ways to smoothen demand levels to match available capacity. Some examples include transportation, lodging, and repair shops.

Importance of the Time Factor

Although convenience of location is often stressed as a key success factor for many services, convenience of scheduling is often just as important. The service must be available when the customers want it as well as where they want it—an important rationale for extending the working hours in many service businesses. A second aspect of timing concerns the duration of service delivery from initial request to final conclusion of the service transaction.

Structure of Distribution Channels

Unlike goods, which require physical distribution channels for moving them from factory to customers, many service businesses either use electronic channels or combine the service factory retail outlet and consumption point into one.

However, a distinction should be drawn between service execution and concept design. As a result of the high capital cost of achieving broad distribution of services to numerous "factories in the field," there is a growing trend for developers of a service concept to contract out execution of that concept to individual entrepreneurs working as franchisees.

ESSENTIAL MARKETING MIX OF SERVICES MARKETING

A service tends to be an experience that a customer holds at a point of purchase. It is highly intangible and perishable in nature. It is inseparable from the point of consumption. Services marketing mix is an intended package of basic elements that make up the product or service, which is presented to the market. Unlike product marketing which deals with the 4 Ps, i.e. Product, Price, Place, and Promotion, services marketing also deals with People, Process, and Physical Evidence. The difference between product marketing and services marketing is given in Table 14.1.

People

The use of appropriate staff and people is an indispensable element of any service provision. To have an edge over other competitors, it is very important to have the right staff at the right time. Training also plays an instrumental role in the service delivery process. Consumers make opinions and convey perceptions of the service based on the employees they deal with. It is very important for the staff to have the right attitude, interpersonal skills, and knowledge of the service offered by

Table 14.1 Product Marketing Versus Services Marketing

Product Marketing	Services Marketing
Marketing is visible	Marketing is invisible
Tangible in nature	Intangible in nature
Deals with the 4 Ps	Deals with the 7 Ps
Standardized product	Heterogeneous product
Production separate from consumption	Simultaneous production and consumption

their company. Singapore Airlines is renowned for its customer service because of its careful selection and training of employees.

Process

Process is the system used to support the organization in delivering the service. When a customer walks into a Kentucky Fried Chicken outlet, orders a meal, and it gets delivered within two minutes, the process involved in delivering the product efficiently and effectively would foster consumer loyalty and satisfaction.

Physical Evidence

The place where the service is being delivered is known to be the physical evidence. It is the constituent of the service mix, which enables the consumer to make a consensus on the enterprise. For example, if a customer walks into a restaurant, he would expect a clean and friendly environment. Physical evidence is an essential ingredient of the service mix. Consumers make perceptions based on their sight of the service provision, which has an impact on the organization's perceptual plan of the service.

KEY SUCCESS FACTORS IN SERVICES MARKETING

What does it take to succeed in marketing? Each situation, of course, has its own specific requirements. However, there are a number of key factors that tend to characterize successful service businesses, as discussed below.

Clearly Articulated Positioning Strategy Once a service firm has selected a positioning strategy, it must articulate this clearly to both prospective customers and its own employees.

Clarifying the Elements of the Product Package Service can be redefined as all actions and reactions that customers perceive they have purchased. The product package can usually be divided into the core service offered by the firm such as transportation of goods between two points, and various supplementary services provided to customers such as acceptance of orders, billing and documentation, problem solving, and other service extras.

Emphasis on Quality Developing a quality service begins with determining the customer's needs (which may vary on a segment-by-segment basis). These needs must be transformed into service specifications, and actual execution of service procedures must then conform to these specifications. It is important that the firm communicates clearly to customers what level of service they should expect and adhere to this level. Failure to meet expectations is almost sure to result in disappointment.

Customer Retention Few service firms rely on one-time sales for the bulk of their business. Getting repeat business is often more important to financial success than winning new customers. This is least because obtaining a repeat sale from an existing customer usually involves only a fraction of the effort required for acquiring a new customer.

Collecting and Using Customer Data Most service firms collect extensive data on their customers for operations and accounting purposes (consider how much a hotel learns about each guest, or how much data a bank collects on a customer's background and use of the bank's services). These databases are potentially marketing goldmines.

Close Relations Among Marketing, Operations, and Human Resources In the services business, operations have a very important role. It not only creates the product but is also responsible for its delivery.

Soliciting Feedback from Customers and Employees Feedback from customers helps the firm determine whether or not it is doing a good job. It may also provide insights into ways of improving the quality of service and even generate ideas for new services not currently offered.

Top Management Commitment Without the support of the chief executive officer and other members of the top management team, it is almost impossible for a service organization to achieve and maintain a strong marketing orientation. In many successful service firms, top executives practice what has been called "management by walking around," by spending time at service delivery locations in an effort to stay close to both their employees and their customers.

DISCUSSION FORUM

- Discuss the differences between product marketing and services marketing.
- Explain the key success factors in services marketing.

MARKETING PROCESS

Marketing is the essence of all enterprises. The activities of marketing products are interrelated with each other and add value to the end customer and to society. The marketing process[3] is illustrated in Figure 14.1 and comprises the following stages:

Market Research

It is an organized activity which enables enterprises to gather pivotal information about the market and customers. Market research facilitates the analysis of customer behaviour, market size, and potential. It acts as a key factor to create an edge over competitors. Marketing research should be a continous process, which involves the collection and evaluation of information from all sources, and results in the modification of the marketing strategy if necessary. It should be a full-scale research project for enterprises. The choice between methods and the scale of research activity will depend on two factors. First, the depth and accuracy of the information required, and second, the budget available. For a majority of firms, keeping their eyes and ears open to what is happening in the market, especially whatever affects their business, and readiness to take an adaptive course of action will suffice. However, one can take note of the trend indicated by secondary information. In any case, it is required to remain very alert and alive to the market situation.

Marketing Planning

A marketing plan is to be developed in detail on the basis of functional plans and programmes. The marketing plan should be formalized as a written document. The marketing planner will define target segments to cater to, the target marketing strategy to be followed, and the positioning of the product in the market in relation to competitors. Segmentation is a process of grouping customers with common needs, behaviours, and desires. After cautiously segmenting the market, enterprises concentrate on their target customers, positioning their products, and branding. Targeting is the

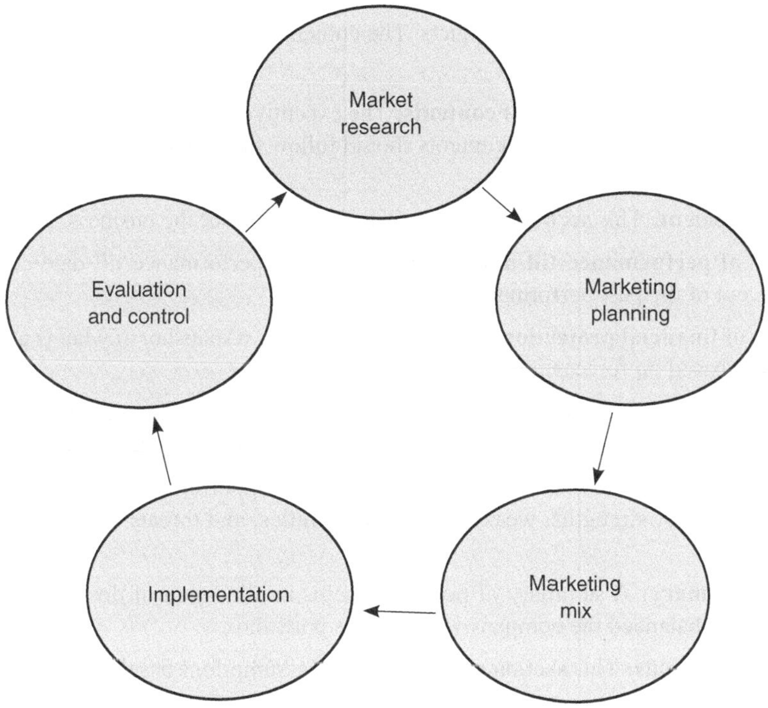

Figure 14.1 The Marketing Process of an Enterprise

selection of actual customers to whom the enterprise wants to cater their products. Positioning helps enterprises to conquer the minds of the customers; it also facilitates people to form a mental image of your product in their minds. According to the American Marketing Association (AMA), a brand is a "name, term, sign, symbol or design, or a combination of them intended to identify the goods and services of one seller or group of sellers and to differentiate them from those of other sellers." A good brand helps enterprises to connect the prospects emotionally and motivates the buyer to be a loyal customer.

The demand for a product, in terms of quality, size, price, performance, and so on may not be uniform throughout the market—it may be segmented. For example, some people will opt for a simple agitator type of washing machine, others semi-automatic, still others for an automatic version.

Customer preferences may be due to differences in economic, demographic, and psychological factors. While selecting a target market this point should be kept in mind—whether to cater to a single segment, or all the segments, depending on the capacity of production and managerial ability to control.

The present Indian scenario is so diverse and full of contrasts and contradictions that you can sell almost anything. It is estimated that 30 crore Indians have enough disposable income to buy an ever-multiplying range of consumer goods. The number is steadily rising. It is not that the rest of the population is lagging far behind. Consumerism is infecting them too. The scenario presents a vast spectrum of paradoxes—at one end are the poor and illiterate with limited needs and at the other end are luxury goods in all their variety and abundance.

At one extreme there are highly knowledgeable and discerning customers, and at the other are the ignorant. On the one hand, the most sophisticated marketing techniques are employed to hook customers, while on the other; primitive modes of marketing still persist.

Take the case of any other product, say cosmetics—talcum powder, nail polish, sunscreen, and so on—available in posh air-conditioned beauty parlours or classy shopping arcades in big cities as well as in remote village roadside shops filled with dust and fleas. The brands are different. It is also true that better brands are making inroads in these areas also. The Reynolds refill, costing many times more than its cheaper cousins, is being sold in the same market. There are innumerable such examples.

Such paradoxical coexistence is likely to endure for a long time. This kind of situation offers unlimited flexibility in the choice of products. The contents of a standard marketing plan are given below;

- **Executive summary and table of contents:** The executive summary provides a synopsis of the overall marketing plan. A table of contents should follow the summary so that readers can easily find more details about each point.
- **Mission statement:** This section should explain the purpose of the business.
- **Summary of performance till date:** The summary of performance till date comes from the projection out of the past performance, if any.
- **Summary of financial projections:** This section provides a snapshot of what is going to happen in the future based on forecasting and past data, if any.
- **Market overview:** This section provides an indicator of the behaviour of the market in the future. A marketer may use a scenario analysis to explain the likely behaviour of the market.
- **SWOT analysis:** SWOT (Strengths, Weaknesses, Opportunities, and Threats) analysis identifies the major strengths, weaknesses, opportunities, and threats which your organization faces.
- **Portfolio summary:** A summary of portfolios helps in allocation of divisions. This summary will show how balanced the company is among its portfolios.
- **Market assumptions:** This section provides a list of assumptions based on which the marketing plan is prepared.
- **Marketing objectives and goals:** This section provides marketing objectives and goals in clear, measurable terms like sales volume, market share, and profit.
- **Financial projections for at least three years:** This section provides financial projections for three years to regulate the market function.
- **Marketing strategy:** This section is the game plan for the market and includes target segments and product positioning in the market in relation to competitors.
- **Marketing action plans:** This section covers the functional plans and will answer questions like, "Who will do it? What will be done? When shall it be done?," the resources required, and what the result of the action is likely to be.

DISCUSSION FORUM

- Discuss the marketing process in small groups.
- Explain the contents of a marketing plan.

Marketing Mix

Business, as a whole, engages in different marketing activities. The combination of all such activities is called a "marketing mix." Although there are many elements, a popular classification consists of the "4 Ps"—product, promotion, price, and place.

Product This is the core element of the marketing mix and consists of tangible products and intangible services offered by an enterprise. It incorporates everything a customer desires such as design, quality, packaging, guarantee, and after-sales service.

There is no ideal or appropriate mix. It all depends on the requirements of the target market. Different market segments require different grades of quality and sophistication. Careful attention should be given to the tangible and intangible elements of the product to create an overall impact in the market.

Promotion Promotion involves various tools to create awareness for the product among customers. Information on the product is a prerequisite for making a purchase. The success or failure of a venture depends mainly on the effectiveness of the promotional efforts made for marketing the product.

Products can be promoted by advertising them on television, newspapers, journals, periodicals, and so on. Eye-catching advertisements loaded with carefully chosen words create a longing for the goods. The sponsorship of regional, national, and international events provides good scope for advertisements. The display of posters, placards, and hoardings during national and international sports events and the participation in exhibitions and fairs are some other avenues for sales promotion.

Modern advertisements aim beyond merely creating awareness. They actively motivate customers to buy. Advertisements during TV serials are included to leave a lingering impression in the minds of the viewers. Often, visuals are addressed to children, who are easily influenced and who compel their parents to purchase.

Database marketing is also making inroads into the country. All information—likes, dislikes, and other predictions—about prospective customers are collected and processed in a computer. Based on this information, a prediction is made about when the customer is likely to feel the need for a particular product.

Advertising is a highly specialized area and highly creative people run the business. To requisition their services will make you substantially poorer. Depending on your capacity and necessity, select the medium you can afford and use it with profit. In any case, advertising is a must, otherwise nobody will come to know about your product.

Price Pricing comprises basic price, discount, and credit policy. Prices should be decided in the light of production costs, demand, and competition. Pricing policy is related to different qualities, and again, to different market segments. One manufacturer may be able to supply a high-quality product at a certain price while another in the same industry offers a cheaper product at a lower price to another market segment.

A good example of this policy would be Nirma. When it was being launched, Surf was the dominant brand in the market targeting the high-price segment. Nirma targeted its detergent at a section of people, which was hesitant to use any brand of washing powder because of its prohibitive price. Most people in this segment used cakes of washing soap. To them, washing powder was used only by the affluent. But when Nirma offered them a quality detergent at an affordable price, many of them made the switch. Not only that, some consumers of Surf switched over to Nirma as well.

Place This is to make the product available to the target market. It includes the physical movement of the product and the type of distribution channels or dealership to be employed.

Big firms have their zonal or regional authorized agents or dealers spread over the entire country. The dealers, in turn, work with sub-agents or distributors and retailers, or directly with the customers, depending on the type of the goods—consumer, industrial, or pharmaceutical. Travelling salesmen book orders from retailers and the consignment follows from the dealers or directly from the manufacturers.

Even if they cannot afford to have zonal offices, firms are devising their own ways of doing business. They also receive regular orders for goods. Entry may seem to be difficult.

Interestingly, it has been observed that many authorized dealers of known brands also stock other unknown or new brands of goods. They also insist on the customer buying the lesser-known brand. The secret is a higher margin of profit. An entrepreneur must be ready to sacrifice a portion of his/her profit in a bid to enter the market. It need not necessarily be a great sacrifice. With fewer overheads and low labour costs coupled with better planning and management, a enterprise may be able to reap good profits.

This does not mean that industries are better managed. That is generally not the case. There is scope for economizing at various stages and optimizing the use of labour and machinery without sacrificing quality and productivity. Adequate attention needs to be paid to this aspect, which has been neglected by entrepreneurs due to ignorance. This drawback can be remedied by equipping entrepreneurs with the necessary information through short-term courses in the required area under EDPs organized by various institutions and agencies.

In order to promote sales, it is necessary to offer better incentives. Offer incentives to local retailers and gradually expand the radius of operation. At present, due to stiff competition, retailers, in most cases, get everything at the point of sale. Employ salespersons on terms and conditions suitable to the unit. It can be on a fixed monthly salary. The person must report daily progress and discuss the strategy for the next day. The salesperson may be given extra commission in addition to the monthly salary if he or she exceeds a certain quota. Nowadays, there is no dearth of young persons looking for such an opportunity.

The Canteen Stores Department (CSD) of the defence services is a big customer of consumer durables and non-durables. It has many branches all over the country and many more are being opened in places where this facility was not available earlier. Shopping by television is also set for expansion in this country.

Quality, packaging, and price will be the deciding factors in case of consumer goods. Performance, durability, and versatility should also be focused on for consumer durables. The entrepreneur can evolve a personal strategy for marketing. It is very important for the survival of an enterprise. The entrepreneur may seek help from government agencies.

Implementation and Control

Marketing implementation involves the execution of the planned strategy and allocation of scarce resources for achieving marketing goals. The marketing manager executes the marketing strategy by translating it into a number of operational plans and short-term programmes, whose time-bound results can be measured. Marketing control is a process of benchmarking the expended efforts and resources with the set of goals.

SNAPSHOT

- The activities in marketing add value to the end customer and to society.
- Market research is an organized activity, which enables the enterprises to gather information.
- Segmentation is a process of grouping customers with common needs, behaviours, and desires.
- Product is the tangible product and intangible service offering of an enterprise. This is the core element of the marketing mix.
- Promotion involves various tools to create awareness for the product among customers. Information on the product is a prerequisite for making a purchase.
- Pricing comprises basic price, discount, and credit policy.
- Place helps to make the product available to the target market. It includes physical movement of the product and the type of distribution channels or dealership to be employed.

COSTING AND PRICING

The cost of a product has two components. One is the fixed cost, which does not vary with the change in production level. The other is the variable cost, which varies according to variations in the level of production. Fixed costs include costs such as factory rent, salary of staff, interest on loan, depreciation charge on machinery, taxes and interest rates, water and power charges, and other miscellaneous expenses. Variable costs are expenses that vary based on production volumes. They include material, labour, utilities, and delivery costs.

The difference between the selling price of a product and its variable cost is known as contribution. Any enterprise should have the total contribution from operations equal to the fixed cost incurred by it to enable it to reach the break-even point—the point of no loss or profits. Any sales below the break-even point will result in a loss for the unit while production/sales above the break-even point will mean profits.

A rudimentary idea of costing can be had by referring to what is known as the cost ladder.

Cost Ladder

Different industries follow different methods of costing because of the differences in the nature of their work. A common method of determining the selling price and marketing price of a product/service is by using a cost ladder, which is in the form of a series of equations as given below.

Direct material cost + Direct labour cost = Principal cost

Principal cost + Overheads = Factory cost

Factory cost + Selling expenses = Ex-factory cost

Ex-factory cost + Profit = Selling price

Selling price + Discount = Market price

The major variables are material, labour costs, and overheads. Direct material cost will vary according to the prevailing market conditions. Direct labour cost will vary according to the skill, efficiency, or productivity of labour. It can be controlled by employing skilled, experienced, quality-conscious, and productive labour and by better supervision and management. The use of the latest technology and machinery will also have a direct bearing on productivity.

Overheads should be kept low, especially in the initial stages, by keeping the managerial and administrative staff to the minimum without affecting the overall operation of the firm. Selling expenses also should be kept within reasonable limits. When the eminent NRI industrialist, Swraj Paul, decided to set up a steel plant in the UK, many of his friends advised him against the decision on the grounds that he would not be able to compete in the market due to high labour costs. However, Swraj Paul did not heed the advice and made a success of his venture. He made it possible not by paying lower wages to the labourers but by improving efficiency and productivity.

The per-unit profit margin has a bearing on the volume of sales. With high volume of sales, the profit margin can be kept low. An attractive discount package to dealers and retailers will motivate them to boost sales. A practical pricing policy should be framed by keeping in mind all the factors mentioned above.

BRANDING

Given the lack of resources and the limited marketing power of entrepreneurial firms, branding gets neglected by many start-up firms. Business plans, however, outline a strategy based on premium pricing. Premium pricing is possible only if the customer places a higher value on the product or service being sold. In this case, branding the product becomes inevitable. At the same time, larger multinational corporations have the luxury of huge brand-building budgets.

A brand is a name, word, mark, symbol, device, or a combination thereof, used to identify a product or service of one seller and to differentiate them from those of competitors. The brand name is a part of a brand consisting of a word, letter, or groups of words or letters that can be vocalized. The brand mark is a part of a brand consisting of a mark, design, distinctive logotype, colouring scheme, or picture used for the purpose of identification. Brand identity consists of a unique set of brand associations that the brand strategist aspires to create or maintain. The perception of a customer about a brand is termed as the brand image. The brand position is that part of the brand identity and value proposition, which is to be actively communicated to the target audience. The brand position demonstrates the advantage that the brand has over competing brands. Brand equity is a set of brand assets and liabilities linked to a brand, its name, and symbol, which add to or subtract from the value provided by a product or service and/or to that firm's customers.

The four important elements in branding are brand identity, brand image, brand position, and brand equity. Brands serve as long-term assets and are vital to the success of an organization. Brands offer a number of benefits to consumers and the owners. In order to build a brand, a number of key decisions need to be taken. Some of these decisions are—whether to brand or not, and if to brand, then the strategy that needs to be followed. Three kinds of branding are possible; namely, single, umbrella, and combined branding. Brand extension strategies help firms to reap the benefits of a successful brand name.

NEW TECHNIQUES OF MARKETING

Every time you include something innovative in marketing attributes to your business, you generate an opportunity for more sales. It also enhances the chances of repeat purchase and thereby increases the horizon of customers. The following section explains new techniques of marketing.

Internet Marketing

Internet marketing is also termed as e-marketing, web marketing, online marketing, and search marketing. The marketing of products through the Internet is known as Internet marketing. It also helps in borderless marketing due to its large scope and penetration power. Internet marketing has been more successful from the aspect of the product meeting the eyes of the customer. Amazon.com is the leading business in Internet marketing.[4]

Internet campaigns help enterprises to design and attract the customers in a cost-efficient manner. It helps enterprises to manage their leads and convert them into opportunities in a seamless process. Investment is very low and captures a huge market. It provides flexibility and gives personalized time space. Experimenting and testing new products or services are feasible in this channel of marketing. Internet marketing, however, has its own limitations. It entails a great deal of effort and work. It needs to be abreast of changes, else it gets outdated within no time. Targeting the right people is relatively a difficult task. It lacks in after-sales service and personalized customer service.

Direct Marketing

This technique helps enterprises to communicate directly with the end consumers. It is adopted by the smallest start-up business to leaders in the industry. A well-planned direct marketing campaign can provide a good return on investment. Direct marketing involves directly reaching a target market, that is, customers and prospects, on a personal level through tele-calling, direct mails, or through sources of mass media like infomercials and magazine advertisements. Pharmaceuticals and tourism services usually go for direct marketing.

This technique offers a distinctive range of benefits because it helps to connect openly with available customers, prospects, or end users. It helps the enterprise to flexibly categorize and isolate its target markets. It is beneficial to assess new markets and trial products. Direct marketing turns out be very cost efficient. Telemarketing as a tool for direct marketing achieves results in a swift and flexible manner. The conversion rates or results can be measured easily with this technique. It helps in planning and forecasting for the future. It is one of the best tools to build a long-term relationship with customers. However, direct marketing has its own limitations as well. Direct mailing as a tool for direct marketing offends consumers and many do not endorse it as they say it hinders their private lives. In case of e-mail marketing, e-mails sent as part of direct marketing are often placed into the spam or trash folders. Customers are also not very happy about receiving voice mails on phone.

Niche Marketing

A niche consists of a narrowly-defined customer group, which seeks a distinctive mix of benefits. Niches can be identified by dividing a segment into sub segments. Customers in a niche have a unique set of needs, and will pay a premium to the firm that best satisfies their needs. Another feature of a niche is that it is not likely to attract other competitors. Sometimes, a concentrated strategy of focusing on a narrow niche market is more profitable than spreading resources over several different segments. The company gains certain economies through specialization and the niche has size, profit, and growth potential.

There are several specialized Indian Web sites focused on niche segments that are performing well. For example, the Web site, www.naukri.com, which focuses on job opportunities in India, has become one of the favoured destinations for people searching for appropriate job opportunities and also offers its services to companies to identify potential candidates. Also, matrimonial Web sites such as www.shaadi.com and www.jeevansathi.com are two popular examples in India. Himalaya Herbal Healthcare specializes in ayurvedic products for general health as well as for specific therapeutic functions. By focusing on ayurvedic medicines and health supplements, Himalaya Herbal Healthcare serves a growing niche market.

Niche marketing has its own benefits and limitations. The benefits are that it can be extremely cost effective; it is not likely to attract other competitors; the company gains certain economies through specialization; and the niche has good growth potential. The limitations are threats of cannibalization due to the smaller market share and the neccessity of skilled marketing techniques.

Ambush Marketing

Ambush is a technique used by enterprises where the advertisers associate themselves with a particular event without any investments. Ambush marketing, a term coined by marketing guru Jerry Welsh, refers to an enterprise's attempt to benefit from the goodwill and reputation of a particular event by creating an association with it, without the agreement or approval of the essential parties. There are various approaches in ambush marketing like direct ambush marketing, indirect ambush marketing, and incidental ambush marketing. The best-known example of ambush marketing in India was during the 1996 cricket World Cup, when Coke paid ₹40 crore to be named as an official sponsor of the event, but Pepsi came out with a counter advertisement, "Nothing official about it," hijacked the World Cup, and clearly occupied the consumer's mind space.

Ambush marketing has its own benefits and limitations. It increases competition, prices of product go down relatively, and it could turn out to be advantageous to customers. This technique helps to target a huge market space. It attracts various segments in one go. The positioning of an enterprise becomes moderately easy. This tool also provides benefits in the sphere of public relations. The limitations are that some events may perhaps go unobserved by the target market. If an enterprise is associated with an unsuccessful event, its brand image may take a beating.

Green Marketing

Green marketing refers to the marketing of products that are assumed to be environmentally friendly. It includes activities like product alteration, changes to the production process, and packaging innovation. The main objective of enterprises using this technique is to improve environmental quality and customer satisfaction. Terms like phosphate-free, recyclable, refillable, ozone friendly, eco-tourism, and environment friendly are some of the terms that consumers most often associate with environmental marketing. Organizations like The Body Shop heavily promote the fact that they are environmentally responsible.

Green marketing has its own benefits and limitations. The benefits are that it saves natural resources; it directly reduces the operational cost of an enterprise; it enhances the relationship with and the loyalty of customers; and helps improve the brand image, goodwill, and identity. The limitations are that it is time consuming and the costs incurred could be colossal. It is also difficult to balance customers' needs and expectations, and the cause may go unnoticed by the customers.

Social Marketing

Social marketing focuses on attaining explicit behavioural goals for a social cause. The chief intent of social marketing is "social well-being." Social marketing is an important technique used to seek specific behavioural changes. Enterprises conduct campaigns for social awareness like the pulse polio programme, family planning, and AIDS awareness. Social marketing has benefits as well as limitations. It is one of the cheapest ways of marketing with a high return on investment. Enterprises using such techniques usually do not require high technical skills. Social marketing increases the visibility of products and the brand as a whole. It educates a large audience in a very short span of time. Enterprises also obtain the opportunity of making a social acquaintance with the customers. However, social marketing is a time-consuming process. Sometimes, a wrong online brand approach could turn out to be bad word-of-mouth publicity for the enterprise.

Relationship Marketing

Relationship marketing focuses on building mutually satisfying, long-term relationships with important stakeholders—customers, suppliers, distributors, and other marketing partners in order to earn and retain their business. Relationship marketing involves cultivating the right kind of relationships with the right constituent groups. As part of relationship marketing, marketers focus on customer relationship management (CRM) as well as partner relationship management (PRM). Unlike other techniques of marketing, it emphasizes customer loyalty and satisfaction with exclusive promotional strategies.

Marketing activities become easier if marketers put in efforts to understand customer behaviour. Customer complaints are never personal—they are usually regarding a product or service or the process involved in making products or planning services. CRM focuses on meeting the individual needs of customers and involves building a customer database and doing data mining to detect trends, segments, and individual needs. For example, BMW's technology now allows buyers to design their own models from 350 variations, 500 options, 90 exterior colours, and 170 trims. The company claims that 80 per cent of the cars bought by individuals in Europe and up to 30 per cent of those in the United States are built to order. British supermarket giant Tesco is outpacing its rival store, Sainsbury, by using its Club Card data to personalize offers according to individual customer attributes.

Relationship marketing has its own benefits and limitations. This technique improves customer experience. It helps in retaining customers and developing loyalty. It enables an enterprise to reach its target audience in a fruitful manner. Using this technique, marketers can easily maintain a database for future use and also respond to customer needs easily. This technique has certain limitations too. The cost incurred in this method is usually very high. It could at times be a misleading or a misguiding technique for the customers because the genuine value of the brand and the product could be hampered.

Viral Marketing

It is a phenomenon that assists and encourages people to pass along a marketing message. Viral marketing, also known as buzz marketing, depends on the message being transmitted from customer to customer at a fast tempo. If a large fraction of recipients forward something to a large number of associates, the overall expansion snowballs very quickly. Hotmail is one of the classic success stories of the benefits of a viral marketing campaign. The founders of Hotmail offered free e-mail to customers, and simply attached a signature at the bottom of each e-mail message that promoted their free service. Every single e-mail sent by a Hotmail user contained this message, thus spreading it like a virus. Recipients would see the advertisement, and as a result, they too signed up for Hotmail.

Viral marketing has its own advantages and limitations. The advantages are that alliances with unknown groups become easier; it is a cost-free method of promotion; and the resources are easily available. Thc limitations are that it might result in the transfer of wrong messages. Marketers can also lose control in their initiatives. It is also a very complex task to measure the marketing campaign.

BREAKTHROUGH ENTREPRENEURSHIP 14.1 CRM Responsible for Magic at Bharti

One of the toughest challenges that a company faces today is the move from a product and sales philosophy to a marketing philosophy. Such a move will give a company a better chance of outperforming competition. The critical feature of a well-conceived marketing orientation is a strong relationship with customers. Customer relationship management is a business philosophy, which places the client in the centre of its processes, its activities, and its culture.

Bharti Tele-Ventures is one of India's leading private-sector telecom operators. Its cellular business, Airtel, is a leading mobile telephony brand. The management at Bharti considers information technology as a key business enabler. "For telecom, IT is like bread and butter. We believe it plays two significant roles—it works as a support system, and it can also be a business driver. Thus, IT is very important to us," says Amrita Gangotra, Director for Information Technology at Bharti Airtel Ltd and a member of the Airtel management board.

When the system was run manually initially, only 40 per cent of customer issues were getting resolved. In order to manage the expectations of its customers and provide them with innovative products and services in a manner which makes them loyal, Bharti opted for a customer relationship management (CRM) solution. After Bharti adopted the CRM tool, 90 per cent of customer issues are getting resolved

Bharti is now successfully using the Oracle CRM platform. This has enabled the company to provide services anywhere and at any time. No matter whichever call centre a customer contacts, the quality of service is the same. Airtel is now able to give its customers more value for money and also able to provide customers different schemes and services depending on airtime usage. Bharti has also managed to segregate workflow with the help of the CRM tool.

Source: www.expresscomputeronline.com/20041011/casestudies14.shtml (last accessed in March 2013).

Rural Marketing

Rural marketing is defined as a marketing process in which one dominant participant is from a rural area. Rural marketing consists of the marketing of inputs (products or services) to the rural markets as well as the marketing of outputs from the rural markets to other geographical areas. Rural markets are free from the shackles of the global meltdown. They exhibit several distinctive characteristics that are different from urban areas. Literacy levels, family structure, occupational patterns, spatial distribution of household settlements, social customs and norms, and several other features are unique to rural India.

With the urban market saturated, FMCG companies are now targeting the rural markets because of the saturation in the urban market. In spite of the income imbalance between urban and rural India, rural India has great potential since 70 per cent of India's population lives in villages. Due to the recent government measures like the waiving of loans, the national rural employment guarantee scheme, and increasing minimum support price, disposable income in rural India has been rapidly increasing. Hindustan Unilever Limited (HUL) has conceived a programme called "Project Shakti" to tap this market.

Rural marketing has its own advantages and disadvantages. It helps in socioeconomic changes and uplifts society. Markets can be tapped at a lower cost. The high costs can be covered if the service and the product are up to the expectations of rural customers. However, transportation and warehousing becomes difficult in the rural market. Some of the other challenges are the difficulties in providing after-sales service; the lack of dealers in the rural market; inadequate banking and credit facilities for customers; and the difficulties to maintain a sales force.

Global Marketing

The evolution of international marketing practices has led to global marketing. Global marketing can be defined as "marketing carried on across national boundaries spanning a number of countries." Global marketing is initializing and then conveying an ultimate product or service globally

WORLD OF ENTREPRENEURS 14.2 **HUL's "Project Shakti"—Changing Lives in Rural India**

In order to tap the rural market in India, Hindustan Unilever Limited (HUL) has conceived "Project Shakti." The Shakti entrepreneur programme was started in 2001 with the aim of increasing the company's rural distribution network reach as well as providing rural women an entrepreneurial opportunity. This is a case where social goals help in the achievement of business goals.

The recruitment of a Shakti *Amma* (SA) begins with the executives of HUL identifying the village not currently covered under the programme. The executives of the company take the help of the village *panchayat* and head to identify the SA. After training, the SA is asked to put up ₹20,000 as investment to buy products for selling. The products distributed include a range of mass-market items especially relevant to rural consumers, such as soap, toothpaste, shampoo, and detergent. The products are then sold door-to-door or through petty shops at home. The company also creates an artificial marketplace with music and promotion so that the SAs are able to sell their products. On an average, an SA makes a ten per cent margin on the products she sells.

The main advantage of Project Shakti for HUL is having more feet on the ground. SAs are able to reach far-flung areas, which were economically unviable for the company to tap. Besides being brand ambassadors for the company, SAs become ready consumers of the products apart from selling them. At the end of 2008, Project Shakti had 45,000 SAs covering more than 100,000 villages across 15 states and reaching 30 lakh homes. This model has been a growth driver for HUL and presently half of HUL's FMCG sales come from rural markets. The Project Shakti programme of HUL has been successful in maintaining its distribution reach advantage over its competitors.

Girija, a leader of a self-help group (SHG), belongs to a small village in the Kadapa district of Andhra Pradesh. The village has 350 households with a total population of 1,200. Girija's six hectares of agricultural land was not sufficient for a five-member family. She attended a meeting of Project Shakti convened by HUL and started her business as an SA with HUL. By 2006, she had a monthly turnover of ₹10,000. Initially, she sold the products door-to-door. In a short span of time, she developed good relationships with the villagers and the customers started visiting her house for products. She says, "I am happy fulfilling my family's requirements and people give me a lot of respect today." Today, Girija has become a key development figure in her village. And she is now very eager to grow her business in the years to come.

Source: www.hul.co.in/careers-redesign/insidehul/oursuccessandchallenges/shaktiprogrammeindia.aspx. (last accesssed in March 2013).

with the hopes of reaching the international marketing society. The concept of the global market considers the whole world as the market and the different countries as its components.

There are two methods of entry into foreign markets—indirect exporting and direct exporting. In case of indirect exports, a producer makes his products and services available in the overseas markets through an intermediate firm and; therefore, gets limited exposure to the international marketing environment. Direct exporting deals with the process of selling the firm's products directly to an importer in the overseas market. A firm may also piggyback on the distribution channels of an overseas firm with a strong marketing network to penetrate into the overseas markets.

A company with a strong production base may opt for the contractual mode or the investment mode for entering overseas markets. The various contractual modes of entering international markets are licensing, franchising, turnkey projects, management contracts, international strategic alliances, and contract manufacturing. The various types of investment modes for entering the international markets are joint ventures and wholly-owned foreign subsidiaries such as acquisition and green field operations. Multinational marketing results in the development of multinational corporations (MNCs). Companies like Unilever, Kodak, and Procter & Gamble are examples of multinational companies. Multinational marketing leads to multi-regional marketing.

Global marketing has its advantages and limitations. The advantages are that it enhances the market size and economies of scale; influences companies to reduce head-on competition; and results in profit sharing. The limitations are that seasonal changes affect the sales of the product; high cost is incurred to customize products; and promotional activities are very difficult to cope with.

SNAPSHOT

- Internet marketing is also called e-marketing, web marketing, online marketing, and search marketing.
- Direct marketing helps enterprises to communicate directly with the end consumers.
- Niche marketing focuses on a narrowly-defined customer group seeking a distinctive mix of benefits.
- Ambush marketing is a technique used by enterprises where the advertisers associate themselves with a particular event without any investments.
- Green marketing refers to the marketing of products that are assumed to be environmentally friendly.
- Relationship marketing is a technique, which involves building a long-term profitable relationship with the customer.
- Viral marketing is a phenomenon that assists and encourages people to pass along a marketing message.
- Rural marketing is defined as a marketing process in which one dominant participant is from a rural area.
- Global marketing is initializing and then conveying an ultimate product or service globally with the hopes of reaching the international marketing society.

INTERNATIONAL TRADE

International trade increases the number of goods that domestic consumers can choose from, decreases the cost of these goods through increased competition, and also allows local enterprises to ship their products to an overseas market. Trade barriers are hindrances to doing international business. Governments usually impose trade barriers to protect the domestic market from competition from outside. The government can impose trade barriers to protect local domestic entrepreneurs and employment in the domestic market in the interest of the nation. Trade barriers are usually of two types: tariff barriers to trade and non-tariff barriers to trade.

Tariff Barriers to Trade

A tariff is a tax on imported goods, which is collected by the domestic government and which raises the price of the good for the consumer. Tariff is also known as import duties. Tariffs are usually levied to limit imports and to raise revenue. Tariffs are often created to protect infant industries, developing economies, domestic employment, consumers from using goods which are injurious to health and which can pollute the environment, and industries that are deemed strategically important such as defense and pharmaceuticals. There are several types of tariff barriers to trade: specific tariffs, tariffs according to value (*ad valorem* tariff), licenses, import quotas, voluntary export restraints, and local content requirements.

Non-tariff Barriers to Trade

Non-tariff barriers (NTB) are trade barriers that restrict imports but are not in the usual form of a tariff. Some types of NTB to trade have the effects of tariffs once they are enacted. NTB to trade are used after the WTO rules led to a very significant reduction in tariff use. The six types of NTB to trade are:

- **Specific limitations on trade:** Quotas, import licensing requirements, proportion restrictions of foreign to domestic goods, minimum import price limits, and embargoes.
- **Customs and administrative entry procedures:** Valuation systems, antidumping practices, tariff classifications, documentation requirements, and fees.

- **Standards:** Standard disparities, inter-governmental acceptances of testing methods and standards, packing, labelling, and marketing.
- **Government participation in trade:** Government trade policies, export subsidies, countervailing duties, and domestic assistance programmes.
- **Charges on imports:** Prior import deposit subsidies, administrative fees, special supplementary duties, import credit discriminations, variable levies, and border taxes.
- **Others:** Voluntary export restraints and orderly marketing arrangements.

Facilitators

National and local governments are active in promoting international trade and development through a number of agencies and departments. Among them is the United States Agency for International Development, which supports the economic development of and trade with developing countries that are politically aligned with the United States. Foreign Trade Zones (FTZ) are tax-free areas in a country that are not considered part of the respective country in terms of import regulations and restrictions.

The Group of Eight is a forum of the most developed countries in the world and addresses economic and financial issues, with trade as a main focus. The International Monetary Fund and the World Bank are two specialized agencies that address the need of global economic development, imposing restructuring standards on aid recipients. There are also other development banks and the different United Nations organizations that promote the economic and financial welfare of developing countries as well as their participation in international trade.

Among the organizations that are most active in and have the greatest impact on promoting international trade are the World Trade Organization (WTO), which provides trade assistance and development assistance to developing countries, promotes trade agreements, and reviews member countries' trade policies to ensure that they conform to the organization's trade requirements.

WORLD OF ENTREPRENEURS 14.3 World Trade Organization (WTO)

The WTO is the largest and most influential international trade organization whose primary goal is to ensure the free flow of trade. The WTO's agreements represent trade rules and regulations and act as contracts guaranteeing countries' trade rights and binding government trade policies. The WTO is run by member governments, and its decisions are made either by the governments' trade ministers, who meet every two years, or by official representatives, who meet regularly at the organization's headquarters in Geneva, Switzerland. Routine issues are addressed by councils, committees, working parties, and negotiating groups.

The WTO came into existence on 1 January 1995 as a successor of the General Agreements on Tariffs and Trade (GATT). The WTO is forever changing the way countries regulate international business on their own territory and beyond. The WTO is often described as a rule-based system. Its main functions are: providing assistance to developing and transitional economies, offering specialized help for export promotion through the international trade centre, promoting regional trade agreement, promoting cooperation in global economic policy-making, reviewing members' trade policies, and engaging in routine notification when members introduce new trade measures or alter old ones.

The WTO agreements cover goods, services, and intellectual property rights. The agreements also address issues such as reducing tariff and non-tariff barriers on specific categories of goods and services; opening service markets to international business; regulating the protection and enforcement of intellectual property rights for trademarks, patents, and copyrights under the agreement on Trade-Related Aspects of Intellectual Property Rights (TRIPS); dealing with antidumping activities; addressing subsidies and trade restrictions designed to safeguard domestic industries such as technical regulations and standards, import licensing, rules origin, and other measures that impede international trade; settling disputes; and regularly reviewing individual countries' trade policies to ensure transparency and compliance with the WTO agreements.

Source: www.wto.org (last accessed in March 2013).

International Marketing Environment

Countries are becoming more and more interconnected by trade, and developments in one region have immediate repercussions in the rest of the world. The transition economies that first opened their markets to multinational firms and privatized national industries experienced the greatest degree of growth and were most successful in developing national industrial sectors that competed effectively with the international firms. The international economy has indeed become one single unit. Major companies simply cannot afford a local home country focus. The market share game is played on a world scale. Countries with emerging markets present great potential for international firms.

There are various ways an entrepreneur can get into international business and market products internationally. The choice of entry method and the mode of operation in the international market depend on the goals of the promoter and the strength and weaknesses of the company. The mode of entering international business is mainly divided into three categories: exporting, non-equity arrangement, and direct foreign investment.

Exporting Usually an entrepreneur starts entering international markets through exporting. Exporting normally involves selling goods made in one country to another country. There are two general types of exporting: direct exporting and indirect exporting.

Non-equity Arrangements In a non-equity arrangement, an entrepreneur can enter international business through an arrangement that does not involve any investment. Non-equity arrangements are of three types: licensing, franchising, management contracts, turn-key projects, and consortiums.

Licensing is the process by which a domestic company allows a foreign company to use its intellectual property such as patents, trademarks, copyright, process technology, design, and specific business skills for a compensation called royalty. Licensing allows an entrepreneur who is a manufacturer (licensee) to give an overseas manufacturer (licensor) the right to use its product, production process, technology, patent or trademark in return for the payment of royalty agreed upon. This process is low risk and most suitable when the entrepreneur has no intention of entering a particular market through direct investment or exporting. Licensing is very common in book publication.

Franchising is a system in which a company grants the right or license to an individual or group to market its products or services in a specific territory. Services firms find it more appropriate to have international franchising as an international market entry mode. International franchising is the process of transfer of intellectual property and other assistance over an extended period of time with greater control compared to licensing. International franchising is a low cost, low risk mode of entry, which provides the opportunity to a firm to penetrate the global market where it has little market knowledge and strengths. In a franchise system, the franchisee takes on the major tasks related to opening the unit such as finding sites, purchasing equipment, and signing the lease. The franchisee is selected by the franchisor, and its eventual replacement is controlled by the franchisor. The franchisor is expected to pass to its franchisees the benefits of its ongoing research programmes as part of the agreement. Although the franchisor does not retain the main goodwill, the franchisee picks up an element of localized goodwill. Some of the major franchisors include McDonald's, Pizza Hut, KFC, and Benetton.

Management contract is another way of entering a foreign market and obtaining a profit without a large equity investment. In this method, an entrepreneur can enter international business by contracting their management skills and techniques. Turn-key project is a special method by which an entrepreneur can gain some international business experience without much risk. Turn-key projects are undertaken by specialist firms and mainly deal with building a factory or other facility, training the workers to operate the equipment, training the management to run the installation, and then turning it over to local promoters once the operation is going. Financing of the project is often provided by the promoters with periodic payments being made over the life of the project. A turn-key project is thus a contract under which a firm agrees to fully design, construct, and equip a manufacturing/business/service facility and turn the project over to the purchaser when it is ready for operation in return for remuneration.

A consortium is a company created with the participation of three or more companies; allowed in underserved markets or in domains where the government and/or the marketplace can control its monopolistic activity. Coopetition is a word coined from cooperation and competition. It is used when companies that are otherwise competitors collaborate in a consortium to cooperate on areas non-strategic for their core business. They prefer to reduce their costs in these non-strategic areas and compete in other areas where they can differentiate better. The World Wide Web Consortium (W3C) is a consortium that standardizes Web technologies like HTML, XML, and CSS. Airbus is an international consortium involving France, the United Kingdom, Germany, and Spain.

Direct Foreign Investment The wholly-owned foreign subsidiary has been the preferred method of ownership for entrepreneurs to use direct foreign investment for doing international business. This may be in the form of joint ventures, mergers or acquisitions, and multinational companies. In India we can see a lot of foreign direct investment entering the information technology sector.

A joint venture can be defined as "an enterprise in which two or more investors share ownership and control over property rights and operation." Joint ventures are a more extensive form of participation than either exporting or licensing. They have the following advantages: sharing of risk and the ability to combine local in-depth knowledge with a foreign partner possessing know-how in technology or process. Joint financial strength may be the only means of entry and may be the source of supply for a third country. They also have disadvantage. Partners do not have full control of management; it may be impossible to recover capital if need be; disagreement on third-party markets to be served may arise; and partners may have different views on expected benefits. Joint ventures are very common in the automobile sector, for example, Hero Honda motorcycle.

Mergers and acquisitions refer to the aspect of corporate strategy, corporate finance, and management dealing with the buying, selling, dividing, and combining of different companies and similar entities that can aid, finance or help an enterprise grow rapidly in its sector or location of origin or a new field or new location without creating a subsidiary, other child entity or using a joint venture. The distinction between a "merger" and an "acquisition" has become increasingly blurred in various respects particularly in terms of the ultimate economic outcome, although it has not completely disappeared in all situations. The best example is from the aviation industry where Air Deccan has merged with Kingfisher Airlines.

Multinational companies operate in many countries. They have centralized control in their country and are sensitive to the local environment. They adapt to the local environment by following the principle of think global and act local. For example, McDonald's and Pizza Hut in India provide an Indian menu to their customers.

Export Procedure and Documentation

Export procedure and documentation is a requirement of international marketing.[5] A number of government regulatory agencies such as the Directorate General of Foreign Trade; export promotion councils; insurance companies; banking institutions; shipping companies; and airlines; facilitate trade transactions between importers and exporters. Apart from that, policy and service support organizations; commodity specialization organizations; training and research institutions; trading/service corporations; financial institutions; and export promotion zones also facilitate exports in India.

The exporter and importer in an export transaction are governed by distinct regulatory frameworks of their own countries. The terms of shipping and delivery are known as the International Commercial Terms (INCOTERMS). For documentation requirements and the procedure for export transactions, the exporter generally utilizes the services of the clearing and forwarding agents at the ports.

In India, international trade transactions are governed by the Foreign Trade Act, 1992; Export–Import Policy; the Customs Act, 1962; the Foreign Exchange Management Act, 1999; the Export Act, 1963; the Insurance Act, 1938; the Marine Insurance Act, 1963; the Central Excise Act, 1944; the Carriage of Goods by Sea Act, 1924; and the International Commercial Terms, 2000. For entering into international markets, an exporter has to identify an importer and strike a deal with him. The export transaction framework is given in Figure 14.2.

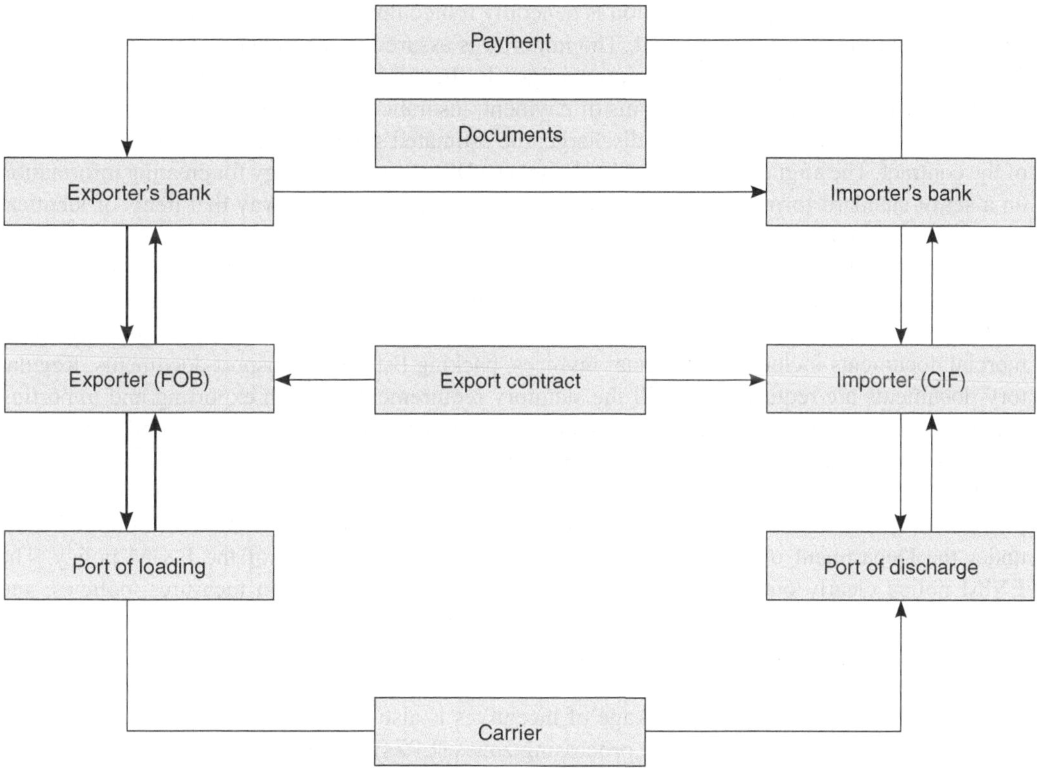

Figure 14.4 Export Transaction Procedure

CHECKLIST FOR ENTREPRENEURS 14.4 ✓ Operations in International Markets

- Operating in international markets is much more complex than in the domestic market. Effective international marketing research is crucial to prevent marketing failures.
- Know that the General Agreement on Tariffs and Trade has been superseded as an international organization by the WTO. An updated general agreement is now one of the WTO's agreements.
- Understand the difference between franchising and licensing. Franchising is also a form of licensing wherein transfer of intellectual property rights takes place. But the two processes are different from each other in a number of ways.
- Know the benefits of strategic alliances for the growth of your enterprise. It is to encourage cooperation with competitors to make use of their specific strengths. A strategic alliance is a shared venture; it reduces the individual risk of the firm especially while operating in international markets.
- Understand the factors affecting the choice of an entry mode into international markets. They are broadly classified as: external factors and internal factors. The external factors include: market size; market growth; government regulations; level of competition; physical infrastructure; level of operational risks. Internal factors include: company objectives; resources; level of commitment; international exposure; and flexibility.
- You have to evaluate various alternatives and choose a mix of international market entry modes as part of a strategic decision in order to serve diverse international markets.

The payment in an export transaction is generally routed through banking channels to assure the exporter about the receipt of payment. The importer is assured of the transfer of the title of goods. The export contract contains the description of goods, the price of each item, net and gross shipping weights, the terms of delivery, the terms of payment, insurance and shipping costs, the currency of sales, the port of loading, the port of discharge, the estimated shipping date, and the validity period of the contract. The aligned documentation system (ADS) is a methodology for creating information on a set of standard forms printed on paper of the same size in such a way that items of identical specifications occupy the same position on each form.

The documents required for export transactions are: commercial documents and regulatory documents. Commercial documents are required to be prepared and used by exporters and importers to discharge their respective legal and other incidental responsibilities under the sales contract. Commercial documents include: commercial invoices, packing lists, and transport documents. Regulatory documents are required to fulfill the statutory requirements of both exporting and importing countries. These documents include: exchange control declaration form; shipping bill; bill of export; bill of entry; and documents for central excise clearance.

The Export–Import (EXIM) policy of India is formulated under the Foreign Trade Act and implemented by the Ministry of Commerce and Industry.[6] The Directorate General of Foreign Trade, under the Department of Commerce, is responsible for the execution of the EXIM policy. The EXIM policy clearly outlines and defines the various export promotion measures, policies, and procedures related to foreign trade. The EXIM policy is published in five volumes and each volume pertains to a specific topic. It offers a variety of schemes for concessional imports by the exporters including the duty exemption scheme, the duty remission scheme, and the export promotion capital goods scheme. A special package of incentives is also given to export and trading houses, export-oriented units (EOUs), export processing zones (EPZs), software technology parks (STPs), electronic hardware technology parks (EHTPs), and agri-export zones (AEZs).

DISCUSSION FORUM

- Discuss the prevailing export environment, formalities, and documentation required for exports.
- Explain the institutions set up in India for promoting export marketing.
- Discuss the EXIM policy of India.

ORGANIZATIONAL LIFE CYCLE

Entrepreneurship is not just about starting a business or remaining content with a particular level of achievement. New ventures pass through transitional stages that present challenges to their founders. These transitional stages are represented by the organizational life cycle. This life cycle requires changes in entrepreneurial behaviour, and because many entrepreneurs cannot adapt to new role responsibilities, their ventures can fail or be terminated. In some cases, the venture survives but the entrepreneur exits. There are many issues to consider for successfully managing ventures during their transition from an embryonic to a mature organization. The organizational life cycle comprises five stages[7]: start-up, survival, expansion, consolidation, and decline.

- **Phase 1—Start-up:** This is the birth stage of the organization, where the emphasis is on creating a product and a market for it. The organization is simple and communication is informal. The organization is, therefore, a personal expression of a single entrepreneur or a few partners. During the start-up phase, entrepreneurs modify their products, change distribution systems, alter services, and experiment with marketing strategies.
- **Phase 2—Survival:** During this stage, the start-up has demonstrated that it is a workable business unit. The goal of the organization continues to be survival. The emphasis shifts to the

viability of the business model. The organization has a structure but the systems have not been fully developed. The entrepreneur is very closely identified with the business.

- **Phase 3—Expansion:** During this stage, the company is reasonably stable and profitable. The rapid growth results in a pattern of success and the organization expands. The concept of a profit centre may be introduced. Systems are being expanded and refined to meet growing requirements, and there is extensive operational and strategic planning. Professional managers are appointed to handle the new and dynamic circumstances.
- **Phase 4—Consolidation:** The stage in the life of a company or an industry in which the components of the company or industry start to merge to form fewer components. These components can include product lines at the company level or companies themselves at the industry level. The consolidation of companies creates new entities.
- **Phase 5—Decline:** Companies in decline are often those that have diversified too widely or created excessively bureaucratic organizations. Successful ventures will not complete the life cycle; they avoid decline.

DISCUSSION FORUM

- What are the various phases in the life cycle of an enterprise?
- What are the important strategies adopted during the stages of the life cycle of an enterprise?

GROWTH STRATEGIES

Growth is a necessary stimulant for most business firms. Growth is the precondition for the survival of a business firm. The reasons that drive business enterprises toward growth are given below:

- For obtaining economies of scale.
- For exploiting business opportunities.
- For facing competition in the market by diversifying the product line.
- For providing protection against adverse business conditions.
- For making optimum utilization of resources.
- For securing subsidies, tax concessions, and other incentives offered by the government.

Generally, the growth strategies adopted by corporates can be classified as:

- Organic growth
- Inorganic growth

Organic Growth

It can also be termed as internal growth. It is the growth from within and can be defined as cost-effective business expansion from within. It is the growth rate that a company can achieve by increasing output and enhancing sales. However, it excludes any profits and growth acquired from takeovers, acquisitions, and mergers as they do not bring about any profits within the company, and therefore are not considered organic. A firm can grow internally by ploughing back its profits into the business. This leads to growth of production and the sales turnover of the business. Internal growth may take place either through increase in the sales of existing products or by adding new products. The various forms of organic growth are discussed below:

Expansion It involves raising the market share, sales revenue, and profit of the present product or services. It is a good strategy for firms with a smaller market share. The expansion strategy is mainly used for market penetration, market development, and product development. Hindustan Unilever Limited used the expansion strategy to penetrate into rural markets (market penetration). Colgate expanded sales by introducing "Colgate Active Salt" (product development). Cadbury expanded the sale of chocolate by including old persons and children (market development).

Diversification It is not feasible for a firm to expand by the expansion strategy beyond a certain point. Therefore, the firm seeks increased sales by developing new products for new markets. This strategy towards growth is called diversification. In case of an expansion strategy, the firm increases the production and sales of its existing products. But in case of diversification, there is the addition of new products and new markets. Diversification is a widely used strategy for growth. For example, LIC, an insurance company initially diversified into mutual funds. McDonald's introduction of the McCafé is an example of diversification.

There are various types of diversification. These are: horizontal integration, vertical integration, concentric diversification, and conglomerate diversification. Horizontal integration involves the addition of parallel new products to the existing product line. For example, seven small cement firms combined together and formed Associated Cement Companies (ACC). In vertical integration, new products or services, which are complementary to the present product line or service, are added. Vertical integration may be of two types, backward and forward. Backward integration involves moving toward the inputs of the present product. For example, Amazon.com vertically integrated backwards when it became not only a bookseller but a book publisher. Starbucks is best known as a chain of coffee shops who went for backward integration by buying coffee farms in China. In forward vertical integration, firms enter the business of distributing or selling its present products. For example, companies such as Bata, Bombay Dyeing, and Raymonds have set up their own retail outlets to sell their fabrics.

A company can use the strategy of concentric diversification when the reputation of the present product or service is high and can be used for new products or services. Therefore, when a firm diversifies into a business, which is related to its present business in terms of marketing, technology, or both, it is called concentric diversification. For example, Amul has added ice creams to its range of milk products. HDFC Bank provides mutual fund services to its customers. When a firm diversifies into a business, which is not related to its existing business both in terms of marketing and technology, it is called conglomerate diversification. Companies such as Reliance, HMT, ITC, and Godrej have grown mainly by conglomerate diversification.

Modernization A firm may use a modernization strategy to achieve growth. A modernization strategy involves upgradation of technology to increase production, to improve quality, and to reduce wastage and the cost of production. Modernization improves the productivity and efficiency of the firm. The growth is systematic and does not affect the normal functioning of the firm. For example, public-sector banks in India used information technology as a modernization strategy in the year 2000.

Inorganic Growth

It can also be termed as external growth. It involves a merger of two or more business firms. A firm may acquire another firm or firms may combine their competitive strength. Inorganic growth is fast and allows immediate utilization of acquired assets. External growth is attempted by enterprises through the following strategies:

Mergers and Acquisitions Merger is an external growth strategy. Mergers and acquisitions involve buying, selling, and combining companies. These help companies to grow rapidly without having to create a new business entity. A merger takes place when two companies combine to form a larger company. It is used by companies to expand their operations and aims to increase their long-term profitability. For example, Air Deccan merged with Kingfisher Airlines and started operating as a single entity. There are various kinds of mergers such as horizontal merger, vertical merger, congeneric merger, and conglomerate merger.

Acquisition refers to the buying of one company by another. It is also known as a takeover. The acquisition can be of two types: a. The acquirer buys only the assets of the target company so that the acquirer has no role in discharging liabilities. b. The acquirer buys the equity of the target company and takes on all assets and liabilities. For example, L. N. Mittal, the owner of Mittal Steel acquired the French steel company Arcelor to achieve global growth in the steel industry.

Distinction Between Mergers and Acquisitions Mergers and acquisitions are often used as though they are synonyms, but they mean different things. Merger and acquisition is a process of combining two or more companies together. Merger is a process when two or more companies come together as a single new company mainly for business expansion. In case of merger, the capital stock of both companies is surrendered and fresh stock is issued. The companies usually share equal profits in the newly created entity. For example, Glaxo Wellcome and SmithKline Beecham merged to become a new company, GlaxoSmithKline. Acquisition is a process when one company buys and takes over another. The buyer company "swallows" the business and stock of the target company, which ceases to exist. For example, Dr Reddy's Laboratories acquired Betapharm through an agreement amounting $597 million.

Strategic Alliances When two or more firms mutually decide to establish a new enterprise by participating in equity capital and in business operations, it is known as strategic alliance or joint venture. It is a mutually beneficial long-term formal relationship formed between two or more parties pursuing a set of goals agreed upon or to meet a critical business need while remaining independent organizations. It is a synergistic arrangement whereby two or more organizations agree to cooperate in the carrying out of a business activity where each brings different strengths and capabilities to the arrangement. Strategic alliances bring enterprises the following benefits:

BREAKTHROUGH ENTREPRENEURSHIP 14.5 Consolidation in the Indian Sky

The airline industry in India has experienced tremendous changes in the past few years. The domestic and international traffic has grown significantly and many players have entered the airline arena. They are: Indian Airlines, Air Sahara, Jet Airways, Air Deccan, Kingfisher, Paramount, Go Air, IndiGo, and Spice Jet. Each airline started its operations at a different period of time and with a different and distinct strategy.

The year 2007 witnessed the mergers between Air India and Indian Airlines, Jet Airways and Air Sahara, and lastly Kingfisher and Air Deccan.

Air India and Indian Airlines merged into a new company—the National Aviation Company of India Ltd, with a combined fleet of 112 carriers. Jet Airways and Air Sahara was renamed JetLite. JetLite had a simple business model catering to price sensitive and first-time flyers.

Kingfisher and Air Deccan merged and decided to operate as a single entity—Kingfisher Aviation, from 2008. The merger was based on recommendations of Accenture, the global consulting firm. After the merger, the company had a combined fleet of 71 aircrafts, connected 70 destinations, and operated 537 flights in a day. The combined entity had a market share of 33 per cent. Through the consolidation, each airline expects synergies to emanate and benefit its operations.

Source: www.dgca.nic.in (last accessed in March 2013).

- Increase in capital for research and product development and yet lower risk (innovations).
- Decrease in product lead times and life cycles (time pressures).
- Ability to bring together complementary skills and assets that neither company could easily develop on its own.
- Access to knowledge and expertise beyond company borders (technology transfer)
- Rapidly achieves scale, critical mass, and momentum (economies of scale—bigger is better).
- Expansion of channels and international market presence (enter a foreign market).
- Building credibility in the industry and brand awareness.
- Providing added value to customers.
- Establishing technological standards for the industry that will benefit the firm.

Strategic alliances come in all shapes and sizes, and include a wide range of cooperation, from contractual to equity forms. Some examples of strategic alliances are Hero Honda, Maruti Suzuki, Kirloskar Toyota, Kirloskar Cummins.

Stages of Alliance Formation[8] A typical strategic alliance formation process involves four steps:

- **Strategy development:** Strategy development involves studying the alliance's feasibility, objectives, and rationale, focusing on the major issues and challenges, and development of resource strategies for production, technology, and people.
- **Partner assessment:** Partner assessment involves analysing a potential partner's strengths and weaknesses, creating strategies for accommodating all partners' management styles, preparing appropriate partner selection criteria, understanding a partner's motives for joining the alliance, and addressing resource capability gaps that may exist for a partner.
- **Contract negotiation:** Contract negotiations involve determining whether all parties have realistic objectives, forming high calibre negotiating teams, defining each partner's contributions and rewards as well as protecting any proprietary information, addressing termination clauses, penalties for poor performances, and highlighting the degree to which arbitration procedures are clearly stated and understood.
- **Alliance operation:** Alliance operations involve addressing senior management's commitment, finding the calibre of resources devoted to the alliance, linking of budgets and resources with strategies priorities, and measuring and rewarding alliance performance.

DISCUSSION FORUM

- Explain the various strategies available for an enterprise to expand the business.
- Elucidate the difference between mergers and acquisitions.

ESSENCE OF BUSINESS ETHICS AND CORPORATE SOCIAL RESPONSIBILITY

Ethics is a branch of philosophy.[9] Its object is the study of both moral and immoral behaviour in order to make well-founded judgements and to arrive at adequate recommendations. A host of

CHECKLIST FOR ENTREPRENEURS 14.6 — Guidelines to Make a Merger Successful

- Identify the objectives, especially economic objectives.
- Specify gains for the shareholders of both the joining companies.
- Be convinced that the acquired company's management is or can be made competent.
- Start the process of merger with the active involvement of the top executives.
- Define business that the company is in clearly.
- Analyse and identify the strengths, weaknesses, and key performance factors for both the combining units.
- Foresee possible problems and discuss them at the initial stage with the other company so as to create a climate of trust.
- Don't threaten the management to be acquired.
- Human considerations should be of prime importance in planning for a merger and designing the organization structure for the new set up.

inventions, improved business organizations, and worldwide commerce have not only changed the way we earn our living, but have also radically changed our whole way of life and even modified our ways of thinking, especially by expanding our perceived needs. These profound changes in our way of life also give rise to a whole range of practical theories concerning the inner functioning and organization of business activities. One of these disciplines is business ethics.

Business ethics concerns the application of general ethical principles and standards to the actions and decisions of companies and the conduct of company personnel. Business ethics evaluates and prescribes moral standards that match a specific sphere in modern society: the business environment. Business is now a prominent part of modern society with its own rules and a relatively independent status. The very basis of business ethics refers to an idea of how business fits into modern society as a whole—a social philosophy of business. More attention is paid to linking strategy with ethical principles and core values in companies headed by moral executives and in companies where ethical principles and core values are a way of life.

Entrepreneurship consists of personal skills as a leader, especially the ability to implement strategic marketing decisions. A highly performing entrepreneur thinks along situation list lines. He or she does not always see marketing activities as a matter of a competitive struggle, with one side emerging the winner and the other side the loser. More specifically, besides competitive warfare for the survival of the fittest, there are other business games that allow for proper exchange of views and real partnerships. Also, morally involved entrepreneurs have great skills in convincing and motivating interlocutors by setting a coherent and appealing example. Entrepreneurs can achieve a higher performance by personally integrating moral demands in corporate policies. Here, the term "higher" refers to a balance among three different moral requirements:

1. Meeting corporate goals, especially medium- and long-term profitability.
2. Ethically motivated job satisfaction.
3. The fostering of durable partnerships.

Ethically valid performance is produced by preventing unnecessary harm and by the ability to build constructive and durable partnerships with employees, consumers, and suppliers. The corporate mission statement articulates the basic objective of ethical entrepreneurial performance. This mission statement should define the balance between two constituents:

1. The strategic vocation of the corporation; and
2. Its commitment to specific corporate responsibilities

Corporate Social Responsibility

Social responsibility applies to business concerns because it is a company's duty to operate without any harm towards stakeholders and the environment. Enterprises who strictly follow social responsibility activities consider the overall betterment of the society in its decisions and actions. Social responsibility comprises duties that every individual or enterprise have to carry out so as to sustain a balance between the economy and the ecosystem.

The notion of social responsibility as it applies to business concerns a company's duty to operate in an honourable manner. It looks to provide good working conditions for employees, be a good steward of the environment, and actively work to better the quality of life in the local communities where it operates and in society at large. Entrepreneurs who want their companies to be regarded as exemplary corporate citizens must see that their companies operate ethically. They must also personally display a social conscience in making decisions that affect employees, the environment, the communities in which they operate, and society at large.

Social Responsibility Strategies of Enterprises

An enterprise's social responsibility strategy[10] is defined by the specific combination of socially beneficial activities it opts to support with its contributions of time, money, and other resources. Many enterprises tailor their strategic efforts to operate in a socially-responsible manner to fit their core values and business mission in order to fulfill their duties towards all stakeholders and society at large. The social responsibility strategies of enterprises comprises the following:

- Operating the business in an ethical way.
- Charitable activities such as community service and helping the needy.
- Actions to protect the environment like "go green" projects, using products that are free from materials harmful for the environment.
- Acting for employee well-being as in helping them in their further studies and creating an awareness of a healthy life.

DISCUSSION FORUM

- Discuss the importance of CSR in today's competitive world.
- Explain the essence of ethics in enterprises.

SNAPSHOT

- Ethics is a branch of philosophy. Business ethics evaluates and prescribes moral standards that match a specific sphere in modern society—the business environment. An ethically valid performance is produced by preventing unnecessary harm and by the ability to build constructive and durable partnerships with employees, consumers, and suppliers.
- Social responsibility applies to business concerns because it is a company's duty to operate without any harm towards its stakeholders and the environment.

BREAKTHROUGH ENTREPRENEURSHIP 14.7 **Temple of Ethics**

Business ethics and corporate social responsibility are the tools used by today's businesses to project their image as an honest, socially-conscious organization. Polyhydron Private Limited (PPL) located in Machhe Industrial Estate, Belgaum, Karnataka, is one of the very few companies in India practising business ethics in its fullest sense. These days many ashrams are run like a business. This is the inspiring story of PPL, a business run like an ashram.

The two units of Polyhydron are appropriately called Temple of Ethics (established in 1986) and Business Ashram (established in 2002). PPL is a corruption-free business enterprise. The factory looks more like an ashram. The campus is spick and span, everyone works quietly, and there is tranquility in the environment. There is a beautiful pond with swans swimming in it with a lot of greenery around. There is a *dhyaan mandir* where workers meditate. There is a well-equipped gymnasium and a place for practising yoga. There is no security at the gate. The system is fully transparent. The financial information is open to all stakeholders.

PPL's mission statement is, "We will nurture an ethically managed organization. We will not exploit our customers, employees, suppliers, government, society, and nature." PPL operates under the overall umbrella of ethical management, which guides all the decisions taken by the organization. The means by which profits are generated are ethical at PPL. "Honesty is not the best policy. It is THE policy and the campus is a place for grooming *karmayogis* based on an experiment of integrating spirituality with business," asserts Suresh Hundre, the CEO of PPL.

Fruits of Ethical Practices at PPL

- Employees: Increase in salary, productivity, bonus, and efficiency.
- Customers: Quality products at minimum cost and in time.
- Suppliers: Single supplier, prompt payment, long-term relationship, and constant assistance.
- Government: Prompt in paying income tax (won an award for the same from the government).
- Society: Liberal donations and continuous financial support to people in need.
- Fellow entrepreneurs: Constant effort to propagate the advantages of ethical business practices.

Polyhydron is known for its ethical management. People from all over India visit the company to understand and analyse the systems. It has become a kind of "pilgrimage centre" for the corporate world in India. It can be said that managing business ethically is no longer an option in the new millennium. To evolve any business into an ethical one requires tremendous effort and commitment at all levels in the organization. This has been proven at PPL.

Sources: www.polyhydron.com (last accessed in March 2013) and interview with Suresh Hundre, CEO, PPL.

SUMMARY

Marketing is a process, which identifies, anticipates, and satisfies customer needs efficiently and profitably in keeping with the objectives of the enterprise. Marketing is a specialized and dynamic area. The enterprise should be conceived as an allied system of marketing processes that can be used to meet the customer's needs. A large-scale business can have its own formal marketing network, media campaigns, and sales force.

The growing competitive market for services means that a marketing orientation has become essential for the competitive survival for service industries too. There are many differences between product and service marketing. A few distinctions of service marketing are: the intangible nature of the service product, the trust and self-confidence aligned with the product, product positioning, more contact between customer and service personnel, customer involvement in production, interaction among marketing, operations, and human resources, problems in controlling product quality and consistency, absence of inventories, importance of the time factor, and structure of distribution channels.

The essential marketing mix of service sectors, which plays an instrumental role in marketing the services to the set consumers are people, process, and physical evidence. The marketing process is the essence of all enterprises. In the marketing process, products are interrelated, and add value to the end customer and to society. The various elements or activities would include market research, segmentation, marketing mix, implementation, and evaluation. The various techniques of marketing are Internet marketing, direct marketing, niche marketing, ambush marketing, green marketing, social marketing, relationship marketing, viral marketing, rural marketing, and global marketing.

Business must face numerous barriers when entering international markets. Barriers to entry can be imposed by local and international competition, by the local channel structure, and by logistics and other firms offering marketing support. Factors in the economic, political, financial, and legal environment can also create barriers for businesses attempting to expand internationally. The reduction in trade barriers constitutes a main concern of multinationals and their representative governments. In addition to participating in numerous regional treaties, governments have joined forces to create forums for the discussion of trade issues and mechanisms for the reduction of trade restrictions. One such organization is the WTO.

The organization's life cycle comprises five stages: start-up, survival, expansion, consolidation, and decline. Business growth means an increase in the size or scale of the operations of a firm usually accompanied by increase in its resources and output. Growth strategy refers to a strategic plan formulated and implemented for expanding a firm's business. Various types of growth can be divided into two broad categories—organic and inorganic growth. Organic growth is an internal growth strategy and includes: expansion, diversification, and modernization. Inorganic growth is an external growth strategy and includes: mergers and strategic alliances.

Ethics is a branch of philosophy. Its object is the study of both moral and immoral behaviour in order to make well-founded judgements and to arrive at adequate recommendations. Business ethics evaluates and prescribes moral standards that match a specific sphere in modern society—the business environment. Corporate social responsibility applies to business concerns because it is a company's duty to operate without any harm towards its stakeholders and the environment.

KEY TERMS

Protectionism: All actions by national and local governments aimed at protecting local markets from foreign competitors

Antidumping: Legislation designed to counter unfair price competition.

Acquisition: Purchase of one organization by another organization.

Ambush Marketing: Is a technique used by enterprises where the advertisers associate themselves with a particular event without any investments.

Backward Integration: It is aimed at moving lower down the production process so that the firm is able to supply its own raw materials or basic components.

Concentric Diversification: A firm diversifies into some business, which is related to its present business in terms of marketing, technology, or both.

Conglomerate Diversification: A firm diversifies into a business, which is not related to its existing business both in terms of marketing and technology.

Consortium: A company created with the participation of three or more companies.

Direct Marketing: Direct marketing focuses on directly reaching a target market.

Diversification Strategy: The firm seeks to grow by developing new products or new markets.

Diversification: The practice of manufacturing a variety of products, investing in a variety of assets, and selling in a number of markets.

Expansion Strategy: It involves raising the market share, sales revenue, and profit of the present product or services.

Forward Integration: It means that firms enter into the business of distributing or selling their present products.

Franchising: A system in which a company grants the right or license to an individual or group to market its products or services in a specific territory.

Global Marketing: Marketing carried out across national boundaries spanning a number of countries.

Green Marketing: Green marketing refers to the marketing of products that are assumed to be environmentally friendly.

Growth Strategy: It refers to a strategic plan formulated and implemented for expanding a firm's business.

Horizontal Integration: It involves the addition of parallel new products to the existing product line.

Inorganic Growth: It can also be termed as external growth.

Internet Marketing: The marketing of products through the Internet is known as Internet marketing.

Licensing: It is an arrangement between two or more enterprises that enter a legal contract for a specific business purpose.

Market Research: A specific market is identified and its size and other characteristics are measured.

Marketing Mix: A planned mix of the controllable elements of a product's marketing plan commonly termed the 4 Ps: product, price, place, and promotion. In service marketing, the marketing mix comprises the 7 Ps (physical evidence, people, and process).

Marketing: A process which identifies, anticipates, and satisfies customer needs efficiently and profitably in keeping with the objectives of the enterprise.

Merger: When two companies combine their resources to form a new company.

Modernization: It involves the upgradation of technology.

Niche Marketing: It involves the concentration of all marketing efforts on a small but specific and well-defined segment of the population.

Organic Growth: It can also be termed as internal growth.

Relationship Marketing: It is a technique that involves building a long term and profitable relationship with customers.

Rural Marketing: Rural marketing is defined as a marketing process in which one dominant participant is from a rural area.

Social Marketing: Social marketing focuses on attaining explicit behavioural goals for a social cause.

Strategic Alliance/Joint Venture: When two or more firms mutually decide to establish a new enterprise by participating in equity capital and in business operations.

Tariffs: Taxes imposed on goods entering a country.

Turn-key Project: One of the special modes of carrying out international business is a turn-key project. It is a contract under which a firm agrees to fully design, construct, and equip a manufacturing/business/service facility and turn the project over to the purchaser when it is ready for operation for remuneration.

Vertical Integration: In vertical integration, new products or services are added, which are complementary to the present product line or service.

Viral Marketing: It is a phenomenon that assists and encourages people to pass along a marketing message.

World Trade Organization (WTO): The largest and most influential international trade organization whose primary goal is to ensure the free flow of trade.

CASE STUDY

Sabki Pasand Nirma!

The success story of Karsanbhai Patel, who founded the Nirma group of companies in Ahmedabad, Gujarat, is one of the most inspirational stories in India's business history. The low-cost washing powder marketed by Patel under the brand name Nirma revolutionized the detergent market in India. Karsanbhai Patel had to overcome many hardships and used many innovative marketing and distribution strategies to ensure the success of his product.

In 1969, Karsanbhai Patel, a chemist at Gujarat Government's Department of Mining and Geology, started manufacturing and selling phosphate-free, synthetic detergent powder from a 100 sq. ft room. Patel named the detergent Nirma after his daughter Nirupama. Initially, he priced his detergent at ₹3.50. The premium detergent powder in the market, Hindustan Unilever's Surf, was being sold at ₹15 per kg at the time. Patel used to sell 15–20 packets on his way back from office. The detergent soon became popular in his hometown of Ruppur in Gujarat.

When business improved, Karsanbhai Patel employed a sales team to promote and market his product. Nirma's salespersons started to approach retailers of multinational brands to stock the company's products. These retailers were reluctant to stock Nirma products. They were willing to keep the stock only on lengthy credit terms and as a special favour to the salesperson. As a result, the huge accumulated credit in the market began to affect the company's operations. Karsanbhai decided to tackle this issue by launching an aggressive advertising campaign and following a no-credit policy. He instructed the sales team to collect cash from retailers or request retailers to return the product. In the meantime, he launched an aggressive print, radio, and television campaign. A television campaign with the jingle, "*Washing powder Nirma, washing power Nirma, doodh si safedi Nirma se aaye, rangeen kapde bhi khil khil jaaye, sabki pasand Nirma*," was developed. This jingle has become one of the most enduring tunes in Indian advertising.

The aggressive advertising strategy adopted by Patel kickstarted demand for Nirma products. Soon customers started asking retailers for the detergent. The retailers did not have stocks with them and started pressurizing Patel to introduce the product in the market again. The popularity of Nirma ensured that Karsanbhai could dictate his own terms—full cash on delivery, no credits, and tight supply. Overnight, the brand was able to provide stiff competition to the leading global brands. The successful marketing mantra followed by Karsanbhai Patel was to "give your consumer what he wants, when he wants, where he wants, and at the price he wants, and selling will be achieved quite automatically."

Nirma took on Hindustan Unilever Limited (HUL) in the low-price detergent segment. In those days, HUL commanded the majority share of 36 per cent in the Indian detergent market. Nirma gave cut-throat competition to HUL and carved a niche for itself in the lower end of the detergents and toilet soap market. The brand name Nirma became almost synonymous with low-priced detergents and toilet soaps. By the end of 1987, Nirma had a 49 per cent share in the detergents market. HUL's share had fallen to eight per cent in 1989.

Nirma tried to replicate its success in the low-price segment by launching toilet soaps for the premium segment. HUL retaliated by launching Wheel, which is today the world's largest detergent in terms of volume. However, unlike Nirma, HUL ensured that it had brands like Rin in the mid-segment and Surf in the premium segment. Meanwhile, Procter and Gamble came out with Tide and Ariel. Surf went from Surf to Super Surf to Surf Excel and changed its technology along the way. Nirma also slowly tried to launch Nirma Blue and Nirma Cake, but the product differentiation was not clearly visible in the market.

Today, Nirma strives to face the challenges that arise out of competing with MNCs like HUL and P&G, which have deep pockets to advertise their wares, well-developed research and development facilities, and a larger distribution channel. The Nirma story is the success story of how an Indian entrepreneur took on MNCs to rewrite the rules of the business. The business is still a profitable one. Nirma has to work towards building economies with a sharp focus on a limited range of complementary products.

Questions:

1. What are the key factors that contributed to Nirma's success?
2. What are the challenges that Nirma faces in the market currently?
3. What recommendations would you make to Nirma's senior marketing executives going forward?

Source: www.nirma.co.in (last accessed in March 2013).

DISCUSSION QUESTIONS

1. Define marketing and explain how marketing plays an important role in an enterprise.
2. Explain the techniques of marketing that have evolved in the modern era.
3. Elucidate the marketing process with reference to the service sector.
4. Why should a company get involved in branding? What benefits will it get by developing a brand? Explain this with examples from the Indian market.
5. Define global marketing and discuss its scope.
6. Briefly explain the barriers and facilitators of international business.
7. Distinguish between domestic marketing and global marketing.
8. What are the different growth strategies available to enterprises? Give an example for each of them.
9. Define business ethics. What do you mean by aligning strategic management to social responsiveness?

ACTIVITY

The Snack Game

Introduction: One of the most basic concepts in marketing is the marketing mix. The marketing mix consists of elements that an organization controls, which can be used to satisfy or communicate with customers. The marketing mix consists of the 4 Ps: Product, Place, Promotion, and Price. In addition to the 4 Ps, three additional Ps are added for service marketing. The 7 Ps of the service marketing mix consist of Product, Place, Promotion, Price, People, Physical Evidence, and Process. The components of each P are given below:

- **Product:** Physical features, quality level, accessories, packaging, warranties, product lines, branding.
- **Price:** Flexibility, price level, terms, differentiation, discounts, allowances.
- **Place:** Channel type, exposure, intermediaries, outlet locations, transportation, storage, managing channels.
- **Promotion:** Sales promotion, advertising, training, salespeople, incentives, publicity.
- **People:** Employees, recruitment, training, motivation, teamwork, rewards, customers.
- **Physical Evidence:** Facility design, equipment, employee dress, business cards, other tangibles
- **Process:** Flow of activities, service delivery, operating systems, customer involvement.

- **Objectives:** To internalize the marketing process among students and in the process understand the 7 Ps of the marketing mix through experiential learning.

Duration: One day

Instructions:

- Students form teams of four to six each and choose a location, preferably where they do not get any reference sales from friends.
- The team needs to choose an edible product to be sold. For example, sandwich, fruit, *mirchi bajji*, *vada pav*, juice, salad, pastries, sweets. The choice is left to them. Now the team can take various decisions such as:
  - Whether to prepare or outsource (make/buy). Whatever may be the decision, the team needs to ensure the right infrastructure needed for the same.
  - Take the necessary permission to keep the stall open for half a day.
  - Start the sales process.
  - The team that makes the highest profit wins the competition.
- Once the game is over, each team should share its experience in front of the class.
- Use the snack game worksheet for recording and documentation.

Rules of the Game:

- While the team that makes the most profit wins, the real objective is to internalize the marketing process among students. Hence, no shortcuts/bloated profits are to be shown by the students and a high level of integrity should be ensured.
- No selling to known friends under obligation.
- Hygiene should be maintained.
- While students are free to sell any edible product, selling non-vegetarian items is discouraged.
- Participants are supposed to record buying prices from the market, record unit sales price, total revenue, profit/loss details, product-wise and in a clear manner.
- Students can choose more than one edible product. There is no limit as such, but total buying cost should not exceed ₹1,000 per team.
- The competition starts at 9 a.m. and ends by 3 p.m.

Learning:

- Understanding the 7 Ps of the service marketing mix.
- Identifying the customer.

Snack Game Worksheet

Team No./Name	Name of Students	Eatery Chosen	Location	Marks out of Ten

PROJECT

1. What are the various export promotion councils in India and how do they help in promoting opportunities for Indian marketers across the globe? Prepare a report on this.
2. Conduct a secondary data analysis to prepare a project report on the changes and evolution of organized retailing in India.
3. A company is planning to launch a branded lantern in the state of Karnataka. Prepare a marketing plan for the launch.

ENDNOTES

1. Kotler, Philip, Kevin Keller, Abraham Koshy, and Mithileswar Jha (2007). *Marketing Management: A South Asian Perspective*. New Delhi: Pearson Education, 13th ed.
2. Zeithaml, Valarie A., A. Parasuraman, and Leonard L. Berry (2001). *Delivering Quality Service: Balancing Customer Perceptions and Expectations*. New York: The Free Press.
3. Panda, Tapan K. (2007). *Marketing Management: Text and Cases*. New Delhi: Excel Books.
4. Linton, Ian (2010). *The Secrets of Success in Marketing*. FT Press.
5. Rathor, B. S. and J. S. Rathor (2010). *Export Marketing*. New Delhi: Himalaya Publishing House, 8th ed.
6. Joshi, Rakesh Mohan (2010). *International Marketing*. New Delhi: Oxford University Press.
7. Roy, Rajeev (2008). *Entrepreneurship*. New Delhi: Oxford University Press
8. Glueck, William F. and Lawrence R. Jauch (1984). *Business Policy and Strategic Management*. New Delhi: Tata McGraw-Hill.
9. Velasquez, Manuel G. (1992). *Business Ethics: Concepts and Cases*. Englewood Cliffs, NJ: Prentice Hall.
10. Kotler, Philip and Nancy Lee (2005). *Corporate Social Responsibility: Doing the Most Good for Your Company and Your Cause*. New York: John Wiley and Sons.

Index

A

accounting, 286–287
  process of, 287
  types of, 288
accounting rate of return (ARR), 142–143
activity/turnover ratios, 300
Aditya Birla Group, 355
agri-tourism, 120
Air Act, 1981, 345–346
Altman's Sickness Prediction Model, 271–272
ambush marketing, 369
angel investing, 148
ArcelorMittal, 259
ARR. *See* accounting rate of return (ARR)
Ash, Mary Kay, 58
Asia, 46
  women entrepreneurs in, 46
assets, 290
Assistance to Rural Women in Non-farm Development (ARWIND), 58
Association of Women Entrepreneurs of Karnataka (AWAKE), 56
average collection period, 300
average payment period, 300
AWAKE. *See* Association of Women Entrepreneurs of Karnataka (AWAKE)

B

balance sheet, 290
  contents of, 290
benefit–cost ratio (BCR), 145
Bikchandani, Sanjeev, 110
Birla, Kumar Mangalam, 356
bookkeeping, 286–287
B-plan software programs, 165
brainstorming, 113
break-even analysis, 298
break-even point, 298
B-schools, 9
Burman, S. K., 70
business plan, 159–173
  contents of, 160–163
  presenting of, 163–164
  procedure for setting up of an enterprise, 166–173
  reasons for failure of, 164–166
business incubators, 223
business strategy, 160
buzz group, 35

C

Cantillon, Richard, 4
capital budgeting, 140
capital market ratios, 302–303
capital structure, 149
case method, 36
cash flow statements, 292–293
cash book, 289
Central Bank of India Credit Schemes, 56–57
Centre for Women's Development Studies (CWDS), 47
Chanel, Coco, 59
Cherukuri, U. Rao, 146
Child Labour Act, 1986, 344
CII. *See* Confederation of Indian Industry (CII)
Cochran, Thomas, 29–30
Coir Board, 207–208
Competition Act, 2002, 252–253
Confederation of Indian Industry (CII), 221
conference, 35
Consortium of Women Entrepreneurs of India (CWEI), 54–55
Consumer Protection Act, 251–252
Contract Labour Act, 1970, 348
cooperative society, 238–239
Copyright Act, 1957, 249–250
corporate social responsibility, 382–384
cost accounting, 288
cost of capital, 149
costing, 366–367
Council of Scientific and Industrial Research (CSIR), 222
creativity, 10
CSIR. *See* Council of Scientific and Industrial Research (CSIR)
current assets, 290
current ratio, 296
CWDS. *See* Centre for Women's Development Studies (CWDS)
CWEI. *See* Consortium of Women Entrepreneurs of India (CWEI)

D

Dabur India Ltd, 70
Dairy Information Services Kiosk (DISK), 248
debentures, 149
debt equity ratio, 301
debt financing, 148
debt ratio, 301
debt solvency ratios, 301
debt-coverage service ratio, 301
debtors' turnover ratio, 296
decision-making ability, 11
demand forecasting, 315–316
detailed project report, 150–151
DIC. *See* District Industries Centre (DIC)
direct marketing, 368
DISK. *See* Dairy Information Services Kiosk (DISK)
District Industries Centre (DIC), 215–216
drone entrepreneur, 8
DuPont analysis, 303

E

e-*choupal*, 248
ecological analysis, 142
economic analysis, 142
EDI. *See* Entrepreneurship Development Institute of India (EDI)
Edward de Bono's Six Thinking Hats, 116
E-governance initiatives, 248
employee engagement, 339
Employees First, Customers Second, 338
Employees Provident Fund and Miscellaneous Provisions Act, 1952, 347
employment generation, 3
EMT. *See* entrepreneurship motivation training (EMT)
entrepreneurial competencies, 10–14
entrepreneurial development, 21–28
  environmental factors affecting, 24–27
  models of, 28–31
  process of, 36–37
entrepreneurial opportunities, 111
entrepreneurs
  advantages of, 7
  capacity building for, 14–15
  differences with manager, 8–9
  mobility of, 118
  types of, 7–8
  ways of becoming, 6–7
Entrepreneurship Development Institute of India (EDI), 210–211
entrepreneurship motivation training (EMT), 32–34
Environment Act, 1986, 345–346

environmental management system, 333–334
  benefits of, 333
EPZ. *See* Export Promotion Zone (EPZ)
Equal Remuneration Act, 1976, 344–345
equity capital, 147
equity financing, 147
exit strategy, 278
Export Promotion Zone (EPZ), 226

F

Fabian entrepreneur, 8
failure, 280
family businesses, 71–84
  challenges faced by, 77–79
  characteristics in India, 74
  improving performance of, 80–81
  roles, responsibilities, and rights of family members in, 75
  stages of development in, 73–74
  succession in, 79
  Three-circle Model of, 75–77
  types of, 74–75
FASSI. *See* Federation of Associations of Small Industries of India (FASII)
Federation of Associations of Small Industries of India (FASII), 221–222
Federation of Indian Women Entrepreneurs (FIWE), 55
FEMA. *See* Foreign Exchange Management Act (FEMA)
FICCI Ladies Organization (FLO), 55
Fields, Debbi, 60
financial accounting, 288
financial analysis, 141–142
financial management, 285–305
  functions of, 285–286
financial ratio analysis, 299–303
financial statements, 289–294
FIWE. See Federation of Indian Women Entrepreneurs (FIWE)
fixed assets, 290
FLO. *See* FICCI Ladies Organization (FLO)
Foreign Exchange Management Act (FEMA), 1999, 253
franchising, 239–241
Frank W. Young's Theory of Group Level Pattern, 30

G

GAAP. *See* Generally Accepted Accounting Principles (GAAP)
Gantt charts, 134–135
GCMMF. *See* Gujarat Cooperative Milk Marketing Federation (GCMMF)
gender and development approach, 63
Generally Accepted Accounting Principles (GAAP), 288
glass ceiling, 65
global entrepreneurship environment, 21–22
global marketing, 371–372
goal orientation, 12
good business opportunity, 111–112
Google, 336
Gordon method, 115
green marketing, 369
growth strategies, 379
Gujarat Cooperative Milk Marketing Federation (GCMMF), 230

H

Housing and Urban Development Corporation (HUDCO), 218–219
Hozelist's sociocultural theory, 29
HUDCO. *See* Housing and Urban Development Corporation (HUDCO)
Huffington, Arianna, 60
human resource development, 263
human resource management, 334–338
  functions of, 335–337
Husain, Shahnaz, 66–67

I

ICSI. *See* Indian Council of Small Industries (ICSI)
imitative entrepreneur, 8
India
  business climate in, 22–24
  business laws in, 241–242
  business opportunities in, 119–120
  contributions of family businesses in, 73
  industrial sickness in, 267–270
  institutions supporting women entrepreneurs in, 54–56
  services sector in, 357–358
  women entrepreneurs in, 46–48
Indian Companies Act, 1956, 245–246
Indian Contract Act, 1872, 243
Indian Council of Small Industries (ICSI), 222
Indian Factories Act, 1948, 341
Indian Partnership Act, 1932, 244–245
Industrial Disputes Act, 1947, 343
Industrial Employment Act, 1946, 342–343
industrial estate, 226
industrial relations, 338
industrial sickness, 263–280
  causes of, 269–270
  definition of, 264–265
  prediction of, 271–272
  process of, 272–273
  symptoms of, 270–271
industry associations, 221
Information Technology Act, 2000, 247
initial public offering, 278–279
innovative entrepreneur, 7
inorganic growth, 380–381
InstaPlan, 138–139
integrated models, 30
Integrated Rural Development Programme (IRDP), 47
intellectual property rights, 249–251
interest cover ratio, 301
internal accruals, 147
internal rate of return (IRR), 144–145
internal–external locus of control theory, 29
international trade, 373–378
Internet marketing, 368
intrapreneurship, 8–9
inventory management, 322–325
inventory turnover ratio, 300
Invert Sugar, 214
investment bank, 280
IRDP. *See* Integrated Rural Development Programme (IRDP)
IRR. *See* internal rate of return (IRR)

J

Jameson, Jenna, 59
joint Hindu family business, 232
joint stock company, 234–237
journal, 288

K

Kadolkar, Rasika, 158
Kakinada experiment, 30
Khadi and Village Industries Commission (KVIC), 207
Kumar, Ritu, 62–63
KVIC. *See* Khadi and Village Industries Commission (KVIC)

L

L. C. Gupta's Sickness Prediction Model, 272
laboratory method, 36
labour laws, 340–349
Laghu Udyog Bharati (LUB), 222
Lauder, Estée, 60
lecture method, 34–35
ledger, 288
liabilities, 290
limited liability partnership (LLP), 233–234
liquidation, 280
liquidity ratios, 300

LLP. *See* limited liability partnership (LLP)
LUB. *See* Laghu Udyog Bharati (LUB)

M

Mahalingam, S., 284
Mahila Vikas Nidhi (MVN), 58
maintenance, 327
management accounting, 288
management deficiency, 262
market analysis, 141
Marketing of Non-farm Products of Rural Women (MAHIMA), 58
marketing process, 362–366
materials management, 320–321
Maternity Benefit Act, 1961, 348
Max Weber's theory of religious beliefs, 29
McClelland's theory of achievement motivation, 28–29
MFO. *See* micro-finance organization (MFO)
micro-finance organization (MFO), 53
Microsoft Project, 138
milestones, 174
Mines Act, 1952, 348
Minimum Wages Act, 1948, 342
Mittal, Lakshmi Niwas, 260
Mother Dairy, 312
MSME–DO (SIDO), 208
Mullins's Seven-domain Framework, 121–123
Murkumbi, Vidya, 48
Murkumbi, Narendra, 276

N

NABARD. *See* National Bank for Agriculture and Rural Development (NABARD)
Narayan, Patrica, 62
National Bank for Agriculture and Rural Development (NABARD), 57–58, 217–218
National Board for Micro, Small and Medium Enterprises (NBMSME), 206
National Company Law Appellate Tribunal (NCLAT), 266
National Company Law Tribunal (NCLT), 266
National Dairy Development Board (NDDB), 312
National Institute for Micro, Small, and Medium Enterprises (NI-MSME), 212–213
National Productivity Council (NPC), 209–210
National Research Development Corporation of India (NRDCI), 211–212, 214
National Safety Council of India (NSCI), 332
National Science and Technology Entrepreneurship Development Board (NSTEDB), 209
National Small Industries Corporation (NSIC), 208–209
NBMSME. *See* National Board for Micro, Small and Medium Enterprises (NBMSME)
NCLAT. *See* National Company Law Appellate Tribunal (NCLAT)
NCLT. *See* National Company Law Tribunal (NCLT)
NDDB. *See* National Dairy Development Board (NDDB)
need for achievement, 32
Negotiable Instruments Act, 1881, 246–247
net asset value, 301
net present value (NPV), 143
network techniques, 135–138
New Designs Act, 2000, 251
NGOs. *See* non-governmental organizations (NGOs)
niche marketing, 368–369
NI-MSME. *See* National Institute for Micro, Small, and Medium Enterprises (NI-MSME)
non-governmental organizations (NGOs), 222
NPC. *See* National Productivity Council (NPC)
NPV. *See* net present value (NPV)
NRDCI. *See* National Research Development Corporation of India (NRDCI)
NSCI. *See* National Safety Council of India (NSCI)
NSIC. *See* National Small Industries Corporation (NSIC)
NSTEDB. *See* National Science and Technology Entrepreneurship Development Board (NSTEDB)

O

occupational health and safety advisory services, 330–333
occupational mobility, 119
OHSAS 18001 registration, 331
operations management, 313–314
operations plan, 174
operations strategy, 314–315
opportunities, 115
  creation of, 115
  identification of, 117
opportunity evaluation, 120–123
organic growth, 379–380
organizational chart, 174
organizational life cycle, 378–379

P

panel discussion, 35
Pareek, Udai, 30
participative methods, 35–36
partnership, 232
Patents Act, 1970, 249
payback method, 146
Payment of Bonus Act, 1965, 342
Payment of Gratuity Act, 1972, 347
Payment of Wages Act, 1936, 341–342
Plantations Labour Act, 1951, 348
PMI. *See* Project Management Institute (PMI)
PMRY. *See* Prime Minister's Rozgar Yojana (PMRY)
PPC. *See* production planning and control (PPC)
preference capital, 147
pricing, 366–368
PRIMAVERA, 139
Prime Minister's Rozgar Yojana (PMRY), 47
PRISM Project Manager, 139
profitability ratios, 301–302
problem solving, 12
product planning, 263
product positioning, 359
production management, 317–319
production planning and control (PPC), 317
productivity, 325
profit and loss account, 292
project analysis, 140–141
project financing, 147–149
project implementation phase, 149
project life cycle, 133–134
Project Management Institute (PMI), 132
project management software, 138–139
project manager, 132–133
project profile, 151
project proposal, 140
project scheduling, 134–138
  using Gantt charts, 134–135
  using network techniques, 135–138
Project Shakti, 372
psychological models, 28–29
  internal–external locus of control theory, 29
  McClelland's theory of achievement motivation, 28–29
  theory of withdrawal of status respect, 29
purchase book, 288

Q

QMS. *See* quality management systems (QMS)

quality management system
(QMS), 327–329
quick ratio, 296

R

Ramakrishnan, C., 289
RAMP Model, 121
Rao, T. V., 30
red herring, 280
redBus, 130
regional development, 4
relationship marketing, 370
reverse brainstorming, 115
Right to Information Act, 2005, 252
risk-taking, 11
Roddick, Anita, 59
role play, 36
Roy, Revathi Siddhartha, 50
RUDSET. *See* Rural Development and Self-Employment Training (RUDSET)
Rural Development and Self-Employment Training (RUDSET), 47
rural marketing, 371

S

Sabala, 54
Sacred Moments, 114
sales book, 289
Sales of Goods Act, 1930, 244
Say, Jean-Baptiste, 5
Schumpeter, Joseph, 5
Science and Technology Applied for Rural Transformation (START), 47
SCXs. *See* Sub-Contracting Exchanges (SCXs)
self-help group (SHG), 65
seminar, 35
services marketing, 360–362
Sexual Harassment of Women at Their Work Place (Prevention) Act, 2003, 345
SEZ. *See* Special Economic Zone (SEZ)
SFC. *See* State Financial Corporation (SFC)
Shaw-Mazumdar, Kiran, 42, 61–62
Shri Mahila Griha Udyog Lijjat Papad (SMGULP), 64
SIADB. *See* State Industries Area Development Board (SIADB)
Sick Industrial Companies Act, 265–266
sick units
  rehabilitation of, 274–275
SIDC. *See* State Industrial Development Corporation (SIDC)
simulation method, 36
Small Industries Development Bank of India, 58
SMGULP. *See* Shri Mahila Griha Udyog Lijjat Papad (SMGULP)
Smith, Adam, 5
social marketing, 369–370
social security laws, 346–347
sociological models, 29–30
  Frank W. Young's theory of group level pattern, 30
  Hozelist's sociocultural theory, 29
  Max Weber's theory of religious beliefs, 29
  Thomas Cochran's theory of entrepreneurial supply, 29–30
sole proprietorship, 231–232
Special Economic Zone (SEZ), 224
START. *See* Science and Technology Applied for Rural Transformation (START)
State Directorate of Industries and Commerce, 215
State Financial Corporation (SFC), 216
State Industrial Development Corporation (SIDC), 216
State Industries Area Development Board (SIADB), 216–217
stock exchange, 280
stock turnover ratio, 296
stock–working capital ratio, 296
Sub-Contracting Exchanges (SCXs), 223
supply chain management, 319–320
survey method, 114–115
Swaraj Tractors, 214
syndicate method, 35–36

T

Takamatsu Corporation, 72
TAT. *See* thematic apperception test (TAT)
Tata Consultancy Services, 284, 306–309
Tata Motors, 289
TCO. *See* Technical Consultancy Organization (TCO)
team building, 10
technical analysis, 141
Technical Consultancy Organization (TCO), 219
technology management, 316–317
term loans, 149
thematic apperception test (TAT), 32
theory of withdrawal of status respect, 29
Thomas Cochran's theory of entrepreneurial supply, 29–30
Three-circle Model, 75–77
total quality management (TQM), 325–327
  benefits of, 326–327
  prerequisites of, 326
TQM. *See* total quality management (TQM)
Trade Unions Act, 1926, 344
Trade Marks Act, 1999, 250–251
turnaround strategy, 275

U

underwriter, 280

V

valuation, 280
value proposition, 174
VC. *See* venture capital (VC)
venture capital (VC), 147–148
venture capital financing, 148
Vidya Vahini, 248

W

WACC. *See* weighted average cost of capital (WACC)
Wadhwani Centre for Entrepreneurship Development, 204
Wadhwani, Ramesh, 204
Walker, Francis, 5
Walker, Madame C. J., 59
WASME. *See* World Association for Small and Medium Enterprises (WASME)
Water Act, 1974, 345
water filter candles, 214
weighted average cost of capital (WACC), 149
window of opportunity, 124
Winfrey, Oprah, 59
WIT. *See* Women's India Trust (WIT)
women entrepreneurs, 43–68
  challenges faced by, 49–50
  strategies for development of, 50–54
women's empowerment, 63
  gender and development approach, 63
Women's India Trust (WIT), 56
working capital management, 294–298
  ratio analysis for, 296
workshop, 35
World Association for Small and Medium Enterprises (WASME), 221
World Trade Organization (WTO), 374
WTO. *See* World Trade Organization (WTO)

Y

Yojana, 139
Young, W. Frank, 30